About This Book

Teach Yourself Game Programming in 21 Days is a unique book that shows you, day by day, how to create action-packed computer games. You'll learn about sprites, sound effects, and simulation. In addition, the accompanying CD illustrates the book's concepts through high-quality, original computer games such as Sim-Pizza and Attank!!!

Who Should Read This Book?

This book is for anyone remotely interested in game programming, from the arcade junkie wanting to test his programming skills to current game programmers looking for new ways to market their games. This book uses a unique day-by-day approach to teach major concepts, industry terms, and little-known secrets about game programming.

How the Book Is Structured

Teach Yourself Game Programming in 21 Days contains 21 chapters, each representing a day of learning and activities. On Day 1, you get an overview of game programming: what it is, where it's been, where it's going, and how you fit into its world. By Day 21, you're learning advanced game-programming concepts, as well as how and where to market your final games.

Conventions

This book contains the following special icons to guide you along your game-programming journey:

 This icon signals some nice-to-know, side information that is relevant to that day's lesson.

 Are you dying to know some insider information about how to make your games and code faster, stronger, better? If so, watch for these icons.

 Careful! This icon highlights possible pitfalls and how to avoid them.

 This icon defines—you guessed it!—new terms that you'll want to be part of your game-programming vocabulary.

In addition, you will see several special icons throughout the book. These icons—Math, Building an Executable, Game Law, Analysis, and Algorithm—point out insider information gleaned from the author's many years of game programming.

Teach Yourself Game Programming

in 21 Days

Teach Yourself
Game
Programming
in 21 Days

André LaMothe

SAMS
PUBLISHING

201 West 103rd Street, Indianapolis, Indiana 46290

Dedication

I dedicate this book to my brother Michael, the hardest working man alive.

Publisher
Richard K. Swadley

Acquisitions Manager
Stacy Hiquet

Managing Editor
Cindy Morrow

Development Editor
Scott Parker

Software Development Specialist
Keith Davenport

Production Editor
Anne Barrett

Editors
Jill Bond
Judy Brunetti
Mary Inderstrodt

Editorial Coordinator
Bill Whitmer

Editorial Assistants
Carol Ackerman
Sharon Cox
Lynette Quinn

Technical Reviewers
Robert Bogue
Edmund DeJesus
William NeSmith
David Reichert

Marketing Manager
Gregg Bushyeager

Cover Designer
Dan Armstrong

Book Designer
Alyssa Yesh

Director of Production and Manufacturing
Jeff Valler

Imprint Manager
Juli Cook

Manufacturing Coordinator
Paul Gilchrist

Production Analysts
Angela Bannan
Dennis Hager
Mary Beth Wakefield

Graphics Image Specialists
Brad Dixon
Becky Beheler
Jason Hand
Clint Lahnen
John Moore
Michael Reynolds
Dennis Sheehan
Craig Small

Production
Georgiana Briggs
Don Brown
Michael Brummit
Cheryl Cameron
Kim Hannel
Donna Harbin
Ayanna Lacey
Shawn MacDonald
Vic Peterson
Casey Price
Brian-Kent Proffitt
Kim Scott
Hillary Smith
SA Springer
Jon Swain
Jackie Thompson
Dennis Wesner
Holly Wittenberg

Indexer
Greg Eldred

Overview

Contents

Acknowledgments

I want to thank Chris Denny for trusting me with a project of this magnitude and for being understanding of my special circumstances as far as time constraints. This seems like *déja vu*, but I'm getting used to not sleeping. I want to also thank Scott Parker for being the greatest development editor on Earth and for letting me air my opinions to him time and time again. Also, Anne Barrett deserves a very honorable mention and apologies for putting her through another 1,000 pages of video-game design! Anne, maybe you'll make the next DOOM!

I want to mention my friends here who gave me support while I was writing: Dion Phillips, Jackie Berry, Mark Bell, Monique Parker, Jim Valentine, Kelly Peacock, and Dennis Duarte. Each one of you contributed in some way to this book; whether it was an idea, a criticism, an eager ear, or a day at the beach, you're all in this book in one way or another…

Finally, I want to thank all the wonderful people at Sams; you should all take a bow because you've done an incredible job!

About the Author

André LaMothe is a native Californian and has lived in the Silicon Valley his entire life. He is versed in mathematics, computer science, and electrical engineering. He has been writing games for computers since the days of the TRS-80 and has worked in every field that the valley has to offer—from Windows programming to virtual reality systems. He is one of the authors of *Tricks of the Game-Programming Gurus* (Sams Publishing) and writes for *Game Developer* magazine.

M T W R F S

As you prepare for the first week of learning how to create PC games, you will need a few things. First, all the programs are written in C with some inline assembly, so you will need a C compiler (preferable Microsoft's). You will also need to use the library manager LIB that comes with your C development system. The Library Manager will be used to create a library of the functions you are to learn. Next, you will next a text editor to edit the programs. You won't need to type in anything, but you will probably want to experiment with all the programs as the days progress. The source code and executables for each day can be found on the CD. Finally, you need to have an open mind because what you're about to learn will change the way you think about computers and programming!

Where You're Going

The first week of study is a "get acquainted with the basics course." On Day 1, "Lights, Camera, Action!," you learn the basics of what goes into a complete game and where the ideas come from. On Day 2, "The Components of a Complete Game—Mech War," you see a complete game torn apart module by module, and you analyze its operation. On Day 3, "Painting the Screen with the VGA Card," you learn to program the VGA card in mode 13h. During Day 4, "Getting Sprite to the Point," you learn about the most basic animation objects used in video games: sprites. Day 5, "Polygon Engines," shows you how lines, polygons, and mathematical transformations are created, as well as how to manipulate these entities. On Day 6, "Real-Time Animation and Effects," you learn more about bit-mapped animation and the techniques needed to make a flicker-free game. Finally, on Day 7, "Reading the Minds of Devices," you learn how to obtain input from all the popular input devices.

Lights, Camera, Action!

Welcome to *Teach Yourself Game Programming in 21 Days*! You're about to embark upon one the most exciting and rewarding learning experiences you've ever had. Game programming is, without a doubt, one of the most difficult areas of computing to understand. However, it's also one of the most satisfying—and, with determination and patience, you *will* conquer it.

Before we do anything, there's one thing I want to say: creating PC-based video games is a highly creative and artistic process. I want us to do this together. You aren't reading this book by yourself; we're reading it together, evolving as we go. We're a team, and together there are no limits to what we can accomplish.

So, let's begin at the very beginning. Today we cover the following topics:

- ☐ What is a PC-based video game?
- ☐ The history of video games
- ☐ Types of video games
- ☐ Architecture of a video game
- ☐ What does the PC offer as a game machine?
- ☐ What you need to write PC-based games
- ☐ Creating the game engine
- ☐ Being creative

What is a PC-Based Video Game?

A PC-based video game is a program that enables a player to interactively interface with a virtual environment simulated using the PC. This "game" has elements of strategy, action, and fantasy. These elements help suspend the player in another place, time, and reality.

We play video games simply for entertainment and fun. Of course, video games can actually increase problem-solving skills, hand/eye coordination, dexterity, and so on. However, most people play them just for the fun of it!

The game designer today is afforded almost unlimited abilities with the recent advances in graphics, sound, and computational power the PC offers. There are still limits, but not many. A clever game programmer can create just about anything using the PC as a tool—a *gateway*—to allow players to see into the programmer's mind.

Video games have evolved over the past few years to the point of almost unimaginable complexity. Most video games written today are highly graphical in nature, meaning that they have the visual aspect of things "pedal-to-the-metal." Entire teams of programmers, artists, and writers are responsible for the major titles with which you're most familiar. This doesn't mean that an individual can't create an incredible game. By no means! It just means that video games are serious business, and their creators know this. With the PC and cartridge game industries bringing in over 10 billion dollars a year, games are serious business by anyone's standard!

There's a semantic perception that I want to clear up before we go much further. This book is about writing video games using an IBM PC or PC-compatible, so I refer to the PC only if it makes any difference. Many concepts and techniques are universal, and the machine you're programming on is irrelevant. Basically, in this book we write code and algorithms for the PC—but they can surely be ported to other platforms.

Now, let's talk a little about the history of video games so we can see where it all began.

A History of Video Games

The IBM PC was one of the late entries into the game market. It wasn't until the late 1980s that any decent games were available for the PC. This was largely because the PC's graphics were extremely slow compared to those of such market leaders as Atari, Commodore, Tandy, and Apple. These computers had graphics hardware that was relatively advanced compared to the PC's. The Atari 800, especially, was the leader in games. Later, the Commodore 64 took over because the people at Commodore knew how to advertise. At any rate, the PC was thought of as a business machine, and kept that stigma for most of the early days.

Then new processors started coming out. The 80286 had finally enough horsepower to give other CPUs a run for their money, even though the aforementioned eight-bit machines all had 6502s. The 6502 was a good processor with which to make games; moreover, each of the eight-bit machines had what you'd now call local buses as part of their graphics hardware. This made them very fast at graphics and rendering. Admittedly, the 8086 and the 80286 could run much faster than a 6502, but the PC just wasn't taking advantage of them properly.

With an 80286 and an EGA card, the PC started becoming a reasonable platform for which to program; some of the larger game companies, which could afford to divert some of their eight-bit talent to PCs, did so. The first PC-based video games were (as you might expect) copies of the games you'd see in the arcades...and they were pretty bad. They were slow. The sound was terrible. They also all seemed to be an order of magnitude lower in quality than the eight-bit versions of the games.

Then something happened. People started realizing that PCs were here to stay, and there were already millions of people who owned them. Game programmers switched to the IBM PC as the computer of choice for which to create games.

Game Law: Write games for the computer that has the most units in the consumer market, no matter how bad the performance of the machine.

The Amiga, the 16-bit versions of the Apple, and the Atari ST slowly fell out of favor— not because of their power or ability as game machines, but simply because there weren't enough units out there for game companies to make profits. Think about it: do you ever see anyone selling Amiga or Atari software anymore? And if they do, how many titles do you see? Not many! The PC has taken over the game world, and today it is a really cool machine to program on. (I remember being *so* reluctant to put my Amiga out to pasture for the PC, but I did and I'm glad.)

The deciding factor that pushed the PC over the top was that game players wanted more than "shoot-'em-up" games. They wanted games that had a little plot. That meant that larger games, and the use of hard drives came into play. This is an area in which the PC was especially strong. Most owners of other machines hadn't bought hard drives because they were so expensive. Hence, many game developers created games for the PC, but not for the other machines.

Today you can walk into any software store and find droves of PC-based video games. Most games today require at least a 386, and prefer a 486. Moreover, most PCs today have sound cards, so all games support sound effects and music. (At least, any game that wants to sell does!)

The funny thing about the PC is that it's still quite slow graphically. It's just that the CPU is so darned fast that people have found ways to get the performance they need, even with the slow graphics. And learning how to do graphics quickly is one of the main points of this book.

Types of Video Games

Now that we know why the PC is the game machine of choice (at least from a marketing perspective), let's look at the dominant types of games we can find for the PC. The PC is a home, or personal, computer, so a game that would normally do well in an arcade

just won't cut it when placed on a PC. However, video-game players still want a lot of depth, complexity, challenge, and overall "texture" to their games.

What's hot and what's not changes so quickly that it's hard to nail down and separate into popular game types. Nonetheless, this section goes through the basic genres of games.

First-Person, Three-Dimensional Walkthroughs

These are games such as Wolfenstein 3-D, DOOM, Blake Stone, and so on. You're in the body of the game character, and you see out of that character's eyes. As you turn your character, the view turns in full 3-D. (In this book I usually shorthand "two-dimensional" as 2-D and "three-dimensional" as 3-D.) Most games of this nature are set in buildings or room-based worlds.

Flying, Driving, or Spaceflight Simulations

These are your standard 2-D or 3-D simulations, such as Microsoft's Flight Simulator, Spectrum Holobyte's Falcon, Origin System's Wing Commander, and so on. These games try to simulate something we can do in reality, such as fly a plane, drive a car, and so on. To make a game out of it, they wrap the simulation around some kind of plot that allows the player to solve some puzzle or achieve some goal.

Sports Games in 2- or 3-D

It doesn't take a molecular-genetic biochemist to know what these are. Any sport you can imagine has, in some manner or form, been implemented on the computer. Some sports games are identical to their real-world counterparts, while others are completely unrealistic. Currently, the most popular games are football and basketball.

If you're going to make a sports game, you'd better make sure to base it on the most popular sport personalities of the day. (Right, Charles!?)

Scrolling Adventure Games

These are games where the universe or environment is larger than what's visible on the computer screen, so the world slowly "scrolls by" as you move the player. Games such as Mario Brothers use scrolling. Most scrolling games are 2-D in nature.

Sideview Combat Games

Combat games have started cropping up in recent years. The most revolutionary game of this type was Street Fighter. Although Street Fighter originally was an arcade game, it can now be found on the PC.

Combat games are usually based on a side view (2-D) with limited scrolling and lots of graphic detail. The factor that attracts most players to these kinds of games is the ability to project themselves into virtual warriors with super strength and abilities.

Role-Playing Fantasy Games in 2- or 3-D

Role-playing games are a spinoff of D&D (Dungeons and Dragons; and, yes, I admit I used to play). Anyway, they are somewhat interactive, but allow minimal arcade-style game play. The players spend most of their time solving puzzles, searching, and exploring. The view on these games isn't true 3-D: the imagery is usually in predrawn plates used as backdrops.

Comparing 2-D and 3-D

Basically, people want to either run around in a realistic world (in games such as DOOM or Falcon), or they want to play something that is simply fun and entertaining (like Mario Brothers). Most players aren't spoiled enough yet that all the games they play *must* be 3-D.

Allow me to digress for a moment and talk about the differences between 2-D and 3-D games. A 2-D game is something like Asteroids or Pong. It's flat and two-dimensional. Even a game with characters that appear to be 3-D, such as Street Fighter, is 2-D. For a game to be truly 3-D, you must be able to move so the image rendered looks as it would in reality, and not simply a top or side view. Figure 1.1 shows a side-by-side comparison of a 2-D game and a 3-D game.

Flight simulators are a perfect example of a 3-D game. As you fly around in the world, you see a view that's fairly realistic.

As we're beginners at this point, let's start with 2-D games. Creating 3-D games is really a matter of more complex math and graphics; however, the same overall techniques are used to create 3-D as 2-D games, so don't worry. We can extend our knowledge later.

A 3-D Game

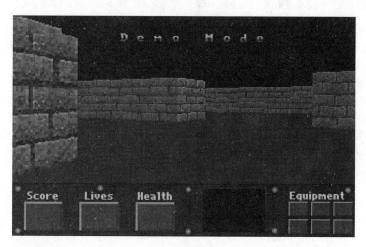

Warlock

A 2-D Game

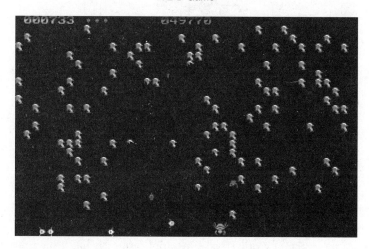

Morphopede

Figure 1.1. *2-D games versus 3-D games.*

Architecture of a Video Game

Now that we have an idea of what a video game is, and the types of games that are prevalent today, let's see what goes into making a game. A video game is so complex, it's hard to even know where to begin. The best way to approach the real architecture is to do it *iteratively*, where we keep adding to the architecture—developing its complexity—with each iteration until we've created a model that encompasses every possible detail. For now, I don't want either of us to get a headache(!), so let's start off with something simple and take a look at an abstract model of all the major video game subsystems. You can refer to Figure 1.2. for this analysis.

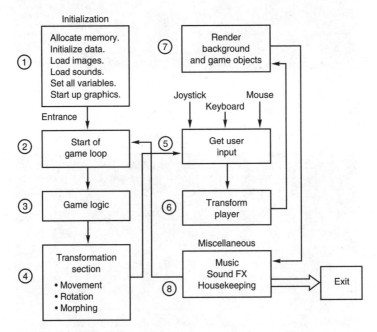

Figure 1.2. *The steps of a game loop.*

A video game is like any other real-time application: it has a main event loop that's executed over and over. This event loop is the heart of the game. Unlike a Microsoft Windows event loop (which normally only responds to events such as mouse clicks and keyboard input), a video-game loop has a kind of heartbeat that's generated using an internal timing reference of some kind. This reference could be one of the timers, the vertical blank, or something else.

The event loop services the screen and the sound devices. Regardless of the player's actions, the event loop tries to draw the screen, play the sounds, move the game objects, and then start all over again. If the player wants to sit still and be terminated, fine: it's up to the individual. However, the event loop doesn't wait for the player to move before executing. The rest of this section talks about the different parts of the game loop.

Section 1: Initialization

The game software is initialized in Section 1 of our illustrated program. This is where you:

- ☐ Allocate memory
- ☐ Clear memory
- ☐ Set variables
- ☐ Open files
- ☐ Load images
- ☐ Load sounds
- ☐ Set up scores

and, in general, get everything ready to play. Take care in the initialization section to leave nothing to chance.

When designing the initialization section, break it into modules. That way, if you want to reset a certain portion of the game during the game, you can reuse code.

 Warning: Even a single improperly set variable can wreak havoc on your game, so assume nothing. Even if a variable doesn't need to be set, set it to zero, NULL, or some other appropriate value.

Section 2: Entrance

Section 2 is where we see some action. This is the entrance into the game loop, and is the loop-back point for every cycle.

A video game has to execute at a reasonable number of cycles each second. Most games run at 15–30 frames per second. That means that the screen is redrawn, over and over, 15–30 times a second. This kind of speed is necessary: your eyes are able to perceive

"flicker" if the screen isn't updated this fast. Moreover, the logic of the game must execute at a rate fast enough to keep up with the player. If your game ran at a single cycle per second, the player would have time to make several input changes—and neither the game nor the objects in it could react fast enough.

Section 3: Game Logic

Section 3 is where most of the game logic, artificial intelligence, collision detection, and related operations are done. This part of the game loop takes relatively little time compared to the rendering, which usually is the bottleneck.

 Game Law: Don't mix game logic and graphics unless absolutely necessary for speed. Try to keep rendering and computation separate.

Section 4: Transformation

Section 4 of the game loop is where the objects are moved, scaled, rotated, and so on. (These movements are called *transformations*, sometimes shortened to *transforms*.) However, we won't draw them yet. We must see what the player is doing first.

Section 5: Input

The user-input section, Section 5, is where the player gets his or her chance to be heard. The input device—whether it be keyboard, mouse, joystick, or whatever—is queried, and the intentions of the player are recorded and, if feasible, acted upon. (We learn much more about input devices on Day 7.)

Section 6: Player Transformation

Section 6 is where the player's character is transformed and any operations pertaining to the player, such as logical decisions, are done.

Section 7: Rendering

Finally, Section 7 is where the screen image is built up. The background is drawn first. Any game objects and the player's character are then rendered on top of the background.

This overlay is done by twiddling bits in the VGA card's memory (more on this on Day 3, in the chapter called "Painting the Screen with the VGA Card.")

Section 8: Music, Sound Effects, and Housekeeping

Section 8 is where all the odds and ends are taken care of, such as updating sound effects, displaying scores, updating global data structures, and so on. The program then jumps back to the entrance to the game loop (Section 2), and the process is repeated.

What Does the PC Offer as a Game Machine?

Today the PC is a formidable computer. You can bank on the following minimum hardware configuration as your base platform:

CPU	A 386 with two megabytes of RAM (with 486s being common)
Video Card	The VGA card is standard, with many PCs having a Super VGA card
Sound Card	A Sound Blaster- or Adlib-compatible sound card
Input Devices	All PCs have keyboards; many have mice, and—if the owner is a gamer—you can count on a joystick

Let's talk about the major components of the PC and see what they offer us. The CPU is a good place to start.

The CPU

Both the 386 and 486 are 32-bit processors that support high clock speeds. The average 386 runs at 25MHz; the average 486 at 33MHz. This means these machines can execute more than 10 MIPS (million instructions per second). This is ample processing power for most video games.

Game Law: You can never have *too much* processing power.

Moreover, both the 386 and 486 have instruction caches to speed things up. The 486 is an order of magnitude more complex in this area, but they have similar technologies.

Finally, the 386 supports a math coprocessor, and the 486 has one that's on board. In general, the math coprocessor and floating-point operations are avoided in video games for speed, but having the ability to do floating-point math in hardware is a great advantage.

We might ask the question, "Why do we need so much processing power for a simple video game?" A video game is a simulation of reality that must respond in real time to user input. It must render high-end graphics, make a bunch of little creatures run around on a screen (and seem smart), and do it in such a way that it seems as though it never misses a beat. This kind of performance on a single-processor machine is possible only with a lot of processing horsepower.

The Video Card

Because graphics performance is the ultimate gauge of a video game's merit, let's discuss the VGA card.

The VGA card is not what you'd call a high-end graphics card. It's slow compared to the graphics subsystems of other computers, and must be carefully programmed. However, it supports a lot of color and high resolutions. In the past, many game programmers had to be VGA gurus to make a video game. Recently, however, the overall performance of the CPU (along with the graphics subsystems of PCs) has reached a point where the video game programmer can relax hardware dependence on the VGA card, and think of it as a simple frame buffer.

We learn what this means on Day 3. For now, rest easy knowing that we really don't need to know much about the VGA card. In the next 21 days we use a special mode called mode 13h: the 320x200 resolution mode with 256 colors. This is the easiest mode to program in, and the performance of this mode is near optimal.

The Sound Card

The next major subsystem to address is the sound system. This is where we can see that the age-old boundaries and restraints with which the PC has been chained are ancient history.

The sound cards produced today are incredibly simple to use and program. They operate independently of the main CPU and permit a form of a parallel execution to take place.

When you want digitized sounds or music to play, you simply tell the sound card where the piece is and what to do with it. The sound card does the rest.

This takes a great burden off the programmer. If sounds had to be made algorithmically by the main CPU, the careful timing and complex techniques necessary would require the programmer to have an understanding of music theory—which most programmers don't!

In this book we talk primarily about Creative Labs' Sound Blaster and compatibles as our base sound card. These cards are inexpensive, reliable, and have more than enough hardware support to create digitized sound effects and music for our games.

That about sums it up for the major pieces of the PC as far as the purpose of writing games. Of course, a large space on the hard drive would be nice, and a joystick can help. All in all, though, the CPU, graphics, and sound card are our main concerns.

Next, let's talk about what we are going to need to write games and work through this book.

What You Need to Write Video Games

In this book we write games on the PC and compatibles. We must consider three areas:

☐ As far as hardware goes, you must have at least a 386 with two megabytes of RAM, a VGA card, and a VGA monitor. A Sound Blaster would be nice if you want to hear anything. Finally, a joystick and mouse come in handy when we cover input devices. You can get by without a 486, joystick, mouse, or Sound Blaster, but a VGA card and 386 are a bare minimum if you want to get the most from this book.

☐ The software requirements are equally flexible. You need a C compiler. I use Microsoft's C/C++ 7.0; if you have that one, we're completely in sync. (If you're using an older or newer version, everything should still be fine.)

Also, it would be to your advantage to have MASM 5.0 or higher. Although we use the in-line assembler if we do any assembly language, you might need the macro assembler for something in your own games. (If you don't have it now, don't worry: I supply the .OBJ files of anything in this book that's in pure assembly language.)

If you're a Borland user, you'll have to make slight changes here and there. However, there shouldn't be a problem with code compiling under Borland's products.

The two other major pieces of software you need when you start writing games yourself are a 320×200×256 painting program and a program to digitize sounds using the Sound Blaster. However, the examples and code in this book are completely self-contained. All programs have already been compiled and, if worse came to worst, you could simply execute them without compiling and experimenting with them.

☐ Finally, you need a lot of patience. Writing a video game from scratch can be overwhelming. There are so many little details to consider, it's amazing that it can be done at all.

Creating the Game Engine

This book is written in a way that calls for creating libraries, which we then build on. We use these libraries later in the book for the games we write. This means that when I supply you with some new function, I may tell you to add it to one of the libraries we already have. Then, of course, when you link and create an executable file, you would make sure to link the "main" program to the proper libraries.

Don't worry if you're not sure what I'm talking about: we deal with it when the time comes. I just want you to realize that one of the goals of this book is to create a library of graphic, sound, and system functions that you can use in the future to write video games. If you want to know more about creating libraries and linking to them, take some time out and read up on the topic. You'll find that it's easy to do and makes life much simpler.

Also, I've elected not to use "make" files and all kinds of related development tools. I find that they blur the purity of what we're trying to do here, which is *learn*. When you write games later, feel free to use anything you like; for now, let's keep everything as simple as possible. Video games are hard enough without having to worry about a lot of little details.

Finally, the C code in the book becomes fairly challenging as the book progresses, just because of the nature of video-game programming (although I comment everything generously). Try to brush up on your C if you're rusty.

Being Creative

1

Well, this is a good one! If creativity is something a person is gifted with, how do I explain *how to be* creative?

First, everyone is creative; some people just need a little push. The most creative people in the world are creative because nothing intimidates them. They come up with ideas and new ways of thinking that would sound absurd to most people. This is the very essence of creativity. Just let yourself go. Don't care what anyone thinks, what's accepted, or what's not. When thinking up ideas for games, I usually talk to myself for a couple hours, watch some science-fiction movies, or take a drive in the country. Whatever it takes to motivate you, you should do.

If you just have no idea where to even begin designing a video game, try to take what someone else has created and change or improve on it. This technique works fine and is a good place to start. To get some ideas, I suggest going to a few arcades, checking out the hundreds of games for the PCs at the software stores, and watching a whole lot of science-fiction and fantasy movies. If there's one game designer on Earth who hasn't seen all the *Star Trek* episodes, the *Alien* movies, and *Real Genius* a thousand times, I'd be surprised! So go out there and use other people's ideas as the seed of your own new idea.

That should get you started on some ideas for games. The other area that we must be extremely creative in is the *programming*. You'd better forget everything you learned about the PC and what's supposedly impossible. Think of programming as a game. It's the greatest game in the world. The object of the game is to do the impossible. Most of the programming a video-game programmer does would seem impossible to a programmer of ordinary applications.

When you're faced with a problem that seems too complex to solve, take a step backward and make a rough stab at it. If anything, this will help you to manage the problem: it won't seem insurmountable. Then, when you try to really solve it, you'll have a much easier time.

 Game Law: There's always someone who can figure out what you think impossible, so beat them to the punch by thinking that *anything* is possible!

Try to be creative in steps. Have a grand plan in your mind, but try to break each problem into smaller problems that can be solved more easily.

And from this point on, never say "It can't be done." There's always a way to make something smaller, faster, better—believe me!

Summary

Today was the first day of class, and things don't seem too bad. We learned what a video game is. We also learned about games on the PC, and the what and why of their existence Then we took a look at some of the popular types of games people play, and decided to stick with 2-D games for our first time out. We even jumped in and looked at a representative game loop that revealed the architecture of most video games. We also learned about the PC itself, and saw what it had to offer us as a game machine.

Next, we took a look at one of the goals of the book: to create a library of functions we can use in the future, and how we implement this library in this book.

Finally, we had a talk about being creative and coming up with ideas for new games and news ways of programming.

That should be enough for the first day.

Q&A

Q What's the difference between a video game and an arcade game?

A A video game is played on a personal computer—in our case, the IBM PC and compatibles. Video games have more depth than arcade games and must be able to keep the player's attention for longer periods of time. Moreover, a video-game developer can create games in which more strategy and thinking are involved, whereas arcade programmers must design their games to cater to the short attention span that is indicative of the physical locations in which arcade games are placed.

Q What was the first video game?

A Good question. The first games were all of the text-adventure type. Then they slowly evolved to having crude graphics and, finally, graphics that surpass arcade-game quality. To answer the question, though: I really don't know. Does anyone?

Q Why are the most popular game titles so…popular?

A Video games and their plots are really extensions of the ideals, feelings, and current beliefs of the day. Today, people who play video games seem to like sports, violence, and fantasy. These are the driving factors that help game designers decide what they will create.

Q If a PC is a single-tasking computer and can do only a single operation at once, how does a PC-based video game seem like it's doing many things at the same time?

A It's true that a PC can do only one thing at a time. Even with a multitasking operating system, such as Windows or OS/2, the PC still only executes a single instruction at a time. The illusion of multitasking, or multiple execution of more than one process, is created by sheer speed. The PC can do calculations millions of times faster than can the human brain. This allows the PC to do hundreds of things in a short stretch of time, while to us it seems as if all these things are happening at once. For instance, the computer screen is drawn 70 times a second by the raster or electron gun. Have you ever seen the tip of the beam trace the screen? (If you have, you must be Robocop!)

Q Does a computer with more memory play video games better than one with less?

A Well, the answer is yes and no. A PC with more memory can store much of the game imagery and sound effects within RAM and access them faster than if they have to be brought in from disk. However, the game logic and artificial intelligence for most games isn't really memory consumptive; it's the imagery and digitized sound effects that eat up memory. Hence, the more space you have in RAM for data, the quicker the data can be accessed and used. Once the data is loaded into RAM, or off disk to RAM, it's up to the CPU to run the software. At that point, the execution speed of the game is related only to the CPU and graphics.

Q I'm a terrible artist and don't know anything about music. Can I still make a video game?

A Yes. First, if you can't draw, you can always find someone who can. Second, most game artwork these days isn't even drawn anymore: the images are digitized with cameras and frame grabbers.

Also, I think there are about five game programmers on Earth who can play an instrument. Most of them use other people's music and or digitized effects, which can be obtained elsewhere.

Q We spoke of creating a "game library." Will I be able to make any game I want with it?

A No. As I said, we concentrate on 2-D games in this book. Furthermore, the library is a starting point only. You'll learn that every function that you create can have many versions that are designed for specific cases of the game you're creating.

Game programming is like no other programming. We must always try and optimize the code for speed.

Q I can't think of any ideas for new games. What should I do?

A You should stop trying so hard, and think instead of what *you* would want to play. Don't worry about other people. There are always people who will like what you like and others who won't, so create games that you want to play.

Workshop

The Workshop section presents quiz questions to help you cement your new knowledge and exercises to give you experience using what you've learned. Try to understand the questions and exercises before moving on to the next lesson. The answers are in Appendix B.

Quiz

1. Name the 8-bit game machines that reigned in the early 1980s.

2. What are the different categories of video games?

3. What's the difference between 2-D and 3-D games?

4. When playing digitized sound on the Sound Blaster, does the programmer have to send each byte of the digitized sample to the Sound Blaster?

5. How many frames per second must we display to have a flicker-free image?

6. Is the 386 a 32-bit processor?

7. If a game designer had to choose between code size or execution speed, which would be the best choice?

8. In the movie *Real Genius*, what was Kent doing when Chris caught him eating Jello?

Exercises

1. List the main categories of game types, and try to think of at least three games that fit into each category.

2. Draw out and annotate a game loop.

3. Play the game DOOM for a couple hours and see what can be done with a PC.

4. Rent a couple science-fiction movies and go spend 10 bucks at an arcade.

5. Read your compiler documentation on building libraries and using the libraries to create executable files.

The Components of a Complete Game: Mech War

The Components of a Complete Game: Mech War

Creating a complete video game is a daunting task. Even the world's best video-game programmers shiver at the amount of code and time it takes to write a professional-quality video game. Today I want us to take a look at a complete game, something indicative of what we're trying to accomplish by the end of this book. The game is called Mech War, and is a classic "shoot-'em-up" game.

Now, I don't want you to think that you'll only be able to write shoot-'em-up games. On the contrary. Mech War is merely a representation of the level of complexity we're shooting for (pun intended). You'll be able to write any kind of game you wish after reading this book; however, a shoot-'em-up is always a good candidate for an illustrative example, and that's why I chose to use one for our discussions.

The object of today's lesson is not to understand the technical aspects of how Mech War works—that's what the rest of the book is for—but to understand in general all the different elements that must be taken into consideration to make a complete game. I want to generate a lot of questions in your mind.

Here's today's hit list:

- ☐ The design of Mech War
- ☐ Starting and playing Mech War
- ☐ The system architecture
- ☐ Drawing the graphics
- ☐ Making the sounds
- ☐ The game introduction
- ☐ The game background
- ☐ The game loop
- ☐ Configuring Mech War
- ☐ The main game elements
- ☐ The mechs
- ☐ Testing for collisions
- ☐ Player input
- ☐ Displaying the game status
- ☐ Screen transitions
- ☐ Synchronization to the video display

□ Wave control

□ Mech War features

□ Testing the game

□ The Mech War challenge

The Design of Mech War

Much of what a game programmer does boils down to *being creative*. Writing games isn't too terribly complex once the fundamentals have been grasped. The hard part about making games is thinking them up! I can't count the number of times I've sat at my desk and tried to think up the ultimate video game. Many times I'd find myself creating games that had already been done. This is the problem: there are so many games out there (literally, thousands) that coming up with a completely new one is hard to do. There are still about 50,000,000,000 good games to be written—they're just harder to come up with.

How Mech War Came to Be

When I started thinking about a game to write for today's discussion I had many things to consider. I wanted to write a game that was familiar to everyone and had many interesting elements on which to base our discussion. Also, the game had to be something that could be implemented using the graphics library we're developing. (Yes, I cheated and used stuff that we haven't seen yet. The actual implementation of a complete game isn't the point yet.) Anyway, after walking around a nearby arcade awhile, I decided to do something that was a cross between Space Invaders, Galaxian, and Phoenix. If you hail from the third planet from the local Sun, you should be familiar with at least one of these titles. I extracted some basic concepts from each, then used these concepts as a foundation to create a really simple game called Mech War, shown in Figure 2.1.

This game took me five days to write, from start to finish. Admittedly, it's simple and crude by today's standards. However, if you were to write something similar and take ten times that amount of time, you'd have a game that would be of shareware quality, and you could probably sell it!

The point is, we're trying to build foundations here. Video games are all made out of the same stuff. If you understand the underlying principles, you can take simple concepts much further. (I'm a firm believer in understanding simple ideas rather than having a fleeting grasp on advanced ones.)

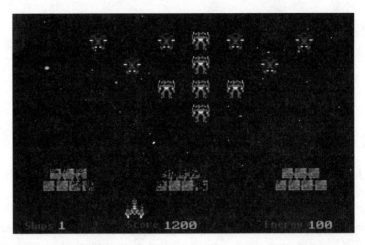

Figure 2.1. *A screen shot of Mech War.*

The idea of the game is that Earth is being invaded by an army of mechanical creatures called *mechs*. These mechs were hibernating within the inner volume of Mars and have been awakened by something. The mechs have become aware of a technologically advanced race on the third planet (that's us) and have decided to enslave the carbon-based units for mining on other worlds. That's the story: basic, simple, and to the point!

Once I'd decided on the idea behind the game, I thought up the *flow* of the game, or the sequence of events presented to the player over time. I decided that the main idea of the game would be to fight wave after wave of these mechs. The player would have a ship that could fire "tachion pulses" at the mechs. I also decided that there would be three different kinds of mechs, all looking similar but with slightly different geometry and colors, as shown in Figure 2.2.

Because I was designing a classic shoot-'em-up game, the layout of the screen would be pretty simple: player at the bottom, mechs at the top. I needed some barriers to block the barrage of torpedoes the mechs would fire, a background image of the galaxy, and a flowing starfield. That would have been enough, but I decided to also throw in a mothership that flew by once in a while to allow the player to score some quick points.

Finally, there's no end to the game. The player plays until his or her game character dies, and that's it.

We go into depth on the thought process behind each of the game's aspects, and more, but for now I think that we're clear and on the same carrier frequency as to what the game is about and what it entails.

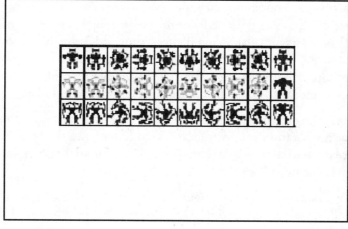

Figure 2.2. *The mechs of Mech War.*

Sound Considerations

Mech War supports Sound Blaster cards and compatibles; if you have a Sound Blaster and your sound card is configured properly, you'll be able to hear the digitized sound effects. The game is set to default at a setting of I/O port 220h and interrupt 5 for sound effects.

If you don't get sound, your sound card may be set differently. You can change the program's settings by altering the configuration file named mechs.cfg. It's an ASCII file, which you can read with the `fscanf()` function to extract two integers:

☐ The first integer is the port number.

☐ The second is the interrupt number.

For example, mechs.cfg looks like this:

```
Dump of the "mechs.cfg" file.

544

5
```

The first number stands for port 220h, which would be 544 in decimal. The second number is the interrupt number. To change either, simply edit the file and save it. Remember, however, that the numbers are in decimal, so don't put hex values in or the program will probably lock up.

One final note on sound: the sound system uses the driver ct-voice.drv, supplied with Creative Labs' Sound Blaster. The driver I've supplied here is version 3.05. It may not work on your particular Sound Blaster sound card. If you have another model of Sound Blaster, use the ct-voice.drv sound driver that came with it. If you don't have the distribution disks that came with your Sound Blaster card, check the companion CD. I've included drivers for all popular models of the Sound Blaster there.

If everything is set right and you still have no sound, try copying your version of the ct-voice.drv file from your particular Sound Blaster into the MECHS directory. The ct-voice.drv file can usually be found on the installation disks that came with your Sound Blaster or compatible.

If you think such detail about sound was a pain to read, imagine implementing the actual sound! Consider this section a brief glimpse of the amount of detail necessary in a complete game.

Starting Mech War

Mech War isn't what you would call a dexterity-challenging game. (I still can't play games like Street Fighter because I just have a hard time controlling all 3,000 of those buttons!) All you need to do is type in mechs and the game executes.

When you start the game, a screen shows the name and then fades away. An instruction screen then pops up briefly telling you how the game functions, and then the game begins.

Playing Mech War

To play, use the arrow keys to move and the spacebar to fire. Your mission is simple: blast as many mechs (and rack up the highest score) as possible before you get vaporized.

To exit the game, press the Q key. You're taken back to DOS (or whatever O/S the game was launched from).

Now, let's take a closer look at all the source code and data modules involved in the game, and their function.

What we want to do now is see how the modules go together to create Mech War, and then take a low-level look at the software architecture of the game.

System Architecture

Mech War is composed of many different modules, including the source code for Mech War, the graphics library, the sound software, the sound data, the bit-map data for the imagery, and the configuration file for mechs (which currently configures sound only). Figure 2.3 shows a graphical layout of the whole thing.

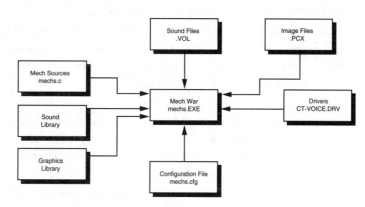

Figure 2.3. *The software layout of Mech War.*

Now let's see what each module is responsible for.

Software Modules

As you see in Figure 2.3, I've been a little nebulous about the names of some of the modules because, technically, they don't exist yet (that is, we haven't made them). However, names are unimportant now; only their function is of consequence.

Mech War source files—The Mech War source files are all the files that make up the actual game itself. The initialization code, logic, artificial intelligence, player control, and so on are included in these files.

The graphics libraries—These libraries are responsible for drawing all the graphics in the game. They were created as a set of tools with which to make games. By the end of the book, your final graphics library will be quite as capable as, and have the functionality of, a commercial graphics library costing hundreds of dollars.

The sound library—The sound driver provided by Creative Labs isn't enough to create sound alone. It's only the interface between the computer and the

Sound Blaster board. Hence, I had to create a sound library to play sound. This library enables you to play digitized sound effects without intervention by the computer. We see the construction of this library later.

The VOC files—The sound effects you hear in the game were created by digitizing real sounds. These sounds, when digitized, are in a standard form called VOC. Mech War has about a half-dozen digitized sounds, including explosions and verbal insults by the mechs.

The PCX files—These files contain all the graphics you see in the game. The background, the imagery for the ship and mechs, the introduction, and the instructions screens are all part of these files. These PCX files are a standard graphic-image file format used on the PC.

The ct-voice.drv sound driver—This is the sound driver responsible for playing sounds on the Sound Blaster and taking care of requests from the PC. It's loaded into memory and used as an interrupt. We learn more about this driver when we talk about sound on Day 9, in the chapter called "Making the PC Rock!"

The configuration file mech.cfg—While Mech War is rather simple, even a game this simple needs some information about its environment. One piece of information that's absolutely necessary is the settings of the sound system. This is contained in this file.

That's all the software involved in Mech War. It's really a paltry amount compared to some of the games I've seen, which actually had gigabytes—that's right, *gigabytes*—of code and data.

The Game Loop

The next topic we want to cover is the general layout of the "game loop." We learned about this concept yesterday, but now we take a little closer look at a real example.

The initialization and main game loop for Mech War have many of the same components we learned about yesterday. Take a look at Figure 2.4 to see the highlights of Mech War's main module.

In Figure 2.4 we see that, as usual, everything is initialized first. The graphics system is then placed into mode 13h, and all subsystems (such as sound and graphics) are initialized. Imagery is loaded, and all the data structures are initialized for all the game objects. Finally, the mouth to the main loop is entered—and that's where the action begins.

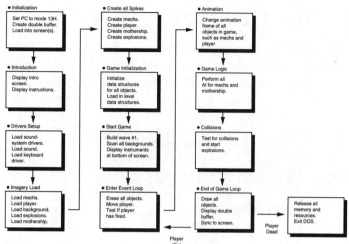

Figure 2.4. *The highlights of Mech War's* `main()` *module.*

The game loop in Mech War consists of three main parts with a few more elements of somewhat lesser importance:

☐ The first thing done in the game loop is to erase all the objects in preparation for the next frame of animation.

☐ The next step is to move all the objects and run through their game logic. This includes both the player's control and the artificial-intelligence logic for the mechs.

☐ After all the objects in the game have been moved and processed, the program draws and displays the next frame of animation.

☐ The loop then executes another iteration from the top.

Of course, there are also the little things: starting the sound effects, obtaining input from the keyboard, blinking the little green lights on the barrier, and so on. For the most part, though, the erase/move/draw components are the most important and dominate the processing time of the game.

Don't worry if you're shaky on the overall architecture of the game and the elements within it at this point: we're just going through the motions here. We go through them many more times in the days to come!

Drawing the Graphics

Mech War consists of many different graphical objects. In addition to the introduction, instruction, and background screens, there are the bit-map images used for the game itself. These bit maps are for the mechs, the player's ship, the explosions, and the mothership. Take a look at Figure 2.5 to see all the bit maps used in the game.

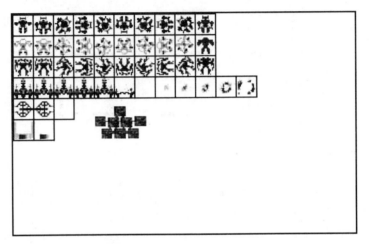

Figure 2.5. *The bit maps for Mech War.*

The bit maps were generated with DPaint, which is a 320×200-pixel, 256-color paint program for the PC. There are many other programs that would work as well (such as Fractal Paint, PC Paintbrush, and so on). However, I'll always have a soft spot in my heart for DPaint from my Amiga 500 days—we used to use DPaint to make games on the Amiga—so I always use DPaint from Electronic Arts.

When you're studying the imagery for the game, pay close attention to the regular matrix within which each bit map is placed. This is called a *template*, and is used to place the bit maps so they can be extracted by software in a logical and predictable manner.

The most interesting bit maps are the explosion frames and the frames of the player's ship. I drew the explosion by first thinking out how something blows up, and then trying, frame by frame, to make bit maps that would look like an explosion. The player's ship has retracting cannons. I found I had to draw a separate frame for each step in the entire retraction process. Also, the retraction has to look like there's some inertia involved: when the cannons are being retracted, they have to look as though they have some real weight and are hard to push back into the retracted position.

Thinking about little things like mass, gravity, and other physical properties helps you create more believable animations and imagery.

The next important part of the data used by Mech War is the sound effects. Let's hear about them.

Making the Sounds

A video game is unacceptably boring without sound effects (which I like to shorthand as *FX*). I can live without music, but I have to have sound FX for things such as engines, explosions, weapons, and so on. To create sound FX, I used one of the most advanced sound-processing elements available on the market today: my vocal cords. That's right, all the sounds you heard were made by...me! I used a piece of software to digitize my voice at some sample rate (usually, 6KHz) and then digital processing software to change my voice into the desired sound. (I don't think my neighbors will ever look at me the same way again after the time I spent trying to synthesize a female voice for the low-energy warning. And then I decided against using it.)

Anyway, this is the standard technique used to create the digitized sound FX for games. Actors, equipment, or both are used to create raw sounds that are then tweaked and massaged using sound-processing software to obtain the perfect effect. Some real-world sounds are hard to come by for recording purposes (like explosions; think about it). However, once you start creating digital sound FX, you soon discover how to make just about any sound with your vocal cords and the help of a few objects made of different materials.

I'm sure you want to know how to make the Sound Blaster play digitized sounds, and we go into that on Day 9. For now, though, I just wanted you to know where I got the sounds in Mech War, and how I made them sound cool.

Taking it Step by Step

We've covered most of the external details of the game. Now let's throw a more-technical light on each step of the game. We're still staying away from detail, though; remember, this is just familiarization.

The Mech War Introduction

The introduction phase of Mech War is quite simple. There are two components to the introduction:

- ☐ First, the title screen comes up and displays the name of the game and other important information. This is just a predrawn PCX file, loaded in for viewing.

- ☐ Second, after a specific amount of time (tracked using the PC's timer), the title screen fades away and the instructions are displayed. The fade-away is done by slowly decreasing the intensity of every color on the screen until all are black.

The instruction screen is just the title screen with the words "Mech War" subtracted and a paragraph of red text (the instructions) added.

The PC waits for the player to press a key by making a call to getch(). (This is a good way to accept a key press before continuing.)

Once a key has been pressed, another screen transition is used: the screen "melts away." This is accomplished by using a set of 320 synthetic *worms* that eat up the vertical strips of the screen at different speeds.

When most of the worms reach the bottom of the screen, the introduction phase is complete and the game continues.

The Background

The first thing you should notice when Mech War starts is a beautiful starfield on top of a distant galaxy of quasars and planets. This is the *background* or *backdrop* of the game, and never changes. It's static and makes the game more pleasing to the eye. However, don't get carried away with artwork to make up for other deficiencies in the game. The technique of using "just for looks" backgrounds and animation to make up for a lack of game play has become an exceedingly common practice.

Game Law: If your game isn't fun with all the added graphics, it just isn't fun. Try again.

Now we come to an interesting topic in animation: saving the background. The background, by nature of its static existence, must not be something that can be destroyed. This means that no matter what happens in the foreground—that is, whatever the game action—the background must not be corrupted. In essence, we must continually save the images under our game objects when we draw them so we can restore that area when the objects move. Otherwise, the objects in the foreground will destroy all the background in no time!

What's good about backgrounds is they're so easy to draw, and they can really add to a good game. I wish I had more time to draw a separate background for each wave of Mech War: maybe a star cluster for one, a nebula for another, and so on. (Who cares that we're supposed to be near Earth? It's a video game, and we can do anything we want.)

Configuring Mechs

The next important event that must take place before the game can really get under way is the configuration of the game itself. All games have some kind of installation sequence, configuration sequence, or both, used to figure out the hardware/software combination of the machine on which the game is running. This configuration information is used by a player to set the game up so it functions in the most appropriate manner for his or her particular machine. Moreover, configuration sequences and data tailor the game to a particular player's liking. For instance, some players may want to redefine the keyboard, screen size, sound card, or difficulty level.

In the case of Mech War, the configuration file is hardly complex. The only thing I had to configure was the sound card. I needed to know what I/O port the sound card was set for, and the interrupt the card uses. These two pieces of information are in an ASCII file that's read by the game at startup. Of course, you have to use an editor to change these pieces of information. The creation of the configuration file could be done just as easily using another program, written specifically for the purpose of creating and updating the configuration file. In a professional quality game, we see such programs.

The Main Game Elements

Now we're getting somewhere! The previous discussions relate to global aspects of the game. At this point, we want to close in on some details of the game. However, I still want to keep the discussion at an abstract level rather than giving specific code and algorithm examples. Therefore, don't worry if something is unclear to you or seems incomplete. Just get out of it what you can for the moment.

I've broken the game down into what I think are the main elements of the action. This division may or may not be the best, but we'll work with it. Let's begin with the player and his or her character's attributes.

The Player

The player is virtually projected into a small ship that's at the bottom of the screen. The player can move the ship by pressing the arrow keys, and can fire weapons using the Spacebar. When I designed the ship, I had to take a few things into consideration:

☐ I wanted to have a flickering engine exhaust that made the ship look like it was moving forward, or at least holding its position.

☐ Also, I wanted the ship to be able to fire its weapons from two side-mounted guns. These guns were to be retractable.

☐ Finally, the ship had to be the same size as all the other objects in the game, which is 16×16 pixels. I chose this size for a couple of reasons:

First, the smaller all the objects are, the more of them I can animate on the screen.

Second, because there is less data, they can be drawn faster.

I also wanted to have a particle-beam weapon that emanated from the fuselage of the ship, but didn't get time to do it.

In a nutshell, that was what I envisioned as the player's ship. With that in mind, let's talk about some of the more interesting points about the actual implementation of some of this functionality.

Animating the Player's Ship

I had to take a couple of factors into consideration to animate the player's ship. For one thing, timing is always important. The game runs at a certain frame rate, just as your TV runs at 30 frames a second and movies run at 24. Based on the frame rate, I had to time any changes to the player's ship so they'd look correct. The ship's animation also had to be done so it fit the timing of other objects in the game.

The main ship animation, going on all the time, is the flickering engines shooting out green flames. I accomplished this by having two different bit maps for the player's ship: one with the engines on and the other with the engines off. During game execution, I randomly select between the two bit maps and use one of them for the current frame of animation.

Randomly selecting one of the bit maps has a visually pleasing look. However, I could have just toggled between the two bit maps. I think the effect would have looked more stable, although I haven't tried it so I don't know for sure.

Retracting Cannons

The next interesting animation that takes place is the retracting tachion cannons. This animation, along with the sound effect for the weapons firing, is *very* cool. I wanted to have the cannons pull back when they fired (as if from the force of the tachion pulse).

Furthermore, I wanted the frames of animation, when played, to look like the cannons had mass and inertia. This I accomplished using basic trial and error, drawing the cannons in different positions for each animation frame. Luckily for me, I got the perfect look on the second try.

The retraction sequence occurs when the player presses the spacebar, firing the cannons. This means that when the cannons are fired we must switch from the normal engine-flickering sequence to the cannon-retraction sequence. This is done using what's called a *state variable*. State variables are used in video games and in many other kinds of software to track the current state of some process. When the cannons are fired, I place the player's ship into a cannon-retraction state. When the retraction state is complete, the ship is placed back into the engine-flickering state.

The frames of animation for the retracting cannons also have to have the engines flickering. (Without this it would look like the engines turned off when the cannon was fired.) Therefore, the retraction animation really has two elements: the retraction of the cannons and the flickering of the engines. A good animator can mix many animations at once into the bit maps to make them seem like they're all happening independently.

Tachion Cannons

The cannons themselves work by starting a process that creates two structures, which are the missiles. These missiles are given an initial color, position, and velocity, and then are moved upward every frame until they hit either the barriers or an enemy.

This is an example of crude multitasking. All video games are multitasking: programmers write software in such a way that many events seem to happen simultaneously. However, things are happening sequentially, just as in Microsoft Windows. The amazing thing about this multitasking is that it's done in DOS. Many people have never done real-time programming, although many argue about what *real time* means. In the context of video games, it means starting and running processes such as missiles and explosions so they seem to be happening simultaneously with the rest of the action in the game.

Getting back to the cannons, the missiles are moved at a rate of about eight pixels per frame. That means that with each frame they move upward eight units of distance. This creates a problem for collision detection, as the missile could possibly skip right over an enemy. However, if we didn't move the missiles this fast they'd appear to move too slow, because the game can only run at so many frames per second. On my PC, the game runs at about 18 frames per second. That means that, if we move an object by a single pixel each frame, it would take it (320/18=) 17 seconds to get across the screen! This would be unacceptable, so we have to cheat a little.

(Did you every wonder why in a game you thought you shot something, but you missed? This kind of "skip" is the culprit.)

The Particle Explosion

At some point one of the missiles from the enemy mechs tags the player's ship. I wanted something spectacular to occur when this happens (at least, something spectacular for a couple of hundred lines of C). My final decision was to do a particle explosion with gravity and cindering effects. This is how I did it:

- ☐ Throughout the explosion, we use a state variable to track the state of the player's ship in the act of exploding.

- ☐ When the program detects that an enemy's missile has hit the player's ship, I have the program place a smashed bit map at the ship's current position and disconnect the controls so the player can't move the ship.

- ☐ The program then creates an array of 30-50 particles with upward velocities, all centered around the player's ship.

- ☐ I then have the program make all the particles bright white. This is the beginning of the explosion.

- ☐ As the explosion runs, each of the particles moves based on its velocity trajectory. Also, I apply a gravity field to each object, altering the object's velocity based on some gravity constant, as follows:

  ```
  velocity = velocity - acceleration of gravity
  ```

  In each frame, the particles slow down until finally they start falling.

- ☐ As this is going on, I also have the program modify the intensity of each of the particles to make it look as though the particles are burning out. I do this by changing the values in the VGA card's color registers, which control what the red, green, and blue (RGB) values for all the 256 displayable colors are. (You'll find more information on this in the chapter for Day 3, "Painting the Screen with the VGA Card.")

- ☐ By the time a few dozen frames play, all the particles hit the ground and burn out. At this point, the explosion sequence is stopped, the current wave is restarted, and the player's original, unsmashed ship is restored.

The Mechs

The most exciting part of the game are the mechs themselves. I designed the mechs to be the enemy of the player. There are three different mechs, each having about 10 frames of animation.

My overall design for the mechs and their functionality included having them start off in a pattern. These patterns are recorded in arrays that have the position of each mech, and the number of mechs for each wave. The mechs then slowly energize onto the screen and then begin their attack. The first phase of their attack is a slow, right-to-left motion. They are, in other words, in a *synchronized flight* state. This is accomplished by moving each mech by the same amount each frame to keep them in synchronization. Then at some point, I wanted them to break away from the group and aggressively attack using some kind of artificial intelligence (AI). When a mech is shot by the player, I wanted it to fizzle away and die.

Animating the Mechs

The mechs have some interesting animation. There are basically two mech states as far as animation is concerned:

- [ ] Marching (in flock state)
- [ ] Flying (in attack state)

When the mechs are marching, they toggle between two frames of animation, frame after frame. The two bit maps for this animation consist of moving the mechs' arms, legs, and heads.

The second interesting animation is done when the mechs attack. I wanted the mechs to look as though they fly in the direction they're moving. To accomplish this, I drew bit maps of the mechs in eight different stages of rotation. Figure 2.6 shows an example of one the mechs in all of its directions.

These eight different bit maps were generated using a single bit map and rotating it in different angles using DPaint. Although bit maps can be rotated algorithmically in real time by the PC, it's a much better idea to pre-rotate and store the bit maps. (The calculations to quickly rotate bit maps are a strain even on a Pentium!) When the mechs attack, the program computes their direction and selects the bit map that would look the most realistic for the direction in which the mech is moving. This makes the mechs look like they're flying toward and away from the player's ship.

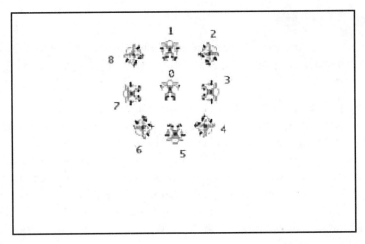

Figure 2.6. *The different rotations of a mech.*

Synthetic Intelligence

The mechs in Mech War have what I call *synthetic intelligence*. The term "artificial intelligence" has, I think, been misused in the past and doesn't do justice to some situations. Synthetic intelligence is real; it's a modeling of something either in nature or based on nature. Artificial intelligence is more of an attempt to trick the player into believing the system is really intelligent. I try to model my game creatures using basic premises of nature: primal instincts, aggression, pain, fear, and so on. I model these elements into algorithms that, when used in a game, create complex behaviors. These behaviors are actually based on simple rules. In Mech War, for example, the mechs follow three simple rules:

☐ Rule 1: Flock together and move in unison.

☐ Rule 2: At a certain time, break off, follow a set of patterns, and attack.

☐ Rule 3: When the attack is done, move back into the flock.

These rules are simple; however, when there are 20 mechs on the screen, it seems as though they're doing much more complex things. In any case, this is the basis of the mechs' intelligence system:

☐ Flocking is accomplished by moving all the mechs the same amount of distance each cycle. When any mech hits the right or left edge of the screen, all mechs are told to reverse their current direction.

☐ Attack mode is implemented by selecting patterns I generated earlier, and then following the instructions in the pattern. The patterns are sequences of directions to take. As the mechs are following the pattern, the code tests to see whether the mech is in the vicinity of the player's ship and if the mech is pointing downward. If both conditions are true, a missile is fired at the player's ship.

Photon Torpedoes

The mechs fire your "run-of-the-mill" photon torpedoes. These torpedoes are blue and move down the screen, toward the player's ship. They're harmless to the mechs themselves, but damaging to both the barriers and the player's ship.

Photon torpedoes are implemented in much the same way as the player's missiles. They move at a certain speed. When they hit an object (or the bottom of the screen), they're removed from the active missile list. The torpedoes are also autonomous: once fired, they execute until stopped, even if the mech that fired the missile in question is destroyed. This brings us to an important point in game design: *object independence*.

Game Law: Make sure that entities that should be self-contained *are* self-contained, and aren't related to the future of the process that started them.

Disintegrating Mechs Without a Mess

All good things must come to an end. This also is true for all bad things (at least, I hope so). At some point, the player is going to hit and destroy a mech. For this I wanted to have an explosion that was more of a disintegration than a blast of particles and fire. I decided to create a function that would fizzle the mechs' bit maps for four frames in randomly selected shades of red. This I accomplished by having the mech's standard bit map filtered

through the following algorithm when a mech is hit:

Algorithm 2.1. Melting a mech away.

```
For (each pixel of the mech's bit map)
{
if the pixel is not black then select a random shade of red
        and plot,
else do nothing.

} // end for
```

That's an easy algorithm! However, the results are visually stunning—at least, I think they are. The melting, or fizzling, occurs for a second or so, and then the mech is taken off the active mech list. In other words, its state becomes "dead."

The Mech Data Structure

The final interesting topic is the data structures used for the mechs. The mechs are fairly simple, and there weren't more than a dozen or so things to track for each mech. For example, we track information such as the position, type, state, velocity, current animation frame, and so on for each mech. Then I created an array with these mech structures that make up the army of mechs.

The interesting aspect of this array is how it's generated. I wanted to somehow start the mechs off in a pattern. I wanted to create a table or array that had the type and position of each mech encoded in some way. In the end, I decided to use a 7×5 array that employs integers to define mechs. I filled the table with the numbers 0–3, where 0 is blank and 1–3 represent the three types of mechs.

The table is processed by a function that computes the position and other data based on the table structure. The mech array is generated from this data. Here's an example of wave 1:

```
int wave_1[PATTERN_X_SIZE*PATTERN_Y_SIZE] = {    0,1,0,0,0,1,0,
                                                 0,0,1,2,1,0,0,
                                                 0,3,3,3,3,3,0,
                                                 0,0,0,0,0,0,0,
                                                 0,0,0,0,0,0,0};
```

If you blur your eyes a bit and look at the table, you can see the mechs in their positions. This is the technique I used to represent all the different waves of mechs.

The Barriers

The barriers are the only thing that stand between the player and the carnage above, as you can see back in Figure 2.1. I designed the barriers for player protection from the onslaught of the mechs. My original idea for the barriers was that they be some kind of orbiting object with little blinking lights (for tracking?), constructed out of pieces of rock connected by some alloy. The final results are OK, but I think they could be better.

The barriers, and their slow destruction, were a bit of a challenge to implement. When a missile strikes the barrier from either side, I wanted a piece of the barrier to be vaporized with a little blast. For that reason, I made sure to draw the barriers using a specific set of colors. The missile program can detect these colors by scanning the area around a missile. If these colors are found to be present, it must mean that the missile has hit a portion of the barrier.

Once a collision between a missile and a barrier is detected, I wanted to have something happen indicating that a chunk of the barrier is destroyed. I did this by randomly plotting 25 black pixels at the point of impact. This had the effect of making each hit look a bit different. Also, to make the hit look more realistic, a little explosion (made out of six frames of animation) also starts at the point of impact. Without this little explosion, it would look funny: a chunk of the barrier would just disappear without fire or debris.

The last neat part about the barriers is the blinking green tracking lights. This is a common effect in video games, and quite cheap computationally. A single color is turned on and off, and anything drawn in this color appears to instantly become visible and then invisible. This is the technique I used: every few frames the lights are toggled, making for a cool effect.

The Starfield

This is really the icing on the cake. The game looked OK, but it needed something to make it look as though it were taking place in outer space. I decided to put a starfield into the game. (I've been on a starfield kick for about six months, so bear with me: throughout the book there are several cases of starfields.) This starfield is implemented by having three collections of moving pixels. Each collection is called a *plane*, and is drawn using a different shade of gray. To simulate the effect of perspective depth, I move each of the star planes at different velocities. This makes the last, darkest plane really look like it's farther away!

The starfield operates completely independent of the game action, no matter what's being shot, blown up, and so on. The stars continue to move, seamlessly. This is important in this kind of animation, which is called *background animation*. Many games have birds flying, or waterfalls, or whatever in the background, which have no purpose other than to increase the realism of the game. However, you must make sure the background animation stops for nothing and doesn't look as though it's linked to the game itself.

The Mothership

The mothership originally was going to be a giant destroyer that came out after each wave was complete. The player would have to destroy the mothership, without being destroyed, to obtain some kind of bonus based on time. However, in the final version of the mothership, and its functionality has been somewhat scaled down—to put it mildly. This is a good example of what happens sometimes in video-game design, or the design of any piece of software. Based on different constraints—time, money, and resources— you may have to deviate from the original plan. But, hey: that's life!

The mothership used in the finished game has the following functionality:

- ☐ It starts at either the right or left side of the screen and progresses at some speed to the opposite side, where it disappears.

- ☐ As the mothership is flying from one edge to another, it follows a sinusoidal pattern. This was accomplished by using the x position, or horizontal position, of the mothership as the parameter for a function that modulates the mothership's y position, or vertical position, by use of a sine wave. In any case, it looks pretty.

The mothership is started during the game play based on a random number. There's roughly a .5-percent chance per frame that a mothership will be started. Moreover, once started, the mothership must complete its cycle or be destroyed before another can start. Therefore there can be only one mothership on the screen at once.

The mothership can be destroyed only by the player, and that takes only a single tachion pulse. When the mothership is hit, a few frames of an explosion are played. That's it.

Testing for Collisions

All collision detection for the entire game is done the same way. These are the collisions that must be tracked:

- ☐ Collisions between a mech's weapons and the player's ship

- ☐ Collisions between the player's weapons and mechs

- ☐ Collisions between the player's weapons and the mothership

- ☐ Barrier collisions with either the player's missile or a mech's missile

Barrier collisions were covered earlier in this chapter, and are done by testing for certain colors used only in composing the barriers. The other forms of collision detection are handled differently.

The basic collision-detection technique used in video games founded on bit-map objects is called the *bounding box technique*. What this means is that we draw an imaginary box around each of the bit maps in the game—such as the player's ship, the missiles, the mechs, and so on—and then do collision tests to see whether these boxes overlap. If they do, there has been a collision.

Using bounding boxes is much easier than using the actual geometry to test for collisions, because object geometry can be quite arbitrary. The only problem with using bounding-box collision detection is that, sometimes, a collision is recorded that didn't really happen, as shown in Figure 2.7.

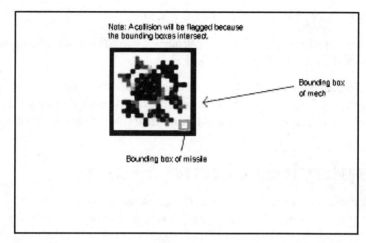

Figure 2.7. *The bounding-box collision problem.*

Here we see a missile that's within the bounding box of a mech, but hasn't hit the mech. However, this was recorded as a hit.

This side effect of bounding boxes is usually acceptable, and hardly ever noticed. If the problem becomes too pronounced, you can artificially make the bounding boxes smaller to help minimize the effect.

 Tip: Testing for collisions of objects in a video game can take much of the processing time that exists in each game cycle. Therefore, your collision-detection algorithms and functions should be as efficient as possible.

Player Input

The input device for Mech War is the keyboard. Although many programmers think reading the keyboard is easy, it's not. Sure, you can use getch(), scanf(), and so on—but not in a video game! We need extremely fast response, and we must be able to track multiple, simultaneous key presses. This can be done only by grabbing the keyboard interrupt and vectoring it to one of our own. In the case of Mech War, we're interested in four keys:

☐ The right and left arrow keys

☐ The spacebar

☐ The Q key

Therefore, I wrote an interrupt routine that would latch onto the keyboard interrupt and track the state of all four of these keys.

Being able to control the keyboard at this level isn't an easy task, and a good understanding of interrupts, timing, and all kinds of other system-level concepts is necessary. We cover them, and master them, in the remainder of this book.

Displaying Game Status

We've covered most of the game elements, but no game is complete without some way to track the score, ships left, energy levels, and so on. In Mech War, there isn't a *lot* to keep track of, but there are a few things. I wanted to track the score and the number of ships left.

This is easy; simply a matter of incrementing or decrementing a variable at the proper time. For instance, when a mech is destroyed, I add 50 to the player's score variable. When the player's ship is destroyed, I decrement the variable that tracks the number of ships. If the player is out of ships, the game is over.

The most interesting status variable is the energy level of the tachion cannons. They can have energy levels from 0–100. When the cannon's energy is at 0, the message CHRG is displayed in red, which means the cannons are charging.

The change in energy level is facilitated by the mean time between weapons discharging. If the player continually fires the weapons, the energy is soon depleted—and the player is left defenseless until the batteries recharge. This is implemented by subtracting a certain number of units from the energy level every time the weapons are fired. Also, when the player isn't firing, the energy level is incremented each frame until it reaches a maximum of 100, which is the upper energy limit.

Finally, all the information is gathered and printed at the bottom of the screen by custom-printing functions that use bit maps for the characters.

Game Law: Never use the C function printf() in a video game unless it's for debugging or something that isn't in the main loop, because printf() is *so slow*.

I had wanted to make the game talk in a sexy voice and say "energy level low" when the energy level reached a certain value. I just couldn't get it to sound right, but it would have been cool!

Screen Transitions

If you've ever watched TV or a movie, you already know what a screen transition is. *Screen transitions* are a pleasing way to change from scene to scene. In Mech War there are two screen transitions:

- [ ] The first screen transition you see is the fading-lights effect at the start of the game (on the introduction screen), used again at the end of the game.

- [ ] The second screen transition is the melting effect that moves from the instructions screen to the game field.

Both these effects were implemented in a dozen or so lines of code. The fading-lights screen transition is implemented by slowly changing all color values on the screen until they all are black. The melting screen transition is done by making a bunch of "worms" march down the screen and eat up the pixels.

The best screen transitions are the ones that are done in the shortest number of lines. We use many different screen transitions in the game we write in this book. One of my favorites is the following. See if you can figure it out:

```
for (index=0; index<300000; index++)
    Plot_Pixel(rand()%SCREEN_WIDTH,rand()%SCREEN_HEIGHT,BLACK);
```

Synchronization to the Video Display

I've been talking in "frames per second" and related phrases. In a video game, the display is updated a certain number of times every second, and that's the maximum speed at which the game will be played. In the case of Mech War, the frame rate is locked at a maximum of 18.2 frames per second. This is done to ensure that, no matter how fast a PC, the game always runs at the same speed.

I accomplished this synchronization using the system timer, which clicks at 18.2 clicks per second. There are other ways to synchronize the video game to the display, such as waiting for the vertical blanking period or using another time base. However, for Mech War, 18.2 frames per second works great.

Wave Control

We've just about covered everything important to your understanding of Mech War now. The last main subject I can think of is the transition from wave to wave, and how that works.

As you know, Mech War is a level-based, or *wave-based*, game. You destroy the mechs on one wave and move to the next. However, there are a few things to consider when changing to the next wave:

- ☐ First, the program must use data structure for the new pattern so the mechs are placed in different starting positions.

- ☐ Second, missiles fired by the player during the start of a wave should be harmless to the mechs because, in terms of the game world, mechs are helpless during their energizing state. The *energizing state* is the phase that you see when the mechs slowly illuminate on the screen, then move into action. This state must continue for a couple of seconds, during which the player can't kill the mechs.

- ☐ Finally, during the start of a wave, a message that displays the current wave number must be placed in the middle of the screen, and then erased when the startup sequence for the wave is complete.

Features of Mech War

To my knowledge, Mech War has no bugs. It's perfect...

Testing the Game

Whenever you write a video game, you should test it to death. (The best testers are young children because they try to make everything in the game do what it's not supposed to do!) I tested Mech War by trying to move the player's ship off the screen, by holding down all the buttons at once, by not shooting any mechs to see what happens, and so on. Simply put, I tried to mess things up as much as possible to see the result.

Another phase of testing is making sure a game runs with different system configurations of drivers and so on. Mech War is so simple it only uses the sound driver ct-voice.drv, and that's about it. Having a bunch of TSR programs installed in your PC during play doesn't seem to bother Mech War at all.

The Mech War Challenge

Well, I hope you've gotten at least a glimmer of what's involved in a small game. Multiply what you've seen here by 1,000 or so, and that's what you face in creating a game such as DOOM from ID Software. However, we have to start somewhere... so I have a little contest for you!

I want you to take Mech War and improve it in any way you wish. Then I want you to take the final game and send it to me. There will be two deadlines each year: June 14 and January 1. I'll take all the submissions and score them for originality and creativity. Then I'll select the version of Mech War I like the best as the winner. I'll send the winner a check for $100. That's right: one hundred dollars!

The complete source and all the libraries and data for Mech War are on the CD-ROM. You can find more information on the structure of the game and where to send your submissions to in Appendix A.

Summary

Wow! There's a lot to a video game, isn't there? (You think this chapter was long? You should see the source code to Mech War!) Anyway, we covered all the main points of a complete video game, one that's at about the same level of complexity as the game we're trying to achieve by the time we complete this book. We discussed all the elements that go into a game, from the artwork and sound to the implementation of all the game elements.

Mech War is just one of the video-game "flavors" that has stood the test of time. There are many more.

Q&A

Q How many lines of code are there in Mech War?

A Mech War has around 5,000 lines of C. This includes the graphics library and the sound library.

Q How long did Mech War take to write, and how long does a seriously awesome game take to write?

A Mech War took about four days to write, with the fifth day for tweaking. A really good video game takes anywhere from three to 18 months to write, and can range from 10,000–200,000 lines of code.

Q **Does Mech War use any assembly language?**

A Yes. It uses some to make calls to the sound library and in a couple of other places, but nothing that couldn't be converted to C without a problem.

Q **Why was the 320×200 mode 13h used for Mech War?**

A It's the easiest and (almost) fastest video mode available to the PC.

Q **You said that you made all the sound effects yourself. How did you make the explosions sound so real?**

A Explosions are just white noise. I would growl and blow into the microphone, record this, and then alter the frequency characteristics of these sounds (along with cutting and pasting) until I had something that sounded like an explosion.

Workshop

The Workshop section presents quiz questions to help you cement your new knowledge and exercises to give you experience using what you've learned. Try to understand the questions and exercises before moving on to the next lesson. The answers are in Appendix B.

Quiz

1. What resolution is Mech War in?

2. What are the functions of PCX files and VOC files?

3. Does Mech War do multitasking?

4. How does the particle explosion for the player's ship work?

5. At how many frames per second does Mech War run?

Exercises

1. Play Mech War until you reach wave 15 and see what happens.

2. Try to edit the PCX files used for Mech War and change some of the imagery for the game. Note: you'll need a program that can read and write 256-color PCX files, such as DPaint.

3. Try to find any bugs in Mech War.

4. If you have a sound editor program that accepts VOC files, try to change the sound effects used in Mech War.

5. Think up an entire game. Write down a list of all the elements in your game, and all their interactions.

2

Painting the Screen
with the VGA Card

Today we delve into the operation and programming of the VGA (Video Graphics Array) card. You must have a good understanding of the major components and operation of the VGA card to create PC games. However, you don't need to know everything about the VGA card or delve too deeply into its internal operations.

The VGA card is so complex that dozens, if not hundreds, of books have been written about it. (I have about 50 of them.) However, we're interested in the VGA card only as an interface to our players. Furthermore, in this book we use mode 13h (the 320×200-pixel, 256-color mode). This mode is easy to understand and program in.

By the end of today you'll have mastered the following topics:

- ☐ Introduction to PC graphics
- ☐ Rendering the screen
- ☐ Inside the VGA card
- ☐ The magical mode 13h
- ☐ Memory configuration
- ☐ Setting the video mode
- ☐ Clearing and filling the video screen
- ☐ Plotting pixels
- ☐ Drawing lines
- ☐ The color palette
- ☐ Programming the color look-up table
- ☐ Color-register effects
- ☐ Bit blitting
- ☐ Text blitting
- ☐ A 3-D starfield
- ☐ Starting our game library
- ☐ Mode X
- ☐ Summary

Introduction to PC graphics

The PC wasn't exactly designed to play video games. As a matter of fact, hardly any of the PC's systems are optimized for real-time graphic simulations such as video games. Although video-game graphics on PCs can seem to be high quality, this is an illusion created through clever use of color and animation.

Not that the PC doesn't have high resolutions available to it. Super VGA systems with appropriate monitors can have resolutions in excess of 1024×1024, with millions of colors. This is great for still images of photorealistic quality and nice-looking user interfaces, but hardly what a video-game programmer needs. For video-game graphics, we need to know only two things:

□ The address of the video buffer

□ How fast we can write to it

A video-game programmer is interested in creating animation. In essence, the game programmer's instructions must update the video screen many times a second while doing the many calculations for the game logic itself. The PC's graphics system isn't designed for this kind of use! When you try to accomplish real-time animation, you quickly realize that the PC can barely hack it. There are many reasons for this, but the factor weighing most is the way the PC's graphics system was designed from the very beginning.

The PC was designed as an open-ended system that allowed many different "feature" cards designed by third parties to be placed in it. One of these feature cards was to be the graphics-adapter card. IBM thought that doing it this way would permit the greatest versatility to the graphics systems. They could have designed a graphics system on the motherboard, but it would probably have become obsolete in time, and would not meet everyone's needs at one time anyway. Alas, they decided to make graphics an add-on feature. This is where the problem occurs. Whatever the graphics adapter may be, from monochrome to Super VGA, it must use the slow AT bus to communicate with the CPU. This means that no matter how fast your PC, you can never write to the video card or update the video screen faster than the AT bus speed.

Recently, local-bus designs have been coming out that allow feature cards to have access to the high-speed bus, and with this configuration graphics are anywhere from 10 to 50 times faster than with the standard AT bus versions. The only problem is, we can't assume that everyone has a local-bus computer and VGA card. We must assume that they have the standard AT bus with a standard VGA card—and we should be grateful for that much! The predecessors to VGA card (CGA and EGA) were nightmares. CGA was a joke, and EGA was nearly impossible to get decent performance out of.

Now let's talk a bit about screen drawing from a hardware point of view.

Rendering the Screen

 Game Law: As a video-game programmer, you must know as much as possible about the hardware for which you're programming. That knowledge can only help you better utilize the computer and extract from it all the performance that's possible.

The VGA card uses a region of memory that holds a special form of the image to be rendered on the screen. This image is drawn on the video screen by the VGA card. The VGA card is connected to the monitor as shown in Figure 3.1.

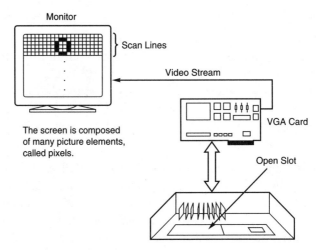

Figure 3.1. *The origins of video.*

Here's how the VGA card and monitor work together to create a final image:

1. The VGA card converts the data in its video memory into electronic signals that are interpreted by the video monitor.

2. The monitor uses this information to render the image on the screen. The image is drawn by an electron gun that excites phosphors on the screen, creating lit pixels.

3. The monitor draws the pixels, one at a time, from left to right and from top to bottom, as shown in Figure 3.2.

The beam scans left to right, then retraces.

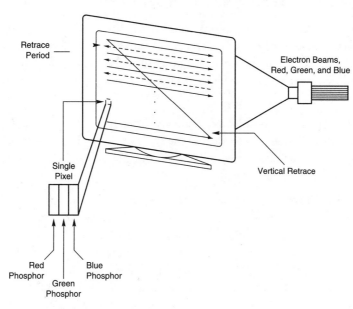

Figure 3.2. *Redrawing the screen.*

Each time a single line of pixels is drawn, the electron gun sweeps back to the left side and draws another line of pixels. The time period the electron gun is sweeping back is called the *horizontal retrace period.*

4. When all the lines of the screen have been rendered, the electron gun retraces all the way back to the top of the screen and starts again. This is called the *vertical retrace period.* In VGA graphics modes, the screen is redrawn 70 times a second, or "at 70Hz."

We're interested in the two retrace periods because when they occur the VGA card is not accessing the video memory. This is a good time to do graphics operations at the best possible speeds. Of course, we can access the video memory any time we wish—but if it's being used by the output hardware at that time, the CPU is put into a "wait state" until the memory becomes available. This is because the CPU and video hardware are both contending for the same region of memory. (We learn more about all this later today, so don't worry if all these new terms and concepts are a little confusing.)

We now know that the VGA card is the hardware responsible for encoding the video memory electronically into an acceptable signal, which the video monitor can use to display the intended image. Now let's see exactly what the VGA card has to offer us.

Inside the VGA Card

The VGA card is fairly complex and has many modes of operation. These modes of operation are based on the way the VGA card accesses video memory, and how the CPU must access video memory. Because the VGA card must be compatible with its predecessors, much of the CGA's and EGA's original architectures were emulated in the VGA card.

Although the VGA card is a completely different beast from the EGA card, its memory-accessing schemes are identical to the EGA card's in all cases—except one, which we get to in a minute. For now, let's cover the general abilities of the VGA card from a programmer's point of view.

The VGA card supports *memory-mapped video*. This means there's a region of memory that you, as the programmer, can alter and then see the results reflected in the video display. The memory starts at address A000:0000h and continues on to A000:FFFFh. That's exactly 64K. However, we know that many VGA cards have at least 256K, and some have up to a megabyte of memory. How is this memory addressed? The answer is that the memory is accessed in *planes*. The EGA card's architecture, which is emulated in the VGA card for upward compatibility, forces a planar memory configuration. Hence, each plane could be 64K, but only 64K of any plane could be accessed at a time. This selectivity is accomplished with a port within the EGA/VGA called the *plane select mask*, shown in Figure 3.3.

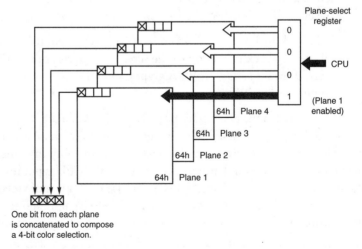

Figure 3.3. *The planar EGA modes.*

We'd really hate to have to write our graphics functions using these modes because the relationship between the image and its planar representation isn't one-to-one.

To get around these planes, we use a special VGA mode called the *chunky bit-map mode*, or mode 13h. This mode supports contiguous video memory, with each pixel being a single byte. We discuss this in a moment, but realize for now that the VGA had to be compatible with the EGA; therefore, there are some features about it that seem inappropriate from a performance point of view.

The next important and interesting asset the VGA card offers is the number of colors it can support. The VGA card is capable of displaying 256 colors at once from a palette of 262,144 colors. Also, the VGA card can initiate interrupts during the horizontal and vertical retrace periods, which is convenient for us.

Finally, the VGA card is a *register-level programmable graphics controller*. This means that you can, if you wish, create new graphics modes and resolutions by programming the internal registers manually. This is beyond the scope of any book I've seen so far (except IBM's own technical reference), and although there have been a few tidbits here and there on creating "hybrid" modes, most people stick with what comes as the standard BIOS video modes.

The Magical Mode 13h

All this talk about planes and slow memory access is starting to depress me. Let's see if there's a bright side to the VGA card. In fact, there is! The VGA card has a special mode that isn't used too often because of its lower resolution. This is mode 13h (also called mode 19, if you like the decimal number system). It's 320×200 pixels and supports 256 colors on the screen at once, as shown in Figure 3.4.

A resolution of 320×200 is grainy by today's standards—but incredible imagery can be rendered with 256 colors. Furthermore, because a video game has lots of animation and movement, it's hard for a player to see this graininess: our brains tend to blur or fix up images that are pixelated. As long as your artwork is good, the 320×200-pixel, 256-color mode is the perfect choice for creating PC-based video games.

Other than all the colors that mode 13h supports, the mode has a memory configuration that's the simplest possible configuration we could ask for. Memory is one long, contiguous array that can be accessed quickly by the CPU. This enables us to write rendering algorithms that are superefficient and fast.

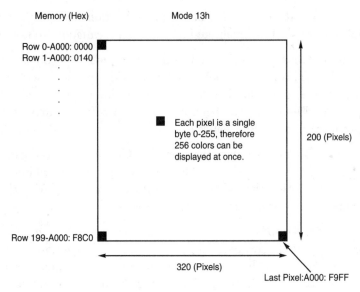

Figure 3.4. *The layout of mode 13h.*

Memory Configuration

The memory configuration of mode 13h is, as we've just learned, one giant array. This array is located at starting address A000:0000h and ends at A000:F9FFh, which is exactly 64,000. The 64,000 is based on the fact that the screen in mode 13h is composed of 200 lines, each being 320 pixels wide. Moreover, each pixel takes exactly one byte. (That's where we get the 64,000: it's the product 320*200.)

So how do we write to video memory? The answer is that we create a FAR pointer to the starting address A000:0000h, and then offset into the video memory to locate the exact pixel we wish to alter. The number you store or retrieve from video memory will always be between 0–255. This is the color of the pixel, which really is an index into a color look-up table. This table has the RGB values that make up the color you see on the screen. This approach is called *color indirection*, shown in Figure 3.5.

More on color indirection later today. I think we're both getting pretty excited over mode 13h, so let's see how we can put the VGA card into that mode.

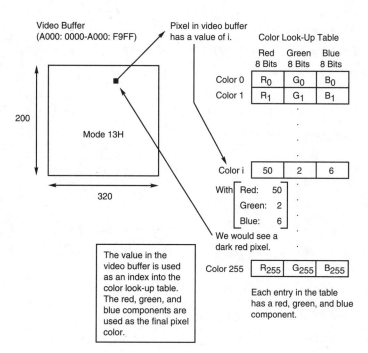

Figure 3.5. *The color-indirection loop.*

Setting the Video Mode

There are numerous ways to put the VGA card into mode 13h:

☐ We can use Microsoft's graphics library.

☐ We could use ROM-BIOS.

☐ We could program all the VGA's registers manually.

I think the easiest way to do it is to use Microsoft's graphics library call `_setvideomode()`, but let's see how to do it using a BIOS call as `setvideomode()` is a Microsoft function. Take a look at Listing 3.1 to see a program that places the VGA card into mode 13h.

Listing 3.1. Setting the video mode (setmodeb.c).

```
// I N C L U D E S ///////////////////////////////////////////

#include <stdio.h>
#include <dos.h>
#include <conio.h>
```

DAY 3

Listing 3.1. continued

```c
// D E F I N E S ///////////////////////////////////////////////

#define VGA256     0x13      // 320x200x256
#define TEXT_MODE 0x03       // The default text mode

// F U N C T I O N S ///////////////////////////////////////////////

void Set_Video_Mode(int mode)
{

// Use video interrupt 10h to set the video mode to the sent
// value.

union REGS inregs,outregs;

inregs.h.ah = 0;                        // Set the video mode
                                        // subfunction.
inregs.h.al = (unsigned char)mode;      // Video mode to which to
                                        // change.

_int86(0x10, &inregs, &outregs);

} // end Set_Video_Mode

/////////////////////////////////////////////////////////////////

void main(void)
{

// Set the video mode to the 320x200, 256-color mode.

Set_Video_Mode(VGA256);

// Wait for a key to be hit.

while(!kbhit()){}

// Put the computer back into text mode.

Set_Video_Mode(TEXT_MODE);

} // end main
```

Setting the video mode is fairly easy with a BIOS call: we simply send the proper mode number and make the call using the C library function _int86().

If you're not familiar with the interrupt function, here's its syntax:

Syntax

If you're not familiar with the interrupt function, here's its syntax:

```
int _int86(int intnum, union _REGS *inregs,
                       union _REGS *outregs);
```

where:

- *intnum* is the interrupt number.

- *inregs* is the values of the 8086 registers on entrance to the call.

- *outregs* is the values of the 8086 registers on exit from the call.

After setting the video mode, you're presented with a black screen. This is hardly exciting, so let's learn how to fill it with something.

Clearing and Filling the Video Screen

The VGA video buffer is nothing more than an array of memory, which we can access as we would any array of memory. To access the video buffer, we merely set a pointer to the start of the video buffer, after which we can do anything we want to the data in the buffer. The following would suffice to get a pointer to the video buffer:

```
char far *video_buffer = (char far)0xA0000000L;
```

This would create a pointer to the video buffer named video_buffer. We can then access the video buffer using the pointer as an array name, such as:

```
video_buffer[offset] = data;
```

If we want to fill the video buffer with a value, all we need do is write a for loop that would set each element in the array to the desired value. This fragment does just that:

```
for (index=0; index<64000; index++)
    video_buffer[index] =color;
```

where *color* is the value with which we want to fill the screen. To clear the screen, we'd usually choose to fill the screen with black (which, traditionally, is 0).

Using a for loop is fine for learning purposes, but hardly the fastest way to do it. We're interested in one thing when it comes to PC-based video games: speed. In all things, we must find a faster way.

We could use pure assembly language, or the in-line assembler, but let's try something a little easier for now. In Listing 3.2 we use one of the memcopy class of functions to clear and set video memory. These functions are translated directly to low-level string- and

memory-move functions, which the 80xxx processor series has specific single instructions to perform. The function in Listing 3.2 fills the video screen.

Listing 3.2. Filling the video screen with a color.

```
#define SCREEN_WIDTH  320
#define SCREEN_HEIGHT 200

void Fill_Screen(int value)
{

// This function uses the "_fmemset" function to fill the video
// buffer with a sent value.

_fmemset(video_buffer,(char)value,SCREEN_WIDTH*SCREEN_HEIGHT+1);

} // end Fill_Screen
```

This function fills the video buffer and, hence, the video screen with any color desired, and does so quickly.

Things are finally getting a bit more exciting! Let's move on to plotting pixels, which is the basis of all graphics engines.

Plotting Pixels

I'm a firm believer in the idea that if you know how to plot a single pixel on the video screen, the rest is easy. To plot pixels on the VGA screen, we must access video memory in such a way that we take into consideration the coordinates we wish to plot. Physically, the VGA system in mode 13h has a resolution of 320×200: that's 320 columns and 200 rows. To plot a pixel, we must be able to calculate the memory address in the video buffer that gets us a pixel plotted in the desired location when we set it. This is easy to do, as shown in Figure 3.6.

Figure 3.7 depicts mode 13h's memory configuration. We see that the coordinate (0,0), or column 0 of row 0, is in the upper-left corner and column 319 of row 199 is in the lower-right corner.

A pixel plotted in the center of the screen would have coordinates (160,100). The layout of the coordinate system in mode 13h is similar to that of quadrant I of the two-dimensional Cartesian coordinate system, except that the y-coordinate is inverted, as shown in Figure 3.8. This is sometimes confusing to newcomers to graphics programming, so keep it in mind.

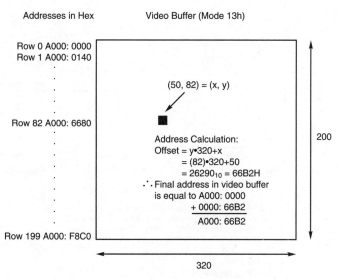

Figure 3.6. *Plotting a pixel in mode 13h with a simple address calculation.*

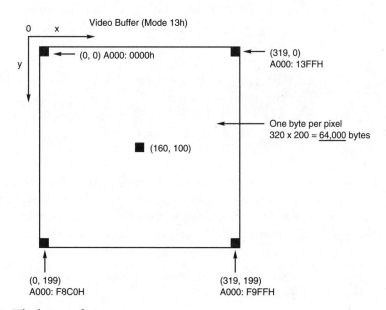

Figure 3.7. *The layout of our universe.*

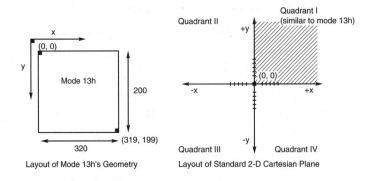

Mode 13h's x- and y- coordinates are almost identical to
Quadrant I of the Cartesian system except that the y-axis
is inverted. The following mapping will suffice to convert
an x and y in the 2-D Cartesian system to Mode 13h.
Given x, y are in 2-D space,

$$\begin{bmatrix} \text{Mode }_{13}(x) = x \\ \text{Mode }_{13}(y) = \max(Y) - y \end{bmatrix}$$

where max(Y) is the largest y coordinate in Mode 13h i.e. 199.

Figure 3.8. *The relationship between mode 13h and the 2-D plane.*

> **Caution:** Many values on computers seem to be off by one. This is called
> the "off-by-one problem." In mode 13h, the screen is 320×200, but the
> actual coordinates are 0–319 and 0–199. If you count from 0–319, you'll
> see that there are 320 values, which is correct.

We know that each pixel on the screen is a single byte. If there are 320 pixels per row,
it would seem reasonable that there are 320 bytes. Therefore, if we multiply the row
number (or y-coordinate) of the desired pixel by 320, we would have a starting address
that began at the desired row. The next question is, what do we do with the column, or
x-coordinate? The answer is to simply add it to the final offset.

Summing up, to plot a pixel on the screen at a position (x,y) with the value of `color`, we
do the following operation:

```
offset = y*320 + x;

video_buffer[offset] = color;
```

That's all there is to it! It's so easy it should be at least a misdemeanor. Now, let's see a
real function that does this. Take a look at Listing 3.3.

Listing 3.3. Plotting a pixel.

```
void Plot_Pixel(int x, int y,char color)
{
// This function plots a pixel on the video screen by
// multiplying the row by 320 and adding the column.

video_buffer[320*y+x] = color;

} // end Plot_Pixel
```

This function does the job. However, we're video-game programmers, and the sight of a multiplication should make your skin crawl! Let's see if we can do something about that. A few days from now we learn a great deal about optimization theory and techniques to use on PC-based video games. For now, though, let's briefly go over little trick to get rid of the multiplication. (Don't worry; we cover it in-depth when we cover fixed-point math. That's on Day 8, in the chapter called "Warp Speed, Anyone?")

Any number can be broken down into a sum of multiples of two. This fact can be used to multiply numbers by using a series of shifts. In this case, we want to multiply y by 320. Noting that 320 is really 256 + 64, we could get the equivalent of y*320 by adding the products of y*256 and y*64.

Now, it may seem as though we have just made the problem more complex. Indeed, we have; however, we have also transformed the multiplicand into a power of 2 and can therefore use a shifting operation to accomplish multiplication.

 Tip: Given an n-digit binary number, shifting to the right by a single bit is equivalent to dividing by 2, and shifting to the left by a single bit is equivalent to multiplying by 2.

Using this interesting mathematical fact, we can now access the screen much faster. Our new pixel plotting function now looks like the one in Listing 3.4

Listing 3.4. Plotting a pixel using shifting.

```
void Plot_Pixel_Fast(int x,int y, char color)
{

// This function plots the pixel in the desired color a little
// quicker using binary shifting to accomplish the
// multiplications.
```

continues

```
// Use the fact that 320*y = 256*y + 64*y = y<<8 + y<<6.

video_buffer[((y<<8) + (y<<6)) + x] = color;

} // end Plot_Pixel_Fast
```

In general, we try to use shifting to accomplish multiplication whenever possible, especially during time-critical operations such as accessing the video buffer.

Drawing Lines

Now that we can plot pixels, the next logical step would be to draw lines. Figure 3.9 shows the representation of a line in mode 13h.

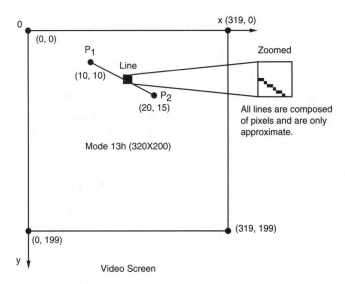

Figure 3.9. *The representation of a line in mode 13h.*

In general, a line is a geometric entity that connects two points in a plane. In our case, a line is a collection of pixels on the screen that approximate a perfect line. The monitor and VGA card have a finite resolution; therefore, they can never render a perfect line, but they can produce a line that is reasonably close to ideal.

Drawing lines on a computer may seem like a simple task; it's not. There was much research done on this topic in the early days of computer graphics. In the end, a computer

scientist named Bresenham conceived an algorithm that would allow a computer to quickly draw a line between any two points. At this point in our studies we're not interested in learning how this algorithm works. When we discuss polygon-based graphics on Day 5 (in the chapter called "Polygon Engines"), we learn the math and implementation details of Bresenham's algorithm.

Another factor to consider when writing PC-based video games is that most of the imagery consists of bit-mapped graphics and is not based on lines. By *bit-mapped graphics* I mean 2-D images drawn as a collection of pixels, not as lines.

In fact, not many video games use lines or polygon-based graphics anymore. Most games are purely bit-mapped. However, 3-D games make a lot of use of polygons, so we cover it. There are two cases of lines that are easy to implement, and we take a look at those right now.

Drawing vertical or horizontal lines is easy because the change in x or y is always constant; that is, the next pixel of the line is either to the right or left of the last pixel, or above or below the last pixel. To write a function that successfully draws horizontal or vertical lines, we must have the function to execute a loop of some kind from the initial point, P1, to the destination point, P2. As the function iterates from one point to another, it uses a pixel-plotting function to plot each pixel along the line from P1 to P2. Listing 3.5 contains functions that draw vertical and horizontal lines.

Listing 3.5. Drawing special cases of lines.

```
//////////////////////////////////////////////////////////////////

H_Line(int x1,int x2,int y,unsigned int color)
{
// This function draws a horizontal line useing the memset
// function. Note: x2 > x1.

_fmemset((char far *)(video_buffer + ((y<<8) + (y<<6)) + x1),
         color,x2-x1+1);

} // end H_Line

//////////////////////////////////////////////////////////////////

V_Line(int y1,int y2,int x,unsigned int color)
{
// Draw a vertical line. Note: y2 > y1.

unsigned int line_offset,
                  index;

// Compute the starting position.
```

continues

Listing 3.5. continued

```
line_offset = ((y1<<8) + (y1<<6)) + x;

for (index=0; index<=y2-y1; index++)
    {
    video_buffer[line_offset] = color;

     line_offset+=320; // Move to the next line.

    } // end for index

} // end V_Line
```

In Listing 3.5, notice how the `H_Line()` function uses the `_fmemset()` function to draw the line. This works in the case of a horizontal line because there's exactly one byte per pixel. As an example, say the line is to be drawn from (10,10) to (20,10). The line would be horizontal and have a y-coordinate of 10. To draw the line on the screen, we'd need to fill in the pixels on row 10 within the video buffer at a starting x of 10 and an ending x of 20. This can be accomplished fastest by using one of the `memset` functions, such as `_fmemset()`. (You must use the FAR version of the function because the pointer to the video buffer is a FAR pointer; that is, a full, 32-bit address composed of both a segment and offset.)

> **Warning:** The PC has *segmented architecture*. This means that the memory is segmented into blocks of 64K each. Many programmers who have used other "flat-model" systems tend to make pointer errors because of this. Remember: for many functions it makes a difference whether you use the NEAR or FAR version of the function.

The function `V_Line()` is a little different. We can't really draw a line vertically by using a memory-movement function because each row differs in the video buffer by 320 bytes, as shown in Figure 3.10.

This is unfortunate, because many games have a lot of vertical symmetry. (I sometimes feel like rotating the monitor 90 degrees and writing a game for the PC that way. Anyway...) The only way to draw a vertical line is to find the starting address in screen memory and then add 320 to it to move to the next pixel to be drawn in the vertical line.

The `V_Line()` function is, unfortunately, as fast as it's going to get for today. We could use registers for the variable and so on, but in general there isn't any magical insight that will speed it up.

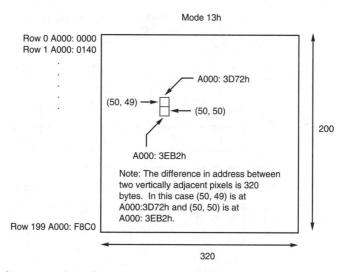

Figure 3.10. *Plotting pixels to draw a vertical line, and the relationship to memory.*

However, the H_Line() function has quite an interesting opportunity hiding within the code. H_Line() uses BYTE-sized memory accesses because it's based on the _fmemset() function. There's no reason we can't use WORD-sized writes to speed things up. To do this we have to realize that writing a WORD to the video buffer is equivalent to writing two pixels. We must take this into consideration when writing an optimized function that draws a horizontal line. Such a function breaks the line up into pairs of two pixels and then deals with the endpoints separately, as shown in Figure 3.11.

If you're wondering why we even care about an issue as insignificant as speeding up our horizontal-line algorithm, consider this: say we have to draw thousands of lines per second. Although the standard H_Line() works fine on a 486 33MHz, on a 386 50MHz it's too slow to run the game at a reasonable rate. If we could get it up to twice the speed, a game that uses the function would run at an acceptable rate. This is the reason for writing fast, efficient code. Sure, most algorithms will run fast on a 586—but we can't count on having a 586. We must program in such a way that our algorithms are as simple and fast as possible. By using WORD-sized writes instead of BYTE-sized writes in the previous example, we should be able to obtain a 100-percent speed increase. That's definitely worth it.

We cover optimizations on Day 8 (in the chapter called "Warp Speed, Anyone?"), but we can't afford to program inefficiently at any time. The new horizontal-line function, shown in Listing 3.6, is called H_Line_Fast(). It uses WORD-sized writes to access the video buffer, and thus is twice as fast as the BYTE version. Study the code carefully and try to understand how the line is drawn.

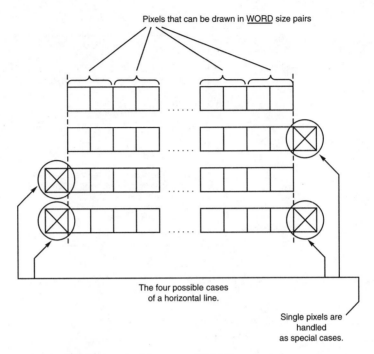

Figure 3.11. *Drawing a horizontal line, one WORD at a time.*

Listing 3.6. A faster `H_Line` function.

```
//////////////////////////////////////////////////////////////

H_Line_Fast(int x1,int x2,int y,unsigned int color)
{
// A fast horizontal line renderer uses WORD-sized writes
// instead of BYTE-sized writes. The only problem is that the
// endpoints of the h line must be taken into account. Test
// whether the endpoints of the horizontal line are on WORD
// boundaries; that is, that they are evenly divisible by 2.
// Basically, we must consider the two endpoints of the line
// separately if we want to write WORDs at a time (or, in other
// words, two pixels at a time). Note: x2 > x1.

unsigned int first_word,
             middle_word,
               last_word,
             line_offset,
                  index;
```

```
// Test the 1's bit of the starting x.

if ( (x1 & 0x0001) )
   {

   first_word = (color<<8);

   } // end if starting point is on a word boundary
else
   {
   // Replicate color into both bytes.
   first_word = ((color<<8) | color);

   } // end else

// Test the 1's bit of the ending x.

if ( (x2 & 0x0001) )
   {

   last_word = ((color<<8) | color);

   } // end if ending point is on a word boundary
else
   {
   // Place color in high byte of word only.

   last_word = color;

   } // end else

// Now we can draw the horizontal line two pixels at a time.

line_offset = ((y<<7) + (y<<5));
// y*160, because there are 160 words/line

// Compute the middle color.

middle_word = ((color<<8) | color);

// Left endpoint

video_buffer_w[line_offset + (x1>>1)] = first_word;

// The middle of the line

for (index=(x1>>1)+1; index<(x2>>1); index++)
    video_buffer_w[line_offset+index] = middle_word;

// Right endpoint

video_buffer_w[line_offset + (x2>>1)] = last_word;

} // end H_Line_Fast
```

In addition to understanding the algorithmic operation of H_Line_Fast(), I want you to note a detail about the program. Instead of accessing the video buffer with a char pointer, the program accesses the video buffer with an int pointer by way of the variable video_buffer_w. This is so the proper pointer arithmetic is done when the variable is indexed as an array.

> **Caution:** Remember that the final memory offset accessed by a pointer that's indexed by a variable is that variable times the size of the element being pointed to. Therefore, if you have an int pointer and you index into the fifth element, you'll really get the tenth byte, because 5*2 = 10!

We learn how to draw general lines in Day 5 (in the chapter called "Polygon Engines"), but for now the two special cases of horizontal and vertical lines demonstrate the tactics to use when accessing the video buffer.

Next, let's move on to the color palette.

The Color Palette

In mode 13h there are 256 displayable colors. These colors are selected from a palette of 262,144 colors by a method called *color indirection*. This is how it works: the VGA card has a set of registers, called *color registers*. Together, these registers form what's called the *color look-up table*. When you plot a pixel on the screen, a value in the range from 0–255 is placed into the video buffer. This value is not the true color you wish displayed. (If it were, there would only be 256 colors available.) The number you stuff into the video buffer, from 0–255, is only the *color index*, not the color itself.

This index tells the VGA card to look in the appropriate color register, take the color in that register, and display it on the screen, as shown in Figure 3.12.

This technique is analogous to having a collection of buckets, each filled with paint. When your hypothetical house painter says, "I want bucket 26," he doesn't mean that he wants the number 26 to be interpreted as some kind of final color value. He just wants to use the paint in bucket 26.

Having this kind of scheme makes a lot of neat effects possible. If we wish to make something glow, instead of manipulating the data in the video buffer (as many other video systems require) we can change the color of the "electronic" paint in the bucket (that is, the color register). During the next video frame anything drawn with that color register or color index changes to the new color!

The VGA card has 256 color registers. Each register is composed of three elements: the red, green, and blue components of the color desired, as shown in Figure 3.13.

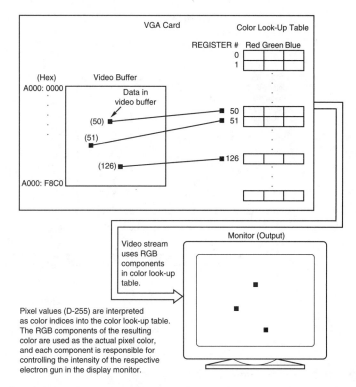

Figure 3.12. *The VGA card interpreting screen data and processing it into a final image.*

If we wanted to have color register 50 be pure blue, we would place a value into the blue element of color register 50, and set the other two elements (which represent the red and green components) to zero.

Together, all the 256 color registers make up what's referred to as the *color palette*. The color palette is used to create all the imagery and objects within a video game. Therefore, you must take care in designing your color palette so your artwork looks its best.

Warning: Although it's possible to reprogram the color palette with a new set of colors as a game is running (for example, to reflect changes in the environment), you must use caution. When a palette register is changed, all imagery drawn with that color register changes based on the new color palette. Undesired effects can occur if you're not careful.

Now that we have a general overview of the color look-up table and its uses, let's see exactly how we can program it and use colors to enhance our games.

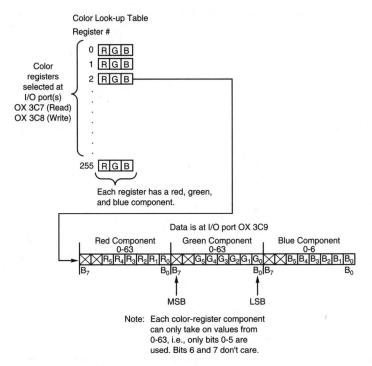

Figure 3.13. *The details of the color look-up table.*

Programming the Color Look-Up Table

The color look-up table is a collection of 256 registers on board the VGA card. Each register is composed of three elements: one element for each of the colors red, green, and blue. (Although these aren't the primary colors, every color you see on the screen is some combination of these, plus black and white.) Each element is, in turn, encoded as a single byte and can therefore take on values from 0–255.

This is a bit misleading. In actuality, there can be only 64 shades each of red, green, or blue. Only the first six bits of each color element are used, as shown in Figure 3.14.

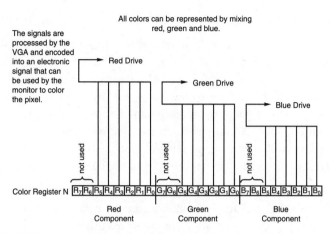

Figure 3.14. *The VGA card encoding the video data in a single color register.*

This is where the total number of 262,144 colors comes from. It's the result of three six-bit registers, or 2^{18}, which is 262,144. Each element is eight bits wide, or a single byte, making the addressing of each color element easier.

It'd be great if we could access these registers at some memory location. We can't. They're accessed by way of I/O ports located on the VGA card. There are four I/O ports with which we must concern ourselves. They are:

```
#define PALETTE_MASK         0x3C6
#define PALETTE_REGISTER_RD  0x3C7
#define PALETTE_REGISTER_WR  0x3C8
#define PALETTE_DATA         0x3C9
```

Remapping the color palette, or a portion of it, is easy. We simply access the color register and change the red, green, and blue components.

To access a register by way of an I/O port, we use the following scheme:

1. Before we do anything, we must place an 0×FFh in the PALETTE_MASK port. This enables us to access all color registers.

2. Next, we tell the VGA card which color register we wish to access. Depending on the operation we're doing (that is, READ or WRITE), we use one of two ports:

   If we wish to write a color register, we place the index of the register we wish to write in the PALETTE_REGISTER_WR port.

   Conversely, if we want to read a color register, we place the index of the color register we want to read in the PALETTE_REGISTER_RD port.

At this point the proper color register is selected for either reading or writing.

The next question is, how do we access the three components of the color register? As we've said, the red, green, and blue components of each register are each a single byte wide. To read or write them in an efficient manner, the VGA card does a little trick. Once we've selected the register to read or write (by naming the `PALETTE_REGISTER_RD` or `PALETTE_REGISTER_WR` port), we can read or write the data a byte at a time—the trick—through the `PALETTE_DATA` port. In the case of writing to a color register, if you had selected register 56 by writing to the `PALETTE_REGISTER_WR` port, you would execute three separate writes to change the elements of the color register.

You would write the red, green, and then blue component to the same place; that is, the `PALETTE_DATA` port. Once you have selected a color register for reading or writing, the VGA card expects you to always write or read three bytes from this port. (I know this seems a little confusing, but that's what we have to work with.)

To reiterate: once you've selected the color register to access, you *must* read three bytes from or write three bytes to the `PALETTE_DATA` register. Otherwise, the VGA card is put into an unpredictable state.

I've written functions that both read and write to a color register. These functions are based on a simple data structure that holds an RGB triple representing a color. Here's the data structure:

```
// This structure holds an RGB triple in three bytes.

typedef struct RGB_color_typ
        {

        unsigned char red;     // Red component of color 0-63
        unsigned char green;   // Green component of color 0-63
        unsigned char blue;    // Blue component of color 0-63

        } RGB_color, *RGB_color_ptr;
```

The two functions that read and write color registers are shown in Listing 3.7.

Listing 3.7. Functions to access the color registers.

```
void Set_Palette_Register(int index, RGB_color_ptr color)
{

// This function sets a single color look-up table value indexed
// by index with the value in the color structure.

// Tell the VGA card we're going to update a palette register.

_outp(PALETTE_MASK,0xff);
```

```
// Tell the VGA card which register we'll be updating.

_outp(PALETTE_REGISTER_WR, index);

// Now update the RGB triple. Note: the same port is used
// each time.

_outp(PALETTE_DATA,color->red);
_outp(PALETTE_DATA,color->green);
_outp(PALETTE_DATA,color->blue);

 // end Set_Palette_Color

/////////////////////////////////////////////////////////////////

void Get_Palette_Register(int index, RGB_color_ptr color)
{

// This function gets the data out of a color look-up register
// and places the data into color

// Set the palette mask register.

_outp(PALETTE_MASK,0xff);

// Tell the VGA card which register we'll be reading.

_outp(PALETTE_REGISTER_RD, index);

// Now extract the data.

color->red   = _inp(PALETTE_DATA);
color->green = _inp(PALETTE_DATA);
color->blue  = _inp(PALETTE_DATA);

} // end Get_Palette_Color
```

The functions in Listing 3.7 take as parameters:

☐ An index to the color register

☐ A pointer to an RGB_color structure that should be used to set a register, or as
an area to receive the elements out of a selected color register.

Warning: Some VGA cards have a problem if you write to the color registers
too fast. This problem usually occurs when an entire palette is updated. Try
to put a few wait states or delays into your palette-update function if you're
reprogramming the entire palette (or large portions of it) at a time.

Now that we know how to access the color registers and change them to any value we wish, let's see why we would want to do this.

Color-Register Effects

Having the ability to change the color registers directly allows many special effects that normally would be impossible to accomplish. For example, say we used color 25 to paint all the eyes of some creatures in a game. Then, if we wanted to make all of them glow, we could simply write a function that periodically changed the value of color register 25. Everything drawn in this color would automatically change instantaneously when the RGB values in the color register changed.

Another effect that can be accomplished with color registers is lighting. Say there's a side view of a street, and within the imagery of the street there's a street lamp shining down on a specific portion of the street. Now imagine that we want the street light to flicker, and we wish to exaggerate this flicker by changing the color of the road under the light to look as though its luminosity has changed as a result of the flickering light. We could accomplish this by using two or more color registers: one for the light itself, and a couple more for the gray-looking asphalt of the road under the light. To do the animation we could write a function that randomly changed the overall intensity of the light's color register along with the color registers used to draw the street.

As another example of the use of color registers, we can do a trick called *color rotation* or *color cycling* to accomplish movement or animation without moving the actual data of the image around. The technique is to draw an object using a specific color register, then draw the object again in a different position using another color register and, finally, draw the object yet again using yet another color register. If each of the color registers had green in them, for example, we'd see three green objects that looked alike in different positions on the screen, as shown in Figure 3.15.

However, what would happen if we sequentially turned each color register on and off? Well, the object would look as though it was moving. This is the premise behind color-register animation, which we go into in depth on Day 6 (in the chapter called "Real-Time Animation and Effects"). For now, know that color registers afford us many interesting effects in video games: blinking lights, fading screens, morphing objects, and more!

To help you get an idea of the sheer number of colors the PC is capable of, I've created a program that builds a palette of reds, greens, blues, and grays. This program, shown in Listing 3.8, then uses the technique of color rotation to make the colors move. Algorithm 3.1 shows the color rotation algorithm.

Algorithm 3.1. A color-rotation algorithm.

```
first_color = Get_Color_Register(start_color);

for (index=start_color; index<end_color; index++)
    {
    // Move the (N+1)th color registerinto the Nth color
    // register.
    Set_Color_Register(index,Get_Color_Register(index+1));
    } // end for

// At this point we moved all the color registers one to the
// left, but we must now place the first saved color register at
// the end so that the cycle is complete.

Set_Color_Register(index,first_color);
```

3

The pseudofunctions `Set_Color_Register()` and `Get_Color_Register()` are set and return the value of the color register sent in the index.

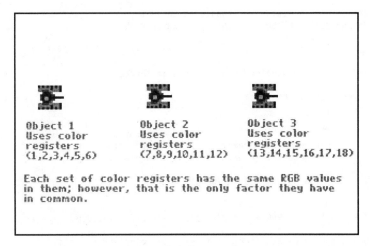

Figure 3.15. *Three tanks, each drawn with different color registers.*

Now, for some action! The program in Listing 3.8 creates the new color palette with all the reds, greens, blues, and grays. It creates a perspective view of a road—well, at least it's supposed to look like a road—and then uses color rotation to cycle the colors. To exit the program, press any key.

Listing 3.8. A color-rotation demo (colorrot.c).

```
// I N C L U D E S ///////////////////////////////////////////////

#include <io.h>
#include <conio.h>
#include <stdio.h>
#include <stdlib.h>
#include <dos.h>
#include <bios.h>
#include <fcntl.h>
#include <memory.h>
#include <math.h>
#include <string.h>

// D E F I N E S ////////////////////////////////////////////////

#define VGA256          0x13
#define TEXT_MODE       0x03

#define PALETTE_MASK        0x3c6
#define PALETTE_REGISTER_RD 0x3c7
#define PALETTE_REGISTER_WR 0x3c8
#define PALETTE_DATA        0x3c9

#define SCREEN_WIDTH    (unsigned int)320
#define SCREEN_HEIGHT   (unsigned int)200

// S T R U C T U R E S /////////////////////////////////////////////

// This structure holds an RGB triple in three bytes.

typedef struct RGB_color_typ
        {

        unsigned char red;    // Red component of color 0-63
        unsigned char green;  // Green component of color 0-63
        unsigned char blue;   // Blue component of color 0-63

        } RGB_color, *RGB_color_ptr;


// P R O T O T Y P E S /////////////////////////////////////////////

void Set_Palette_Register(int index, RGB_color_ptr color);

void Get_Palette_Register(int index, RGB_color_ptr color);

void Create_Cool_Palette(void);

void H_Line(int x1,int x2,int y,unsigned int color);

// G L O B A L S ////////////////////////////////////////////////

unsigned char far *video_buffer = (char far *)0xA0000000L;
// vram byte ptr
```

```
// F U N C T I O N S ///////////////////////////////////////////////

void Set_Palette_Register(int index, RGB_color_ptr color)
{

// This function sets a single color look-up table value indexed
// by index with the value in the color structure.

// Tell the VGA card we're going to update a palette register.

_outp(PALETTE_MASK,0xff);

// Tell the VGA card which register we'll be updating.

_outp(PALETTE_REGISTER_WR, index);

// Now update the RGB triple. Note: the same port is used
// each time.

_outp(PALETTE_DATA,color->red);
_outp(PALETTE_DATA,color->green);
_outp(PALETTE_DATA,color->blue);

} // end Set_Palette_Color

/////////////////////////////////////////////////////////////////

void Get_Palette_Register(int index, RGB_color_ptr color)
{

// This function gets the data out of a color look-up register
// and places the data into color

// Set the palette mask register.

_outp(PALETTE_MASK,0xff);

// Tell the VGA card which register we'll be reading.

_outp(PALETTE_REGISTER_RD, index);

// Now extract the data.

color->red   = _inp(PALETTE_DATA);
color->green = _inp(PALETTE_DATA);
color->blue  = _inp(PALETTE_DATA);

} // end Get_Palette_Color

/////////////////////////////////////////////////////////////////

void Create_Cool_Palette(void)
{
// This function creates a nifty palette: 64 shades of gray, 64
// of red, 64 of green, and 64 of blue.
```

continues

Listing 3.8. continued

```
RGB_color color;

int index;

// swipe through the color registers and create four banks
// of 64 colors each.

for (index=0; index < 64; index++)
    {
    // These are the grays:

    color.red   = index;
    color.green = index;
    color.blue  = index;

    Set_Palette_Register(index, (RGB_color_ptr)&color);

    // These are the reds:

    color.red   = index;
    color.green = 0;
    color.blue  = 0;

    Set_Palette_Register(index+64, (RGB_color_ptr)&color);

    // These are the greens:

    color.red   = 0;
    color.green = index;
    color.blue  = 0;

    Set_Palette_Register(index+128, (RGB_color_ptr)&color);

    // These are the blues:

    color.red   = 0;
    color.green = 0;
    color.blue  = index;

    Set_Palette_Register(index+192, (RGB_color_ptr)&color);

    } // end index

// Make color 0 black.

color.red   = 0;
color.green = 0;
color.blue  = 0;

Set_Palette_Register(0, (RGB_color_ptr)&color);

} // end Create_Cool_Palette

/////////////////////////////////////////////////////////////////
```

```
void Set_Video_Mode(int mode)
{

// Use video interrupt 10h to set the video mode to the sent
// value.

union REGS inregs,outregs;

inregs.h.ah = 0;                    // Set the video mode
                                    // subfunction.
inregs.h.al = (unsigned char)mode;  // Video mode to which to
                                    // change.

_int86(0x10, &inregs, &outregs);

} // end Set_Video_Mode

/////////////////////////////////////////////////////////////////

void H_Line(int x1,int x2,int y,unsigned int color)
{
// Draw a horizontal line using the memset function. Note:
// x2 > x1.

_fmemset((char far *)(video_buffer + ((y<<8) + (y<<6)) + x1),
         color,x2-x1+1);

} // end H_Line

//M A I N /////////////////////////////////////////////////////

void main(void)
{

int index,          // Loop var.
    x1=150,         // x1 and x2 are the edges of the current
                    // piece of the road.
    x2=170,
    y=0,            // y is the current y position of the piece
                    // of the road.
    curr_color=1;   // The current color being drawn.

RGB_color color,color_1;

// Set the video mode to the 320x200, 256-color mode.

Set_Video_Mode(VGA256);

// Create the color palette.

Create_Cool_Palette();

printf("Press any key to exit.");

// Draw a road to nowhere.
```

continues

Listing 3.8. continued

```
for (y=80; y<200; y++)
    {
    // Draw the next horizontal piece of road.

    H_Line(x1,x2,y,curr_color);

    // Make the road wider.

    if (-x1 < 0)
       x1=0;

    if (++x2 > 319)
       x2=319;

    // Next color, please.

    if (++curr_color>255)
       curr_color=1;

    } // end for

// Wait for the user to press a key.

while(!kbhit())
    {
    Get_Palette_Register(1,(RGB_color_ptr)&color_1);

    for (index=1; index<=254; index++)
        {
        Get_Palette_Register(index+1,(RGB_color_ptr)&color);
        Set_Palette_Register(index,(RGB_color_ptr)&color);

        } // end for

        Set_Palette_Register(255,(RGB_color_ptr)&color_1);

    } // end while

// Put the computer back into text mode.

Set_Video_Mode(TEXT_MODE);

} // end main
```

Building an Executable: To make an executable file of the program in Listing 3.8, you can type it in or use the source on the companion CD. The name of the source is colorrot.c. The precompiled executable is named colorrot.exe. I suggest the following compile line for Microsoft C:

```
cl -AM -Zi -c  -Fc -Gs -G2 colorrot.c
```

> This tells the compiler to use the MEDIUM memory model (which we always use), include debugger information, remove stack probes, allow 286 in-line instructions, and use the default warning level.
>
> After compiling the program in this manner you can link it to the standard libraries to create an executable file.

Notice that the program in Listing 3.8 uses many of the functions that we've seen and built up today. Soon we'll have to figure out a plan to place these functions into a general library, to which we can keep adding, so that things don't start getting out of hand!

The next topic of discussion is bit blitting.

Bit Blitting

Bit blitting is the main technique used to draw images in a video game. (The term *blitting* is taken from "block image transferring.") A long time ago, games were more vector- or line-based than bit-map based. This was because of the slow speed of *pixel-blasting* operations (that is, actually drawing the dots on the screen). Today, everything we see on the video display is usually a bit map of some sort, and video games are no different. The game objects and backgrounds are bit maps of differing sizes.

These bit maps are really 2-D matrices with the color information for each row of the object encoded in some manner. In the case of mode 13, there's a single byte for each pixel. Hence, if we wanted a bit map of a creature that was 32×32 pixels, it would take up 32*32, or 1024, bytes per image.

Bit maps are usually represented by one-dimensional arrays of memory, because using a 2-D array would be too slow. Therefore, storing bit maps is easy. This code fragment creates an abstract bit-map structure for an object 16×16 pixels in size:

```
#define BITMAP_HEIGHT 16
#define BITMAP_WIDTH 16

unsigned char far *bitmap;

bitmap = (unsigned char far *)
         _fmalloc(BITMAP_WIDTH * BITMAP_HEIGHT);
```

Once we have a pointer to a region of allocated memory, we can load into it the data for the appropriate bit map.

Figure 3.16 shows an example bit map (this one of a robot) and the associated data.

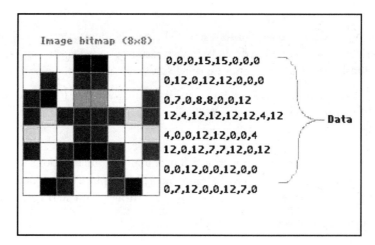

Figure 3.16. *An 8×8 bit-mapped object and its data.*

After deciding on the data structures for bit maps, we'd like to be able to do a few things with them. We want to be able to both paste a bit map on the screen and scan one from the screen. These two operations are all we need to accomplish animation, which we discuss on Day 4 ("Getting Sprite to the Point").

The theory and practice of bit maps and bit blitting are so important to a video-game programmer that a term has been given to the objects that are bit blitted in a video game. That term is *sprites*, and we cover sprites in depth (along with how to animate them) tomorrow and on Day 6 in "Real-Time Animation and Effects." For now, you need only understand the general use of bit blitting.

To refresh your memory, bit blitting is the movement of pixel-based data to or from the video buffer. This data is usually some kind of image or object that we wish displayed or scanned from the video buffer. In the case of a video game, we're mostly interested in moving around and displaying game objects, so this is the main purpose of writing code to do bit blitting.

Text Blitting

Bit blitting is a general technique of drawing a matrix of pixels on the video screen, but it can be used for images other than game objects. For example, bit blitting is used to draw characters on the screen so we can print out text to display game status. Remember that when we're in graphics mode and the game is running, we can't just use printf() to display text; we must do it ourselves. We must learn where we get the bit maps for the ASCII character, and then how to print them on the screen.

Before we discuss how text is drawn on the screen in a graphics mode, let's consider how it's drawn in a text mode. When the VGA card is in a text mode, such as the one you see in DOS's command-line editor, the video buffer is set up differently from the way it is in a graphics mode. In a text mode, the screen is defined as a 2-D matrix of characters and attributes. As an example, let's analyze the standard 80×25-character mode DOS operates in.

In the 80×25 text mode, there are two bytes for each displayed character:

☐ One byte describes the ASCII code of the character to be displayed.

☐ The other byte in the pair describes the color and style attributes of the character.

Therefore, there are 160 bytes per row of characters. The organization of the video buffer for a text mode is shown in Figure 3.17.

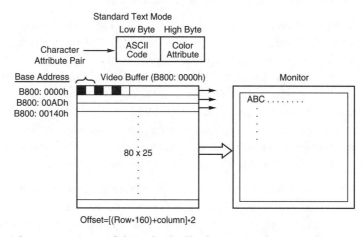

Figure 3.17. *The organization of the video buffer for text modes.*

Note that the text-video buffer is at a different base memory location than the buffer for the pixel-based graphics modes. I'm belaboring text mode to get the point across that letters you see in graphics mode are merely bit maps that look like the desired characters. Neither the operating system nor the VGA card has a clue that you're printing alphabetic characters.

When the VGA card is in a character mode, it *does* know you're printing characters, and interprets the data in the video buffer as ASCII codes along with attributes. It's wonderful that the VGA card has pure text modes; it allows us to write applications that can render text fast—if text is all we need.

Now, let's dig a little deeper into how the text modes work. When the VGA card begins to draw the screen at the beginning of a frame, it looks into the video buffer and gets the next row of characters to be printed. The problem is that the VGA card has no idea what any of the ASCII codes look like. The VGA card just knows that it needs to print each character represented by the ASCII codes.

Ultimately, the VGA card needs to have a pixel-based or bit-mapped representation of each character in the ASCII set so that it can create the proper video stream to send to the monitor. This is where things get interesting.

We could go ahead and draw out all of the characters in the ASCII set in our own font, and this is what's done in many applications. For now, though, it'd be nice if we could somehow find where the bit maps for the character sets are located in memory. Once we found the data, we could write a function that could "draw" a character in a graphics mode, pixel by pixel, by using this data. Then we could use the function that draws a single character to draw strings of characters, and so on.

It so happens that the data for the 8-point ASCII font (the 8×8 ROM character set) can be found in ROM at base address 0×F000:FA6E. We need only figure out how the data is stored, and then come up with an algorithm to access it in such a way that we can bit blit a character quickly on the screen in any color. It turns out that the data is in ASCII order and, because each character is 8×8, each character takes exactly eight bytes of storage (each row is encoded as a single byte). To find a particular character, we simply multiply the ASCII code by 8 and add that to the base offset of 0×F000:FA6E. The eight bytes starting at the resulting location are the data bytes that make up the bit map of the character. Take a look at Figure 3.18 to see this graphically.

In a text-based mode, you can only print characters at specific boundaries, because characters cannot overlap. In a graphics mode, there are no such constraints. Moreover, because the characters are bit maps, we can make them any color(s) we want, and do weird things to them (such as stretching and so on). We need only two functions to be able to print text in a graphics mode: one to print a single character and another to call the single character function with the characters of a whole string. Listing 3.9 contains the function to print a single character.

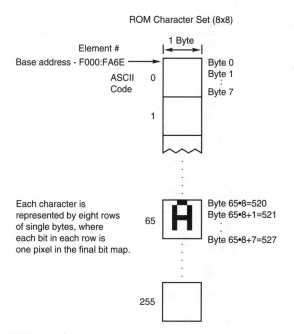

ROM Character Set (8x8)

Figure 3.18. *The 8×8 ROM character set.*

Listing 3.9. Printing a single character in mode 13h.

```
// "Defines" are used for width and height so that different
// character sizes can be used in the future.

#define CHAR_HEIGHT 8
#define CHAR_WIDTH 8

void Blit_Char(int xc,int yc,char c,int color,int trans_flag)
{
// This function uses the ROM 8x8 character set to blit a
// character on the video screen. Notice the trick used to
// extract bits out of each character byte that comprises
// a line.

int offset,x,y;
char far *work_char;
unsigned char bit_mask = 0x80;

// Compute the starting offset in the ROM character look-up
// table.

work_char = rom_char_set + c * CHAR_HEIGHT;

// Compute the offset of the character in the video buffer.
```

continues

Listing 3.9. continued

```
offset = (yc << 8) + (yc << 6) + xc;

for (y=0; y<CHAR_HEIGHT; y++)
    {
    // Reset the bit mask.

    bit_mask = 0x80;

    for (x=0; x<CHAR_WIDTH; x++)
        {
        // Test for a transparent pixel; that is, 0. If the
        // pixel is not transparent, draw it.

        if ((*work_char & bit_mask))
            video_buffer[offset+x] = color;

        else if (!trans_flag)  // Takes care of transparency.
            video_buffer[offset+x] = 0;

        // Shift the bit mask.

        bit_mask = (bit_mask>>1);

        } // end for x
    // Move to the next line in the video buffer and in the ROM
    // character data area.
    offset      += SCREEN_WIDTH;
    work_char++;

    } // end for y

} // end Blit_Char
```

The `Blit_Char()` function in Listing 3.9 needs a little explaining, so let's take a look at the parameters:

```
void Blit_Char(int xc,int yc,char c,int color,int trans_flag);
```

where:

☐ *xc* is the x position at which to display the character.

☐ *yc* is the y position at which to display the character.

☐ *c* is the ASCII character to display.

☐ *color* is the color, from 0–255, to make the character.

☐ *trans_flag* makes the background of the character either opaque or transparent.

To use `Blit_Char()`, call it with the appropriate parameters. You instantly see the desired character rendered on the video screen.

The function is worth taking a look at, especially the way I tested to see whether a pixel should be drawn. Because the eight pixels of each row are encoded as bits in a single byte, it's hard to test whether a pixel should be drawn at the current column location. To solve this problem, I use a shifting mask and a logical AND operation with the current row data. If the result is true, there must be a visible bit at the current pixel column that needs to be drawn. Otherwise, we shift the mask and continue to the next pixel, as shown in Figure 3.19.

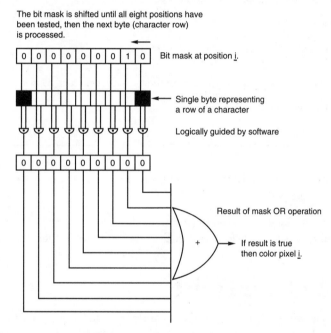

Figure 3.19. *The schematic representation of an algorithm to blit a character.*

The characters are drawn from left to right and from top to bottom; hence, there are a total of 64 iterations through the loop.

Tip: It might be worth the extra memory to encode characters as 64 bytes rather than eight bytes, where each row is encoded as bits. This would allow the character blitter to be sped up by a factor of nearly eight, because we could blast an entire row of pixels at a time into the video buffer without doing the bit test to see whether a pixel was lit.

The next logical function to write would be to draw an entire string of text on the screen. This is easy; we need only pass a function a pointer to the string of interest, along with its starting position and color. The function then makes calls to the lower-level function `Blit_Char()`, generating the appropriate parameters for each character. Listing 3.10 contains the string printing function.

Listing 3.10. Printing a string to the video screen.

```
void Blit_String(int x,int y,int color, char *string,int trans_flag)
{
// This function blits an entire string on the screen with fixed
// spacing between each character. It calls blit_char.

int index;

for (index=0; string[index]!=0; index++)
    {

    Blit_Char(x+(index<<3),y,string[index],color,trans_flag);

    } /* end while */

} /* end Blit_String */
```

(I can never get over how simple graphics programming is once you understand how to plot a single pixel.)

We've covered a great deal of ground today and it's time to see what can be done with the functions we've been writing. Prepare for some serious graphics!

A 3-D Starfield

When learning a new language it's customary to learn how to print something as the first lesson. Traditionally, the string printed is "hello world!" I want to suggest a new tradition: whenever we learn a new graphics system, we should write a program that animates a 3-D starfield of some kind on the screen. (I think I mentioned yesterday that I've been on a starfield kick lately.) This is what the next program does.

The program in Listing 3.11 demonstrates a couple of points about animation and timing. The starfield program creates three planes of stars. Each plane moves with a different velocity to simulate perspective depth.

In general, computer animation is accomplished by drawing the objects on the screen then erasing, moving, and drawing them again. This is done repeatedly to accomplish motion or *animation*, as shown in Figure 3.20.

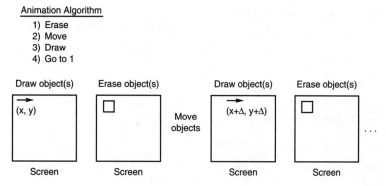

Figure 3.20. *The steps of animation.*

The starfield works in much the same manner:

1. A data structure is created that holds within it the position, velocity, and color of each star.

2. A loop is then executed for each star in the data structure. The loop erases where the star was last cycle, moves the star based on its velocity, and then redraws the star at its new position.

These operations are done for each star in the structure until they're all drawn.

In a regular video game there would be about a million other factors to consider—such as timing, foreground objects, and so on—but for now let's just see if we can draw some stars and get them to move. You can slow down or speed up the starfield by pressing the plus (+) and minus (-) keys. To exit, press the Q key. Here's the source code for the program that creates the starfield. Study the main() closely, as it's important that you get a grip on the general event loops used in real-time animation programs (such as video games).

Listing 3.11. A controllable starfield (strfield.c).

```
// I N C L U D E S /////////////////////////////////////////////

#include <dos.h>
#include <bios.h>
#include <stdio.h>
#include <stdlib.h>
#include <math.h>
#include <conio.h>


// D E F I N E S /////////////////////////////////////////////
```

Listing 3.11. continued

```c
#define NUM_STARS   75

#define PLANE_1     1
#define PLANE_2     2
#define PLANE_3     3

#define VGA256      0x13
#define TEXT_MODE   0x03

#define ROM_CHAR_SET_SEG 0xF000
// Segment of 8x8 ROM character set.
#define ROM_CHAR_SET_OFF 0xFA6E
// Beginning offset of 8x8 ROM character set.

#define CHAR_WIDTH        8
      // The size of the characters.
#define CHAR_HEIGHT       8

#define SCREEN_WIDTH      (unsigned int)320
// Mode 13h screen dimensions.
#define SCREEN_HEIGHT     (unsigned int)200

// P R O T O T Y P E S /////////////////////////////////////////

void Blit_Char(int xc,int yc,char c,int color,int trans_flag);

void Blit_String(int x,int y,int color,
                 char *string,int trans_flag);

void Plot_Pixel_Fast(int x,int y,unsigned char color);

void Init_Stars(void);

void Set_Video_Mode(int mode);

void Delay(int clicks);

// S T R U C T U R E S /////////////////////////////////////////

// Data structure for a single star.

typedef struct star_typ
        {
        int x,y;    // Position of star.
        int plane;  // Which plane the star is in.
        int color;  // The color of the star.

        } star, *star_ptr;


// G L O B A L S ///////////////////////////////////////////////

unsigned char far *video_buffer = (char far *)0xA0000000L;
// vram byte ptr
```

```
unsigned char far *rom_char_set = (char far *)0xF000FA6EL;
// ROM characters 8x8

int star_first=1;   // Flags the first time into starfield.

star stars[NUM_STARS]; // The starfield

int velocity_1=2,       // The speeds of each plane
    velocity_2=4,
    velocity_3=6;


// F U N C T I O N S ////////////////////////////////////////////

void Blit_Char(int xc,int yc,char c,int color,int trans_flag)
{
// This function uses the ROM 8x8 character set to blit a
// character on the video screen. Notice the trick used to
// extract bits out of each character byte that comprises
// a line.

int offset,x,y;
char far *work_char;
unsigned char bit_mask = 0x80;

// Compute the starting offset in the ROM character look-up
// table.

work_char = rom_char_set + c * CHAR_HEIGHT;


// Compute the offset of the character in the video buffer.

offset = (yc << 8) + (yc << 6) + xc;

for (y=0; y<CHAR_HEIGHT; y++)
    {
    // Reset the bit mask.

    bit_mask = 0x80;

    for (x=0; x<CHAR_WIDTH; x++)
        {
        // Test for a transparent pixel; that is, 0. If the
        // pixel is not transparent, draw it.

        if ((*work_char & bit_mask))
            video_buffer[offset+x] = color;

        else if (!trans_flag)  // Takes care of transparency.
            video_buffer[offset+x] = 0;

        // Shift the bit mask.

        bit_mask = (bit_mask>>1);
```

continues

Listing 3.11. continued

```
        } // end for x

    // Move to the next line in the video buffer and in the ROM
    // character data area.

    offset      += SCREEN_WIDTH;
    work_char++;

    } // end for y

} // end Blit_Char

///////////////////////////////////////////////////////////////

void Blit_String(int x,int y,int color,
                 char *string,int trans_flag)
{
// This function blits an entire string on the screen with fixed
// spacing between each character. It calls blit_char.

int index;

for (index=0; string[index]!=0; index++)
    {

    Blit_Char(x+(index<<3),y,string[index],color,trans_flag);

    } /* end while */

} /* end Blit_String */

///////////////////////////////////////////////////////////////

void Plot_Pixel_Fast(int x,int y,unsigned char color)
{

// Plots the pixel in the desired color a little quicker using
// binary shifting to accomplish the multiplications.

// Use the fact that 320*y = 256*y + 64*y = y<<8 + y<<6.

video_buffer[((y<<8) + (y<<6)) + x] = color;

} // end Plot_Pixel_Fast

///////////////////////////////////////////////////////////////

void Init_Stars(void)
{

// This function initializes the starfield.

int index;

// For each star, choose a position, plane, and color.
```

```
for (index=0; index<NUM_STARS; index++)
    {
    // Initialize each star to a velocity, position, and color.

    stars[index].x      = rand()%320;
    stars[index].y      = rand()%180;

    // Decide what star plane the star is in.

    switch(rand()%3)
        {
        case 0: // Plane 1: the farthest star plane.
            {
            // Set the velocity and color.

            stars[index].plane = 1;
            stars[index].color = 8;

            } break;

        case 1: // Plane 2: the mid-distance star plane.
            {

            stars[index].plane = 2;
            stars[index].color = 7;

            } break;

        case 2: // Plane 3: the nearest star plane.
            {

            stars[index].plane = 3;
            stars[index].color = 15;

            } break;

        } // end switch

    } // end for index

} // end Init_Stars

///////////////////////////////////////////////////////////////

void Set_Video_Mode(int mode)
{

// Use video interrupt 10h to set the video mode to the sent
// value.

union REGS inregs,outregs;

inregs.h.ah = 0;                    // Set the video mode
                                    // subfunction.
inregs.h.al = (unsigned char)mode;  // Video mode to which to
                                    // change.
```

continues

Listing 3.11. continued

```c
    _int86(0x10, &inregs, &outregs);

} // end Set_Video_Mode

/////////////////////////////////////////////////////////////////

void Delay(int clicks)
{
// This function uses the internal timekeeper (the one that runs
// at 18.2 clicks/sec to time a delay). You can find the 32-bit
// value of this timer at 0000:046Ch.

unsigned int far *clock = (unsigned int far *)0x0000046CL;

unsigned int now;

// Get the current time.

now = *clock;

// Wait until the time has gone past the current time plus the
// amount we wanted to wait. Note that each tick is
// approximately 55 milliseconds.

while(abs(*clock - now) < clicks){}

} // end Delay

// M A I N /////////////////////////////////////////////////////

void main(void)
{

int done=0, // Exit flag
    index;  // Loop index

// Set the video mode to the 320x200, 256-color mode.

Set_Video_Mode(VGA256);

// Initialize the starfield data structure.

Init_Stars();

// Begin the main event loop.

while(!done)
    {

    // Test whether the user is trying to do something.

    if (kbhit())
        {
        // What key was pressed?
```

```
            switch(getch())
                {
                case '-': // Slow the starfield down
                       {
                       // Decrease the velocity of each plane.

                       velocity_1-=1;
                       velocity_2-=2;
                       velocity_3-=3;

                       } break;

                case '=': // Speed the starfield up.
                       {
                       // Increase the velocity of each plane.
                       velocity_1+=1;
                       velocity_2+=2;
                       velocity_3+=3;

                       } break;

                case 'q': // The user is exiting.
                       {
                       done=1;
                       } break;

                default:break;

                } // end switch

       } // end if kbhit

// Move the starfields.

for (index=0; index<NUM_STARS; index++)
       {

       // Erase the star.

       Plot_Pixel_Fast(stars[index].x,stars[index].y,0);

       // Move the star and test for off-screen condition.

       // Each star is in a different plane, so test which
       // plane the star is in so that proper velocity can
       // be used.

       switch(stars[index].plane)
                {
                case PLANE_1: // The slowest (farthest) plane.
                       {
                       stars[index].x+=velocity_1;
                       } break;

                case PLANE_2: // The mid-speed plane.
                       {
```

continues

Listing 3.11. continued

```
                    stars[index].x+=velocity_2;
                    } break;

               case PLANE_3: // The fastest (nearest) plane.
                    {
                    stars[index].x+=velocity_3;
                    } break;

            } // end switch

    // Test whether the star went off screen.

    if (stars[index].x > 319 ) // Off right edge?
       stars[index].x=(stars[index].x-320);
       // Wrap around
    else
    if (stars[index].x < 0) // Off left edge?
       stars[index].x = (320+stars[index].x);
       // Wrap around

    // Draw the star at the new position.

    Plot_Pixel_Fast(stars[index].x,stars[index].y,
                    stars[index].color);

    } // end for

// Draw the directions again.

Blit_String(0,0,1, "Press '+' or '-' to change speed.",1);

Blit_String(88,180,2, "Press 'Q' to exit.",1);

// Wait a second so we can see the stars; otherwise, it'll
// look like warp speed!

Delay(1);

} // end while

// Put the computer back into the 320x200, 256-color mode
Set_Video_Mode(TEXT_MODE);

} // end main
```

Building an Executable: To make an executable of the program in Listing 3.12, you can type it in or use the source on the companion CD. The name of the source is `strfield.c`. The precompiled executable is named `strfield.exe`. As before, use the following compile line for Microsoft C:

```
cl -AM -Zi -c -Fc -Gs -G2 strfield.c
```

After compiling the program in this manner, you can link it to the standard libraries to create an executable file.

You should be noticing that the programs are beginning to get big. The simple starfield program in Listing 3.12 is a couple of hundred lines long, and it doesn't even do anything! Many video games can be tens of thousands of lines of C code. (I wrote a version of Centipede on the Atari 800 years ago, and even something that simple was over 9,000 lines of assembly...yuck!)

To be able to manage such huge amounts of code, we must take some time and create a general library on which we can build. And that's our next topic.

Starting Our Game Library

We already have about a dozen graphics functions. These functions, and others to come in the near future, are the basis of many of the calls we make throughout the code we write. For that reason, we should agree on some way to build a library so that we need not include the source code for all the functions with every new program. To accomplish this task I've decided on the following: every day we write some new functions for our game library, I'll place all the functions and header information into two files, called graph#.c and graph#.h, where the "#" is the day number to help keep track of the module. For instance, the functions we created today have been cleaned up a little and placed into the two files graph3.c and graph3.h. (Because we didn't do any coding on Days 1 and 2, we won't have files called graph1.c or graph2.c.)

I then took the source module graph3.c (which, by the way, has no main()) and compiled it into an object. We could just link the object in and include the header file graph3.h in any of our new programs that need the functions, but this would get out of hand once we had many of the source modules (that is, soon). Therefore, we can create a library called gamelib.lib. We'll then insert into the library graph3.obj, created (of course) by compiling graph3.c. Once we've created the library graphlib.lib, we can link it to any of our programs and have access to the functions in it. The only thing we need do in the source code of our main program is to be sure to include the file graph3.h with the other include files.

By the end of the book, we'll have many source modules that together comprise the entire library of functions we need in order to write the games. All of these functions will be accessible through the library gamelib.lib, which we'll keep adding to as we go. To see a graphical description of the overall process, take a look at Figure 3.21.

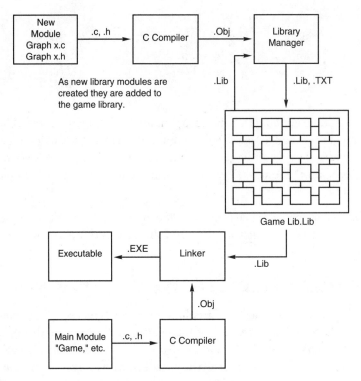

Figure 3.21. *The architecture of gamelib.lib.*

Let's step through an example of how we'd create the graphics library, add the first module (graph3.obj) to it, and then create a small program that would use the graphics library. Let's write a program that plots 10,000 randomly colored pixels on the screen using the functions in graph3.c. Here are the steps we must take before we begin writing the dot program:

1. Compile graph3.c with the following compile line:

   ```
   cl -AM -Zi -c  -Fc -Gs -G2 graph3.c
   ```

   This results in the object graph3.obj, which we must insert into our new library, gamelib.lib.

2. Take the object graph3.obj and create with it a new library using the Microsoft Library Manager. Name the new library graphlib.lib, and insert graph3.obj into the new library.

   Here's a screen shot of me creating the game library and adding graph3.obj to it. I also create a list file so I can see the functions and variables that are within the library.

```
Microsoft (R) Library Manager Version 3.20.010

Copyright (C) Microsoft Corp 1983-1992. All rights reserved.

Library name: gamelib.lib

Library does not exist. Create (y/n) y

Operations: +graph1.obj

List file: gamelib.txt
```

Here is a dump of the file gamelib.txt:

```
_Blit_Char.......graph3          _Blit_String......graph3
_Delay..........graph3          _Get_Palette_Register..graph3
_H_Line.........graph3          _H_Line_Fast......graph3
_Plot_Pixel......graph3          _Plot_Pixel_Fast..graph3
_rom_char_set....graph3          _Set_Palette_Register..graph3
_Set_Video_Mode..graph3          _video_buffer.....graph3
_video_buffer_w..graph3          _V_Line..........graph3


graph3          Offset: 00000010H  Code and data size: 1485H
  _Blit_Char      _Blit_String  _Delay        _Get_Palette_Register
  _H_Line         _H_Line_Fast  _Plot_Pixel  _Plot_Pixel_Fast
  _rom_char_set  _Set_Palette_Register       _Set_Video_Mode
  _video_buffer  _video_buffer_w   _V_Line
```

We now have a library we can link with our main source module to create a final executable. We get to exactly how to do this in a moment but, for now, let's write the program that displays 10,000 colored dots on the screen. This program is shown in Listing 3.13.

Listing 3.13. Blasting pixels to the video screen with our new library (dots.c).

```c
// I N C L U D E S ///////////////////////////////////////////////

#include <stdio.h>
#include <stdlib.h>
#include <conio.h>
#include "graph3.h" // This is all we need to include so the
                    // program knows all the #defines,
                    // structures, prototypes, and so on.

// M A I N ///////////////////////////////////////////////////////

void main(void)
{

int done=0, // Exit flag
    index; // Loop index
```

continues

105

Listing 3.13. continued

```
// Set the video mode to the 320x200, 256-color mode.

Set_Video_Mode(VGA256);

// Plot 10,000 dots

for (index=0; index<10000; index++)
    Plot_Pixel_Fast(rand()%320, rand()%200,rand()%256);

// Wait for the user to press a key.

while(!kbhit()){}

// Reset the video mode to the 320x200, 256-color mode.
Set_Video_Mode(TEXT_MODE);

} // end main
```

Building an Executable: We now have a main program that uses a couple of the functions in our game library. To make a final, functioning executable, we first must compile the source code for the dots.c program into an object. Use the standard compile line we've been using:

```
cl -AM -Zi -c -Fc -Gs -G2 colorrot.c
```

As usual, you can type in the source, copy the file dots.c off the companion CD, or use the precompiled object dots.obj. Whichever way you decide to do it, come up with an object named dots.obj.

We're now ready to create a final executable, composed of the library, gamelib.lib, and the main program, dots.c. Use a link line similar to the following to create a final executable named dots.exe:

```
link /ST:8192 /CO dots,,,graphics.lib+gamelib.lib,,
```

This tells the linker to create a stack that's 8,192 bytes in size, add debugger information, and link the object module dots.obj with the functions in graphics.lib and gamelib.lib. The library graphics.lib is Microsoft's, and isn't really needed here, but I wanted to show how you could have more than one library in the linking process. (Of course, the executable is also on the companion CD if you can't wait!)

Run the program dots.exe. Press any key to exit the program.

This discussion on creating a library and using it as a resource to build a main program may seem unnecessary if you're using Programmer's Workbench or some other development tool. Personally, I don't use any development tool that does my work for me. I like to know exactly what's going on with my source code and so on. (I once lost 2,500 lines of wicked C code to a development system, so I'm a little biased!) Although development tools are great, and have their place, I like to keep things simple by using the bare minimum of tools. These include an editor, compiler, linker, library manager, and debugger. (Remember, the more cooks in the kitchen the easier it is to mess up the recipe!)

We continue to create new library modules and add them to the main library gamelib.lib as the days pass, so make sure you understand how this is done. We don't want any problems with incorrect versions of functions and the like. Because I plan for us to have quite a few modules, let's keep them organized from the very start. (This will also cause the people who put this book together fewer nightmares, because I probably had about 15,000 lines of C code in my last book.)

Finally, I supply an executable of any program in the book, so you can see what it does before you compile it or do any development on it.

Mode X

This was really a last minute addition to today's topics, but I feel we should talk about it so you know what mode X is. Mode X is just about the most nebulous computer word I've ever heard. It describes an undocumented mode of the VGA card. Actually, it's really a new mode of the VGA card, one that can be programmed to create a modified version of mode 13h that supports multiple pages and a slightly higher resolution.

The VGA card is a programmable controller, and thus can support about a million modes that you've never seen (and probably never will see). While mode 13h is great, and is the simplest mode to program in, mode X is faster. Mode X is a mix of the timing parameters from mode 13h with some of the parameters for the higher-resolution modes.

The resolution of mode X is 320×240: a hybrid between the 320×200 mode and the 640×480 mode. Its memory mapping is a bit different from that of mode 13h. The memory configuration is somewhat planar, like the EGA modes. The attractive asset of mode X is its ability to use multiple video pages and do what's called *page flipping*. Page flipping is a technique where there exist two or more areas of memory to which we can write, but only one page is visible to the user. Using page flipping, we can display one page while updating another, and then switch to the new page. This instantaneously updates the screen image at the fastest possible speed.

3

Although this mode is probably the best, the paged-memory configuration makes using mode X more complex than using mode 13h—and, for our purposes, would dilute some of the purity of our functions. Moreover, to really see mode X shine it's necessary to use protected-mode programming along with reprogramming the local descriptor table (LDT) to simulate better memory configuration. Both of these concepts are beyond the scope of this book; and, anyway, they're optimizational topics, which we aren't as interested in as we are the overall design of video games.

Summary

Today we learned the essence of the VGA card and its capabilities, which we need to know as video-game programmers. The VGA card is really an extremely complex graphics controller, and I probably haven't done it justice. However, we know enough to do what we need to. We can place the VGA card into mode 13h, plot pixels, remap the color palette, draw lines, and more. If we knew nothing more than the information is this chapter, we could probably make a decent game. However, we're going to learn much, much more. When you're done with this book, there will be very little you can't make the VGA card do.

We learned that graphics and game programming require tons of code, and we must keep it all organized. We learned how to create a library and in so doing made our first installment, called graph3.c, to the game library. We continue to create more library modules and add them as we progress until we have a complete graphics, sound, and I/O library that we can use to write just about any 2-D game there is—not to mention, maybe, we could sell the library and make some money...?

Q&A

Q Why are some VGA cards faster than others?

A The VGA card is like any other piece of computer hardware you can purchase. Based on the price, the quality of the card will be high or low. Furthermore, some VGA cards have more efficient hardware than others. However, most of the speed difference is related to the internal memory configuration of the VGA card. Some VGA cards have quite advanced memory systems that are dual-ported and have been optimized so that writes and reads are as fast as possible. Nevertheless, the deciding factor—the governor of the maximum rendering speed of the VGA card—is the system bus. This is why local-bus VGAs are much faster. The memory bandwidth, or speed of access, is many times greater than the standard system bus and, hence, the video memory can be manipulated.

Q What's a pixel?

A That's a fairly *atomic* question! It's just a dot on the computer monitor. (The word *pixel* is derived from PICture ELement.) The screen is composed of a matrix of these pixels. The pixels are lit by electrons striking them and exciting them to give off photons of light. Each pixel is a triangle or rectangle composed of a triad of the three main colors: red, green, and blue. These colors are created by different materials of which each pixel is composed. These materials are referred to as *picture phosphors*, and can be engineered to glow different colors when excited by electrons.

Q Why is mode 13h the easiest mode in which to program?

A Mode 13h has a linear memory map instead of a planar memory map. This means the video buffer is one long region of memory, like an array. If we used one of the planar video modes for our graphics, we would be inundated by all the manipulations of the plane-select registers to access the different bits that make up a single pixel in the display.

Q The 386 and 486 are 32-bit computers. Why can't I write four bytes at a time to the video buffer and speed up such things as clearing the screen or bit blitting?

A It's true that the 386 and 486 are 32-bit, but the VGA card is either 8- or 16-bit, and is plugged into an 8- or 16-bit slot—so no matter what you do the results are always 8- or 16-bit writes at a single time.

Q Why are only six bits used in each of the RGB elements of a color register?

A Because each component can have six bits of definition, or 64 shades. That means there are a total of 262,144 colors available. If we used eight bits for each color component, which the hardware could easily do, there would be 2^{24}, or 16,777,216, colors. This is called *true color* or *24-bit color*. The only reason this isn't common on the VGA card is that earlier monitors couldn't support all those colors. Today you can buy 24-bit Super VGA cards along with monitors that can support all those colors.

Q Is using the `_fmemset()` function the fastest way to clear or fill the video screen?

A No! `_fmemset()` uses only BYTE-sized writes, which is half as fast as using WORD-sized writes. Assuming you have a 16-bit VGA card (which is common today), you could write a small program using the in-line assembler that would clear or fill the video buffer a WORD at a time, which is optimal. (Of course, if you have a VLBUS video card or a PCI card, you can use 32-bit writes. However, it's best to stay with the common denominator when writing games.)

Q **When printing text on the video screen, what if I want another font?**

A You're on your own. You'd have to create your own font, character by character, and then store the characters in memory somewhere. You'd then write a new text-blitting function that could print out the new characters. Before going to this extreme, I suggest experimenting with the current ROM font and making a few changes to the text blitter, such as vertical or horizontal stretching and color tricks. For instance, I've used the internal ROM 8×8 font with the simple change of drawing each character in two colors: the top half dark and the lower half bright. This looks *very* cool.

Workshop

The Workshop section presents quiz questions to help you cement your new knowledge and exercises to give you experience using what you've learned. Try to understand the questions and exercises before moving on to the next lesson. The answers are in Appendix B.

Quiz

1. What does VGA stand for?

2. What's the resolution of mode 13h, and how many colors does it support?

3. What do each of the color register I/O ports do?

4. Given that the VGA video buffer starts at A000:0000h, what is the pixel address of (100,100)?

5. In your own words, define color rotation.

6. Why is video memory slower than normal memory?

7. What's the minimum refresh rate a video game must maintain to keep the image from flickering?

8. What is meant by *bit blitting*?

9. What's the resolution of mode X?

10. What is the *horizontal retrace*?

Exercises

1. Using the game library, write a program that plots a pixel on the screen and makes it glow red.

2. Profile the difference between the two pixel-plotting functions `Plot_Pixel()` and `Plot_Pixel_Fast()`. Hint: write a program that plots 1,000,000 or so pixels with each version, and record their speed difference.

3. Rewrite the `Blit_Char()` function so it draws each character in two colors.

4. Write a program that slowly decreases the intensity of all the colors in each color register until each color register has all zeros in it.

5. Try to make `Plot_Pixel_Fast()` even faster!

6. Using the keyboard as an input device, try to make a crude drawing program that allows the user to change colors and move a pen on the screen.

7. Write a program that bounces a single pixel around on the screen without leaving a trail.

8. Close this book and watch a rerun of *Star Trek: The Next Generation*!

Getting Sprite to the Point

1

Admittedly, a sprite is well-known to be a little elven creature from mythology. In the context of video games, however, it's something entirely different. Loosely defined, a *sprite* is an object within a game that can move around the screen and is part of the action. The name might have been adapted by an unknown game programmer, writing some weird game late at night. Perhaps that programmer noticed how the game objects on the screen moved and jumped around like little sprites...but it's only a guess.

We're beginning to learn that most video games are collections of moving and animated bit maps on the video screen. A video game has so many of these little objects moving around and participating in the game that it would be wise to create a library of functions to manipulate bit-mapped images, with the premise that sprites are game objects and not just pictures. This is where a *sprite engine* comes into play. We want to build up some functions to create sprites, move them, animate them, and more. This is what we work on today.

When you've mastered today's material, you should be able to write simple video games. Such games wouldn't be at a professional level just yet, but they would be playable.

Here's what we cover today:

- ☐ What sprites are
- ☐ The operations we'd like to perform on sprites
- ☐ A sprite data structure
- ☐ Bit-map editors
- ☐ Loading PCX files
- ☐ Extracting bit maps from PCX files
- ☐ Creating and destroying sprites
- ☐ Drawing sprites
- ☐ Scanning the background under a sprite
- ☐ Erasing sprites
- ☐ Moving sprites
- ☐ Scaling a sprite
- ☐ Rotating a sprite
- ☐ Transparency encoding sprite data for speed and size

- [ ] Testing for sprite collision
- [ ] Sprite animation and timing
- [ ] Adding to the graphics library
- [ ] A demo: Attank!!!
- [ ] Flicker and double buffering

What are Sprites?

Sprites are the video-game objects that perform the game action, and are the main focus of the game itself. Sprites can be cars, creatures, missiles, explosions, humans, aliens, or what-have-you. The image a sprite represents is, really, irrelevant: a sprite is a bit map that can be placed on the screen and animated. The bit map itself can be anything. Figure 4.1 shows an example of a sprite.

Figure 4.1. *An image of a sprite.*

Later today we see a demo called Attank!!!. Attank!!! is a simple program that loads in a background image of a military outpost and then allows you to drive a tank around while the computer drives another tank. The tanks are sprites. The background is a stationary bit map (that is, the background is not a sprite). Figure 4.2 shows a screen shot of the demo.

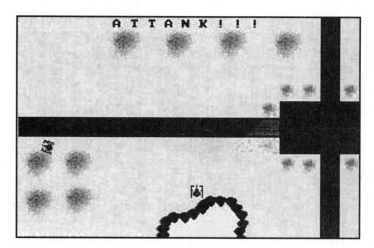

Figure 4.2. *A screen shot of Attank!!!*

The word *sprite*, and the techniques used to draw and animate sprites, usually are relevant only in bit-mapped graphics systems. For instance, say you decided to write a new version of Asteroids and draw the asteroids out of polygons, not bit maps. In such a case, the asteroids wouldn't be called sprites because they'd be based on lines, not pixels. This is a generalization, and could be argued, but most of the time sprites are bit-mapped images and not line- or polygon-based images.

The bit-mapped quality of sprites also has to do with the early game machines, such as the Atari 800, Commodore 64, and TRS-80 Color Computer. These machines all had some kind of sprite mechanism that was based on bit-mapped imagery, not polygon- or line-based imagery. This, I suspect, is where the tradition of sprites being bit maps evolved.

If we make a simplification and think of the graphics in a video game being composed of a background with objects moving around in the foreground, we quickly come to the conclusion that we only need a couple of things to make a video game:

- ☐ We need a *sprite engine* that enables us to create and animate sprites on the screen.

- ☐ We need a library of graphics functions that allow us to draw or load backgrounds for the sprites to move around on.

That's really the essence of a video game. Of course, there are about 50 million or so more details, but this is a beginning.

The sprite engine is what we concern ourselves with today. We are about to create a "first generation" of sprite functions, which we may or may not need to add to or alter later. However, they can be a starting point. Fortunately, there aren't that many things you can do to a sprite. We *could* get a little crazy and make a sprite engine that might turn heads at LucasFilms, but I'll be satisfied with just the basics. Let's see what we need.

Operations We'd Like to Perform on Sprites

A sprite is an *abstract data type* (or ADT, for those of you with a computer science degree). We want to encapsulate the qualities of the sprite within a data structure, and then write functions that operate on this data structure. The language C++ is perfect for this kind of thing, but C will suffice (and is still the language of choice for game programmers, although the tides are turning).

Today we draw the sprites on the video screen. On Day 6 (in the chapter called "Real-Time Animation and Effects") we learn another way of drawing them in a temporary buffer, and we'll need to create modified functions at that point. For now, however, let's assume that the video buffer is where the action takes place.

In a moment we get into the data structure I've created for our sprites, but for now let's see what we might want to do to a sprite (and why). Sprites are bit maps; therefore, we have to obtain this bit-map data from somewhere. This means we need a way to load in predrawn images from a paint program or graphics package.

Once we have the data for the sprite loaded, we want to be able to perform a few basic operations with it. These operations can be better understood if we briefly review the basic animation cycle first.

The following algorithm animates a sprite in a video buffer:

Algorithm 4.1. The steps in animating a sprite.

```
1.      Erase the sprite by restoring the background that was under it.
2.      Move and animate the sprite.
3.      Scan the background where the sprite will be placed, so that it
        can be replaced.
4.      Draw the sprite.
5.      GOTO 1
```

These steps can be somewhat condensed because some steps can be done simultaneously. However, each step must be done for the sprite to move and animate without destroying the background.

The most important concept to grasp about animation is that, if there's a background and you draw something on top of it, you'd better make some provision for restoring the background when the object moves. Otherwise, the background is obliterated. This goes for sprites, as well. Steps 1 and 3 of Algorithm 4.1 are there to avoid trashing the background of your game.

If you've ever used Microsoft Windows and moved a window around the screen, you'll probably have noticed that when you moved the window, what was under it was restored. This is important. If this operation wasn't done by Windows, the video buffer would become a visual nightmare. As video-game programmers, we don't have the luxury of updating the video screen as slowly as Windows does: we must do it so fast it's almost as if it didn't happen.

At this point, we know that we must be able to somehow grab the background under a sprite, replace this background, and draw the sprite itself. These are all such easy operations, I'll leave writing the whole sprite engine to you...

Just kidding! I felt your heart stop there for a second. We see exactly how we do all this scanning and drawing in a moment.

Now that we've got the animation cycle down, let's talk about the things we want to be able to do to a sprite. We can start at a fairly high level of abstraction and then decide how we would actually implement each action. Here are the things we want to be able to do:

- ☐ Create the sprite
- ☐ Load bit maps into the sprite's data structure
- ☐ Draw the sprite
- ☐ Erase the sprite
- ☐ Scan the background under the sprite
- ☐ Scale a sprite (make it larger or smaller)
- ☐ Rotate the sprite
- ☐ Test whether the sprite has collided with another sprite
- ☐ Delete the sprite from memory

There are few more minor actions that we might want to perform, but these are the main ones to work on. If we can write functions to do all these operations, we're really in a good position to start writing simple games.

Now, I know you might still be a little uneasy with the concept of a sprite, and might not know yet exactly what is or isn't a sprite and what they're used for. This is because sprites

are kind of primal knowledge: we must define them with themselves. (Know what I mean?) Anyway, don't despair: they become more understandable as we progress throughout the day.

A Sprite Data Structure

Now that we've decided on some of the operations and capabilities of sprites, let's take a stab at a data structure for them. The data structure we create must take a lot of information into account. We have yet to cover some of this information—so, if you don't see why we need so many fields, don't worry; be happy.

Let's begin with the basics. We need to know:

- [ ] Where the sprite is
- [ ] The sprite's size
- [ ] The current frame of animation (remember, a sprite can animate)
- [ ] The data area for all the bit maps
- [ ] The area to hold the background under a sprite
- [ ] The state of the sprite (alive, dead, or what-have-you)
- [ ] Some timing information that enables us to move and animate the sprite in more realistic ways

The code fragment in Listing 4.1 shows the sprite data structure we use as our foundation.

Listing 4.1. A sprite data structure.

```
// The sprite data structure:

typedef struct sprite_typ
        {
        int x,y;              // Position of the sprite
        int x_old,y_old;      // Old position of the sprite
        int width,height;     // Dimensions of the sprite,
                              //    in pixels
        int anim_clock;       // The animation clock
        int anim_speed;       // The animation speed
        int motion_clock;     // The motion clock
        int motion_speed;     // The motion speed

// An array of pointers to the images
        char far *frames[MAX_SPRITE_FRAMES];
```

continues

Listing 4.1. continued

```
// The current frame being displayed
        int curr_frame;
// The total number of frames
        int num_frames;
// The state of the sprite: alive, dead...
        int state;
// What's under the sprite
        char far *background;
// An auxiliary pointer to more data, if needed
        void far *extra_data;

        } sprite, *sprite_ptr;
```

As you can see, the sprite structure is fairly simple. (I like simple.) All the fields are simple data types and fairly self-explanatory, but let's cover each of them anyway to see why they all exist.

☐ The variables int x,y hold the x and y positions of the sprite on the video screen.

☐ Sometimes it helps to know where the sprite was before it was moved. The two variables int x_old,y_old make such calculations more convenient; otherwise, a local variable in the game logic might have to track the old position of the sprite.

☐ The variables int width,int height are the size of the sprite, in pixels. It's handy for computing collisions and memory requirements.

☐ The int anim_clock variable is used as a counter to help with the rate at which the frames of animation are cycled, if we need to cycle them. For example, we may define a sprite that has five frames of animation and find that we want these frames to be cycled through every three seconds. This variable and int anim_speed, discussed next, help encapsulate the process.

☐ The int anim_speed variable is used as the threshold for the animation clock. When the animation clock hits this value, the animation clock is reset and the current frame is advanced.

☐ The int motion_clock variable is used as a clock to count the number of cycles before the sprite should be moved. This variable is compared against the int motion_speed variable, which we discuss next, to determine whether it's time to move the sprite.

☐ The int `motion_speed` variable is analogous to the animation variables, but used for motion. This variable is used as a threshold for the motion clock. When the motion clock hits this threshold, the sprite can be moved.

☐ The char far `*frames[MAX_SPRITE_FRAMES]` variable is an array of pointers, each of which points to a region of memory that holds a bit map. These are the bit maps to which the sprite has access for animation.

☐ The int `curr_frame` variable keeps track of the frame currently being displayed for the sprite.

☐ The int `num_frames` variable is the total number of frames, or *animation cells*, that have been loaded into the `frames[]` array.

☐ The int `state` variable is a general-state variable that can be used to track the current "state" of the sprite; for example, whether the sprite is alive, dying, dead, or whatever.

☐ The char far `*background` variable is a pointer to a region of memory used to hold the background under a sprite so the background can be replaced when the sprite moves from its last position.

☐ The void far `*extra_data` variable is a fairly advanced field. It lets us add onto the sprite structure without changing all the functions that access the structure. For instance, if we want to add an entirely new element to the sprite structure, but have already written too much code with the old structure, we could just point this field to the new structure. This enables us to implement a form of data abstraction. Because the pointer is void, we don't care what it points to; the function(s) that use this field must take care of that themselves.

The data structure in Listing 4.1 is probably more than we need, but it's better to be safe than sorry! We discuss shortly how all the functions we've covered are implemented. Now, however, we must digress momentarily and talk about where we get the art—the bit maps themselves—and how we load this data into our game programs.

Bit-Map Editors

Unless you want to algorithmically generate images for your games, you'll have to draw them using some kind of bit-map paint program that works with mode 13h. My favorite is Deluxe Paint (Dpaint) and Deluxe Animation (DA), both from Electronic Arts. Figure 4.3 shows a screen shot from Deluxe Animation.

Figure 4.3. *A screen shot of Deluxe Animation from Electronic Arts.*

These programs are two of the few on the market that have just the right degree of capability to get the job done without having so many options you get a headache. Moreover, both programs were originally designed to operate in mode 13h and run under DOS, so they're simple to use—and what you see is what you get, as they run in the video mode in which the images are to be used (mode 13h, or the 320x220-pixel, 256-color mode).

Although I recommend Dpaint, you can use any paint program you like. Whatever you use, the imagery you create for the objects in your game requires some planning. As we discussed during Day 3 (Chapter 3, "Painting the Screen with the VGA Card"), the object's color is a consideration—but only one. You also must take into account the number of frames of animation required to make the motion of the objects look realistic, which we discuss in detail on Day 6 (Chapter 6, "Real-Time Animation and Effects").

Remember, too, that there are only 256 colors you can use at a time. You must draw all the images in the same 256 colors unless you plan to load multiple color palettes throughout the game.

Also, you must make your images in rectangular *templates*. I find that most games can be made with sprites that are 8×8, 16×16, 32×32, and 48×48 pixels. These are common image sizes in video games. To create images of these sizes, you'd create one rectangular template for each size using your paint program. Make sure each bit map you draw fits within the rectangle of the template, including any animation cells.

Your templates can be any size you wish, but the bigger they are, the more memory the bit maps take—and the slower they'll be rendered, because there's more data in a larger

object. I suggest you make most of your game objects square: keep the horizontal and vertical dimensions the same. Take a look at Figure 4.4 to see a sample template that would accommodate 16 objects.

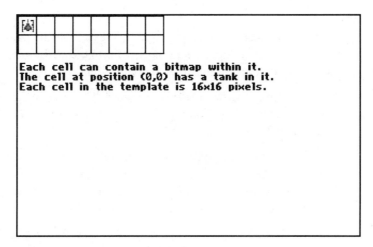

Figure 4.4. *A template used for holding 16×16-pixel bit-map images.*

As an example, let's take a look at the imagery used for the demo at the end of the chapter, called Attank!!!. I drew 32 little tanks, each 16×16 pixels, and then placed them in a regular manner on the paint program's screen. Basically, I thought of the paint program's screen as a matrix of animation cells, each $m \times n$. Each cell in the case of Attank!!! is 16×16 pixels. Figure 4.5 shows the animation cells for Attank!!!.

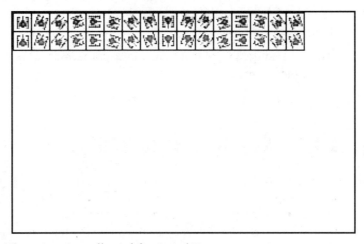

Figure 4.5. *The animation cells used for Attank!!!.*

Once I'd drawn the cells for the animation, they could be saved and imported into my game or application. The file format we use is called *PCX*, and is the original paint-program format invented for PC Paintbrush by Zsoft a long time ago.

To reiterate:

1. We draw the images in a paint program. We can use any paint program (preferably, one that operates in mode 13h) to create the game imagery and draw the sprites, including sprite animation cells.

   The foreground objects, or sprite bit maps, all have some dimension in pixels: $m \times n$. If possible, make m and n equal (such as 8×8 or 16×16 pixels) to accommodate Step 2.

2. We order the images by placing them in "cell" positions, creating a regular matrix of cells on the paint program's screen. Each bit map's cell location is based on the width and height of that bit map—an excellent reason to give your bit maps regular dimensions—in left-to-right, top-to-bottom order.

   We must place all graphic images on a full, 320×200-pixel screen image. For instance, we'd save a single 16×16 bit map by saving the entire paint-program screen with that single, 16×16 bit map in the upper-left corner. This facilitates the bit-map extraction process of Step 4.

3. We next save the whole screen as a PCX file.

4. We write a function that can access each bit map's cell coordinates, along with the size of each cell, and extract the bit map from the proper location.

   In the example in Step 2, our bit-map extraction program would extract that isolated, 16×16 bit map from the larger, 320×220-pixel image by accessing cell (0,0): the upper-left corner.

5. We then load the PCX file into memory and use our extraction function to extract the bit maps.

That last step is easier said than done! Therefore, it's the topic of the next section.

Working with PCX Files

Details, details, details. Everything would be so easy without details. (My taxes, especially!) Well, the harsh reality of life is that PCX files are *not* magical and they won't load themselves into a region of memory so we can extract the bit maps from them. We must write software to load the PCX file in and do the right thing with it. Hence, let's first talk about what exactly a PCX file is.

PCX File Content

A *PCX file* is a graphics exchange file format created by Zsoft Corporation for the graphic images generated by PC Paintbrush. It quickly became the standard on the IBM PC, and is the file format we use throughout this book.

PCX files are basically the stored bit map of some image, so let's take inventory on what makes up an image in the 320×200-pixel, 256-color mode:

☐ First, as with any file, there's some header information. PCX files have impor-tant information in the header portion, which we get to in a moment. For now, we can anticipate a need for 128 bytes for the header.

☐ Next, there's the image itself. This means there should be 320*200, or 64,000, bytes of data that describe the screen image.

☐ The 64,000 bytes of data are the pixel values, but not the actual colors of the image. This means that we must include the palette in which the image was drawn. There are 256 color registers, each with three components (one each for red, green, and blue). Each component is one byte; hence, a total of 768 more bytes must be placed in the file somewhere.

This all comes to about 65,000 bytes (in the worst case). This rough estimate of what we need to save a 320×200-pixel, 256-color image isn't bad. It left out one little detail: *compression*! No matter what you draw in a paint program, from a single pixel to a whole screen, the program saves the whole screen. (It does seem like a waste to save 64,000 bytes of information to describe a single pixel!) PCX files are therefore compressed to save space. The method PCX files use for compression is called *run-length encoding*, or RLE.

RLE Encoding

RLE works because graphical images have a lot of *coherence*, meaning they contain many pixels of the same value in neighboring regions. Most images you might see on a paint-program screen have long, horizontal runs of the same color. We can compress such runs this way:

1. We count how many pixels there are of the same color in a continuous stream.

2. We then encode the pixel value itself, along with the number of times it occurs. These two pieces of information are later used to decompress the original run of pixels.

This is the technique used by PCX files: runs of horizontal pixels are encoded as pixel values along with the number of pixels in the run. The only problem with this method

is that is works only in the horizontal dimension. If an image has a lot of vertical coherence, there's little compression. However, it seems to do well with most computer graphic images.

PCX File Headers

As we said during our image inventory a moment ago, the PCX file has a header section that describes the file and some attributes about it. The header for a PCX file is exactly 128 bytes long. Listing 4.2 shows an example PCX file header.

Listing 4.2. The structure of a PCX header.

```
typedef struct pcx_header_typ
        {
        char manufacturer;
                // Always 10
        char version;
                // 0-Ver 2.5 Paintbrush, 2-Ver 2.8 with
                // palette, 3-Ver 2.8 use the default palette,
                // 5 - Ver 3.0 or higher of Paintbrush
        char encoding;
                // Always 1, meaning RLE encoding
        char bits_per_pixel;
                // Bits per pixel; in our case, eight
        int x,y;
                // Upper-left corner of the image
        int width,height;
                // Size of the image
        int horz_res;
                // Pixels in the x direction
        int vert_res;
                // Pixels in the y direction
        char ega_palette[48];
                // The EGA palette; we can ignore it
        char reserved;
                // Nothing
        char num_color_planes;
                // The number of planes in the image
        int bytes_per_line;
                // Bytes per one horizontal line
        int palette_type;
                // Don't worry about it
        char padding[58];
                // Extra bytes for a rainy day

        } pcx_header, *pcx_header_ptr;
```

Compressed-Image Data in a PCX File

After the header information comes the compressed-image data. This data is encoded RLE style, but (as you'll see) decoding it is a little twisted: after reading in the first 128 bytes (the header), the next section of data consists of image data.

This is where the 64,000 pixels that make up the final image come from. This data is assumed to be image data until 64,000 pixels have been decompressed. We might read five bytes, 40,000 bytes, or 64,000 bytes; we don't know. All we know is that when our code has decompressed a complete image of 320×200, or 64,000, bytes, we're done.

This doesn't necessarily mean that if we read more than 64,000 data bytes from the raw file we're can be sure of being done. It's actually possible for the file to be much larger than 64,000 bytes in the case of expansion, which can happen sometimes when a graphics file with little spatial coherence is being compressed.

Now, here's how we decode the image data:

1. When a byte between 0–191 is read, we place it into the buffer at the next location.

2. If the byte read is in the range from 192 to -255, it's an RLE run and we must decompress it. To decompress it, we subtract 192 from the number just read. Call the result R. If we read a 199, for example, R is 7.

3. We then read the next byte after the RLE run-length byte from the file and replicate it R times in the buffer.

For example, if we read a 195, we then read the next byte (say, 233) and replicate it 195-192=3, or three times, in the buffer. (I have no idea why 192 is the cutoff, but I bet I could make one up!)

The only problem with this scheme is: how do we encode pixel values from 192 to -255 if they're always interpreted as RLE runs? The answer is: to encode the pixels from 192 to -255, make sure they're encoded as RLE runs of 1. For example, if we wanted to encode a 192, we'd place a 193 and *then* a 192 in the data file. The 193 would be read and interpreted as a run of 1. The 192 would be read next and used for the run data placed in the buffer without any interpretation. This may seem contrived, but it works pretty well.

Palette Data in a PCX File

After we have decompressed exactly 64,000 pixels we're ready to load the palette data, which is the next 768 bytes in the file. Algorithm 4.2 is the decompression algorithm, written out step by step.

Algorithm 4.2. Decompressing a PCX file.

1.   *Open the PCX file in raw binary mode.*
2.   *Read in the first 128 bytes of the PCX file. This is the header information.*
3.   *Allocate a 64,000-byte buffer that will hold the data to be decompressed from the PCX file.*
4.   *Set a counter that represents how many bytes have been decom pressed to the value of zero. This counter is used to flag when the decompression is complete.*
5.   *Read the next byte in the PCX file.*
6.   *If the byte just read is between 0-191, store the byte unchanged at the next location in the decompression buffer.*
        If the decompression buffer is not full (that is, if 64,000 bytes have not been decompressed), repeat step 5; otherwise, go to step 8.
7.   *The byte read must have been from 192-255; therefore, it's an RLE run and must be decompressed. To do the decompression, read the next byte from the PCX file and repeat it unchanged in the decompression buffer a number of times equal to the byte read in step 5 minus 192.*
        At this point, if the decompression buffer is not full, repeat step 5; otherwise, go to the palette-load section starting in step 8.
8.   *At this point we've read in the header information for the PCX file and we have decompressed the image data itself. We are now ready to load in the VGA palette. To do this, we simply load in the next 768 bytes from the PCX file. We read 768 bytes as there are 256 color registers, each composed of three bytes. This makes up a total of 768 bytes that must be read. The color registers are in order; that is, the first three bytes are for the red, green, and blue components of color register 0, and so on.*
9.   *Close the PCX file.*

I decided to create a set of functions that enable us to:

☐ Load a PCX file.

☐ Display it on the screen, if we wish.

☐ Load the VGA's palette registers with the palette of the PCX file.

☐ Destroy the PCX file and deallocated the buffer that was used by it. (Remember, we must allocate a 64,000-byte buffer to load the PCX file into!)

PCX File Functions

Once we have the PCX file loaded and decompressed into a buffer, we can extract bit maps from the buffer and use them for our sprites or other game imagery. Before we see how to do that, let's take a look at all the PCX file functions and their purpose, shown in Listing 4.3.

Listing 4.3. The PCX file functions and associated data structures.

```
// The data structure for PCX file

typedef struct pcx_picture_typ
        {
        pcx_header header;
                    // The header
        RGB_color palette[256];
                    // The VGA palette
        char far *buffer;
                    // The 64,000 byte buffer to hold the image

        } pcx_picture, *pcx_picture_ptr;


// PCX functions

void PCX_Init(pcx_picture_ptr image)
{
// This function allocates the buffer region needed to load a
// PCX file.

if (!(image->buffer = (char far *)
                    _fmalloc(SCREEN_WIDTH * SCREEN_HEIGHT + 1)))

    printf("\ncouldn't allocate screen buffer");

} // end PCX_Init

/////////////////////////////////////////////////////////////////

void PCX_Load(char *filename,
            pcx_picture_ptr image,int enable_palette)
{
// This function loads a PCX file into a picture structure. The
// actual image data for the PCX file is decompressed and
// expanded into a secondary buffer within the picture
// structure. The separate images can be grabbed from this
// buffer later. Also, the header and palette are loaded.

FILE *fp;
int num_bytes,index;
long count;
unsigned char data;
char far *temp_buffer;

// Open the file

fp = fopen(filename,"rb");

// Load the header

temp_buffer = (char far *)image;
```

continues

129

Listing 4.3. continued

```
for (index=0; index<128; index++)
    {
    temp_buffer[index] = (char)getc(fp);
    } // end for index

// Load the data and decompress it into the buffer.

count=0;

while(count<=SCREEN_WIDTH * SCREEN_HEIGHT)
    {
    // Get the first piece of data.

    data = (unsigned char)getc(fp);

    // Is this an RLE?

    if (data>=192 && data<=255)
        {
        // How many bytes in the run?

        num_bytes = data-192;

        // Get the actual data for the run.

        data  = (unsigned char)getc(fp);

        // Replicate the data in the buffer num_bytes times.

        while(num_bytes-->0)
            {
            image->buffer[count++] = data;

            } // end while

        } // end if rle
    else
        {
        // Actual data; just copy it into the buffer at the
        // next location.

        image->buffer[count++] = data;

        } // end else not rle

    } // end while

// Move to the end of the file, then back up 768 bytes to the
// beginning of the palette.

fseek(fp,-768L,SEEK_END);

// Load the palette into the VGA's palette registers.
```

```
for (index=0; index<256; index++)
    {
    // Get the red component.

    image->palette[index].red=(unsigned char)(getc(fp) >> 2);

    // Get the green component.

    image->palette[index].green = (unsigned char)(getc(fp) >> 2);

    // Get the blue component.

    image->palette[index].blue  = (unsigned char)(getc(fp) >> 2);

    } // end for index

fclose(fp);

// Change the palette to the newly loaded palette if commanded
// to do so.

if (enable_palette)
    {

    // For each palette register, set to the new color values.

    for (index=0; index<256; index++)
        {

        Set_Palette_Register(index,
                    (RGB_color_ptr)&image->palette[index]);

        } // end for index

    } // end if change palette

} // end PCX_Load

//////////////////////////////////////////////////////////////

void PCX_Delete(pcx_picture_ptr image)
{
// This function deallocates the buffer region used for the PCX
// file load.

_ffree(image->buffer);

} // end PCX_Delete

//////////////////////////////////////////////////////////////

void PCX_Show_Buffer(pcx_picture_ptr image)
{
// Just copy the PCX buffer into the video buffer.

char far *data;
```

continues

Listing 4.3. continued

```
data = image->buffer;

_asm
   {
   push ds                     ; save the data segment
   les di, video_buffer        ; point es:di to video buffer
   lds si, data                ; point ds:si to data area
   mov cx,320*200/2            ; move 32000 words
   cld                         ; set direction to forward
   rep movsw                   ; do the string operation
   pop ds                      ; restore the data segment
   }

} // end PCX_Show_Buffer
```

You can use the functions in Listing 4.3 to load, display, and delete PCX files. Let's understand the usage of the functions in Listing 4.3 and review a small demo that loads a PCX file and displays it.

As you see, there are only four functions:

☐ We use the first function, PCX_Init(), before loading a PCX file. Use PCX_Init() to initialize a previously defined pcx_picture structure and allocate the appropriate memory for the decompression buffer.

☐ The next function of interest is the file-loading function itself, PCX_Load(). This is the workhorse of all the functions. PCX_Load() opens the PCX file you requested to load, loads it into the decompression buffer, and loads and installs the new VGA palette (if you so desire). The function then closes the file and exits.

☐ Once a PCX file has been loaded, you may want to view it or use it as a background for your game. You can accomplish this using the PCX_Show_Buffer() function. PCX_Show_Buffer() transfers the data from the pcx_picture data structure's decompression buffer to the video buffer, and hence to the video screen.

☐ The final function we need is something that deallocates the memory used by the decompression buffer. The function that frees up the buffer memory is PCX_Delete(), and is equivalent to freeing the buffer field of the pcx_picture structure back to the heap.

Caution: These functions are all easy to use, but they all have one little shortcoming that may or may not disturb you: they have very little error checking. If the calling function makes calls to them thinking they're bulletproof, magical things may happen to your PC.

The reason they have so little error checking is that I've left such common-sense topics up to you. Implement error checking however you wish. We have so much to cover, I don't feel it necessary to belabor such common things as checking file names and NULL pointers. I'd rather supply you with clean code so you can focus on the video-game aspects of the code and not some general error-handling scheme.

Now that we have an overall view of each of the functions, let's take a look at their syntax and parameters. All these functions take a pointer to a pcx_picture; in the case of PCX_Load(), the function also takes a file name and a palette-load flag. There's a demo after the syntax explanations.

4

Syntax

The syntax for the PCX_Init() function is

```
void PCX_Init(pcx_picture_ptr image);
```

where *image* is a pointer to a pcx_picture structure.

The syntax for the PCX_Load() function is

```
void PCX_Load(char *filename, pcx_picture_ptr image,
              int enable_palette);
```

where:

☐ *filename* is a pointer to a DOS filename that holds the PCX file to be loaded.

☐ *image* is a pointer to the pcx_picture structure you wish used as the recipient of the data.

☐ The enable_palette variable is a flag that denotes whether or not the color palette at the end of the PCX file should be loaded into the VGA card's color registers.

The syntax for the PCX_Show_Buffer() function is

```
void PCX_Show_Buffer(pcx_picture_ptr image);
```

where *image* is a pointer to the pcx_picture structure you wish displayed on the video screen.

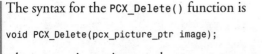

The syntax for the `PCX_Delete()` function is

```
void PCX_Delete(pcx_picture_ptr image);
```

where *image* is a pointer to the `pcx_picture` structure you wish deallocated.

Time for a demo program! I've written a small program that uses the new PCX file functions along with a couple of functions from our evolving library, gamelib.lib. The demo program is called pcxshow. It enables you to display a 320x200-pixel, 256-color PCX file by supplying the file name as a command-line parameter.

Listing 4.4 contains the source code for the program.

Listing 4.4. A PCX file-display program (pcxshow.c).

```
// I N C L U D E S /////////////////////////////////////////////

#include <io.h>
#include <conio.h>
#include <stdio.h>
#include <stdlib.h>
#include <dos.h>
#include <bios.h>
#include <fcntl.h>
#include <memory.h>
#include <malloc.h>
#include <math.h>
#include <string.h>

#include "graph3.h"  // Our graphics functions from Day 3

// S T R U C T U R E S /////////////////////////////////////////

typedef struct pcx_header_typ
        {
        char manufacturer;
        char version;
        char encoding;
        char bits_per_pixel;
        int x,y;
        int width,height;
        int horz_res;
        int vert_res;
        char ega_palette[48];
        char reserved;
        char num_color_planes;
        int bytes_per_line;
        int palette_type;
        char padding[58];

        } pcx_header, *pcx_header_ptr;
```

```
typedef struct pcx_picture_typ
        {
        pcx_header header;
        RGB_color palette[256];
        char far *buffer;

        } pcx_picture, *pcx_picture_ptr;

// P R O T O T Y P E S ///////////////////////////////////////////

void PCX_Init(pcx_picture_ptr image);

void PCX_Load(char *filename,
              pcx_picture_ptr image,int enable_palette);

void PCX_Delete(pcx_picture_ptr image);

void PCX_Show_Buffer(pcx_picture_ptr image);

// F U N C T I O N S ///////////////////////////////////////////

void PCX_Init(pcx_picture_ptr image)
{
// This function allocates the buffer region needed to load a
// PCX file.

if (!(image->buffer = (char far *)
                    _fmalloc(SCREEN_WIDTH * SCREEN_HEIGHT + 1)))

   printf("\ncouldn't allocate screen buffer");

} // end PCX_Init

/////////////////////////////////////////////////////////////////

void PCX_Load(char *filename,
              pcx_picture_ptr image,int enable_palette)
{
// This function loads a PCX file into a picture structure. The
// actual image data for the PCX file is decompressed and
// expanded into a secondary buffer within the picture
// structure. The separate images can be grabbed from this
// buffer later. Also, the header and palette are loaded.

FILE *fp;
int num_bytes,index;
long count;
unsigned char data;
char far *temp_buffer;

// Open the file.

fp = fopen(filename,"rb");

// Load the header.
```

continues

Listing 4.4. continued

```c
temp_buffer = (char far *)image;

for (index=0; index<128; index++)
    {
    temp_buffer[index] = (char)getc(fp);
    } // end for index

// Load the data and decompress it into the buffer.

count=0;

while(count<=SCREEN_WIDTH * SCREEN_HEIGHT)
    {
    // Get the first piece of data.

    data = (unsigned char)getc(fp);

    // Is this an RLE?

    if (data>=192 && data<=255)
        {
        // How many bytes are in the run?

        num_bytes = data-192;

        // Get the actual data for the run.

        data  = (unsigned char)getc(fp);

        // Replicate the data in the buffer num_bytes times.

        while(num_bytes-->0)
            {
            image->buffer[count++] = data;

            } // end while

        } // end if rle
    else
        {
        // Actual data; just copy it into the buffer at the
        // next location.

        image->buffer[count++] = data;

        } // end else not rle

    } // end while

// Move to the end of the file, then back up 768 bytes to the
// beginning of the palette.

fseek(fp,-768L,SEEK_END);

// Load the pallete into the VGA's palette registers.
```

```
for (index=0; index<256; index++)
    {
    // Get the red component.

    image->palette[index].red
         =(unsigned char)(getc(fp) >> 2);

    // Get the green component.

    image->palette[index].green=(unsigned char)(getc(fp) >> 2);

    // Get the blue component.

    image->palette[index].blue=(unsigned char)(getc(fp) >> 2);

    } // end for index

fclose(fp);

// Change the palette to the newly loaded palette if commanded
// to do so.

if (enable_palette)
    {

    // For each palette register, set to the new color values.

    for (index=0; index<256; index++)
        {

        Set_Palette_Register(index,
                    (RGB_color_ptr)&image->palette[index]);

        } // end for index

    } // end if change palette

} // end PCX_Load

//////////////////////////////////////////////////////////////////

void PCX_Delete(pcx_picture_ptr image)
{
// This function deallocates the buffer region used for the
// PCX file load.

_ffree(image->buffer);

} // end PCX_Delete

//////////////////////////////////////////////////////////////////

void PCX_Show_Buffer(pcx_picture_ptr image)
{
// Just copy the PCX buffer into the video buffer.
```

continues

137

Listing 4.4. continued

```c
char far *data;

data = image->buffer;

_asm
    {
    push ds              ; save the data segment
    les di, video_buffer ; point es:di to video buffer
    lds si, data         ; point ds:si to data area
    mov cx,320*200/2     ; move 32000 words
    cld                  ; set direction to forward
    rep movsw            ; do the string operation
    pop ds               ; restore the data segment
    }

} // end PCX_Show_Buffer

// M A I N //////////////////////////////////////////////////////

void main(int argc, char **argv)
{
long index;                  // Loop counter.
pcx_picture background_pcx;  // This PCX structure holds the
                             // background imagery.
FILE *fp;                    // Used to see whether the file
                             // exists.

// Make sure there's a file name.

if (argc<2)
    {
    printf("\nUsuage: pcxshow filename.pcx");
    return;

    } // end if

// Test whether the file exists, but not for the PCX extension.

if (!fopen(argv[1],"rb"))
    {
    printf("\nFile:%s - not found!",argv[1]);
    return(1);
    } // end if not found
else
    {
    fclose(fp);
    } // end else found

// Set the video mode to the 320x200, 256-color mode.

Set_Video_Mode(VGA256);

// Load in the background.

PCX_Init((pcx_picture_ptr)&background_pcx);
```

```
PCX_Load(argv[1], (pcx_picture_ptr)&background_pcx,1);

PCX_Show_Buffer((pcx_picture_ptr)&background_pcx);

PCX_Delete((pcx_picture_ptr)&background_pcx);

// Wait for the user to press a key.

while(!kbhit()){}

// Dissolve the screen...in one line, might I add!

for (index=0; index<=300000; index++,
    Plot_Pixel_Fast(rand()%320, rand()%200, 0));

// Go back to text mode.

Set_Video_Mode(TEXT_MODE);

} // end main
```

Building an Executable: To make an executable of the program in Listing 4.4, you can either type it in or use the source on the companion CD. The name of the source is pcxshow.c. The precompiled executable is named pcxshow.exe. As before, use the following compile line for Microsoft C:

```
cl -AM -Zi -c -Fc -Gs -G2 pcxshow.c
```

After compiling the program in this manner you can link it to the standard libraries and to our previously generated game library, gamelib.lib, with a link line such as:

```
link /ST:8192 /CO pcxshow,,,graphics.lib+gamelib.lib,,
```

This creates a final executable named pcxshow.exe.

To run the program, type in pcxshow with the file name of a PCX image you wish displayed. As an example, typing

```
pcxshow outpost.pcx
```

displays the background for the Attank!!! demo at the end of today's chapter.

If you don't want to type the program in, you can find the C code on the companion CD under the name pcxshow.c.

4

Analysis The program functions in a straightforward manner:

1. First, the command-line parameters are tested to see whether the user has typed in a second parameter; that is, if there's a file name to load.

2. The program then performs a test on the file name to see if it's in the local directory. Note that there are no further tests to check whether the file has a PCX extension or any other kind of error-checking facilities.

3. After setting the video mode to mode 13h, the program initializes the PCX structure `background_pcx`.

4. The filename that was sent on the command line (the PCX file to load) is loaded into the PCX structure's decompression buffer. At this point the file is fully decompressed and waiting to be displayed.

5. The call to `PCX_Show_Buffer()` displays the PCX file.

6. The call to `PCX_Delete()` deallocates the memory buffer used by the PCX file load so that it can be used by other processes.

Even though we've deleted the memory buffer, the PCX image is still visible. This is because the bit map was copied from the PCX buffer to the video buffer. This is a common technique used in video games: we load a PCX image into an off-screen buffer, sit on it for a while, copy it into the video buffer before, and discard the original PCX image in memory because it's no longer needed. Finally, the program waits for a key press. It then does a pixel-dissolve of the screen and returns to DOS.

Listing 4.4 shows us how to load a PCX file and display it on the screen. This ability is great for backgrounds and full-screen animation, but what about loading in smaller bit maps for our sprites? That's our next topic.

Extracting Bit Maps from PCX Files

As we discussed earlier, we load an entire PCX file and scan small cells out of it for the imagery used as the animation cells for our sprites. We must write a function that takes as parameters:

☐ A PCX structure

☐ The cell location we wish to "grab"

☐ The sprite itself, in which we place the animation cells extracted from the PCX file

The function should use the width and height of a sprite, along with the cell location, to compute the pixel location within the PCX bit map from which to extract the sprite image, as shown in Figure 4.6.

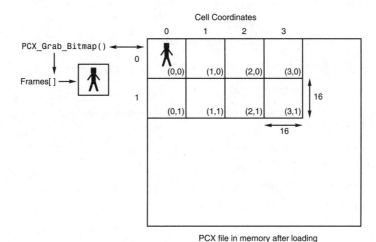

PCX_Grab_Bitmap() uses the cell coordinates
to compute where the bit map should be
extracted from the loaded .PCX file. The cell
coordinates are multiplied by the size of the
cell in pixels to obtain a final position in the
PCX bit map.

Figure 4.6. *Extracting a sprite from a PCX file.*

The function must scan each pixel row of the requested cell and store it in a continuous region of memory within the sprite structure itself. This region of memory is one of the pointer locations within the frames field of the sprite structure.

The function to extract a sprite is shown in Listing 4.5.

Listing 4.5. Extracting a sprite from a loaded PCX file.

```
void PCX_Grab_Bitmap(pcx_picture_ptr image,
                     sprite_ptr sprite,
                     int sprite_frame,
                     int grab_x, int grab_y)

{
// This function grabs a bit map from the PCX frame buffer. It
// uses the convention that the 320x200-pixel matrix is
// subdivided into a smaller matrix of nxn adjacent squares.
```

continues

Listing 4.5. continued

```
int x_off,y_off, x,y;
char far *sprite_data;

// First, allocate the memory for the sprite in the sprite
// structure.

sprite->frames[sprite_frame] = (char far *)_fmalloc(sprite_width * sprite_height + 1);

// Create an alias to the sprite frame for ease of access.

sprite_data = sprite->frames[sprite_frame];

// Now load the sprite data into the sprite frame array from the
// PCX picture.

x_off = (sprite_width+1)  * grab_x + 1;
y_off = (sprite_height+1) * grab_y + 1;

// Compute the starting y address.

y_off = y_off * 320;

for (y=0; y<sprite_height; y++)
    {

    for (x=0; x<sprite_width; x++)
        {

        // Get the next byte of the current row and place it
        // into the next position in the sprite frame data
        // buffer.

        sprite_data[y*sprite_width + x]
                    = image->buffer[y_off + x_off + x];

        } // end for x

        // Move to the next line of the picture buffer.

        y_off+=320;

    } // end for y

// Increment the number of frames.

sprite->num_frames++;

// Done! Let's bail!

} // end PCX_Grab_Bitmap
```

Once a sprite structure has been initialized and a PCX file loaded, you can use the PCX_Grab_Bitmap() function in Listing 4.5 to load in the frames of animation for a sprite.

The function is self-contained: it not only scans the image out of the PCX file, but also allocates the memory needed for the sprite image itself, based on the size of the sprite image being extracted. Let's see what the parameters of the function do. The following code fragment defines the calling syntax of the function

```
void PCX_Grab_Bitmap(pcx_picture_ptr image,
                     sprite_ptr sprite,
                     int sprite_frame,
                     int grab_x, int grab_y);
```

where:

> *image* is a pointer to the PCX file structure, already loaded.
>
> *sprite* is a pointer to the sprite to which you wish the images loaded.
>
> *sprite_frame* is the frame or cell number of the image you wish loaded into the frames array. The first sprite bit map would be 0, the second would be 1, and so on.
>
> *grab_x* is the x-cell location you wish scanned out of the PCX image.
>
> *grab_y* is the y-cell location you wish scanned out of the PCX image.

Now let's see how the function works. The PCX_Grab_Bitmap() function isn't optimized at all because it's not time critical. This is because the function is used during the initialization section of the game, when imagery and data structures are being loaded and processed. The function is not used during the game loop, and can therefore be written using less-complex techniques than the sprite-rendering functions we see shortly. With that in mind, let's discuss the main points of the function.

1. First, the function allocates the memory for the bit map by using the width and height of the sprite (which are globals named sprite_width and sprite_height) and multiplying them together. The result of the multiplication is the number of bytes needed to allocate for the sprite bit map. This is true because in mode 13h there's exactly one byte per pixel.

2. During the next phase of the function, the starting pixel location of the requested bit map in the PCX image is computed. This is used as the upper-left corner for the extraction loop, which follows.

3. Finally, using the computed starting position, the function scans the specified rectangle out of the PCX image, a row at a time, using two for loops. As the data is retrieved from the PCX image, it's placed unchanged into the sprite structure at the desired sprite-frame location indexed by sprite_frame.

4. When the function completes, it increments the number of frames in the sprite structure and returns.

It may seem as though we jumped the gun a bit by explaining how to extract a bit map image from a PCX file and store it in a sprite structure when we haven't even written the software to create sprites. The fact is, I wanted you to see all the PCX functions in the same place. Anyway, now let's see what's needed to create a sprite.

Creating and Destroying Sprites

Creating a sprite is simple: we need only define a sprite using the proper data structure, and then write some functions that either fill in the data structures to create a sprite, or free up any memory used by a sprite to delete one. For the following discussion, let's assume we have the following definition:

```
sprite toy;  // Create a sprite named toy.
```

Also we need a couple of global variables, `sprite_width` and `sprite_height`, that store the width and height of the sprite currently being manipulated. Let's assume that we've defined these as follows:

```
int sprite_width = 16;
int sprite_height = 16;
```

We could make the sprite any size we wish. However, this is a traditional size, and works well for our purposes here. Let's write a function that initializes a sprite structure. The code for this function, `Sprite_Init()`, is shown in Listing 4.6.

Listing 4.6. Initializing a sprite structure.

```
void Sprite_Init(sprite_ptr sprite,
                 int x,int y,int ac,int as,int mc,int ms)
{
// This function initializes a sprite with the sent data.

int index;

sprite->x            = x;
sprite->y            = y;
sprite->x_old        = x;
sprite->y_old        = y;
sprite->width        = sprite_width;
sprite->height       = sprite_height;
sprite->anim_clock   = ac;
sprite->anim_speed   = as;
sprite->motion_clock = mc;
sprite->motion_speed = ms;
sprite->curr_frame   = 0;
sprite->state        = SPRITE_DEAD;
sprite->num_frames   = 0;
sprite->background   =
        (char far *)_fmalloc(sprite_width * sprite_height+1);
```

```
// Set all bit-map pointers to null.

for (index=0; index<MAX_SPRITE_FRAMES; index++)
    sprite->frames[index] = NULL;

} // end Sprite_Init
```

Analysis The `Sprite_Init()` function doesn't do anything magical: it simply takes as parameters a pointer to the sprite and each of the fields in the sprite structure, which we've seen previously. As an example, to create a sprite that has all its fields initialized to zero using the sprite we've defined as toy, we would make the following call:

```
Sprite_init((sprite_ptr)&toy,0,0,0,0,0,0);
```

This would initialize toy, set its position to (0,0) and place a zero in each of its animation and timing fields.

This is actually how I define most of the sprites in the games we explore in the remaining days of study. If I want to change one of the fields, I usually do it during runtime. However, we may as well have the functionality to set fields of a sprite to some known value during creation of the sprite.

The next function we need is one to destroy a sprite. This function would be called at the end of a game, or when the images loaded into a sprite were no longer needed. The latter could occur when the sprite was changing into something else because of the game flow, or when the sprite was just killed and will no longer be in the game. In any case, we should write a function to deallocate all the memory that sprite used up. A function to do just that, called `Sprite_Delete()`, is shown in Listing 4.7.

Listing 4.7. Deleting a sprite.

```
void Sprite_Delete(sprite_ptr sprite)
{
// This function deletes all the memory associated with
// a sprite.

int index;

_ffree(sprite->background);

// Now deallocate all the animation frames.

for (index=0; index<MAX_SPRITE_FRAMES; index++)
    _ffree(sprite->frames[index]);

} // end Sprite_Delete
```

 As usual, the function takes a pointer to the sprite and not the sprite itself. The function operates by freeing up all the sprite imagery and the memory buffer used for the background under a sprite. (Remember: when moving objects around a screen, we must scan the background under a sprite before placement and then replace the background when moving the sprite, or the screen image will become garbled.)

 Warning: As a rule, whenever you allocate memory, make sure you have a mechanism to deallocate it when it's no longer needed—unless you really know what you're doing and don't care.

Now that we can create, destroy, and load imagery into a sprite structure, let's see how we would draw a sprite on the screen.

Drawing Sprites

Drawing a sprite on the video screen is easy with the setup we have now (along with the fact that we're using mode 13h). We need only copy the bit map in the sprite structure to the video buffer at the requested location. This is done row by row, taking a pixel at a time from the frame to be displayed and placing it in the appropriate position in the video buffer. The data for these frames of animation is, of course, in the frames field of the sprite structure. Each frame or bit map of the sprite is accessed by dereferencing a FAR pointer. These pointers are what's contained within the frames field of the sprite structure. Figure 4.7 shows a graphical representation of this.

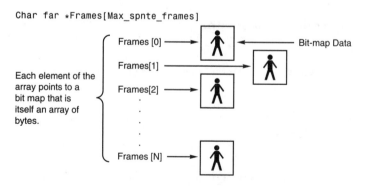

Figure 4.7. *A graphical representation of the sprite* frames *array.*

It looks as though all we need to know to draw the sprite is the position of the sprite and the sprite frame—and that's about it. That'll do it; however, there's one thing we must take into consideration before we write the function to draw the sprite: *transparency!*

Transparency

The sprite images we draw typically will have holes in them, and regions that are supposed to be transparent. How do we accomplish this transparency?

We accomplish transparency by selecting a transparent pixel value or color. Traditionally, this value is black (or color 0). Therefore, any part of a sprite that is color 0 is supposed to be transparent, and hence not copied to the video buffer.

Having the ability to create transparent regions is necessary if the sprite doesn't take up the entire rectangle and is not completely opaque. Take a look at Figure 4.8 to see what would happen if a sprite were placed on a background without transparency.

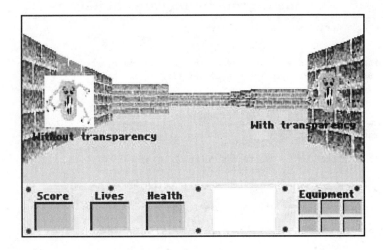

Figure 4.8. *The effects of transparency.*

Implementing transparency is simple. However, it consumes time in a really time-critical portion of the rendering code. We must test each pixel for transparency—that is, the value of 0—before plotting it on the video screen. This means that for a 16×16-pixel image there are 256 added `ifs` to test for transparent pixels. This is a real bummer, but we can work around it using a technique called *transparency encoding*, which we get into shortly.

There are some cases where the sprite is actually completely rectangular and opaque. You can make a special version of the sprite-drawing function to take advantage of these special cases.

Game Law: A video game's performance is the conglomeration of special cases that are handled in such a way that it seems that they're all the same case.

Getting back to the topic of drawing sprites, we see that we simply need to access the sprite structure properly (taking transparency into consideration), and then plot the sprite pixel by pixel. That seems good enough to me, so let's see some code! Listing 4.8 contains code to draw a sprite to the video buffer.

Listing 4.8. Drawing a sprite to the video buffer.

```
void Draw_Sprite(sprite_ptr sprite)
{

// This function draws a sprite on the screen, row by row,
// really quickly. Note the use of shifting to implement
// multiplication.

char far *work_sprite;
int work_offset=0,offset,x,y;
unsigned char data;

// Alias a pointer to the sprite for ease of access.

work_sprite = sprite->frames[sprite->curr_frame];

// Compute the offset of the sprite in the video buffer.

offset = (sprite->y << 8) + (sprite->y << 6) + sprite->x;

for (y=0; y<sprite_height; y++)
    {
    // Copy the next row into the screen buffer using memcpy
    // for speed.

    for (x=0; x<sprite_width; x++)
        {

        // Test for a transparent pixel; that is, 0. If the
        // pixel is not transparent, draw it.

        data=work_sprite[work_offset+x];
```

```
        if (data)
             video_buffer[offset+x] = data;

        } // end for x

    // Move to the next line in the video buffer and in the
    // sprite bit-map buffer.

    offset      += SCREEN_WIDTH;
    work_offset += sprite_width;

    } // end for y

} // end Draw_Sprite
```

 The Draw_Sprite() function in Listing 4.8 takes a single parameter: a pointer to the sprite. (Isn't that a nice interface!?) The function operates this way:

1. First, the function computes the starting location in the video buffer to which the sprite will be blitted. (We covered blitting on Day 3.)

2. At that point a double for loop begins. The for loop draws the sprite, pixel by pixel, a row at a time. Note how each pixel is tested for transparency.

3. When a row is completely drawn, the pointer into the video buffer is moved down a scan line: 320 bytes are added to it, and the process is repeated.

4. This continues until each row of the sprite has been drawn into the video buffer.

Scanning the Background Under a Sprite

As we've been learning, you can't just draw a sprite on the screen without taking into consideration what was under it. You must scan the background under a sprite if you wish to restore it.

It's necessary to scan the background under a sprite before the sprite is positioned if the background is to ever be restored. Without this step in the animation cycle, the background under game objects is slowly eaten alive.

Scanning the background is easy to do. We can use Draw_Sprite() as the basis for a new function, which I've named Behind_Sprite(). This new function works in a manner similar to Draw_Sprite(), except its source data is the video buffer and its destination is the background buffer within the sprite structure. The Draw_Sprite() function is shown in Listing 4.9.

Listing 4.9. Scanning the background from the video buffer.

```
void Behind_Sprite(sprite_ptr sprite)
{

// This function scans the background behind a sprite so that,
// when the sprite is drawn, the background isn't obliterated.

char far *work_back;
int work_offset=0,offset,y;

// Alias a pointer to the sprite background for ease of access.

work_back = sprite->background;

// Compute the offset of the background in the video buffer.

offset = (sprite->y << 8) + (sprite->y << 6) + sprite->x;

for (y=0; y<sprite_height; y++)
    {
    // Copy the next row out of the screen buffer into the
    // sprite background buffer.

    _fmemcpy((char far *)&work_back[work_offset],
            (char far *)&video_buffer[offset],
            sprite_width);

    // Move to the next line in the video buffer and in the
    //sprite background buffer.

    offset     += SCREEN_WIDTH;
    work_offset += sprite_width;

    } // end for y

} // end Behind_Sprite
```

As usual, the function takes a single parameter: a pointer to the sprite that's about to be placed on the screen. Here's what happens:

1. The function begins (as does Draw_Sprite()) by computing the starting offset into the video buffer from which the image should be scanned.

2. The function then takes a simple approach and scans out the data row by row. This scanning is accomplished at warp speed through the use of the _fmemcpy() function, which is superfast.

3. When each row of the rectangular region has been scanned and placed into the background buffer, the function is complete and it exits.

 Tip: Although the memcpy() functions would seemingly be the fastest way to move memory in and out of the video buffer, they can be improved upon. They're all based on byte-wide data movements and can be rewritten to use WORD-wide data movements. This increases the speed of most video operations by almost 100 percent.

We can draw sprites and scan the background under them, but what about replacing the background when we're ready to move them? That's the next topic of discussion.

Erasing Sprites

The phrase "erasing sprites" is a bit misleading, but it's the best way I can generalize the terminology until we learn more advanced ways of rendering sprites, which happens on Day 6 (in the chapter called "Real-Time Animation and FX"). In any case, in erasing a sprite what we really want is to replace the background that was under the sprite. In essence, this erases or removes the sprite image, and makes the original bit map in the sprite's position visible again.

To implement a sprite eraser we must blit the scanned background bit map that was stored in the background buffer in the sprite structure. This can be accomplished in a manner similar to that used by the Draw_Sprite() function, except that the source data isn't a sprite frame but the background data. Moreover, it's unnecessary to test for transparency in the case of replacing the background, because the concept of transparency has no meaning for the background.

The code to erase a sprite is shown in Listing 4.10.

Listing 4.10. Erasing a sprite by replacing its background.

```
void Erase_Sprite(sprite_ptr sprite)
{
// Replace the background that was behind the sprite.

// This function replaces the background that was saved from
// where a sprite was going to be placed.

char far *work_back;
int work_offset=0,offset,y;

// Alias a pointer to the sprite background for ease of access.

work_back = sprite->background;
```

continues

Listing 4.10. continued

```
// Compute the offset of the background in the video buffer.

offset = (sprite->y << 8) + (sprite->y << 6) + sprite->x;

for (y=0; y<sprite_height; y++)
    {
    // Copy the next row out of the screen buffer into the
    // sprite background buffer.

    _fmemcpy((char far *)&video_buffer[offset],
             (char far *)&work_back[work_offset],
             sprite_width);

    // Move to the next line in the video buffer and in the
    // sprite background buffer.

    offset     += SCREEN_WIDTH;
    work_offset += sprite_width;

    } // end for y


} // end Erase_Sprite
```

Analysis At this point, you should be able to analyze the function in a millisecond or so. It begins, like all the others, by computing the starting address in the video buffer, and then proceeds to copy a row at a time into the video buffer, and using the _fmemcpy() function.

We now have a good portion of a sprite engine completed. There are, of course, many things more that we can add. However, with the functions we currently have, we could actually create something decent.

Let's switch gears and talk some about moving the sprites.

Moving Sprites

Sprite movement is a form of animation. Theoretically, to move an object we must *translate* its position. This is achieved by adding values to the object's current position. In the case of a sprite, the current location is stored within the structure as a pair of coordinates, named x and y. With our previous declaration of a sprite named toy, we could access these elements of the structure with the following:

```
toy.x =
toy.y =
```

where the right side of the equation would, of course, be the value or expression to which we want to equate the position variables.

Accomplishing motion is a matter of adding on a constant or variable value to the position variables, such as:

```
toy.x += delta_x;
toy.y +=delta_y;
```

where `delta_x` and `delta_y` are the translation factors by which we'd like to move the object or sprite. These variables can also be interpreted as the *velocity* of the sprite if they're continually added to the sprite's position every cycle through the game loop.

In any case, applying the previous operation to the position elements of the sprite structure moves the sprite. However, you must take care to change the position variables at the right time in the animation cycle, which usually falls between the erasing and drawing phases.

As we learned yesterday, the animation cycle consists of a few major steps. As a change of pace, here they are, illustrated as a partial C-language algorithm that moves a sprite on the screen.

Algorithm 4.3. Animating a sprite.

```
// Scan what's under the sprite before entering the event loop.
// This must be done, or the first call the Erase_Sprite() will
// be invalid!

Behind_Sprite((sprite_ptr)&toy);

// The event loop

while(!done)
{
// First, erase the old sprite.

Erase_Sprite((sprite_ptr)&toy);

// Move the sprite.

toy.x += dx;
toy.y_+=dy;

// Change the frame of the sprite, if we so desire.

toy.curr_frame = new_frame;

// Scan the background under the sprite.

Behind_Sprite((sprite_ptr)&toy);

// Draw the sprite.

Draw_Sprite((sprite_ptr)&toy);

} // end while
```

This animation algorithm is simple. It consists of only three sections:

☐ The first section is where we erase the sprite.

☐ Next, we move and animate the sprite.

☐ Finally, we scan the background and draw the sprite.

We then loop back and do it again. This is called the *erase-move-draw* cycle, and is the most common technique used in a non-buffered video system. By *non-buffered*, I mean one in which we do all of our drawing and animation right in the video buffer in deference to another, off-screen buffer. (We actually learn about using an off-screen buffer later today, but for now let's stick to the system of using the video buffer itself as the work area.)

You may have noticed a section in the algorithm that changes the frame of the sprite. This is where we accomplish visual changes to the shape of the sprite. We might have four frames of a little man walking. We would cycle through them by changing the frame in the sprite structure. This would result in the bit-map image of the sprite changing as a function of time, looking as if it were animated like a cartoon.

Actually, animation takes much more than simply changing frames. You must take into consideration factors such as the direction of the sprite's movement, the timing of the animation cells, and so on if a professional-quality game is to emerge, and we discuss those issues on Day 6 ("Real-Time Animation and FX"). Changing the frame in this way, however, results in a crude form of animation.

We're almost ready to see the Attank!!! demo. First, though, let's touch upon a few advanced topics that we cover fully in a couple of days—just so we're not taken by surprise then!

Scaling Sprites

Scaling a sprite means to make the sprite's bit-map image larger or smaller. Figure 4.9 shows a bit map scaled to a few different sizes.

To accomplish bit-map scaling is no easy task. If you take a brute-force approach, the result will be really slow execution time. To implement a sprite scaler that has the performance we need, we must use some advanced concepts, such as look-up tables, fixed-point math, and more. These concepts (and others) are covered later, when we discuss optimization techniques on Day 8 (in the chapter called "Warp Speed, Anyone?"). For now, I just want you to know that being able to scale a sprite is an important feature that can add more options to the complexity of a PC game.

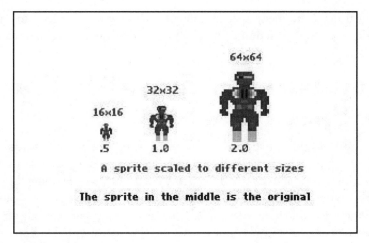

Figure 4.9. *The results of scaling.*

Rotating Sprites

Sprite rotation means to rotate the sprite parallel to some imaginary axis, as if the sprite were a 3-D object instead of flat. This axis could be the x-axis, the y-axis, or the z-axis. (You can imagine the z-axis as one piercing the screen.)

In the case of rotating the sprite on the z-axis, parallel to the screen plane, the rotation *can* be done algorithmically, but seldom is. For example, the Attank!!! demo at the end of the chapter uses sprite rotation; however, I pre-rotated the tank images using Dpaint. That is, I drew the tank in one position and then generated 15 other bit maps by slowly rotating the tank bit map. These rotated images were then loaded into the sprite structure and used to simulate rotation of the sprite. We use precomputed rotations because rotating the sprite in real time would take too much computational power, and it's better to use memory to hold the pre-rotated bit maps of the image.

In the case in which the bit map is rotated on some arbitrary axis, we can't do this algorithmically because the bit map is 2-D. The only way to accomplished this is by taking snapshots of a real 3-D image, either physically (using a video camera and a video-capture board) or by using some piece of 3-D rendering software, such as Autodesk's 3D Studio. In any case, as before, the rotated imagery is stored in the frames of the sprite. As each frame is displayed, the sprite looks like it's rotating.

As an example of sprite rotation along with scaling, there's a program on the companion CD called shuttle.exe. The program displays a shuttle and lets you fly it around the screen

by using the numeric keypad. The software to write this program is beyond what we've done so far, so you don't get any source code; you only get to see what's in store!

Transparency Encoding Sprite Data for Speed and Size

Up to this point I've tried to steer away from optimizational topics. However, we're starting to write some of the more important graphics functions, and I want to start acclimating you to always try to figure out a better way of doing things. When we wrote the sprite-drawing function Draw_Sprite(), we uncovered an unfortunate fact: the function had to be able to implement transparency, and the only way to do this was test each pixel before it was drawn. This was time-consuming; a simple calculation showed that 256 ifs would be executed for a simple 16×16-pixel bit map. There's got to be a faster way to draw sprites that somehow deals with transparency better, right?

Well, of course there is. There are about a million ways to draw sprites faster. We briefly discuss one of them next, and I'll leave the other 999,999 for you as an exercise.

If we didn't have to take into consideration transparency, we could draw the sprite row by row and make use of the _fmemcpy() function. This would make the function orders-of-magnitude faster. The question is, how can we do this and support transparency at the same time? The answer is to do some preprocessing of the image data and encode it in a way that's more applicable to sprite drawing with transparency effects. Let's take a look at a typical sprite image; see Figure 4.10.

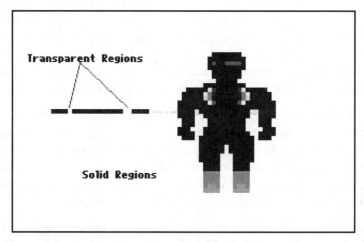

Figure 4.10. *Solid and transparent components of a strip of pixels.*

As you see, if we look at the image as horizontal *strips*, we see that the image has longs runs of solid, opaque pixels and transparent pixels. Why don't we somehow encode these runs of solid and transparent into the image data itself? Then, during the drawing algorithm, we can use this information to figure out ahead of time how many continuous pixels in any given row are solid or transparent. This is the basis of *transparency encoding*. We won't be implementing a function to draw sprites using this technique because I'm not sure that we even need it for the games we create in this book, but let's look at it anyway. You may want to use this method someday.

As an example let's see a hypothetical compression and decompression system we could use to do transparency encoding. For the system to work we'd have to write a function that takes the extracted bit map (using `PCX_Grab_Bitmap()`) and encodes the transparent and solid runs in the image data somehow. Then we could rewrite the `Draw_Sprite()` function so it knows about the new encoding scheme, and can use the information to speed up the rendering process by drawing large horizontal strips instead of single pixels.

We could use the following scheme to encode transparency in bit-map data:

A standard bit map is a continuous array of pixel values ranging from 0–255. As our first premise, we no longer allow the numbers 254 or 255. We are going to use these to denote solid and transparent runs, respectively. The encoding works this way:

1. The bit map is scanned row by row by the transparency encoder.

2. When a run of solid pixels is found, the encoder writes a 254 to a destination buffer that holds the encoded bit map. The coder also writes the number of solid bytes and the data bytes themselves to the buffer.

3. When a run of transparent zeros is found, the encoder writes a 255 to the buffer along with the number of transparent pixels.

    There's no need to place a number of zeros in the destination buffer as this would be redundant.

Figure 4.11 shows this encoding process graphically.

4. We would then rewrite the sprite drawing function to look for a 254 or 255. When it found it, it would read the next byte, which is the run length. The run length can represent either a run of solid or transparent. In the case of transparent then the offset of the current video position is advanced. If the run is solid then the bytes following the run length byte are copied using the `_fmemcpy()` function into the video buffer.

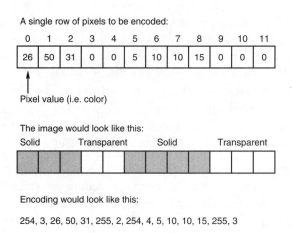

Figure 4.11. *Encoding a row of pixels for more efficient drawing.*

Of course, details such as the video-buffer offset would have to be changed with care. However, the basic steps are as we have discussed. This technique has only two shortcomings:

☐ First, the numbers 254 and 255 are no longer valid colors.

☐ Second, the largest runs that can be encoded are 255.

Neither of these problems are overwhelming concerns and would pose little restraint on a game.

Testing for Sprite Collision

Collision is one of the most important things in a video game. (Most of a video game is just testing whether you hit something or it hit you!) Accommodating sprite collision is easy and can be done in a few lines. However, let's talk for a moment about the theoretical aspects of collision detection in general.

In the real world, collision between two objects occurs when some of the volume of one object tried to occupy the same space as some of the volume from another object. As this is impossible (at least, the Pauli Exclusion Principle says it is), a collision occurs, and the objects either deform or bounce off each other. In the 2-D space that is the computer screen, objects collide when a portion of their imagery overlaps. Figure 4.12 shows two objects that have collided.

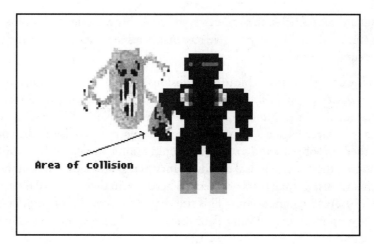

Figure 4.12. *Two sprites colliding.*

Testing correctly for collision is time consuming, and becomes more complex as the shapes we're testing become more complex. For example, testing two squares for collision is much simpler than testing the two arbitrary polygons shown in Figure 4.13.

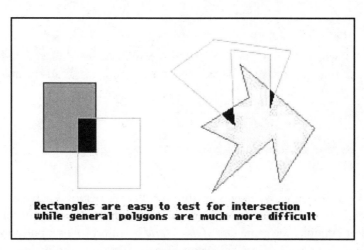

Figure 4.13. *A comparison of rectangular and polygonal intersections.*

This is because the number of tests and the testing algorithm itself are closely related to the geometry of the objects being tested for collision. I'm sure you've played a game before and thought that you weren't hit—as your character was blown into a billion subatomic particles. In some cases, you probably were right! Collision detection in video games is done in a way to give reasonable results—most of the time at the expense of accuracy, but at the gain of speed.

Why do we have to be able to test collisions so quickly? The reason is that collision testing is a *quadratic problem*, meaning that, in the worst case, the number of tests increases as the square of the number of objects. As an example, if there were 10 objects, we'd have to test object 1 against the remaining nine objects for collision, then object 2 against the other nine objects, and so on. This would result in a total of 10*9=90 collision tests. Of course, there's a great deal of redundancy here, and a closer look at the problem dictates that we test only all pairs of objects. Therefore, in the case of 10 objects we need only do C(10,2)=45 computations. This still requires quite a bit of computational time, so we must optimize the collision algorithms as much as possible to minimize the amount of math done.

Note: The notation C(*n,r*) means "how many ways can *n* items be chosen *r* at a time?" This is from a field of mathematics called *combinatorics*, and not for the weak-hearted. The formula to compute C(*n,r*) is:

$$\frac{n!}{(n-r)!\ r!}$$

where ! means "factorial," and is computed by a descending product of the number to which the factorial is being applied. As an example,

```
5!=5*4*3*2*1
```

Also, as a convention, 0!=1.

In a video game, we may want to test collisions between polygon-based objects. This might occur in a situation where the objects on the screen were not composed of bit maps. (For example, the game *Out of this World* by Interplay uses polygon-based graphics, as does *Alone in the Dark*.) Polygon-based collision detection can be complex, and we discuss it later, when we cover polygon graphics on Day 5, in the chapter called "Polygon Engines." For now, we can consider bit-map based or sprite-based collision.

The first problem we encounter when trying to write a sprite-collision algorithm is that we don't know what the sprite looks like, because it's a bit map. It could be a man, a monster, or a flower. To test for collision between sprites, we might be tempted to test each solid pixel between each sprite to see whether they intersect. However, you'd quickly come to the conclusion that this would take so many calculations that you might be waiting for years for your game to test all the collisions!

The solution to all our problems is to use the *bounding box* of the sprites. This means that we place an imaginary rectangle around the sprite based on the sprite's size, as shown in Figure 4.14.

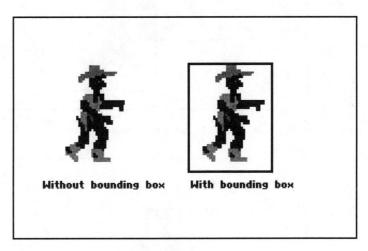

Without bounding box   With bounding box

Figure 4.14. *Placing a bounding box around a sprite.*

Hence, each sprite is a rectangle as far as collision detection is concerned, and testing rectangles for collision is easy. We need only test whether the rectangles overlap in both the x- and y-axes, and *presto!* We've tested for collision.

The drawback to this technique is invalid collisions. Figure 4.15 shows the problem graphically; we see two sprites and their bounding boxes. The bounding boxes overlap and a collision would be flagged. However, the sprites themselves do not intersect!

This is the problem with using bounding-box collision detection. One heuristic solution, and the one most commonly used, is to shrink the size of the bounding box around the sprite, because most of the sprite's "mass" is in the center of the sprite's bit map anyway. This seems to give better results, as shown in Figure 4.16.

Figure 4.15. *An invalid collision caused by bounding boxes.*

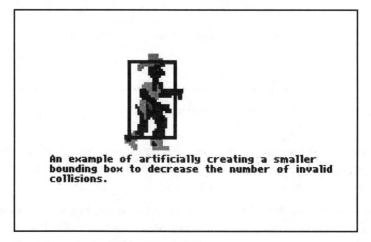

Figure 4.16. *Making the bounding box smaller.*

Now that we've a background for the problem and its possible solutions, let's write a function that tests whether two sprites have collided. This function, `Sprite_Collide()`, is shown in Listing 4.11.

Listing 4.11. A sprite collision-detection function.

```
int Sprite_Collide(sprite_ptr sprite_1, sprite_ptr sprite_2)
{
// This function tests the bounding boxes of each sprite to see
// whether a collision has occured. If so, a 1 is returned;
// otherwise, a 0 is returned.

int dx,dy;

// Compute the amount of overlap, if any.

dx = abs(sprite_1->x - sprite_2->x);
dy = abs(sprite_1->y - sprite_2->y);

// Test the x and y extents. Note how the width and height are
// decreased by a percentage of the actual width and height.
// This is to make the bounding box a little more realistic, as
// very seldom will an object be rectangular. This helps to
// ensure that there's a solid collision.

if (dx<(sprite_width-(sprite_width>>3)) && dy<(sprite_height-(sprite_height>>3)))
   {

   return(1);

   } // end if collision occured
else
   {

   return(0);

   } // end else

} // end Sprite_Collide
```

 The function takes as parameters two pointers to the two sprites we wished tested for collision. The function tests the bounding boxes for collision and returns a 1 if there was a collision, or a 0 otherwise.

The only thing interesting about the function is that, when it tests the objects to see whether their x- and y-extents overlap, it tests with bounding boxes that are the original size minus 12.5 percent of the sprites' real size. This is to ensure that, if a collision is flagged, there was a solid collision!

You may want to play with this subtraction factor and make it smaller or larger depending on the general shapes of your sprites. If your sprite bit maps take up the whole sprite, you may be able to bypass it altogether. If, on the other hand, the sprite bit maps are smaller than the size of the sprite, you may want to increase the subtraction factor and, in essence, scale down the bounding box.

Sprite Animation and Timing

We've already learned what the word "animation" means in general. Loosely defined, it means to change or transform an object in some way. In the case of video games, *animation* means to change what our sprites look like as a function of time, along with moving them around the screen. We're a long way from understanding all the idiosyncrasies of animation timing yet, but we need to start somewhere. I just want to brief you on concepts we cover over several later days.

When we animate a sprite, we change the cell or bit map that's displayed. This is done by using another bit map, predrawn and previously stored in the frames array of the sprite structure. Imagine that we've written a game and we want to make a game creature walk across the screen. We have a few cells drawn of the creature walking. Now, remember that on Day 1 we learned about game loops and the steps that a game loop goes through every game cycle. We know how to move an object: we simply add a constant to its position. To animate it, we could change frames every game cycle and then start over when the frames of animation were done. This works, but it may look artificial. There might be objects in the game that you want to animate faster than others, such as objects that move faster than others, and so on. However, each object gets only one iteration per game cycle—so how can we accomplish this kind of relative animation?

We can accomplish relative animation speeds and velocities by using timing parameters and counters. Because the PC is a single-tasking computer (on which we're trying to simulate multiple events in a single stream), we don't have the luxury of multiple processes running at their own speeds. All objects in a game run at the same speed. If we want one sprite to animate faster or slower than another, therefore, we must use a counter that counts up to a value. When the counter reaches some pre-set threshold value, the sprite frame is changed or the sprite is moved, or whatever. This way, some sprites seem to be on different time scales than other sprites.

Implementing these kinds of abilities is the reason I added the extra fields to the sprite structure. To refresh your memory, here are those extra fields again:

```
int anim_clock;     // The animation clock
int anim_speed;     // The animation speed
int motion_clock;   // The motion clock
int motion_speed;   // The motion speed
```

I placed these variables into the structure for one reason: to help with these kinds of timing problems. We use them later in the book as we write different games, but now you know what they're for and how they're used.

Adding to the Graphics Library

We've touched on many different sprite-related topics thus far. Now let's take everything we know and put it all into one big program that shows off all the different functions and their use.

On the companion CD I've supplied all the functions we've created today in the form of a single C module and a header file. As per our convention, the name of today's module is graph4.c, and the header is graph4.h. Let's compile the new module and add it to our graphics library gamelib.lib. Take these steps to compile graph4.c and add it to our library:

1. Compile graph4.c with the following compile line:

   ```
   cl -AM -Zi -c  -Fc -Gs -G2 graph4.c
   ```

   This would result in the object graph4.obj, which we want to insert into our library gamelib.lib.

2. Take the object graph4.obj and, using the Microsoft Library Manager, add the object to the library gamelib.lib.

   Now when we print out the functions within the graphics library, we should see something like this:

   ```
   _Behind_Sprite....graph4      _Blit_Char........graph3
   _Blit_String......graph3      _Delay............graph3
   _Draw_Sprite......graph4      _Erase_Sprite.....graph4
   _Get_Palette_Register..graph3 _Get_Pixel........graph4
   _H_Line...........graph3      _H_Line_Fast......graph3
   _PCX_Delete.......graph4      _PCX_Grab_Bitmap..graph4
   _PCX_Init.........graph4      _PCX_Load.........graph4
   _PCX_Show_Buffer..graph4      _Plot_Pixel.......graph3
   _Plot_Pixel_Fast..graph3      _rom_char_set.....graph3
   _Set_Palette_Register..graph3 _Set_Video_Mode...graph3
   _Sprite_Collide...graph4      _Sprite_Delete....graph4
   _sprite_height....graph4      _Sprite_Init......graph4
   _sprite_width.....graph4      _video_buffer.....graph3
   _video_buffer_w...graph3      _V_Line...........graph3

   graph3 Offset: 00000010H Code and data size: 1485H
     _Blit_Char        _Blit_String        _Delay
   _Get_Palette_Register
     _H_Line           _H_Line_Fast      _Plot_Pixel       _Plot_Pixel_Fast
     _rom_char_set     _Set_Palette_Register               _Set_Video_Mode
     _video_buffer     _video_buffer_w   _V_Line
   graph4            Offset: 00001b20H  Code and data size: 1caeH
     _Behind_Sprite    _Draw_Sprite      _Erase_Sprite     _Get_Pixel
     _PCX_Delete       _PCX_Grab_Bitmap  _PCX_Init         _PCX_Load
     _PCX_Show_Buffer  _Sprite_Collide   _Sprite_Delete    _sprite_height
     _Sprite_Init      _sprite_width
   ```

4

As you can see, we now have all the functions from Day 3 and today in the library gamelib.lib. Isn't that cool!? Now let's use our new library to make a demo program.

Attank!!!

Maybe it was all those years of playing that tank game on the Atari 2600, but I still have a warm spot in my heart for tank games. Anyway, I thought I'd just write a tank demo that uses all the functions we've created thus far. The program is called Attank!!!. It uses the PCX file functions along with all the sprite functions. If you comprehend this program, you're on your way to writing games.

There's an executable of the program named attank.exe on the companion CD. I suggest running it and playing Attank!!! for a couple of minutes so you can better value out of the analysis section. To run the program just enter attank. You'll see two tanks, one red and one blue. You are the blue tank. Use the numeric keypad to move your tank, and try to avoid the renegade red tank that's controlled by the computer. When you're done, press the Q key to quit.

Now that you've seen the program operate, let's see the source code that comprises the program. Listing 4.12 contains the source code.

Listing 4.12. Attank!!! the demo program (attank.c).

```
// I N C L U D E S //////////////////////////////////////////////

#include <io.h>
#include <conio.h>
#include <stdio.h>
#include <stdlib.h>
#include <dos.h>
#include <bios.h>
#include <fcntl.h>
#include <memory.h>
#include <malloc.h>
#include <math.h>
#include <string.h>

#include <graph.h>    // Microsoft's stuff, if we need it.

#include "graph3.h"  // The module from Day 3
#include "graph4.h"  // The module from Day 4

// D E F I N E S //////////////////////////////////////////////

#define TANK_SPEED  4
#define PI          (float)3.14159
```

```
// M A I N ////////////////////////////////////////////////////////

void main(void)
{


long index;
                  // Used as a loop index

sprite tank1,       // The player's sprite
       tank2;       // The enemy sprite

pcx_picture background_pcx,
                  // This PCX structure holds the background
                  // imagery.
           objects_pcx;
                  // This PCX structure holds the foreground
                  // imagery.


int tank1_direction=0,
                  // The tank's current direction; also the
                  // current frame.
    tank2_direction=0,
                  // 0 is straight up North.
    done=0;
                  // The system exit flag


float dx,         // Motion variables
      dy,
      angle;

// S E C T I O N  1 ////////////////////////////////////////////////

// Set the video mode to the 320x200, 256-color mode.

Set_Video_Mode(VGA256);

// Load in the background.

PCX_Init((pcx_picture_ptr)&background_pcx);

PCX_Load("outpost.pcx", (pcx_picture_ptr)&background_pcx,1);

PCX_Show_Buffer((pcx_picture_ptr)&background_pcx);

// Put up the title.

Blit_String(90,2,7,"A T T A N K ! ! !",1);

PCX_Delete((pcx_picture_ptr)&background_pcx);

// Load the PCX file with the tank cells.

// Load in the player's imagery.
```

continues

Listing 4.12. continued

```
PCX_Init((pcx_picture_ptr)&objects_pcx);

PCX_Load("tanks.pcx", (pcx_picture_ptr)&objects_pcx,0);

// S E C T I O N  2 /////////////////////////////////////////////

// Initialize the sprite size and data structure.

sprite_width  = 16;
sprite_height = 16;

// Place tank1 (the player) at the bottom of the screen.

Sprite_Init((sprite_ptr)&tank1,160,150,0,0,0,0);

// Grab all 16 images from the tank's PCX picture.

for (index=0; index<16; index++)
    {

    PCX_Grab_Bitmap((pcx_picture_ptr)&objects_pcx,
                    (sprite_ptr)&tank1,index,index,0);

    } // end for index

// Place tank2 (the enemy) at the top of the screen.

Sprite_Init((sprite_ptr)&tank2,160,50,0,0,0,0);

// Grab all 16 images from the tank's PCX picture.

for (index=0; index<16; index++)
    {

    PCX_Grab_Bitmap((pcx_picture_ptr)&objects_pcx,
                    (sprite_ptr)&tank2,index,index,1);

    } // end for index

// Kill the PCX memory and buffers now that we're done with them.

PCX_Delete((pcx_picture_ptr)&objects_pcx);

// S E C T I O N  3 /////////////////////////////////////////////

// Point the tanks straight up.

tank1.curr_frame = tank1_direction;
tank2.curr_frame = tank2_direction;

// Scan the background under the tanks on the first iteration.

Behind_Sprite((sprite_ptr)&tank1); // The player
Behind_Sprite((sprite_ptr)&tank2); // The enemy
```

```
// Wait for exit; this is the main event loop.

while(!done)
     {

// S E C T I O N  4 //////////////////////////////////////////

     // Erase the player's tank.

     Erase_Sprite((sprite_ptr)&tank1);

     // Erase the enemy tank.

     Erase_Sprite((sprite_ptr)&tank2);

// S E C T I O N  5 //////////////////////////////////////////

     // Test whether the user wants to translate or rotate
     // the tank.

     if (kbhit())
        {

        // Reset translation factors.

        dx=dy=0;

        // Test what key was pressed.

        switch(getch())
             {

             case '6': // Rotate to the right.
                  {
                  // Change the direction of the tank; make
                  // sure to wrap around.

                  if (++tank1_direction > 15)
                     tank1_direction=0;

                  } break;

             case '4': // Rotate to the left.
                  {
                  // Change the direction of the tank; make
                  // sure to wrap around.

                  if (--tank1_direction < 0)
                     tank1_direction=15;

                  } break;

             case '8': // Move forward.
                  {
                  // Based on the direction variable, compute
                  // the translation factors.
```

continues

Listing 4.12. continued

```
                        // Compute the angle in radians.

                        angle = (90+360-22.5*(float)tank1_direction);

                        // Compute factors based on angle and speed.

                        dx = TANK_SPEED * cos(PI*angle/180);
                        dy = TANK_SPEED * sin(PI*angle/180);

                        } break;

                case '2': // Move backward.
                        {
                        // Based on the direction variable, compute
                        // the translation factors.

                        // Compute the angle in radians.

                        angle = (90+360-22.5*(float)tank1_direction);

                        // Compute factors based on angle and speed.

                        dx = TANK_SPEED * cos(PI*angle/180);
                        dy = TANK_SPEED * sin(PI*angle/180);

                        } break;

                case 'q': // Quit
                        {
                        // Set the exit flag to true.

                        done=1;

                        } break;

                default:break;

                } // end switch

// S E C T I O N  6 ///////////////////////////////////////////////

        // Do the translation.

        tank1.x+=(int)(dx+.5);
        tank1.y-=(int)(dy+.5);

        // Test whether the player bumped into edge. If so, push
        // the player's tank back.

        // Set the frame based on the new direction.

        tank1.curr_frame = tank1_direction;

        } // end if kbhit
```

```
// S E C T I O N  7 ///////////////////////////////////////////

    // Now move the enemy tank.

    // Test whether it's time to turn.

    if (rand()%10==1)
        {

        // Select the direction to turn.

        switch(rand()%2)
            {

            case 0: // Turn to the right.
                {

                if (++tank2_direction > 15)
                    tank2_direction=0;

                } break;

            case 1: // Turn to the left.
                {

                if (--tank2_direction < 0)
                    tank2_direction=15;

                } break;

            default:break;

            } // end switch

        // Set the frame based on the new direction.

        tank2.curr_frame = tank2_direction;

        } // end if

// S E C T I O N  8 ///////////////////////////////////////////

    // Compute the angle in radians.

    angle =  (90+360-22.5*(float)tank2_direction);

    // Compute factors based on angle and speed.

    dx = (TANK_SPEED+rand()%2) * cos(PI*angle/180);
    dy = (TANK_SPEED+rand()%2) * sin(PI*angle/180);

    // Do the translation.

    tank2.x+=(int)(dx+.5);
    tank2.y-=(int)(dy+.5);
```

4

continues

Listing 4.12. continued

```c
// S E C T I O N  9 /////////////////////////////////////////////

// Test whether enemy has hit an edge. If so, wrap to the
// other side.

if (tank2.x > (320-(int)sprite_width) )
   tank2.x = 0;

else
if (tank2.x < 0 )
   tank2.x = 319-(int)sprite_width;

if (tank2.y > (200-(int)sprite_height) )
   tank2.y = 0;

else
if (tank2.y < 0 )
   tank2.y = 199-(int)sprite_height;

// S E C T I O N  10 /////////////////////////////////////////////

// Scan the background under the player's tank.

Behind_Sprite((sprite_ptr)&tank1);

// Scan the background under the enemy tank.

Behind_Sprite((sprite_ptr)&tank2);

// Draw the player's tank.

Draw_Sprite((sprite_ptr)&tank1);

// Draw the enemy tank.

Draw_Sprite((sprite_ptr)&tank2);

// Test for collision.

if (Sprite_Collide((sprite_ptr)&tank1,(sprite_ptr)&tank2))
   {
   // Do something spectacular!


   } // end if collision

// Delay the main loop for a second so the user can see a
// solid image.

Delay(2); // Wait approximately 55ms (1/18.2 of a second).

} // end while

// S E C T I O N  11 /////////////////////////////////////////////

// Dissolve the screen...in one line, might I add!
```

```
for (index=0; index<=300000; index++,
    Plot_Pixel_Fast(rand()%320, rand()%200, 0));

// Go back to text mode.

Set_Video_Mode(TEXT_MODE);

} // end main
```

Building an Executable: To make an executable of the program in Listing 4.10, you can either type it in or use the source on the companion CD. The name of the source is attank.c. The precompiled executable is named attank.exe. As before, use the following compile line for Microsoft C:

```
cl -AM -Zi -c  -Fc -Gs -G2 attank.c
```

After compiling the program in this manner, you can link it to the standard libraries and to our game library, gamlib.lib.

4

You're probably saying, "The program is so big and it doesn't even do anything!" I used to say things like that—until I started writing games and realized what complex programs they are. You think this program is big!? Remember, it uses functions in our library, so it's really bigger! The main portion of the program is delineated into sections so we can analyze the function of each section.

1. The Section 1 variable is the initialization portion of the code. Here we load up the PCX files and display the title message.

2. Section 2 is where is the sprites are initialized. Their imagery is extracted from the previously loaded PCX files. Also, the PCX file that held the imagery for the sprites is now deleted: it's no longer needed.

3. Section 3 is the point right before the entrance to the game loop. Here we set up the tanks and scan what's under them for the first time. If this first time scanning isn't done, garbage is placed down on the first iteration through the game loop.

4. Section 4 begins the animation cycle. Here we erase the objects; in this case, the tanks. Erasure is done by replacing their backgrounds.

5. Section 5 is where some action takes place. We test the keyboard for input and then, based on that, move the tank either forward or backward or rotate it. In the case of rotation, we simply increment or decrement the tank's direction variable. The motion computation is more complex. To move the tank forward or backward, the direction of the tank is determined based on the direction variable. The direction variable is scaled and converted into an angle and used as the input to the trig functions `sine` and `cosine`. The results are used as the translation factors for the tank.

6. Section 6 is where the actual translation takes place, along with the updating of the current animation frame. Also, note how the translation factors are rounded and then truncated during the cast to integer. It's usually wise to round floating-point integers up when assigning them to nonfloating-point data types.

7. Section 7 is where a new direction is computed for the computer-controlled, enemy tank. The program uses a random number to select a new direction and, based on that, rotates the enemy tank either right or left one click. The program then updates the current frame of the enemy tank.

8. Section 8 is where the enemy tank's direction is used to compute translation factors. Using these translation factors, the enemy tank is then moved. Note that the enemy tank is always in motion.

9. The code in Section 9 is something we haven't directly talked about yet. These few lines of code make sure that when the enemy tank hits a screen border, it appears on the opposite side. This calculation is done by comparing the enemy tank's position to the screen boundaries.

10. Section 10 is the end of the game loop. Here we scan the backgrounds where the sprites are about to be blitted. We then draw the sprites and, finally, check for collision. Note that nothing happens when a collision occurs; you're going to add this later!

    After the collision there's a curious call to `Delay()`. I've been keeping this function quiet for now, but it was actually in the function within graph3.c. It uses the PC's internal timer, which clicks at 18.2 times per second, to create a time delay. (We learn more about this function and the timer in later chapters.) The reason for the call to the function is to slow the game down and lock it to a maximum operational rate of 18.2 frames/second. Without it, each PC would run the demo at different speeds because each PCX has faster or slower hardware. (See why timing is important?)

11. Section 11 is the end of the road. We dissolve the screen by plotting a zillion black pixels, restore the screen mode back to 80x25 text, and exit to DOS.

Getting Rid of the Flicker: Double Buffering

If you watch the Attank!!! demo closely, you should notice that every so often the imagery seems to flicker. This is actually a problem that occurs in many video games, and there's an elegant solution.

Within a video game, images on the screen can flicker if they're updated in a time span that's longer than 16 milliseconds. You see, 16 milliseconds is the smallest amount of time it takes an (average) human to perceive visual changes. Therefore, in a video game you must make sure that, if you're going to erase and draw something, you do it faster than 16 milliseconds. In the Attank!!! demo we see flicker because of two reasons:

☐ First, the drawing of the video image takes place completely out of synchronization with the video display. The best time to update the video screen is during the vertical retrace, when the screen image can't be disturbed with updates to the video buffer.

☐ Second, there's flicker because we erase the objects, then do some processing, and then redraw the objects. Hence, there's a time period in which there's nothing on the screen! This time period is sometimes longer that 16 milliseconds.

There are many techniques to decrease flicker, such as page flipping, double buffering, using longer-persistence phosphors on the video screen, and using dedicated video hardware. In this book we stick to programming solutions, so let's look first at double buffering. Page flipping is similar, and we cover that in a moment.

Double buffering is a technique in which the screen image is drawn in an off-screen buffer and then the entire screen is drawn or moved into the video buffer at once, as shown in Figure 4.17.

Using this technique, there's never a time when the screen image is blank and the objects are invisible. Another nice thing about this technique is that, once screen has been built up in another buffer, the game can wait for the vertical retrace and then copy the entire off screen buffer into the video buffer. The image appears to be rock steady; moreover, it's locked to the refresh rate of the monitor.

All of our games in this book use double buffering, and in the near future we create modified versions of the sprite functions and everything else that writes directly to the video buffer.

4

Page flipping is a twist on double buffering. Page flipping uses two pages that are really two video buffers, supported by the VGA card. While one video page is being displayed, the other is being updated. When it's time for another frame of animation, the updated frame is "paged to" and, instantly, the new image is displayed on the screen. This technique also gives a perfect image without flicker. The only problem is that the VGA card supports only one video page in mode 13h. Bummer!

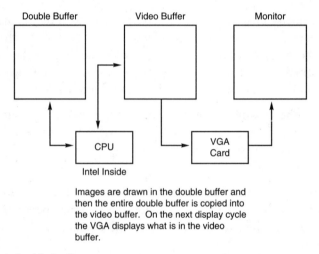

Images are drawn in the double buffer and
then the entire double buffer is copied into
the video buffer. On the next display cycle
the VGA displays what is in the video
buffer.

Figure 4.17. *A double buffer system.*

Summary

Today we learned quite a bit of information. If you got it all, you could probably close this book now and write some cool games.

We learned about sprites, including how to draw and animate them. We also learned about PCX files: how the data is encoded in them and how to load them. We then covered some advanced topics, such as collision and double buffering. Finally, we saw some code for a complete demo—and got a look at how big a video game can be!

Q&A

Q What is a sprite?

A A sprite is an object in a video game that moves around—and doesn't disturb the background. Sprites are usually based on bit-mapped imagery.

Q **Describe the erase-move-draw cycle.**

A When trying to accomplish animation of any kind, the object being moved or animated (or both) must first be erased, then moved, and, finally, redrawn in its new location. This entire process must be done without destroying the background.

Q **What is double buffering?**

A Double buffering is the technique of using a second, off-screen memory region to build up the screen display. Then, when an entire frame is built up, the whole image is copied into the video buffer.

Q **What is the `extra` field in the sprite data structure for?**

A It's used for anything that wasn't originally placed in the data structure. For example, it could point to another structure. Without it, changes to the original data structure would entail recompilation of all the programs and libraries.

Q **Why must the bit maps for the sprites be drawn in a regular matrix of cells?**

A So the `PCX_Grab_Bitmap()` function can figure out where you want the bit map for the sprite extracted. Otherwise, you'd have to give the function screen coordinates and the dimensions of the sprite. In video games, all sprites in a class of sprites usually have the same dimensions, and the animation frames of any particular sprite all have the same dimensions.

Q **What is RLE encoding?**

A RLE stands for run-length encoding, and is a method of compression used to encode long runs of similar values into smaller amounts of data. RLE encoding is the technique used in PCX files.

Workshop

The Workshop section presents quiz questions to help you cement your new knowledge and exercises to give you experience using what you've learned. Try to understand the questions and exercises before moving on to the next lesson. The answers are in Appendix B.

Quiz

1. In the `Draw_Sprite()` function, how many `if` statements would be executed for a sprite that was 64×64 pixels?

2. What is a bounding box?

3. Why is the `Delay()` function called at the end of the game loop in Attank!!!?

4. How are sprites rotated?

5. What is meant by *flickering*?

6. Describe transparency encoding.

7. Why is it important to compress graphical images?

Exercises

1. Write a function that scales a sprite.

2. Write a program that places a PCX file on the screen and then fades to black when a key is pressed.

3. Write a function named `Sprite_Fizz()` that makes a sprite fizzle away in 25 cycles.

4. When the tanks collide in the Attank!!! demo, nothing happens. Make something spectacular happen when the tanks collide.

5. Create a starfield that looks like the one in the shuttle.exe program; that is, one that swings around. Then place a sprite of a spaceship with glowing engines in the center of the starfield. (Hint: use color-register animation to make the engines glow.)

Polygon Engines

Traditionally, arcade and video games have been produced by means of bit-mapped graphics (although vector graphics were used in games such as Asteroids, Battlezone, and Star Wars—in prehistoric times). We've become familiar with this type of technology. However, there's another technique used in video games, called *polygon-based graphics*. This technique is based on modeling the objects in the game world as collections of triangles, squares, and general n-sided objects.

Polygon graphics are mostly used in the arena of flight simulation and 3-D games. However, in light of the improved speed of PCs and the increasing power of graphics cards, many 2-D games based on polygon graphics have hit the streets. A favorite game of mine is called Out of This World by Interplay, and is one of the most impressive exhibits I've ever seen of polygon-based graphics applied to a 2-D game.

Anyway, today we learn about polygon-based graphics and add some key functions to our graphics library. We may use polygon-based graphics later in the book—and then again, we may not. Nevertheless, I don't want to leave any calcium carbonate or quartzite crystalline matrices unturned. Here are the main topics for today:

- ☐ Polygon preliminaries
- ☐ The 2-D plane
- ☐ Two-dimensional entities
- ☐ Introduction to polygons
- ☐ Polygon transformations
- ☐ Clipping polygons to the view port
- ☐ High-performance polygon engines
- ☐ Adding to the game library

Polygon Preliminaries

Polygon-based graphics is a technique of drawing on the computer screen using the simple assumption that anything can be modeled with a polygon or a collection of polygons. A polygon is just a closed, multisided object. If we look at the etymology of the word *polygon*, you find it means "multiple sided" or "many sided."

You've already worked with polygons. Rectangles, squares and triangles are polygons, although they're special cases. A rectangle is a polygon with four sides, where each side makes a 90-degree angle with the other. A square not only has the properties of a rectangle, it has the extra condition that the length of each of the sides be equal. The

triangle is a three-sided polygon where the internal angles always add up to 180 degrees. Figure 5.1 shows a few 2-D polygons.

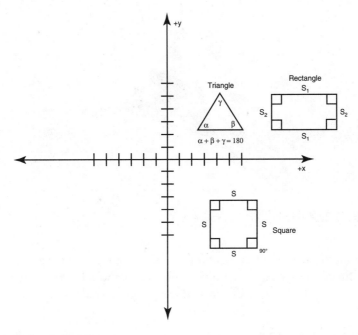

Figure 5.1. *A few 2-D polygons.*

In general, you can think of a polygon as a flat object drawn in two-dimensional space, as on a piece of paper. However, there's no need to adhere to this metaphor. We can, if we wish, think of polygons as three-dimensional entities. For example, Figure 5.2 shows a triangle drawn in three-dimensional space.

Today, however, we're concerned only with 2-D polygons and two-dimensional graphics.

The first question that might come to mind is, "Why even learn about polygon-based graphics?" There are many reasons, but here are the most important:

☐ First, polygon-based graphics are important to understand if you wish to create 3-D games.

☐ Second, bit-mapped graphics are a special case of polygon graphics in which all the polygons are rectangular and a texture or image is mapped on them.

☐ Finally, polygon graphics lend themselves easily to mathematical transformations such as scaling, translation, rotation, and more, all discussed today.

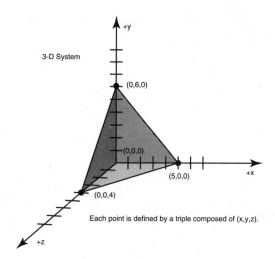

Figure 5.2. *A triangle in 3-D space.*

We want to create a collection of functions that build from the ground up, and then use these functions to create a primitive polygon engine, which we can use to draw images on the computer screen differently than with our standard, bit-mapped methods.

The 2-D Plane

The 2-D plane, or the two-dimensional Cartesian coordinate plane, is just a representation of two-dimensional space. We can use it to draw objects in and perform various operations within. The 2-D plane has two axes:

☐ The x-axis

☐ The y-axis

Figure 5.3 shows a representation of the 2-D Cartesian plane.

As you can see, the x-axis runs horizontally and the y-axis runs vertically: they're perpendicular to each other. Also, the 2-D plane is broken up into four *quadrants* by the axes themselves. These quadrants are named quadrants I, II, III, and IV, increasing numerically in a counter-clockwise direction, as you can see in Figure 5.3.

The aspects of the 2-D plane that make it so attractive for polygon-based graphics is that it's so similar to the computer screen. As we've learned on previous days, mode 13h is laid out as a 2-D matrix with the origin at the upper-left corner of the screen. If you think about it for a moment, you'll realize that mode 13h is really quadrant I of the 2-D

Cartesian coordinate system, save one detail: the y-axis is inverted. This is of little consequence, and can be almost disregarded. See Figure 5.4 for a comparison of quadrant I of the 2-D plane and mode 13h's layout.

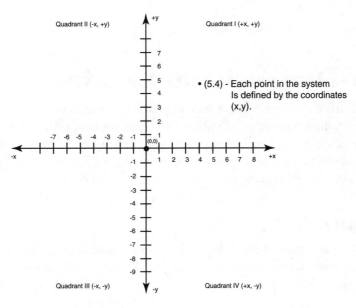

Figure 5.3. *The 2-D Cartesian plane.*

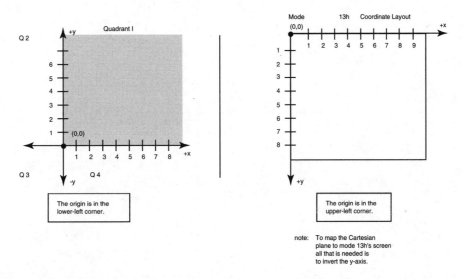

Figure 5.4. *A comparison between mode 13h and the Cartesian plane.*

In general, all the graphic modes of the EGA, VGA, and SVGA cards have their coordinate origins at the upper-left corner of the screen, and are all almost directly mappable to quadrant I of the 2-D Cartesian coordinate system (with the inversion of the y-axis).

Now let's talk about some of the objects that can be drawn in a 2-D plane.

Two-Dimensional Entities

We learned on Days 3 and 4 how to plot points and draw special lines. We were, in essence, drawing on the 2-D plane. However, we were taking more of a bit-mapped approach to things then: looking at all computer images as being composed as a collection of pixels. Although this is true, it's sometimes a good idea to think of the images on the computer screen as being composed of slightly more complex entities.

Points

We have seen points before: they're finite positions on the 2-D plane or on the computer screen. If we plotted a point at location (50,50) on the 2-D Cartesian plane, it would look like Figure 5.5.

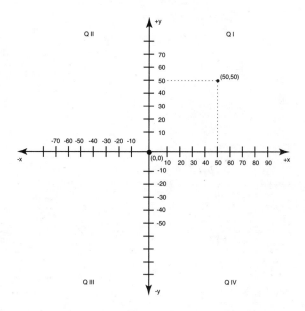

Figure 5.5. *A plot of the point (50,50) on the Cartesian 2-D plane.*

On the other hand, if we plotted a point on the computer screen in mode 13h, it would look like Figure 5.6.

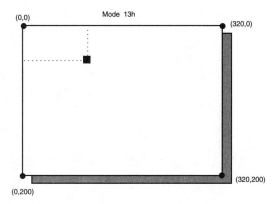

Figure 5.6. *The point (50,50) plotted on mode 13h's screen.*

There's not much difference, actually; hence, we can think of the computer screen as a 2-D plane without any loss of generality. The only thing to remember is that the positive x-axis runs from left to right and the positive y-axis runs from top to bottom.

Lines

The point by itself is pretty boring: it just sits there! However, if we take two points and draw a line between them we have a *line*. (Sorry, I had to use the word "line" to define "line." Sometimes an idea is so simple that it's hard to define and explain without complex logic and mathematics.)

> **Note:** Did you know that it took one of the world's most brilliant mathematicians a whole lifetime and thousands of pages to prove that 1+0 = 1!? Believe it or not, some of the most basic things we take for granted assume almost primal knowledge. (This brings up the question of genetically coded intelligence...)

A line is defined by two points in the 2-D plane, P1 and P2, as shown in Figure 5.7.

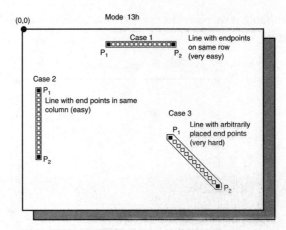

Figure 5.7. *Drawing lines on the video screen.*

In the case of mode 13h, we must draw a line between these two points by plotting pixels that approximate the true line. This necessity stems from the fact that mode 13h, unlike the real 2-D Cartesian coordinate system, has a finite resolution of 320×200. To draw lines, we must build them out of pixels, which always lie on integral boundaries. For example, if one of the points on the line must be at (12.5,120.8), we can plot it at (13,121) if we round the coordinates or (12,120) if we truncate them. In either case, though, there's an error.

Drawing horizontal or vertical lines is easy because we just fill the pixels in a specific row or column. The problem comes in doing this when each of the endpoints of the line isn't in the same row or column, as in Figure 5.7.

Drawing lines between any two endpoints is a rather complex task when the points do not lie in the same row or column. We must look at the mathematical form of a line to gain some insight into how to do this.

A line can be mathematically described by two things:

☐ Its slope

☐ A point on the line and its intercept

The slope of a line is the easiest to understand, so let's begin there.

Slope

You can think of a line as having *slope* relative to the x-axis. Lines with large slopes are quite steep, and lines with gentle slopes are almost be parallel to the x-axis, as shown in Figure 5.8.

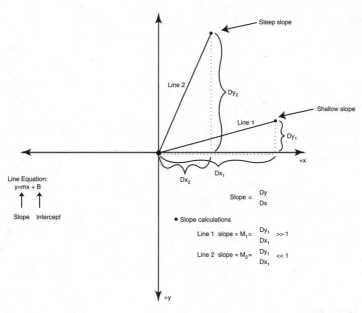

Figure 5.8. *The slope of lines.*

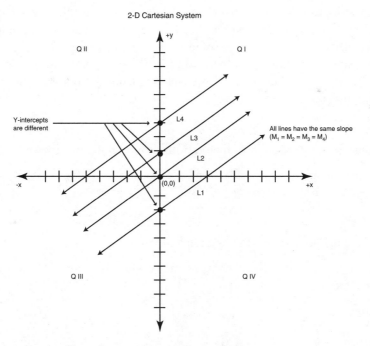

Figure 5.9. *A family of lines having slope 1/2.*

The slope of a line is defined by:

```
         change in y
slope = _____
         change in x
```

In other words, it's the rate at which the y-coordinate changes relative to the x-coordinate. Now we're getting somewhere.

If the two endpoints of a line are (x1,y1) and (x2,y2), the slope would be calculated like this:

```
            (y2-y1)
slope =m = _____
            (x2-x1)
```

Note: Traditionally, the slope of a line is called *m*.

Intercept

The other component that differentiates one line from another is the *intercept*. You see, many lines can have the same slope, as shown in Figure 5.9. Lines having the same slope are said to be *from the same family*. However, notice that each line intercepts the y-axis in a different place. This piece of information, along with the slope, is enough to define a unique line. Hence, the derivation of the point-slope form is complete with the intercept we just defined. (We cover point-slope forms in a moment.) Here's the equation for the slope-intercept form of a line:

```
y = mx+b
```

where *x* and *y* are the coordinates of the points along the line and *b* is the intercept.

As an example of a line, take a look at Figure 5.10. It's the plot of the following line on the 2-D Cartesian plane.

```
y = 2x+4
```

where the slope is 2 and the y-intercept is 4.

If we were to plot the line on the computer screen in mode 13h, the y-axis would just be inverted.

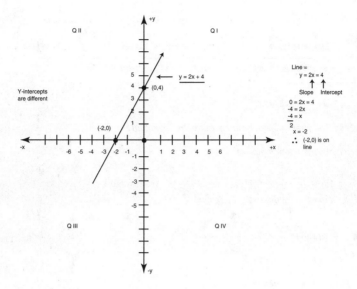

Figure 5.10. *The plot of the line y=2x+4.*

The Point-Slope Form

Before moving on to how we use the equation of a line, we must look at yet another form of the line. This other form is called the *point-slope form*. This is my favorite form because it lends itself to computation more easily when you have the endpoints but not the y-intercept. The point-slope form works in much the same way as the slope-intercept form, but defines a line using the slope of the line along with one point on the line. The point-slope form of a line with endpoints (x1,y1) and (x2,y2) can be written as:

```
y = m(x - x1) + y1
or
y = m(x -x2) + y2
```

where *m* is the slope of the line, which is just (y2-y1)/(x2-x1).

Drawing Lines

We've discussed the formalities of the line. Now, how can we use this information to draw one? The answer is that we must somehow use one of the equations of the line to generate the points along the line. As an example, let's look at an algorithm that works based on the point-slope form of a line.

Algorithm 5.1. Drawing a line the hard way.

```
Given the endpoints of the line are (x1,y1) and (x2,y2):
// Begin

m = (y2-y1) / (x2-x1)

// Test whether x components must be swapped.

if (x1 > x2) then swap(x1,x2)

// Draw the line.

for (index=x1; index<x2; index++)
    {
    // Compute the y coordinate.
    y = m(index - x1) + y1;

    // Plot the point.

    Plot_Pixel(index,y);
    } // end fors
```

Algorithm 5.1 seems simple enough. However, when you're drawing thousands of lines a second, this method won't suffice. We must find a better way. If we analyze Algorithm 5.1, we see that it contains a lot of floating-point operations, which are slower than integer-based operations. The trick is to get rid of them. Unless we both want to get a headache figuring out a way to do this, I suggest we look through one of the hundreds of graphics books available and see if anyone else has solved this problem. Just one minute; let me check...cool! We're in luck. It so happens that a mathematician named Bresenham worked for IBM in the 1960s. It also happens that he figured out a way to draw lines really fast using integers only, and wrote of it in a 1965 paper. Let me see if I can translate the magical inscriptions.

It looks like Bresenham's algorithm works like this. If we take a look at a matrix of pixels with a line drawn on it from P1 to P2, the pixels themselves are not the exact pixel locations that should be drawn, but the nearest ones to the "true line," as shown in Figure 5.11.

If we could somehow figure out which pixel was the nearest one without figuring out which was the exact one, we'd be able to draw a line between two points. The question is, how is this going to help us with floating-point calculations? The answer is that Bresenham's algorithm uses what's called a *decision variable* to decide whether or not to draw the next pixel above or below (or to the right or left) of the previous pixel.

Allow me to clarify. We can speak of two kinds of lines:

- ☐ Lines with |slopes| of greater than 1
- ☐ Lines with |slopes| of less than 1

These lines are shown in Figure 5.12.

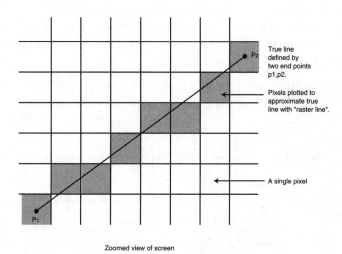

Figure 5.11. *Approximating the "true line" with pixels.*

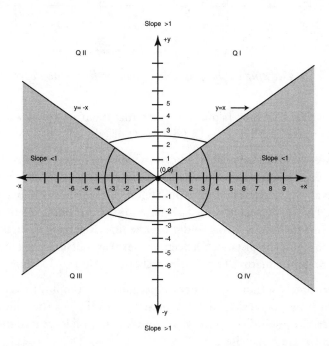

Figure 5.12. *The distribution of slopes.*

The final function we write today breaks these two cases into separate cases. The reason for this is that lines that have a |slope| of less than 1 (expressed as <1) can be drawn using a for loop to increment the x-coordinate, while using a decision variable to change the y-coordinate. Similarly, lines that have a |slope| of greater than 1 (expressed as >1) can be drawn using a for loop that increments the y-coordinate and uses a decision variable to change the x-coordinate. The question is, how do we arrive at this mysterious decision variable? The answer is that the decision variable is based on a single premise, which can be formulated in the following manner:

☐ For lines that have |slopes| <1, given that the pixel (xi,yi) was just drawn, the next pixel is at (xi+1,yi+1), (xi+1,yi-1) or (xi+1,yi), as shown in Figure 5.13.

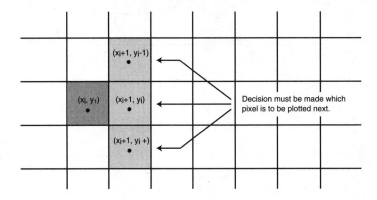

Zoomed view of screen

Figure 5.13. *Deciding on the next pixel to plot for lines with slopes of less than 1.*

☐ For lines that have |slope| >1, given that the pixel (xi,yi) was just drawn, the next pixel is at (xi+1,yi+1), (xi-1,yi+1) or (xi,yi+1), as shown in Figure 5.14.

In essence, the decision variable indicates which way to bias the pixel location. Moreover, because Bresenham's algorithm is inherently iterative, we always know the last pixel—which is always (xi,yi)—and we simply figure out which way to bias the next pixel to be plotted. This can be accomplished by analyzing the true line in relationship to the integral matrix on which we're trying to digitize the line. Referring to Figure 5.15, we see that we can compute the distance between the next two possible pixel locations and the true line we're approximating. (The horizontal case of |slope| <1 is shown is in this example.)

If we can somehow transform the two equations that compute the length into a form that has no floating-point calculation, we are victorious. This can be done using some algebra. However, the result is still somewhat complex, and I'll leave it to those of you who like punishment as an exercise.

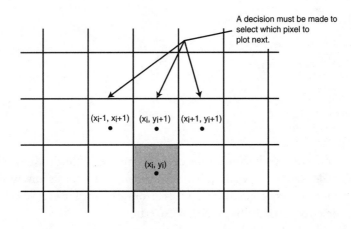

Figure 5.14. *Deciding of the next pixel to plot for lines with |slopes| greater than 1.*

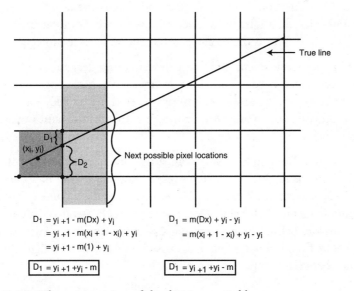

Figure 5.15. *The computation of the decision variables.*

Using the results of the distance decision variable as a foundation, yet another insight can make the algorithm even more efficient. Let me use the case of a line with $|slope| < 1$ for discussion. We know that we can use a for loop to draw the line by calculating the next x-coordinate iteratively, and then computing the next y-coordinate based on some decision variable. The loop looks something like this:

```
y = y1; // Starting point is (x1,y1).

// Draw the (x1,y1) - (x2,y2).

for (x=x1; x<=x2; x++)
    {
    if (decision is up)
       Plot_Pixel(x,y—);
    else
       Plot_Pixel(x,y++);
    } // end for
```

This fragment draws the line for the case of |slope| <1. The decision part is the last piece of the puzzle. We create what's called an *error term*. This tracks how well the line is fitting the true line. We continually adjust this error term until it overflows. At that point, we adjust the error term so that it doesn't overflow.

Now, this next part is important, so pay close attention! The error term is based on comparing the current accumulating slope with that of the true slope and using this as an indicator of when to draw the next pixel above or below the last pixel. In a way, we've normalized the y-component of the slope to the x-component so that, instead of |slope| being a number less then 1, it's been scaled relative to the x-component, or dx, of the slope (slope = dy/dx-M). This is the single fact that allows us to use integers.

To put it in another way, imagine that you were using decimal numbers that had two decimal places. You'd need to take these decimal places into consideration during your calculation. However, if you were to multiply everything by 100, you'd no longer need to do this and you could work solely in integers. In a roundabout way, this is how the error term works.

If the workings of Bresenham's algorithm still seem elusive, there are many text books that go into much further detail. I suggest obtaining a copy of *Computer Graphics: Principles and Practice* by Foley, van Dam, Feiner, and Hughes. It has a much more detailed (not to mention a more mathematical) look at Bresenham's algorithm. Anyway, the math and idea behind Bresenham's algorithm may be complex, but the program to do it isn't. The function in Listing 5.1 is based on Bresenham's algorithm and quickly draws a line between two points in mode 13h.

Listing 5.1. Bresenham's line algorithm modified to write directly into the video buffer.

```
void Bline(int xo, int yo, int x1,int y1, unsigned char color)
{
// This function uses Bresenham's algorithm (IBM 1965) to draw a
// line from (xo,yo) - (x1,y1).

int dx,          // Difference between one x and another.
    dy,          // difference between one y and another.
```

```
      x_inc,          // Amount in pixel space to move during
                      // drawing.
      y_inc,          // Amount in pixel space to move during
                      // drawing.
      error=0,        // The discriminant (i.e., error; i.e,
                      // decision variable).
      index;          // Used for looping.


// Access the video buffer directly for speed.
unsigned char far *vb_start = video_buffer;


// S E C T I O N  1 ///////////////////////////////////////////

// Precompute the first pixel address in the video buffer.
// Use shifts for multiplication.


vb_start = vb_start + ((unsigned int)yo<<6) +
                      ((unsigned int)yo<<8) +
                      (unsigned int)xo;

// Compute the deltas.

dx = x1-xo;
dy = y1-yo;

// S E C T I O N 2 ///////////////////////////////////////////

// Test which direction the line is going in; i.e., the
// slope angle.

if (dx>=0)
   {
   x_inc = 1;

   } // end if line is moving right
else
   {
   x_inc = -1;
   dx    = -dx;  // Need the absolute value.

   } // end else moving left

// S E C T I O N 3 ///////////////////////////////////////////

// Test the y component of the slope.

if (dy>=0)
   {
   y_inc = 320; // 320 bytes per line.

   } // end if line is moving down
else
```

continues

Listing 5.1. continued

```
{
y_inc = -320;
dy   = -dy;  // Need the absolute value.

} // end else moving up

// S E C T I O N 4 /////////////////////////////////////////////

// Now, based on which delta is greater, we can draw the line.

if (dx>dy)
   {

   // Draw the line.

   for (index=0; index<=dx; index++)
       {
       // Set the pixel.

       *vb_start = color;

       // Adjust the discriminate.

       error+=dy;

       // Test if error overflowed.

       if (error>dx)
          {

          error-=dx;

          // Move to the next line.

          vb_start+=y_inc;

          } // end if error overflowed

       // Move to the next pixel.

       vb_start+=x_inc;

       } // end for

   } // end if ¦slope¦ <= 1
else
   {

// S E C T I O N 5 /////////////////////////////////////////////

   // Draw the line.

   for (index=0; index<=dy; index++)
       {
       // Set the pixel.
```

```
        *vb_start = color;

        // Adjust the discriminate.

        error+=dx;

        // Test if error overflowed.

        if (error>0)
           {

           error-=dy;

           // Move to the next line.

           vb_start+=x_inc;

           } // end if error overflowed

        // Move to the next pixel.

        vb_start+=y_inc;

        } // end for

    } // end else ¦slope¦ > 1

} // end Bline
```

We've covered the general mathematical formulation of Bresenham's algorithm and found it to be relatively complex. However, the implementation itself isn't that bad. Let's take a look at the Bline() function. The Bline() function takes five parameters:

☐ The first two pairs of parameters are the (x,y) endpoint coordinates of the line to be drawn.

☐ The last parameter is the color of the line.

Using this information and Bresenham's algorithm, the function draws a line between the two points. Note that one key feature of this function is that it operates directly with the video buffer. In other words, it doesn't make calls to a pixel-plotting function. Rather, it calculates pixel addresses itself for increased speed.

1. Section 1 is the beginning of the function, and where some of the initial important values are computed. The starting address of the video buffer is calculated here, and the x- and y-components of the slope are computed.

2. In Section 2 the function must compute which way the line is to be drawn relative to the x-axis. This information is used later to help move the current pixel location, and is therefore stored in variables used for incrementing the pixel location in the main drawing loop.

Polygon Engines

3. Section 3 is similar to Section 2, except that it makes decisions on the y-component of the slope and creates appropriate variables to track it.

4. In Section 4 the function decides which type of line is being drawn; that is, for a |slope| greater or lesser than 1. Based on this, one of two code segments is entered to draw the line with a particular slope. In the case of Section 4, lines of |slope| less than 1 are processed.

   The algorithm works like this. The x-position of the next pixel is incremented either in the positive or negative direction based on the precomputed variable x_inc. The y-component of the next pixel is the tricky part: the code continually adds to the error term the y-component of the slope. When the error term has exceeded the x-component of the slope (that is, dx), it's time to change the vertical component of the next pixel to be plotted. This is done using y_inc, which is added to the current video-buffer location. Note that y_inc is [+-] 320, because there are 320 bytes per row in the video buffer.

   When the error term has been flagged as overflowed, it's reset by subtracting dx, and the process continues.

5. Section 5 is identical to Section 4 except that Section 5 supports the case of |slope| >1.

Being able to draw a line is one of the most important graphics primitives in a polygon-based system; we wouldn't get very far without it. The line algorithm presented in Listing 5.2 (Bresenham's algorithm with my modifications) is fast; however, it can be made at least four times faster by using symmetry and prediction, which are discussed in advanced graphics texts (such as the aforementioned *Computer Graphics: Principles and Practice*). This kind of speed won't be necessary for our usage, but you should know that there are better ways to do it and each day someone figures out a way to make line drawing a little faster.

As an example of using the line drawing function, I've created a demo program that draws random lines then, when a key is pressed, switches to a familiar-looking screen saver based on the line algorithm. The name of the program is linedemo.exe. The source code is named linedemo.c. The source is shown in Listing 5.2.

Listing 5.2. A demonstration program using the new line drawing function. (linedemo.c)

```
// I N C L U D E S ///////////////////////////////////////////////

#include <io.h>
#include <conio.h>
#include <stdio.h>
#include <stdlib.h>
```

```
#include <dos.h>
#include <bios.h>
#include <fcntl.h>
#include <memory.h>
#include <malloc.h>
#include <math.h>
#include <string.h>

#include "graph3.h"  // Include our graphics stuff.
#include "graph4.h"

// D E F I N E S /////////////////////////////////////////////

// S T R U C T U R E S ///////////////////////////////////////

// P R O T O T Y P E S ///////////////////////////////////////

void Bline(int xo, int yo, int x1,int y1, unsigned char color);

void Bounce(void);

// G L O B A L S //////////////////////////////////////////////

// F U N C T I O N S //////////////////////////////////////////

void Bounce(void)
{
// This function makes use of the bline function to bounce a
// line around.

int xo,yo,x1,y1,x2,y2,x3,y3;
int dxo,dyo,dx1,dy1,dx2,dy2,dx3,dy3;
long counter=0;
int color=9;

// Starting positions of lines.

xo=x2=rand()%320;
yo=y2=rand()%200;
x1=x3=rand()%320;
y1=y3=rand()%200;

// Velocities of lines.

dxo=dx2=2+rand()%5;
dyo=dy2=3+rand()%5;
dx1=dx3=2+rand()%5;
dy1=dy3=2+rand()%5;

// Animation loop

while(!kbhit())
    {
    // Draw the leader.

    Bline(xo,yo,x1,y1,color);
```

5

continues

Listing 5.2. continued

```
// Move the line.

if ((xo+=dxo)>=315 || xo<5)
  dxo=-dxo;

if ((yo+=dyo)>=195 || yo<5)
  dyo=-dyo;

if ((x1+=dx1)>=315 || x1<5)
  dx1=-dx1;

if ((y1+=dy1)>=195 || y1<5)
  dy1=-dy1;

// Test whether it's time to follow the leader.

if (++counter>50)
  {

  Bline(x2,y2,x3,y3,0);

  // Move the line.

  if ((x2+=dx2)>=315 || x2<5)
    dx2=-dx2;

  if ((y2+=dy2)>=195 || y2<5)
    dy2=-dy2;

  if ((x3+=dx3)>=315 || x3<5)
    dx3=-dx3;

  if ((y3+=dy3)>=195 || y3<5)
    dy3=-dy3;

  } // end if time to follow.

// Wait a while so humans can see it.

Delay(1);

// Update the color.

if (counter>250)
  {
  if (++color>=16)
    color=1;
  counter = 51;

  } // end if time to change color

} // end while

} // end Bounce
```

```
/////////////////////////////////////////////////////////////////

void Bline(int xo, int yo, int x1,int y1, unsigned char color)
{
// This function uses Bresenham's algorithm (IBM 1965) to draw a
// line from (xo,yo) - (x1,y1).

int dx,          // Difference between one x and another.
    dy,          // difference between one y and another.
    x_inc,       // Amount in pixel space to move during
                 // drawing.
    y_inc,       // Amount in pixel space to move during
                 // drawing.
    error=0,     // The discriminant (i.e., error; i.e,
                 // decision variable).
    index;       // Used for looping.


// Access the video buffer directly for speed.
unsigned char far *vb_start = video_buffer;

// S E C T I O N 1 /////////////////////////////////////////

// Precompute the first pixel address in the video buffer.
// Use shifts for multiplication.


vb_start = vb_start + ((unsigned int)yo<<6) +
                      ((unsigned int)yo<<8) +
                      (unsigned int)xo;

// Compute the deltas.

dx = x1-xo;
dy = y1-yo;

// S E C T I O N 2 /////////////////////////////////////////

// Test which direction the line is going in; i.e., the
// slope angle.

if (dx>=0)
   {
   x_inc = 1;

   } // end if the line is moving right.
else
   {
   x_inc = -1;
   dx    = -dx;  // Need the absolute value.

   } // end else moving left

// S E C T I O N 3 /////////////////////////////////////////

// Test the y component of the slope.
```

Listing 5.2. continued

```
if (dy>=0)
   {
   y_inc = 320; // 320 bytes per line.

   } // end if line is moving down
else
   {
   y_inc = -320;
   dy   = -dy;  // Need the absolute value.

   } // end else moving up

// S E C T I O N 4 /////////////////////////////////////////////

// Now, based on which delta is greater, we can draw the line.

if (dx>dy)
   {

   // Draw the line.

   for (index=0; index<=dx; index++)
       {
       // Set the pixel.

       *vb_start = color;

       // Adjust the discriminate.

       error+=dy;

       // Test if error overflowed.

       if (error>dx)
          {

          error-=dx;

          // Move to the next line.

          vb_start+=y_inc;

          } // end if error overflowed

       // Move to the next pixel.

       vb_start+=x_inc;

       } // end for

   } // end if |slope| <= 1
else
   {

// S E C T I O N 5 /////////////////////////////////////////////
```

```
    // Draw the line.

    for (index=0; index<=dy; index++)
        {
        // Set the pixel.

        *vb_start = color;

        // Adjust the discriminate.

        error+=dx;

        // Test if error overflowed.

        if (error>0)
            {

            error-=dy;

            // Move to the next line.

            vb_start+=x_inc;

            } // end if error overflowed

        // Move to the next pixel.

        vb_start+=y_inc;

        } // end for

    } // end else ¦slope¦ > 1

} // end Bline

// M A I N ////////////////////////////////////////////////////

void main(void)
{
// Set the video mode to the 320x200, 256-color mode.

Set_Video_Mode(VGA256);

// Draw a couple of lines.

while(!kbhit())
    {
    // Plot a line between a random start and endpoint.

    Bline(rand()%320,rand()%200,
        rand()%320,rand()%200,rand()%256);

    } // end while

getch();
```

5

continues

Listing 5.2. continued

```
// Clear the screen.

Set_Video_Mode(VGA256);

// Show off a little screen saver.

Bounce();

// Reset the video mode back to text.

Set_Video_Mode(TEXT_MODE);


} // end main
```

Building an Executable: To make an executable of the program in Listing 5.2, you can either type it in or use the source on the companion CD. The name of the source is linedemo.c. The precompiled executable is named linedemo.exe. As before, use the following compile line for Microsoft C:

```
cl -AM -Zi -c -Fc -Gs -G2 linedemo.c
```

After compiling the program in this manner, you can link it to the standard libraries and to our previously generated game library, gamelib.lib, with a link line such as:

```
link /ST:8192 /CO linedemo,,,graphics.lib+gamelib.lib,,
```

This creates a final executable named linedemo.exe.

The linedemo.exe program is a good example of more for less, meaning a cool-looking display can be made with just a few functions. The program is rudimentary and we won't take time to look at the operation of the main() or subfunctions. Basically, the first part of the demo was created by selecting two random points and drawing a line between them in a random color. The second part of the demo bounces a line segment off the screen boundaries, while a second eraser line follows.

We have a long way to go, so let's move on to polygons.

Introduction to Polygons

Now that we have lines under control, let's use them to create the next level of geometrical abstraction. This would be the polygon. A polygon is simply a closed, multisided object constructed of lines, as shown in Figure 5.16.

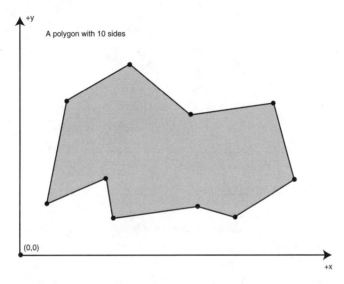

Figure 5.16. *A garden-variety polygon.*

Using our line algorithm and some data structures, we can create a library of functions to draw polygons, transform them, and clip them against a view port.

In a graphics system, polygons can either be filled (solid) or unfilled (hollow or wire frame). We're writing a function that's based on the latter type: unfilled. Filling polygons at reasonable rates is quite a task, and I'm not sure we need to do it for the games we're trying to make. (If we find it necessary to draw filled polygons, rest assured that you'll have the code to do it!) Nevertheless, when we create our polygon data structures we assume that, in the future, the polygons may be filled—so we have a field to record this.

So a polygon is an n-sided object created from a set of connecting lines. In other words, a polygon is a set of points, which we connect with lines. These points are referred to as *vertices*. For example, a triangle has three vertices, as shown in Figure 5.17.

5

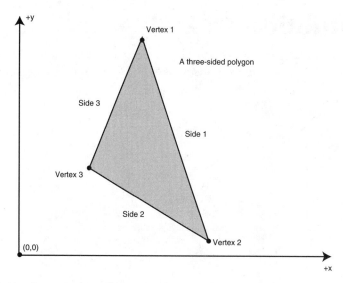

Figure 5.17. *A triangular polygon.*

Hence, we must design a data structure that enables us to represent a collection of vertices for the polygon. We then always connect them in the same order (that is, clockwise or counterclockwise). Also, polygons by definition are always closed, meaning the last vertex is connected to the first vertex with a line to close the polygon, as shown in Figure 5.18.

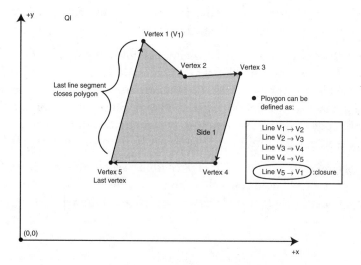

Figure 5.18. *A polygon must be closed to be called a polygon.*

There's no reason to force this attribute on our graphics engine as we may want to create an open polygon for some reason. Therefore, we also want to have a field in our data structure that records whether the polygon is open or closed. (If a polygon isn't closed, it's not really a polygon. However, we may not want to draw the last line segment that closes the polygon. Therefore, we include this closure field.)

The final two pieces of information we need about the polygon are its colors and where it is in the universe, or its position on the video screen. We call the latter its *local origin*.

Just because the screen is 320×200 doesn't mean we can't have a polygon at location 5000,5000. We just wouldn't be able to see it. The polygons, and all the objects in our video games, are in *world coordinates*. This means they can be anywhere in the universe. The *screen coordinates* are for 0–319 on the x-axis and 0–199 on the y-axis, so an object within these ranges is visible. See Figure 5.19 for a comparison of screen versus world coordinates.

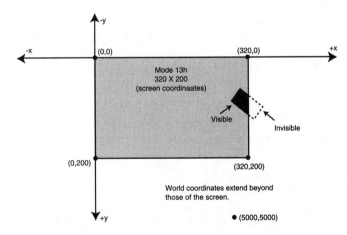

Figure 5.19. *The relationship between screen and world coordinates.*

Because the polygon has a local origin or a position somewhere in 2-D space, we must define its vertices relative to its center, or origin, which we think of as always being (0,0). This doesn't necessarily mean that in a triangle defined by three vertices, at (-5,0), (+5,5), and (-5,5), the polygon vertices are actually at those locations: they're relative to the location or position of the polygon, which is at its local origin. For example, if we moved the polygon to (100,100), the three vertices would be at (95,100), (105,105) and (95,105).

We know the aspects of a polygon that must be recorded in a data structure, so let's try to come up with a reasonable structure to suit our needs. Listing 5.3 contains the structures and definitions we need for polygons.

Listing 5.3. A vertex structure.

```c
#define MAX_VERTICES        16
// Maximum number of vertices in a polygon.

// A vertex structure.

typedef struct vertex_typ
        {

        float x,y;          // The vertex in 2-D.

        } vertex, *vertex_ptr;

// The polygon structure.

typedef struct polygon_typ
        {

// Border color
        int b_color;

// Interior color
        int i_color;

// Is the polygon closed?
        int closed;

// Is this polygon filled?
        int filled;

// Local origin of the polygon
        int lxo,lyo;

// Number of defined vertices
        int num_vertices;

// The vertices of the polygon
        vertex vertices[MAX_VERTICES];

        } polygon, *polygon_ptr;
```

Notice that there are two structures:

☐ One for a vertex

☐ One for the polygon itself

Also, notice that the vertices of the polygon are stored in an array of size MAX_VERTICES. In general, using arrays to hold vertices and other geometrical data isn't the most memory-efficient way to do things; however, we're trying to understand the aspects of

writing video games along with the graphics needed to render them. A little wasted space isn't going to kill us. If you wish, you can modify everything to use linked lists. I don't feel it's worth the large amount of work it would take to make all the functions use linked lists, though.

Note: This will be my philosophy throughout the book. I tend to shy away from complex data structures when possible so you can visualize the purest form of the material at hand without a lot of abstract data structures in the way.

All right, we now have a polygon data structure that can hold a polygon representation. The next important issue is to write functions that draw them and transform polygons.

Drawing a polygon is fairly easy: we simply access the data structure and then draw lines from vertex to vertex. As an example, let's define a polygon and then write a function to draw it. The code in Listing 5.4 defines a square.

Listing 5.4. Defining a square.

```
polygon square;   // Our square

square.b_color     = 1;   // Make the square blue.
square.i_color     = 1;
square.closed      = 1;   // This is a closed polygon.
square.filled      = 0;   // Don't fill it.
square.lxo         = 160; // Place the square in the center of
                          // the screen.
square.lyo         = 100;
square.num_vertices = 4;  // There are four vertices in a
                          // square.

// Define the vertices of a square; that is, 20x20.

square.vertices[0] =-10;
square.vertices[0] = 10;

square.vertices[0] = 10;
square.vertices[0] = 10;

square.vertices[0] = 10;
square.vertices[0] = -10;

square.vertices[0] = -10;
square.vertices[0] = -10;
```

Now that we've defined a square, let's see how we would draw it. Basically, we must draw lines between each of the vertices, in order, and then (if the polygon is to be closed) draw a line from the last vertex to the first vertex to close it. Because each polygon has a local origin, defined by lxo and lyo, we must add the contents of these variables to each of the (x,y) coordinates of each vertex that make up the polygon. This is how we map the polygon onto the view screen, which is 320×200. We use the polygon's vertice definition, which is relative to the local origin of the polygon; that is, (lxo,lyo).

There's one more detail we must consider before drawing the polygon: what if the extents of the polygon exceed the extents of the viewing screen, which has a finite of dimension 320×200? The answer is that the polygon must be clipped, as shown in Figure 5.20.

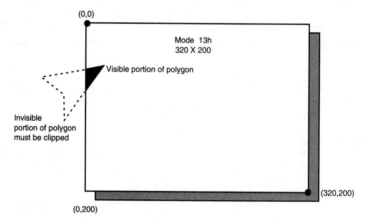

Figure 5.20. *Clipping in action.*

In essence, we only draw the portions of the polygon that are visible. This translates to clipping the lines that make up the polygon against the viewing region, which itself is a rectangle that bounds the screen (although sometimes the clipping region is smaller than the screen, or even a nonrectangular shape). In any case, we must take clipping into consideration, but we do this later today. For now, let's start off without clipping and build up, shall we? The function shown in Listing 5.5 draws a polygon into the video buffer.

Listing 5.5. Drawing a polygon on the screen.

```
void Draw_Polygon(polygon_ptr poly)
{
// This function draws a polygon on the screen without clipping.
// The caller should make sure that vertices are within bounds
// of the clipping rectangle. The polygon will always be
// unfilled regardless of the fill flag.
```

```
    int index,xo,yo;

    // Extract the local origin.

    xo = poly->lxo;
    yo = poly->lyo;

    // Draw the polygon.

    for (index=0; index<poly->num_vertices-1; index++)
        {

        Bline(xo+(int)poly->vertices[index].x,
              yo+(int)poly->vertices[index].y,
              xo+(int)poly->vertices[index+1].x,
              yo+(int)poly->vertices[index+1].y,
              poly->b_color);

        } // end for index

    // Close the polygon?

    if (!poly->closed)
        return;

    Bline(xo+(int)poly->vertices[index].x,
          yo+(int)poly->vertices[index].y,
          xo+(int)poly->vertices[0].x,
          yo+(int)poly->vertices[0].y,
          poly->b_color);


} // end Draw_Polygon
```

5

As you can see, the function takes a single parameter: the polygon to draw. (Actually, it takes a pointer to the polygon we wish drawn.)

 Tip: When passing parameters, if the parameter is a structure it's usually better to send a pointer to the structure. This is faster, and also allows the function to alter the contents of the structure.

Using our previously defined square polygon, we would use the following call to draw the square:

```
Draw_Polygon(polygon_ptr)&square);
```

That's all there is too it. Of course, you'd better make sure the polygon fits on the screen. Otherwise, weird things happen because there's no clipping yet.

Analysis The function in Listing 5.5 is straightforward, and the comments should explain its operation. The only interesting thing about the function is that the last segment of it tests the "closed" flag, which indicates whether the polygon should be closed.

We now have a simple polygon engine. With it we could probably write some games that didn't have many moving or transforming objects. However, the whole idea of a video game is to have a lot of moving objects. Therefore, we must learn how to move and transform the polygons.

Polygon Transformations

A polygon is a set of vertices. These vertices represent a collection of edges that make up the polygon. Furthermore, each polygon has a position in the world, defined by the coordinates (lxo,lyo). If we want to see any excitement with our polygon engine, we must write some functions that, at the very least, translate, rotate, and scale polygons. There's a little math involved here, but nothing you haven't seen before (even if many years ago!!).

Translation

Translation is the simplest of the transformations. *Translation* means to move an object from one point to another. If we consider an object to be located at the point (x,y), we can use the following math to move the object an amount dx in the x-axis and amount dy in the y-axis:

```
x = x + dx
y = y + dy
```

The results are that the point (x,y) is moved to another location, as shown in Figure 5.21.

If we generalize this to our polygon structure, we see that to move a polygon we must move every vertex of the polygon. Luckily for us, we've defined the polygon in reference to a position (lxo,lyo). If we want to move the polygon, we need only move (lxo,lyo). Hence, we can use the simple function shown in Listing 5.6 to translate a polygon:

Listing 5.6. Translating a polygon.

```
void Translate_Polygon(polygon_ptr poly, int dx,int dy)
{

// Translate the origin of the polygon.

poly->lxo+=dx;
poly->lyo+=dy;
```

```
// That was easy!

} // end Translate_Polygon
```

Wow! That was hard. The function takes as parameters three things:

☐ The polygon we wish translated

☐ The translation factor in the x direction

☐ The translation factor in the y direction

Writing a translation function was easy! Let's continue with the next important transformation, which is scaling.

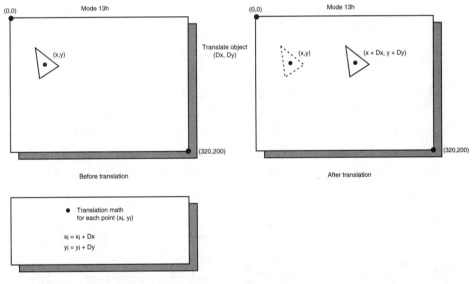

Figure 5.21. *Translating an object.*

Scaling

Scaling isn't what you used to do about fences when you were getting away from Mr. Peabody after picking apples from his orchard. In the context of computer graphics, *scaling* means to change the size of an object, as shown in Figure 5.22.

213

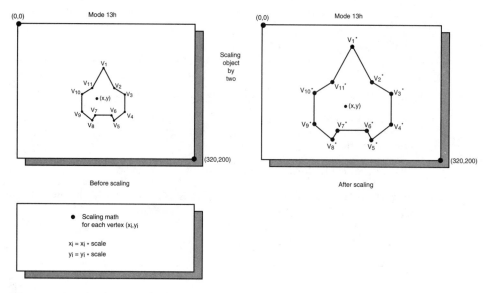

Figure 5.22. *Scaling an object.*

Here we see a square scaled to half its original size and to twice its original size. Scaling is basically a multiplication of size by some factor, called the *scaling factor*. The problem is, how do we accomplish scaling given the representation of the polygon we're using?

The answer is to multiply the scaling factor with each one of the vertices of the polygon and store the result back in each of the vertices. Mathematically, we can write this as:

```
scaled (x,y) = s*(x,y) = (sx,sy)
```

where *s* is the scaling factor and `(x,y)` is a single vertex.

 Tip: Scaling can also be thought of in the following manner: each vertex of the polygon is really a vector from the polygon's local origin to the vertex in question. Therefore, we can think of every vertex as a vector. Hence, the standard scalar multiplication defined in vector mathematics is a scaling operation when mapped back to the polygon definition.

The scaling operation on an entire polygon can be achieved by scaling each vertex by the scaling factor, which can be done in a simple loop. The function in Listing 5.7 does that.

Listing 5.7. Scaling a polygon.

```c
void Scale_Polygon(polygon_ptr poly, float scale)
{

int index;

// Scale each vertex of the polygon.

for (index=0; index<poly->num_vertices; index++)
    {
    // Multiply by the scaling factor.

    poly->vertices[index].x*=scale;
    poly->vertices[index].y*=scale;

    } // end for

} // end Scale_Polygon
```

The function `Scale_Polygon()` takes two parameters:

☐ The first parameter is the polygon to be scaled.

☐ The second parameter is the scale factor itself, which is a floating-point number to support nonintegral scaling factors such as 0.3.

There's one important thing to remember about scaling: once the object has been scaled, it has been changed. Therefore, the actual vertices are different.

5

Note: Sometimes a polygon engine may keep track of the scaling factor in the polygon structure itself and only scale during rendering instead of beforehand. This difference is application-dependent.

Translation and scaling are simple, and I doubt if you even had to use more than three or four neurons to understand them. However, the next topic—rotation—is a bit more complex, and its real basis of operation takes quite a bit to really understand.

Rotation

This is always the hard part. The second people see trig functions, they freak. There's really nothing complex about trig functions such as sine and cosine; they're just tools used to measure triangles. However, we can use them to help rotate a polygon about a single point.

First, let's make sure we're all talking about the same kind of rotation. Because we're dealing with two-dimensional space, the only rotation that can be performed is "in the plane." In other words, we can think of all objects in our game universe as being flat, and then think of rotation as spinning or turning them on the screen, as shown in Figure 5.23.

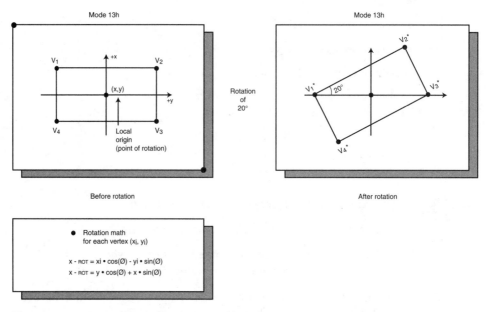

Figure 5.23. *Rotating an object.*

I'm not going to derive the rotation equations for you because we only need the end result, which is the proper linear combination (the sum of products) that rotate a point (x,y) a given angle (theta) about a center (xo,yo). However, we at least take a look at some of the geometry involved in rotation.

Let's take a look at sine and cosine and see what those things are, anyway.

The right triangle is one of the most famous geometrical entities and, I'm sure, gave Euclid and his friends many hours of enjoyment. A right triangle, shown in Figure 5.24, is defined as a polygon having three sides, where two of the sides meet at a 90-degree angle.

In this figure we see that the three sides of the triangle are named the *hypotenuse* and the *adjacent* and *opposite sides* relative to the labeling of the angle (theta). We also see that sine and cosine are defined as quotients of these values. The sin and cosine functions are defined as follows:

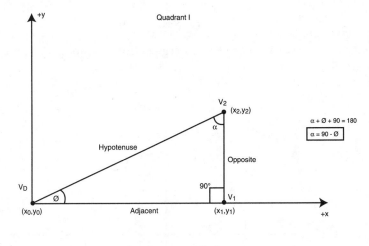

$$\sin\ q = \frac{\text{opposite}}{\text{hypotenuse}}$$

$$\text{cosine}\ q = \frac{\text{adjacent}}{\text{hypotenuse}}$$

$$\text{Sin}\ \varnothing = \frac{\text{Opposite}}{\text{Hypotenuse}} = \frac{y_2 - y_1}{\sqrt{(x_2 - x_0)^2 + (y_2 - y_0)^2}}$$

$$\text{Cos}\ \varnothing = \frac{\text{Adjacent}}{\text{Hypotenuse}} = \frac{x_1 - x_0}{\sqrt{(x_2 - x_0)^2 + (y_2 - y_0)^2}}$$

$$\tan \varnothing = \frac{\text{Sin}\ \varnothing =}{\text{Cos}\ \varnothing =} = \frac{y_2 - y_1}{x_1 - x_0} = \frac{D_y}{D_x} = M$$

Figure 5.24. *The right triangle demystified.*

Also, the sine and cosine of any angle have absolute value less than or equal to one. In other words, the range of sine and cosine is [-1,1]. (And the range of an MX missile is about 5,000 miles...) Anyway, it so happens that sine and cosine can be used to compute the points around a perfect *unit circle* (a circle with a radius of 1). For instance, if we wanted to know the exact point on a unit circle that was 20 degrees from the horizontal, we could compute it as follows:

```
x = cos(20);
y = sin(20);
```

 Warning: Many math books use both degrees and radians to measure angles, as do calculators. However, C uses only radians. There are 2 radians in a circle, or 360 degrees. You can use this information to convert between the two.

The result of the calculation would be a point (x,y) that was exactly one unit of distance from the origin (0,0) at an angle of 20 degrees from the horizontal, or x-axis, as shown in Figure 5.25.

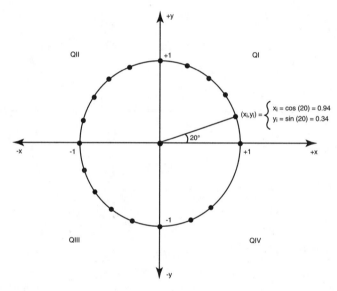

Figure 5.25. *Computing the points along a circle.*

Isn't this interesting!? It seems that we can compute the points along a unit circle with sine and cosine. Actually, a C program to do this is so simple I can't help but throw it in. Listing 5.8 is coming up.

Listing 5.8. A C fragment to draw a circle.

```
for (angle=0; angle<=360; angle++)
    {
    Plot_Pixel(radius * cos(angle*PI/180),
               radius * sin(angle*PI/180));
    } // end for
```

The `radius` factor makes the circle bigger or smaller. Also, notice the use of `PI/180` to convert degrees to radians for use with the C math library. The fact is, with a bit of higher math, equations can be derived to rotate a point (x,y) about any other point (xo,yo) by an angle (theta).

We see those equations in a moment. However, let's talk about the polygon engine again and what we may need. We need a function that can rotate a polygon around its own local center of (lxo,lyo). We could make a function to rotate a polygon around any point—but, nine times out of 10, objects are rotated around their geometrical or *mass centroids* (centers of interest), so we follow this easier trend.

To rotate a polygon, we must rotate each point in the polygon structure the same amount, and that's about it. The technique is similar to scaling, except the equations are different. Here are the mysterious rotation equations:

```
Given the point (x,y) and the angle q in radians, the new
rotated point (x_new, y_new) is:

x_new = x*cos(q) -   y*sin(q);
y_new = y*cos(q) + x*sin(q);
```

Notice that there are four multiplications and two calculations of sine and cosine. This is not acceptable: we must strive to optimize this a little. We're going to jump a bit ahead of ourselves here and use a *look-up table* that has the values of sine and cosine precomputed so they don't have to be computed during runtime. Listing 5.9 contains the polygon-rotation function, along with its support function and data structure for the look-up tables.

Listing 5.9. A function to rotate a polygon.

```
float sin_look[361],    // Look-up tables for sine and cosine
      cos_look[361];


void Create_Tables(void)
{
// This function creates the sine and cosine look-up tables.

int index;

// Create the tables.

for (index=0; index<=360; index++)
    {

    cos_look[index] = (float)cos((double)(index*3.14159/180));
    sin_look[index] = (float)sin((double)(index*3.14159/180));

    } // end for
```

continues

219

Listing 5.9. continued

```
} // end Create_Tables

/////////////////////////////////////////////////////////////////

void Rotate_Polygon(polygon_ptr poly, int angle)
{

int index;     // Loop index

float si,cs,   // Balues of sine and cosine.
      rx,ry;   // Rotated points

// Rotate each point of the poly gon around its local origin.
// Note: angle is an integer and ranges from -360 to +360.

// Compute the sine and cos of the angle to be rotated.

if (angle>=0)
    {
    // Extract the sine and cosine from the look-up table.

    si = sin_look[angle];
    cs = cos_look[angle];


    } // end if positive angle
else
    {
    // Angle is negative to convert to positive

    // Convert negative angle to positive angle and extract
    // values.

    si = sin_look[angle+360];
    cs = cos_look[angle+360];

    } // end else

// Using values for sine and cosine, rotate the point.

for (index=0; index<poly->num_vertices; index++)
    {
    // Compute rotated values using rotation equations.

    rx  = poly->vertices[index].x *
          cs -  poly->vertices[index].y * si;
    ry  = poly->vertices[index].y *
          cs +  poly->vertices[index].x * si;

    // Store the rotated vertex back into structure.
```

```
        poly->vertices[index].x = rx;
        poly->vertices[index].y = ry;

      } // end for

} // end Rotate_Polygon
```

The `Rotate_Polygon()` function uses the rotation equations with the precomputed look-up table to rotate each vertex in the polygon structure, which is straightforward. However, there are a couple important details in the function we should address:

- [ ] The first is that the angle of rotation sent to the function is in degrees, not radians. This is because the look-up table is indexed by integers and not radians.

- [ ] Second, it's possible that the caller may want to rotate by a negative angle. (A positive angle rotates the object counterclockwise; a negative angle rotates it clockwise.) This is taken care of by an `if` statement that converts negative angles into positive ones using the rule:

```
a negative angle = 360+itself
```

The final result of a call to the function is a rotated polygon.

There's an issue we must address again, just as we did with the scaling function: the rotation function actually changes the vertex values. They *will* be different after the call to the function, so beware.

Transformations aren't so bad once you've got the hang of them—actually, they're kind of fun. We can now translate, scale, and rotate, which is more than enough for a first draft of a polygon engine. However, we must revisit an important topic that I swept under the CPU tower a few minutes ago: clipping.

Clipping Polygons to the View Port

I'm sure that you have seen clipping before in many video games. *Clipping* is simply cutting off portions of objects that extend past the visible display of the screen. This is necessary because drawing a pixel at (400,300) in mode 13h doesn't make sense: the resolution is only 320×200. Therefore, we must somehow filter portions of objects so they stay within the clipping region.

For an example of clipping take a look at Figure 5.26.

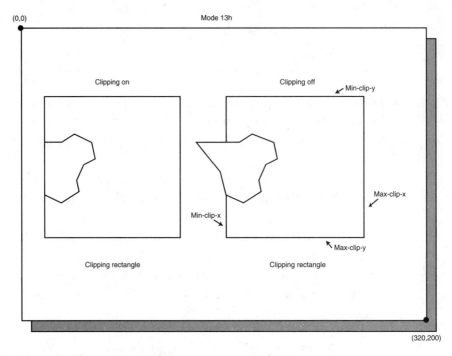

Figure 5.26. *Clipping a spaceship against a rectangle.*

Here we see a space ship drawn within a clipping rectangle. In one case, clipping is on. In the other case, clipping is off. In this example the clipping region or window is quite small. Sometimes this is true, sometimes it's not. The only thing we have to be able to accomplish is to clip our polygons to a rectangular region of any size less than or equal to the physical size of the screen.

Let's begin talking about clipping using some variables to define our clipping region, also referred to as a *view port*. We use a set of variables that determine the rectangular region to which all images must be clipped. This rectangular region is defined by the following variables:

```
int poly_clip_min_x,
    poly_clip_min_y,
    poly_clip_max_x,
    poly_clip_max_y;
```

By equating these variables to constants, we can define a rectangular clipping region. For example, if we want a clipping region that's the exact size of the video screen in mode 13h, we'd use the following constants:

```
poly_clip_min_x = 0;
poly_clip_min_y = 0;
poly_clip_max_x = 319;
poly_clip_max_y = 199;
```

On the other hand, if we want a clipping region that's a 100×100 square, centered in the middle of the screen, we'd use the following values:

```
poly_clip_min_x = 160-50;
poly_clip_min_y = 100-50;
poly_clip_max_x = 160+50-1;
poly_clip_max_y = 100+50-1;
```

To clip our polygons we must somehow filter out all pixel values that lie beyond the range of the clipping window. Figure 5.27 shows an abstract polygon filter.

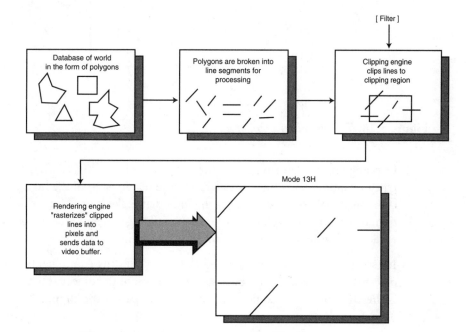

Figure 5.27. *A polygon-clipping filter.*

This operation can be accomplished in either of two ways:

☐ The first way is called *image-space clipping*. In image-space clipping we force all graphics functions to use the same pixel-plotting function, and within the pixel-plotting function there's a test to see whether the pixel is within the clipping region. If the pixel is within the region, it's plotted; otherwise, it isn't. This is graphically represented in Figure 5.27.

This method works great in pure hardware; however, software implementations are less efficient because each pixel in an object is tested to see whether it's in the clipping region—which can be a waste of computing time. For example, if we're drawing a line and know that both endpoints of the line are far away from the clipping region, there's no need to clip, or trivially reject, the pixels in the line because the whole line is invisible, as shown in Figure 5.28.

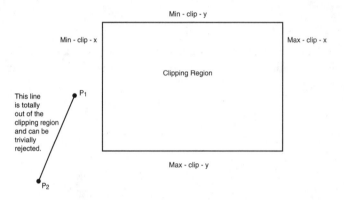

Figure 5.28. *The trivial rejection of a line.*

☐ Clipping objects based on their geometry is called *object-space clipping*. This type of clipping takes into consideration the relationship of the high-level components of an object, such as the lines that make it up. Using this information, object-space clipping tries to pass or fail large segments of the object to the renderer without the renderer caring about clipping.

In essence, an object-space clipping algorithm clips the components of the objects mathematically and passes a new version of the object. This new version is already clipped and couldn't possibly extend passed the clipping region. Therefore, there's no need to separately test each pixel, and the rendering engine runs faster—which is the name of the game.

Now let's concentrate on the details of implementing a clipping algorithm for polygons. First, we can think of polygons as a set of lines, so our algorithm is concerned only with clipping lines against the clipping region. Although it's possible to create a clipping algorithm that uses the polygon as a whole for clipping, we don't want to get into that subject as it's mathematically more complex. Furthermore, we aren't going to be drawing solid polygons at this point because filling them would take a scan-line conversion algorithm, which is beyond the scope of this book.

We're assuming we can clip any object composed of lines by clipping the lines themselves against the clipping region. This is true, and works in all cases, so we have to solve only

one problem: how to clip a line defined by two endpoints, p1 and p2, against a rectangle. We begin by trying to enumerate all possible cases. Figure 5.29 shows graphically all the cases that can occur when trying to clip a line against a rectangle.

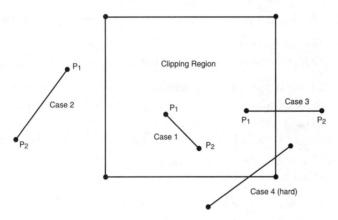

Figure 5.29. *Cases that must be considered to clip a line.*

Let's look at these. The cases are listed here from easiest to hardest:

- ☐ Case 1—Both endpoints of the line (p1,p2) are within the clipping region.

   Action—Draw the line without any changes.

- ☐ Case 2—Both endpoints are on the far side of one of the halfplanes created by the four sides of the clipping region.

   Action—The line is invisible; don't draw it.

- ☐ Case 3—One endpoint is in the clipping region and the other is outside the clipping region.

   Action—Find where the line intersects the clipping region. Then draw a line from the point that was within the clipping region to this point of intersection.

- ☐ Case 4—Both points are outside the clipping region; however, the line enters into the clipping region and exits it at some point.

   Action—Find the two points where the line enters and exits the clipping region and draw a line between them.

It turns out that all these cases can be determined with a whole lot of `if` statements and conditional logic. Granted, there are some tricks to consider. In general, though, the hardest thing to do from a mathematical standpoint is find the intersection of the line and one of the sides of the clipping region.

Finding an intersection is easy if we recall the point-slope form of the line from earlier in this chapter:

☐ We know the slope of the line we're clipping because we have both endpoints.

☐ We also know a point on the line because, again, we have both endpoints.

☐ Finally, we know where we want the intersection to be calculated, which is one of the horizontal or vertical lines that define the clipping region.

Taking all these factors into consideration and rearranging the point-slope form of the line equations, we come up with two equations to find the point of intersection of a line and the clipping region. Given that the endpoints of the line are (x1,y1) - (x2,y2) and the slope is (y2-y1)/(x2-x1), the following equations solve for the points of intersection:

```
x_clipped = m-1(y_boundary - y1) + x1;
y_clipped = m(x_boundary - x1) + y1;
```

where x_boundary and y_boundary are either the x- or y-clipping minimum or maximum values respectively.

We now have everything we need to write a polygon-clipping algorithm. The only thing we need to be careful of is that we make sure to cover all cases and take into consideration when we have asymptotic lines that are totally vertical or totally horizontal; otherwise, we get floating-point errors. I've implemented the algorithm for you; however, there are a couple points about implementation that I want to cover before we get to it.

☐ First, the algorithm is a "brute force" thing so that it's more understandable. There are better ways to encode all the cases (for example, using bit fields).

☐ The function uses floating-point numbers for its calculations. This isn't wise in general, because floating-point math is slower than pure integer math. However, we haven't covered enough ground yet to write fixed-point algorithms.

Nevertheless, the function is still fast and efficient, and almost transparent as far as speed goes. Listing 5.10 contains the function that clips a line.

Listing 5.10. The line-clipping function.

```
int Clip_Line(int *x1,int *y1,int *x2, int *y2)
{
// This function clips the sent line using the globally defined
// clipping region.

// Track whether each endpoint is visible or invisible.
int point_1 = 0, point_2 = 0;
```

```
int clip_always = 0;    // Used for clipping override.

int xi,yi;              // Point of intersection

int right_edge=0,       // Which edges are the endpoints beyond?
    left_edge=0,
    top_edge=0,
    bottom_edge=0;


int success = 0;        // Was clipping successfull?

float dx,dy;            // Used to hold slope deltas.

// S E C T I O N 1 //////////////////////////////////////////

// Test whether the line is completely visible.

if ( (*x1>=poly_clip_min_x) && (*x1<=poly_clip_max_x) &&
     (*y1>=poly_clip_min_y) && (*y1<=poly_clip_max_y) )
    point_1 = 1;


if ( (*x2>=poly_clip_min_x) && (*x2<=poly_clip_max_x) &&
     (*y2>=poly_clip_min_y) && (*y2<=poly_clip_max_y) )
    point_2 = 1;

// S E C T I O N 2 //////////////////////////////////////////

// Test endpoints.

if (point_1==1 && point_2==1)
    return(1);

// S E C T I O N 3 //////////////////////////////////////////

// Test whether the line is completely invisible.

if (point_1==0 && point_2==0)
    {

    // Must test to see whether each endpoint is on the same side
    // of one of the bounding planes created by each clipping·
    // region boundary.

// To the left
    if ( ((*x1<poly_clip_min_x) && (*x2<poly_clip_min_x)) ||
// To the right
        ((*x1>poly_clip_max_x) && (*x2>poly_clip_max_x)) ||

// Above
        ((*y1<poly_clip_min_y) && (*y2<poly_clip_min_y)) ||
// Below
        ((*y1>poly_clip_max_y) && (*y2>poly_clip_max_y)) )
        {
```

continues

227

Polygon Engines

Listing 5.10. continued

```
            // No need to draw the line.

            return(0);

            } // end if invisible

    // If we got here, we have the special case where the line
    // cuts into and out of the clipping region.

    clip_always = 1;

    } // end if test for invisibly

// S E C T I O N  4 ////////////////////////////////////////////////

// Take care of the case where either endpoint is in the
// clipping region.

if (( point_1==1) || (point_1==0 && point_2==0) )
    {

    // Compute the deltas.

    dx = *x2 - *x1;
    dy = *y2 - *y1;

    // Compute what boundary line must be clipped against.

    if (*x2 > poly_clip_max_x)
        {
        // Flag the right edge.

        right_edge = 1;

        // Compute intersection with the right edge.

        if (dx!=0)
            yi = (int)(.5+(dy/dx)*(poly_clip_max_x-*x1)+*y1);
        else
            yi = -1;  // Invalidate the intersection.

        } // end if to right
    else
    if (*x2 < poly_clip_min_x)
        {
        // Flag the left edge.

        left_edge = 1;

        // Compute intersection with the left edge.

        if (dx!=0)
            yi = (int)(.5+(dy/dx)*(poly_clip_min_x-*x1)+*y1);
        else
```

```
              yi = -1;   // Invalidate the intersection.

         } // end if to left

    // Horizontal intersections

    if (*y2 > poly_clip_max_y)
       {
       // Flag the bottom edge.

       bottom_edge = 1;

       // Compute intersection with the right edge.

       if (dy!=0)
          xi = (int)(.5+(dx/dy)*(poly_clip_max_y-*y1)+*x1);
       else
          xi = -1;   // Invalidate the intersection.

       } // end if bottom
    else
    if (*y2 < poly_clip_min_y)
       {
       // Flag the top edge.
       top_edge = 1;

       // Compute intersection with the top edge.

       if (dy!=0)
          xi = (int)(.5+(dx/dy)*(poly_clip_min_y-*y1)+*x1);
       else
          xi = -1;   // Invalidate the intersection

       } // end if top

// S E C T I O N 5 ///////////////////////////////////////////////

    // Now that we know where the line passed through, compute
    // which edge is the proper intersection.

    if (right_edge==1 &&
       (yi>=poly_clip_min_y && yi<=poly_clip_max_y) )
       {

       *x2 = poly_clip_max_x;
       *y2 = yi;

       success = 1;

       } // end if intersected right edge
    else
    if (left_edge==1 &&
       (yi>=poly_clip_min_y && yi<=poly_clip_max_y) )
       {

       *x2 = poly_clip_min_x;
```

continues

Listing 5.10. continued

```
        *y2 = yi;

        success = 1;

        } // end if intersected left edge

    if (bottom_edge==1 &&
        (xi>=poly_clip_min_x && xi<=poly_clip_max_x) )
        {

        *x2 = xi;
        *y2 = poly_clip_max_y;

        success = 1;

        } // end if intersected bottom edge
    else
    if (top_edge==1 &&
        (xi>=poly_clip_min_x && xi<=poly_clip_max_x) )
        {

        *x2 = xi;
        *y2 = poly_clip_min_y;

        success = 1;

        } // end if intersected top edge

    } // end if point_1 is visible

// S E C T I O N  6 ///////////////////////////////////////////////
// Reset the edge flags.

right_edge = left_edge= top_edge = bottom_edge = 0;

// Test the second endpoint.

if ( (point_2==1) ¦¦ (point_1==0 && point_2==0))
    {

    // Compute the deltas.

    dx = *x1 - *x2;
    dy = *y1 - *y2;

    // Compute what boundary line must be clipped against.

    if (*x1 > poly_clip_max_x)
        {
        // Flag the right edge.

        right_edge = 1;

        // Compute intersection with the right edge.

        if (dx!=0)
```

```
        yi = (int)(.5+(dy/dx)*(poly_clip_max_x-*x2)+*y2);
   else
      yi = -1;  // Invalidate the intersection.

   } // end if to right
else
if (*x1 < poly_clip_min_x)
   {
   // Flag the left edge.

   left_edge = 1;

   // Compute intersection with the left edge.

   if (dx!=0)
      yi = (int)(.5+(dy/dx)*(poly_clip_min_x-*x2)+*y2);
   else
      yi = -1;  // Invalidate the intersection.

   } // end if to left

// Horizontal intersections

if (*y1 > poly_clip_max_y)
   {
   // Flag the bottom edge.

   bottom_edge = 1;

   // Compute intersection with the right edge.

   if (dy!=0)
      xi = (int)(.5+(dx/dy)*(poly_clip_max_y-*y2)+*x2);
   else
      xi = -1;  // Invalidate the intersection.

   } // end if bottom
else
if (*y1 < poly_clip_min_y)
   {
   // Flag the top edge.

   top_edge = 1;

   // Compute intersection with the top edge.

   if (dy!=0)
      xi = (int)(.5 + (dx/dy) * (poly_clip_min_y - *y2) + *x2);
   else
      xi = -1;  // Invalidate the intersection.

   } // end if top

// Now that we know where the line passed through, compute
// which edge is the proper intersection.

if (right_edge==1 &&
```

Listing 5.10. continued

```
              (yi>=poly_clip_min_y && yi<=poly_clip_max_y) )
              {

              *x1 = poly_clip_max_x;
              *y1 = yi;

              success = 1;

              } // end if intersected right edge
         else
         if (left_edge==1 &&
              (yi>=poly_clip_min_y && yi<=poly_clip_max_y) )
              {

              *x1 = poly_clip_min_x;
              *y1 = yi;

              success = 1;

              } // end if intersected left edge

         if (bottom_edge==1 &&
              (xi>=poly_clip_min_x && xi<=poly_clip_max_x) )
              {

              *x1 = xi;
              *y1 = poly_clip_max_y;

              success = 1;

              } // end if intersected bottom edge
         else
         if (top_edge==1 &&
              (xi>=poly_clip_min_x && xi<=poly_clip_max_x) )
              {

              *x1 = xi;
              *y1 = poly_clip_min_y;

              success = 1;

              } // end if intersected top edge


         } // end if point_2 is visible

// S E C T I O N  7 ////////////////////////////////////////////

return(success);

} // end Clip_Line
```

Analysis The function is rather long because of all the cases and conditional testing. This is typical of many complex algorithms in computer graphics. (That's why no one ever gives a working implementation of anything! I have dozens of computer graphics books that have pages of pseudo code, but no complete working algorithms. I guess that's the trick that separates the graphics gurus from...???)

The Clip_line() function takes four parameters, which are the endpoints of the line to be clipped. Note that the parameters are pointers so the function can alter the endpoints itself and doesn't have to return them on the stack. This means that the calling function must consider this alteration as a side effect and send parameters that can be altered without corrupting any data structures.

Let's take a look at the different components of the line-clipping function.

1. The function begins with Section 1, testing to see where each of the endpoints of the line are. This information is needed to speed the reset of the test and to determine whether the line is completely inside or outside the clipping region.

2. In Section 2 we test for the *trivial rejection cases* of totally visible polygons (that is, cases in which no clipping is necessary). If the line is totally visible, the sent parameters are untouched and a value of true is returned, which instructs the calling function to draw the line unchanged.

3. Section 3 tests the case of the line being invisible. The information from Section 1, along with some conditional statements, determines whether the line is on the far side of one of the cutting planes created by the clipping region. If so, a zero is returned signifying not to draw the line.

4. The fun starts in Section 4. At this point the line has either one endpoint within the clipping region or both endpoints outside the clipping region, so this section of the code takes care of the case when endpoint 1 is within the clipping region and endpoint 2 is out of the clipping region.

   This section also executes if both endpoints are outside the clipping region but the line intersects the clipping region, and is therefore visible.

   In any case, Section 4 determines which side the line intersects and then computes the intersection of the line with both possible edges. Based on these intersections, the code determines which one is valid and then updates the endpoint appropriately.

5. Section 5 uses the information from Section 4. This section of the code does the actual updating of the parameters so they can be used by the calling function.

5

233

6. Section 6 is identical to section 4. However, it takes care of the case when endpoint 2 is within the clipping region and endpoint 1 is outside the clipping region, or if both endpoints are outside the clipping region.

7. Section 7 returns the status of the clipping operation so that the calling function can decide to draw the line or not.

The Clip_line() function may seem contrived but, believe me, it could be much worse!

As we decided early on, we'll use the line-clipping algorithm to draw polygons, so we need to somehow place the line clipper inside the polygon-drawing function as a filter. This is easy to do, and can be done by altering our original function with just a few lines of code. Listing 5.11 contains the version of the polygon-drawing function with clipping installed.

Listing 5.11. A polygon drawing function that supports clipping.

```
void Draw_Polygon_Clip(polygon_ptr poly)
{

// This function draws a polygon on the screen with clipping.
// The polygon will always be unfilled, regardless of the fill
// flag in the polygon structure.

int index,  // Loop index
    xo,yo,  // Local origin
    x1,y1,  // Endpoints of the line currently being processed.
    x2,y2;

// Extract the local origin.

xo = poly->lxo;
yo = poly->lyo;

// Draw the polygon.

for (index=0; index<poly->num_vertices-1; index++)
    {

    // Extract the line.

    x1 = (int)poly->vertices[index].x+xo;
    y1 = (int)poly->vertices[index].y+yo;

    x2 = (int)poly->vertices[index+1].x+xo;
    y2 = (int)poly->vertices[index+1].y+yo;

    // Clip the line to the viewing screen and draw it, unless
    // the line is totally invisible.

    if (Clip_Line(&x1,&y1,&x2,&y2))
```

```
            {
            // The line was clipped, and now can be drawn.
            Bline(x1,y1,x2,y2,poly->b_color);

            } // end if draw line

    } // end for index

    // Close the polygon?

    if (!poly->closed)
       return;

    // Extract the line.

    x1 = (int)poly->vertices[index].x+xo;
    y1 = (int)poly->vertices[index].y+yo;

    x2 = (int)poly->vertices[0].x+xo;
    y2 = (int)poly->vertices[0].y+yo;

    // Clip the line to the viewing screen and draw it, unless
    // the line is totally invisible.

    if (Clip_Line(&x1,&y1,&x2,&y2))
       {

       // The line was clipped and now can be drawn.

       Bline(x1,y1,x2,y2,poly->b_color);

       } // end if draw line

} // end Draw_Polygon_Clip
```

Analysis   The polygon-drawing function Draw_Polygon_Clip() has the same interface as Draw_Polygon(). The difference in the functions is that one clips and the other doesn't. Also, note how the function uses local variables to hold the endpoints of the lines being drawn, because they could possibly be changed by the line-clipping function.

We now have a fairly functional polygon engine. Later in the book, if we decide we need more power, we'll create extensions to it.

I'm sure you want to see a demo of clipping and the clipping engine. I've therefore written a program called polydemo.c, which creates a little spaceship and clips it to a really small rectangle on the screen. Use the numeric keypad (with NumLock down) to move the ship, and the T key to toggle the clipping engine. The name of the executable is polydemo.exe. Listing 5.12 contains the source.

5

235

Listing 5.12. A demo of the clipping engine. (polydemo.c)

```c
// I N C L U D E S ///////////////////////////////////////////////

#include <io.h>
#include <conio.h>
#include <stdio.h>
#include <stdlib.h>
#include <dos.h>
#include <bios.h>
#include <fcntl.h>
#include <memory.h>
#include <malloc.h>
#include <math.h>
#include <string.h>

#include "graph3.h"   // Include our graphics stuff.
#include "graph4.h"

// D E F I N E S ///////////////////////////////////////////////

// Global clipping region default value

#define POLY_CLIP_MIN_X    (160-30)
#define POLY_CLIP_MIN_Y    (100-30)

#define POLY_CLIP_MAX_X    (160+30)
#define POLY_CLIP_MAX_Y    (100+30)

// Maximum number of vertices in a polygon
#define MAX_VERTICES        16

// S T R U C T U R E S ///////////////////////////////////////////////

typedef struct vertex_typ
        {

        float x,y;        // The vertex in 2-D

        } vertex, *vertex_ptr;

///////////////////////////////////////////////////////////////////

typedef struct polygon_typ
        {

// Border color
        int b_color;

// Interior color
        int i_color;

// Is the polygon closed?
        int closed;

// Is this polygon filled?
```

```
        int filled;


// Local origin of polygon
        int lxo,lyo;

// The number of defined vertices
        int num_vertices;

// The vertices of the polygon
        vertex vertices[MAX_VERTICES];

        } polygon, *polygon_ptr;

// P R O T O T Y P E S /////////////////////////////////////////

void Bline(int xo, int yo, int x1,int y1, unsigned char color);

// G L O B A L S  /////////////////////////////////////////////

float sin_look[361],    // Look-up tables for sin and cosine
     cos_look[361];

// The clipping region; set it to default on start up

int poly_clip_min_x = POLY_CLIP_MIN_X,
    poly_clip_min_y = POLY_CLIP_MIN_Y,

    poly_clip_max_x = POLY_CLIP_MAX_X,
    poly_clip_max_y = POLY_CLIP_MAX_Y;


// F U N C T I O N S ////////////////////////////////////////////

void Create_Tables()
{
// This function creates the sine and cosine look-up tables.

int index;

// Create the tables.

for (index=0; index<=360; index++)
    {

    cos_look[index] = (float)cos((double)(index*3.14159/180));
    sin_look[index] = (float)sin((double)(index*3.14159/180));

    } // end for

} // end Create_Tables

////////////////////////////////////////////////////////////////

void Rotate_Polygon(polygon_ptr poly, int angle)
```

continues

Listing 5.12. continued

```
{

int index;     // Loop index

float si,cs,   // Values of sine and cosine
      rx,ry;   // Rotated points

// Rotate each point of the polygon around its local origin.
// Note: the angle is an integer and ranges from -360 to +360.

// Compute the sine and cos of the angle to be rotated.

if (angle>=0)
   {
   // Extract the sine and cosine from the look-up table.

   si = sin_look[angle];
   cs = cos_look[angle];


   } // end if positive angle
else
   {
   // Angle is negative to convert to positive

   // Convert negative angle to positive angle and extract
   // values.

   si = sin_look[angle+360];
   cs = cos_look[angle+360];

   } // end else

// Using values for sine and cosine, rotate the point.

for (index=0; index<poly->num_vertices; index++)
    {
    // Compute rotated values using rotation equations.

    rx=poly->vertices[index].x*cs-poly->vertices[index].y * si;
    ry=poly->vertices[index].y*cs+poly->vertices[index].x * si;

     // Store the rotated vertex back into the structure.

     poly->vertices[index].x = rx;
     poly->vertices[index].y = ry;

     } // end for

} // end Rotate_Polygon

///////////////////////////////////////////////////////////////

void Scale_Polygon(polygon_ptr poly, float scale)
```

```
{

int index;

// Scale each vertex of the polygon.

for (index=0; index<poly->num_vertices; index++)
    {
    // Multiply by the scaling factor.

    poly->vertices[index].x*=scale;
    poly->vertices[index].y*=scale;

    } // end for

} // end Scale_Polygon

////////////////////////////////////////////////////////////////

void Translate_Polygon(polygon_ptr poly, int dx,int dy)
{

// Translate the origin of the polygon.

poly->lxo+=dx;
poly->lyo+=dy;

// That was easy!

} // end Translate_Polygon

////////////////////////////////////////////////////////////////

void Draw_Polygon(polygon_ptr poly)
{
// This function draws a polygon on the screen without clipping.
// The caller should make sure that vertices are within bounds
// of the clipping rectangle. The polygon will always be
// unfilled regardless of the fill flag.

int index,xo,yo;

// Extract the local origin.

xo = poly->lxo;
yo = poly->lyo;

// Draw the polygon.

for (index=0; index<poly->num_vertices-1; index++)
    {

    Bline(xo+(int)poly->vertices[index].x,
          yo+(int)poly->vertices[index].y,
          xo+(int)poly->vertices[index+1].x,
          yo+(int)poly->vertices[index+1].y,
```

continues

Listing 5.12. continued

```
                poly->b_color);

      } // end for index

      // Close the polygon?

      if (!poly->closed)
         return;

      Bline(xo+(int)poly->vertices[index].x,
            yo+(int)poly->vertices[index].y,
            xo+(int)poly->vertices[0].x,
            yo+(int)poly->vertices[0].y,
            poly->b_color);


} // end Draw_Polygon

///////////////////////////////////////////////////////////////

int Clip_Line(int *x1,int *y1,int *x2, int *y2)
{
// This function clips the sent line using the globally defined
// clipping region.

// Track whether each endpoint is visible or invisible
int point_1 = 0, point_2 = 0;

int clip_always = 0;    // Used for clipping override

int xi,yi;              // Point of intersection

int right_edge=0,       // Which edges are the endpoints beyond?
    left_edge=0,
    top_edge=0,
    bottom_edge=0;


int success = 0;        // Was clipping successfull?

float dx,dy;            // Used to hold slope deltas.

// S E C T I O N 1 /////////////////////////////////////////////

// Test whether the line is completely visible.

if ( (*x1>=poly_clip_min_x) && (*x1<=poly_clip_max_x) &&
     (*y1>=poly_clip_min_y) && (*y1<=poly_clip_max_y) )
    point_1 = 1;


if ( (*x2>=poly_clip_min_x) && (*x2<=poly_clip_max_x) &&
     (*y2>=poly_clip_min_y) && (*y2<=poly_clip_max_y) )
    point_2 = 1;

// S E C T I O N 2 /////////////////////////////////////////////
```

```
// Test the endpoints.

if (point_1==1 && point_2==1)
   return(1);

// S E C T I O N 3 ///////////////////////////////////////////////

// Test whether the line is completely invisible.

if (point_1==0 && point_2==0)
   {

   // Must test to see whether each endpoint is on the same side
   // of one of the bounding planes created by each clipping-
   // region boundary.

// To the left
   if ( ((*x1<poly_clip_min_x) && (*x2<poly_clip_min_x)) ¦¦
// To the right
      ((*x1>poly_clip_max_x) && (*x2>poly_clip_max_x)) ¦¦

// Above
      ((*y1<poly_clip_min_y) && (*y2<poly_clip_min_y)) ¦¦
// Below
      ((*y1>poly_clip_max_y) && (*y2>poly_clip_max_y)) )
      {

      // No need to draw the line.

      return(0);

      } // end if invisible

   // If we got here, we have the special case where the line
   // cuts into and out of the clipping region.

   clip_always = 1;

   } // end if test for invisibly

// S E C T I O N 4 ///////////////////////////////////////////////

// Take care of the case where either endpoint is in the
// clipping region.

if (( point_1==1) ¦¦ (point_1==0 && point_2==0) )
   {

   // Compute the deltas.

   dx = *x2 - *x1;
   dy = *y2 - *y1;

   // Compute what boundary line must be clipped against.

   if (*x2 > poly_clip_max_x)
```

5

Listing 5.12. continued

```
            {
            // Flag the right edge.

            right_edge = 1;

            // Compute intersection with the right edge.

            if (dx!=0)
               yi = (int)(.5+(dy/dx)*(poly_clip_max_x-*x1)+*y1);
            else
               yi = -1;  // Invalidate the intersection.

            } // end if to right
        else
        if (*x2 < poly_clip_min_x)
            {
            // Flag the left edge.

            left_edge = 1;

            // Compute intersection with the left edge.

            if (dx!=0)
               yi = (int)(.5+(dy/dx)*(poly_clip_min_x-*x1)+*y1);
            else
               yi = -1;  // Invalidate the intersection.

            } // end if to left

    // Horizontal intersections

    if (*y2 > poly_clip_max_y)
        {
        // Flag the bottom edge.

        bottom_edge = 1;

        // Compute intersection with the right edge.

        if (dy!=0)
           xi = (int)(.5+(dx/dy)*(poly_clip_max_y-*y1)+*x1);
        else
           xi = -1;  // Invalidate the intersection.

        } // end if bottom
    else
    if (*y2 < poly_clip_min_y)
        {
        // Flag the top edge.

        top_edge = 1;

        // Compute intersection with the top edge.

        if (dy!=0)
```

```
            xi = (int)(.5+(dx/dy)*(poly_clip_min_y-*y1)+*x1);
        else
            xi = -1;   // Invalidate the intersection.

        } // end if top

// S E C T I O N 5 ///////////////////////////////////////////

    // Now that we know where the line passed through, compute
    // which edge is the proper intersection.

    if (right_edge==1 &&
        (yi>=poly_clip_min_y && yi<=poly_clip_max_y) )
        {

        *x2 = poly_clip_max_x;
        *y2 = yi;

        success = 1;

        } // end if intersected right edge
    else
    if (left_edge==1 &&
        (yi>=poly_clip_min_y && yi<=poly_clip_max_y) )
        {

        *x2 = poly_clip_min_x;
        *y2 = yi;

        success = 1;

        } // end if intersected left edge

    if (bottom_edge==1 &&
        (xi>=poly_clip_min_x && xi<=poly_clip_max_x) )
        {

        *x2 = xi;
        *y2 = poly_clip_max_y;

        success = 1;

        } // end if intersected bottom edge
    else
    if (top_edge==1 && (xi>=poly_clip_min_x && xi<=poly_clip_max_x) )
        {

        *x2 = xi;
        *y2 = poly_clip_min_y;

        success = 1;

        } // end if intersected top edge

    } // end if point_1 is visible

// S E C T I O N 6 ///////////////////////////////////////////
```

5

Listing 5.12. continued

```
// Reset the edge flags.

right_edge = left_edge= top_edge = bottom_edge = 0;

// Test the second endpoint.

if ( (point_2==1) || (point_1==0 && point_2==0))
   {

   // Compute the deltas.

   dx = *x1 - *x2;
   dy = *y1 - *y2;

   // Compute what boundary line must be clipped against.

   if (*x1 > poly_clip_max_x)
      {
      // Flag the right edge.

      right_edge = 1;

      // Compute intersection with the right edge.

      if (dx!=0)
         yi = (int)(.5+(dy/dx)*(poly_clip_max_x-*x2)+*y2);
      else
         yi = -1;  // Invalidate the intersection.

      } // end if to right
   else
   if (*x1 < poly_clip_min_x)
      {
      // Flag the left edge.

      left_edge = 1;

      // Compute intersection with the left edge.

      if (dx!=0)
         yi = (int)(.5+(dy/dx)*(poly_clip_min_x-*x2)+*y2);
      else
         yi = -1;  // Invalidate the intersection.

      } // end if to left

   // Horizontal intersections

   if (*y1 > poly_clip_max_y)
      {
      // Flag the bottom edge.

      bottom_edge = 1;

      // Compute intersection with the right edge.

      if (dy!=0)
```

```
            xi = (int)(.5+(dx/dy)*(poly_clip_max_y-*y2)+*x2);
        else
            xi = -1;  // Invalidate the intersection.

        } // end if bottom
    else
    if (*y1 < poly_clip_min_y)
        {
        // Flag the top edge.

        top_edge = 1;

        // Compute intersection with the top edge.

        if (dy!=0)
            xi = (int)(.5+(dx/dy)*(poly_clip_min_y-*y2)+*x2);
        else
            xi = -1;  // Invalidate the intersection.

        } // end if top

    // Now that we know where the line passed through, compute
    // which edge is the proper intersection.

    if (right_edge==1 &&
        (yi>=poly_clip_min_y && yi<=poly_clip_max_y) )
        {
        *x1 = poly_clip_max_x;
        *y1 = yi;

        success = 1;

        } // end if intersected right edge
    else
    if (left_edge==1 &&
        (yi>=poly_clip_min_y && yi<=poly_clip_max_y) )
        {
        *x1 = poly_clip_min_x;
        *y1 = yi;

        success = 1;

        } // end if intersected left edge

    if (bottom_edge==1 &&
        (xi>=poly_clip_min_x && xi<=poly_clip_max_x) )
        {
        *x1 = xi;
        *y1 = poly_clip_max_y;

        success = 1;

        } // end if intersected bottom edge
    else
```

Listing 5.12. continued

```
if (top_edge==1 &&
    (xi>=poly_clip_min_x && xi<=poly_clip_max_x) )
    {

    *x1 = xi;
    *y1 = poly_clip_min_y;

    success = 1;

    } // end if intersected top edge


    } // end if point_2 is visible

// S E C T I O N 7 ///////////////////////////////////////////////

return(success);

} // end Clip_Line

///////////////////////////////////////////////////////////////////

void Draw_Polygon_Clip(polygon_ptr poly)
{

// This function draws a polygon on the screen with clipping.
// The polygon will always be unfilled regardless of the fill
// flag in the polygon structure.

int index,  // Loop index
    xo,yo,  // Local origin
    x1,y1,  // Endpoints of line currently being processed.
    x2,y2;

// Extract the local origin.

xo = poly->lxo;
yo = poly->lyo;

// Draw the polygon.

for (index=0; index<poly->num_vertices-1; index++)
    {

    // Extract the line.

    x1 = (int)poly->vertices[index].x+xo;
    y1 = (int)poly->vertices[index].y+yo;

    x2 = (int)poly->vertices[index+1].x+xo;
    y2 = (int)poly->vertices[index+1].y+yo;

    // Clip the line to the viewing screen and draw it, unless
    // the line is totally invisible.

    if (Clip_Line(&x1,&y1,&x2,&y2))
```

```
      {
      // The line was clipped and now can be drawn.
      Bline(x1,y1,x2,y2,poly->b_color);

      } // end if draw line

   } // end for index

   // Close the polygon?

   if (!poly->closed)
      return;

   // Extract the line.

   x1 = (int)poly->vertices[index].x+xo;
   y1 = (int)poly->vertices[index].y+yo;

   x2 = (int)poly->vertices[0].x+xo;
   y2 = (int)poly->vertices[0].y+yo;

   // Clip the line to the viewing screen and draw it, unless
   // the line is totally invisible.

   if (Clip_Line(&x1,&y1,&x2,&y2))
      {

      // The line was clipped and now can be drawn.

      Bline(x1,y1,x2,y2,poly->b_color);

      } // end if draw line

} // end Draw_Polygon_Clip

////////////////////////////////////////////////////////////

void Bline(int xo, int yo, int x1,int y1, unsigned char color)
{
// This function uses Bresenham's algorithm (IBM 1965) to draw a
// line from (xo,yo) - (x1,y1).

int dx,            // Difference between one x and another.
    dy,            // difference between one y and another.
    x_inc,         // Amount in pixel space to move during
                   // drawing.
    y_inc,         // Amount in pixel space to move during
                   // drawing.
    error=0,       // The discriminant (i.e., error; i.e,
                   // decision variable).
    index;         // Used for looping.


// Access the video buffer directly for speed.
```

continues

Listing 5.12. continued

```c
unsigned char far *vb_start = video_buffer;


// S E C T I O N 1 /////////////////////////////////////////////

// Precompute the first pixel address in the video buffer.
// Use shifts for multiplication.


vb_start = vb_start + ((unsigned int)yo<<6) +
                      ((unsigned int)yo<<8) +
                      (unsigned int)xo;

// Compute the deltas.

dx = x1-xo;
dy = y1-yo;

// S E C T I O N 2 /////////////////////////////////////////////

// Test which direction the line is going in; i.e., the
// slope angle.

if (dx>=0)
   {
   x_inc = 1;

   } // end if line is moving right
else
   {
   x_inc = -1;
   dx    = -dx;   // Need the absolute value.

   } // end else moving left

// S E C T I O N 3 /////////////////////////////////////////////

// Test the y component of the slope.

if (dy>=0)
   {
   y_inc = 320; // 320 bytes per line.

   } // end if line is moving down
else
   {
   y_inc = -320;
   dy    = -dy;   // Need the absolute value.

   } // end else moving up

// S E C T I O N 4 /////////////////////////////////////////////

// Now, based on which delta is greater, we can draw the line.

if (dx>dy)
```

```
    {
    // Draw the line.

    for (index=0; index<=dx; index++)
        {
        // Set the pixel.

        *vb_start = color;

        // Adjust the discriminate.

        error+=dy;

        // Test if error overflowed.

        if (error>dx)
            {

            error-=dx;

            // Move to the next line.

            vb_start+=y_inc;

            } // end if error overflowed

        // Move to the next pixel.

        vb_start+=x_inc;

        } // end for

    } // end if ¦slope¦ <= 1
else
    {

// S E C T I O N 5 //////////////////////////////////////////////

    // Draw the line.

    for (index=0; index<=dy; index++)
        {
        // Set the pixel.

        *vb_start = color;

        // Adjust the discriminate.

        error+=dx;

        // Test if error overflowed.

        if (error>0)
            {

            error-=dy;
```

Listing 5.12. continued

```
                // Move to the next line.

                vb_start+=x_inc;

                } // end if error overflowed

            // Move to the next pixel.

            vb_start+=y_inc;

            } // end for

        } // end else |slope| > 1

} // end Bline

///////////////////////////////////////////////////////////////

void Draw_Boundary(int color)
{
// Draws in the clipping boundary, if the user is interested in
// seeing it.

Bline(poly_clip_min_x,poly_clip_min_y,
      poly_clip_max_x,poly_clip_min_y,color);


Bline(poly_clip_max_x,poly_clip_min_y,
      poly_clip_max_x,poly_clip_max_y,color);

Bline(poly_clip_max_x,poly_clip_max_y,
      poly_clip_min_x,poly_clip_max_y,color);

Bline(poly_clip_min_x,poly_clip_max_y,
      poly_clip_min_x,poly_clip_min_y,color);

} // end Draw_Boundary

// M A I N ////////////////////////////////////////////////////

void main(void)
{

// Track whether the clipping engine is on.
int clip_on = 1;

polygon p1;              // The working polygon

int done=0;              // The system exit flag

// Set the video mode to the 320x200, 256-color mode.

Set_Video_Mode(VGA256);

// Draw some instructions.

Blit_String(0,0 ,7,"Press Q - To quit.",1);
```

```
Blit_String(0,10,7,"Press T - To toggle clipping engine.",1);
Blit_String(0,20,7,"Use Numeric keypad to translate.",1);

// Create look-up tables for polygon engine.

Create_Tables();


// Build up a little spaceship polygon.

p1.vertices[0].x = 3;
p1.vertices[0].y = -19;

p1.vertices[1].x = 12;
p1.vertices[1].y = -1;

p1.vertices[2].x = 17;
p1.vertices[2].y = 2;

p1.vertices[3].x = 17;
p1.vertices[3].y = 9;

p1.vertices[4].x = 8;
p1.vertices[4].y = 14;

p1.vertices[5].x = 5;
p1.vertices[5].y = 8;

p1.vertices[6].x = -5;
p1.vertices[6].y = 8;

p1.vertices[7].x = -8;
p1.vertices[7].y = 14;

p1.vertices[8].x = -17;
p1.vertices[8].y = 9;

p1.vertices[9].x = -17;
p1.vertices[9].y = 2;

p1.vertices[10].x = -12;
p1.vertices[10].y = -1;

p1.vertices[11].x = -3;
p1.vertices[11].y = -19;

p1.vertices[12].x = -3;
p1.vertices[12].y = -8;

p1.vertices[13].x = 3;
p1.vertices[13].y = -8;

// Set the position of the spaceship.

p1.lxo = 160;
p1.lyo = 100;
```

continues

Polygon Engines

Listing 5.12. continued

```c
// Fill in important fields.

p1.num_vertices=14;
p1.b_color = 1;
p1.closed=1;


// Main event loop

while(!done)
    {

    // Erase the polygon.

    p1.b_color = 0;

    if (clip_on==1)
       Draw_Polygon_Clip((polygon_ptr)&p1);
    else
       Draw_Polygon((polygon_ptr)&p1);

    // Erase the origin of the polygon.

    Plot_Pixel_Fast(p1.lxo,p1.lyo,0);

    // What is the user doing?

    if (kbhit())
        {
        switch(getch())
            {
            case '8':   // Move the ship left.
                {
                p1.lyo—;

                } break;

            case '2':  // Move the ship right.
                {
                p1.lyo++;

                } break;

            case '6':   // Move the ship down.
                {
                p1.lxo++;

                } break;

            case '4':   // Move the ship up.
                {
                p1.lxo—;

                } break;
```

```
                    case 't':    // Toggle the clipper.
                        {
                        clip_on=-clip_on;
                        } break;

                    case 'q':    // It's coming now, Khan!!!
                        {
                        done=1;
                        } break;

                    default:break;

                    } // end switch

            } // end if kbhit

    // Rotate the polygon 5 degrees.

    Rotate_Polygon((polygon_ptr)&p1,5);

    // Draw the polygon.

    if (clip_on==1)
        {
        p1.b_color = 1;
        Draw_Polygon_Clip((polygon_ptr)&p1);
        Blit_String(10,100,7,"Clipping on. ",0);
        }
    else
        {
        p1.b_color = 12;
        Draw_Polygon((polygon_ptr)&p1);
        Blit_String(10,100,7,"Clipping off.",0);
        }

    // Draw a point at origin of polygon

    Plot_Pixel_Fast(p1.lxo,p1.lyo,15);

    // Let the user see the clipping region.

    Draw_Boundary(10);

    // Just chill here for 1/18.2 th of a second.

    Delay(1);

    } // end while

// Reset the video mode back to text.

Set_Video_Mode(TEXT_MODE);

} // end main
```

Building an Executable: To make an executable of the program in Listing 5.12, you can either type it in or use the source on the companion CD. The name of the source is polydemo.c. The precompiled executable is named polydemo.exe. As before, use the following compile line for Microsoft C:

```
cl -AM -Zi -c -Fc -Gs -G2 polydemo.c
```

After compiling the program in this manner, you can link it to the standard libraries and to our previously generated game library, gamelib.lib, with a link line such as:

```
link /ST:8192 /CO polydemo,,,graphics.lib+gamelib.lib,,
```

This creates a final executable named polydemo.exe.

The polydemo program is a good demonstration of what clipping is and why it is needed; moreover, it's a good example of some of the other functions we have created for rotation and translation.

High-Performance Polygon Engines

Many times during today's lesson I've alluded to different ways to improve the functions we've created and create functions for more advanced techniques, such as filling. In the competitive world of today's game makers, polygon-based graphics have to be anywhere from two to 10 times more complex than what we have. The engines must support solid or shaded polygons and high-speed rendering and transformations—and, of course, most of the engines are 3-D. However, we've seen the foundation of polygon engines and now know the jargon and some of the algorithms.

The next step to improving our polygon engine would be to implement shaded polygons. This would bring another level of realism to our graphics. Shading isn't that complex, but is does take a complex algorithm to do it which is relatively long and we will not go into at this juncture. (Maybe we could do it in *Teach Yourself Advanced Video-Game Programming in 210 Days*!)

In most of the polygon implementations I write, I like to break all polygons up into triangles and then render the triangles. This is a good approach: drawing filled triangles is much easier than drawing filled, general *n*-sided polygons. This approach is so successful that many graphics hardware makers, such as Silicon Graphics, build into the hardware triangle-based graphics engines that only work with triangles.

In any case, as a final example of the polygon engine in a role that is easy for it to fill, I present you with the program in Listing 5.13, which is also the source of many of the questions in the Q&A section of today's lesson. The program is a skeleton of an Asteroids game based on our polygon engine. The game has a collection of tumbling asteroids and a ship that can fly around with gravity effects. Finally, all the asteroids are rotating and moving at different rates. The name of the program is rockdemo.c; the executable is rockdemo.exe. Press the A and S keys to turn the ship and the L key for thrust.

Listing 5.13. An appropriate use of the polygon engine. (rockdemo.c)

```
// I N C L U D E S //////////////////////////////////////////////

#include <io.h>
#include <conio.h>
#include <stdio.h>
#include <stdlib.h>
#include <dos.h>
#include <bios.h>
#include <fcntl.h>
#include <memory.h>
#include <malloc.h>
#include <math.h>
#include <string.h>

#include "graph3.h"  // Include our graphics stuff.
#include "graph4.h"

// D E F I N E S //////////////////////////////////////////////

// Global clipping region default value

#define POLY_CLIP_MIN_X    0
#define POLY_CLIP_MIN_Y    0

#define POLY_CLIP_MAX_X    319
#define POLY_CLIP_MAX_Y    199

// Maximum number of vertices in a polygon
#define MAX_VERTICES       16




// Number of rocks in asteroid field
#define NUM_ROCKS          10

#define FRICTION           .2
    // Friction in space: yes, believe it or not! Space applies
    // friction to both energy and matter. Even in deepest space
    // there are approximately four hydrogen atoms per cubic cm,
    // and the wave impedence, or energy friction, is 377 ohms.
    // That's why light maxes out at 186,300 miles per second.

// S T R U C T U R E S //////////////////////////////////////////////
```

5

Polygon Engines

Listing 5.13. continued

```c
typedef struct vertex_typ
        {

        float x,y;          // The vertex in 2-D

        } vertex,*vertex_ptr;

////////////////////////////////////////////////////////////////

// The polygon structure

typedef struct polygon_typ
        {

// Border color
        int b_color;

// Interior color
        int i_color;

// Is the polygon closed?
        int closed;

// Is this polygon filled?
        int filled;

// Local origin of the polygon
        int lxo,lyo;

// Number of defined vertices
        int num_vertices;
// The vertices of the polygon
        vertex vertices[MAX_VERTICES];

        } polygon, *polygon_ptr;

// A moving object

typedef struct object_typ
        {
        int state;          // State of the rock

        int rotation_rate;  // Angle to rotate object per frame

        int xv,yv;          // Velocity vector

        polygon rock;       // One polygon per rock

        } object, *object_ptr;

// P R O T O T Y P E S /////////////////////////////////////////

void Bline(int xo, int yo, int x1,int y1, unsigned char color);
```

256

```
// G L O B A L S /////////////////////////////////////////////

float sin_look[361],    // Look-up tables for sine and cosine
     cos_look[361];

// The clipping region; set it to default on start up.

int poly_clip_min_x = POLY_CLIP_MIN_X,
    poly_clip_min_y = POLY_CLIP_MIN_Y,

    poly_clip_max_x = POLY_CLIP_MAX_X,
    poly_clip_max_y = POLY_CLIP_MAX_Y;

// The asteroid field

object rocks[NUM_ROCKS];

// F U N C T I O N S ///////////////////////////////////////////

void Create_Tables()
{
// This function creates the sine and cosine look-up tables.

int index;

// Create the tables.

for (index=0; index<=360; index++)
    {

    cos_look[index] = (float)cos((double)(index*3.14159/180));
    sin_look[index] = (float)sin((double)(index*3.14159/180));

    } // end for

} // end Create_Tables

///////////////////////////////////////////////////////////////

void Rotate_Polygon(polygon_ptr poly, int angle)
{

int index;     // Loop index

float si,cs,   // The values of sine and cosine
      rx,ry;   // Rotated points

// Rotate each point of the polygon around its local origin.
// Note: the angle is an integer and ranges from -360 to +360.

// Compute the sine and cos of the angle to be rotated.

if (angle>=0)
    {
    // Extract the sine and cosine from the look-up table.
```

Listing 5.13. continued

```
        si = sin_look[angle];
        cs = cos_look[angle];


        } // end if positive angle
    else
        {
        // Angle is negative to convert to positive

        // Convert negative angle to positive angle and extract
        // values.

        si = sin_look[angle+360];
        cs = cos_look[angle+360];

        } // end else

// Using values for sine and cosine, rotate the point.

for (index=0; index<poly->num_vertices; index++)
    {
    // Compute rotated values using rotation equations.

    rx  = poly->vertices[index].x*cs-poly->vertices[index].y*si;
    ry  = poly->vertices[index].y*cs+poly->vertices[index].x*si;

    // Store the rotated vertex back into the structure.

    poly->vertices[index].x = rx;
    poly->vertices[index].y = ry;

    } // end for

} // end Rotate_Polygon

/////////////////////////////////////////////////////////////////

void Scale_Polygon(polygon_ptr poly, float scale)
{

int index;

// Scale each vertex of the polygon.

for (index=0; index<poly->num_vertices; index++)
    {
    // Multiply by the scaling factor.

    poly->vertices[index].x*=scale;
    poly->vertices[index].y*=scale;

    } // end for

} // end Scale_Polygon
```

```
//////////////////////////////////////////////////////////////

void Translate_Polygon(polygon_ptr poly, int dx,int dy)
{

// Translate the origin of the polygon.

poly->lxo+=dx;
poly->lyo+=dy;

// That was easy!

} // end Translate_Polygon

//////////////////////////////////////////////////////////////

void Draw_Polygon(polygon_ptr poly)
{
// This function draws a polygon on the screen without clipping.
// The caller should make sure that vertices are within bounds
// of the clipping rectangle. The polygon will always be
// unfilled regardless of the fill flag.

int index,xo,yo;

// Extract the local origin.

xo = poly->lxo;
yo = poly->lyo;

// Draw the polygon.

for (index=0; index<poly->num_vertices-1; index++)
    {

    Bline(xo+(int)poly->vertices[index].x,
          yo+(int)poly->vertices[index].y,
          xo+(int)poly->vertices[index+1].x,
          yo+(int)poly->vertices[index+1].y,
          poly->b_color);

    } // end for index

    // Close the polygon?

    if (!poly->closed)
       return;

    Bline(xo+(int)poly->vertices[index].x,
          yo+(int)poly->vertices[index].y,
          xo+(int)poly->vertices[0].x,
          yo+(int)poly->vertices[0].y,
          poly->b_color);


} // end Draw_Polygon
```

continues

Listing 5.13. continued

```c
/////////////////////////////////////////////////////////////////

int Clip_Line(int *x1,int *y1,int *x2, int *y2)
{
// This function clips the sent line using the globally defined
// clipping region.

// Track whether each endpoint is visible or invisible
int point_1 = 0, point_2 = 0;

int clip_always = 0;    // Used for clipping override

int xi,yi;              // Point of intersection

int right_edge=0,       // Which edges are the endpoints beyond?
    left_edge=0,
    top_edge=0,
    bottom_edge=0;


int success = 0;        // Was clipping successful?

float dx,dy;            // Used to hold slope deltas.

// S E C T I O N 1 //////////////////////////////////////////////

// Test whether the line is completely visible.

if ( (*x1>=poly_clip_min_x) && (*x1<=poly_clip_max_x) &&
     (*y1>=poly_clip_min_y) && (*y1<=poly_clip_max_y) )
    point_1 = 1;


if ( (*x2>=poly_clip_min_x) && (*x2<=poly_clip_max_x) &&
     (*y2>=poly_clip_min_y) && (*y2<=poly_clip_max_y) )
    point_2 = 1;

// S E C T I O N 2 //////////////////////////////////////////////

// Test the endpoints.

if (point_1==1 && point_2==1)
   return(1);

// S E C T I O N 3 //////////////////////////////////////////////

// Test whether the line is completely invisible.

if (point_1==0 && point_2==0)
   {

   // Must test to see if each endpoint is on the same side of
   // one of the bounding planes created by each clipping-region
   // boundary.
```

```
// To the left
    if ( ((*x1<poly_clip_min_x) && (*x2<poly_clip_min_x)) ||
// To the right
        ((*x1>poly_clip_max_x) && (*x2>poly_clip_max_x)) ||

// Above
        ((*y1<poly_clip_min_y) && (*y2<poly_clip_min_y)) ||
// Below
        ((*y1>poly_clip_max_y) && (*y2>poly_clip_max_y)) )
        {

        // No need to draw the line.

        return(0);

        } // end if invisible

    // If we got here, we have the special case where the line
    // cuts into and out of the clipping region.

    clip_always = 1;

    } // end if test for invisibly

// S E C T I O N 4 /////////////////////////////////////////////

// Take care of the case where either endpoint is in the
// clipping region.

if (( point_1==1) || (point_1==0 && point_2==0) )
    {

    // Compute the deltas.

    dx = *x2 - *x1;
    dy = *y2 - *y1;

    // Compute what boundary line must be clipped against.

    if (*x2 > poly_clip_max_x)
        {
        // Flag the right edge.

        right_edge = 1;

        // Compute intersection with the right edge.

        if (dx!=0)
            yi = (int)(.5+(dy/dx)*(poly_clip_max_x-*x1)+*y1);
        else
            yi = -1;  // Invalidate the intersection.

        } // end if to right
    else
    if (*x2 < poly_clip_min_x)
        {
        // Flag the left edge.
```

Listing 5.13. continued

```
            left_edge = 1;

            // Compute intersection with the left edge.

            if (dx!=0)
               yi = (int)(.5+(dy/dx)*(poly_clip_min_x-*x1)+*y1);
            else
               yi = -1;  // Invalidate the intersection.

            } // end if to left

        // Horizontal intersections

        if (*y2 > poly_clip_max_y)
            {
            // Flag the bottom edge.

            bottom_edge = 1;

            // Compute intersection with the right edge.

            if (dy!=0)
               xi = (int)(.5+(dx/dy)*(poly_clip_max_y-*y1)+*x1);
            else
               xi = -1;  // Invalidate the intersection.

            } // end if bottom
        else
        if (*y2 < poly_clip_min_y)
            {
            // Flag the top edge.

            top_edge = 1;

            // Compute intersection with the top edge.

            if (dy!=0)
               xi = (int)(.5+(dx/dy)*(poly_clip_min_y-*y1)+*x1);
            else
               xi = -1;  // Invalidate the intersection.

            } // end if top

    // S E C T I O N 5 //////////////////////////////////////////////

        // Now that we know where the line passed through, compute
        // which edge is the proper intersection.

        if (right_edge==1 &&
            (yi>=poly_clip_min_y && yi<=poly_clip_max_y) )
            {

            *x2 = poly_clip_max_x;
            *y2 = yi;

            success = 1;
```

```
      } // end if intersected right edge
   else
   if (left_edge==1 &&
       (yi>=poly_clip_min_y && yi<=poly_clip_max_y) )
       {

       *x2 = poly_clip_min_x;
       *y2 = yi;

       success = 1;

       } // end if intersected left edge.

   if (bottom_edge==1 &&
       (xi>=poly_clip_min_x && xi<=poly_clip_max_x) )
       {

       *x2 = xi;
       *y2 = poly_clip_max_y;

       success = 1;

       } // end if intersected bottom edge
   else
   if (top_edge==1 &&
       (xi>=poly_clip_min_x && xi<=poly_clip_max_x) )
       {

       *x2 = xi;
       *y2 = poly_clip_min_y;

       success = 1;

       } // end if intersected top edge

   } // end if point_1 is visible

// S E C T I O N 6 /////////////////////////////////////////////

// Reset the edge flags.

right_edge = left_edge= top_edge = bottom_edge = 0;

// Test the second endpoint.

if ( (point_2==1) ¦¦ (point_1==0 && point_2==0))
   {

   // Compute the deltas.

   dx = *x1 - *x2;
   dy = *y1 - *y2;

   // Compute what boundary line must be clipped against.

   if (*x1 > poly_clip_max_x)
       {
       // Flag the right edge.
```

Listing 5.13. continued

```c
        right_edge = 1;

        // Compute intersection with the right edge.

        if (dx!=0)
            yi = (int)(.5+(dy/dx)*(poly_clip_max_x-*x2)+*y2);
        else
            yi = -1;   // Invalidate the intersection.

        } // end if to right
    else
    if (*x1 < poly_clip_min_x)
        {
        // Flag the left edge.

        left_edge = 1;

        // Compute intersection with the left edge.

        if (dx!=0)
            yi = (int)(.5+(dy/dx)*(poly_clip_min_x-*x2)+*y2);
        else
            yi = -1;   // Invalidate the intersection.

        } // end if to left

    // Horizontal intersections

    if (*y1 > poly_clip_max_y)
        {
        // Flag the bottom edge.

        bottom_edge = 1;

        // Compute intersection with the right edge.

        if (dy!=0)
            xi = (int)(.5+(dx/dy)*(poly_clip_max_y-*y2)+*x2);
        else
            xi = -1;   // Invalidate the intersection.

        } // end if bottom
    else
    if (*y1 < poly_clip_min_y)
        {
        // Flag the top edge.

        top_edge = 1;

        // Compute intersection with the top edge.

        if (dy!=0)
            xi = (int)(.5+(dx/dy)*(poly_clip_min_y-*y2)+*x2);
        else
```

```
        xi = -1;  // Invalidate the intersection.

    } // end if top

// Now that we know where the line passed through, compute
// which edge is the proper intersection.

if (right_edge==1 &&
    (yi>=poly_clip_min_y && yi<=poly_clip_max_y) )
    {

    *x1 = poly_clip_max_x;
    *y1 = yi;

    success = 1;

    } // end if intersected right edge
else
if (left_edge==1 &&
    (yi>=poly_clip_min_y && yi<=poly_clip_max_y) )
    {

    *x1 = poly_clip_min_x;
    *y1 = yi;

    success = 1;

    } // end if intersected left edge

if (bottom_edge==1 &&
    (xi>=poly_clip_min_x && xi<=poly_clip_max_x) )
    {

    *x1 = xi;
    *y1 = poly_clip_max_y;

    success = 1;

    } // end if intersected bottom edge
else
if (top_edge==1 &&
    (xi>=poly_clip_min_x && xi<=poly_clip_max_x) )
    {

    *x1 = xi;
    *y1 = poly_clip_min_y;

    success = 1;

    } // end if intersected top edge


    } // end if point_2 is visible

// S E C T I O N 7 /////////////////////////////////////////////

return(success);
```

Listing 5.13. continued

```c
} // end Clip_Line

/////////////////////////////////////////////////////////////////

void Draw_Polygon_Clip(polygon_ptr poly)
{

// This function draws a polygon on the screen with clipping.
// The polygon will always be unfilled regardless of the fill
// flag in the polygon structure.

int index,  // Loop index
    xo,yo,  // Local origin
    x1,y1,  // Endpoints of the line currently being processed
    x2,y2;

// Extract the local origin.

xo = poly->lxo;
yo = poly->lyo;

// Draw the polygon.

for (index=0; index<poly->num_vertices-1; index++)
    {

    // Extract the line.

    x1 = (int)poly->vertices[index].x+xo;
    y1 = (int)poly->vertices[index].y+yo;

    x2 = (int)poly->vertices[index+1].x+xo;
    y2 = (int)poly->vertices[index+1].y+yo;

    // Clip the line to the viewing screen and draw it, unless
    // the line is totally invisible.

    if (Clip_Line(&x1,&y1,&x2,&y2))
        {
        // The line was clipped and now can be drawn.
        Bline(x1,y1,x2,y2,poly->b_color);

        } // end if draw line

    } // end for index

    // Close the polygon?

    if (!poly->closed)
        return;

    // Extract the line.

    x1 - (int)poly->vertices[index].x+xo;
    y1 = (int)poly->vertices[index].y+yo;
```

```
    x2 = (int)poly->vertices[0].x+xo;
    y2 = (int)poly->vertices[0].y+yo;

    // Clip the line to the viewing screen and draw it, unless
    // the line is totally invisible.

    if (Clip_Line(&x1,&y1,&x2,&y2))
       {

       // The line was clipped and now can be drawn.

       Bline(x1,y1,x2,y2,poly->b_color);

       } // end if draw line

} // end Draw_Polygon_Clip

/////////////////////////////////////////////////////////////////

void Bline(int xo, int yo, int x1,int y1, unsigned char color)
{
// This function uses Bresenham's algorithm (IBM 1965) to draw a
// line from (xo,yo) - (x1,y1).

int dx,              // Difference between one x and another.
    dy,              // difference between one y and another.
    x_inc,           // Amount in pixel space to move during
                     // drawing.
    y_inc,           // Amount in pixel space to move during
                     // drawing.
    error=0,         // The discriminant (i.e., error; i.e,
                     // decision variable).
    index;           // Used for looping.


// Access the video buffer directly for speed.
unsigned char far *vb_start = video_buffer;


// S E C T I O N 1 /////////////////////////////////////////////

// Precompute the first pixel address in the video buffer.
// Use shifts for multiplication.


vb_start = vb_start + ((unsigned int)yo<<6) +
                      ((unsigned int)yo<<8) +
                      (unsigned int)xo;

// Compute the deltas.

dx = x1-xo;
dy = y1-yo;

// S E C T I O N 2 /////////////////////////////////////////////
```

continues

5

Listing 5.13. continued

```c
// Test which direction the line is going in; i.e., the
// slope angle.

if (dx>=0)
   {
   x_inc = 1;

   } // end if line is moving right
else
   {
   x_inc = -1;
   dx    = -dx;  // Need the absolute value.

   } // end else moving left

// S E C T I O N 3 /////////////////////////////////////////

// Test the y component of the slope.

if (dy>=0)
   {
   y_inc = 320; // 320 bytes per line

   } // end if line is moving down
else
   {
   y_inc = -320;
   dy    = -dy;  // Need the absolute value.

   } // end else moving up

// S E C T I O N 4 /////////////////////////////////////////

// Now, based on which delta is greater, we can draw the line.

if (dx>dy)
   {

   // Draw the line.

   for (index=0; index<=dx; index++)
      {
      // Set the pixel.

      *vb_start = color;

      // Adjust the discriminate.

      error+=dy;

      // Test if error overflowed.

      if (error>dx)
         {

         error-=dx;
```

```
            // Move to the next line.

            vb_start+=y_inc;

            } // end if error overflowed

        // Move to the next pixel.

        vb_start+=x_inc;

        } // end for

    } // end if ¦slope¦ <= 1
else
    {

// S E C T I O N 5 ///////////////////////////////////////////

    // Draw the line.

    for (index=0; index<=dy; index++)
        {
        // Set the pixel.

        *vb_start = color;

        // Sdjust the discriminate.

        error+=dx;

        // Test if error overflowed.

        if (error>0)
            {

            error-=dy;

            // Move to the next line.

            vb_start+=x_inc;

            } // end if error overflowed

        // Move to the next pixel.

        vb_start+=y_inc;

        } // end for

    } // end else ¦slope¦ > 1

} // end Bline

/////////////////////////////////////////////////////////////

void Draw_Boundary(int color)
```

Listing 5.13. continued

```
{
// Draws in the clipping boundary if the user is interested in
// seeing it.

Bline(poly_clip_min_x,poly_clip_min_y,
      poly_clip_max_x,poly_clip_min_y,color);


Bline(poly_clip_max_x,poly_clip_min_y,
      poly_clip_max_x,poly_clip_max_y,color);

Bline(poly_clip_max_x,poly_clip_max_y,
      poly_clip_min_x,poly_clip_max_y,color);

Bline(poly_clip_min_x,poly_clip_max_y,
      poly_clip_min_x,poly_clip_min_y,color);

} // end Draw_Boundary

/////////////////////////////////////////////////////////////////

void Initialize_Rocks(void)
{

// This function initializes all rocks in the asteroid field.

int index;       // Loop index

float scale;     // Used to change scale of each rock

// Initialize all rocks in the asteroid field.

for (index=0; index<NUM_ROCKS; index++)
    {

    // Build up each rock and add a little noise to each vertex
    // to make them look different.

    rocks[index].rock.vertices[0].x = 4.0 + rand()%2;
    rocks[index].rock.vertices[0].y = 4   + rand()%2;
    rocks[index].rock.vertices[1].x = 9   + rand()%2;
    rocks[index].rock.vertices[1].y = -3  - rand()%2;
    rocks[index].rock.vertices[2].x = 6   + rand()%2;
    rocks[index].rock.vertices[2].y = -5  - rand()%2;
    rocks[index].rock.vertices[3].x = 2   + rand()%2;
    rocks[index].rock.vertices[3].y = -3  - rand()%2;
    rocks[index].rock.vertices[4].x = -4  - rand()%2;
    rocks[index].rock.vertices[4].y = -6  - rand()%2;
    rocks[index].rock.vertices[5].x = -3  - rand()%2;
    rocks[index].rock.vertices[5].y = 5   + rand()%2;

    // Set the number of vertices.

    rocks[index].rock.num_vertices = 6;

    rocks[index].rock.b_color      = 10;
```

```
        rocks[index].rock.i_color    = 10;
        rocks[index].rock.closed     = 1;
        rocks[index].rock.filled     = 0;
        rocks[index].rock.lxo        = rand()%poly_clip_max_x;
        rocks[index].rock.lyo        = rand()%poly_clip_max_y;

        // Compute the velocity.

        rocks[index].xv = -5 + rand()%10;
        rocks[index].yv = -5 + rand()%10;

        // Set the state of the rock to alive, and set the
        // rotation rate.

        rocks[index].state = 1;

        rocks[index].rotation_rate = -10 + rand() % 20;

        // Compute the scale.

        scale = ((float)(5 + rand()%15))/10;

        // Scale the rock to make it look different.

        Scale_Polygon((polygon_ptr)&rocks[index].rock,scale);

        } // end for index

} // end Initialize_Rocks

//////////////////////////////////////////////////////////////

void Draw_Rocks(void)
{
// This function draws all the asteroids.

int index;  // Loop variable

// loop through all rocks and draw them.

for (index=0; index<NUM_ROCKS; index++)
    {

    rocks[index].rock.b_color = 10;
    Draw_Polygon_Clip((polygon_ptr)&rocks[index].rock);

    } // end for

} // end Draw_Rocks

//////////////////////////////////////////////////////////////

void Erase_Rocks(void)
{
// This functions erases all the asteroids.

int index;  // Loop variable
```

Listing 5.13. continued

```
// Loop through all rocks and draw them.

for (index=0; index<NUM_ROCKS; index++)
    {

    rocks[index].rock.b_color = 0;
    Draw_Polygon_Clip((polygon_ptr)&rocks[index].rock);

    } // end for

} // end Erase_Rocks

//////////////////////////////////////////////////////////////////

void Move_Rocks(void)
{

// This funnction moves and rotates all the asteroids.

int index;  // Loop variable

// Loop through all rocks and draw them.

for (index=0; index<NUM_ROCKS; index++)
    {

    // Translate the polygon.

    Translate_Polygon((polygon_ptr)&rocks[index].rock,
                    rocks[index].xv,rocks[index].yv);

    // Rotate the rock.

    Rotate_Polygon((polygon_ptr)&rocks[index].rock,
                    rocks[index].rotation_rate);

    // Test for collision of edges.

    if (rocks[index].rock.lxo > 310)
        rocks[index].rock.lxo = 10;
    else
    if (rocks[index].rock.lxo < 10)
        rocks[index].rock.lxo = 310;

    if (rocks[index].rock.lyo > 190)
        rocks[index].rock.lyo = 10;
    else
    if (rocks[index].rock.lyo < 10)
        rocks[index].rock.lyo = 190;

    } // end for

} // end Move_Rocks

// M A I N /////////////////////////////////////////////////////////
```

```
void main(void)
{

int done=0;              // System exit flag

polygon ship;

float xv=0,              // Initial velocity of the ship
      yv=0;

int   angle=90,          // Initial angle of the ship
      engines=0;         // Tracks whether engines are on

// S E C T I O N 1 /////////////////////////////////////////////

// Set the video mode to the 320x200, 256-color mode.

Set_Video_Mode(VGA256);

// Create look-up tables for the polygon engine.

Create_Tables();

// S E C T I O N 2 /////////////////////////////////////////////

// Build up a little spaceship polygon.

ship.vertices[0].x = 3;
ship.vertices[0].y = -19;

ship.vertices[1].x = 12;
ship.vertices[1].y = -1;

ship.vertices[2].x = 17;
ship.vertices[2].y = 2;

ship.vertices[3].x = 17;
ship.vertices[3].y = 9;

ship.vertices[4].x = 8;
ship.vertices[4].y = 14;

ship.vertices[5].x = 5;
ship.vertices[5].y = 8;

ship.vertices[6].x = -5;
ship.vertices[6].y = 8;

ship.vertices[7].x = -8;
ship.vertices[7].y = 14;

ship.vertices[8].x = -17;
ship.vertices[8].y = 9;

ship.vertices[9].x = -17;
ship.vertices[9].y = 2;
```

continues

Listing 5.13. continued

```
ship.vertices[10].x = -12;
ship.vertices[10].y = -1;

ship.vertices[11].x = -3;
ship.vertices[11].y = -19;

ship.vertices[12].x = -3;
ship.vertices[12].y = -8;

ship.vertices[13].x = 3;
ship.vertices[13].y = -8;

// Set the position of the spaceship.

ship.lxo = 160;
ship.lyo = 100;

// Sill in important fields.

ship.num_vertices = 14;
ship.b_color     = 1;
ship.closed      = 1;

// Make the ship a little smaller.

Scale_Polygon((polygon_ptr)&ship,0.75);

// Create the asteroid field.

Initialize_Rocks();

// main event loop

// S E C T I O N 3 /////////////////////////////////////////////////

while(!done)
    {
    // Erase all the rocks.

    Erase_Rocks();

    // Erase the player's ship.

    ship.b_color = 0;

    Draw_Polygon_Clip((polygon_ptr)&ship);

    // Move everything.

    engines=0;

// S E C T I O N 4 /////////////////////////////////////////////////

    if (kbhit())
```

```
{
// Get the key.

switch(getch())
      {
      case 's':
         {

         Rotate_Polygon((polygon_ptr)&ship,5);

         // Adjust the angle.

         angle+=5;

         if (angle>360)
            angle=0;

         } break;
      case 'a':
         {

         Rotate_Polygon((polygon_ptr)&ship,-5);

         // Adjust the angle.

         angle-=5;

         if (angle<0)
            angle=360;

         } break;
      case 'l':
         {

         // Adjust the velocity vector based
         // on direction

         xv = xv - cos(angle*3.14159/180);
         yv = yv - sin(angle*3.14159/180);

         // Flag that engines are on

         engines = 1;

         // Control the upper throttle limit.

         if (xv>10)
            xv=10;
         else
         if (xv<-10)
            xv=-10;

         if (yv>10)
```

Listing 5.13. continued

```
                                yv=10;
                       else
                       if (yv<-10)
                                yv=-10;

                       } break;

                   case 'q':      // Is the user trying to exit?
                       {
                       done=1;
                       } break;

                   } // end switch

           } // end if kbhit

// S E C T I O N 5 ///////////////////////////////////////////////

       // Decelerate the engines if they're off.

       if (!engines)
          {

          // Tend the x and y components of velocity toward 0.

          if (xv>0)
             xv-=FRICTION;
          else
          if (xv<0)
             xv+=FRICTION;

          if (yv>0)
             yv-=FRICTION;
          else
          if (yv<0)
             yv+=FRICTION;

          } // end if

       // Test whether the ship went offscreen.

       if (ship.lxo > 310)
          ship.lxo = 10;
       else
       if (ship.lxo < 10)
          ship.lxo = 310;

       if (ship.lyo > 190)
          ship.lyo = 10;
       else
       if (ship.lyo < 10)
          ship.lyo = 190;

// S E C T I O N 6 ///////////////////////////////////////////////

       // Do the actual translation.
```

```
    Translate_Polygon((polygon_ptr)&ship,xv,yv);

    // Now move the rocks.

    Move_Rocks();

// S E C T I O N 7 /////////////////////////////////////////////////

    // Draw everything.

    Draw_Rocks();

    ship.b_color = 9;

    Draw_Polygon_Clip((polygon_ptr)&ship);

    // Draw instructions.

    Blit_String(0,190,15,"
                    (A,S)-Rotate, (L)-Thrust, (Q)-Exit",1);

    // Just chill here for 1/18.2 th of a second.

    Delay(1);

    } // end while

// Reset the video mode back to text.

Set_Video_Mode(TEXT_MODE);

} // end main
```

5

Building an Executable: To make an executable of the program in Listing 5.13, you can either type it in or use the source on the companion CD. The name of the source is rockdemo.c. The precompiled executable is named rockdemo.exe. As before, use the following compile line for Microsoft C:

```
cl -AM -Zi -c  -Fc -Gs -G2 rockdemo.c
```

After compiling the program in this manner, you can link it to the standard libraries and to our previously generated game library, gamelib.lib, with a link line such as:

```
link /ST:8192 /CO rockdemo,,,graphics.lib+gamelib.lib,,
```

This creates a final, executable file named rockdemo.exe.

Analysis

Because the whole idea of this book is to learn to write video games, it may seem funny that we're learning about many other topics also. However, as you're learning, we basically need to know everything. One of the main reasons for today's material was to show you an example of an Asteroids-type, polygon-based game, but we needed to create a whole polygon engine to even begin with the game!

Most of the new functions in Listing 5.13 are related to the asteroids and the player's ship itself. We concentrate our discussion on the `main()` function because it's where most of the action takes place. The most important thing to remember in this discussion is that to accomplish animation we must always erase-move-draw. If we do that, and put some game logic in-between, we'll have a game!

The demo doesn't do much except let you fly around the asteroid field with a gravity field in flux, so the gravity and a couple of other points are all we're interested in understanding. You've seen almost everything else before. Let's begin with the analysis of the `main()`. As usual, I sectioned it off so we can discuss it in pieces.

1. In Section 1 the video system is set to mode 13h, and all the tables that must be created for the polygon engine are built up.

2. Section 2 is where the polygon definition of the ship is placed into the polygon structure, vertex by vertex. Also, the position of the ship and other attributes are set. Finally, the ship is scaled down a little to make it look more realistic compared to the asteroids, and the asteroids themselves are initialized. This initialization consists of defining the vertices of each asteroid, along with their position and velocity in space.

3. Section 3 is the entrance into the main event loop, where the erasing of all objects is done. In this case, the ship and the asteroids are erased.

4. Section 4 is where player inputs are tested and the player's ship is transformed accordingly. Note how the player's ship uses its current angle to compute velocity factors to add onto its current velocity. This is part of the gravity algorithm. The ship is thrust in the direction in which it's pointed until it reaches maximum speed. Then, when the thrust is released, the velocity is slowly decreased until the ship is stationary.

5. Section 5 is where the friction or deceleration of the ship takes place. Note that deceleration occurs only if the player is not applying thrust.

   Friction is usually implemented in the following manner: two variables contain the current velocity of a ship object. Each game cycle, the deceleration or frictional factor is subtracted from the current velocity, in essence slowing down the object. Also, we test to see whether the ship has hit a boundary of the screen and, if so, warp the ship to the other side.

6. Section 6 is where all the objects are actually moved. First, the ship is translated. Then a call to Move_Rocks() moves each one of the asteroids in the field and tests them for boundary collisions as well.

7. Section 7 is the point at which all images are drawn in the scene, which completes the erase-move-draw cycle. Also, a small delay is used here to make sure that the game runs at the same speed on all machines.

There's nothing in rockdemo that should confuse you at this point. There are, of course, about 1,000 ways to improve it—but one thing at a time!

Adding to the Game Library

The functions that we've created today must be placed into our graphics library. The name of the library modules are graph5.c and graph5.h. You can compile them or use the ones I've supplied on the CD, inserting them into the graphics library gamelib.lib. We have seen how to do this a couple times, so I won't cover it again. However, if you're having trouble, take a look at what we did yesterday to add to the game library.

Once you've added graph5.c to the graphics library, simply include the file graph5.h in your C source to use the functions.

Summary

This is one of the largest chapters we've seen yet. However, we had to cover a lot of information. We learned about the 2-D plane, line algorithms, and polygons, including how to clip them. We also learned how to transform polygons and some of the mathematics involved in doing this. Finally, we wrote a few demo programs that visualized what we covered, and saw a skeleton game—that you add to yourself in the next lesson!

Q&A

Q Why are polygon-based graphics important in video games?

A Many video games use bit-mapped graphics. However, most 3-D games, and some 2-D games, use polygon-based graphics. Using polygons is sometimes the only way to render certain types of objects. Also, polygons have a completely different look that can be quite pleasing to the eye.

Q **Why is the origin of the video screen at the upper-left corner instead of the lower-left corner (as it is in a normal Cartesian coordinate system)?**

A The first reason is that the screen is drawn from top to bottom and from left to right. The upper-left corner seemed to be the most logical place at which to start the screen memory. However, there's no technological barrier that would stop hardware engineers from making the start of video RAM at the bottom-left—other than they feel it can be done in software and don't want to address memory backward relative to the raster scan. (At least, that sounds like a good excuse to me!)

Q **What's considered a high-performance polygon rendering rate?**

A Well, this is a hard question as it depends on the kinds of polygons being drawn. Details such as type of shading, texturing, and the average size of the polygons all must be taken into consideration. However, a good speed is 25,000 flat, shaded triangles per second, with clipping where each triangle fits into a 5×5 grid of pixels.

Q **Can bit-mapped and polygon-based graphics be mixed in a single game?**

A Yes. Remember: bit maps are just rectangular polygons with textures on them.

Q **Is it possible to create a polygon engine that uses only integers?**

A Yes. Most retail games use integer-based polygon engines for performance reasons. We learn how to do this when we talk about optimization theory, on Day 8.

Workshop

The Workshop section presents quiz questions to help you cement your new knowledge and exercises to give you experience using what you've learned. Try to understand the questions and exercises before moving on to the next lesson. The answers are in Appendix B.

Quiz

1. What is a polygon?

2. When was Bresenham's algorithm invented, and what is it used for?

3. Write down the point-slope form of a line and solve for the slope.

4. What cases must be considered when clipping a line against a rectangular clipping region?

5. What are the differences between image-space and object-space clipping?

6. What's a unit circle, and how does it relate to the rotation formulas?

7. What's the difference between filled and wire-frame polygons?

Exercises

1. Write a function that draws a circle of any radius.

2. Write a function that scales polygons differently on each axis; that is, there's a separate scaling factor for both the x- and y-axis.

3. Time and analyze the difference in performance between `Draw_Polygon()` and `Draw_Polygon_Clip()`.

4. Make the ship in rockdemo fire missiles.

5. Place a black hole into rockdemo by creating a local gravity field somewhere on the screen.

6. *Extra Credit*: see if you can derive the rotation equations.

5

6

Real-Time Animation and Effects

The graphics functions we've created thus far are usable and have value. However, we must create a next generation of functions that are higher performance and can be used in professional-quality video games. Also, we must talk about some philosophical topics, such as special effects, screen transitions, and background animation. Although we definitely add to our game library today, the point of our discussions are more informational than implementational. What I'm trying to say is that I want you to think *creatively*! Here's today's hit list:

- ☐ Using double buffering to eliminate flicker
- ☐ Sprite clipping
- ☐ Sprite scaling
- ☐ Transitioning from screen to screen
- ☐ Scrolling the game field
- ☐ Mixing animation and motion
- ☐ Bringing games to life with background animation
- ☐ Context-sensitive animation
- ☐ Putting color in motion
- ☐ Locking onto the vertical retrace
- ☐ Adding to the game library

Using Double Buffering to Eliminate Flicker

This is the most important part of today's lesson. *Double buffering* is a method of rendering our graphics in an off-screen buffer before we draw them on the screen. Double buffering is a must if we want flicker-free animation. Figure 6.1 shows the architecture of a double buffer.

There's no reason we can't use a 64,000-byte buffer that has the same configuration as mode 13h (that is, a continuous array as a secondary drawing surface). Even though drawing on it won't have visible results, we can take our time when we access the secondary, or double, buffer because the player can't see what we're doing. This is the basis of using double buffers to create flicker-free animation.

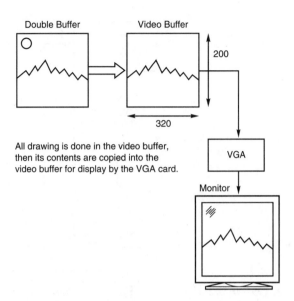

Double Buffer   Video Buffer

200

320

All drawing is done in the video buffer,
then its contents are copied into the
video buffer for display by the VGA card.

VGA

Monitor

Figure 6.1. *The architecture of a double buffer.*

Here's the theory behind the double buffer:

1. A double buffer—an off-screen work area—is created.

2. The imagery for the current frame is drawn in the double buffer.

3. Once the image is complete, the entire double buffer is copied to the video RAM and instantaneously becomes visible. No matter how many blitting operations we do, the image seen by the player seems to just *appear*.

4. A delay or some kind of synchronization takes place so that the viewer can see the image for a second.

   While the next frame of imagery is being drawn in the double buffer, the player still is viewing a solid image that's not being altered in real time.

5. When the next image in the double buffer is ready to be displayed, it's copied to the video RAM and thus becomes visible to the player.

By drawing in the double buffer and copying it to video RAM over and over, a frame-based animation takes place, just like a movie. This is how most video games are made.

Figure 6.2 shows the operational flow of a double buffer.

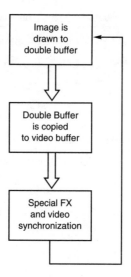

Figure 6.2. *Operational flowchart of a double-buffered animation system.*

Before we start writing the functions to create double buffers and draw in them, I want to direct your attention to the fact that the double buffer does not necessarily need to be as big as the screen. You may write a game that uses only the first 150 video lines for animation and the last 50 for controls, as shown in Figure 6.3.

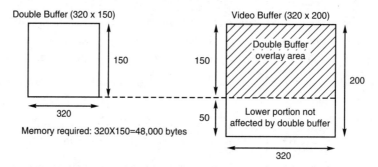

Figure 6.3. *A double buffer with size smaller than that of the video buffer.*

In that case, you may only want to have a double buffer that's 150 lines tall or 320*150 bytes in size, because you only need to update the active portions of the game area, which are in the upper 150 lines. The lower section of the screen, which contains the controls, can be updated directly in the video buffer because in most cases the controls are only text and lights, and need not be flicker-free.

Warning: Many programmers create double-buffer systems and then write into the double buffer past its size limit. This can cause strange bugs. Remember: the double buffer is an allocated region of memory in the heap. If you write past its initial size, the results can be unpredictable.

I'm not sure what functions we will be using from yesterday's lesson in the games. (We may not use any of them because the game we make today is mostly bit-mapped.) Therefore, for now, let's convert the bare minimum of functions to work with a double buffer, and add more as the days pass. The functions we definitely need to convert are:

☐ The sprite functions

☐ The text functions

☐ The pixel-plotting functions

We also must write a few new functions to do the following:

1. Create a double buffer of a specific size.

2. Copy the double buffer to the video buffer.

3. Clear the double buffer or fill it with a specific color.

4. Delete the double buffer's memory.

We might find a couple more utility functions coming in handy, but this list covers the major functions.

Before we write any code for these functions, let's agree on some conventions. Just as the video buffer is pointed to by a pointer variable named `video_buffer`, we create a similar variable today called `double_buffer` that points to the double buffer. Also, we define a couple of variables to track the size of the double buffer in WORDs. Furthermore, I've decided to allow the double buffer to be of different heights instead of supporting only the vertical extent of the screen, which is 200 lines. This information must be tracked, as well.

Note: The buffer_size variable is in WORDs instead of bytes for two reasons:

First, the double buffer always contains a number of bytes that is divisible by 2.

Second, another function uses WORD-sized moves to copy the double buffer into the video buffer, and having `buffer_size` in terms of WORDs is more convenient.

Here are the variable definitions that will be used by the double-buffer functions:

```
unsigned char far *double_buffer = NULL;

unsigned int buffer_height        = SCREEN_HEIGHT;

unsigned int buffer_size = SCREEN_WIDTH*SCREEN_HEIGHT/2;
```

With these declarations as a foundation, let's look through Listing 6.1. This listing contains the functions we need to create and manipulate a double buffer.

Listing 6.1. The double-buffer functions.

```
// F U N C T I O N S //////////////////////////////////////////////

int Create_Double_Buffer(int num_lines)
{

// Allocate enough memory to hold the double buffer.

if ((double_buffer =
(unsigned char far *)_fmalloc(SCREEN_WIDTH
                           *(num_lines + 1)))==NULL)
   return(0);

// Set the height of the buffer and compute its size.

buffer_height = num_lines;

buffer_size = SCREEN_WIDTH * num_lines/2;

// Fill the buffer with black.

_fmemset(double_buffer, 0, SCREEN_WIDTH * num_lines);

// Everything was OK.

return(1);

} // end Create_Double_Buffer

////////////////////////////////////////////////////////////////////

void Fill_Double_Buffer(int color)
{
// This function fills in the double buffer with the sent color.
```

```
_fmemset(double_buffer, color, SCREEN_WIDTH * buffer_height);

} // end Fill_Double_Buffer


//////////////////////////////////////////////////////////////////

void Show_Double_Buffer(char far *buffer)
{
// This function copies the double buffer into the
// video buffer.

_asm
   {
   push ds                 ; Save ds on stack.
   mov cx,buffer_size      ; This is the size of buffer in WORDs.
   les di,video_buffer     ; es:di is the destination of the
                           ; memory move
   lds si,buffer           ; ds:si is the source of the memory
                           ; move
   cld                     ; Make sure to move in the right
                           ; direction.
   rep movsw               ; Move all the WORDs.
   pop ds                  ; Restore the data segment.
   } // end asm

} // end Show_Double_Buffer

//////////////////////////////////////////////////////////////////

void Delete_Double_Buffer(void)
{
// This function frees up the memory allocated by the double
// buffer. Be sure to use FAR version.

if (double_buffer)
   _ffree(double_buffer);

} // end Delete_Double_Buffer

//////////////////////////////////////////////////////////////////
```

As you can see, there are four functions, each composed of less than a dozen lines:

☐ The Create_Double_Buffer() function creates a double buffer. In essence, it allocates a block of memory that is 320*num_lines. This block of memory is in the FAR heap.

☐ The Fill_Double_Buffer() function fills the double buffer with a color.

☐ The Show_Double_Buffer() function copies the contents of the double buffer into the video buffer so that it becomes visible.

☐ The `Delete_Double_Buffer()` function takes no parameters. It simply frees the memory allocated by the double buffer.

Let's talk about the syntax and use of each function. Then I think we should cover the `Show_Double_Buffer()` function in detail, as it's in in-line assembly language.

Syntax

The syntax for the `Create_Double_Buffer()` function is

```
int Create_Double_Buffer(int num_lines);
```

where *num_lines* is the height of the double buffer in lines. Each line is 320 pixels.

The syntax for the `Fill_Double_Buffer()` function is

```
wvoid Fill_Double_Buffer(int color);
```

where *color* is the color, from 0-255, you wish to fill the double buffer.

The syntax for the `Show_Double_Buffer()` function is

```
void Show_Double_Buffer(char far *buffer);
```

where **buffer* is a pointer to the double buffer you wish copied into the video buffer. (In our case this parameter is always `double_buffer`). The `Show_Double_Buffer()` function is parameterized for expansibility in the near future.

The syntax for the `Delete_Double_Buffer()` function is

```
void Delete_Double_Buffer(void);
```

Analysis These functions are all you need to implement a double-buffered graphics system. Although we must create graphics functions that write to the double buffer so we can see some action, we soon see that this is a matter of a changing a single variable name. The operation of each of the functions is quite basic: there are no tricks. The only function that might give you a problem is the `Show_Double_Buffer()` function. Let's cover it in detail.

The `Show_Double_Buffer()` function copies the double buffer to the video buffer. This operation has to be done as fast as possible because the video buffer is so slow; video RAM is much slower than normal memory. We could have used an ordinary `memcpy` function, but then only one byte at a time would be transferred from the double buffer to the video buffer. To obtain the best speed possible, we should move WORDs. We can accomplish this by using `movsw`, one of the 80xxx WORD-movement string functions.

The purpose of the `Show_Double_Buffer()` function is simple: move the entire contents of the double buffer into the video buffer at high speed. It happens like this:

1. The function begins by saving the `ds` register, which we need for part of the source operand of the `movsw` instruction.

2. The function then moves into `cx` the number of WORDs to be moved from the double buffer to the video buffer. At this point, the destination and source pointers are set up with the two instructions:

```
les di,video_buffer     ; es:di is destination of memory move
lds si,buffer           ; ds:si is source of memory move
```

3. The function must reset the direction flag to forward with the `cld` instruction.

4. The function then moves the data with the `rep movsw` instruction, and that's it.

5. After the function executes, the `ds` register is restored and the function exits.

It's becoming difficult to keep thinking up "cute" demos that use the functions we create! This time I've created a kaleidoscope program to do the following:

1. Create a double buffer.

2. Clear the double buffer.

3. Plot random dots in random colors with biaxial symmetry.

4. Copy the double buffer to the video buffer.

5. Wait 100 milliseconds before going back to Step 2.

The name of the program that does this is buffer.exe. This program can be found on the companion CD. The source code is shown in Listing 6.2. It's mostly an encore presentation of the functions we've just seen—except for one: a new pixel-plotting function. I took the old pixel-plotting function, `Plot_Pixel_Fast()`, and modified it to write into the double buffer instead of the video buffer.

To exit the program, press any key.

Listing 6.2. A demo of double buffering (buffer.c).

```
// I N C L U D E S /////////////////////////////////////////////

#include <io.h>
#include <conio.h>
#include <stdio.h>
#include <stdlib.h>
#include <dos.h>
#include <bios.h>
#include <fcntl.h>
```

continues

291

Listing 6.2. continued

```c
#include <memory.h>
#include <malloc.h>
#include <math.h>
#include <string.h>

#include "graph3.h"
#include "graph4.h"

// G L O B A L S  ///////////////////////////////////////////

unsigned char far *double_buffer = NULL;

unsigned int buffer_height        = SCREEN_HEIGHT;

unsigned int buffer_size = SCREEN_WIDTH*SCREEN_HEIGHT/2;

// F U N C T I O N S ///////////////////////////////////////////

void Show_Double_Buffer(char far *buffer)
{
// This function copies the double buffer into the video
// buffer.

_asm
   {
   push ds               ; Save ds on stack.
   mov cx,buffer_size    ; This is the size of buffer in WORDs.
   les di,video_buffer   ; es:di is the destination of the
                         ; memory move
   lds si,buffer         ; ds:si is the source of the memory
                         ; move
   cld                   ; Make sure to move in the right
                         ; direction.
   rep movsw             ; Move all the WORDs.
   pop ds                ; Restore the data segment.
   } // end asm

} // end Show_Double_Buffer

///////////////////////////////////////////////////////////////

int Create_Double_Buffer(int num_lines)
{

// Allocate enough memory to hold the double buffer.

if ((double_buffer =
   (unsigned char far *)
      _fmalloc(SCREEN_WIDTH * (num_lines + 1)))==NULL)
   return(0);

// Set the height of the buffer and compute its size.

buffer_height = num_lines;
```

```
buffer_size = SCREEN_WIDTH * num_lines/2;

// Fill the buffer with black.

_fmemset(double_buffer, 0, SCREEN_WIDTH * num_lines);

// Everything was OK.

return(1);

} // end Init_Double_Buffer

//////////////////////////////////////////////////////////////

void Fill_Double_Buffer(int color)
{
// This function fills in the double buffer with the sent color.

_fmemset(double_buffer, color, SCREEN_WIDTH * buffer_height);

} // end Fill_Double_Buffer

//////////////////////////////////////////////////////////////

void Delete_Double_Buffer(void)
{
// This function frees up the memory allocated by the double
// buffer. Be sure to use FAR version.

if (double_buffer)
  _ffree(double_buffer);

} // end Delete_Double_Buffer

//////////////////////////////////////////////////////////////

void Plot_Pixel_Fast_DB(int x,int y,unsigned char color)
{

// This function plots the pixel in the desired color a little
// quicker using binary shifting to accomplish the
// multiplications.

// Use the fact that 320*y = 256*y + 64*y = y<<8 + y<<6.

double_buffer[((y<<8) + (y<<6)) + x] = color;

} // end Plot_Pixel_Fast_DB

//////////////////////////////////////////////////////////////

void main(void)
{
// This program creates a kaleidoscope of colors.

int x,y,fcolor=1,index;
```

continues

Listing 6.2. continued

```
// Set the video mode to the 320x200, 256-color mode.

Set_Video_Mode(VGA256);

// Create a double buffer.

if (!Create_Double_Buffer(SCREEN_HEIGHT))
    {
    printf("\nNot enough memory to create double buffer.");

    } // end if

// Main event loop

while(!kbhit())
    {

    // Clear out the double buffer with black.

    Fill_Double_Buffer(0);

    // Next color

    if (++fcolor>15) fcolor=1;

    // Draw something in it.

    for (index=0; index<200; index++)
        {
        // Make a kaleidoscope of color.

        x = rand()%(SCREEN_WIDTH/2);
        y = rand()%(SCREEN_HEIGHT/2);

        Plot_Pixel_Fast_DB(x,y,fcolor);
        Plot_Pixel_Fast_DB((SCREEN_WIDTH-1)-x,y,fcolor);
        Plot_Pixel_Fast_DB(x,(SCREEN_HEIGHT-1)-y,fcolor);
        Plot_Pixel_Fast_DB((SCREEN_WIDTH-1)-x,
                           (SCREEN_HEIGHT-1)-y,fcolor);

        } // end for

    // Copy the double buffer to the video buffer.

    Show_Double_Buffer(double_buffer);

    // Wait a bit so the user can see it.

    Delay(2);

    } // end while

// Reset the video mode back to text.

Set_Video_Mode(TEXT_MODE);
```

```
// Free the double buffer.

Delete_Double_Buffer();

} // end main
```

Building an Executable: To make an executable of the program in Listing 6.2, you can either type it in or use the source on the companion CD. The name of the source is buffer.c. The precompiled executable is named buffer.exe. As before, use the following compile line for Microsoft C:

```
cl -AM -Zi -c -Fc -Gs -G2 buffer.c
```

After compiling the program in this manner you can link it to the standard libraries and to our previously generated game library, gamelib.lib, with a link line such as:

```
link /ST:8192 /CO buffer,,,graphics.lib+gamelib.lib,,
```

This creates a final executable named buffer.exe.

There isn't anything spectacular about the demo program; it shows the basic operation of a double buffer and how to implement one with our functions. As I said a moment ago, there's a new version of the pixel plotting function: Plot_Pixel_Fast_DB(). The DB at the end of the function name stands for "double buffer," and is used as a naming convention throughout.

The video buffer and double buffer work in much the same way. The major difference is that the video buffer is visible and on the VGA card while the double buffer is invisible and exists within main memory. However, they're accessed the same way and have the same layout.

For a function to work properly with the double buffer, we must convert the function. Because the double buffer and video buffer have the same size and format, functions designed to work with video buffer can, in most cases, be modified to work with the double buffer simply by changing one line of code. This one line is the line that accesses the memory in the function.

Each graphics function we've written thus far has either written to or read from the video buffer. When using a double buffer, we need only make a change so the function writes

to or reads from the double buffer. To make this change, any reference to `video_buffer` in the functions previously written must be changed to `double_buffer`—and that's it!

As an example, let's look at the `Plot_Pixel_Fast()` and `Plot_Pixel_Fast_DB()` functions to see the difference. I have highlighted the areas of interest.

Listing 6.3. Pixel-plotting functions compared.

```
void Plot_Pixel_Fast(int x,int y,unsigned char color)
{

// This function plots the pixel in the desired color a little
// quicker using binary shifting to accomplish the
// multiplications.

// Use the fact that 320*y = 256*y + 64*y = y<<8 + y<<6.

video_buffer[((y<<8) + (y<<6)) + x] = color;

} // end Plot_Pixel_Fast

//////////////////////////////////////////////////////////////

void Plot_Pixel_Fast_DB(int x,int y,unsigned char color)
{

// This function plots the pixel in the desired color a little
// quicker using binary shifting to accomplish the
// multiplications.

// Use the fact that 320*y = 256*y + 64*y = y<<8 + y<<6.

double_buffer[((y<<8) + (y<<6)) + x] = color;

} // end Plot_Pixel_Fast_DB

//////////////////////////////////////////////////////////////
```

If you inspect each function you see that the only difference is what region of memory is accessed.

The games we write in this book mostly use sprites as the main objects in the games. Although we might have some pixel-based or polygon-based effects, we do most of our animation with sprites and bit blitting. Therefore, let's convert all sprite functions to work with the double buffer.

We can use the following process to create the double buffer versions of the sprite functions:

1. Make a copy of the standard sprite function and rename it with the _DB extension at the end of the function name.

2. Change all references from video_buffer to double_buffer.

Using these steps I've created new, double-buffered versions of all the sprite functions thus far. They're shown in Listing 6.4.

Listing 6.4. Double-buffered versions of the sprite functions.

```
void Behind_Sprite_DB(sprite_ptr sprite)
{

// This function scans the background behind a sprite so that,
// when the sprite is drawn, the background isn't obliterated.

char far *work_back;
int work_offset=0,offset,y;

// Alias a pointer to sprite background for ease of access.

work_back = sprite->background;

// Compute the offset of the background in the video buffer.

offset = (sprite->y << 8) + (sprite->y << 6) + sprite->x;

for (y=0; y<sprite_height; y++)
    {
    // Copy the next row out of the screen buffer into sprite-
    // background buffer.

    _fmemcpy((char far *)&work_back[work_offset],
            (char far *)&double_buffer[offset],
            sprite_width);

    // Move to the next line in the double buffer and in the
    // sprite-background buffer.

    offset      += SCREEN_WIDTH;
    work_offset += sprite_width;

    } // end for y

} // end Behind_Sprite_DB

///////////////////////////////////////////////////////////////

void Erase_Sprite_DB(sprite_ptr sprite)
{
// Replace the background that was behind the sprite.

// This function replaces the background that was saved from
// where a sprite was going to be placed.
```

continues

Listing 6.4. continued

```c
char far *work_back;
int work_offset=0,offset,y;

// Alias a pointer to sprite background for ease of access.

work_back = sprite->background;

// Compute the offset of the background in the double buffer.

offset = (sprite->y << 8) + (sprite->y << 6) + sprite->x;

for (y=0; y<sprite_height; y++)
    {
    // Copy the next row out of the screen buffer into the sprite-
    // background buffer.

    _fmemcpy((char far *)&double_buffer[offset],
            (char far *)&work_back[work_offset],
            sprite_width);

    // Move to the next line in the video buffer and in the
    // sprite-background buffer.

    offset       += SCREEN_WIDTH;
    work_offset += sprite_width;

    } // end for y


} // end Erase_Sprite_DB

/////////////////////////////////////////////////////////////

void Draw_Sprite_DB(sprite_ptr sprite)
{

// This function draws a sprite on the screen, row by row,
// quickly.  Note the use of shifting to implement
// multiplication.

char far *work_sprite;
int work_offset=0,offset,x,y;
unsigned char data;

// Alias a pointer to the sprite for ease of access.

work_sprite = sprite->frames[sprite->curr_frame];

// Compute the offset of the sprite in the video buffer.

offset = (sprite->y << 8) + (sprite->y << 6) + sprite->x;

for (y=0; y<sprite_height; y++)
    {
```

```
    // Copy the next row into the double buffer using memcpy
    // for speed.

    for (x=0; x<sprite_width; x++)
        {

        // Test for a transparent pixel; that is, 0. If the
        // pixel is not transparent, draw it.

        if ((data=work_sprite[work_offset+x]))
            double_buffer[offset+x] = data;

        } // end for x

    // Move to the next line in the double buffer and in the
    // sprite bit-map buffer.

    offset      += SCREEN_WIDTH;
    work_offset += sprite_width;

    } // end for y

} // end Draw_Sprite_DB
```

//

Analysis The functions in Listing 6.4, along with the double-buffer functions themselves, are all you need to make sprites work with the double buffer. However, you probably noticed that the sprite initialization and deletion functions are not present. This is because those functions don't access the video buffer, and there's no need for redundant copies of them.

Later today I supply you with a complete library module, graph6.c, that contains all these new functions, definitions, and structures.

Sprite Clipping

We briefly spoke about sprite clipping on Day 4, and we covered polygon-based clipping yesterday. Today I want us to write a version of the Draw_Sprite() function that takes into consideration a clipping rectangle. We won't yet write a complete set of sprite functions that perform clipping, because we may not need them for any of the games that we create in the book. We may learn better ways to implement sprites, or we may find that we can get away without clipping all together. The latter would be a plus because every operation a sprite must do takes up more time, and that's a commodity we don't have a lot of. We must always make our graphic functions as fast as possible—and if they don't need a specific functionality, why put it in?

Clipping a sprite against a rectangle is easy, because the sprite itself is a rectangle. There a many cases of a sprite lying partially within the clipping rectangle, as shown in Figure 6.4.

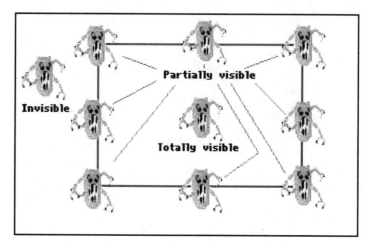

Figure 6.4. *The possibilities of clipping.*

Here we see that the sprite's bounding rectangle can be on eight different edges, along with being completely visible and invisible. The cases of complete invisibility and visibility are the easiest to take care of. The problem lies in cases in which the sprite is partially visible (for example, lying on an edge).

The basic algorithm to clip a sprite is shown in Algorithm 6.1.

Algorithm 6.1. Clipping a sprite against a rectangular boundary.

```
if (sprite is invisible)
   don't draw it and exit.

else
if (sprite is totally visible)
   draw the sprite normally and exit.

else
    the sprite must be clipped. Compute its new bounding
     rectangle and draw it.
```

Algorithm 6.1 tests for the two simple cases and assumes that clipping is necessary if they fail. In that case, the sprite must be clipped against the viewing boundaries and then drawn with new x and y extents.

I've written a function based on Algorithm 6.1 and the old `Draw_Sprite()` function. The new function, `Draw_Sprite_Clipped_DB`, has almost the same interface as `Draw_Sprite()` except that the clipping rectangle is sent as a set of four integers. The function is shown in Listing 6.5.

Listing 6.5. A new sprite drawing function with clipping.

```c
void Draw_Sprite_Clipped_DB(sprite_ptr sprite,
                int min_x,int min_y, int max_x, int max_y)
{

// This function draws a sprite into the double buffer and clips
// it to the sent clipping boundary. The function is drawn out
// to show each step clearly.

char far *work_sprite;
int work_offset=0,
    offset,x_off,
    x,y,xs,ys,
    xe,ye,
    clip_width,clip_height;
unsigned char data;

// Extract the sprite position.

xs = sprite->x;
ys = sprite->y;

// Compute the end of the sprite bounding box in screen
// coordinates.

xe = xs + sprite_width  - 1;
ye = ys + sprite_height - 1;

// Test whether the sprite is totally invisible; that is,
// whether the sprite is beyond the screen boundaries.

if ( (xs >= max_x) || (ys >= max_y) ||
     (xs <= (min_x-sprite_width)) ||
     (ys <= (min_y-sprite_height)) )
    {
    return;
    } // end if sprite invisible

// The sprite must be partially visible. Therefore, compute the
// region that must be drawn.

// Clip in the x direction.

if (xs < min_x)
   xs=min_x;

else
if (xe >= max_x)
    xe=max_x-1;
```

6

Listing 6.5. continued

```
          // Clip in the y direction.

          if (ys < min_y)
             ys=min_y;

          else
          if (ye >= max_y)
              ye=max_y-1;

          // Compute the new width and height.

          clip_width  = xe - xs + 1;
          clip_height = ye - ys + 1;

          // Compute the working offsets based on the new starting y.

          work_offset = (sprite->y - ys) * sprite_width;

          x_off = (xs-sprite->x);

          // Now render the clipped sprite.

          // Alias a pointer to the sprite for ease of access.

          work_sprite = sprite->frames[sprite->curr_frame];

          // Compute the offset of the sprite in the video buffer.

          offset = (ys << 8) + (ys << 6) + xs;

          for (y=0; y<clip_height; y++)
              {
              // Copy the next row into the screen buffer using memcpy
              // for speed.

              for (x=0; x<clip_width; x++)
                  {

                  // Test for a transparent pixel; that is, 0. If the
                  // pixel is not transparent, draw it.

                  if ((data=work_sprite[work_offset+x + x_off]))
                      double_buffer[offset+x+x_off] = data;

                  } // end for x

              // Move to the next line in the double buffer and in the
              // sprite bit-map buffer.

              offset      += SCREEN_WIDTH;
              work_offset += sprite_width;

              } // end for y

       } // end Draw_Sprite_Clipped_DB
```

Let's take a look at the syntax of the function and see what the parameters are for.

The syntax for the `Draw_Sprite_Clipped_DB()` function is

```
void Draw_Sprite_Clipped_DB(sprite_ptr sprite,
                  int min_x, int min_y,
                  int max_x, int max_y);
```

where:

☐ `sprite` is a pointer to the sprite you wish clipped and drawn into the double buffer.

☐ `min_x` is the x component of the upper left corner of the clipping region.

☐ `min_y` is the y component of the upper left corner of the clipping region.

☐ `max_x` is the x component of the lower right corner of the clipping region.

☐ `max_y` is the y component of the lower right corner of the clipping region.

Analysis The `Draw_Sprite_Clipped_DB()` function implements Algorithm 6.1 almost verbatim. The only difference in the actual C implementation is all the details that must be taken into consideration. Many variables must be tracked to clip the sprite properly. Furthermore, the function draws the sprite only into the double buffer.

If you wish, you can base a complete set of sprite functions on the `Draw_Sprite_Clipped_DB` function. However, I suggest you wait until you actually need them before writing them.

Sprite Scaling

Sprite scaling means to make a sprite object larger or smaller. Figure 6.5 shows three versions of the same sprite scaled by the factors 0.5, 1.0, and 2.0.

We learned yesterday that scaling is accomplished by multiplying each vertex in a polygon by the scaling factor—and, *voila!* The object is scaled properly. Theoretically, this is the correct technique. In the context of bit-mapped images, though, this technique doesn't lend itself well to implementation.

To begin with, bit maps have no vertices; they are a collection of points. Therefore, we don't have any vertices to scale! We must try another approach. Let's say we want to scale an 8×8 bit map by 2.0. This means we want twice the number of pixels in each dimension. Because there's both an x- and a y-axis, the resulting, scaled bit map would be 16×16.

Take a look at Figure 6.6. In it we see that each pixel has been replicated twice in each direction; in other words, there are four pixels in the 16×16 bit map for each pixel in the 8×8 bit map.

6

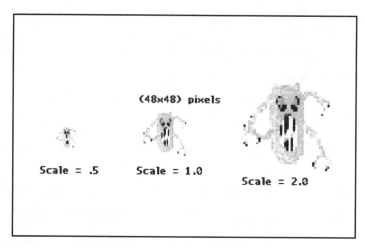

Figure 6.5. *Scaling a sprite to different sizes.*

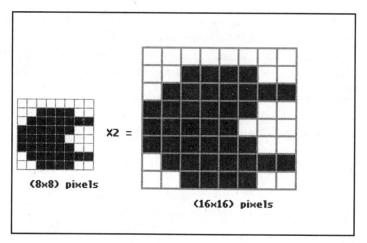

Figure 6.6. *Scaling a 8x8 bit map by 2.*

This brings us to the conclusion that we must scale our sprites in both the x-axis and the y-axis to make the entire sprite scale properly.

Now, it's easy to scale a sprite by multiples of 2. I think you could write an algorithm right now to do such a thing. Let's see how we'd do something like that:

1. We can begin by thinking of the bit map as a collection of horizontal or vertical strips. Let's choose horizontal.

2. If the scaling factor is four, for example, we can then replicate each pixel in each horizontal row four times. If the image was 8×8, then, each row would be 32 pixels long when we were done scaling. That's shown in Figure 6.7.

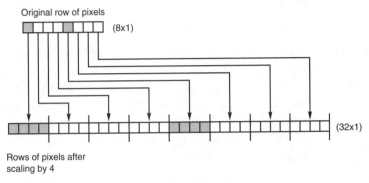

Figure 6.7. *The results of scaling a single row of pixels.*

3. We then can copy that row four times to take care of the vertical scaling. Therefore, the final object would be 32 pixels wide by 4*8 pixels high, which is 32×32 or 4*(8×8). This is exactly what we want.

Writing a scaler based on a multiple of two is simple, but we aren't going to need one. Today, though, we're just interested in learning how to scale to any size. This is no easy task, and you have to start with the proper point of view. That point of view (first discussed on Day 4) is to think of the sprite or bit map as being composed of horizontal or vertical *strips*. For our discussion, let's think of a sprite bit map as being composed of horizontal strips. You scale the entire bit map using the same technique as on a single strip, so we can concentrate on scaling a single horizontal strip to begin with.

Scaling can be thought of as a conversion, or *mapping*, of one length to another. In our case, we want to scale a row of pixels to some size. This new size may be smaller or larger than the row's original size. We can restate this formally in the following way: we want to stretch a 1-D bit map from some source size, s, in pixels, to some destination size, d, in pixels.

The previous sentence contains all you need to know to write a sprite scaler: we must stretch a source row of pixels to a destination row of pixels. In the case of a scaling factor of 2, this means we want to stretch the source row to be twice as big. In other words, we need to replicate each pixel twice.

Now, let's get a bit mathematical. You can scale a bit map by copying a number of source pixels to the destination size. We may replicate pixels or (in the case of shrinking) actually skip pixels. In any case, the operation is pixel-based. We must figure a way of determining either:

☐ The number of pixels from the source row that should be copied to the destination row in the case of scaling down

☐ How many of each source pixel should be copied, in the case of scaling up

We can make this determination by creating a scaling factor that describes how the source row is to be sampled to create the destination row. For example, in the case of scaling an object by 2, we want to sample each source pixel twice to create the destination row. If the source row had eight pixels and we sampled each pixel twice, plotting them as the destination row, the result would be 16 pixels. Therefore, if we create a variable that indexes into the source row, and the data extracted from the source row with that index is used as the destination pixel, we're done.

So, how do we create this index? Easy: the index is a variable, which we start at 0 and increment by the inverse of the scaling factor.

What's the inverse of the scaling factor? Good question! Given that the source object is 16x16 and the requested destination object is 80×80, the scaling factor is 80/16, or 5. Hence, the inverse of the scaling factor (and the index we'd use) would be 1/5, or 0.2. This means it would take the index variable five iterations before it's bumped up to the next pixel in the source row. In other words, it would replicate each pixel in the source row five times—which is exactly what we want.

To solidify this explanation, I've written a demo that loads in a PCX file and extracts an object from it, which is then scaled using the keys on the keyboard. To get the most out of it, let's take a look at the scaling operation in its simplest form, in Algorithm 6.2.

Algorithm 6.2. Scaling a 1-D bit map.

```
scale_index=0;
scale_step = source_size / destination_size;

for (index=0; index<destination_size; index++)
    {
    destination_bitmap[index] = source_bitmap[scale_index];
    scale_index+=scale_step;

    } // end for
```

Algorithm 6.2 is the basis of all sprite scaling. Its single downfall is...speed. It's super slow. It can be sped up by using fixed-point math and look-up tables, but we aren't going to worry about that now. (You can write a faster scaler if you need one.) Listing 6.6 contains

the program I promised, called scalar.exe. This program scales a character called Robopunk, whom you see in action later today. Here's the source code.

Listing 6.6. A demonstration of bitmapped scaling (scalar.c).

```c
// I N C L U D E S /////////////////////////////////////////////

#include <io.h>
#include <conio.h>
#include <stdio.h>
#include <stdlib.h>
#include <dos.h>
#include <bios.h>
#include <fcntl.h>
#include <memory.h>
#include <malloc.h>
#include <math.h>
#include <string.h>

#include "graph3.h" // Include our graphics library.
#include "graph4.h" // Include our graphics library.


// G L O B A L S /////////////////////////////////////////////

unsigned char far *double_buffer = NULL;

unsigned int buffer_height      = SCREEN_HEIGHT;

unsigned int buffer_size = SCREEN_WIDTH*SCREEN_HEIGHT/2;

sprite object;

pcx_picture imagery_pcx;

// F U N C T I O N S /////////////////////////////////////////////

void Show_Double_Buffer(unsigned char far *buffer)
{
// This function copies the double buffer into the video
// buffer.

_asm
   {
   push ds                 ; Save ds on stack.
   mov cx,buffer_size      ; This is the size of buffer in WORDs.
   les di,video_buffer     ; es:di is the destination of the
                           ; memory move
   lds si,buffer           ; ds:si is the source of the memory
                           ; move
   cld                     ; Make sure to move in the right
                           ; direction.
   rep movsw               ; Move all the WORDs.
   pop ds                  ; Restore the data segment.
   } // end asm
```

continues

307

Listing 6.6. continued

```
} // end Show_Double_Buffer

////////////////////////////////////////////////////////////////

int Create_Double_Buffer(int num_lines)
{

// Allocate enough memory to hold the double buffer.

if ((double_buffer =
    (unsigned char far *)_fmalloc(SCREEN_WIDTH *
    (num_lines + 1)))==NULL)
    return(0);

// Set the height of the buffer and compute its size.

buffer_height = num_lines;

buffer_size = SCREEN_WIDTH * num_lines/2;

// Fill the buffer with black.

_fmemset(double_buffer, 0, SCREEN_WIDTH * num_lines);

// Everything was OK.

return(1);

} // end Init_Double_Buffer

////////////////////////////////////////////////////////////////

void Fill_Double_Buffer(int color)
{
// This function fills in the double buffer with the sent color.

_fmemset(double_buffer, color, SCREEN_WIDTH * buffer_height);

} // end Fill_Double_Buffer

////////////////////////////////////////////////////////////////

void Delete_Double_Buffer(void)
{
// This function frees up the memory allocated by the double
// buffer. Be sure to use FAR version.

if (double_buffer)
  _ffree(double_buffer);

} // end Delete_Double_Buffer

////////////////////////////////////////////////////////////////
```

```
void Scale_Sprite(sprite_ptr sprite,float scale)
{

// This function scales a sprite by computing the number of
// source pixels needed to satisfy the number of destination
// pixels. Note: this function works in the double buffer.

char far *work_sprite;

int work_offset=0,
    offset,
    x,
    y;

unsigned char data;

float y_scale_index,
      x_scale_step,
      y_scale_step,
      x_scale_index;

// Set the first source pixel.

y_scale_index = 0;

// Compute the floating-point step.

y_scale_step = sprite_height/scale;
x_scale_step = sprite_width/scale;

// Alias a pointer to the sprite for ease of access.

work_sprite = sprite->frames[sprite->curr_frame];

// Compute the offset of the sprite in the video buffer.

offset = (sprite->y << 8) + (sprite->y << 6) + sprite->x;

// Scale the object row by row

for (y=0; y<(int)(scale); y++)
    {
    // Copy the next row into the screen buffer using memcpy
    // for speed.

    x_scale_index=0;

    for (x=0; x<(int)scale; x++)
        {

        // Test for a transparent pixel; that is, 0. If the
        // pixel is not transparent, draw it.

        if ((data=work_sprite[work_offset+(int)x_scale_index]))
            double_buffer[offset+x] = data;
```

continues

Listing 6.6. continued

```
          x_scale_index+=(x_scale_step);

        } // end for x

    // Using the floating scale_step, index to the next source
    // pixel.

    y_scale_index+=y_scale_step;

    // Move to the next line in the video buffer and in the
    // sprite bit-map buffer.

    offset      += SCREEN_WIDTH;
    work_offset = sprite_width*(int)(y_scale_index);

    } // end for y

} // end Scale_Sprite

// M A I N //////////////////////////////////////////////////////

void main(void)
{
int done=0;        // Exit flag
char buffer[128];  // Used to build up info string

float scale=32; // Initial scale of object

// Set the video mode to the 320x200, 256-color mode.

Set_Video_Mode(VGA256);

// Set the sprite system size so functions use the correct
// sprite size.

sprite_width = sprite_height = 32;

// Initialize the PCX file that holds all the animation cells

PCX_Init((pcx_picture_ptr)&imagery_pcx);

// Load the PCX file that holds the cells.

PCX_Load("robopunk.pcx", (pcx_picture_ptr)&imagery_pcx,1);

Sprite_Init((sprite_ptr)&object,0,0,0,0,0,0);

// Grab the bit map.

PCX_Grab_Bitmap((pcx_picture_ptr)&imagery_pcx,
                (sprite_ptr)&object,0,3,0);

// Create a double buffer.
```

```
if (!Create_Double_Buffer(SCREEN_HEIGHT))
    {
    printf("\nNot enough memory to create double buffer.");

    } // end if

// Initialize the sprite.

object.curr_frame = 0;
object.x          = 160-(sprite_width>>1);
object.y          = 100-(sprite_height>>1);

// Clear the double buffer.

Fill_Double_Buffer(0);

// Show the user the scaled texture.

Scale_Sprite((sprite_ptr)&object,scale);

Show_Double_Buffer(double_buffer);

Blit_String(0,190,10,"Press 'Q' to Quit,'<' '>' to Scale.",1);

// Main loop

while(!done)
    {

    // Has the user hit a key?

    if (kbhit())
        {
        switch(getch())
            {
            case '.': // Scale the object larger.
                {
                if (scale<180)
                    {
                    scale+=4;
                    object.x-=2;
                    object.y-=2;
                    } // end if ok to scale larger

                } break;

            case ',': // Scale the object smaller.
                {
                if (scale>4)
                    {
                    scale-=4;
                    object.x+=2;
                    object.y+=2;
                    } // end if OK to scale smaller

                } break;
```

continues

6

Listing 6.6. continued

```
                    case 'q': // Let's go!
                            {
                            done=1;
                            } break;

                default:break;

                } // end switch


        // Create a clean slate.

        Fill_Double_Buffer(0);

        // Scale the sprite and render it into the double
        // buffer.

        Scale_Sprite((sprite_ptr)&object,scale);

        // Show the double buffer.

        Show_Double_Buffer(double_buffer);

        Blit_String(0,190,10,
                    "Press 'Q' to Quit,'<' '>' to Scale.",1);

        sprintf(buffer,"Current scale = %f   ",scale/32);

        Blit_String(0,8,10,buffer,1);


        }// end if

    } // end while

// Delete the PCX file.

PCX_Delete((pcx_picture_ptr)&imagery_pcx);

// Reset the video mode back to text.

Set_Video_Mode(TEXT_MODE);

// Delete the double buffer.

Delete_Double_Buffer();

} // end main
```

Building an Executable: To make an executable of the program in Listing 6.6, you can either type it in or use the source on the companion CD. The name of the source is scalar.c. The precompiled executable is named scalar.exe. As before, use the following compile line for Microsoft C:

```
cl -AM -Zi -c  -Fc -Gs -G2 scalar.c
```

After compiling the program in this manner you can link it to the standard libraries and to our previously generated game library, gamelib.lib, with a link line such as:

```
link /ST:8192 /CO scalar,,,graphics.lib+gamelib.lib,,
```

This creates a final executable named scalar.exe.

The program in Listing 6.6 simply implements a single function that we haven't seen thus far. It's called Scale_Sprite(). The Scale_Sprite() function scales the sent sprite and draws it into the double buffer. The function uses Algorithm 6.2 to scale the sent sprite in both the x- and y-axes.

The most interesting thing about the entire program is its speed—or, I should say, lack of it. We could never use such an algorithm in a professional-quality video game; it would be just too slow. Also, notice how the sprite looks as it's scaled larger. It gets very "blocky." This is because of the pixel scaling. It could be fixed with advanced image-processing algorithms, but they're beyond the scope of this book. (Such algorithms "smooth" the edges and use interpolation techniques to get rid of the "jaggies.")

Transitioning from Screen to Screen

Screen transitions are simple things, but they can really add to the overall punch of a video-game presentation. With interesting screen transitions, a game looks more professional and has the "feel" of a movie instead of a video game. In this section we look at a few screen transitions and see how to implement them using the library functions we already have.

A screen transition is just some visually pleasing way of clearing the screen besides blasting it with black or some other color. The common screen transitions you see in the movies are fades and swipes:

☐ *Fades* are when the image seems to darken to black or illuminate to white. Either way, the image blurs and becomes invisible at some point.

☐ The second effect, called a *swipe*, occurs when the image "walks" off the screen.

Because we have a computer at our fingertips (and can do just about anything we like with the screen image), we can create some neat screen transitions and then call them as functions. These transitions always affect the video buffer directly, so if there's something in the buffer you want saved—and the screen transition is one that gobbles up the image—you'd better save what's there.

Creating screen transitions is easy: most of them only take a few lines of code. To show you a few examples of screen transitions, I've created a program called transfx.exe, which loads a PCX file, displays it, and enables you to transition between screens in any of four different methods. Later, we extract the screen-transition functions and place them in the library we're building. Listing 6.7 contains the program.

Listing 6.7. A screen transition demo (transfx.c).

```
// I N C L U D E S ////////////////////////////////////////////////

#include <io.h>
#include <conio.h>
#include <stdio.h>
#include <stdlib.h>
#include <dos.h>
#include <bios.h>
#include <fcntl.h>
#include <memory.h>
#include <malloc.h>
#include <math.h>
#include <string.h>

#include "graph3.h"
#include "graph4.h"

// D E F I N E S ////////////////////////////////////////////////

#define NUM_WORMS 320

// S T R U C T U R E S ////////////////////////////////////////////

typedef struct worm_typ
        {
        int y;        // Current y position of worm.
        int color;    // Color of worm
        int speed;    // Speed of worm
        int counter;  // Counter

        } worm, *worm_ptr;
```

```
// G L O B A L S ////////////////////////////////////////////////

pcx_picture screen_fx; // Our test screen

/////////////////////////////////////////////////////////////////

void Fade_Lights(void)
{
// This function fades the lights by slowly decreasing the
// color values in all color registers.

int pal_reg,index;
RGB_color color;

for (index=0; index<30; index++)
    {

    for (pal_reg=1; pal_reg<255; pal_reg++)
        {
        // Get the color to fade.

        Get_Palette_Register(pal_reg,(RGB_color_ptr)&color);

        if (color.red   > 5) color.red-=3;
        else
           color.red = 0;

        if (color.green > 5) color.green-=3;
        else
           color.green = 0;
        if (color.blue  > 5) color.blue-=3;
        else
           color.blue = 0;

        // Set the color to a diminished intensity.

        Set_Palette_Register(pal_reg,(RGB_color_ptr)&color);

        } // end for pal_reg

    // Wait a bit...

    Delay(2);

    } // end fade for

} // end Fade_Lights

/////////////////////////////////////////////////////////////////

void Disolve(void)
{
// Dissolve the screen by plotting zillions of black pixels.

unsigned long index;
```

continues

Listing 6.7. continued

```
for (index=0; index<=300000; index++,
    Plot_Pixel_Fast(rand()%320, rand()%200, 0));

} // end Disolve

///////////////////////////////////////////////////////////////

void Melt(void)
{

// This function "melts" the screen by moving little worms at
// different speeds down the screen. These worms change to the
// color they're eating.

int index,ticks=0;

worm worms[NUM_WORMS]; // The array of worms used to make the
                       // screen melt.

// Initialize the worms.

for (index=0; index<160; index++)
    {

    worms[index].color   = Get_Pixel(index,0);
    worms[index].speed   = 3 + rand()%9;
    worms[index].y       = 0;
    worms[index].counter = 0;

    // Draw the worm.

    Plot_Pixel_Fast((index<<1),0,(char)worms[index].color);
    Plot_Pixel_Fast((index<<1),1,(char)worms[index].color);
    Plot_Pixel_Fast((index<<1),2,(char)worms[index].color);


    Plot_Pixel_Fast((index<<1)+1,0,(char)worms[index].color);
    Plot_Pixel_Fast((index<<1)+1,1,(char)worms[index].color);
    Plot_Pixel_Fast((index<<1)+1,2,(char)worms[index].color);

    } // end index

// Do the screen melt.

while(++ticks<1800)
    {

    // Process each worm.

    for (index=0; index<320; index++)
        {
        // Is it time to move the worm?

        if (++worms[index].counter == worms[index].speed)
```

```
        {
        // Reset the counter.

        worms[index].counter = 0;

        worms[index].color =
            Get_Pixel(index,worms[index].y+4);

        // Has the worm hit bottom?

        if (worms[index].y < 193)
            {
            Plot_Pixel_Fast((index<<1),worms[index].y,0);
            Plot_Pixel_Fast((index<<1),worms[index].y+1,
                            (char)worms[index].color);
            Plot_Pixel_Fast((index<<1),worms[index].y+2,
                            (char)worms[index].color);
            Plot_Pixel_Fast((index<<1),worms[index].y+3,
                            (char)worms[index].color);

            Plot_Pixel_Fast((index<<1)+1,worms[index].y,0);
            Plot_Pixel_Fast((index<<1)+1,worms[index].y+1,
                        ➥(char)worms[index].color);
            Plot_Pixel_Fast((index<<1)+1,worms[index].y+2,
                        ➥(char)worms[index].color);
            Plot_Pixel_Fast((index<<1)+1,worms[index].y+3,
                        ➥(char)worms[index].color);

            worms[index].y++;

            } // end if worm isn't at bottom yet

        } // end if time to move worm

    } // end index

// Accelerate the melt.

if (!(ticks % 500))
    {

    for (index=0; index<160; index++)
        worms[index].speed--;

    } // end if time to accelerate melt

} // end while

} // end Melt

/////////////////////////////////////////////////////////////////

void Sheer(void)
{
// This program "shears" the screen (for lack of a better word).
```

continues

Listing 6.7. continued

```
long index;
int x,y;

// Select the starting point of the shear.

x=rand()%320;
y=rand()%200;

// Do it a few times to make sure the whole screen is destroyed.

for (index=0; index<100000; index++)
    {

    // Move the shear.

    x+=17; // Note the use of prime numbers.
    y+=13;

    // Test whether shears are of boundaries. If so, roll them
    // over.

    if (x>319)
       x = x - 319;

    if (y>199)
       y = y - 199;

    // Plot the pixel in black.

    Plot_Pixel_Fast(x,y,0);

    } // end for index

} // end Sheer

// M A I N /////////////////////////////////////////////////////

void main(void)
{
int done=0,                     // Exit flag
    index=0;                    // Current position in
                                // instruction string

static char instructions[256]=""; // Holds the instruction
                                  // string

char buffer[41];

// Build up the instruction string.

strcat(instructions,".................................................");
strcat(instructions,"Press 1 to fade the lights, ");
strcat(instructions,"Press 2 to dissolve the screen, ");
strcat(instructions,"Press 3 to melt the screen, ");
```

```
strcat(instructions,"Press 4 to sheer the screen.");
strcat(instructions,"...............................................");

// Set the video mode to the 320x200, 256-color mode.

Set_Video_Mode(VGA256);

// Load in a background picture.

PCX_Init((pcx_picture_ptr)&screen_fx);

PCX_Load("screenfx.pcx", (pcx_picture_ptr)&screen_fx,1);

PCX_Show_Buffer((pcx_picture_ptr)&screen_fx);

PCX_Delete((pcx_picture_ptr)&screen_fx);

// Main event loop

while(!done)
    {

    // Wait for a keyboard press

    if (kbhit())
        {

        // Which special effects did the user want to see?

        switch(getch())
            {
            case '1':  // Dim the lights.
                {

                    Fade_Lights();

                } break;

            case '2': // Dissolve the screen.
                {
                Disolve();

                } break;

            case '3': // Melt the screen.
                {

                    Melt();

                } break;

            case '4': // Shear the screen.
                {

                    Sheer();
```

continues

Listing 6.7. continued

```
                        } break;

              default:break;

              } // end switch

      // Set the exit flag.

      done=1;

      } // end if keyboard press */

   // Extract the substring to be displayed.

   memcpy(buffer,&instructions[index],40);

   // Put a NULL terminator at the end.

   buffer[40]=0;

   Blit_String(0,23*8+6,15,buffer,0);

   // Increment the instruction index.
   // Roll over if at end of instructions.

   if (++index>180)
      index=0;

   // Assume the user can read at only 1,000,000 words
   // a second...

   Delay(2);

   } // end while

// Reset the video mode back to text.

Set_Video_Mode(TEXT_MODE);

} // end main
```

Building an Executable: To make an executable of the program in Listing 6.7, you can either type it in or use the source on the companion CD. The name of the source is transfx.c. The precompiled executable is named transfx.exe. As before, use the following compile line for Microsoft C:

```
cl -AM -Zi -c -Fc -Gs -G2 transfx.c
```

After compiling the program in this manner you can link it to the standard libraries and to our previously generated game library, gamelib.lib, with a link line such as:

```
link /ST:8192 /CO transfx,,,graphics.lib+gamelib.lib,,
```

This creates a final executable named transfx.exe.

The program in Listing 6.7 consists of a `main()` that loads in a PCX file, does some initializations, and then waits for you to select a screen transition, 1 through 4. Notice that the text scrolls at the bottom of the screen. This is a neat effect that's simple to accomplish. We go into how it's done after covering the important points of each of the screen transitions.

All four screen transitions together took me less than an hour to complete, so they aren't that spectacular. Let's see how each one works.

Light Fade

The fading-light transition is called by the single function `Fade_Lights()`. It takes no parameters and returns nothing. It operates by accessing all the color registers in the color look-up table and decreasing their values in a loop. As the loop executes, the values in each of the color registers are decremented until the red, green, and blue component in each register has a value of 0. This has the effect of making the screen image look as though it's fading away.

The fading-light transition is one possible use of the color registers. There are many others. For example, you could increase the intensities of all the color registers until they all were saturated and the screen looked white. Another neat effect might be to first kill all the red components of each color register, then the green, and finally the blue. The possibilities are endless.

Dissolve

The dissolve has got to be the simplest screen transition known to mankind. The function is called by `Disolve()` and works by pixelating the screen image with black dots. These dots are placed randomly on the surface of the screen. If enough of these randomly positioned pixels are plotted, sooner or later the screen image is "dissolved." A twist on this method might be to use a color other than black to plot the dots. The color could be sent as a parameter to the `Disolve()` function.

Meltdown

This is the most complex of these screen transitions. (I was trying to imitate the screen transition used in DOOM. I had some success, but it doesn't look as good as DOOM's.) The function operates on the following premise: a collection of 320 "worms" eat up the screen, beginning at the top and ending at the bottom. Each worm has its own velocity and acceleration. Here's the structure for the worms:

```
// The worm structure

typedef struct worm_typ
        {
        int y;       // Current y position of the worm
        int color;   // Color of the worm
        int speed;   // Speed of the worm
        int counter; // Counter

        } worm, *worm_ptr;
```

The meltdown algorithm works by starting each worm off at the top of the screen and then moving it downward on the screen, erasing what's behind (or above) the worm. To make it look more like it's "eating" or "absorbing" the screen pixels, the pixels around the worm are averaged and used as the pixel the worm is drawn with.

When an arbitrary number of cycles is complete, the worms stop. This arbitrary number of cycles was chosen to give a pleasing result and can be changed by altering the constant in this fragment of the meltdown main loop:

```
// Do a screen melt.

while(++ticks<1800) // Change the 1800 to make the worms last
                    // longer.
    {
    ...
```

Finally, if any of the worms hit the bottom of the screen, they just sit there in their own space.

Shear

This screen transition is called a "shear" because I can't think of a better word for it. It looks as though the image on the screen is cleaved away at 45 degree angles—and, from materials engineering, you should recall that the maximum shear plane force in a crystal lattice is at 45 degrees. (That's how my mind works; I don't try to understand anymore.) The Sheer() function is only a few lines long and works by plotting a pixel located at (x,y), where (x,y) is generated by a running sum that wraps around at the screen edges. The premise that makes the shear look good is based on the following algorithm, which generates all possible integers from O to I:

Algorithm 6.3. An algorithm to generate all integers in an interval without using a unity increment.

```
Given I, C, and X are integers and I>0 and 0<C<I, make x range
from 0 to I, but not necessarily in integral order.

Let X=0

1. Add C to X and store the result back in X.
2. Test if X > I, if so then X equals the amount that X exceeded I or X=X-I.
3. Use X in some way.
4. GOTO 1.
```

This algorithm is used for both the x- and y-coordinates of the pixel to be plotted—and, if allowed to run long enough, eventually fills the screen with black. By changing the size of the constant added to the (x,y) coordinate, you can create different slopes.

Now that we know how to make the screen disappear, let's learn how to make the game field seem bigger than it really is.

Scrolling the Game Field

Scrolling, sometimes referred to as *panning*, means to move the video window over an amount of data that's larger than what can be displayed on the screen at once, as shown in Figure 6.8.

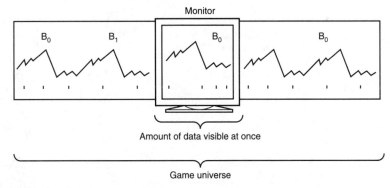

Figure 6.8. *A universe larger than what can be displayed on the screen at once.*

Many video games have more than one screen of playing area. In fact, some video games have hundreds of screens' worth of data. This data is usually scrolled by moving a viewing window over the entire game universe so the player can see only a specific portion of the

universe at a time. For example, Mario Brothers is a scrolling game. So is Sonic the Hedgehog. In both games, the characters run across the screen from right to left and *vice versa* as the screen scrolls with them, showing more graphics as they go. These kinds of scrolling games are usually referred to as *side scrollers*, as their main scrolling axis is horizontal. However, there are games that scroll vertically, or even in both directions.

Scrolling is basically bit blitting of really large surfaces: anything up to the entire screen, in fact. However, a scrolling game need not scroll the *entire* screen image. For example, a game may have a lot of control panels and indicators, making the active game area only a small percentage of the entire screen size. Alternatively, the scenery could scroll past a window on a wall. A demonstration we see shortly has a scrolling area that occupies only 25 percent of the screen.

The PC is capable of hardware scrolling. This means the VGA card can actually scroll the screen image for us. However, this is practical only when using one of the planar video modes. Because we're using VGA mode 13h, we can't use hardware scrolling—but that isn't a big loss. For our discussions, we can assume that we want to scroll the entire screen over 10 screens laid out horizontally, as shown in Figure 6.9.

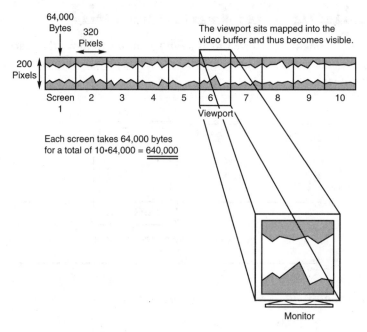

Figure 6.9. *A ten-screen wide game universe.*

Now that we have a decent grasp on what scrolling is, let's talk about the two main types of scrolling used in video games, and how to implement them. The two types are:

☐ Smooth scrolling

☐ Paged scrolling

Let's start with smooth scrolling.

Smooth Scrolling

The first method of scrolling is called *smooth scrolling* and occurs when the screen image smoothly scrolls in some direction a few pixels at a time. Smooth scrolling is accomplished either by having the entire game universe predrawn or by drawing it "on the fly." If the universe were predrawn, we'd need 640,000 bytes of memory for the example of a moment ago (the one with 10 screens laid out horizontally). This is because each screen is exactly 64,000 bytes in mode 13h, as you saw in Figure 6.9. This is a ton of memory. For a moment, though, let's pretend the PC has more than 640K available to DOS, and that this large demand for memory wouldn't pose a problem.

To scroll the image, we would have a current window position that would be tracked based on the position of the player's character. As the player's character moves right or left, we update this window position and then move the image data from the 10-screen game universe to the video buffer, as shown in Figure 6.10.

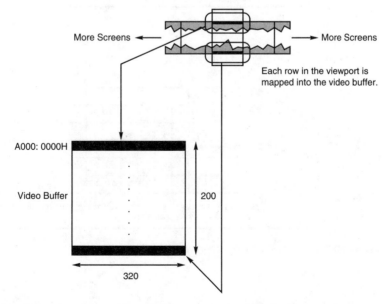

Figure 6.10. *Mapping the scrolling view port into the video buffer.*

This isn't so bad; we could use a `memcpy` function or assembly language, and the movement would be analogous to moving a double buffer to the video buffer. This is exactly what's done to accomplish scrolling when large amounts of memory are available on a computer:

1. The entire universe is drawn somewhere else in memory.

2. Then a window is moved around on it, and the contents of the window are moved into the video buffer each game cycle.

While this works great if you have a machine with a lot of memory, the PC isn't such a machine. We can't use up hundreds of kilobytes of RAM for such purposes when we're writing DOS-based games. We must come up with another plan. That plan is this: instead of having the entire game universe predrawn and stored elsewhere in memory, we can generate it "on the fly" from some database. This means that, as the player's character moves around on the screen, we compute where the view window would be in the universe. Then, usually from a database composed of cells that represent bit maps, we draw the screen in an off-screen buffer. Finally, we copy the image into the video buffer.

Having a cell-based universe is a way of using little memory to represent a lot of information. We may decide to have each screen composed of a matrix of 32×32 bit maps. That means the screen is really a matrix of 10×6, where each element is a 32×32-pixel bit map. Figure 6.11 shows such a cell-based world.

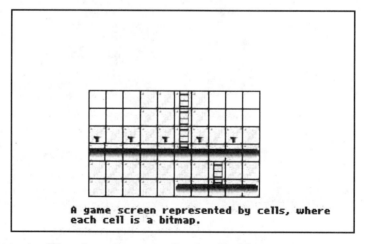

A game screen represented by cells, where each cell is a bitmap.

Figure 6.11. *A cell-based representation of a game world.*

Using this technique, we can create a small data structure that holds the information for an entire screen in 10*6 integers, or 60 bytes. This data structure works by creating a 10x6 matrix and filling it with integers that represent the bit-map IDs of the bit maps that should be placed in each cell location, as shown in Figure 6.12.

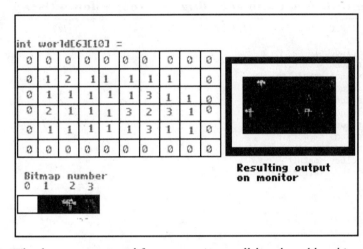

Figure 6.12. *The data structure used for representing a cell-based world and its output.*

We might have three different bit maps: one bit map could be the ground, another could be a tree, and the third could be a rock. Then we would tag each bit map with an ID, and use these IDs in the cell-based representation of the universe. To render any screen we would load all the bit maps and then, cell by cell, blit the bit map located in that cell of the matrix to the screen.

There are two problems with this technique:

☐ First, the action of drawing each screen from a collection of bit-map cells takes a lot of time.

☐ Second, as each screen is drawn with a collection of cells, the image can't be as complex as a completely pre-rendered game universe.

However, this technique is usually the one used—and, with enough bit maps, the screen can look quite realistic.

As a demo of smooth scrolling, I've created a program called lscape.exe. This program scrolls a landscape horizontally on the screen. The landscape is 640×100 pixels and is shown in a smaller window that's only 160×100. Therefore, there are a total of 640/160, or four, full screens of information. This demo uses predrawn screens because this is easier

to implement than the cell-based method. Of course, the resulting universe is quite small; making it larger would take a ton of memory. The program is shown in Listing 6.8. You can also find it on the companion CD.

Listing 6.8. A smooth scrolling landscape demo (lscape.c).

```c
// I N C L U D E S ////////////////////////////////////////////////

#include <io.h>
#include <conio.h>
#include <stdio.h>
#include <stdlib.h>
#include <dos.h>
#include <bios.h>
#include <fcntl.h>
#include <memory.h>
#include <malloc.h>
#include <math.h>
#include <string.h>

#include <graph.h>

#include "graph3.h"
#include "graph4.h"

#define SCROLL_WIDTH  (unsigned int)640
#define SCROLL_HEIGHT (unsigned int)100

// G L O B A L S ////////////////////////////////////////////////

// Pointer to the scrolling buffer, which is 640x100 pixels.
unsigned char far *scroll_buffer = NULL;

// F U N C T I O N S ////////////////////////////////////////////////

void Show_View_Port(char far *buffer,int pos)
{
// Copy a portion of the scrolling buffer to the video buffer.

unsigned int y,scroll_off, screen_off;

// There are 100 rows that must be moved.
// Move the data row by row.

for (y=0; y<100; y++)
    {

    // Compute the starting offset into scroll buffer
    // y * 640 + pos

    scroll_off = ((y<<9) + (y<<7) + pos );

    // Compute the starting offset in video RAM
    // y * 320 + 80
```

```
        screen_off = ( ( (y+50)<<8) + ( (y+50)<<6) + 80 );

    // Move the data.

    _fmemmove((char far *)&video_buffer[screen_off],
              (char far *)&buffer[scroll_off],160);

    } // end for y

} // end Show_View_Port



/////////////////////////////////////////////////////////////////

void Plot_Pixel_Scroll(int x,int y,unsigned char color)
{
// This function plots pixels into the scroll buffer with our
// new virtual screen size of 640x100.

// Use the fact that 640*y = 512*y + 128*y = y<<9 + y<<7.

scroll_buffer[((y<<9) + (y<<7)) + x] = color;

} // end Plot_Pixel_Scroll

/////////////////////////////////////////////////////////////////

void Draw_Terrain(void)
{

// This function draws the terrain into the scroll buffer
// (which, in this case, is 640x100 pixels).

int x,y=70,y1,index;

// Clear out memory first.

_fmemset(scroll_buffer,0,SCROLL_WIDTH*SCROLL_HEIGHT);

// Draw a few stars.

for (index=0; index<200; index++)
    {
    Plot_Pixel_Scroll(rand()%640,rand()%70,15);
    } // end for index

// Draw some mountains.

for (x=0; x<640; x++)
    {

    // Compute the offset.

    y+=-1 + rand()%3;
```

6

continues

329

Listing 6.8. continued

```
        // Make sure the terrain stays within a reasonable boundary.

        if (y>90) y=90;
        else
        if (y<40) y=40;

        // Plot the dot in the double buffer.

        Plot_Pixel_Scroll(x,y,2);

        for (y1=y+1; y1<100; y1++)
            Plot_Pixel_Scroll(x,y1,10);

        } // end for x

} // end Draw_Terrain

// M A I N ////////////////////////////////////////////////////////

void main(void)
{

int done=0, // Exit flag
    sx=0;    // Scrolling view port position

// Set the video mode to the 320x200, 256-color mode.

_setvideomode(_MRES256COLOR);

// Put up some information.

_settextposition(0,0);

printf("Use < > to move. Press Q to quit.");

// Draw a little window.

_setcolor(1);

_rectangle(_GBORDER, 80-1,50-1,240+1,150+1);

// Allocate memory for the scrolling buffer.

scroll_buffer=(char far *)_fmalloc(SCROLL_WIDTH*SCROLL_HEIGHT);

// Draw the mountains.

Draw_Terrain();

// Show the initial view.

Show_View_Port(scroll_buffer,sx);

// Main loop
```

```
while(!done)
    {

    // Has the user pressed a key?

    if (kbhit())
        {

        switch(getch())
              {
              case ',': // Move the window to the left, but
                        // don't go too far.
                        {
                        sx-=2;

                        if (sx<0)
                            sx=0;

                        } break;

              case '.': // Move the window to the right, but
                        // don't go too far.
                        {
                        sx+=2;

                        if (sx > 640-160)
                            sx=640-160;

                        } break;

              case 'q': // Is the user trying to bail?
                        {
                        done=1;

                        } break;

              } // end switch

        // Copy the view port to the screen.

        Show_View_Port(scroll_buffer,sx);

        _settextposition(24,0);

        printf("Viewport position = %d  ",sx);

        } // end if

    } // end while

// Reset the video mode back to text.

_setvideomode(_DEFAULTMODE);

} // end main
```

Building an Executable: To make an executable of the program in Listing 6.8, you can either type it in or use the source on the companion CD. The name of the source is lscape.c. The precompiled executable is named lscape.exe. As before, use the following compile line for Microsoft C:

```
cl -AM -Zi -c -Fc -Gs -G2 lscape.c
```

After compiling the program in this manner you can link it to the standard libraries and to our previously generated game library, gamelib.lib, with a link line such as:

```
link /ST:8192 /CO lscape,,,graphics.lib+gamelib.lib,,
```

This creates a final executable named lscape.exe. Also, make sure to link it to Microsoft's graphics library; we used a couple of their functions this time.

Unfortunately, the demo program we just saw was just that: a demo. There aren't any functions or extra software to add to our library from it. The only thing we can extract from the lscape program is understanding.

The `main()` is where most of the action takes place, so let's see what's happening there.

1. First, the VGA is put into mode 13h, and some text is placed on the screen to tell the player what to do.

2. Next, the scrolling buffer is allocated. It's similar to a double buffer: an off-screen area we can write to and read from, which is separate from the video buffer. The scrolling buffer is 640x100 pixels, or 64,000 bytes, of information.

3. After the scrolling buffer is a allocated, the terrain is drawn in the buffer by a call to the function `Terrain()`. This function uses a modified version of `Plot_Pixel()` to draw into the scrolling buffer. The terrain is generated using a random-number generator that decides whether the mountain should go up or down at each pixel across its entire width.

4. Now we're ready to scroll. Scrolling is accomplished in a main loop that tracks the keyboard and tests whether the player is pressing the lesser-than (<) or greater-than (>) keys. If so, the window position (tracked in a variable) is updated and passed to a function called `Show_View_Port()`. This function, which works much the same way as `Show_Double_Buffer()`, copies a rectangular region out of the scrolling buffer into the video buffer.

5. Once the new view has been displayed, the event loop jumps back up to the top and waits for another key press until you press the Q key, whereupon it exits.

The important concepts to extract from this demo are the use of a predrawn game universe, which could have as easily been a street scene or whatever, and the use of bit blitting to move large chunks of memory around. This movement is accommodated by the fact that we're using mode 13h, and would be much harder in one of the planar memory modes.

Paged Scrolling

The second type of scrolling is called *paged scrolling*. Paged scrolling is employed in many VGA video games that use mode 13h. Paged scrolling works in the following manner: when the player's character hits the right or left edge of the screen (in a horizontal scrolling game), the entire screen is paged to the next scene—in other words, the image is scrolled an entire screen. This technique is a bit rough and can cause a bit of disorientation for the player when the next screen is instantly placed on the screen. However, it's much easier to do than smooth scrolling because speed is no longer an issue. Moreover, because the game universe is viewed one screen at a time, it opens up the possibility of using the hard drive to hold extremely detailed screens, as the load time would be so small the player wouldn't mind too much.

Let's discuss how we'd implement paged scrolling in a game. One way would be to use the same kind of cell-based world representation we spoke of earlier. We could say that each screen is composed of a collection of 32x32-pixel bit maps. The position of these bit maps is stored in a matrix that holds the IDs of the bit maps for each position of the real image. To draw a screen, the program refers to the matrix along with the actual bit maps as data, and draws the real image by looping through the matrix and drawing each bit map at the proper position.

As an example of paged scrolling, I've created a demo with a character I call Robopunk. He's a cyborg. Robopunk has been placed in a world that's six screens long. Each screen is composed of a matrix of 10x6 cells, where each cell has an ID number. The screen is built from a set of bit maps that I created just for this demo. You can see these bit maps, along with the animation cells for Robopunk, in Figure 6.13.

The upper row of images is, of course, Robopunk. The lower row of images is the bit maps used to draw the screen.

6

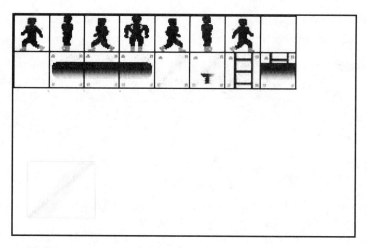

Figure 6.13. *The bit maps used for Robopunk.*

The demo works like this:

1. First, there's an array of six matrices, as shown in Figure 6.14.

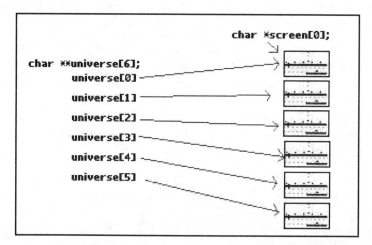

Figure 6.14. *The data structure used to represent the universe in the Robopunk demo.*

Each matrix holds the 2-D cell representation of IDs used to draw the screen image with the background bit maps. As Robopunk moves from screen to screen by reaching the right or left edge of the screen, the appropriate matrix is accessed and its data used to generate a new background scene in a double buffer.

2. This image is then copied to the video screen for viewing.

3. The movement for Robopunk is created by stepping through his animation frames each game-loop cycle.

That's about all there is to know. To see the program run, you can use the precompiled executable called robo.exe. Listing 6.9 contains the source code.

Listing 6.9. A demonstration of paged scrolling (robo.c).

```c
// I N C L U D E S ///////////////////////////////////////////

#include <io.h>
#include <conio.h>
#include <stdio.h>
#include <stdlib.h>
#include <dos.h>
#include <bios.h>
#include <fcntl.h>
#include <memory.h>
#include <malloc.h>
#include <math.h>
#include <string.h>

#include "graph3.h"  // Include our graphics stuff.
#include "graph4.h"

#define CELL_COLUMNS   10  // Size of cell-based matrix
#define CELL_ROWS      6

#define CELL_WIDTH     32  // Width of a cell, in pixels
#define CELL_HEIGHT    32  // Height of a cell, in pixels

#define NUM_SCREENS    6   // Number of screens in game

#define ROBO_MOVE      8   // Speed at which the player moves

// G L O B A L S ///////////////////////////////////////////

pcx_picture imagery_pcx,    // Used to load in the imagery for
                            // Robopunk
            intro_pcx;      // The intro screen

sprite back_cells,  // Background cells sprite
       robopunk;    // Robopunk

unsigned char far *double_buffer = NULL;

unsigned int buffer_height       = SCREEN_HEIGHT;

unsigned int buffer_size = SCREEN_WIDTH*SCREEN_HEIGHT/2;

// Use an array of 2-D matrices to hold the screens.
```

continues

Listing 6.9. continued

```c
char **universe[NUM_SCREENS] = {NULL,NULL,NULL,NULL,NULL,NULL};

// Here's screen 1. Note: its 10x6 cells, where each cell is
// represented by an ASCII character. (This makes it easier to
// draw each screen by hand). Later, the ASCII characters are
// translated to bit map IDs so the screen image can be drawn.

char *screen_1[CELL_ROWS] = {"          ",
                             "##*###*####",
                             "##########",
                             "<=========",
                             "######:####",
                             "####<=;=>##"};


char *screen_2[CELL_ROWS] = {"    ###   ",
                             "    #:#   ",
                             "#######:###",
                             "=======;===",
                             "#<==>#####",
                             "##########"};


char *screen_3[CELL_ROWS] = {"      ##<=>",
                             "  #*##<==>#",
                             "####*######",
                             "==========",
                             "##########",
                             "##########"};


char *screen_4[CELL_ROWS] = {"###       ",
                             "#<=>##    ",
                             "####<==>###",
                             "==========",
                             "##########",
                             "#<==>######"};


char *screen_5[CELL_ROWS] = {"   #<=># ",
                             " #:#***#:##",
                             "##:#####:##",
                             "==;=====;==",
                             "##########",
                             "##########"};


char *screen_6[CELL_ROWS] = {"          ",
                             "##        ",
                             "#*#*##     ",
                             "========>  ",
                             "########  ",
                             "########  "};
```

```
// F U N C T I O N S //////////////////////////////////////////

void Show_Double_Buffer(unsigned char far *buffer)
{
// This function copies the double buffer into the video
// buffer.

_asm
   {
   push ds                  ; Save ds on stack.
   mov cx,buffer_size       ; This is the size of buffer in WORDs.
   les di,video_buffer      ; es:di is the destination of the
                            ; memory move
   lds si,buffer            ; ds:si is the source of the memory
                            ; move
   cld                      ; Make sure to move in the right
                            ; direction.
   rep movsw                ; Move all the WORDs.
   pop ds                   ; Restore the data segment.
   } // end asm

} // end Show_Double_Buffer

/////////////////////////////////////////////////////////////////

int Create_Double_Buffer(int num_lines)
{

// Allocate enough memory to hold the double buffer.

if ((double_buffer =
    (unsigned char far *)_fmalloc(SCREEN_WIDTH *
    (num_lines + 1)))==NULL)
    return(0);

// Set the height of the buffer and compute its size.

buffer_height = num_lines;

buffer_size = SCREEN_WIDTH * num_lines/2;

// Fill the buffer with black.

_fmemset(double_buffer, 0, SCREEN_WIDTH * num_lines);

// Everything was OK.

return(1);

} // end Init_Double_Buffer

/////////////////////////////////////////////////////////////////

void Fill_Double_Buffer(int color)
{
// This function fills in the double buffer with the sent color.
```

6

continues

Listing 6.9. continued

```c
    _fmemset(double_buffer, color, SCREEN_WIDTH * buffer_height);

} // end Fill_Double_Buffer

////////////////////////////////////////////////////////////////////

void Delete_Double_Buffer(void)
{
// This function frees up the memory allocated by the double
// buffer. Be sure to use FAR version.

if (double_buffer)
  _ffree(double_buffer);

} // end Delete_Double_Buffer

////////////////////////////////////////////////////////////////////

void Plot_Pixel_Fast_DB(int x,int y,unsigned char color)
{

// This function plots the pixel in the desired color a little
// quicker using binary shifting to accomplish the
// multiplications.

// Use the fact that 320*y = 256*y + 64*y = y<<8 + y<<6.

double_buffer[((y<<8) + (y<<6)) + x] = color;

} // end Plot_Pixel_Fast_DB

////////////////////////////////////////////////////////////////////

void Behind_Sprite_DB(sprite_ptr sprite)
{

// This function scans the background behind a sprite so that,
// when the sprite is drawn, the background isn't obliterated.

char far *work_back;
int work_offset=0,offset,y;

// Alias a pointer to the sprite background for ease of access.

work_back = sprite->background;

// Compute the offset of the background in the video buffer.

offset = (sprite->y << 8) + (sprite->y << 6) + sprite->x;

for (y=0; y<sprite_height; y++)
    {
    // Copy the next row out of screen buffer into the sprite-
    // background buffer.
```

```
    _fmemcpy((char far *)&work_back[work_offset],
            (char far *)&double_buffer[offset],
            sprite_width);

    // Move to the next line in the double buffer and in the
    // sprite-background buffer.

    offset      += SCREEN_WIDTH;
    work_offset += sprite_width;

    } // end for y

} // end Behind_Sprite_DB

///////////////////////////////////////////////////////////////////

void Erase_Sprite_DB(sprite_ptr sprite)
{
// Replace the background that was behind the sprite.

// This function replaces the background that was saved from
// where a sprite was going to be placed.

char far *work_back;
int work_offset=0,offset,y;

// Alias a pointer to the sprite background for ease of access.

work_back = sprite->background;

// Compute the offset of the background in the double buffer.

offset = (sprite->y << 8) + (sprite->y << 6) + sprite->x;

for (y=0; y<sprite_height; y++)
    {
    // Copy the next row out of screen buffer into sprite-
    // background buffer.

    _fmemcpy((char far *)&double_buffer[offset],
            (char far *)&work_back[work_offset],
            sprite_width);

    // Move to the next line in the video buffer and in the
    // sprite-background buffer.

    offset      += SCREEN_WIDTH;
    work_offset += sprite_width;

    } // end for y


} // end Erase_Sprite_DB

///////////////////////////////////////////////////////////////////
```

6

continues

Listing 6.9. continued

```c
void Draw_Sprite_DB(sprite_ptr sprite)
{

// This function draws a sprite on the screen, row by row,
// quickly. Note the use of shifting to implement
// multiplication.

char far *work_sprite;
int work_offset=0,offset,x,y;
unsigned char data;

// Alias a pointer to the sprite for ease of access.

work_sprite = sprite->frames[sprite->curr_frame];

// Compute the offset of the sprite in the video buffer.

offset = (sprite->y << 8) + (sprite->y << 6) + sprite->x;

for (y=0; y<sprite_height; y++)
    {
    // Copy the next row into the double buffer using memcpy
    // for speed.

    for (x=0; x<sprite_width; x++)
        {

        // Test for a transparent pixel; that is, 0. If the
        // pixel is not transparent, draw it.

        if ((data=work_sprite[work_offset+x]))
            double_buffer[offset+x] = data;

        } // end for x

    // Move to next line in the double buffer and in the sprite
    // bit-map buffer.

    offset     += SCREEN_WIDTH;
    work_offset += sprite_width;

    } // end for y

} // end Draw_Sprite_DB

//////////////////////////////////////////////////////////////

void Draw_Screen(char **screen)
{
// This function draws a screen by using the data in the
// universe array. Each element in the universe array is a 2-D
// matrix of cells. These cells are ASCII characters that
// represent the requested bit map that should be placed in the
// cell location.
```

```
char *curr_row;

int index_x, index_y, cell_number;

// Translation table for screen database, used to convert the
// ASCII characters into ID numbers

static char back_cell_lookup[] =

   { 0,0, 0, 4,0,0,0,0,0,0,5,0,0,0,0,
     0,0,0,0,0,0,0,0,0,0,0,6,7,1,2,3,0,
// SP!"#$%&'()*+,-./0123456789:;<=>?

     0,0,0,0,0,0,0,0,0,0, 0,0,0,0, 0,0, 0,
     0,0,0,0,0 ,0,0,0,0,0,0 ,0, 0,0,0};
// @ABCDEFGHIJKLMNOPQRSTUVWXYZ[\]^_

// Clear out the double buffer.

Fill_Double_Buffer(0);

// Now draw the screen, row by row.

for (index_y = 0; index_y<CELL_ROWS; index_y++)
    {

    // Get the current row for speed.

    curr_row = screen[index_y];

    // Do the row.

    for (index_x = 0; index_x<CELL_COLUMNS; index_x++)
        {
        // Extract the cell out of the data structure and blit
        // it onto the screen.

        cell_number = back_cell_lookup[curr_row[index_x]-32];

        // Compute the screen x and y.

        back_cells.x = index_x * sprite_width;
        back_cells.y = index_y * sprite_height;

        // Figure out which bit map to draw.

        back_cells.curr_frame = cell_number;

        // Draw the bit map.

        Draw_Sprite_DB((sprite_ptr)&back_cells);

        } // end for index_x

    } // end for index_y
```

continues

6

Listing 6.9. continued

```
} // end Draw_Screen

/////////////////////////////////////////////////////////////////

void Rotate_Lights(void)
{

// This function uses color rotation to move the walkway lights.
// Three color registers are used.
// Note: this function has static variables, which track timing
// parameters and also whether the function has been entered yet.

static int clock=0,entered_yet=0;   // Used for timing.
                                    // Note: they're static!

RGB_color color,
          color_1,
          color_2,
          color_3;

// This function blinks the running lights on the walkway.

if (!entered_yet)
   {

   // Reset the palette registers 96,97,98 to red, black, black.

   color.red   = 255;
   color.green = 0;
   color.blue  = 0;

   Set_Palette_Register(96,(RGB_color_ptr)&color);

   color.red = color.green = color.blue = 0;

   Set_Palette_Register(97,(RGB_color_ptr)&color);
   Set_Palette_Register(98,(RGB_color_ptr)&color);

   // The system has initialized, so flag it.

   entered_yet=1;

   } // end if first time into function

// Try to rotate the light colors; that is, color rotation.

   if (++clock==3)  // Is it time to rotate?
      {
      // Get the colors.

      Get_Palette_Register(96,(RGB_color_ptr)&color_1);
      Get_Palette_Register(97,(RGB_color_ptr)&color_2);
      Get_Palette_Register(98,(RGB_color_ptr)&color_3);

      // Set the colors.
```

```
    Set_Palette_Register(97,(RGB_color_ptr)&color_1);
        Set_Palette_Register(98,(RGB_color_ptr)&color_2);
        Set_Palette_Register(96,(RGB_color_ptr)&color_3);

        // Reset the clock.

        clock=0;

        } // end if time to rotate

} // end Rotate_Lights

//////////////////////////////////////////////////////////////////

void Disolve(void)
{
// Dissolve the screen by plotting zillions of black pixels.

unsigned long index;

for (index=0; index<=300000; index++,
     Plot_Pixel_Fast(rand()%320, rand()%200, 0));

} // end Disolve

// M A I N ///////////////////////////////////////////////////////

void main(void)
{

int index,
    curr_screen=0,
    done=0;

// S E C T I O N    1 ///////////////////////////////////////////

// Set the video mode to the 320x200, 256-color mode.

Set_Video_Mode(VGA256);

// Create a double buffer.

if (!Create_Double_Buffer(SCREEN_HEIGHT))
    {
    printf("\nNot enough memory to create double buffer.");

    } // end if

// S E C T I O N    2 ///////////////////////////////////////////

// Load the intro screen and display it for a few seconds.

PCX_Init((pcx_picture_ptr)&intro_pcx);

PCX_Load("roboint.pcx", (pcx_picture_ptr)&intro_pcx,1);
```

continues

Listing 6.9. continued

```
PCX_Show_Buffer((pcx_picture_ptr)&intro_pcx);

// Let the user see it.

Delay(50);

PCX_Delete((pcx_picture_ptr)&intro_pcx);

// S E C T I O N   3 //////////////////////////////////////////

// Load in the background and animation cells.

PCX_Init((pcx_picture_ptr)&imagery_pcx);

PCX_Load("robopunk.pcx", (pcx_picture_ptr)&imagery_pcx,1);

// Initialize the sprite size.

sprite_width  = 32;
sprite_height = 32;

// Create a sprite for Robopunk.

Sprite_Init((sprite_ptr)&robopunk,0,0,0,0,0,0);

// Create a sprite to hold the background cells.

Sprite_Init((sprite_ptr)&back_cells,0,0,0,0,0,0);

// Extract animation cells for Robopunk.

PCX_Grab_Bitmap((pcx_picture_ptr)&imagery_pcx,
                (sprite_ptr)&robopunk,0,3,0);
PCX_Grab_Bitmap((pcx_picture_ptr)&imagery_pcx,
                (sprite_ptr)&robopunk,1,5,0);
PCX_Grab_Bitmap((pcx_picture_ptr)&imagery_pcx,
                (sprite_ptr)&robopunk,2,4,0);
PCX_Grab_Bitmap((pcx_picture_ptr)&imagery_pcx,
                (sprite_ptr)&robopunk,3,5,0);
PCX_Grab_Bitmap((pcx_picture_ptr)&imagery_pcx,
                (sprite_ptr)&robopunk,4,6,0);
PCX_Grab_Bitmap((pcx_picture_ptr)&imagery_pcx,
                (sprite_ptr)&robopunk,5,1,0);
PCX_Grab_Bitmap((pcx_picture_ptr)&imagery_pcx,
                (sprite_ptr)&robopunk,6,2,0);
PCX_Grab_Bitmap((pcx_picture_ptr)&imagery_pcx,
                (sprite_ptr)&robopunk,7,1,0);
PCX_Grab_Bitmap((pcx_picture_ptr)&imagery_pcx,
                (sprite_ptr)&robopunk,8,0,0);


// Extract background cells.

for (index=0; index<8; index++)
    {
```

```
      PCX_Grab_Bitmap((pcx_picture_ptr)&imagery_pcx,
                    (sprite_ptr)&back_cells,index,index,1);

   } // end for index

// We're done with the PCX file, so obliterate it.

PCX_Delete((pcx_picture_ptr)&imagery_pcx);

// S E C T I O N   4  /////////////////////////////////////////////

// Set up the universe data structure.

universe[0] = (char **)screen_1;
universe[1] = (char **)screen_2;
universe[2] = (char **)screen_3;
universe[3] = (char **)screen_4;
universe[4] = (char **)screen_5;
universe[5] = (char **)screen_6;

Draw_Screen((char **)universe[curr_screen]);
Show_Double_Buffer(double_buffer);

// Place Robopunk

robopunk.x = 160;
robopunk.y = 74;

robopunk.curr_frame = 0;

// Scan the background under Robopunk.

Behind_Sprite_DB((sprite_ptr)&robopunk);

// S E C T I O N   5  /////////////////////////////////////////////

// Main event loop

while(!done)
    {

// S E C T I O N   6  /////////////////////////////////////////////

    // Erase Robopunk.

    Erase_Sprite_DB((sprite_ptr)&robopunk);

    // Test whether the user has pressed key.

    if (kbhit())
       {
       // Get the key.

// S E C T I O N   7  /////////////////////////////////////////////

       switch(getch())
```

continues

Listing 6.9. continued

```
        {

     case 'a': // Move the player to the left.
            {
            // Advance the animation frame and move
            // the player

            // Test whether the player is moving to
            // the right. If so, show the player
            // turning before moving.

            if (robopunk.curr_frame > 0 &&
               robopunk.curr_frame < 5)
               {
               robopunk.curr_frame = 0;
               } // end if player going right
            else
            if (robopunk.curr_frame == 0 )
               robopunk.curr_frame = 5;
            else
               {
               // The player is already in leftward
               // motion, so continue.

               if (++robopunk.curr_frame > 8)
                  robopunk.curr_frame = 5;

               // Move the player to the left.

               robopunk.x-=ROBO_MOVE;

               // Test whether the edge was hit.

               if (robopunk.x < 8)
                  {
                  // Test whether there's another
                  // screen to the left.

                  if (curr_screen==0)
                     {
                     robopunk.x += ROBO_MOVE;
                     }//end if at end of universe
                  else
                     {
                     // Warp robopunk to the other
                     // edge of the screen, and change
                     // screens.

                     robopunk.x = SCREEN_WIDTH - 40;

                     // Scroll to the next screen to
                     // the left.

                     curr_screen--;

                     Draw_Screen((char **)
```

```
                    universe[curr_screen]);

                            } // end else move to the left

                        } // end if hit left edge of screen

                    } // end else

                } break;


        case 's': // Move the player to the right.
                {

                    // Advance the animation frame and move
                    // the player.

                    // Test whether player is moving to the
                    // left. If so, show the player turning
                    // before moving.

                    if (robopunk.curr_frame > 4)
                        {
                        robopunk.curr_frame = 0;
                        } // end if player going right
                    else
                    if (robopunk.curr_frame == 0 )
                        robopunk.curr_frame =1;
                    else
                        {
                        // The player is already in rightward
                        // motion, so continue.

                        if (++robopunk.curr_frame > 4)
                            robopunk.curr_frame = 1;

                        // Move the player to the right.

                        robopunk.x+=ROBO_MOVE;

                        // Test whether the edge was hit.

                        if (robopunk.x > SCREEN_WIDTH-40)
                            {
                            // Test whether there's another
                            // screen to the left.

                            if (curr_screen==5)
                                {
                                robopunk.x -= ROBO_MOVE;
                                } // end if already at end of
                                  // universe
                            else
                                {
                                // Warp robopunk to the other
                                // edge of the screen and change
```

6

continues

Listing 6.9. continued

```
                                // screens

                                    robopunk.x = 8;

                                    // Scroll to the next screen to
                                    // the right.

                                    curr_screen++;

                                    Draw_Screen((char **)
                                        universe[curr_screen]);

                                    } // end else move to the right

                                } // end if hit right edge of screen

                            } // end else

                    } break;

            case 'q': // Exit the demo
                    {
                    done=1;

                    } break;

            default:break;

            } // end switch

        } // end if keyboard hit

// S E C T I O N   8   //////////////////////////////////////////////

    // Scan the background under Robopunk.

    Behind_Sprite_DB((sprite_ptr)&robopunk);

    // Draw him.

    Draw_Sprite_DB((sprite_ptr)&robopunk);

    // Do any background animation.

// S E C T I O N   9   //////////////////////////////////////////////
    // Move the walkway lights.

    Rotate_Lights();

    // Show the double buffer.

    Show_Double_Buffer(double_buffer);

    // Wait a bit...

    Delay(1);
```

```
    } // end while

// S E C T I O N   10 //////////////////////////////////////////

// Use one of the screen effects as the exit.

Disolve();

// Reset the video mode back to text.

Set_Video_Mode(TEXT_MODE);

// Free the double buffer.

Delete_Double_Buffer();

} // end main
```

Building an Executable: To make an executable of the program in Listing 6.9, you can either type it in or use the source on the companion CD. The name of the source is robo.c. The precompiled executable is named robo.exe. As before, use the following compile line for Microsoft C:

```
cl -AM -Zi -c -Fc -Gs -G2 robo.c
```

After compiling the program in this manner you can link it to the standard libraries and to our previously generated game library, gamelib.lib, with a link line such as:

```
link /ST:8192 /CO robo,,,graphics.lib+gamelib.lib,,
```

This creates a final executable named robo.exe.

6

(I'll bet that you think robo.c is a long program! Hardly. Actually, robo.c is jokingly short and simple. A complete, professional video game can have tens of thousands of lines of code with million line programs becoming common. I just thought I'd mention that; I want to make sure you understand the mammoth amount of software and data that goes into a video game.)

Before we analyze the program, let's talk about a couple of details relating to the overall operation of robo.c so the analysis sections make more sense.

First, the overall purpose of robo.c is to demonstrate paged scrolling, which is a coarse-version of scrolling based on redrawing the entire screen as the player's character

(Robopunk) moves from screen to screen. In the case of robo.c, there are six screens. As Robopunk (the hero) walks around on a walkway, he can either move off the right or left edge of the screen. When this happens, the screen he should walk into (which is currently out of view) is drawn in the double buffer and then copied to the video buffer.

Although the point of this demo is scrolling, not animation, the next important aspect of robo.c is the animation of Robopunk. Robopunk has seven frames of animation, broken up as follows:

☐ Three frames for right motion

☐ Three frames for left motion

☐ A single frame for Robopunk standing still

These animation frames are shown in Figure 6.15.

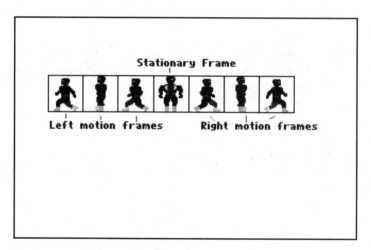

Figure 6.15. *The animation frames of Robopunk.*

The animation of Robopunk is done by cycling through these frames of animation based on the direction Robopunk is walking. When the end of the sequence is reached, the animation cycle starts over. This creates the illusion of seamless animation. When Robopunk is stationary, he's drawn looking at you (frame 0).

The logic to animate Robopunk properly is fairly complex, and I could have implemented it more easily with look-up tables. However, I think using if-based logic is more illustrative of the animation logic and what went into it.

To further clarify the operation of the main() function, I've created a flowchart so you can see the function's operation graphically. This flowchart is shown in Figure 6.16.

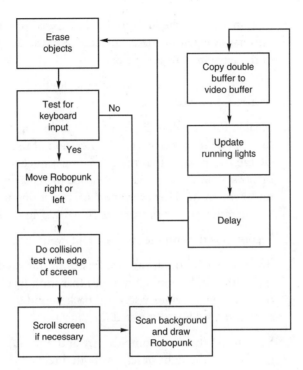

Figure 6.16. *A flowchart of Robopunk's event loop.*

Now, onto analysis of the main().

Analysis The program uses the double-buffer functions and the versions of the sprite functions modified to use the double buffer. Other than that, there are only a couple of extra functions that do anything. Most of the program is in the main() function; therefore we can concentrate our analysis there.

1. Section 1 sets the video mode to 320×200×256 and allocates the double buffer. If there's a problem, the main() is exited.

2. Section 2 loads the introduction screen image, which is a PCX file, then waits for a couple of seconds, and then deletes it.

3. Section 3 loads in the imagery for the background bit maps and the animation cells for Robopunk as a single PCX file. The images for the backgroundand animation are then extracted and placed into sprite structures.

6

4. Section 4 makes the links to the six screens comprising the demo's universe by equating the array elements of the `universe []` array to each of the separate screen matrices.

    The first screen is then drawn in the double buffer, and the double buffer is displayed.

    Finally, Robopunk is displayed and the background under him scanned so it can be replaced on the first iteration of the main game loop. (Recall from Day 2 that the animation sequence is *erase-move-draw*, and in our system erasing is accomplished by replacing the background under the sprite. However, there isn't anything under the sprite on the first iteration, so we must make sure to do an initial scan.)

5. Section 5 is the entrance to the main event loop.

6. In Section 6 all the sprites are erased. In this case, there's only one sprite (that is, Robopunk himself) that must be erased. This is done by replacing the previously scanned background under him. Also, in this section the keyboard is tested for a key press.

7. Section 7 is the most complex part of the `main()`: it's where Robopunk is moved to the right or left. As both directions are done the same way, let's cover motion to the left.

    First, Robopunk is tested to see whether he was already moving to the left. If he was, his current frame is changed to that of the next frame in his animation cycle.

    On the other hand, if he was moving to the right, we want him to turn forward before beginning his motion to the left. This added step in the animation makes him look more realistic (instead of instantly turning 180 degrees).

    After the program draws some conclusion about direction, Robopunk is moved, or translated. This is done by subtracting `ROBO_MOVE` from his current position.

    Finally, his position on the screen is tested against the left edge. If Robopunk has reached the edge of the screen, the next screen is drawn and Robopunk is moved to the right edge of the screen.

8. Now that Robopunk has moved and the screen (possibly) has been updated, Section 8 scans the background under Robopunk and draws him.

9. At this point we're at the end of the animation cycle: the screen image has been updated in the double buffer. In Section 9 we copy the image in the double buffer into the video buffer for viewing.

   This section also is where all background animation should be done; hence the call to `Rotate_Lights()`, a function that uses color rotation to make the lights on the walkway look like they're moving. (We cover background animation in more detail in a moment.)

Game Law: You can never have too many blinking lights in a video game.

   Finally, a delay is created for synchronization purposes. This is done using a call to `Delay()`. This makes the PC wait a specific amount of time, ensuring that Robopunk operates at the same speed on any PC.

10. In Section 10 the player is done being impressed and has pressed the Q key, so we deallocate all resources, set the video mode back to the 80×25 text mode, and exit.

Mixing Animation and Motion

The Robopunk demo is a good example of paged scrolling; however, there's another lesson we can learn from it: *animotion*. This is a term I coined to describe the proper merging of animation and motion so that realistic animation takes place.

We've been learning that animation is accomplished by drawing a collection of frames and then sequencing through them at some rate. If the frames happened to be steps of a walking motion, the object will look like it's walking...almost. When we see an object on the screen going through the motions of walking, we expect it to move. To accomplish this motion, we cycle through the frames of animation and also move, or translate, the object at each iteration.

The result of this is a character that looks as though it's walking. However, the "friction" of its feet and its translation look somewhat synthetic and unreal. Given we're talking about video games, where things can look unreal—that's the whole idea!—when we're trying to make something look as though it's walking or jumping, or whatever, we want it to look as real as possible. This is the problem: when animating a creature and then translating it, we must not only animate the frames of animation at a specific rate, but also take into consideration the current frame of animation when doing the motion.

As an example, when Robopunk moves he's always translated an amount equal to `ROBO_MOVE`, regardless of the current animation frame. This makes him look a bit unreal. Because he has so few animation frames, this distortion isn't terribly noticeable. If there were more frames of animation, it would become more apparent. This is because Robopunk is an example of a biped: a two-legged creature that moves by using each foot as a frictional anchor and shifting its weight forward. We've digitized this smooth motion into only a few frames, but if we had many frames of animation we'd have to be more careful about taking into account the current frame of animation when moving him.

In general, when a biped walks there are times when its position is stationary because it's shifting its mass and not its final position relative to the ground. Moreover, there are times when there is little motion and other times when there's a great deal of motion. Therefore, to animate a biped walking—or to animate anything that's supposed to look real—we must create a data structure that holds how much the object should be translated for each frame of animation. Doing this increases the realism by an order of magnitude.

As an example, I've created a program called animate.exe. There is no source code for this, because there would be nothing to gain. I only want you to run the program so you can see what I'm talking about. The program animates a little stick figure and makes it walk across the screen. The stick figure moves at a constant velocity normally, and looks as though it's moonwalking. However, when you hit the Spacebar the demo toggles into animotion mode and uses a look-up table for the amount of translation to perform for each animation cell. You'll notice a great improvement. Run the program and then come back.

It's interesting how such a simple insight can give such improved results, isn't it?

Now let's see how animotion is accomplished. Keep in mind that this technique can be used for any motion or object; it's up to you. The main idea of animotion is to take a look at your frames of animation and then, based on them, decide how much the object should be moved during each frame. In the animate program there are 12 frames of animation, shown in Figure 6.17.

(Each frame was generated by watching my friend Ash Patel walk in slow motion over an over.) Once I had the frames of animation, I guessed heuristically how much the stick man should translate for each frame, and came up with a look-up table that contains this data. Here it is:

```
// The motion look-up table has a separate entry for each frame
// of animation so a more realistic movement can be made based
// on the current frame.

int object_vel[] = {17,0,6,2,3,0,17,0,6,2,3,0};
```

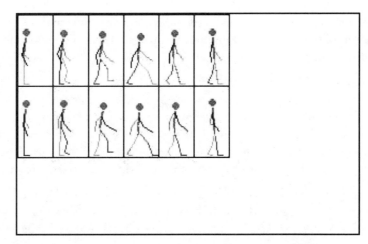

Figure 6.17. *The frames of animation for the animotion demo, animate.exe.*

As you can see, there are 12 entries: one for each frame of animation. Using the table is easy. In the animate.exe program you just looked at, the current frame of animation is called `curr_frame`. During the portion of the program that takes care of translation, this information is used to translate the stick man. Here's the code to do this:

```
stick_man.x += object_vel[curr_frame];
```

The current frame is used as an index into the motion look-up table, and the resulting value is used as the translation factor. When the program is not in animotion mode, the following line of code is used in deference to the look-up table:

```
stick_man += STICK_MOVE;
```

This has the effect of always moving the stick man by a constant value instead of one that takes into consideration the relationship between animation and motion.

Bringing Games to Life with Background Animation

As you're learning, a video game is a collection of backgrounds and game objects that participate in the game itself. This brings us to the topic of background animation. *Background animation* simply means that some kinds of action(s) are taking place in the background. Although we're writing 2-D games for the most part, it doesn't mean that our background must be stale and stagnant. For example, many combat games are staged

6

in front of a group of people (or creatures), and from time to time you see a camera flash, or one of the people move his head or change expression. This is a form of background animation.

Many times the background for a level of a game is simply a picture. However, there's no reason we can't animate small portions of the picture to make the still image look a little more lifelike. As another example, imagine you're playing a side-scroller game and you walk by a store. The store has a window in which, all of a sudden, you see a neon light illuminate. Even though the light has nothing to do with the game, it adds to the texture of the game and makes the environment, which is 2-D, seem more alive.

Finally, there's no reason we can't also use sprites as background animation. Strictly speaking, "background" could mean anything that isn't part of the player's interaction with the game. Hence, having some bird sprites fly by, or maybe a shooting-star sprite once in a while, is fine.

In general, you should add background animation to the game near the end of the development cycle. This is because a game programmer could add so many cool things that do nothing, the background might consume too much development time. The best thing to do is complete the game, at least for the most part, and then sit down and play it and think up things that would be cool but simple to implement in a few minutes to a few hours.

Context-Sensitive Animation

Context-sensitive animation is the technique of changing the frames of animation using different imagery, or using different colors, depending on the time, setting level, or action taking place. For instance, imagine that the player in a side-scrolling adventure can press the Spacebar to kick. Therefore, the programmer would have a set of, say, six frames to create the animation. However, a real person would probably kick at different levels of height based on the height of the target. This means if a character in a game kicks at the same height regardless of whether the target is a midget or a giant, that character is going to look pretty stupid. If there's a context-sensitive animation system in place, the computer takes factors such as what the player is doing and selects a more appropriate animation—if one exists. This can add to the realism of the game.

As another example, you may have created frames of animation for the player's character in the game to look as though he or she is walking. However, the game also allows the player to pick up objects. If you really wanted to have a good, context-sensitive animation system, you might create three different walking sequences to be used based on how many

objects the player had picked up and, hence, proportional to the weight of all the objects the character was carrying. If a player had picked up nothing, the player's character should have a quick, springy step. However, if the character is carrying a laser cannon and 5,000 gold pieces, it should behave as though more labor is involved.

Putting Color in Motion

We've already discussed how it's possible to remap the VGA card's color registers and set them to any value. We've also talked about a technique called color rotation, which is a method of cycling a set of color registers in a linear fashion. For example, you could use Algorithm 6.4 to rotate five color registers that begin at register i.

Algorithm 6.4. Rotating five colors.

```
temp = color i
color i = color i+1
color i+1 = color i+2
color i+2 = color i+3
color i+3 = color i+4
color i+4 = temp
```

You can use color rotation to simulate many effects. For example, back in the old days programmers would use color-rotation effects to simulate the movement of water, or sometimes even the movement of the environment. In the Robopunk demo, I used color rotation to rotate a set of three colors. There was only one color on at any one time, but rotating the three colors had the effect of making the lights move. These moving lights were the ones on the walkway Robopunk walked on. The moving lights made the walkway look more realistic.

Let's look at another effect you can accomplish with color rotation: movement. Imagine, if you will, drawing an object in many different positions on the screen, using a different color register each time. If we were to place blue in all the color registers, we'd see a collection of blue objects on the screen. But what if we were to set all the color registers to black? The result would be...invisibility. We wouldn't be able to see any of the objects.

Now imagine that we set one of the color registers to red. We would instantly see an object appear. The object was always there; it was merely invisible because it was black. Now, if we turn off the color register we just turned on and turn on another, we'd see the object "jump," or move instantly. This is the premise behind movement with color registers. Using this technique, large images can be moved with hardly any processing time.

6

This effect can be used in many ways, and I'll leave it up to you to figure out creative uses for it. However, I've written a demo that shows a set of paper airplanes drawn on the screen. There are 14 of them. I drew each paper airplane using a different color register. The color registers I used were numbers 17–30. The program functions by sequentially illuminating a single color register in that range while turning the rest off. This makes the paper airplane look as though it's moving. The name of the program, shown in Listing 6.10, is paper.exe.

Listing 6.10. A demonstration of color rotation uses to simulate movement (paper.c).

```
// I N C L U D E S //////////////////////////////////////////////

#include <io.h>
#include <conio.h>
#include <stdio.h>
#include <stdlib.h>
#include <dos.h>
#include <bios.h>
#include <fcntl.h>
#include <memory.h>
#include <malloc.h>
#include <math.h>
#include <string.h>

#include "graph3.h" // Include our graphics library.
#include "graph4.h" // Include our graphics library.

// D E F I N E S //////////////////////////////////////////////

#define PLANE_START_COLOR_REG 17
#define PLANE_END_COLOR_REG   30

// G L O B A L S //////////////////////////////////////////////
// 18.2 clicks/sec

pcx_picture plane;

////////////////////////////////////////////////////////////////

void Animate_Plane(void)
{
// This function animates a paper plane drawn with 14 different
// colors by illuminating a single color and turning off all the
// others in sequence.

RGB_color color_1, color_2;
int index;

// Clear out each of the color registers used by the plane.

color_1.red   = 0;
```

```
     color_1.green = 0;
     color_1.blue  = 0;

     color_2.red   = 0;
     color_2.green = 63;
     color_2.blue  = 0;

     // Clear all the colors out.

     for (index=PLANE_START_COLOR_REG;
               index<=PLANE_END_COLOR_REG; index++)
        {

        Set_Palette_Register(index, (RGB_color_ptr)&color_1);

        } // end for index

     // Make the first plane green, and then rotate the colors.

     Set_Palette_Register(PLANE_START_COLOR_REG,
                          (RGB_color_ptr)&color_2);

     // Animate the colors.

     while(!kbhit())
         {
         // Rotate the colors.

         Get_Palette_Register(PLANE_END_COLOR_REG,
                              (RGB_color_ptr)&color_1);

         for (index=PLANE_END_COLOR_REG-1;
                  index>=PLANE_START_COLOR_REG; index--)
             {

             Get_Palette_Register(index,(RGB_color_ptr)&color_2);
             Set_Palette_Register(index+1,(RGB_color_ptr)&color_2);

             } // end for

             Set_Palette_Register(PLANE_START_COLOR_REG,
                              (RGB_color_ptr)&color_1);

         // Wait a while...

         Delay(3);

         } // end while

     } // end Animate_Plane

     // M A I N //////////////////////////////////////////////////

     void main(void)
     {
```

6

continues

359

Listing 6.10. continued

```
// Set the video mode to the 320x200, 256-color mode.

Set_Video_Mode(VGA256);

// Initialize the PCX file that holds the plane.

PCX_Init((pcx_picture_ptr)&plane);

// Load the PCX file that holds the cells.

PCX_Load("paper.pcx", (pcx_picture_ptr)&plane,1);

PCX_Show_Buffer((pcx_picture_ptr)&plane);

PCX_Delete((pcx_picture_ptr)&plane);

Blit_String(8,8,15,"Hit any key to see animation.",0);

getch();

Blit_String(8,8,15,"Hit any key to exit.          ",0);

Animate_Plane();

// Reset the video mode back to text.

Set_Video_Mode(TEXT_MODE);

} // end main
```

 Building an Executable: To make an executable of the program in Listing 6.10, you can either type it in or use the source on the companion CD. The name of the source is paper.c. The precompiled executable is named paper.exe. As before, use the following compile line for Microsoft C:

```
cl -AM -Zi -c  -Fc -Gs -G2 paper.c
```

After compiling the program in this manner you can link it to the standard libraries and to our previously generated game library, gamelib.lib, with a link line such as:

```
link /ST:8192 /CO paper,,,graphics.lib+gamelib.lib,,
```

This creates a final executable named paper.exe.

 The program in Listing 6.10 doesn't do anything we haven't seen already.

1. It begins by setting the video mode and loading a PCX file with the paper-airplane images.

2. The program then waits for a key press. When it gets one it calls `Animate_Plane()`. This function basically implements Algorithm 6.4 using the color registers 17–30.

That's all there is to it. Personally, I like to use color rotation for waterfalls, rain, moving lights, and small animations, but if you want to base an entire animation system on it, the choice is yours. There's no doubt that you'll have enough color registers, with 256 of them at your disposal!

Locking On to the Vertical Retrace

We've learned that using a double buffer can eliminate flickering during screen updates. This is only partially true. Granted, the entire screen is copied from the double buffer to the video buffer in one transaction. However, this movement of data is not synchronized in any way with the video display. This lack of synchronization can result in an effect called *shearing*. Shearing occurs when the video buffer is updated with a new data after the electron gun has already partially updated the screen. This can be rectified by only updating the video buffer while the electron gun is not actively drawing the image on the video screen, which is called the *vertical blank*.

It's possible to detect this time interval and synchronize with it so video updates occur only while the electron gun is not drawing the screen. As we learned on Day 4, the video image is drawn 70 times a second in mode 13h. That means that there are 70 vertical retrace periods per second. If we can somehow track when each of these periods occurs and wait for it before we update the video buffer, we'll have solved our problem. Luckily, there's a way to do this.

The VGA card has a register called the *input status word* register, located at I/O port address 0X3DA. Each bit in the input status word tracks a specific aspect of the VGA card's status. The bit we're interested in is d3, or the fourth bit from the right. This bit tracks the vertical retrace period as follows:

☐ If bit 4 is 1, there's a retrace in progress.

☐ If bit 4 is 0, there's no retrace, meaning the screen is being drawn.

We can use this knowledge to write a function that waits for a vertical retrace. However, I want to first direct your attention to another opportunity that exists with the vertical

retrace period. Because we can track when the vertical retrace is occurring, we can use this as another timing event. However, this new timing event has the resolution of 1/70th of a second (in contrast to the system timer, which has a resolution of roughly 1/18th of a second). This enables us to do finer-grained temporal event tracking. Although we ultimately learn to reprogram the internal timer (on Day 11, in the chapter called "Out of Time"), it's nice to know we have another timing source available.

Now, to the problem at hand. We must write a function that waits for the vertical retrace. This seems easy: we simply write a function that waits for bit 4 of the input status word to become 1. However, even if this bit is 1, we still don't know how far into the retrace the monitor is! It could have just begun, or it could be almost complete. We must take this into consideration, as we want the function to wait for the beginning of the vertical retrace and not just start anywhere in between. We can use Algorithm 6.5 to do this:

Algorithm 6.5. Waiting for the vertical retrace.

```
while(bit 4 is equal to 1)
    {
    // Wait for the end of the current vertical retrace.
    } // end while

while(bit 4 is equal to 0)
    {
    // Wait for the end of the active display time.
    } // end while

// At this point, we're guaranteed to be at the beginning of a
// vertical retrace.
```

Implementing Algorithm 6.5 into a complete C function is a snap. We simply add a couple of "defines" and then translate the algorithm into C. Listing 6.11 contains a complete program that shows the use of such a function. The program locks on to the vertical retraces and counts their occurrences while plotting a randomly positioned dot during every retrace period. The name of the program is vertical.exe; its source and executable can be found on the companion CD.

Listing 6.11. A program that locks onto the vertical retrace (vertical.c).

```
// I N C L U D E S //////////////////////////////////////////////

#include <io.h>
#include <conio.h>
#include <stdio.h>
#include <stdlib.h>
```

```c
#include <dos.h>
#include <bios.h>
#include <fcntl.h>
#include <memory.h>
#include <malloc.h>
#include <math.h>
#include <string.h>

#include "graph3.h"
#include "graph4.h"


// D E F I N E S ///////////////////////////////////////////////

#define VGA_INPUT_STATUS_1   0x3DA
// VGA status reg 1, bit 3 is the vsync:
    // when 1 - retrace in progress
    // when 0 - no retrace

#define VGA_VSYNC_MASK 0x08        // Masks off unwanted bit of
                                   // the status reg.



// F U N C T I O N S ///////////////////////////////////////////

void Wait_For_Vsync(void)
{
// This function waits for the start of a vertical retrace. If a
// vertical retrace is in progress, it waits until the next one.

while(_inp(VGA_INPUT_STATUS_1) & VGA_VSYNC_MASK)
     {
     // Do nothing: VGA is in retrace.
     } // end while

// Now wait for vysnc and exit.

while(!(_inp(VGA_INPUT_STATUS_1) & VGA_VSYNC_MASK))
     {
     // Do nothing: wait for the start of retrace.
     } // end while

// At this point a vertical retrace is occurring, so return to
// the caller.

} // end Wait_For_Vsync

// M A I N ///////////////////////////////////////////////////////

void main(void)
{
char buffer[128];        // Used as temporary string buffer.
long number_vsyncs=0;    // Tracks the number of retrace cycles.

// Set the video mode to the 320x200, 256-color mode.
```

continues

6

Listing 6.11. continued

```
Set_Video_Mode(VGA256);

// Wait until the user presses a key.

while(!kbhit())
    {

    // Wait for a vsync.

    Wait_For_Vsync();

    // Do graphics or whatever now that we know electron gun is
    // retracing. We have only 1/70 of a second, though!
    // Usually, we would copy the double buffer to the video
    // RAM.

    Plot_Pixel_Fast(rand()%320, rand()%200,rand()%256);

    // Tally the vsyncs.

    number_vsyncs++;

    // Print to the screen.

    sprintf(buffer,"Number of Vsync's = %ld    ",number_vsyncs);

    Blit_String(8,8,9,buffer,0);

    } // end while

// Reset the video mode back to text.

Set_Video_Mode(TEXT_MODE);

} // end main
```

Building an Executable: To make an executable of the program in Listing 6.11, you can either type it in or use the source on the companion CD. The name of the source is vertical.c. The precompiled executable is named vertical.exe. As before, use the following compile line for Microsoft C:

```
cl -AM -Zi -c  -Fc -Gs -G2 vertical.c
```

After compiling the program in this manner you can link it to the standard libraries and to our previously generated game library, gamelib.lib, with a link line such as:

```
link /ST:8192 /CO vertical,,,graphics.lib+gamelib.lib,,
```

This creates a final executable named vertical.exe.

Analysis
There isn't much to analyze here. The program places the VGA card in mode 13h, goes into an event loop, and plots a randomly positioned pixel on the screen every time there's a vertical retrace. The program locks onto the vertical retrace by calling Wait_For_Vsync() each cycle. There are no parameters sent and none received. The function is a timing function only. It waits for the beginning of the vertical retrace and returns.

The Vertical Interrupt

There's one more related topic that we should take a moment to discuss: the *vertical interrupt*. It's possible to trigger an interrupt based on the vertical retrace period and perform some action during the retrace by using an interrupt-service routine. However, this is usually left alone because it isn't exactly compatible with all VGA cards, and the interrupt the vertical interrupt uses, if enabled, is the same one used for a hardware fault.

Having the ability to initiate a vertical interrupt is definitely a plus. However, we can accomplish the same effect in other ways, such as using the system timer.

Adding to the Game Library

Today we covered a plethora of topics, and the software we developed must be collected and put into a single library module so we can use the functions in the near future. I've created a library module, graph6.c, along with its appropriate header, graph6.h. These files contain all the important functions we've written and covered today. You should compile graph6.c and then add it to our game library, gamelib.lib. If you don't want to compile the module, I've done so for you. You can find graph6.obj on the companion CD.

6

Summary

Wow! We've learned *so much* today. We learned about double buffers and rewrote our sprite functions. The topics of scaling and clipping were further covered. We also wrote some neat screen transitions. Then we covered scrolling and learned about the two main methods to do it. Also, we took another look at using color registers to accomplish animation and, finally, learned to synchronize the PC to the vertical retrace.

Q&A

Q What is a double buffer?

A A double buffer is a secondary region of memory, used to render an image. This memory region is then copied into the video buffer to be viewed.

Q How can look-up tables be used to scale a sprite?

A It's possible to precompute the results of running the scaling algorithm for all possible scales. For example, to precompute the scaling indices for all scales from 1–200, it would take $200+199+198+...+3+2+1 = 200(201)/2 = 20,100$ bytes of memory for such a table—which is well worth it.

Q How would you write a screen transition that moved from one image to another?

A You could select a pixel from the new screen and then copy it on top of the screen being viewed. If you selected the pixels at random or with some other algorithm, the new image would slowly become discernible.

Q How can color rotation be used to move objects that have more than a single color?

A Instead of using a single color for each object, use a set of colors. For example, draw the object in position 1 with the colors $(i,i+1,i+2)$, then in position 2 with the colors $(i+3,i+4,i+5)$, and so on. The function responsible for color rotation would know that the object is composed of three colors, not one, and would move the colors in triples, as in: $i= i+3$, $i+1=i+4$, $i+2=i+5$, and so on.

Q Is using a cell-based data structure the only way to represent multiple screens in a scrolling game?

A No. There are as many representations of universes as there are universes. However, one of the next most popular systems is called a *display list*, which is a list of instruction to a display processor or function that says things such as, "Draw a house," "Draw a bridge," and so on. It uses high levels of abstraction to generate images.

Q Is it possible to synthesize excited bromide in an argon matrix?

A Yes. I've done it with household appliances.

Workshop

The Workshop section presents quiz questions to help you cement your new knowledge and exercises to give you experience using what you've learned. Try to understand the questions and exercises before moving on to the next lesson. The answers are in Appendix B.

Quiz

1. What is the purpose of a double buffer?

2. In most cases a change is required to a single variable reference to modify a normal screen-based function to work with a double buffer. What is that change?

3. What are the I/O port and the bit used for tracking the vertical retrace?

4. Describe *animotion*.

5. What's the relationship between the inverse of the scaling factor and the scaling index in the context of the sprite-scaling function?

6. When implementing color rotation on a set of colors, what happens to the colors at the end points of the set? Are they thrown away each cycle?

7. Why is locking onto the vertical retrace so important?

8. How many times a second does the vertical retrace occur in mode 13h?

9. Name the two types of scrolling.

10. Describe paged scrolling.

Exercises

1. Modify the text-blitting functions to work with a double buffer.

2. Modify the robo.c program so that when Robopunk walks all the way to the right edge of the universe, he falls downward instead of floating mid-air.

3. Write a function that adds a starfield to robo.c.

4. Modify the Disolve() screen transition function so that it dissolves the screen with any color.

5. Modify the fading-light function so it increases the intensity of all the color registers until they're saturated.

6. *Extra Credit:* Try to make Robopunk jump in a parabolic path. (*Hint:* use the fact that position = yo + velocity * time + 1/2 * acceleration * time2.)

Reading the Minds of Devices

Video games are interactive adventures. The player interacts with a virtual world within the computer. This interaction takes place between the player and the computer, with each party participating in his, her, or its own way. The computer is responsible for generating the video display and the sounds, while the player is responsible for supplying the input to drive the game. This input is what we're interested in now: we must learn how to obtain input from the most popular game input devices. Here are the topics for today:

- [ ] Understanding input devices
- [ ] Punching it out with the keyboard
- [ ] Pulling up with the joystick
- [ ] Squeezing the mouse
- [ ] Ergonomical algorithms
- [ ] Adding to the game library

Understanding Input Devices

Input devices aren't that hard to understand. They all perform the same function, which is to convert some type of information from the user into a form of data that is palatable to the computer. Throughout time there have been many input devices invented for the computer, from the most popular (the keyboard) to the not-so-popular light pen. On the PC, the three most popular input devices used with games are

- [ ] The keyboard
- [ ] The joystick
- [ ] The mouse

(Probably in that order, also.) The keyboard is, of course, the most complex of all three. It allows a full, textual conversation to go on between the user and the computer in a somewhat symbolic form (that is, the keys of the keyboard).

The joystick, on the other hand, was designed, and is used almost solely, for games. It's a mechanical device that enables the player to point a yoke in the direction he or she would like to go, and to press one or more firing button(s). Although most games designed on other game machines use the joystick as the sole input device, it seems that it isn't as popular on the PC. Many people really like the keyboard because they can use both hands and, usually, can define the keys as they wish.

The mouse is a really interesting device. As an input device for video games, it isn't that useful (unless the game is a strategy or non-action game). As far as being an intuitive input device for games that need a lot of directional control, the mouse falls short. The mouse was designed to help people "point and click" in a graphical user interface such as Microsoft's Windows, not as an input device for video games.

Because we're video-game programmers, we must be able to communicate with any of these devices. Even though there are twists on the generic versions (such as floating mice, flying yokes, and modified keyboards), the techniques to interface with them are all similar. Interfacing with nongeneric versions usually is only a matter of adding a few more dozen lines of code to the software that we write today.

Without further ado, then, let's begin with the input device that everyone has: the keyboard.

Punching It Out With the Keyboard

Of all input devices supported by computers, keyboards have definitely stood the test of time as quality input devices that get the job done. The keyboard is, without doubt, the most complex input device the PC has to offer. You may think all it does is return the keys that are pressed and have some neat lights. On the contrary, the PC keyboard is a marvel of technology and "black box" interfacing. Did you know the PC's keyboard has a computer in it? That's right; the keyboard is so complex it needs a small processor to take care of all the details of pressing keys simultaneously, "reapeat-amatic" functions, indicator lights, transmission of information, and overall transparency of operation that the keyboard supplies us.

An entire book could be written on the operation and use of the keyboard. (However, we only get a few pages, so we should get to the point!) The perfect interface for a video game would allow the player to select whatever input device he or she wishes to play with. We shouldn't argue if the device chosen is appropriate or not; we should blindly supply the functionality to support it. That means we must not only be able to use the keyboard as a normal text-input device, but as a control panel on which the player presses keys to control the action in the game. Moreover, these key presses may occur at a fast rate, such as you would see in a shoot-'em-up game where the spacebar or something was being used as a firing button. Also, we must learn how to deal with two or more keys being pressed simultaneously. This could happen in a two-player game using the same keyboard for both players, or in a game where the player is pressing the motion keys and the firing button(s) at the same time.

7

371

The keyboard is broken up into two sets of keys:

☐ The control keys

☐ The qwerty keys

Let's look at them each.

Control Keys

Control keys are just like buttons: they can be read all the time without complex software code. These are the control keys:

☐ Right shift key

☐ Left shift key

☐ Ctrl key

☐ Alt key

☐ Scroll Lock key

☐ Num Lock key

☐ Caps Lock key

☐ Insert key

☐ Sys Request (SysRq) key

The current state of these keys, called the *shift state*, is kept in an area of memory at location 417h and 418h. The shift state tracks what these keys are doing and what they have been doing. This information is needed so that when the player presses the A key we can decide whether it's a lowercase "a" or uppercase "A," whether the control key was down, and so on. If we wished, we could look into the two memory locations, 417h and 418h, and decipher the shift state ourselves. For now, however, we can use a C library function that's based on a call to BIOS. As a rule you shouldn't use BIOS in PC game programs because it is so slow. However, in the case of reading the shift state, it suffices and is not going to make a difference.

We get to the code that reads the shift state in a minute, but now let's talk about getting normal, "qwerty" input from the keyboard.

Qwerty Keys

When you press a key on the keyboard, a million things happen. ("Qwerty," incidentally, is just a word made up of the first six letters at the top left of the alphabetical section of

most keyboards.) The result of these million things is that a *scan code* is created and sent to the PC. This scan code represents the key that was pressed, and has nothing to do with the ASCII code that represents that key. Table 7.1 shows the scan codes for the PC keyboard.

Table 7.1. The scan codes for the PC's keyboard.

Key	Scan Code	Key	Scan Code	Key	Scan Code
Esc	1	Y	21	Tilde	41
1	2	U	22	Left shift	42
2	3	I	23	Backslash	43
3	4	O	24	Z	44
4	5	P	25	X	45
5	6	Left bracket	26	C	46
6	7	Right bracket	27	V	47
7	8	Enter	28	B	48
8	9	Ctrl	29	N	49
9	10	A	30	M	50
0	11	S	31	Comma	51
MINUS	12	D	32	Period	52
EQUALS	13	F	33	Foward slash	53
BKSP	14	G	34	Right shift	54
TAB	15	H	35	Print Scrn	55
Q	16	J	36	Alt	56
W	17	K	37	Spacebar	57
E	18	L	38	Caps Lock	58
R	19	Semicolon	39	F1	59
T	20	Apostrophe	40	F2	60

7

continues

Table 7.1. continued

Key	Scan Code	Key	Scan Code	Key	Scan Code
F3	61	F12	134	Center (keypad 5)	76
F4	62	Num Lock	69		
F5	63	Scroll Lock	70	Right arrow	77
F6	64	Home	71	Numerical plus	78
F7	65	Up arrow	72	End	79
F8	66	PgUp	73	Down arrow	80
F9	67	Numerical minus	74	PgDn	81
F10	68			Ins	82
F11	133	Left arrow	75	Del	83

Note: There is exactly one scan code for each key, not one for each symbol. For instance, there's a single scan code for the colon (:) key, which has two symbols on it. The way the PC figures out which symbol was intended by the player is by looking at the shift state.

Scan codes are hardware-dependent and must be converted into ASCII codes. Therefore, an ASCII 65 is not sent when you press the A key; instead, a 30 is sent by the keyboard. This 30 is sent whether you press 'a' or 'A'. (See why the shift state is needed? Without it, the PC wouldn't be able to figure out whether a key was meant to be lower- or uppercase.)

Writing a Keyboard Interface

Now, I'm sure you've used the `getch()` functions from C and realized that they're just about worthless. The C I/O functions are, in general, quite simple and don't do anyone any good. (They have their uses when it comes to writing programs for computer classes in school—and that's about it!) We must learn to write functions that have the same functionality as the standard C functions and more. Here are the fundamental operations we must be able to perform to do this:

☐ We want to be able to detect a key press.

☐ When we receive a key press, we may want to convert the key we receive into an ASCII code. This may or may not be necessary. In the case of a video game, we may just want to know if the F key were pressed and could care less about the ASCII code for it.

Anyway, we see shortly how to use C library functions to receive an ASCII key. Then we use BIOS to get closer to the hardware and receive scan codes.

Game Law: When writing input functions always assume the player will press everything at the same time and try to crash your program.

Let's begin writing our keyboard interface with the function that returns the shift state. We use a C library function, along with some #defines to make the decoding easier. The code is shown in Listing 7.1.

Listing 7.1. Reading the shift state.

```
// Bitmasks for control keys/shift status

#define SHIFT_R            0x0001
#define SHIFT_L            0x0002
#define CTRL               0x0004
#define ALT                0x0008
#define SCROLL_LOCK_ON     0x0010
#define NUM_LOCK_ON        0x0020
#define CAPS_LOCK_ON       0x0040
#define INSERT_MODE        0x0080
#define CTRL_L             0x0100
#define ALT_L              0x0200
#define CTRL_R             0x0400
#define ALT_R              0x0800
#define SCROLL_LOCK_DWN    0x1000
#define NUM_LOCK_DWN       0x2000
#define CAPS_LOCK_DWN      0x4000
#define SYS_REQ_DWN        0x8000

unsigned int Get_Control_Keys(unsigned int mask)
{
// Return the status of all requested control keys.

return(mask & _bios_keybrd(_KEYBRD_SHIFTSTATUS));

} // end Get_Control_Keys
```

Analysis

The function in Listing 7.1 takes a single parameter, which is one of the #defines. The parameter is used as a mask to test the state of the key in question. The result of this test is returned and decisions can be made on this.

As I said before, we could have just looked into memory locations 417h and 418h and figured out which bits represent what. However, the C function does exactly that, and I don't think we'd be able to do it any better than Microsoft (at least in this case).

Now, let's move on to reading an ASCII key.

Reading an ASCII Key

Reading an ASCII key can be done at a low level by obtaining the scan code (which we haven't gone over yet) and, based on the shift state, translating the scan code into an ASCII character. We don't do this ourselves; instead, we use yet another C library function. Listing 7.2 contains the code.

Listing 7.2. Reading the ASCII code of a key press.

```
unsigned char Get_Ascii_Key(void)
{

// If there's a normal ASCII key waiting, return it;
// otherwise, return 0.

if (_bios_keybrd(_KEYBRD_READY))
 return(_bios_keybrd(_KEYBRD_READ));
else return(0);

} // end Get_Ascii_Key
```

Analysis

The Get_Ascii_Key() function takes no parameters. It simply tests the keyboard to see whether a character is waiting and, if so, returns the ASCII code for the character. If there isn't a character waiting, the function returns a 0.

Personally, I use the real ASCII codes once in a blue moon. They're only needed when the player is supposed to type something into the computer that's supposed to be in English, like a name. We're more interested in using the keyboard as a set of buttons, similar to what you see on the console of an arcade game such as Street Fighter. Therefore, let's see how to read the raw scan codes from the keyboard using BIOS.

Reading Scan Codes

The PC's BIOS has a few functions that allow us to directly communicate with the keyboard. These functions are called through interrupt 16h, more appropriately referred to as INT 16h. Table 7.2 details the functions we have to work with.

> **Warning:** Because we're using the BIOS routines to access the keyboard, we still notice keyboard buffering and the "beeping" that occurs when the 13-character keyboard buffer is full. This can wreak havoc on a video game. We learn how to deal with this later today.

Table 7.2. The ROM BIOS keyboard functions.

Interrupt 16h—Keyboard interrupt.

Function 00h—Read character from keyboard.

Inputs:	AH:00h
Outputs:	AH:The scan code for the key
	AL: The ASCII character for the key

Function 01h—Read keyboard status.

Inputs:	AH:01h
Outputs:	AH: The scan code for the key
	AL: The ASCII character for the key
	Z-flag:0—Character waiting
	1—Queue empty

Function 02h—Read the shift state.

Inputs:	AH:02h
Outputs:	AL: The shift state encoded as bits
	Bit 0 = Right shift key down
	Bit 1 = Left shift key down
	Bit 2 = Ctrl key down

continues

Table 7.2. continued

Interrupt 16h—Keyboard interrupt.

Bit 3 = Alt key down

Bit 4 = Scroll lock on

Bit 5 = Num lock on

Bit 6 = Caps lock on

Bit 7 = Insert on

As you can see, BIOS gives us just about everything we need. It falls a little short in the shift state because it doesn't fully qualify which Alt or Ctrl key is down. However, in addition to BIOS, we're using the C library functions to query the shift state. These C library functions do support this further functionality.

Now that we know what BIOS has to offer, let's write the function that reads the scan code out of the keyboard. We use the in-line assembler for this one, but we could have used the _int86() call if we wished. (I just like to mix things up so you feel comfortable with assembly language.) Listing 7.3 contains the code to read the scan code from the keyboard. The #defines the caller of the function would use to decide what physical key was pressed follow later today, in a demo program and library module. (Believe me, you wouldn't want to type them all in and make a mistake!)

Listing 7.3. Reading a scan code from the keyboard.

```
unsigned char Get_Scan_Code(void)
{
// Get the scan code of a key press. Because we have to look at
// status bits, let's use the in-line assembler.

// Is a key ready?

__asm
    {
    mov ah,01h          ; Function 1: is a key ready?
    int 16h             ; Call the interrupt.
    jz empty            ; There was no key, so exit.
    mov ah,00h          ; Function 0: get the scan code, please.
    int 16h             ; Call the interrupt.
    mov al,ah           ; The result was in ah, so put it
                        ; into al.
    xor ah,ah           ; Zero out ah.
    jmp done            ; The data's in ax...let's blaze!
```

```
empty:
    xor ax,ax              ; Clear out ax (0 means no key)
done:

    } // end asm

// Data is returned properly because it's in ax.

} // end Get_Scan_Code
```

Analysis The Get_Scan_Code() function works the same way as the Get_Ascii_Key() function. It returns the scan code of the key pressed, and a 0 if no key is pressed. Note how the return value is placed in AX. This is how you return data from a C function: within the AX register (at least for BYTE and WORD values).

Break Codes

There's one more detail about the keyboard I've waited to tell you: when you release a key, another scan code is sent. This scan code is called the *break code*. Therefore, there are two codes sent by the keyboard to the PC when a key is pressed:

☐ One scan code made when the key is pressed is called the *make code*.

☐ The scan code made when the key is released is called the *break code*.

Together, these two codes can be used to turn the keyboard into a fully functional set of switches that can be pressed simultaneously and as fast as we like. However, we cover this on Day 11 (in the chapter called "Out of Time").

A Word about Multitasking and Interrupts

We have a fairly complete keyboard input library now except for one little detail, which we take up on Day 11 (when we discuss multitasking and interrupts). That detail is: we still don't have a way to completely take over the keyboard and receive two or more key presses at the same time. This kind of functionality is absolutely necessary in a video game. The way it's done is to take over the keyboard interrupt and process the key presses ourselves.

A Demo

As usual, I like to put all our functions together into a demo of some kind so you can see their operation. I've created a small demo that uses a couple of the functions to read the shift state and the scan code of the key pressed by the player. Listing 7.4 contains the source code.

Listing 7.4. A keyboard demo (keytst.c).

```c
// I N C L U D E S ///////////////////////////////////////////////

#include <dos.h>
#include <bios.h>
#include <stdio.h>
#include <math.h>
#include <conio.h>
#include <graph.h>

// D E F I N E S ///////////////////////////////////////////////

// bitmasks for control keys/shift status

#define SHIFT_R              0x0001
#define SHIFT_L              0x0002
#define CTRL                 0x0004
#define ALT                  0x0008
#define SCROLL_LOCK_ON       0x0010
#define NUM_LOCK_ON          0x0020
#define CAPS_LOCK_ON         0x0040
#define INSERT_MODE          0x0080
#define CTRL_L               0x0100
#define ALT_L                0x0200
#define CTRL_R               0x0400
#define ALT_R                0x0800
#define SCROLL_LOCK_DWN      0x1000
#define NUM_LOCK_DWN         0x2000
#define CAPS_LOCK_DWN        0x4000
#define SYS_REQ_DWN          0x8000

// Scan code values. Note: keys with two symbols on them are the
// same, so I use the lower symbol. For example, the 1 key also
// has a ! above it, but we would just call it the SCAN_1 key.

#define SCAN_ESC             1
#define SCAN_1               2
#define SCAN_2               3
#define SCAN_3               4
#define SCAN_4               5
#define SCAN_5               6
#define SCAN_6               7
#define SCAN_7               8
#define SCAN_8               9
#define SCAN_9               10
#define SCAN_0               11
#define SCAN_MINUS           12
#define SCAN_EQUALS          13
#define SCAN_BKSP            14
#define SCAN_TAB             15
#define SCAN_Q               16
#define SCAN_W               17
#define SCAN_E               18
#define SCAN_R               19
#define SCAN_T               20
```

```
#define SCAN_Y              21
#define SCAN_U              22
#define SCAN_I              23
#define SCAN_O              24
#define SCAN_P              25
#define SCAN_LFT_BRACKET    26
#define SCAN_RGT_BRACKET    27
#define SCAN_ENTER          28
#define SCAN_CTRL           29

#define SCAN_A              30
#define SCAN_S              31
#define SCAN_D              32
#define SCAN_F              33
#define SCAN_G              34
#define SCAN_H              35
#define SCAN_J              36
#define SCAN_K              37
#define SCAN_L              38

#define SCAN_SEMI           39
#define SCAN_APOS           40
#define SCAN_TILDE          41

#define SCAN_LEFT_SHIFT     42
#define SCAN_BACK_SLASH     43
#define SCAN_Z              44
#define SCAN_X              45
#define SCAN_C              46
#define SCAN_V              47
#define SCAN_B              48
#define SCAN_N              49
#define SCAN_M              50
#define SCAN_COMMA          51

#define SCAN_PERIOD         52
#define SCAN_FOWARD_SLASH   53
#define SCAN_RIGHT_SHIFT    54
#define SCAN_PRT_SCRN       55
#define SCAN_ALT            56
#define SCAN_SPACE          57
#define SCAN_CAPS_LOCK      58
#define SCAN_F1             59
#define SCAN_F2             60
#define SCAN_F3             61
#define SCAN_F4             62
#define SCAN_F5             63
#define SCAN_F6             64
#define SCAN_F7             65
#define SCAN_F8             66
#define SCAN_F9             67
#define SCAN_F10            68
#define SCAN_F11            133
#define SCAN_F12            134
#define SCAN_NUM_LOCK       69
#define SCAN_SCROLL_LOCK    70
```

continues

381

Listing 7.4. continued

```c
#define SCAN_HOME          71
#define SCAN_UP            72
#define SCAN_PGUP          73
#define SCAN_NUM_MINUS     74
#define SCAN_LEFT          75
#define SCAN_CENTER        76
#define SCAN_RIGHT         77
#define SCAN_NUM_PLUS      78
#define SCAN_END           79
#define SCAN_DOWN          80
#define SCAN_PGDWN         81
#define SCAN_INS           82
#define SCAN_DEL           83


// F U N C T I O N S /////////////////////////////////////////////

unsigned char Get_Ascii_Key(void)
{
// If there's a normal ASCII key waiting, return it;
// otherwise, return 0.
if (_bios_keybrd(_KEYBRD_READY))
 return(_bios_keybrd(_KEYBRD_READ));
else return(0);

} // end Get_Ascii_Key

///////////////////////////////////////////////////////////////////

unsigned int Get_Control_Keys(unsigned int mask)
{
// Return the status of all requested control keys.

return(mask & _bios_keybrd(_KEYBRD_SHIFTSTATUS));

} // end Get_Control_Keys

///////////////////////////////////////////////////////////////////

unsigned char Get_Scan_Code(void)
{
// Get the scan code of a key press. Because we have to look at
// status bits, let's use the in-line assembler.

// Is a key ready?

__asm
   {
   mov ah,01h          ; Function 1: is a key ready?
   int 16h             ; Call the interrupt.
   jz empty            ; There was no key, so exit.
   mov ah,00h          ; Function 0: get the scan code, please.
   int 16h             ; Call the interrupt.
   mov al,ah           ; The result was in ah, so put it
                       ; into al.
```

```
        xor ah,ah              ; Zero out ah.
        jmp done               ; The data's in ax...let's blaze!

empty:
        xor ax,ax              ; Clear out ax (0 means no key)
done:

        } // end asm

// Data is returned properly because it's in ax.

} // end Get_Scan_Code

//  M A I N /////////////////////////////////////////////////////

void main(void) // Keyboard demo
{
unsigned char key;
int done=0;

_clearscreen(_GCLEARSCREEN);

// Show some info.

printf("Press a key and look at the scan code it generates.");
printf("\nTo exit the program press the 'q' key.");

// Wait until the user presses the Q key.

while(!done)
    {

    _settextposition(4,0);

    // Has the user pressed a key?

    if ( (key = Get_Scan_Code()) )
        {
        printf("Scan Code = %d   ",key);
        printf("\nScan code interpretted as ASCII = %c",key);
        } // end if key pressed

    // Test for ctrl and alt keys.

    if (Get_Control_Keys(CTRL))
        printf("\ncontrol key pressed                        ");

    if (Get_Control_Keys(ALT))
        printf("\nalt key pressed                        ");

    if (key==16) done=1; // 16 is the scan code for q.

    } // end main

} // end main
```

Building an Executable: To make an executable of the program in Listing 7.4, you can either type it in or use the source on the companion CD. The name of the source is keytst.c. The precompiled executable is named keytst.exe. As before, use the following compile line for Microsoft C:

```
cl -AM -Zi -c -Fc -Gs -G2 keytst.c
```

After compiling the program in this manner you can link it to the standard libraries and to our previously generated game library, gamelib.lib, with a link line such as:

```
link /ST:8192 /CO keytst,,,graphics.lib+gamelib.lib,,
```

This creates a final executable named keytst.exe.

Now that we've got a clue on interfacing with the keyboard, let's see how the joystick works!

Pulling Up with the Joystick

The joystick is the icon of input devices for video games. While it really works best as an input device in flight simulation games, people who own joysticks do so for the single purpose of playing games on the PC.

The joystick is implemented as an add-on card on the PC, and because of that, the design and operation aren't as smooth as they could be. Moreover, because of the technology available at the time the joyport was designed for the PC, the designers had to use techniques that today would seem crude and primitive. (Frankly, I think that the joyport is crude and primitive for any time period, even Precambrian!)

In any case, the PC's joysticks are implemented as analog devices. *Analog* means the joystick has a contiguous range of motion values. Analog joysticks are different from the more common digital joysticks we see on old Atari and Commodore computers. Digital joysticks work on the premise that when the player moved the joystick to the right, to the left, up, or down, a switch was activated. This switch would be interpreted as the direction the player wanted to go. Take a look at Figure 7.1 to see a side-by-side view of an analog and a digital joystick.

Analog joysticks, on the other hand, are implemented as two potentiometers (variable resistors) that can track how much the joystick is deflected in either the x or y direction.

This allows a much smoother control of the position of whatever the player is trying to position. In essence, an analog joystick allows a player to say how much to travel in a specific direction, while a digital joystick allows only the direction.

Now, let's see what the analog joystick is made of, and how it operates on a PC.

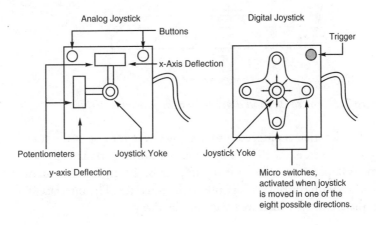

Figure 7.1. *A comparison of analog and digital joysticks.*

What Makes a Joystick

Figure 7.2 shows the layout of the joystick hardware we use for our operational discussions in this section.

As you see, the PC supports two joystick ports, numbered 1 and 2. (Some literature calls them A and B.) Each PC joystick is fitted with two buttons, named button 1 and button 2. So, how do we read the values of the joysticks? Let's begin by taking a look at what each joystick offers, and then discuss how to read the joystick positions and buttons. Each joystick is the same, so I discuss only one of them.

As I said a moment ago, the joystick has two potentiometers. These potentiometers are connected to the x and y direction of the joystick yoke mechanically. When the joystick is deflected in either of the directions (or both), the resistance of these potentiometers changes. By running an electrical current through the potentiometers and using a type of analog-to-digital (A/D) converter, the amount of deflection in each axis can be computed.

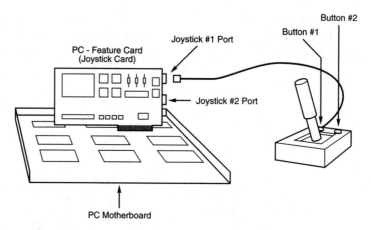

Figure 7.2. *The connection diagram for the joystick interface.*

The PC's joystick is plugged into a *joyport,* which most of the time is an add-on card plugged into one of the PC's slots. (One or more joyports actually exist as an extra option on many floppy controller cards and I/O cards.) In any case, for our discussions we aren't concerned with the physical nature of the interface. The interface is always compatible with the circuitry, which we cover momentarily.

The buttons on each joystick are simple switches and can be read through a simple port read. There are two buttons per joystick and a total of two joysticks, so a total of four bits are needed to determine the state of all the buttons. The port through which all the action takes place is I/O port 201h. This is where we can read the buttons and the position of the joystick.

Take a look at Table 7.3 to see the bit layout of port 201h:

☐ The first bits, 0–3, are used to read the value of the joystick.

☐ The second bank of bits, 4–7, are used to read the buttons themselves.

Table 7.3. The bit designations for the joystick port 201h.

Bit 0—Joystick 1's x-axis

Bit 1—Joystick 1's y-axis

Bit 2—Joystick 2's x-axis

Bit 3—Joystick 2's y-axis

Bit 4—Joystick 1's first button

Bit 5—Joystick 1's second button

Bit 6—Joystick 2's first button

Bit 7—Joystick 2's second button

If you were to write a program right now that just scanned port 201h and printed it out, you'd find that bits 4–7 toggle from 1 to 0 when buttons are pressed; in other words, they're inverted. This is no big deal: we can write code that extracts each bit and inverts it so we get a 1 when one of the buttons is pressed and a 0 when it's released.

We must talk about how the joystick positions are read; that is, how potentiometer deflections are converted into digital words. Back in the old days, real A/D converters where expensive and slow. Many hardware designers therefore had to be creative to achieve A/D conversion. One way to convert an analog voltage into a digital word is by the following system:

1. Use a potentiometer as the sensing unit.

2. Place the potentiometer in series with a capacitor.

3. Apply a constant voltage.

Based on the time constant of the circuit, the capacitor takes a longer or shorter amount of time to charge depending on the value of the potentiometer. You can see this set up in Figure 7.3.

We start charging the capacitor at some time, T0, and count how long it takes for the capacitor to come to a full charge. We can call this time T1. T1–T0 is proportional to the value of the resistance to which the potentiometer is set, which is also proportional to the amount of deflection of the joystick (its position).

So all we need do is place the potentiometer(s) of the joystick into charging circuits, apply a voltage, start counting and, when the capacitor in the charging circuit hits a threshold, stop and look at the counter. This is exactly how the joystick operates on the PC. There is one problem though: the counting!

We can write code that starts the charging circuit and we can detect when the capacitor is charged. The problem is that when we count during the process, the same potentiometer deflection—the same joystick position—gives two different readings on two different PCs if those PCs run at different speeds! This is a serious problem. Imagine: a 486 will count to about a gillion in the milliseconds the capacitor takes to charge, while an XT will only be able to count to a few hundred thousand. The result of the count would be interpreted as the position of the joystick, and would be wrong!

7

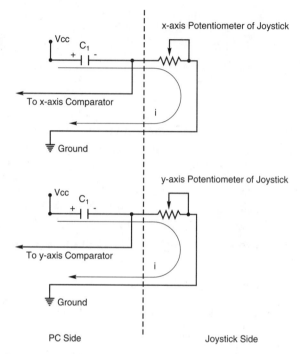

Figure 7.3. *The charging circuit for the joystick.*

So how do we deal with this problem? (Buy an Amiga! Just kidding.) We must calibrate the joysticks, or in some way figure out the maximum and minimum charging times of the charging circuit. This is exactly what's done on many video games: there's a calibration phase of the configuration.

Note: There *are* joysticks available that do not work in this manner, such as Gravis and others. These joysticks have their own proprietary hardware and work the same on any speed machine.

Warning: Some nonstandard PC joysticks only work on certain-speed CPUs. Be sure to check this out before buying one.

This calibration problem is really no big deal: we can write code that tells the player to move the joystick around, and we can figure out its maximum and minimum deflection in both axes. Using this information we can then figure out where the joystick yoke actually is.

(I'll bet you that the few paragraphs we've just seen are the most that's ever been written about the PC joystick in the same book! It's one of those mysteries of the universe, just like how Jimmy Carter became president!)

Now that we've talked about how joysticks work and can be read, I want to let you know that you can also use BIOS routines to read the joystick. BIOS routines are reliable; moreover, I actually use them in some of my games. (I know, I know: we aren't supposed to use BIOS. In this case it's all right.) Let's take a look at what BIOS has to offer in the department of joystick functions.

The BIOS `devices` interrupt 15h has a function 84h that gives joystick support. Table 7.4 shows the subfunctions we use.

Table 7.4. Joystick functions supported by BIOS interrupt 15h.

Interrupt 15h—devices interrupt	
Function 84h—Joystick support	
Subfunction 00h—Read switch status.	
Inputs:	AH:84h
	DX:00h
Outputs:	AL: Button States
Subfunction 01h—Read joystick positions.	
Inputs:	AH:84h
	DX:01h
Outputs:	AX: Joystick 1's x-axis
	BX: Joystick 1's y-axis
	CX: Joystick 2's x-axis
	DX: Joystick 2's y-axis

7

In this table we see that BIOS supports both the reading of the joystick buttons and the position of the joysticks.

We've laid the framework for communicating with the joystick, so let's write some code to read button states and joystick positions.

Reading Joystick Buttons

For starters, we a need routine to read the state of the joystick buttons. Listing 7.5 contains two functions to do this. One is based on BIOS. The other is based on direct comunications with the joystick port.

Listing 7.5. Joystick button-reading functions.

```
// D E F I N E S ////////////////////////////////////////////

#define JOYPORT        0x201  // Joyport is at 201 hex

#define BUTTON_1_1   0x10   // Joystick 1, first button
#define BUTTON_1_2   0x20   // Joystick 1, second button
#define BUTTON_2_1   0x40   // Joystick 2, first button
#define BUTTON_2_2   0x80   // Joystick 2, second button

#define JOYSTICK_1   0x01   // Joystick 1, in general
#define JOYSTICK_2   0x02   // Joystick 2, in general

#define JOYSTICK_1_X 0x01   // Joystick 1, x-axis
#define JOYSTICK_1_Y 0x02   // Joystick 1, y-axis
#define JOYSTICK_2_X 0x04   // Joystick 2, x-axis
#define JOYSTICK_2_Y 0x08   // Joystick 2, y-axis

#define JOY_1_CAL      1    // Command to calibrate joystick #1
#define JOY_2_CAL      2    // Command to calibrate joystick #2

// F U N C T I O N S ////////////////////////////////////////

unsigned char Buttons(unsigned char button)
{
// Read the joystick buttons by peeking the port to which the
// switches are attached.

outp(JOYPORT,0); // Clear the latch and request a sample.

// Invert buttons, then mask with request.

return( ~inp(JOYPORT) & button);

} // end Buttons
```

```
/////////////////////////////////////////////////////////////

unsigned char Buttons_Bios(unsigned char button)
{
// BIOS version of buttons read

union _REGS inregs, outregs;

inregs.h.ah = 0x84; // Joystick function 84h
inregs.x.dx = 0x00; // Read buttons subfunction 0h

// Call DOS

_int86(0x15,&inregs, &outregs);

// Invert buttons, then mask with request.

return( (~outregs.h.al) & button);

} // end Buttons_Bios
```

You can use either `Buttons()` or `Buttons_Bios()` to retrieve the state of the joystick button switches. The input and output of the functions are identical; the difference is in their internal operations:

☐ The `Buttons()` function operates by directly accessing the joystick port at I/O address 201h.

☐ The `Buttons_Bios()` functions uses the BIOS call to retrieve the status of the buttons (which, in the end, also access the joystick port).

In any case, the functions operate by using the sent parameter as a mask to select which joystick button is requested. As we learned a few moments ago, the values of the buttons are inverted. Therefore, the requested button state is inverted by software so that "down" translates to a binary 1 and "up" (or "release") translates to a binary 0.

For example, we could use the following code to use the `Buttons()` function to see whether joystick 1 has the first button down:

```
if (Buttons(BUTTON_1_1))
    {
    ...do something cool!
    } // end if
```

As you can see, using the buttons functions couldn't be any simpler. Now let's move on to the position-reading functions.

Reading Joystick Positions

Reading the position of the joystick using BIOS is easy: it takes no more than a call to the BIOS function. However, we must know how to read the position of the joysticks ourselves to be complete. This can only help us in the future, when we must write device drivers ourselves for other input devices that might not have a nice BIOS interface. Many input devices use the same charge/discharge hardware found in the PC's joystick, so the exercise of writing code to read the joysticks is well-founded. You can use Algorithm 7.1 to read a joystick.

Algorithm 7.1. Reading the position of a joystick.

1. Reset a counter variable that will count during the process.

2. Strobe the joystick port with any number.

3. Increment the counter variable.

4. Test whether the required bit has been set in the joystick port, this means that the charge is complete and the time that it took is proportional to the position of the joystick.

5. If the test in part 4 is true then exit and the counter is proportional to the joystick position, else GOTO 3

Obviously, Algorithm 7.1 must be used for both the x- and y-axes of the joystick so a complete 2-D position can be computed. However, the algorithm contains the necessary steps for joystick reading. Using Algorithm 7.1 as a basis for a real function, let's write a function that actually reads the joystick. This function is shown in Listing 7.6.

Listing 7.6. Reading the joystick using assembly language.

```
unsigned int Joystick(unsigned char stick)
{
// This function reads the joystick values manually by counting
// how long the capacitors take to charge/discharge.
// Let's use the in-line assembler. It's cool!

__asm
   {
   cli                      ; Disable interrupts.

   mov ah, byte ptr stick ; Get mask into ah to select the
                            ; joystick to read.
   xor al,al                ; Zero out al, xor is a trick.
   xor cx,cx                ; Same with cx, which we will use as
                            ; a counter.
   mov dx,JOYPORT           ; dx is used by inp and outp.
```

```
        out dx,al               ; Write 0s to the port.

discharge:
        in al,dx                ; Read the data back from the port.
        test al,ah              ; Has the bit in question changed?
        loopne discharge        ; If the stick isn't ready, --cx and
                                ; loop.

        sti                     ; Reenable interrupts.
        xor ax,ax               ; Zero out ax.
        sub ax,cx               ; ax now holds the position of the
                                ; axis switch.

        } // end asm

// The function returns properly because ax has the result.

} // end Joystick
```

We've been cutting down on the number of analyses we do because (I hope) you're frosty and wide awake. However, the above function is written completely in assembler and deserves some explanation.

First, the function uses the in-line assembler and had to be written using assembly because we were timing a hardware event. Although C may have been fast enough, I feel that using assembler is the best bet in this situation and insulates us on slower machines. Anyway, let's see how the function works.

1. The function begins by zeroing out CX and AL. CX is used to count the amount of time the charge event takes, while AL is used as a strobe value to send the joystick port. We could have sent any value; however, 0 is a nice number. Also, note that AH holds the bitmask for the requested joystick. This is used continuously as the test pattern to see whether the requested joystick has completed its cycle.

2. The next step in the code is the charge loop. The loop tests the bitmask against the joystick bits and checks whether the bit representing the requested joystick axis has been set to 1. If the bit isn't set to 1, the loop continues and the counter CX is decremented.

   There's a little trick we need to discuss because it isn't so obvious. When the loopne instruction is executed, it decrements CX for us and updates the counter. Therefore, when the loop exits we must subtract CX from 0 to get the real count, because the value in CX at the loop exit is really negative.

3. Finally, the function leaves the result in the AX register which is the C standard for returning BYTE and WORD values.

7

In addition to the Joystick() function I've supplied another version based on the BIOS. We see it in a moment in a final demo program. Before that, though, let's talk briefly about joystick detection and calibration.

Joystick Detection and Calibration

Detecting whether a joystick is present can be done in many ways, some more reliable than others. One way is to use BIOS to test whether a joystick card is even present. However, knowing a card is present doesn't tell us whether or not there's a joystick plugged into it. I've found that the best way to determine whether a joystick is present is to read the position of the stick's x- and y-axes. If both return zeroes, you're almost assured that a joystick is not plugged in. I've supplied a function to do this, shown in Listing 7.7.

Listing 7.7. Determining whether a joystick is present.

```
int Joystick_Available(int stick_num)
{
// This function tests whether the joystick the user is
// requesting be tested is plugged in.

if (stick_num == JOYSTICK_1)
    {
    // Test whether joystick 1 is plugged in by testing the port
    // values. If there's no stick, they're 0,0.

return(Joystick_Bios(JOYSTICK_1_X)+Joystick_Bios(JOYSTICK_1_Y));

    } // end if joystick 1
else
    {
    // Test whether joystick 2 is plugged in by testing the port
    // values. If there's no stick, they're 0,0.

    return(Joystick_Bios(JOYSTICK_2_X)+Joystick_Bios(JOYSTICK_2_Y));

    } // end else joystick 2

} // end Joystick_Available
```

 The Joystick_Available() function takes as a parameter the joystick you're testing for, returning a 1 if the joystick is plugged in and a 0 otherwise.

As we discussed earlier today, calibrating the joysticks is really a method of figuring out the minimum and maximum deflection of the particular joystick plugged into the PC on which we're running. This is necessary so that we may divide the analog travel into regions that give the most freedom of the joystick.

To put together all the ideas we've talked about relating to joysticks, I've written another demo that uses the functions and displays the status of joystick 1. The program is called joytst.exe, and you can find it on the companion CD. The program begins by testing for joystick 1's existence, then allows you to calibrate the joystick. Finally, the program displays the joystick's position and button status in real-time. Listing 7.8 contains the code for joytst.exe.

Listing 7.8. A joystick demo program. (joytst.c).

```
// I N C L U D E S ///////////////////////////////////////////////

#include <dos.h>
#include <bios.h>
#include <stdio.h>
#include <math.h>
#include <conio.h>
#include <graph.h>


// D E F I N E S ///////////////////////////////////////////////

#define JOYPORT       0x201   // Joyport is at 201 hex

#define BUTTON_1_1    0x10    // Joystick 1, button 1
#define BUTTON_1_2    0x20    // Joystick 1, button 2
#define BUTTON_2_1    0x40    // Joystick 2, button 1
#define BUTTON_2_2    0x80    // Joystick 2, button 2

#define JOYSTICK_1    0x01    // Joystick 1, in general
#define JOYSTICK_2    0x02    // Joystick 2, in general

#define JOYSTICK_1_X  0x01    // Joystick 1, x-axis
#define JOYSTICK_1_Y  0x02    // Joystick 1, y-axis
#define JOYSTICK_2_X  0x04    // Joystick 2, x-axis
#define JOYSTICK_2_Y  0x08    // Joystick 2, y-axis

#define JOY_1_CAL        1    // Command to calibrate joystick #1
#define JOY_2_CAL        2    // Command to calibrate joystick #2


// G L O B A L S ///////////////////////////////////////////////

unsigned int joy_1_max_x,   // Global joystick calibration
                            // variables
             joy_1_max_y,
             joy_1_min_x,
             joy_1_min_y,
             joy_1_cx,
             joy_1_cy,
             joy_2_max_x,
             joy_2_max_y,
             joy_2_min_x,
             joy_2_min_y,
             joy_2_cx,
             joy_2_cy;
```

continues   395

Listing 7.8. continued

```c
// F U N C T I O N S /////////////////////////////////////////

unsigned char Buttons(unsigned char button)
{
// Read the joystick buttons by peeking the port to which the
// switches are attached.

outp(JOYPORT,0); // Clear the latch and request a sample.

// Invert buttons, then mask with request.

return( ~inp(JOYPORT) & button);

} // end Buttons

///////////////////////////////////////////////////////////////

unsigned int Joystick(unsigned char stick)
{
// This function reads the joystick values manually by counting
// how long the capacitors take to charge/discharge.
// Let's use the in-line assembler. It's cool!

   __asm
      {
      cli                      ; Disable interrupts.

      mov ah, byte ptr stick   ; Get mask into ah to select the
                               ; joystick to read.
      xor al,al                ; Zero out al, xor is a trick.
      xor cx,cx                ; Same with cx, which we will use as
                               ; a counter.
      mov dx,JOYPORT           ; dx is used by inp and outp.
      out dx,al                ; Write 0s to the port.

discharge:
      in al,dx                 ; Read the data back from the port.
      test al,ah               ; Has the bit in question changed?
      loopne discharge         ; If the stick isn't ready, --cx and
                               ; loop.

      sti                      ; Reenable interrupts.
      xor ax,ax                ; Zero out ax.
      sub ax,cx                ; ax now holds the position of the
                               ; axis switch.

      } // end asm

// The function returns properly because ax has the result.

} // end Joystick

///////////////////////////////////////////////////////////////
```

```
unsigned int Joystick_Bios(unsigned char stick)
{
// BIOS version of joystick read.

union _REGS inregs, outregs;

inregs.h.ah = 0x84; // Joystick function 84h
inregs.x.dx = 0x01; // Read joystick subfunction 1h

// Call DOS.

_int86(0x15,&inregs, &outregs);

// Return the proper value depending on the sent command.

switch(stick)
     {
     case JOYSTICK_1_X:
          {
          return(outregs.x.ax);
          } break;

     case JOYSTICK_1_Y:
          {
          return(outregs.x.bx);
          } break;

     case JOYSTICK_2_X:
          {
          return(outregs.x.cx);
          } break;

     case JOYSTICK_2_Y:
          {
          return(outregs.x.dx);
          } break;

     default:break;

     } // end switch stick

} // end Joystick_Bios


///////////////////////////////////////////////////////////////

unsigned char Buttons_Bios(unsigned char button)
{
// BIOS version of buttons read

union _REGS inregs, outregs;

inregs.h.ah = 0x84; // Joystick function 84h
inregs.x.dx = 0x00; // Read button subfunction 0h

// Call DOS

_int86(0x15,&inregs, &outregs);
```

7

Listing 7.8. continued

```
// Invert buttons, then mask with request.

return( (~outregs.h.al) & button);

} // end Buttons_Bios

//////////////////////////////////////////////////////////////////

void Joystick_Calibrate(int stick)
{
// This function calibrates the joystick by finding the minimum
// and maximum deflections in both the x- and y-axis, then
// stores it in a global data structure for future use.

unsigned int x_new,y_new; // Temporary joystick positions

// Set vars so we can find their actual values.

if (stick==JOY_1_CAL)
   {

   printf("\nCalibrating Joystick #1: ")
   printf("Swirl stick then release and press fire");

   // Set calibrations to impossible values.

   joy_1_max_x=0;
   joy_1_max_y=0;
   joy_1_min_x=10000;
   joy_1_min_y=10000;

   // Now the user should swirl the joystick, let the stick fall
   // neutral, and then press any button.

   while(!Buttons(BUTTON_1_1 ¦ BUTTON_1_2))
        {
        // Get the new values and try to update calibration.
        x_new = Joystick_Bios(JOYSTICK_1_X);
        y_new = Joystick_Bios(JOYSTICK_1_Y);

        // Process the x-axis.

        if (x_new >= joy_1_max_x)
           joy_1_max_x = x_new;

        if (x_new <= joy_1_min_x)
           joy_1_min_x = x_new;

        // Process the y-axis.

        if (y_new >= joy_1_max_y)
           joy_1_max_y = y_new;
```

```
        if (y_new <= joy_1_min_y)
            joy_1_min_y = y_new;

        } // end while

        // The user has let the stick go to center, so that must
        // be the center.

        joy_1_cx = x_new;
        joy_1_cy = y_new;

    } // end calibrate joystick #1
else
if (stick==JOY_2_CAL)
    {
    printf("\nCalibrating Joystick #2: ")
    printf("Swirl stick then release and press fire");

    // Set calibrations to impossible values.

    joy_2_max_x=0;
    joy_2_max_y=0;
    joy_2_min_x=10000;
    joy_2_min_y=10000;

    // Now the user should swirl the joystick, let the stick fall
    // neutral, and then press any button.

    while(!Buttons(BUTTON_2_1 ¦ BUTTON_2_2))
        {
        // Get the new values and try to update calibration.
        x_new = Joystick(JOYSTICK_2_X);
        y_new = Joystick(JOYSTICK_2_Y);

        // Process the x-axis.

        if (x_new >= joy_2_max_x)
            joy_2_max_x = x_new;
        else
        if (x_new <= joy_2_min_x)
            joy_2_min_x = x_new;

        // Process the y-axis.

        if (y_new >= joy_2_max_y)
            joy_2_max_y = y_new;
        else
        if (y_new <= joy_2_min_y)
            joy_2_min_y = y_new;

        } // end while

        // The user has let the stick go to center, so that must
        // be the center.

        joy_2_cx = x_new;
```

7

continues

Listing 7.8. continued

```
            joy_2_cy = y_new;


    } // end calibrate joystick #2

printf("\nCalibration Complete...hit any key to continue.");

getch();

} // end Joystick_Calibrate

/////////////////////////////////////////////////////////////

int Joystick_Available(int stick_num)
{
// Test whether the joystick the user is requesting tested is
// plugged in.

if (stick_num == JOYSTICK_1)
    {
    // Test whether joystick 1 is plugged in by testing the port
    // values. If there's no stick, they're 0,0.

    return(Joystick_Bios(JOYSTICK_1_X)+Joystick_Bios(JOYSTICK_1_Y));

    } // end if joystick 1
else
    {
    // Test whether joystick 2 is plugged in by testing the port
    // values. If there's no stick, they're 0,0.

    return(Joystick_Bios(JOYSTICK_2_X)+Joystick_Bios(JOYSTICK_2_Y));

    } // end else joystick 2

} // end Joystick_Available


/////////////////////////////////////////////////////////////

void main(void) // Test the joystick interface.
{

// Test whether the joy stick is plugged in.

if (!Joystick_Available(JOYSTICK_1))
    {
    printf("\nThere is not a joystick plugged into port #1.");
    return;

    } // end if joystick not installed

// Calibrate the joystick.
```

```
Joystick_Calibrate(JOY_1_CAL);

_clearscreen(_GCLEARSCREEN);

// Let the user fiddle with the joystick.

while(!kbhit())
    {

    _settextposition(2,0);

    printf("Joystick 1 = [%u,%u]    ",
            Joystick_Bios(JOYSTICK_1_X),
            Joystick_Bios(JOYSTICK_1_Y));

    if (Buttons_Bios(BUTTON_1_1))
       printf("\nButton 1 pressed    ");
    else
    if (Buttons_Bios(BUTTON_1_2))
       printf("\nButton 2 pressed    ");
    else
       printf("\nNo Button Pressed   ");
    } // end while

// Let the user know what the calibrations turned out to be.

printf("\nThe calibration data was:");

printf("\nmax x=%u, max y=%u,min x=%u,min y=%u,cx=%u,cy=%u",
       joy_1_max_x,
       joy_1_max_y,
       joy_1_min_x,
       joy_1_min_y,
       joy_1_cx,
       joy_1_cy);

// Later!

} // end main
```

 Building an Executable: To make an executable of the program in Listing 7.8, you can either type it in or use the source on the companion CD. The name of the source is joytst.c. The precompiled executable is named joytst.exe. As before, use the following compile line for Microsoft C:

```
cl -AM -Zi -c  -Fc -Gs -G2 joytst.c
```

7

> After compiling the program in this manner you can link it to the standard libraries and to our previously generated game library, gamelib.lib, with a link line such as:
>
> ```
> link /ST:8192 /CO joytst,,,graphics.lib+gamelib.lib,,
> ```
>
> This creates a final executable named joytst.exe.

At the end of today's lesson we take the functions in joytst.c and build up a joystick library that we can insert into our game library, gamelib.lib (along with the keyboard functions and the mouse functions to follow).

Squeezing the Mouse

The mouse is one of the most user-friendly input devices a person could ask for. You simply "point and click" and, magically, your will is acted out by the computer. However, the mouse is so simple it really doesn't do much. For that reason it has limited use in video games.

The mouse was primarily designed to be used in a window-based graphical interface to help people who were completely computer illiterate by supplementing the command-line interface found on so many computers. I don't think that anyone ever intended the mouse as a video-game input device; although it makes an excellent pointing device, it isn't suited for use in video games (unless, of course, you like moving the mouse around vigorously and getting a workout).

Although some games are perfectly matched for a mouse—strategy games, for example, or pick-and-place games such as chess—I really don't like mice as game-input devices. Nevertheless, we learn how to tame the mouse and program its driver to meet our needs. I wouldn't want to leave out fundamental mouse operation because you may not be able to easily find it elsewhere. Even though mouse operation is published more often than the operation of the joystick, the mouse is still something of a mystery to many.

Let's cover the brief history of mice and the types of mice available for the PC. The mouse was invented by PARC, the Xerox Research Facility in Palo Alto, California (isn't everything good invented in California?). The mouse idea was quickly picked up and implemented by Apple Computer in the late 1970s to early 1980s—and the rest you know.

There are two major methods mice use to interpret motion:

☐ The first method is to use two disks that are perpendicularly mounted within the mouse housing to detect motion, as shown in Figure 7.4.

A small ball held within the mouse housing is then used as the frictional interface and, when moved by the user, rotates the disks within. This disk rotation is measured by light pulses generated from the holes in the disks. The number of pulses per second is converted into distance units, from which the relative motion of the mouse can be computed.

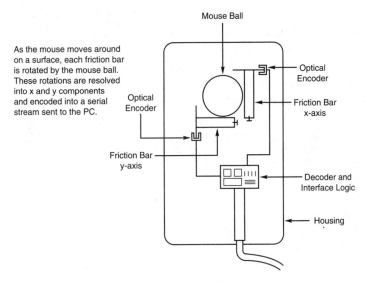

Figure 7.4. *The workings of a mechanical mouse.*

☐ The second way PC mice work is with a photo-optical system that uses a mouse pad grated with a darkened grid pattern. A light-emitting diode (L.E.D.) and a detector are used to compute which direction the mouse is moving, as shown in Figure 7.4. As the mouse moves, the emitter diode's light beam is absorbed and reflected by the pattern on the mouse pad. This information is used to compute the motion vector of the mouse.

Whichever mouse technology is used, the information is collected and built up into a packet and sent from the mouse to the PC as a serial stream. We could write software that

7

breaks down the serial stream and interprets the information—but I'm not into self-inflicted torture, so we use a driver.

Most mice produced today are Microsoft-compatible. (If they aren't, they probably won't be produced tomorrow!) All Microsoft-compatible mice generate serial streams that have the same format and, therefore, can always be read using the Microsoft-compatible mouse driver.

Finding Mouse Position and Status

So how do we, as programmers, obtain the position of the mouse and status of the buttons? We do so by means of the mouse library supported by the mouse driver. We can communicate with the mouse library through interrupt 33h. This interrupt has about 50 or so subfunctions that enable you to do about anything you wish to do to the mouse. However, we're only interested in a few of them. Table 7.5 contains the mouse functions we use.

Table 7.5. Mouse functions supported by interrupt 33h.

Function Number	Function Description
0	Mouse Reset and Status
1	Show Cursor
2	Hide Cursor
3	Get Button Status and Mouse Position
11	Read Mouse Motion Counters
26	Set Mouse Sensitivity

To communicate with the mouse driver we could use the in-line assembler and call the interrupt directly. However, I decided to keep it simple and use the C function _int86(). You can use this function to execute interrupts (software) and to pass and receive parameters in the CPU registers. These registers are accessed by using a UNION structure that holds both the input and output registers. The name of the function I've created, which allows our game programs to interface with the mouse driver, is Squeeze_Mouse(). You call this function with a command that specifies what mouse driver function you want executed. Then, using a simple interface, the function receives and sends back the values of interest. Listing 7.9 contains the Squeeze_Mouse() function, along with #defines it uses.

Listing 7.9. The mouse function.

```c
// D E F I N E S  //////////////////////////////////////////

// Mouse subfunction calls

// Mouse interrupt number
#define MOUSE_INT               0x33

// Reset the mouse.
#define MOUSE_RESET             0x00

// Show the mouse.
#define MOUSE_SHOW              0x01

// Hide the mouse.
#define MOUSE_HIDE              0x02

// Get buttons and position.
#define MOUSE_BUTT_POS          0x03

// Set the sensitivity of the mouse 0-100.
#define MOUSE_SET_SENSITIVITY   0x1A

// Query motion counters to compute relative motion.
#define MOUSE_MOTION_REL        0x0B

// Definitions to make reading buttons easier:
#define MOUSE_LEFT_BUTTON       0x01 // Left button mask
#define MOUSE_RIGHT_BUTTON      0x02 // Right button mask
#define MOUSE_CENTER_BUTTON     0x04 // Center button mask


// F U N C T I O N S //////////////////////////////////////

int Squeeze_Mouse(int command, int *x, int *y,int *buttons)
{
// Mouse interface. We use _int86 instead of the in-line asm.
// (Why? No real reason...)

// What function is the caller requesting?

union _REGS inregs, outregs;

switch(command)
      {

      case MOUSE_RESET:
          {

          inregs.x.ax = 0x00;
           // Subfunction 0: reset
          _int86(MOUSE_INT, &inregs, &outregs);
          *buttons = outregs.x.bx;
           // Return the number of buttons
          return(outregs.x.ax);
```

continues

Listing 7.9. continued

```
                // Return overall success/failure

            } break;

    case MOUSE_SHOW:
            {
            // This function increments the internal show-mouse
            // counter. When it's equal to 0, the mouse is
            // displayed.

            inregs.x.ax = 0x01;
             // Subfunction 1: increment show flag
            _int86(MOUSE_INT, &inregs, &outregs);

            return(1);

            } break;

    case MOUSE_HIDE:
            {
            // This function decrements the internal show-mouse
            // counter. When it's equal to -1, the mouse is
            // hidden.

            inregs.x.ax = 0x02;
             // Subfunction 2: decrement show flag
            _int86(MOUSE_INT, &inregs, &outregs);

            return(1);

            } break;

    case MOUSE_BUTT_POS:
            {
            // This functions gets the buttons and returns the
            // absolute mouse positions in the vars x,y, and
            // buttons.

            inregs.x.ax = 0x03;
             // Subfunction 3: get position and buttons
            _int86(MOUSE_INT, &inregs, &outregs);

            // Extract the info and send it back to the caller
            // by using pointers.
            *x       = outregs.x.cx;
            *y       = outregs.x.dx;
            *buttons = outregs.x.bx;

            return(1);

            } break;

    case MOUSE_MOTION_REL:
            {
```

```
        // This function gets the relative mouse motions from
        // the last call and puts them in the vars x,y.

        inregs.x.ax = 0x03;
         // Subfunction 11: get relative motion
        _int86(MOUSE_INT, &inregs, &outregs);

        // Extract the info and send it back to caller by
        // using pointers.
        *x        = outregs.x.cx;
        *y        = outregs.x.dx;

        return(1);

        } break;

    case MOUSE_SET_SENSITIVITY:
        {
        // This function sets the overall "sensitivity" of
        // the mouse. Each axis can have a sensitivity of
        // from 1-100, so the caller should put 1-100 in both
        // x and y before calling. Also, "buttons" is used to
        // send in the doublespeed value, which also ranges
        // from 1-100.

        inregs.x.bx = *x;
        inregs.x.cx = *y;
        inregs.x.dx = *buttons;

        inregs.x.ax = 0x1A;
         // Subfunction 26: set sensitivity
        _int86(MOUSE_INT, &inregs, &outregs);

        return(1);

        } break;

    default:break;

    } // end switch

} // end Squeeze_Mouse
```

Syntax

The syntax of the function call and its operation are worth describing in detail, so let's take a look.

```
int Squeeze_Mouse(int command, int *x, int *y,int *buttons);
```

where:

- *command* is the function you want issued to the mouse driver. It can be any one of the predefined #defines I've supplied in the code.

7

☐ *x is a pointer to an integer you wish to be used as the x-coordinate of the operation to be performed by the mouse driver. It can either be read or written depending on the mouse driver operation.

☐ *y is a pointer to an integer you wish to be used as the y-coordinate of the operation to be performed by the mouse driver. It can either be read or written, depending on the mouse-driver operation.

☐ *buttons is used to retrieve the status of the mouse buttons, which can then be used in a logical AND operation with one of the #defines to compute which button is down.

As an example of using the Squeeze_Mouse() function, I've created a demo called mousetst.exe, which you can find on the companion CD. This demo puts the PC into a graphics mode and then allows you to draw on the screen by pressing the mouse buttons. Listing 7.10 contains the code.

Listing 7.10. A demonstration of the mouse library. (mousetst.c)

```
// I N C L U D E S /////////////////////////////////////////////

#include <dos.h>
#include <bios.h>
#include <stdio.h>
#include <math.h>
#include <conio.h>
#include <graph.h>

// D E F I N E S /////////////////////////////////////////////

// Mouse subfunction calls

// Mouse interrupt number
#define MOUSE_INT               0x33

// Reset the mouse.
#define MOUSE_RESET             0x00

// Show the mouse.
#define MOUSE_SHOW              0x01

// Hide the mouse.
#define MOUSE_HIDE              0x02

// Get buttons and position.
#define MOUSE_BUTT_POS          0x03

// Set the sensitivity of the mouse 0-100.
#define MOUSE_SET_SENSITIVITY   0x1A
```

```
// Query motion counters to compute relative motion.
#define MOUSE_MOTION_REL        0x0B

// Definitions to make reading buttons easier

#define MOUSE_LEFT_BUTTON       0x01 // Left button mask
#define MOUSE_RIGHT_BUTTON      0x02 // Right button mask
#define MOUSE_CENTER_BUTTON     0x04 // Center button mask


// G L O B A L S ///////////////////////////////////////////


// F U N C T I O N S ///////////////////////////////////////

int Squeeze_Mouse(int command, int *x, int *y,int *buttons)
{
// Mouse interface. We use _int86 instead of the in-line asm.
// (Why? No real reason...)

// What function is the caller requesting?

union _REGS inregs, outregs;

switch(command)
      {

      case MOUSE_RESET:
            {

            inregs.x.ax = 0x00;
             // Subfunction 0: reset
            _int86(MOUSE_INT, &inregs, &outregs);
            *buttons = outregs.x.bx;
             // Return number of buttons
            return(outregs.x.ax);
             // Return overall success/failure

            } break;

      case MOUSE_SHOW:
            {
            // This function increments the internal show-mouse
            // counter. When it's equal to 0, the mouse is
            // displayed.

            inregs.x.ax = 0x01;
             // subfunction 1: increment show flag
            _int86(MOUSE_INT, &inregs, &outregs);

            return(1);

            } break;
```

continues

Listing 7.10. continued

```
case MOUSE_HIDE:
    {
    // This function decrements the internal show-mouse
    // counter. When it's equal to -1, the mouse is
    // hidden.

    inregs.x.ax = 0x02;
     // Subfunction 2: decrement show flag
    _int86(MOUSE_INT, &inregs, &outregs);

    return(1);

    } break;

case MOUSE_BUTT_POS:
    {
    // This function gets the buttons and returns the
    // absolute mouse positions in the vars x,y, and
    // buttons.

    inregs.x.ax = 0x03;
     // Subfunction 3: get position and buttons
    _int86(MOUSE_INT, &inregs, &outregs);

    // Extract the info and send it back to the caller by
    // using pointers.
    *x       = outregs.x.cx;
    *y       = outregs.x.dx;
    *buttons = outregs.x.bx;

    return(1);

    } break;

case MOUSE_MOTION_REL:
    {

    // This function gets the relative mouse motions
    // from the last call and puts them in the vars x,y.

    inregs.x.ax = 0x03;
     // Subfunction 11: get relative motion
    _int86(MOUSE_INT, &inregs, &outregs);

    // Extract the info and send it back to the caller by
    // using pointers.
    *x       = outregs.x.cx;
    *y       = outregs.x.dx;

    return(1);

    } break;
```

```
        case MOUSE_SET_SENSITIVITY:
            {
            // This function sets the overall "sensitivity" of
            // the mouse. Each axis can have a sensitivity of
            // from 1-100, so the caller should put 1-100 in both
            // x and y before calling. Also, "buttons" is used to
            // send in the doublespeed value, which also ranges
            // from 1-100.

            inregs.x.bx = *x;
            inregs.x.cx = *y;
            inregs.x.dx = *buttons;

            inregs.x.ax = 0x1A;
             // Subfunction 26: set sensitivity
            _int86(MOUSE_INT, &inregs, &outregs);

            return(1);

            } break;

        default:break;

        } // end switch

} // end Squeze_Mouse

////////////////////////////////////////////////////////////////

void main(void)
{

int x,y,buttons,num_buttons;
int color=1;

// Put the computer into graphics mode.

_setvideomode(_VRES16COLOR);
// 640x480 in 16 colors; use Microsoft's stuff

// Initialize the mouse.

Squeeze_Mouse(MOUSE_RESET,NULL,NULL,&num_buttons);

// Show the mouse.

Squeeze_Mouse(MOUSE_SHOW,NULL,NULL,NULL);

// Exit the main loop when the user presses a key.

while(!kbhit())
```

7

continues

Listing 7.10. continued

```
    {
    // Display some info.
    _settextposition(2,0);

    Squeeze_Mouse(MOUSE_BUTT_POS,&x,&y,&buttons);

    printf("Mouse x=%d y=%d    ",x,y);
    printf("\nButtons=%d   ",buttons);
    printf("\nColor = %d   ",color);

    // Video easel

    _settextposition(40,0);

    printf("V I D E O   E A S E L - Press any key to exit.");


    if (buttons==1) // Draw
        {
        _setcolor(color);
        _setpixel(x-1,y-2);
        _setpixel(x,y-2);
        _setpixel(x-1,y-1);
        _setpixel(x,y-1);
        } // end if draw on

    if (buttons==2) // Change color
        {
        if (++color>15) color=0;

        // Wait for mouse release.

        while(buttons==2)
            {
            Squeeze_Mouse(MOUSE_BUTT_POS,&x,&y,&buttons);
            } // end while

        } // end if draw on

    } // end while

// Place the computer back into text mode

_setvideomode(_DEFAULTMODE);

} // end main
```

Building an Executable: To make an executable of the program in Listing 7.10, you can either type it in or use the source on the companion CD. The name of the source is mousetst.c. The precompiled executable is named mousetst.exe. As before, use the following compile line for Microsoft C:

```
cl -AM -Zi -c -Fc -Gs -G2 mousetst.c
```

After compiling the program in this manner you can link it to the standard libraries and to our previously generated game library, gamelib.lib, with a link line such as:

```
link /ST:8192 /CO mousetst,,,graphics.lib+gamelib.lib,,
```

This creates a final executable named mousetst.exe.

Analysis

The mouse demo shows you all the important points of using the mouse functions, and their results.

1. The program begins by initializing the mouse.

2. The program then falls into a loop in which a test is continually performed to see whether the buttons are down.

   If the left button is down, the current color is used to draw a pixel on the screen at the current mouse position.

   If the right button is down, the current color is incremented and then reset to 0 if it exceeds 15.

Mouse Sensitivity

That's almost all there is to the mouse functions. However, there's one more small point you should be aware of.

The mouse is a mechanical, or optimechanical, device that moves around on a physical surface. This surface is supposed to represent the surface of the computer screen in a linear, 1:1 fashion. Therefore, if you move the mouse an inch in the real world, the mouse should move two inches on the computer screen, as shown in Figure 7.5.

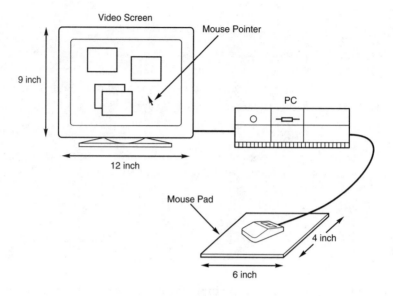

The motion of the mouse must be scaled so the
entire surface of the video screen can be traversed.
In this case, for every 1 inch the mouse moves, the
mouse pointer must move approximately 2 inches.

Figure 7.5. *The relationship between mouse space and visual monitor space.*

Although this would seem ideal, it's somewhat impractical. Imagine what would happen if you had a 40-inch monitor. You'd have to move your mouse around on the floor! We need the ability to scale mouse motion. This is accomplished by setting the sensitivity of the mouse. The sensitivity controls how many *mickeys*, or ratio of units of motion to pixels, to which the mouse is set. The mouse driver enables you to set the sensitivity separately for the x- and y-axes. Currently, when the mouse driver is reset the sensitivity is set for an amount such that the entire video display can be covered by moving the mouse a few inches in both directions.

To change the sensitivity of the mouse, you would send the `Squeeze_Mouse()` function the command `MOUSE_SET_SENSITIVITY`, along with the proper x- and y-axes sensitivities in the appropriate variables. The input to these variables can range from 1–100—and the meaning of the number is somewhat arbitrary, so experiment with it.

Before closing up shop today, we're going to touch upon a topic that's hardly ever mentioned or implemented in today's software: ergonomical algorithms.

Ergonomical Algorithms

Ergonomical algorithms, when applied to input devices, means software algorithms used in a way to somehow make a specific input device more intuitive for the task at hand. For example, an input device's data is usually taken to be literal: what the PC receives is exactly what the user told the input device to do. However, many humans try to accomplish something with an input device that it can't make happen: either the person doesn't have the physical dexterity to operate the device that way or the input device can't respond fast enough. With an ergonomical algorithm, if a player is stuck using a keyboard for a driving game (for instance), the software might have some added code that would filter or enhance the keyboard input to help the player do more what was intended than what was directed.

As another example, a player might be trying to pick an object on the screen but keeps missing, while your game keeps receiving the button clicks. Apparently, the player is trying to tell your game something but is having a hard time doing so. At this point, your software should try to do what it *thinks* the player is trying to accomplish. Perhaps there's an object so small that it's hard to click on. If there are no other objects in the area, chances are the player wanted to click the only object in the area.

Small observations such as the ones illustrated by these two examples can make the input interface much easier to swallow. Many input interfaces write a small amount of code so they can work with any input device. However, if the game was originally designed to work with a specific device, such as a joystick, other input devices are going to be hard to use. Rather them make a terrible interface, try to use more software to "map" the other input devices into the one that the game is best suited for. For instance, a joystick has a linear travel line that, as you move farther in one direction, might turn a ship farther. If a keyboard is used instead of a joystick, there's no way to make this turn with analog input. The player can either turn, or not. Perhaps a solution would be to give the player the ability to add an acceleration factor to the key press: the longer the player holds the key, the farther the turn.

There's nothing worse than a good game with a bad interface and bad interface software, so take your time when designing your input software.

Adding to the Game Library

We've covered all the input devices we need to interface with within our games. We could clump all the functions together into the same module; however, I think it's better to keep the keyboard, joystick, and mouse functions in separate modules. For that reason, we

415

should further qualify our module names. On the companion CD you'll find the following files:

☐ graph7j.c—The C module for the joystick functions

☐ graph7j.h—The header file for the joystick functions

☐ graph7k.c—The C module for the keyboard functions

☐ graph7k.h—The header file for the keyboard functions

☐ graph7m.c—The C module for the mouse functions

☐ graph7m.h—The header file for the mouse functions

To add these to our gamelib.lib game library, compile the modules and add them to gamelib.lib using the library manager. You've done this a few times in the past few days, and today is no different except that there are three different modules. To use the functions in your code, simply include in the proper header file and make sure to link to the game library, gamelib.lib. Everything should be fine.

Summary

Wow, I never thought we would get through this chapter! We covered *so much* material it could have filled a whole book. We learned about the input devices used in video games: the keyboard, mouse, and joystick. We wrote libraries to communicate with all these devices, and even learned how they worked internally. Finally, we had a little talk about good interfacing and bad, and I hope that you paid attention because that portion of today's material was probably the most important of all.

Q&A

Q Name five PC input devices.

A The keyboard, the mouse, the joystick, the light pen, and the graphics tablet.

Q Can joypads (found on the Nintendo and Sega game systems) be plugged into the PC?

A No. They may have the same DB-9 female connector, but they are digital in nature and not analog. However, there *are* manufactures that produce joypads for use on the PC. These pads look and feel similar to the ones found on console game machines.

Q How many joysticks can the PC accommodate?

A The PC can have only two joysticks plugged in at once, but this condition holds only when using IBM-compatible joysticks with an IBM-compatible joyport. There's no reason why other manufacturers couldn't make multijoystick cards. However, the market for such cards would be quite small. This is why we don't see such products.

Q I have a non-Microsoft mouse, but it's supposed to be compatible. Should I use the driver that comes with the mouse or the one supplied with Microsoft?

A Try the driver supplied with the mouse first. If it works well with the software we've written, stick with it; otherwise, try the Microsoft mouse driver.

Q What's a mickey?

A A mickey is a unit of measure, used within the mouse driver to set the sensitivity of the mouse motion.

Q I've seen flying mice before. What are they?

A Maybe you should go in for drug testing. Just kidding! Flying mice are multidimensional input devices with special drivers. They enable the player to input coordinates in 3-D, with some flying mice allowing for full, 6-D position systems. By the way, the other three dimensions in 6-D are yaw, pitch, and roll.

Q How can I take over the keyboard so the player can press Ctrl-Break or Ctrl-Alt-Delete?

A Taking over the keyboard is simple: you do it by linking into the keyboard interrupt and not allowing the operating system access to the keypresses. We learn to do this on Day 11, when we talk about interrupts and timing.

Workshop

The Workshop section presents quiz questions to help you cement your new knowledge and exercises to give you experience using what you've learned. Try to understand the questions and exercises before moving on to the next lesson. The answers are in Appendix B.

Quiz

1. What is the port address of the joystick port?

2. What are the addresses 417h and 418h used for?

3. How is the mouse interrupt used?

4. What are the differences between "control keys" and "qwerty keys"?

5. How do joysticks work?

6. Is the data stream a mouse sends serial or parallel?

7. Why is joystick calibration necessary?

8. How can the existence of joysticks be tested?

9. What is a scan code?

10. *Extra Credit*: Given a resistance R, a capacitance C, and a voltage applied to R and C in series, what is the charging time of C? (*Hint*: there's an exponential in the answer somewhere.)

Exercises

1. Write a program that prints out the bit pattern in memory locations 417h and 418h. Use the output to figure out which bit represents what part of the shift state.

2. Write another version of the Video-Easel program that uses the keyboard instead of the mouse; however, make a pointer that resembles the mouse pointer using sprites.

3. Experiment with the mouse sensitivity until one inch on your mouse pad is equivalent to one inch on your computer screen.

4. See if you can figure out a technique to detect whether a joystick(s) is present that differs from the technique we implemented earlier today (`Joystick_Available()`).

M T W **1** F S

1
2
3
4
5
6
7

We've covered a tremendous amount of ground this week! Let's revisit the highlights of each day's lessons, and then take a look at our game library thus far.

Day 1

On this day, we were introduced to PC-based games and video games in general. We learned where the ideas for games come from and the different components that go into a game. Finally, we learned about the unbelievable complexity of writing a complete, marketable PC-based video game.

Day 2

During Day 2 we jumped right into the fire and took a look at a complete game called Mech War. We looked at the different elements that went into the game and, for the first time, saw the structure of a PC-based video game at the software level. Also, I told you of a contest that's going to be held, with the person who creates the best version of Mech War winning $100.00. This contest will be held twice a year.

Day 3

The VGA card and its inner workings were the topic of discussion on the third day. Amazingly, we learned that the VGA isn't so bad when it's programmed in mode 13h (the 320×200 pixel, 256-color mode so popular with video game programmers). We learned to do just about everything with the VGA—from plotting pixels and changing colors to blitting images at high speed.

Day 4

This is where we starting locking in on video game-related graphics functions and learned about the abstract concept of a sprite (the main animation unit in a video game). We learned how to create sprites, animate them, and test them for collision. Furthermore, we learned about PCX files and how to extract them from disk.

Day 5

This was a tough day! We jumped into the fairly mathematical realm of polygon-based graphics and rendering. However, we came out unscathed—and learned how to draw lines and polygons, as well as how to clip them. We also learned how to perform mathematical operations on polygons, such as translation, scaling, and rotation. We topped the day off with some fun demos and a skeleton asteroids game.

Day 6

This is where we started getting serious about performance and learning the real methods and techniques used by video-game gurus to create realistic animation and graphics. We covered sprite scaling, animation synchronization, scrolling, and many other fascinating topics that will help put the edge on your games.

Day 7

This day might have seemed oddball; however, we learned quickly just how much we need to know about input devices! We covered all the important input devices used in PC-based video games, such as the mouse, keyboard, and joystick. (There's still more to learn about the keyboard!)

The Game Library

Throughout the past week we've been creating modules that contain all the important functions and structures we use to write PC-based video games. Let's take a look at what we have thus far. Here, I've dumped the contents of my library file (which should have the same things in it that yours does now) for your review:

Listing WR.1. What your library file contents should look like at this point.

```
_Behind_Sprite....graph4          _Behind_Sprite_DB..graph6
_Bline...........graph5           _Blit_Char.......graph3
_Blit_Char_DB.....graph6          _Blit_String......graph3
_Blit_String_DB...graph6          _buffer_height....graph6
_buffer_size......graph6          _Buttons.........graph7j
_Buttons_Bios.....graph7j         _Clip_Line.......graph5
_Create_Double_Buffer..graph6     _Create_Tables....graph5
_Delay...........graph3           _Delete_Double_Buffer..graph6
_Disolve.........graph6           _double_buffer....graph6
_Draw_Boundary....graph5          _Draw_Polygon.....graph5
_Draw_Polygon_Clip..graph5        _Draw_Sprite......graph4
_Draw_Sprite_DB...graph6          _Erase_Sprite.....graph4
_Erase_Sprite_DB..graph6          _Fade_Lights......graph6
_Fill_Double_Buffer..graph6       _Get_Ascii_Key....graph7k
_Get_Control_Keys..graph7k        _Get_Palette_Register..graph3
_Get_Pixel.......graph4           _Get_Scan_Code....graph7k
_H_Line..........graph3           _H_Line_Fast......graph3
_Joystick........graph7j          _Joystick_Available..graph7j
_Joystick_Bios....graph7j         _Joystick_Calibrate..graph7j
_Melt............graph6           _PCX_Delete.......graph4
_PCX_Grab_Bitmap..graph4          _PCX_Init........graph4
_PCX_Load........graph4           _PCX_Show_Buffer..graph4
_Plot_Pixel......graph3           _Plot_Pixel_Fast..graph3
_Plot_Pixel_Fast_DB..graph6       _poly_clip_max_x..graph5
_poly_clip_max_y..graph5          _poly_clip_min_x..graph5
_poly_clip_min_y..graph5          _rom_char_set.....graph3
_Rotate_Polygon...graph5          _Scale_Polygon....graph5
_Scale_Sprite.....graph6          _Set_Palette_Register..graph3
_Set_Video_Mode...graph3          _Sheer...........graph6
_Show_Double_Buffer..graph6       _Sprite_Collide...graph4
_Sprite_Delete....graph4          _sprite_height....graph4
```

continues

Week 1 in Review

Listing WR.1. continued

```
_Sprite_Init......graph4        _sprite_width.....graph4
_Squeeze_Mouse....graph7m       _Translate_Polygon..graph5
_video_buffer.....graph3        _video_buffer_w...graph3
_V_Line...........graph3        _Wait_For_Vsync...graph6


graph3          Offset: 00000010H  Code and data size: 1485H
  _Blit_Char      _Blit_String     _Delay             _Get_Palette_Register
  _H_Line         _H_Line_Fast     _Plot_Pixel        _Plot_Pixel_Fast
  _rom_char_set   _Set_Palette_Register               _Set_Video_Mode
  _video_buffer   _video_buffer_w  _V_Line


graph4          Offset: 00001b20H  Code and data size: 1caeH
  _Behind_Sprite  _Draw_Sprite     _Erase_Sprite      _Get_Pixel
  _PCX_Delete     _PCX_Grab_Bitmap _PCX_Init          _PCX_Load
  _PCX_Show_Buffer _Sprite_Collide _Sprite_Delete     _sprite_height
  _Sprite_Init    _sprite_width


graph5          Offset: 0000a1e0H  Code and data size: 244fH
  _Bline          _Clip_Line       _Create_Tables     _Draw_Boundary
  _Draw_Polygon   _Draw_Polygon_Clip                  _poly_clip_max_x
  _poly_clip_max_y _poly_clip_min_x _poly_clip_min_y  _Rotate_Polygon
  _Scale_Polygon  _Translate_Polygon


graph6          Offset: 00007330H  Code and data size: 2257H
  _Behind_Sprite_DB                 _Blit_Char_DB      _Blit_String_DB
  _buffer_height  _buffer_size      _Create_Double_Buffer
  _Delete_Double_Buffer             _Disolve           _double_buffer
  _Draw_Sprite_DB _Erase_Sprite_DB  _Fade_Lights       _Fill_Double_Buffer
  _Melt           _Plot_Pixel_Fast_DB                  _Scale_Sprite
  _Sheer          _Show_Double_Buffer                  _Wait_For_Vsync


graph7k         Offset: 000040e0H  Code and data size: a87H
  _Get_Ascii_Key  _Get_Control_Keys                   _Get_Scan_Code


graph7m         Offset: 00004e50H  Code and data size: b2bH
  _Squeeze_Mouse


graph7j         Offset: 00005c50H  Code and data size: ff2H
  _Buttons        _Buttons_Bios    _Joystick          _Joystick Available
  _Joystick_Bios  _Joystick_Calibrate
```

As you can see, we've written quite a few functions. I would say that by the time we're done with this book you'll have a formidible game library!

During Week Two, we take a high-tech roller coaster ride. You learn all the advanced techniques needed to make a professional-quality game. You learn all the dark secrets of video-game design and of the PC. The highlights of the week are artificial intelligence, sound, multitasking, optimization theory, and physics modeling.

Where You're Going

Here's the layout of this week. On Day 8, "Warp Speed, Anyone?," you learn how to make your games faster and how to look for possible optimizations in your code. On Day 9, "Making the PC Rock!," you learn how to play music and sound FX on the PC using a Sound Blaster or compatible card. During Day 10, "Playing Dr. Franken-stein," you learn the basics of artificial intelligence, synthetic intelligence, state machines, and fuzzy logic to bring the objects in your game to life! On Day 11, "Out of Time," you learn about *Back to the Future*-type time travel: stopping, speeding, and slowing time on the PC. During Day 12, "Laying out the Universe," you learn the different techniques and data structures used to represent the game grid in a video game. Day 13, "The Physics of Games," teaches you to create simple physical models of the objects in your games to synthesize acceleration, friction, and collisions. Finally, on Day 14, "Tools of the Trade," you learn all the tools that video game programmers wear on their belts to make the job easier.

Warp Speed, Anyone?

If there's any one piece of software that must use the PC's capabilities to the fullest and run as fast as possible, it's a video game. In the past days we've learned much about the PC's graphics abilities and how to evoke them. However, we haven't spent much time discussing *optimization theory*. This is the topic of today's lesson. We want to learn how to get the most out of each PC. This means learning how to optimize specific areas to gain speed. Although your programming style in general dictates how fast and efficient your code is, knowing a few tricks definitely helps you in coding video games. Here's what we cover today:

- [ ] Where optimization begins
- [ ] Optimizing compilers in regard to 16- and 32-bit code
- [ ] Memory models
- [ ] Stacking up data
- [ ] Global variables
- [ ] Pointer and structure aliasing
- [ ] Unrolling the loop
- [ ] The internal CPU registers
- [ ] Looking up data
- [ ] Multiplication by shifting
- [ ] Fixed-point math
- [ ] Using assembly language and the in-line assembler
- [ ] DOS extenders
- [ ] Adding to the game library

Optimization Begins With You

The word *optimize* can mean many different things. We can talk about optimizing space, speed development time, and so on—but the kind of optimization we care about most here is speed! Space is important; however, I'd rather have a lightning-fast game that requires two megabytes than a slow game that runs with one megabyte.

Optimization and good coding go hand in hand. The ability to write fast code develops through years of...trying to write fast code. (You could have 20 years of programming experience and still not know how to write fast code!) However, the information in the following pages are some basic guidelines to get you started on a path of optimization.

Video games are the most demanding application you can run on a PC, and you must write them in ways that may seem improper, illogical, or unethical from the standard practices you have learned. The kinds of optimizations we learn in this chapter are *local optimizations*. This means that a program could be analyzed by any person, piece by piece, and certain obvious optimizations made. Such local optimizations aren't related to many of the other factors of the program.

On the other hand, there are *global optimizations* that involve the general architecture of the program itself—and which only creativity and imagination can optimize. Global optimizations have to do with the whole program. If you wanted to change one thing, you might have to alter 20–50 different interrelated variables or functions. In any case, global optimizations are up to you. However, global optimizing is based on local optimizing, which can give you good results if you understand and know where to apply it.

As an example of how optimized a program can be, let me tell you a little story. In college we had to write a encryption program that would encrypt and decrypt an ASCII file. Each student had to write his or her own program. Most of the students turned in programs that were 2,000–5,000 lines long. This was too much for such a simple program. My program was about 500 lines and used an encryption algorithm I invented (which was very cool, but that's another story). The most interesting program was written by a friend of mine who did the program in a single page! Admittedly, there were about five people on earth who could have understood it, and it was terribly documented. However, it was one of the most clever programs I'd ever seen. He received a C because the program was so messy and complex, but the moral of the story is this: people think that something is impossible until someone does it. No one thought he could mash it into a single page. (I guess that's why he writes video games in his mansion in Hawaii and works three months a year now.)

Game Law: A program can always be made faster...always!

Optimizing Compilers: 16- and 32-Bit Code

Because we're writing games using the C language for the most part, we must talk about optimizing compilers and the difference between 16- and 32-bit code.

First, many compilers (such as Microsoft's C/C++ compiler) are *optimizing compilers*. This means that the compiler itself tries to optimize your code on a local basis. For example, it may see that you're doing something like this:

```
var_3 = var_1+var_2;

... more lines of code

var_3 = var_1+var_2;
```

If the compiler can ascertain that the value of var_1 and var_2 doesn't change, there's no reason to add them again and store the result in var_3. The compiler might create a temporary variable on the stack that can store the precomputed result of var_1 + var_2 and use that for the second assignment, such as:

```
var_3 = var_1 + var_2;
 // The compiler assigns this to a local variable called sum_1.

... more lines of code

 // var_3 = var_1 + var_2; this line is exchanged for the next
 // line, which is faster.

var_3 = sum_1;
```

The compiler can make one further optimization here: if the value of var_3 is not altered by the time of the next assignment to it, and the value of var_1 and var_2 have not been changed, there's no reason to even make the assignment. Therefore, the final version of the code may look like this:

```
var_3 = var_1 + var_2;

.... more lines of code
```

In general, optimizations like this are fine and the compiler does a good job. However, we can't rely on the compiler optimizing our code for us; it can only do so much. Moreover, if we tell it to do aggressive optimization, the compiler is likely to corrupt any but the simplest code.

In conclusion, using the optimization abilities of the C/C++ compiler is fine, but keep the optimization setting low and non-aggressive.

Warning: Avoid using aggressive compiler optimization in software as complex as a video game. It may introduce impossible-to-find bugs.

Now let's talk about 16- and 32-bit object code. Most C\C++ compilers that produce DOS executables produce only 16-bit code. This is really too bad, because most games

are now run on a 386/486/586, and 32-bit code (or at least the use of the 32-bit registers) would speed the execution of many video games by 50–100 percent. For example, when a 16-bit compiler adds two LONGs it must break the LONG into two words and do two separate additions: one for the lower 16 bits of the LONG and one for the upper 16 bits of the LONG. Listing 8.1 is an assembly language dump of just such an addition.

Listing 8.1. A dump of a .COD file showing the addition of two LONGs.

```
; File addl.c
;
; #include <math.h>
; #include <stdio.h>
;
;
;
; void main(void)
; {
; Line 8
                        _main:
*** 000000  c8 00 00 00    enter  OFFSET L00271,OFFSET 0
    *** 000004    56         push si
    *** 000005    57         push di
; x = fffa
; y = fff6
; z = fff2
;
; long x,y,z;
; Line 10
;
; // Add the longs and see what assembly language is generated.
;
; z = x+y;
; Line 14
    *** 000006    8b 46 fa   mov  ax,WORD PTR -6[bp]
    *** 000009    8b 56 fc   mov  dx,WORD PTR -4[bp]
    *** 00000c    03 46 f6   add  ax,WORD PTR -10[bp]
    *** 00000f    13 56 f8   adc  dx,WORD PTR -8[bp]
    *** 000012    89 46 f2   mov  WORD PTR -14[bp],ax
    *** 000015    89 56 f4   mov  WORD PTR -12[bp],dx
;
; } // end main
; Line 16
; Line 16
                        L00267:
    *** 000018    5f         pop  di
    *** 000019    5e         pop  si
    *** 00001a    c9         leave
    *** 00001b    cb         ret  OFFSET 0
Local Size: 14
; Line 0
```

As you can see at line 14 of the dump in Listing 8.1, there are two additions and four moves necessary to add two 32-bit LONGs together. If the compiler generated full 32-bit code, we'd see something like this:

```
mov   eax,DWORD PTR -6[bp]
add   eax,DWORD PTR -10[bp]
mov   DWORD PTR -14[bp],eax
```

The 32-bit addition uses half as many instructions and is (almost) twice as fast. What this means is that it would be nice to have a 32-bit compiler along with a 32-bit operating system. This is a bit of a problem for DOS, and later today we talk about a solution called DOS extenders, which allow DOS programs to run in 32-bit mode and memory beyond the 640K barrier. However, the lesson to learn here is that the PC works best with 16-bit data when it's in 16-bit mode, so try to use integers where possible instead of LONGs or FLOATs.

Memory Models

The next area we can squeeze some performance out of is *memory models*. As you may know, the PC has a segmented architecture. (Actually, the PC doesn't, but the CPU does.) All of Intel's early processors used in the PC had segmented architecture. This means that data and code are segmented by hardware into different regions of memory. This was a good idea, and still is. However, the problem is that the segment sizes for the PC were designed in the late 1970s and early 1980s, and were only 64K long. Back then it seemed more than enough, but today it's hardly enough to hold a sound file!

This was a hardware flaw and the number-one problem for the PC in the past, present, and maybe even the future. Although the new 386/486/586 processors can operate in flat memory mode (that is, without segments), there are so many DOS applications that rely on this hardware quirk that it's hard to shake.

How does this relate to us as far as optimization is concerned? Well, there are many areas in which segments affect us, and we must try to resolve how we can use the PC in 16-bit mode, with its segmented architecture, to write games that are impacted as little as possible by segmentation.

I want to direct your attention to a few important areas in which segments and memory models come into play. The overall best memory model to use is the MEDIUM memory model. This allows multiple code segments and a single data segment. Our programs will be so big that we can't avoid multiple code segments. However, we can get around needing more than one data segment. The performance hit we take for having multiple code segments is that jumps to functions must be either FAR or full, 32-bit addresses composed of a segment and an offset. If there was only one segment, all jumps can be NEAR (that is, composed of only an offset).

This is not a killer as a couple more pushes and pops per function call is not going to hurt too much. (Besides, it's something we can't avoid.) Having a single data segment is a must, and it's something we can work around if we need more data. Most of the time a program is going to have more than 64K of data; in a video game there's definitely more than 64K. This means we have to access data in the FAR heap no matter what. If we were to use the LARGE memory model, which has multiple data segments, during variable loads, there could be possible segment register updates slowing the access to data. On the other hand, if we use the MEDIUM memory model with one data segment, we know two things:

- [ ] All global variables are in the same segment.
- [ ] The DS register always is pointing to the data segment.

This allows us to write assembler functions that can access the variables in a C program much easier than if they were in multiple segments. This is absolutely necessary for efficient, mixed-language programming (using C and assembly language): there must be a common data segment pointed to by DS.

As we're stuck with using the MEDIUM memory model, we know that if we want large chunks of data we have to allocate them in the FAR heap and access them with a FAR pointer. For instance, if you wanted to allocate 10 chunks of 40K each, you could do the following:

```
int far *chunks[10];

for (t=0; \t<10; t++)
    chunks[t] = malloc(40*1024);
```

This fragment allocates 400K from the FAR heap, much more than you could access in the NEAR local data segment. The only setback to this scheme is that all accesses to chunks[] is done with FAR pointers, which is slower.

This brings us to a possible insight into optimization. If we're going to create frequently accessed data structures, we should try to fit them into the NEAR data segment because access of the data is slower if it's in a FAR segment. For example, if an array had important values that were needed 10,000 times per game cycle, it would be wise to fit this array into the local NEAR data segment with the following simple line:

```
int table[10000];
```

Granted, it may not fit—but you should design your data structures and algorithms knowing that the NEAR data segment is precious for time-critical data access. Of course, if you can fit your whole program and data into a single, 64K segment, that's great. You could use the SMALL, COMPACT, or TINY models in that case.

Stacking Up Data

The next optimization technique has to do with the usage of the stack and parameter passing. Passing parameters on the stack is not free. When parameters are passed on the stack there are one to two pushes and one to two pops per parameter, depending on parameter type. Each push and pop takes time, and therefore slows down the execution of the code. As an example, take a look at the graphics function we wrote a few days ago, Plot_Pixel_Fast(), shown in Listing 8.2.

Listing 8.2. The pixel-plotting function revisited.

```
void Plot_Pixel_Fast(int x,int y,unsigned char color)
{

// This function plots the pixel in the desired color a little
// quicker using binary shifting to accomplish the
// multiplications.

// Use the fact that 320*y = 256*y + 64*y = y<<8 + y<<6.

double_buffer[((y<<8) + (y<<6)) + x] = color;

} // end Plot_Pixel_Fast
```

You may not think at first that there's much here to optimize. On the contrary: lurking within this function is a good optimization. The function takes three parameters that are each 16 bits wide when pushed. (The unsigned char is extended into 16 bits when pushed.) There are therefore three pushes and three pops, for a total of six stack accesses, just to get the variables into and out of the function. This is fine if the function is 1,000 lines long and the overhead of parameter passing is insignificant. In this case, however, parameter passing could possibly take longer than the access to the double buffer! Parameter passing is, at the least, 10-20 percent of the time spent in the function.

Passing parameters with this big a performance hit doesn't cut it; there has to be a better way to do things. There is. We can always use global variables instead of parameters. True, it could be dangerous—but video games are serious business and my middle name is danger, so let's check it out.

Global Variables

Global variables are, by definition, supposed to be global, which means they're values that must be accessed by many functions and are (to put it metaphorically) in the public domain. In a video game we try to get high performance, and to do this we sometimes may have to use more global variables than normally necessary (especially for functions that are called by the graphics engine hundreds or thousands of times per game cycle). As we saw in Listing 8.2, the Plot_Pixel_Fast() function was spending a relatively long time just passing parameters back and forth to the function.

Imagine, if you will, having the plotting function called 50,000 times. There would be 300,000 pushes and pops! It really adds up, doesn't it? What if we were to use global variables instead of pushing parameters? For example, we could define a global plotting position and color in the following manner:

```
int g_x,g_y;            // Global x,y pixel position
unsigned char g_color;  // Global pixel color
```

With this definition, pixels could be plotted without passing parameters. Furthermore, many times the same color is used for hundreds of pixels. Once the global pixel color is set, it doesn't have to be changed again unless the color had to change. The only drawback to using globals is that the caller must set the globals before the call, which can be as bad as the initial pushing onto the stack if variables were passed. Despite that, in the best case globals can be almost transparent.

If we modify our pixel-plotting function to use globals instead of passed parameters, it would look like Listing 8.3.

Listing 8.3. A pixel plotter that uses global variables.

```
void Plot_Pixel_Global(void)
{

// This function plots the pixel in the desired color a little
// quicker using binary shifting to accomplish the
// multiplications.

// Use the fact that 320*y = 256*y + 64*y = y<<8 + y<<6.

double_buffer[((g_y<<8) + (g_y<<6)) + g_x] = g_color;

} // end Plot_Pixel_Fast
```

As a second performance bonus, using global variables in general can be faster than variables on the stack. This is because of the way the compiler works. Accessing stack variables, which is what local function variables are, can be slower than accessing global variables—which can make a difference in the body of the called function that uses the variable for calculations.

As a rule, use globals to enhance performance in areas in which parameter passing takes a considerable amount of the overall execution time of a function. Of course, the function should be one that's called many times so that this waste of time becomes visible in the program execution. For example, if a function is called once in a program and has 100 variables passed to it, who cares? It's not worth making the variables global because the function is called only once.

Pointer and Structure Aliasing

As John Conner said to the Terminator, "Are we learning yet?" I hope you're starting to get the hang of this stuff. It's not terribly hard; you just have to always keep these little tips on hand as you code. The next topic is *aliasing*, which is a means of representing or accessing one variable with another name.

Many times in a program you want to access a field of a data structure or dereference a pointer. In either case, the action isn't free. Every time you access a data structure or dereference a pointer, the compiler has to write a few instructions to access the final data. The problem with this is that it's a waste of time. For example, assume we had the following data structures:

```
typedef struct point_typ
    {
    int x,y;
    } point, *point_ptr;

typedef struct triangle_typ
    {
    point p1,p2,p3;
    int color;
    } triangle, *triangle_ptr;
```

Now let's create a pointer to a triangle, like this:

```
triangle_ptr t1;

t1 = (triangle_ptr)malloc(sizeof(triangle));
```

We could access the x and y components of the triangle with the following code:

```
a = t1->p1.x;
b = t1->p1.y;
```

If we analyze this situation, we see that it's unavoidable if we want to access the x and y components of a field. However, once we *have* accessed this data there's no reason to keep doing it over and over. So here's the optimization: if you access complex data structures that are read-only, and you use the data in a comparison or in the body of a loop, assign the value to a temporary variable and use the temporary variable as an alias to the real data. As an example, take a look at the following fragment:

8

```
for (index=0; index<t1->p1.x; index++)
    {
    if (t1->p2.y>10)
        printf("\nextrema found at %d", index);
    } // end for
```

This code doesn't do much except flag when a value in the structure is greater than 10. However, it does access the structure and do a lot of pointer and structure dereferencing. If the value in t1->p1.x is large, the code fragment could do hundreds of complex pointer calculations—which would kill the performance of the simple test. Let's see if we can change this situation around by means of aliasing:

```
int count, threshold; // Temporary alias variables

// Alias the data.

count = t1->p1.x;
threshold = t1->p2.y;

// Now use the aliases in the code instead of the
// real variables.

for (index=0; index<counrt index++)
    {
    if (threshold>10)
        printf("\nextrema found at %d", index);
    } // end for
```

Not only is the new code fragment faster, it's easier to understand! In general, you should alias variables that are accessed more than twice and that are of complex types, meaning they must be dereferenced by pointers and so on. However, don't alias a variable that is changed in the code unless you store the result back into the original storage place.

Unrolling the Loop

This type of optimization is an old classic from the days of the 6502 processor and when the Atari 2600 reigned supreme. The days of the 6502, and maybe even those of the Atari, are gone forever, but the legacy of techniques learned from programming 8-bit games lives on.

Much of what's done in a computer program is the execution of loops. These loops may execute a few times to millions of times per game cycle. This brings an interesting optimization possibility to light. Let's use a typical loop structure for our discussion:

```
// Sum up the elements of an array.

for (index=0; index<100; index++)
    {
    sum=sum+data[index];
    } // end for index
```

435

The code above seems harmless enough. However, lurking in it is a cycle eater. You see, we must sometimes take a step back and look at how the compiler will actually compile this code. The body of the loop is unimportant; it's the loop itself we need to look at.

To implement a loop:

1. The code must first load the initial value into the variable index.

2. The code then must make a comparison.

3. Finally, the code increments the variable index at the end of each iteration.

4. At the end of each iteration there's a jump back to the top of the loop body for the next cycle.

When the loop is complete, the code falls out of the loop to the next instruction in the instruction stream.

The initialization of the index variable and the incrementing of the variable isn't too bad, but the comparison of the loop variable and the jump are wasting our time! The answer is to *unroll the loop*, or undo it. I know this seems weird: the whole reason the loop structure was created was to automate repetitive tasks. However, when performance is necessary we have to do things that may seem to go against the grain.

As an example, let's take another look at the example above. That code executes the loop comparison `index<100` and the increment instruction `index++` 100 times. These two processes take almost as much time as the code in the body of the loop that does the work! We can decrease the number of comparisons and the number of jumps by unrolling the loop a bit. Take a look:

```
// Sum up the elements of an array with unrolling.

for (index=0; index<100; index+=10;)
    {
    sum=sum+data[index];
    sum=sum+data[index+1];
    sum=sum+data[index+2];
    sum=sum+data[index+3];
    sum=sum+data[index+4];
    sum=sum+data[index+5];
    sum=sum+data[index+6];
    sum=sum+data[index+7];
    sum=sum+data[index+8];
    sum=sum+data[index+9];
    } // end for index
```

The results of this loop are the same as the previous, unrolled loop. However, this loop executes much faster. Table 8.1 displays the number of operations of each technique so we can see the difference.

Table 8.1. The difference between a standard loop and an unrolled loop.

	Assignments	Comparisons	Index additions	Jumps
Standard loop	1	100	100	99
Unrolled Loop	1	10	10	9

As you can clearly see, the unrolled loop beats out the standard loop in three out of four areas—clearly an improvement, but there's a price to pay for this performance: code size. If you unroll all your loops, you'll surely create thousands of extra lines of code. Therefore, as a rule of thumb, you should unroll each loop four to eight times, and that's it. Unrolling each loop four to eight times isn't going to do much more than add a few more statements, but the performance will go up markedly.

Using loop unrolling to speed up your programs is a quick and easy way to extract performance from time-dependent code. (I've actually unrolled loops 16,000 times in old 6502 games!)

The Internal CPU Registers

If you know anything about the PC's CPU, you know it has a set of internal registers that are used to process programs. These registers include the data registers, segment registers, flag registers, instruction pointer, and so on. The processor works only with these registers, so all C programs you write are compiled into assembly language that use these registers (and whatever memory is required to perform the task you've written your program to accomplish).

Because these registers are internal to the processor, they can be accessed much faster than external memory (RAM). With the advent of internal and external caches today, this difference is becoming less noticeable. However, today's internal registers are still faster than pure external memory.

Having this piece of knowledge, should we make all our variables use registers? Well, that would be nice. However, the 80xxx family only has about a dozen registers that we can use for data, so that isn't going to work. We can only use registers in specific places in our C code.

The question is, how can we tell the C compiler to use a register for a variable? The answer is to use the REGISTER keyword to define the variable. For example, if you wanted to define an integer named fast_var using a register, you would do the following:

```
register fast_var;
```

This informs the compiler that you'd like `fast_var` to be a register. However, it's only a request. The compiler might not be able to accommodate you.

Warning: Some compilers may produce a bug by allowing you to use a register variable, so if you have a function that doesn't work, take out all register variables in it and see if that helps.

Personally, I think using registers is tricky and might put constraints on the code further down that drown out any speed gained by the use of the register variable in the first place. Nevertheless, register variables can be quite handy and are good optimizations in some cases.

Note: Microsoft compilers use the `SI` and `DI` registers for register variables.

Looking Up Data

This is a hot area, and one I feel can be used to create video games that are unbelievably fast. Look-up tables are nothing new; they're basically tables containing precomputed values that are to be used during run time. These precomputed values are the same for every run of the software and are complex to compute; therefore, there's no need to compute them during run time of the program if they can be computed and stored in a table during the initialization part of a program.

For instance, a classic look-up table is a sine/cosine table. As you know, computing trigonometric functions on the PC is slow, so what typically is done is to create a table that has 360 entries, where each entry has the sine or cosine stored in it. Once this table is built, a program that needs the sine or cosine of an angle can access the *i*th element instead of doing the calculation.

The only drawback to this technique is that it can consume a great deal of memory if the tables are large. However, this kind of concern is becoming less important when the average PC today has a 386SX with two megabytes of RAM.

Look-up tables can be used for anything that can be precomputed and takes up a lot of time to compute. The idea of the look-up table is that once it has been computed, it never has to be computed again. For instance, if you've ever played Wolfenstein 3-D by ID Software, you've seen look-up tables being created and didn't even know it. When you

resize the screen in Wolfenstein 3-D, calculations are done to compute scaling tables and other tables for the new screen size. This process takes a couple of seconds, but once done, the game can continue at lightning speed. If look-up tables weren't used in games, they wouldn't be one-tenth as fast as they are today!

Game Law: Precompute everything you can and put it in a table.

As an example of look-up tables, let's write a set of functions that use the standard sine and cosine to draw 1,000 circles, and another set of functions that use a look-up table to draw 1,000 circles and compare their speeds. The name of the program is lookup.c. Listing 8.4 contains the source code. (You can find an executable of it on the companion CD.)

Listing 8.4. Drawing circles with and without look-up tables (lookup.c).

```
// I N C L U D E S ///////////////////////////////////////////

#include <io.h>
#include <conio.h>
#include <stdio.h>
#include <stdlib.h>
#include <dos.h>
#include <bios.h>
#include <fcntl.h>
#include <memory.h>
#include <malloc.h>
#include <math.h>
#include <string.h>

#include "graph3.h"   // Include our graphics stuff.
#include "graph4.h"

// D E F I N E S ///////////////////////////////////////////

#define NUM_CIRCLES 1000
#define FULL_CIRCLE 360

// G L O B A L S ///////////////////////////////////////////

float sin_table[360], cos_table[360];

// M A I N ///////////////////////////////////////////////

void main(void)
{

int index,x,y,xo,yo,radius,ang;
```

Listing 8.4. continued

```
// Create look-up tables

for (index=0; index<FULL_CIRCLE; index++)
    {

    sin_table[index]= sin(index*3.14159/180);
    cos_table[index] = cos(index*3.14159/180);

    } // end for index

// Set the video mode to the 320x200, 256-color mode.

Set_Video_Mode(VGA256);

printf("\nHit any key to draw circles with")
printf("internal sine and cosine.");
getch();

// Draw circles using the built-in sine and cosine.

for (index=0; index<NUM_CIRCLES; index++)
    {

    // Get a random circle.

    radius = rand()%50;
    xo     = rand()%320;
    yo     = rand()%200;

    for (ang=0; ang<360; ang++)
        {
        x = xo + cos(ang*3.14159/180)*radius;
        y = yo + sin(ang*3.14159/180)*radius;

        // Plot the point of the circle with a little image-
        // space clipping.

        if (x>=0 && x<320 && y>=0 && y<200)
            Plot_Pixel_Fast(x,y,9);

        } // end for ang
    } // end for index

// Done. Halt the system and wait for the user to press a key.

printf("\nHit any key to see circles drawn with look-up.");
getch();

// Set the video mode to the 320x200, 256-color mode.

Set_Video_Mode(VGA256);

// Draw circles using look-up tables
```

```
for (index=0; index<NUM_CIRCLES; index++)
    {

    // Get a random circle.

    radius = rand()%50;
    xo     = rand()%320;
    yo     = rand()%200;

    for (ang=0; ang<FULL_CIRCLE; ang++)
        {

        x = xo + cos_table[ang]*radius;
        y = yo + sin_table[ang]*radius;

        // Plot the point of the circle with a little image-
        // space clipping.

        if (x>=0 && x<320 && y>=0 && y<200)
            Plot_Pixel_Fast(x,y,12);

        } // end for ang
    } // end for index

// Let the user press a key to exit.

printf("\nWow! Hit any key to exit.");
getch();

// Reset the video mode to text.

Set_Video_Mode(TEXT_MODE);

} // end main
```

Building an Executable: To make an executable of the program in Listing 8.4, you can either type it in or use the source on the companion CD. The name of the source is lookup.c. The precompiled executable is named lookup.exe. As before, use the following compile line for Microsoft C:

```
cl -AM -Zi -c -Fc -Gs -G2 lookup.c
```

After compiling the program in this manner you can link it to the standard libraries and to our previously generated game library, gamelib.lib, with a link line such as:

```
link /ST:8192 /CO lookup,,,graphics.lib+gamelib.lib,,
```

This creates a final executable named lookup.exe.

The lookup.c program really shows the gains that can be made by the use of look-up tables, especially for complex calculations such as transcendental functions. Of course, you might argue, what if you want to know the sine of 34.6 degrees? You could do either of two things:

☐ First, you could make the look-up table bigger.

☐ Second, you could interpolate two values in the table to compute one in-between value.

Interpolation is a method of estimating a value between two known values using a linear basis as the interpolating function. Many functions aren't interpretable by linear functions, although for small deltas between adjacent data-points, interpolation gives results that are better than rounding or truncation. In general, to interpolate a value C that lies in the interval $[a_1, a_2]$:

```
F(C) = F(a₁)+ (F(a₂)-F(a₁))*(C-a₁)/(a₂- a₁)
```

where $F(x)$ is the look-up table function and elements exist at a_1 and a_2, but not at C.

We're becoming quite knowledgeable about optimization. Let's move on to a mathematical topic next.

Multiplication by Shifting

The decimal number system we're accustomed to using is base 10. To multiply or divide any number by 10, we can simply shift the decimal place to the right or left, respectively. For example, if we wanted to multiply 1,204.456 by 10, we would shift the decimal once to the right. The result would be 12,044.56. Division works in the same manner.

This is an intriguing mathematical tidbit we can apply to any closed numerical system that doesn't have any weird gaps in it. The binary system works fine. Let's take a look at the representation of a binary number. Binary numbers are base 2. This means that each digit grows in magnitude twice the previous digit; or, in general, the nth digit has weight 2^N, where N is the digit place counting from right to left. This is illustrated in Figure 8.1.

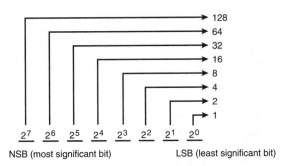

2^7 2^6 2^5 2^4 2^3 2^2 2^1 2^0

NSB (most significant bit)   LSB (least significant bit)

In general the nth digit of a binary word will
have value 2^n and an n-digit binary word
will have unsigned range of (2^n - 1).
For example, a 16-bit word would have range of
2^{16} - 1 = 65536 - 1 = 65535

Figure 8.1. *The magnitudes of bits.*

For example, if we use an 8-bit binary number to represent data, the number 24 would look like this:

```
00011000%%%2 = 24₁₀
```

This is true because there's a 1 in both the 8's place and the 16's place. We can use shifting of the decimal point to multiply and divide binary numbers by 2 just as we did decimal numbers. The only problem is, where's the decimal point? Well, it's implied to be to the right of the *least significant bit* (LSB). Moreover, we can't really move the decimal point; therefore, we must shift the binary number itself relative to an imaginary decimal point.

This means that shifting to the right is division while shifting to the left is multiplication, which is backward from the decimal example. Well, almost; it only seems backward. In the decimal example we shifted the decimal point rather than the number. If we were to shift the number relative to the decimal point, things would reverse. To multiply a binary number by 2, we shift it once to the left. Division by 2 is accomplished by shifting once to the right. Therefore, if we wanted to multiply a binary number by 4, we would shift it twice to the left. If we wanted to multiply it by 8 we would shift it 3 times. Each shift multiplies the previous multiple by another factor of 2, so to multiply a binary number by 1,024 we would shift it 10 times to the left.

This is great, but how can we multiply a binary number by 25, or something else that isn't a power of 2? The answer is to use partial products and sum them up. As an example, 24 can be written as 16+8. If we want to multiply a binary number by 24, we could first shift

443

it by 3 and then add that to the number shifted once more. Take a look below:

```
int x=24;

// Multiply x*24.

x = x<<4 + x<<3; // x* 16 + x*8
```

This code multiplies x by 24.

Binary shifting is better than using straight multiplication because:

☐ The shifting can be done faster by the CPU.

☐ There's very little logic involved.

☐ There's only a shift register!

Not only can shifting be used to multiply and divide binary numbers, it can be used to simulate a decimal point (and, therefore, decimal numbers), but without the use of floating-point numbers. Let's see how next.

Fixed-Point Math Primer

Fixed-point mathematics is a method of representing numbers using a decimal point that is not allowed to move as computations are performed. The number system we're used to using is based on a floating decimal point, and so is not fixed-point. A computer could use integers alone if the decimal portion of a calculation wasn't necessary. However, we must be able to record the decimal results of many calculations and cannot arbitrarily truncate the decimal portion of the calculation. As an example, imagine we wanted to multiply .1 * 100. Using floating-point calculation, the result would be 10. However, if we were to first throw away the decimal portion of the numbers so we could use an integer representation, we'd have the product 0 * 100 = 0!. This is clearly not acceptable, and we definitely wouldn't want to do something like that in our software.

The question should be raised, "Why try to use integers in the first place?" The answer is that floating-point numbers permit much more complexity in carrying out computations. That's why people have invented entire co-processors: just to take care of floating-point calculations so the main CPU is relieved of this task. The reason for this complexity stems from the representation of the floating-point numbers themselves. They're not in a simple binary format, but in a special, encoded format. This special format, called *IEEE format*, uses binary to represent different portions of the floating-point number, such as the exponent and mantissa.

The problem with this special format is that it's extremely hard to work with, and calculations using it take much more time than doing it in straight binary. What we'd like to do is somehow use straight binary integers to represent numbers that have a decimal portion, and then use the simple CPU operations of addition, subtraction, multiplication, and division to operate on them quickly while still keeping the decimal portions intact. It may seem impossible; but there is a way to do this, and it's called fixed-point math.

Let's see if we can come up with a scheme to facilitate the use of decimals with standard integers. As an example, imagine what would happen if we were to take a 16-bit number and use it as our new fixed-point type. Normally, we can represent 0–65535 with this number if the number we want to represent is unsigned. For a moment let's pretend that we can only represent a number from 0–255 with it, and that we do this by placing the 0–255 in the upper eight bits while leaving the lower eight bits alone. As long as we kept this in mind, we can add and subtract these numbers with the upper eight bits representing 0–255. Here's the interesting part: we can think of the lower eight bits as the decimal portion of the number, as shown in Figure 8.2.

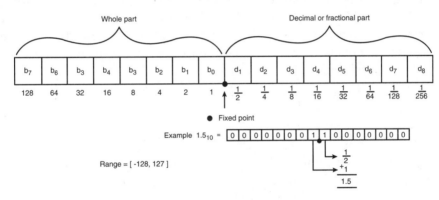

Figure 8.2. *The layout of a 16-bit fixed-point number with the decimal point in the middle.*

In this figure we see that each bit now has a magnitude, and the bits to the right of the imaginary decimal are inverse powers of 2. Just as in decimal we have the 1/10th's place, the 1/100th's place, and so on, we have the same setup in binary except that decimal places are in inverse powers of two. For example, the first decimal place to the right of the decimal is 1/2, the next place is the 1/4 place, and so on. Using the model just described, we create a floating-point data type that uses the largest standard integral data type C has to offer: the LONG data type, which is 32 bits. We can place the decimal anywhere we wish. If we want to have large numbers with only a couple of decimal places, we would tend to move the decimal to the right. On the other hand, if we wanted to have small numbers with a lot of decimal places, we would place the decimal to the left, as shown in Figure 8.3.

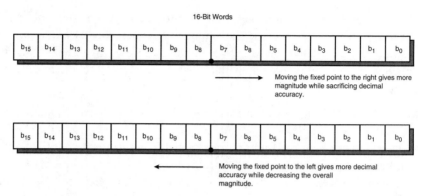

Figure 8.3. *The results in accuracy when the fixed-point is moved.*

The placement of the decimal is up to you, and can be placed to best suit your needs for the type of data you're processing. As a rule, I usually place the decimal either smack in the middle (16 bits whole part, 16 bits decimal part) or eight bits from the LSB. In either case, fixed-point numbers are always manipulated the same way. (Don't worry if this is a little confusing; we see next exactly how to create fixed-point numbers and how to manipulate them.)

Using a LONG as the base type of a fixed-point number, we can create the following type definition:

```
typedef long fixed;    // Fixed is an alias for long.
```

Creating a fixed-point number is easy; all we do is create a fixed variable:

```
fixed f1=0, f2=0;  // This creates two fixed-point numbers,
                   // and both would contain 0.0.
```

We've decided to use the lower eight bits of the fixed type as the decimal, so we must create a #define that reflects that. We use the #define to assign numbers to our fixed-point type so we can do something with them. The two #define lines we need are as follows:

```
#define FP_SHIFT        8     // Number of decimal digits
#define FP_SHIFT_2N   256 // The result of taking 2 to the
                        // FP_SHIFT power.
```

To assign an integer to the fixed-point type, we must shift it into the portion of the number that holds the whole part. Remember, the first eight bits are decimal and the remaining 24 bits are the whole part. To assign a decimal whole number to a fixed-point type we could write:

```
f1 = 34 <<FP_FP_SHIFT;
```

The result of this operation would be to shift the whole part of the number into the upper 24 bits of the fixed type without altering the lower eight bits. Therefore, the value of f1 in binary would look like this:

```
f1 = 000000000000000000100010.0000000₂;  // 34.0₁₀
```

If we were to interpret this number in straight binary it would be 8704_{10}, but we're pretending that it's a fixed-point number.

Now, let's talk about manipulating fixed-point numbers and see some of the rules involved.

Because fixed-point numbers are really binary numbers in disguise, the CPU has no clue where the decimal place is; it's imaginary. Therefore, the CPU adds, subtracts, multiplies, and divides fixed-point numbers as if they were normal LONGs. It just so happens this is exactly what we want. In the case of addition and subtraction we can directly add or subtract fixed-point numbers as if they were normal integers, as shown here:

```
// Create a couple of fixed-point numbers.

fixed f1,f2, f3;

// Assign some values to the fixed-point numbers.

f1 =     24 << FP_SHIFT; // 24.0
f2 =  10 << FP_SHIFT; // 10.0
```

To add them, we would write:

```
f3 = f1 + f2;
```

To subtract them, we would write:

```
f3 = f2 - f1;
```

Note that because the LONG base type is signed, so is the fixed type. All calculations are thus signed, which is perfect.

The most complex operations are multiplication and division. Accomplishing them is straightforward except for one caveat: when you multiply fixed-point numbers, you must shift the result back down to the right. This is because the fixed-point numbers were created by shifting to the left (to place the whole part to the left of the fixed point), and an extra factor of FP_SHIFT_2N is multiplied when we multiply two fixed-point numbers. We can remedy this situation by simply shifting the final result back to the right using FP_SHIFT. Take a look at this example:

```
f3 = (f1 * f2) >> FP_SHIFT;
 // Multiply and shift the result to renormalize it.
```

Also, if you want to multiply many fixed-point numbers together, you can hold the final shift until the end of the calculation:

```
f3 = (f1 * f2 * f4 * f5 *.....* fn) >> FP_SHIFT;
```

Performing division is a little harder, but is based on the same premise: an unwanted factor of FP_SHIFT_2N is introduced in one form or another during the operation. In the case of division, we must first shift the dividend to the left FP_SHIFT times before the calculation—and that's it. Take a look:

```
f3 = ( (f1<<FP_SHIFT) / f2);   // The result will be f1/f2.
```

You see, the division divides an extra factor of FP_SHIFT_2N out of the quotient, so we must multiply by this factor before the division, which is accomplished by the shift to the left of FP_SHIFT.

We can now perform floating-point calculations, and access the results by extracting either:

☐ The upper bits to the left of the fixed-point (the whole part)

☐ The lower bits to the right of the decimal (the decimal part)

However, how can we assign a floating-point number to the fixed-point number? This isn't too hard, but we must revisit, for a little insight, how we assigned integers. If you recall from a few moments ago, we assigned integers to the fixed-point type by shifting the integer so that it was in the upper portion of the fixed-point type (which, in our case, was the upper 24 bits). This means we would shift to the left FP_SHIFT, which in our number system is 8.

Shifting the integer eight times to the left is the same as multiplying it by 256, or 2^8. This is what we must do to a floating-point number. We simply need to multiply it by 256, which has been defined as FP_SHIFT_2N. Unfortunately, we can't use shifting because that would make no sense to the floating-point representation. Therefore, we must do brute-force multiplication and then cast the result into a fixed-point type. The following code does this:

```
fixed f1;

f1 = (fixed)(34.56 * 256);   // f1 = 34.56 in fixed-point.
```

Obviously, the multiplication by 256 is going to take a bit of processor time. Once the number is converted to fixed-point, however, that doesn't matter.

We've covered almost everything you need to know about fixed-point numbers to at least work with them. To truly understand all their subtleties would be quite challenging mathematically (and really isn't important for us because we're not doing dissertations on number theory). Nevertheless, there are two more points I want to cover before we move on to a demo of fixed-point numbers. These points are *errors* and *maximum representable values* using our system. Let's use our system of fixed-point numbers, which has eight bits of decimal precision and 24 bits of whole precision, for the analysis. Analyzing other setups is similar.

Maximum Representable Numbers

First, let's talk about the maximum and minimum numbers that can be represented. There are eight bits of decimal precision. That means the smallest number we can represent would be one that looked like this:

```
00000000000000000000000000.00000001
```

This is equivalent to 1/256 = .0039.

On the other hand, the largest number we can represent looks like this:

```
01111111111111111111111.11111111
```

which is equivalent to 8388608.996.

Both of the numbers can be positive or negative so the total range of our system becomes [-8388608.996, 8388608.996].

Errors

Errors begin to occur if you overflow the maximum value representable or try to represent a number smaller than the smallest number representable. In general, the smallest number representable can be viewed as the decimal accuracy of the system.

A Demo

Now that we've covered everything I can think of about fixed-point numbers, let's see a demo and some of the functions. I've created a demo called fixdemo.c, which uses the fixed-point representation along with all the math functions we've talked about to manipulate some fixed-point numbers and show you the results. When you run the program, notice how errors are large in some cases (when doing multiplication and division) and small in others (when doing addition and subtraction). The reasoning behind these errors is beyond the scope of this book, but you get a feel for the practical accuracy of our representation. Finally, I've created another function that prints out a fixed-point number. It does this by simply extracting the decimal and whole part of the number and printing them out with a decimal point between them. Listing 8.5 contains the source code.

Listing 8.5. A demonstration of fixed-point mathematics (fixdemo.c).

```
/// I N C L U D E S ///////////////////////////////////////////////

#include <math.h>
#include <stdio.h>

// D E F I N E S /////////////////////////////////////////////////

#define FP_SHIFT        8    // Number of binary decimal digits
#define FP_SHIFT_2N     256  // 2^FP_SHIFT, used during
                             // conversion of floats

// S T R U C T U R E S ///////////////////////////////////////////

// Define our new, magical fixed-point data type.

typedef long fixed;

// F U N C T I O N S /////////////////////////////////////////////

fixed Assign_Integer(long integer)
{
// This function assigns an integer to a fixed-point type by
// shifting.

return((fixed)integer << FP_SHIFT);

} // end Assign_Integer

///////////////////////////////////////////////////////////////////

fixed Assign_Float(float number)
{
// Ghis function assigns a floating-point number to a fixed-
//point type by multiplication, because it makes no sense to
// shift a floating-point data type.

return((fixed)(number * FP_SHIFT_2N));

} // end Assign_Float

///////////////////////////////////////////////////////////////////

fixed Mul_Fixed(fixed f1,fixed f2)
{
// This function mulitplies two fixed-point numbers and returns
// the result. Notice how the final result is shifted back.

return((f1*f2) >> FP_SHIFT);

} // end Mul_Fixed

///////////////////////////////////////////////////////////////////

fixed Div_Fixed(fixed f1,fixed f2)
{
// This function divides two fixed-point numbers and returns
```

```
// the result. Notice how the dividend is preshifted before the
// division.

return((f1<<FP_SHIFT)/f2);

} // end Div_Fixed

//////////////////////////////////////////////////////////////

fixed Add_Fixed(fixed f1,fixed f2)
{

// This function adds two fixed-point numbers and returns the
// result. Notice how no shifting is necessary.

return(f1+f2);

} // end Add_Fixed

//////////////////////////////////////////////////////////////

fixed Sub_Fixed(fixed f1,fixed f2)
{

// This function subtracts two fixed-point numbers and returns
// the result. Notice how no shifting is necessary.

return(f1-f2);

} // end Sub_Fixed

//////////////////////////////////////////////////////////////

void Print_Fixed(fixed f1)
{
// This function prints out a fixed-point number. It does this
// by extracting the portion to the left of the imaginary
// decimal point and then extracting the portion to the right of
// the imaginary decimal point.

printf("%ld.%ld",f1 >> FP_SHIFT,
       100*(unsigned long)(f1 & 0x00ff)/FP_SHIFT_2N);

} // end Print_Fixed


//M A I N //////////////////////////////////////////////////////

void main(void)
{

fixed f1,f2,f3; // Defines some fixed-point numbers.

f1 = Assign_Float((float)15.00);
f2 = Assign_Float((float)233.45);

printf("\nf1:=");
```

Listing 8.5. continued

```c
Print_Fixed(f1);

printf("\nf2:=");
Print_Fixed(f2);

printf("\nf1+f2:=");
f3 = Add_Fixed(f1,f2);
Print_Fixed(f3);

printf("\nf1-f2:=");
f3 = Sub_Fixed(f1,f2);
Print_Fixed(f3);

printf("\nf1*f2:=");
f3 = Mul_Fixed(f1,f2);
Print_Fixed(f3);

printf("\nf2/f1:=");
f3 = Div_Fixed(f2,f1);
Print_Fixed(f3);

} // end main
```

Building an Executable: To make an executable of the program in Listing 8.5, you can either type it in or use the source on the companion CD. The name of the source is fixdemo.c. The precompiled executable is named fixdemo.exe. As before, use the following compile line for Microsoft C:

```
cl -AM -Zi -c  -Fc -Gs -G2 fixdemo.c
```

After compiling the program in this manner, you can link it to the standard libraries and to our previously generated game library, gamelib.lib, with a link line such as:

```
link /ST:8192 /CO fixdemo,,,graphics.lib+gamelib.lib,,
```

This creates a final executable named fixdemo.exe.

Analysis The program adds, subtracts, multiplies, and divides a pair of fixed-point numbers and prints out the results. In general, you wouldn't use separate functions to do your fixed-point math; you would perform the calculation right in the code itself. However, this was just a demonstration so we could clearly separate each function.

Using Assembly Language and the In-Line Assembler

This is the ultimate optimization: write the whole video game in assembly. It would definitely be faster than if it were in C. In fact, this used to be the only way video games could be written for the PC. However, all the techniques we've learned apply to assembly language, and using assembly alone is not the answer. If your coding is clumsy, you'll get a speed-up using assembly—but at some point the inefficiency of your code will reach a break-even point. The trick is to program efficiently in all languages and get the most out of each.

It's true that almost all video games for the PC were written in pure assembly just a few years ago, but with today's faster compilers and CPUs, C/C++ is the choice of most PC-based video-game programmers. Nevertheless, there are times when the C code is optimized to the hilt and we just have to use assembly language. Today's C compilers are good, but they still can't outprogram an average assembly programmer. The difference is becoming smaller and smaller, but it's still there. (Personally, I think that assembly should only be used for low-level programming, such as device-driver programming and when accessing the video display.)

Usually, if we want to use assembly language in our C programs we have to write an assembly program and then assemble it with an assembler such as MASM. At that point we take the object file, link it to our C program, and call it as if it were a C function, as shown in Figure 8.4.

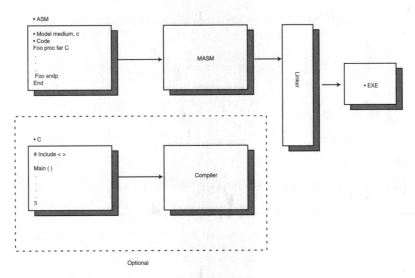

Figure 8.4. *Creating an executable from an assembly language module.*

This works fine and is a valid technique, but not the easiest. Doing mixed-language programming takes quite a bit of knowledge that is wholly unnecessary in most cases. There's a solution, though: the new in-line assembler. In-line assemblers are the latest addition to all the new compilers. Microsoft, Borland, and Symantec (to name a few) all support in-line assemblers.

An in-line assembler is a way of placing assembly language directly into your C code with access to all the variables to which C has access. The advantage of in-line assembly language is that it can be placed anywhere in the C source and you don't have to worry about all the details of mixed-language programming. The only downside to using the in-line assembler is that it isn't as powerful as using a complete, full-featured macro assembler such as MASM. This doesn't really matter, though, as most of the time only a few dozen lines of assembly are needed in key positions in the C code.

If you aren't familiar with assembly language, you'll be at a slight disadvantage in the rest of our discussions here, but stay with me anyway.

Invoking the in-line assembler is easy: we use the keyword _asm and then enclose the in-line assembly in curly braces (kinda like curly fries, but different). As an example, we might have something like the code shown in Listing 8.6.

Listing 8.6. Adding two numbers using the in-line assembler.

```
#include <stdio.h>

int Add_Numbers(int x,int y)
{
// Add two 16-bit numbers using the in-line assembler.
_asm
    {
    clc             ; Clear the carry
    mov ax, x            ; Do the addition
    adc ax,y            ; Leave the result in ax, as this is
                        ; standard for WORD.
            ; Size return values in C
    } // end assembly

} // end Add_Numbers

void main(void)
{
printf("\n1 + 2 = %d",Add_Numbers(1,2));
} // end main
```

I haven't supplied source for this program on the companion CD because I want you to type something in! If you type this program in, compile it, and then run it, you should see the following result:

```
1+2 = 3
```

This proves that the in-line assembler works and adds the numbers correctly. If you don't see these results, your PC's CPU has been infiltrated by nano-machines from deep space. (Someone who cared less about you than I do would probably suggest you send a power surge through your PC to cleanse them out.)

Adding a couple of numbers is great; however, we're interested in seeing how we can use the in-line assembler to improve time-critical graphics operations such as bit blitting, pixel blasting, and so on. With that in mind, let's try and convert a simple function used in the graphics library to in-line assembly language. The perfect candidate for this example function is the Fill_Double_Buffer() function. (If you recall, I pulled a fast one on you and wrote the Show_Double_Buffer() function in in-line assembly, but never really said much about it.) The Fill_Double_Buffer() is in C and uses the _fmemset() function to fill a region of memory. The only problem is that this function is an 8-bit function; in other words, it only moves eight bits of data at a time. We can double this by using WORD-sized moves using the in-line assembler. Let's see how in Listing 8.7.

Listing 8.7. An in-line version of the buffer fill using WORD moves.

```
void Fill_Double_Buffer_I(unsigned char color)
{

_asm
   {
   mov ax, 160
                    ; Multiply buffer_height * SCREEN_WIDTH/2.
   mul buffer_height
   mov cx,ax         ; CX holds the number of words to set.
   mov ah,color      ; Move the color into both ah and al.
   mov al,ah
   les di,double_buffer
                    ; es:di is the destination of memory move.
   cld               ; Be sure to move in the right direction.
   rep stosw         ; Move all the words.

   } // end asm

} // end Fill_Double_Buffer_I
```

This function, `Fill_Double_Buffer_I()`, can replace the C version `Fill_Double_Buffer()`. The only difference is the in-line version is faster and uses WORD-sized moves instead of BYTE-sized moves. The `Fill_Double_Buffer_I()` function operates this way:

1. The `Fill_Double_Buffer_I()` function first computes the total number of words that must be filled in the double buffer, which is equal to `(SCREEN_WIDTH/2 * buffer_height)`.

2. The function then places the color into the high and low part of the `AX` register.

3. Finally, the starting address of the memory fill is stored into `ES:DI`, and t fill initiated with `rep stosw`.

Note: Even though most VGA cards are 16-bit, older ones are 8-bit, and moving 16 bits at a time does not increase the speed because the data bus of the VGA card itself is only eight bits wide.

This is a good example of the in-line assembler. We can obtain up to a 100 percent increase in speed by using the in-line assembler in this case.

The in-line assembler is a useful tool; however, you should take care when using it for two reasons:

☐ Your C code will become more and more Intel-CPU dependent.

☐ Your programs will become harder to debug.

Additionally, you should only use the in-line assembler, and assembly language in general, for small, time-critical portions of your games, never for the game logic itself.

We've covered all the optimizations we can do ourselves with what we have. Now let's talk about using other tools to push the PC to the 32-bit envelope.

DOS Extenders

DOS extenders are an advanced topic, and one I'm sure I won't do justice to in a couple pages. However, a knowledge of them is necessary if you're going to write advanced games that take advantage of the advanced processing capabilities of Intel's 286, 386, 486, and 586 processors, and the extended memory above one megabyte. The purpose of this discussion is not to explain how DOS extenders work in detail, nor to cover all

the different types that are made and how they're used. I simply want to make you aware that there's a 32-bit platform sitting under a 16-bit DOS facade, and that we can uncover it with the use of a DOS extender.

Let's begin by taking a look at DOS as an operating system and see what the problem is with it. DOS is a 16-bit operating system that was designed in the 1970s. (That's right: the 1970s. DOS is really a conversion of CP/M.) DOS was originally designed to operate on the Intel 8088 in the IBM PC. The operating system had been designed to access one megabyte of RAM, had an interrupt structure, was open-ended, and (for its time) was a great breakthrough in technology. Alas, time marched on and newer versions of the 8088 were designed. The 8086 came out and was a full, 16-bit version of the 8088. This didn't make much of a difference to DOS because the 8086 could only address one megabyte, and was relatively the same.

Then Intel came out with the 80286, and this is where things started changing. The 80286 could directly address a total of 16 megabytes. This was unheard of! At the time, the real power of the new 286 hadn't yet been realized. It had extra instructions, hardware for multitasking, and could operate in a new mode called *protected mode*. Then, too, the cost of memory was decreasing, and more and more PCs were fitted with the full one megabyte of RAM a PC could access.

This was the point when DOS should have been put to rest and DOS II should have been created as the next generation. However, as we all know, this isn't what happened. Intel started creating processors (like they were cheese sandwiches) that were extremely advanced. These new processors—the 386, 486, and now the Pentium—could access gigabytes of RAM and had all kinds of added hardware for internal caching, multitasking, and so forth. However, DOS stayed more or less its 16-bit self. Even though the processors that began with the 386 had enhanced capabilities, DOS didn't answer these challenges—so other manufacturers did. Beginning with the introduction of the 80286, companies started creating what were called *DOS extenders*. These were mini-operating systems that could place the processor into what was called *protected mode*. This new mode of the processor allowed it to use more instructions and address its full memory space.

When the first DOS extenders came out for the 80286, the performance increase wasn't that noticeable. The added memory addressing ability was, though. At this point DOS programs could access whatever amount of memory was in the PC and do it in a straightforward way. The difference in performance didn't arise until the release of the 80386. Here was truly a next-generation processor with all kinds of features. However, when the 80386 was plugged into a PC and run under DOS, it was just a fast 8086 running in what was called *real mode* or *8086 emulation mode*. The 80386 was a full, 32-bit processor that was being held back by DOS.

Of course, manufacturers created DOS extenders for the 80386 that allowed it to operate in protected mode, address the full four-gigabyte address space, and use 32-bit instructions. The one challenge was that someone had to supply a compiler for the 80386 that would produce 32-bit code for it to be used in conjunction with the DOS extender. That wasn't a problem; many manufacturers did so.

Finally we saw the release of the 486 and the 586 Pentium. These processors are even more advanced than the 80386, and the extenders work with them also.

Summing up, DOS extenders allow us to use the advanced CPUs (such as the 286, 386, 486, and 586) in their native protected mode, which is 32-bit in the case of the 386 on up, and allow access to much more memory than the one megabyte barrier of standard DOS. The question is, "Why doesn't everyone use a DOS extender?" The answer is *compatibility*. For instance, if you develop on a 486 and use a 32-bit DOS extender along with 486-specific instructions, your program will only run on a 486 or a 586! We also need completely new development tools, such as compilers, linkers, and so on. However, while we must be careful when using DOS extenders, all this is really insignificant when we look at the power of 32-bit programming. For instance, the game DOOM by ID software was written using DOS extenders and 32-bit code. DOOM works on a minimum of a 386, but today it's been said that the average PC is a 386SX/25 with two megabytes of RAM, so this isn't a problem.

The next question is, "Where do we get a DOS extender and what else do we need?" First, I suggest that we only concern ourselves with 32-bit DOS extenders that need a minimum of a 386; the 286 will be lucky if it can be used in calculators anymore! We need a DOS extender, a 32-bit compiler and linker, and development tools.

The most popular DOS extenders are made by the following manufacturers:

- [ ] **Ergo** makes both 16-bit and 32-bit DOS extenders. The only problem is that you must purchase a license to sell any product that uses their extender.

- [ ] **Flash-Tek** produces a 32-bit DOS extender that has advanced features such as virtual memory.

- [ ] **Phar Lap** is probably the best-known manufacturer of DOS extenders. They make a full line of both 16- and 32-bit extenders, along with all kinds of development tools.

- [ ] **Rational Systems** makes the favorite DOS extender among PC-based video-game programmers, and the one I recommend. Their extender is 32-bit, compatible with most 32-bit compilers, and allows the programmer to break rules (important when making games). Also, there's no licensing fee to use their extender in your games.

8

To go along with the DOS extender, you need some development tools: compilers, debuggers, linkers, and so forth. Here are the main vendors of 32-bit products.

☐ **MetaWare** makes the High C/C++ compiler, which is quite powerful. The only problem is that the version of C that's supported by MetaWare isn't all that ANSI- or Microsoft-compatible. However, that's not that important as being ANSI- or Microsoft-compatible isn't that important for game programming.

☐ **Watcom** makes the 32-bit compiler of choice for game developers. This compiler is highly Microsoft-compatible and comes with a full line of tools, such as a debugger, linker, profiler, and librarian. Also, some versions of the compiler come with Rational Systems' DOS extender!

☐ **Symantec** makes a 32-bit compiler and tools that are really the old Zortech products. (Zortech was one of the first companies to make a C++ compiler a few years ago. Actually, a single programmer wrote the original Zortech C++ compiler.) The product is well supported and produces excellent code.

In conclusion, if you're going to be serious about making PC games, you need a DOS extender and a 32-bit compiler. I suggest Rational Systems for the DOS extender and Watcom for the compiler and tools.

Adding To the Game Library

There wasn't much code in today's lesson. The only useable functions I foresee us doing anything with are the fixed-point functions and the in-line assembly version of the screen fill, so these are the only functions in today's installment of the game library. The source and header files are graph8.c and graph8.h, as expected, and are on the companion CD. Compile the library module and insert it into gamelib.lib, or use the precompiled version, graph8.obj, on the companion CD. In either case, to use the functions in your programs, include the header file graph8.h and link to the game library gamelib.lib.

Summary

Today we have learned a great deal about optimization theory on the PC. We looked at many techniques, from classics (such as loop unrolling and assembly language) to the not-so-classic (parameter passing, pointer aliasing, and memory-model use). We also covered the rather complex, though powerful, concept of fixed-point mathematics. Finally, we talked about DOS extenders and their role in PC-based video games of the 1990s.

Q&A

Q Why is optimization important?

A Optimization is important because, as video-game programmers on the PC, we don't have the luxury of being able to program in an inefficient manner. We must push the PC to its limit if want to be able to make great games.

Q Why don't we just use assembly language all the time?

A Even if we did, we'd still have to optimize. Furthermore, assembly language is too hard to understand, debug, and maintain—and development time in assembler is two to 10 times longer than that of C programs.

Q Why is fixed-point math better than floating-point math?

A Fixed-point math is based on integers, which are quite fast when used for computations on the PC. Floating-point numbers, on the other hand, are slow because of the internal IEEE representation. We can no longer use simple binary operations on floating-point numbers; there must be encoding and decoding phases during calculations.

Q What are the advantages of having a single data segment?

A The DS segment register always is pointing to the data segment; therefore, we can write assembly routines to access C variables, and global variables can be accessed quite fast. This is important if look-up tables are placed in the data segment. Because it's NEAR, accessing is fast.

Q Why are FAR function calls slower than NEAR ones?

A The CPU must do a segment load and a 32-bit jump. If the CPU knows that the function is NEAR, it can jump within 64K and find the function's address, which is faster.

Q What is an internal CPU cache?

A The CPU cache is where the most recently used instructions are copied so that main memory doesn't have to be accessed again in small loops.

Workshop

The Workshop section presents quiz questions to help you cement your new knowledge and exercises to give you experience using what you've learned. Try to understand the questions and exercises before moving on to the next lesson. The answers are in Appendix B.

Quiz

1. What are the differences between the MEDIUM and LARGE memory models?

2. In a function, where are local variables created?

3. Why is floating-point math slow?

4. What is the maximum address range of a 80286?

5. When using the register keyword to request the use of an internal CPU register, what registers are used (if the compiler can accommodate you)?

6. What's the difference between a 16-bit and 32-bit DOS extender?

7. In general, how many times should a loop be unrolled?

Exercises

1. Modify the fixed-point library to use a fixed-point number format that has 16 bits of whole part and 16 bits of decimal part.

2. Write a test program that creates two fixed-point numbers and then adds them together 10,000 times. Compare this to using floating-point numbers.

3. Compare the difference in speed between the C and in-line two versions of `Fill_Double_Buffer()`.

4. *Extra Credit* (really hard): Try to figure out how to perform general binary division of any divisor using shifting.

Making the PC Rock!

In the past week and a half we've concentrated our discussions on graphics and animation programming. It's time to talk about the sound capabilities of the PC. Well, there aren't any! The PC alone is incapable of creating sound (I refuse to acknowledge that internal clicker as a sound device). However, third-party hardware vendors have created plug-in cards that allow the PC to make incredibly sophisticated sound effects and music. The most popular of these sound cards are those made by Creative Labs and Media Vision. The Creative Labs Sound Blaster card has become an industry standard. Even the cards that are produced by other manufacturers are all Sound Blaster-compatible. Hence, our discussion focuses on Creative Labs' Sound Blaster and compatibles.

There are two main things the Sound Blaster can do:

☐ Synthesize sounds

☐ Playback digitized sounds

Synthesizing sound is used for sound effects and for playing music. Digitized sounds are also used for sound effects. However, digitized sounds are used in cases where synthesis is hard, impractical, or impossible to do for the required sound.

The topic of programming the Sound Blaster is a book in itself, and we aren't going to learn everything about it in one chapter. (There are some good books on the topic listed in the bibliography.) While not biting off more than we can chew, though, we must get into both digitized sound and music today. The main points of our discussion are digitized sounds and how to play them. With that in mind, here are the topics:

☐ Sound fundamentals

☐ The Sound Blaster family

☐ The FM synthesizer

☐ The DSP chip

☐ The CMS chips

☐ Playing music

☐ Digitized sound

☐ Creating a sound library

☐ Manipulating sound files

☐ The use of sound in PC games

☐ Adding to the game library

Sound Fundamentals

Before we can start unraveling the complexities of the Sound Blaster, we must understand what sound really is. A sound is something that you hear with your ears. OK; that's a good start. However, the better question may be, "Why do we hear sound?" The answer to that is that sound is composed of waves that travel through air. These are called *mechanical waves* because they're propagated by matter and not energy. You see, whenever an object moves around in air, it displaces the air and sends out a shock wave of sorts from the origin of the disturbance, as shown in Figure 9.1.

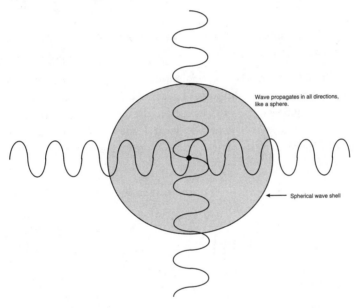

Figure 9.1. *A sound wave propagating from its origin.*

This shock wave propagates through the air by means of elastic collisions between air molecules. In other words, sound is a disturbance in a medium (usually, air) propagated by a mechanical wave, which is really composed of air molecules transferring their kinetic energy from one to the next in the direction of the wave propagation, as shown in Figure 9.2.

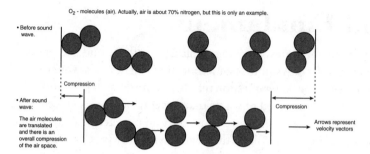

Figure 9.2. *A mechanical wave propagating at the molecular level.*

The reason we can hear sound is that our ears have sensors in them than can detect these kinds of mechanical waves.

There are a few details about the transmission or propagation of sound waves that we can talk about. For one thing, sound waves have *frequency*. This means that the sound is said to have a number of beats, or *cycles*, per second. Remember, a sound wave is a disturbance in the air that propagates from a specific point. If these disturbances continue to emanate from the same point, a pulse or *wave train* is created. Figure 9.3 shows a wave train.

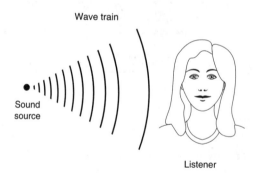

Figure 9.3. *A wave train.*

This wave train has a mean time between pulses, which is interpreted as the frequency. For example, when you hear an orchestra tuning to A, which is 440Hz, that means that the sound wave is hitting your ear 440 times per second.

The next question is, "What, mathematically, does sound look like?" All sounds are based on sinusoidal waves, or *sine waves*. For example, a pure tone of 1,000Hz would look like Figure 9.4. If we look at Figure 9.4, we see that it takes exactly one millisecond per cycle. In other words, the sound is 1,000Hz.

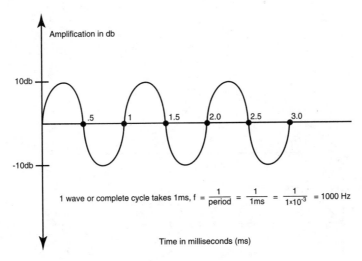

Figure 9.4. *A graphical representation of a 1,000Hz tone.*

In Figure 9.4 we also see that the sound wave looks like a single sine wave. If you were to listen to this sound wave it would sound...well, boring. The other aspect of the sound wave that we can see in Figure 9.4 is its *amplitude*, which is its overall height. The amplitude of the sound is related to how loud we perceive it when we listen to it. The intensity of the sound—its loudness—is proportional to how much air is being moved or propagated by the mechanical sound wave. This is the amplitude of the sound.

The single sine wave shown in Figure 9.4 is interesting; however, we should add something to make things more exciting. We can add another sine wave if we wish, with the result being the sum of the two. This is how complex sounds such as music and voice are created: they are sums of sinusoids. (It was proven by a brilliant French mathematician, Fourier, that all waveforms—including sound—can be represented by a summation of sinusoids.) As far as we're concerned as sound programmers, this means that complex sounds can be created by adding sine waves of different frequencies and amplitudes. In a sense, this is exactly what's done by the Sound Blaster. The Sound Blaster is capable of creating *harmonics*, or multiples, of a pure tone and then mixing them back with the original tone. For example, the tone 1,000Hz has harmonics at 2,000Hz, 3,000Hz, and so forth. There are subharmonics of 1,000Hz at 500Hz, 250Hz, an so on. This is represented in Figure 9.5.

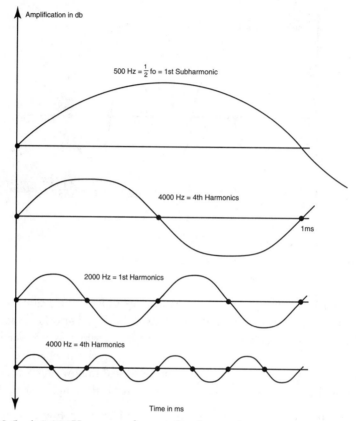

Figure 9.5. *A 1,000Hz tone and some of its harmonics.*

If we take a pure tone and add a few harmonics, the result is a *textured sound*. If we were to add all possible harmonics until infinity, the result would be a square wave, as shown in Figure 9.6.

 Math: The Fourier series is an infinite series that's basically a linear combination of all sine waves using a base frequency of F as the fundamental, or starting, frequency. If the series is summed up to infinity, the result is a perfect square wave. Therefore, the inverse Fourier transform of a square wave is a series of sine waves. Each sine wave has a different frequency that's a harmonic of the fundamental.

By carefully adding different sine waves to a signal, it's possible to create any sound. This is the basis for sound synthesis, which we talk about next.

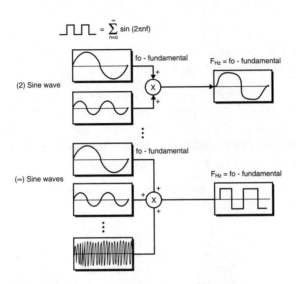

Figure 9.6. *Combining sine waves to create a square wave.*

The Sound Blaster Family

The Sound Blaster is a sound-synthesis card that was created in the late 1980s. It was actually the second mainstream card built in that generation; another sound standard was created and supported by a company called Adlib. With a little effort, the Sound Blaster card was compatible with the Adlib card. However, while the Adlib card slowly disappeared, the Sound Blaster kept much of this compatibility (just as Media Vision and others make their cards compatible with the Sound Blaster today).

What we want to do now is get an overview of the Sound Blaster family of sound cards, including their capabilities and differences.

The original Sound Blaster was called the Sound Blaster version 1.0. It had a Yamaha OPL2 FM synthesizer, a direct-memory access (DMA) chip, and an option for a pair of CMS chips:

☐ The OPL2 FM synthesizer was a chip used in musical keyboard synthesizers to create sound effect and music.

☐ The DMA chip allowed the Sound Blaster to directly access the computer's memory so that it could play digitized sound effects without the intervention of the system CPU.

☐ The CMS chips made the Sound Blaster compatible with the Adlib card and allowed the Sound Blaster to play music in stereo. However, most Sound Blasters didn't have these chips installed when shipped.

Today, while the Sound Blaster has come a long way, much of the original architecture is still in place. This has allowed games and programs to be upwardly compatible with new versions of the Sound Blaster. This means that a game written on Sound Blaster 1.0 still works on the most advanced Sound Blaster (the new Sound Blaster AWE 32 with wave-table synthesis), but not the other way around.

Let's take a look at the different models of the Sound Blaster and their associated capabilities, shown in Table 9.1.

Table 9.1. The different Sound Blasters.

Function	Sound Blaster V2.0	Sound Blaster Pro V2.0	Sound Blaster 16	Sound Blaster 16 ASP
Sample Rates	4-15KHz	4-44.1KHz	4-44.1KHz	4-44.1KHz
Playback Rates	4-44.1KHz	4-44.1KHz	4-44.1KHz	4-44.1KHz
Stereo	No	Yes	Yes	Yes
DSP	8-Bit	8-Bit	8/16-Bit	8/16-Bit
FM Voices	11	20	20	20
Mic In	Yes, Mono	Yes, Mono	Yes, Mono	Yes, Mono
Mic Auto Gain	No	Yes	Yes	Yes
Line In	Yes	Yes	Yes	Yes
Speaker Out	Yes	Yes	Yes	Yes
Line Out	No	Yes, Internal	Yes, Internal	Yes, Internal
CD Audio In	No	Yes	Yes	Yes

Function	Sound Blaster V2.0	Sound Blaster Pro V2.0	Sound Blaster 16	Sound Blaster 16 ASP
CD-ROM Connector	No	Yes	Yes	Yes
Mixer	No	Yes	Yes	Yes
Tone Control	No	No	Yes	Yes
Voice Recognition	No	No	No	Yes
Hardware Compression	No	No	No	Yes

As you can see, each of the different models has a little more than its predecessor. However, all models have the ability to play music and to digitize and play sounds, and all have DSP chips.

Because we're trying to create PC-based video games that are playable on the greatest number of platforms, use the Sound Blaster V2.0 as your basic target. We won't use the capabilities of the other models, which many users won't have. This doesn't mean that we can't write our games to take advantage of the advanced features of the newer cards. However, we should always support the older versions of the Sound Blaster, because sound cards are still a relatively scarce commodity on the average computer.

 Game Law: It's better to be downwardly compatible than not to be.

Now that we have a general overview of the Sound Blaster, let's discuss each of its subsystems.

The FM Synthesizer

As we learned earlier, all sounds can be created by adding together harmonics of a fundamental frequency. Normally, this is quite a hardware-expensive task to accomplish, because a separate sine wave would have to be created for each harmonic and then finally mixed, as shown in Figure 9.7.

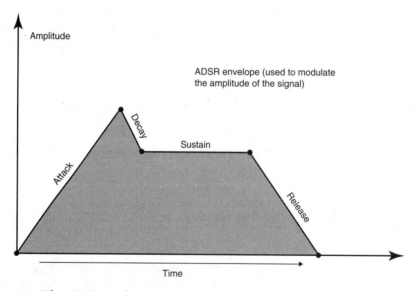

Figure 9.7. *Mixing sine waves manually.*

This works, but is seriously limited to simple sounds and nothing that could compete with real instruments. In fact, this is how the early organs were made. That's why they sounded like organs (that is, really bad).

This synthesis system was improved slightly by adding what's called an *envelope* to the sound. An envelope is a way of modulating the sound's amplitude as a function of time. Sound engineers and musicians came up with an envelope that had four components and called it the attack-decay-sustain-release (ADSR) envelope, shown in Figure 9.8.

Figure 9.8. *The ADSR envelope in action.*

The ADSR envelope allowed the amplitude of a sound to change over a period of time. For instance, a drum would have the ADSR envelope shown in Figure 9.9: a quick attack followed by no decay, no sustain, and ending with an abrupt release.

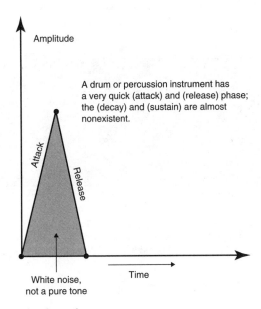

Figure 9.9. *The ADSR of a drum beat.*

On the other hand, Figure 9.10 shows an ADSR of a typical piano key being pressed. Notice the long sustain, which is dependent on how long the key is held down and the quality of the musician's "after touch."

At some point in history, a sound synthesizer engineer realized that complex sounds could be created in much the same way FM radio transmissions are encoded. It's possible to synthesize complex waveforms by modulating a basic carrier wave. The heart of the Sound Blasters's music synthesis is the FM synthesizer, a piece of hardware based on either the OPL2 or OPL3 FM synthesizer from Yamaha.

In the case of a radio transmission, the *modulating signal* is the voice or music and the *carrier wave* is the signal the transmission is sent on, such as 97.7MHz (one of my favorite stations). This concept can be generalized to music synthesis: it's exactly what the Sound Blaster's FM chip does. To accomplish this synthesis, the Sound Blaster has a collection of *operator cells* that can be programmed to oscillate at different frequencies. Each operator cell can have its own ADSR envelope.

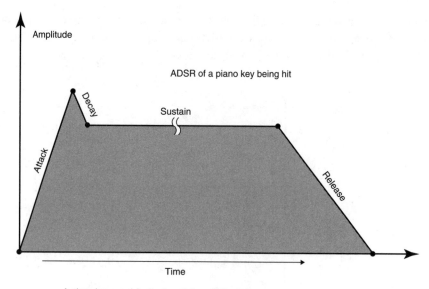

A piano has a quick attack and decay followed
by a long sustain (based on how long the key is held down),
terminating with an abrupt release that also depends on any
"after touch."

Figure 9.10. *The ADSR of a piano key being hit.*

Operator cells can be fed into one another to create sounds. There are two basic ways
operator cells can be connected:

- [ ] Additive synthesis
- [ ] Frequency modulation synthesis

We look at these next.

Additive Synthesis

The first method, *additive synthesis*, is much like the old synthesizers. Additive synthesis
is shown in Figure 9.11.

With this method, multiple sine waves can be added and the result will be heard. The
formula that dictates the final output is what we would think it would be: the sum of two
sine waves. This formula is shown in Formula 9.1.

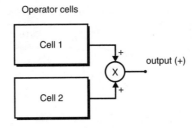

Figure 9.11. *Additive synthesis.*

Formula 9.1. Additive synthesis formula.

```
Output(t) = Operator₁(t) + Operator₂(t)
```

```
Operatorᵢ = ADSRᵢ(t) * sin(2*PI*f*t+shift)
```

where:

- t is time.

- f is the fundamental frequency in hertz.

- $ADSR_i(t)$ is the envelope of operator i.

- $shift$ is the phase shift for operator i.

Frequency Modulation Synthesis

The more intriguing form of connecting operators, called *frequency modulation synthesis*, is capable of creating startlingly real sounds. Take a look at Figure 9.12 to see the connection path.

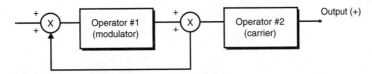

Figure 9.12. *Frequency modulation synthesis.*

Here we see that the output of the modulator operator cell is fed back into its own input. This is what creates all the harmonics, and hence the texture, in the output sound. The formula for the final output is shown in Formula 9.2.

Formula 9.2. Frequency modulation synthesis.

```
Output_M(t) = ADSR_M(t) * sin(2*PI*f*t+shift * Output_M(t))

Output_C(t) = ADSR_C(t) * sin(2*PI*f*t+Output_M(t))  .
```

where:

- t is time.

- f is the fundamental frequency in hertz.

- $ADSR_M(t)$ is the envelope of the modulator operator.

- $ADSR_C(t)$ is the envelope of the carrier operator.

- $shift$ is the phase shift for the modulator operator.

By programming each of the operators with the required parameters and connecting them in the desired way, we can synthesize musical instruments—and even human voice!

Programming the FM Chip

Programming the FM chip is complex and I just want you to have an overview, so we aren't going to cover it in depth. However, you should know that we communicate with the FM chip through the I/O ports shown in Table 9.2.

Table 9.2. The Sound Blaster FM synthesizers I/O ports.

Adlib-compatible ports
388h—Index and status port (read and write)
389h—Data port (write only)
Sound Blaster-specific ports
2x8h—Index and status port (read and write)
2x9h—Data port (write only)

where x is a hex digit based on the base address of the Sound Blaster, which is set by the jumpers or software.

9

Using these I/O ports, we can index, or select, a register and then read or write to it. This is how we program the FM synthesizer. For each operator, there's a bank of similar registers that can be programmed. The registers on the FM synthesizer are detailed in Table 9.3.

Table 9.3. The FM registers.

Register	Bit 7	Bit 6	Bit 5	Bit 4	Bit 3	Bit 2	Bit 1	Bit 0
01H	Test							
02H	Fast Counter							
03H	Slow Counter							
04H	IRQ	Mask					Start/Stop	
		st Cnt	SI Cnt				SI Cnt	Fst Cnt
08H	CSM	SEL						
20H-35H	AM	VIB	EG-TYP	KSR	MULTI			
40H-55H	KSL		Total Level (TL)					
60H-75H	ATTACK RATE (AR)				DECAY RATE (DR)			
80H-95H	SUSTAIN LEVEL (SL)				RELEASE RATE (RR)			
A0H-A8H	F-NUMBER							
B0H-B8H			KEY	BLOCK			F-NUMBER	
BDH	Intensity AM VIB		Rhythm	BASS	SNARE	TOM	TOP CYMBAL	HI HAT
C0H-C8H					FEEDBACK			FM
E0H-F5H							WS	

Instruments and the FM Synthesizer Chip

Before we continue, let's talk about instruments. The Sound Blaster can, as we all know, synthesize instruments. Moreover, different musical pieces have within them information about the instruments themselves that are to be used in the piece. An instrument on the Sound Blaster is really a specific set of values for a pair of operators. These values are used to program the FM synthesizer chip. The data for each instrument is in a format called SBI, which stands for Sound Blaster Instrument. This file format is composed of header information, along with 16 bytes used to program the FM chip for each instrument.

If you feel a little bewildered by all this stuff, don't worry. I think that most game programmers are in the same boat as far as sound is concerned. It's like networking: there's just a lot of information on formats and conventions that we have to learn to do it!

The DSP Chip

Along with the FM synthesizer, the Sound Blaster has a *digital signal processor* (DSP) chip. This chip helps process the sound signals the Sound Blaster creates, and also processes inputs the Sound Blaster may be fed, such as musical instruments digital interface (MIDI) and voice information. A DSP chip is a specialized version of a microprocessor, used to process signals or information at quite high rates. These rates must be high because DSP chips are used in real-time applications, such as speech recognition and so forth.

In the case of the Sound Blaster, the DSP chip is used for internal processing and for interpreting MIDI signals. Although software vendors have finally figured out how to do real-time voice recognition with the DSP chip, many programmers don't really use it as yet. For our purposes as video-game programmers, we won't be using the DSP chip directly. However, the possibility of doing speech recognition with it sounds like something you might want to look into!

The CMS Chips

CMS chips are an old appendage from the days when the Sound Blaster was Adlib-compatible. The CMS chips are a set of two chips that could be placed into the Sound Blaster card that would allow it to be fully compatible with Adlib. This meant that the Sound Blaster would be able to play stereo sound (that is, have a separate data stream for the right and left speakers).

The use of the CMS chips is nonexistent; after version 2.0 of the Sound Blaster, there aren't even any chip sockets to put them into anymore. The reason for this is that newer versions of the Sound Blaster have this stereo functionality built in.

Playing Music

One of the most impressive features of the Sound Blaster is its ability to play music in the background of a game without interfering with the game itself. This is accomplished using an interrupt routine that's called a specific number of times per second. Control is given to a sound driver program that plays the proper instruments for the piece and then returns control to the program that was interrupted. The sound driver latches on to the timer interrupt and is called every time there's a timer interrupt, which normally is 18.2 times a second. However, when the sound driver is loaded the timer is reprogrammed to tick at 96 clicks per second. This permits the music to make enough note and instrument changes per second that it doesn't seem choppy.

Today we write code only to play digitized sounds. However, we're going to take a brief look at the overall function of the music driver on the Sound Blaster. Playing music on the Sound Blaster is quite complex: not only must you be a programmer, you must be somewhat familiar with the properties of sound and with music theory. What we're going to do is take a look at all the pieces that fit together to create a music system to play music. You'll then be better equipped to learn the details of playing music at some later date.

Let's begin with the music we wished played. Music is stored in many file formats on the PC, but we're interested in only one format. This format is CMF. This is the official data format for the Sound Blaster, and the one used by the music driver. Of course, all other formats can be converted to this format. However, this format is almost a perfect replica of the MIDI format, which is a world standard for musical compositions on computers and synthesizers.

If we look inside a CMF file we find three things:

- ☐ The header information
- ☐ The instrument data
- ☐ The music itself

Figure 9.13 shows the layout of a CMF file.

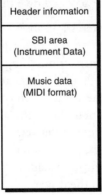

Figure 9.13. *The layout of a CMF file.*

The header information tracks things such as:

☐ Versions

☐ The number of instruments

☐ Timing parameters for the music

☐ The length of the music

☐ Other related pieces of information

At some point in the file is the instrument data block. This isn't at a specific place in the CMF file; it can be anywhere. (It's located in the header file at an offset from the beginning of the file, so it can be in different places.) With the instrument data block are all the register setting, for the FM synthesizer chip. There are 16 bytes for each instrument needed in the musical piece.

Finally, there's the musical data itself, which is in MIDI format (which still confuses me) and is a temporal description of the notes to be played.

Once we have a CMF file, we can use it as a source of data to have the Sound Blaster play music. As I said, the Sound Blaster has a driver that interprets CMF files and plays them for us without our intervention (other than the initial set up of the file to be played). However, to use this driver, we must load it in! The name of the driver is sbfmdrv.com. It's an executable program that automatically loads itself as a terminate-and-stay-resident (TSR) program and waits to be accessed by either you or the timer interrupt.

Now, here's where things get interesting: after you've loaded the driver by simply typing in its name at the DOS prompt, your C programs still have no clue as to how to access it. (Maybe we should leave such mysterious things alone...) When the driver is loaded and becomes a TSR, it scans through all the interrupt vectors from 0x80h to 0xBFh and latches itself into one of these interrupts. Then you, as a programmer, must scan all these interrupts and see what they point to. From the starting offset of the vector to which each interrupt points, you then scan for the characters FMDRV at offset 0x103h. When you find these characters, you've found the proper interrupt to use to call the music driver. (How do you like that? I think they could have made it harder by encrypting the characters, too!) At any rate, that's how you find the driver.

At this point we have a CMF file we want to play and we know how to access the driver. To play the music, we must:

1. Load the CMF file.

2. Extract the instrument data and send it to the FM chip.

3. Set a pointer to the beginning of the actual music data.

All these functions (and more) are accomplished using the music driver interface, which we access by passing variables in CPU registers, and then by calling the interrupt on which the driver is installed—that is, the interrupt you previously identified.

If you can keep that all straight in your neural cortex, let's take a look at the driver functions in Table 9.4.

Table 9.4. The sbfmdrv.com music-driver functions.

Function	Description
0	Get FM Drive Version
1	Set Music Status Byte Address
2	Set Instrument Table
3	Set System Clock Rate
4	Set Driver Clock Rate
5	Transpose Music
6	Play Music
7	Stop Music
8	Reset FM Driver
9	Pause Music
10	Resume Music
11	Set User-Defined Trap for System Exclusive

You can access the driver by using the AX, BX, CX, and DX registers as parameter-passing areas and then making an INT XXh call, where XXh is the interrupt the music driver has latched onto after the driver was installed with SBFMDRV.COM.

Playing music on the Sound Blaster is quite involved and there are a lot of little details that we must take into consideration. However, with the previous description, you should be in a far better position to understand the overall architecture of the music system.

Now that we've seen the overall method used to control the Sound Blaster, let's blast into playing digitized sound effects.

Digitized Sound

Digitizing sound is a method of sampling a sound signal at a predetermined rate per second. This can be done with an analog to digital (A/D) converter, a lot of memory, and some extra support hardware (such as control logic and filters). The hardware layout of a digitizer is shown in Figure 9.14.

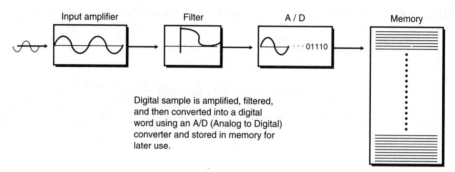

Digital sample is amplified, filtered, and then converted into a digital word using an A/D (Analog to Digital) converter and stored in memory for later use.

Figure 9.14. *The hardware layout of a digitizer.*

A digitized sample is basically a digital version of an analog signal. This digital version is represented by data WORDs, where each WORD is the magnitude, or amplitude, of a sample at some specific point in time. The Sound Blaster usually samples sounds using eight or 16 bits of data (commonly, eight bits). This means that each sample can take on 256 different values, which is a paltry amount compared to the infinite range of an analog signal. Nevertheless, eight bits of resolution is acceptable and is usually the WORD size used.

A digitized sample resembles the original; however, it has a discontinuous look to it, which is a function of the sample data WORD size. The more bits per sample, the smoother the sample.

The problem with sampling is that it can take a lot of memory. Not only does the sample need enough bits per data WORD to obtain a reasonable amplitude spectrum of the sample signal, but there must be enough samples per second to capture the frequency spectrum of the signal. You see, a sound is composed of many sinusoidal waves (as we learned earlier). For a digital sample to be able to completely reproduce all the frequency components of a sound, the digitizing hardware must digitize the sample at twice the highest frequency component of the sample signal to be sampled.

As an example, humans have a hearing range of 20-20,000Hz. However, our voices only can make sounds in the 0-3,000Hz range. This means that if you want to properly reproduce a human voice, you'd better sample it at a minimum of twice the maximum frequency of 3,000Hz, or a total of 6,000 samples per second. Of course, musical instruments create frequencies up to and beyond 20,000Hz. That's why CD players use a sample rate of 44.1KHz at 16 bits. This means a CD has stored an amazing 26.46 megabytes for just a five-minute song! The sample rate used on a CD is too much for PC-based video games, and that kind of memory use is unwarranted for explosions and laser blasts. Nevertheless, we still have to monitor our sample rate and sample WORD size.

Note: In actuality, CD disks are compressed so that much more can be encoded on each disk.

Typically, digitized sound effects for video games are sampled at four to eight kilohertz using a single a byte per sample. (Incidentally, I prefer to use the term *FX* for "sound effects.") This means that a 10-second sample consumes, on average, 60K of memory! Therefore, we must take care in managing the memory requirements of the digital samples and the sampling of the samples themselves.

We now know what digital samples are, so now we must figure out how to create them.

Creating digital samples is easy; any sound source can be used by the sampler: microphones, CD players, your vocal cords, and so on. However, how do we do the actual sampling? Well, we could write a sampler ourselves that used the DSP processor and the DMA chip, and totally controlled the Sound Blaster...or we could use a piece of software that's already been written. (Sounds like a plan.) There are tons of programs that digitize sound FX for you. New and old versions of the Sound Blaster come with sound-digitizer programs that enable you not only to digitize sounds, but to alter and change the shapes of the sounds. Personally, I like to use a really simple Shareware program called Blaster Master. It enables you to digitize sounds at any sample rate, along with providing the capability to alter the shape of the sound. Effects such as volume increase, pitch change, echoing, fading, and more are all included in this package. I've included a copy of it on the companion CD for you to experiment with. To run the program just type in `blaster.exe`. The program guides you through its operation.

The output of Blaster Master or any similar sound-digitization program is a digitized sample that can be played by the Sound Blaster (or any other sound card). There are many different digitized sample formats: IFF, SND, WAV, VOC, and (I'm sure) several others. The one we use is called VOC, the native format of the Sound Blaster. The VOC file

contains a header section and then instruction blocks, with sound data following them. These VOC files can be passed directly to the Sound Blaster, which plays them using direct-memory access (DMA) without you having to send each byte to the Sound Blaster. This means you can tell the Sound Blaster to play a digitized sound effect and then continue with other game-related processing. The sound plays and then terminates when it's complete, without you having to monitor it.

"So," you're probably asking, "what's the magical driver that can play digitized sounds?" The answer is the ct-voice.drv driver. Once loaded and initialized, it's almost too easy to play digitized sound FX. (I guess Creative Labs felt bad after creating such a complex music driver!) Let's see how the driver works, and write a library to control it.

Creating a Sound Library

First, a few words about the library. Our main goal is to create a library of C functions that interface to the sound driver ct-voice.drv. Using these C functions, we can play digitized samples with the Sound Blaster.

Before we start writing these functions, we should take a look at some of the functions we think we need. This is part of the design process when creating software. I admit that I've never used flow charts or written software on paper; however, I always write down or type a list of functions I wish to implement. This is like creating an outline for a report. Granted, we may change things around. In general, though, an outline or functional listing is a good place to start. With that in mind, here are the main areas for which we must write functions:

- ☐ Loading the sound driver ct-voice.drv into memory
- ☐ Loading a pre-recorded sound sample
- ☐ Playing, pausing, and stopping a sound sample
- ☐ Obtaining the status of the sound card
- ☐ Unloading the sound driver from memory

Of course, the final library will be more specific than the list above. These items are, in general, a minimum of what we need to implement.

Before we start writing software to accomplish the needed functions, let's take a look at ct-voice.drv's internal functions and their usage.

The ct-voice.drv Driver

The ct-voice.drv driver, unlike the SBFMDRV.COM driver, is not loaded as a TSR. Instead, we load it manually into a region of memory starting on a segment boundary, and then vector to it with an assembly language CALL instruction. Therefore, we don't call the driver functions with an interrupt; we call them by setting up a parameter in the proper registers, and then calling the driver at the address at which it was loaded into memory. Basically, we're emulating the functionality of the DOS loader, just as the DOS loader finds a free region of memory and then loads and executes a program, which you furnish through the command line. We are, in essence, doing the same thing.

Before we start writing all the required functions to interface to the sound driver, we should take a look at the functions of the driver itself and see what it has to offer. These are shown in Table 9.5.

Table 9.5. The ct-voice.drv driver functions.

Function	Description
0	Get Driver Version
1	Set Base I/O Address
2	Set DMA Interrupt
3	Initialize Driver
4	Toggle Speaker
5	Set Status Word Address
6	Start Voice Output
8	Stop Voice Output
9	Terminate Driver
10	Pause Voice Output
11	Continue Voice Output
12	Break Voice Output Loop
13-28	Advanced Functions

 Note: We won't be using functions 13-28 because they're of an advanced nature, and most of them are only supported by newer models of the Sound Blaster.

You can call each of the functions in Table 9.5 by first passing some key parameters into the CPU registers, and then calling the driver function by means of vectoring to its starting address, wherever it was loaded in memory.

Let's take a closer look at the inputs and outputs of each function.

Function 0: Get Driver Version

This function queries the driver version number from the driver itself.

Entry	BX = 0
Exit	AH = Major Version Number
	AL = Minor Version Number

Function 1: Set Base I/O Address

This function sets the base I/O address used by the driver and the card. Therefore, the number to which you set the card should match the selected I/O port on the card itself. If you don't call this function, the driver defaults to I/O port 220h.

Entry	BX = 1
	AX = Base I/O address
Exit	None

Function 2: Set DMA Interrupt

This function sets the interrupt number the driver uses to flag that a DMA transfer is completed by the Sound Blaster.

Entry	BX = 2
	AX = Interrupt Number
Exit	None

Function 3: Initialize Driver

This function initializes and starts up the sound driver. Note: You must call Functions 1 and 2 prior to calling this one.

Entry	BX = 3
Exit	AX = 0 Driver Initialized Successfully
	1 Incorrect Driver Version
	2 I/O Read-Write Failure
	3 DMA Interrupt Failure

Function 4: Toggle Speaker (Sound Blaster Base Model Only)

This function turns on or off the digitizer speaker output.

Entry	BX = 4
	AL = 0 For Off, 1 For On
Exit	None

Function 5: Set Status Word Address

This function tells the driver the address of a variable to be used as storage area for the current status of the driver. Therefore, you would define a variable and then pass the segment and offset to this function, so the driver can convey to you important information and status.

Entry	BX = 5
	ES:DI = The segment and offset of the variable you want to use for status.
Exit	None

Function 6: Start Voice Output

This function is the one that does the work. It plays a VOC file using DMA to the speaker. However, we must point a pointer to the data.

Entry	BX = 6
	ES:DI = The segment and offset of the beginning of the VOC data you want played. Note: we must be careful to pass the address of the actual data; that is, we must skip the header information. (More on this later today.)
Exit	AX = 0 if successful, nonzero otherwise

Function 7: Record Sample

Not used in this book.

Function 8: Stop Voice I/O

This function stops all I/O operations and sets the ct_voice_status variable to 0.

Entry	BX = 8
Exit	None

Function 9: Terminate Driver

This function kills the drivers and stops all processing. However, it does not unload the driver from memory. You must do that yourself.

Entry	BX = 9
Exit	None

Function 10: Pause Voice Output

This function pauses the voice output. You can restart the sound using the continue command.

Entry	BX = 10
Exit	AX = 0 if successful, 1 if the voice output is not active.

Function 11: Continue Voice Output

This function continues a previously paused sound.

Entry	BX = 11
Exit	AX = 0 if successful, 1 if voice output is not paused.

Function 12: Break Voice Output Loop

This function breaks a sound *loop* in the digitized data.

Entry	BX = 12
	AX = 0 Leave voice loop and end of current cycle.
	1 Leave voice loop immediately.
Exit	AX = 0 if successful, 1 if voice loop is not active

Creating an Interface

The functional descriptions in the last section are quite simple, and 99 percent of the work has already been done for us. All we have to do is create a simple interface that calls each function as if it were a C function. We accomplish this by enclosing each of the driver calls in a C function that wraps up the details of the CPU registers and parameter passing in in-line assembly code.

Even if you aren't that familiar with assembly language, you should have no problem understanding what's going on in each call. The functions are well-documented and consist of only a few instructions each. (Actually, this is a really good way to ease yourself into assembly language if you've never programmed in it. Viewing and understanding simple programs can help you get a firmer grasp on it.)

There are a couple of functions that are written completely in C. These are the functions that load the driver itself and load VOC sound files. Let's begin with loading the ct-voice.drv driver.

Loading the ct-voice.drv Driver

To load the sound driver:

1. Open the ct-voice.drv file on the disk.

2. Compute its size so we can allocate enough memory to hold it.

3. Allocate the memory for ct-voice.drv using a memory allocation function that can allocate a region of memory that starts with an offset of 0000h. We use `_dos_allocmem()` for this purpose.

Loading the driver into a memory region that doesn't have an offset of 0000h wreaks havoc on the driver. If we were to use the `malloc()` memory allocation function to allocate memory, we couldn't be assured that the segment:offset of the returned memory would have a 0000h offset. In other words, we must make sure that the driver is loaded on a 16-byte boundary (or page boundary), which means there's only one address for its starting location.

3. Load the bytes of the driver into memory as if we were loading data into a buffer.

4. Once the driver is loaded into memory, we must assign a pointer to it so we can vector to this driver. The pointer, which is global, is called `driver_ptr`.

Listing 9.1 contains the code to load the driver.

Listing 9.1. Loading the ct-voice.drv sound driver into memory at a paragraph boundary.

```
void Voc_Load_Driver(void)
{
// This function loads the ct-voice.drv, which allows digitized
// effects to be played.

int driver_handle;

unsigned segment,num_para,bytes_read;

// Open the driver file.

_dos_open("CT-VOICE.DRV", _O_RDONLY, &driver_handle);

// Allocate the memory.

 num_para = 1 + (filelength(driver_handle))/16;

_dos_allocmem(num_para,&segment);

// Point the driver pointer to data area.

_FP_SEG(driver_ptr) = segment;
_FP_OFF(driver_ptr) = 0;

// Load in the driver code.

data_ptr = driver_ptr;
```

```
do
 {
 _dos_read(driver_handle,data_ptr, 0x4000, &bytes_read);
 data_ptr += bytes_read;

 } while(bytes_read==0x4000);

// Close the file.

_dos_close(driver_handle);

} // end Voc_Load_Driver
```

The Voc_Load_Driver() takes no parameters and returns nothing. As usual, the function does no error handling. (For the most part, I leave error checking to you.)

About the only thing that can go wrong in this function is if the ct-voice.drv file can't be found on the disk or the memory couldn't be allocated, so you may want to check for these situations in your own code. (Then again, you may not.) The Voc_Load_Driver() function loads the driver into memory and then assigns the pointer named driver_ptr to the starting address of the driver in memory. We can then use the assembly language instruction CALL driver_ptr to call the driver and, depending on the parameters in the various registers, the driver will perform the proper function.

Loading a Sound File

Before we start writing driver interface functions, we should think about writing a function that loads a sound file! To load a sound file, we do much the same thing as in the driver-loading function:

1. Open the VOC sound file to be loaded (which will be passed as a string).

2. Allocate enough memory for the file.

3. Load the file into memory.

4. Set a pointer to the file.

5. Return this pointer to the calling function so it can be used later as an address of the data for a particular sound.

Now, there's one little catch to loading a sound into memory and then playing it later. We don't have to do anything as brutal as making sure the VOC file has been loaded into a paragraph boundary (although we did, for kicks). We do, however, have to take note of the length of the header portion of the sound file. This is because the ct-voice.drv sound driver needs to know where the header for the sound file ends and the actual sound

data starts. To compute this, we can look in the 20th byte of the sound file. It always has the length of the header portion of the sound file. We can use this later to compute an offset from the beginning of the loaded sound file to find the actual start of the data, as shown in Figure 9.15.

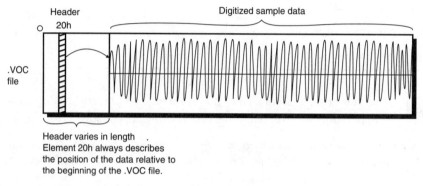

Figure 9.15. *The structure of a .VOC file.*

So now let's write the function to load a sound. We must open the sound file, allocate the memory for it, and load it into memory. When we're done loading the sound, we must compute the size of the header portion of the sound file and return it to the caller, along with the starting memory address of the sound itself. Listing 9.2 contains the code that does all this.

Listing 9.2. Loading a .VOC sound file into memory from disk.

```
char far *Voc_Load_Sound(char *filename,
                         unsigned char *header_length)
{
// This function loads a sound off disk into memory and returns
// a pointer to the data.

char far *temp_ptr;
char far *data_ptr;

unsigned int sum;

int sound_handle;

unsigned segment,num_para,bytes_read;

// Open the sound file.

_dos_open(filename, _O_RDONLY, &sound_handle);
```

```
// Allocate the memory.

num_para = 1 + (filelength(sound_handle))/16;

_dos_allocmem(num_para,&segment);

// Point data pointer to the allocated data area.

_FP_SEG(data_ptr) = segment;
_FP_OFF(data_ptr) = 0;

// Load in the sound data.

temp_ptr = data_ptr;

do
 {
 _dos_read(sound_handle,temp_ptr, 0x4000, &bytes_read);
 temp_ptr += bytes_read;

 sum+=bytes_read;

 } while(bytes_read==0x4000);

// Make sure it's a VOC file.

   if ((data_ptr[0] != 'C') || (data_ptr[1] != 'r'))
      {
      printf("\n%s is not a voc file!",filename);
      _dos_freemem(_FP_SEG(data_ptr));
      return(0);

      } // end if voc file

   *header_length = (unsigned char)data_ptr[20];

// Close the file.

_dos_close(sound_handle);

return(data_ptr);

} // end Voc_Load_Sound
```

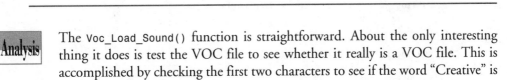 The Voc_Load_Sound() function is straightforward. About the only interesting thing it does is test the VOC file to see whether it really is a VOC file. This is accomplished by checking the first two characters to see if the word "Creative" is at the beginning of the file.

The function returns a FAR pointer to the region of memory into which the VOC file was loaded. This an important detail: all VOC files are loaded into the FAR regions of memory.

The parameters of the function are worth taking a look at.

Syntax

Here's the syntax of the `Voc_Load-Sound()` function:

```
char far *Voc_Load_Sound(char *filename,
                         unsigned char *header_length)
```

where:

- `filename` is a pointer to an ASCII filename of the VOC file to be loaded.

- `header_length` is a pointer to a variable in which the function will place the length of the header section, so this information can be used later to compute the actual start of real digitized data relative to the header portion of the VOC file.

We have now loaded the device driver along with a sound file, so we're ready to start implementing each of the driver functions. We walk through only a few of the implementations of the functions here because they're all similar. Let's begin with implementing function 3, which initializes the driver itself.

All we need do is place a 0×03h in the BX register and call the driver function using an assembly language CALL driver_ptr. The result of the function is returned in the AX register, which is used by C as the byte- and word-sized holder of return values. Listing 9.3 contains the code.

Listing 9.3. Initializing the sound driver.

```
int Voc_Init_Driver(void)
{
// This function initializes the driver and returns the status.

_asm
   {
   mov bx,3          ; Function 3: initialize the driver
   call driver_ptr   ; Call the driver.
   mov status,ax     ; Store in version variable

   } // end in-line asm

// Return the status.

printf("\nDriver Initialized");

return(status);

} // end Voc_Init_Driver
```

 As you can see, the `Voc_Init_Driver()` function doesn't do much except place a 0×03h in the `BX` register, call the driver, and return—but there's a little point here that I've purposely added to the code. The `mov status,ax` is unnecessary because the result is automatically returned in `AX` if there isn't a formal return statement. However, if you define a function as returning an `INT`, and then don't return anything with the `return()` statement, the C compiler gives you a warning. (Personally, I ignore the C compiler—but many others might find this warning annoying.) In general, then, if you write an in-line assembly language function and the result is already in the `AX` register, you don't have to do anything—but you do get a compiler warning. To remedy this, add an instruction that moves the `AX` register into a dummy variable and then return the dummy variable in the final return statement. This shuts the compiler up.

When the `Voc_Init_Driver()` function returns, the return value has an error code as defined in Table 9.5. You can use this information to make the decision to proceed, for example.

The next important and slightly tricky function we want to implement is the status variable. You see, the driver has all kinds of good internal information that we, as programmers, would like to get hold of. However, as the driver is loaded into memory, it doesn't have a place to store these goodies. Thus, we must give the driver a place in memory to store all of its results. We can accomplish this by declaring a global variable and then sending the segment and offset of this variable to the driver using Function 5. Listing 9.4 contains the code to accomplish this.

Listing 9.4. Setting the sound driver's status word.

```
void Voc_Set_Status_Addr(char far *status)
{

// This function sets the address of the global status word in
// the driver.

unsigned segm,offm;

// Extract the segment and offset of the status variable.

segm = _FP_SEG(status);
offm = _FP_OFF(status);

_asm
   {
   mov bx,5          ; Function 5: set the status variable
                     ; address
   mov es, segm      ; es gets the segment.
   mov di, offm      ; di gets the offset.
   call driver_ptr   ; Call the driver.
```

continues

495

Making the PC Rock!

Listing 9.4. continued

```
    } // end in-line asm
} // Voc_Set_Status_Addr
```

 The operation of the `Voc_Set_Status_Addr()` is simple. The only interesting part of it is how the segment and offset of the global status variable are extracted. In general, you can use the macros `_FP_SEG()` and `_FP_OFF()` to extract the segment and offset, respectively, of any variable.

Follow these steps to set the global status word:

1. Extract the segment and offset of a global variable named `status`.
2. Place the results in `ES:DI`.
3. Then place a `0x05h` in `BX`, which specifies the set status word function to the driver.
4. Call the driver itself.

All the functions in the library are created in much the same way as the few we've covered.

The most important function we need to complete our implementational discussions is the function that actually plays the sound that's in memory. We look at that now.

Playing a Sound from Memory

To play a sound from memory, we must implement the function 0x06h, which is called "start voice output." The only parameters we need to set up are the function request itself (in `BX`) and the `ES:DI`, which points to the data buffer of the digitized sample. The only caveat here is that we must use the saved header length that was returned from the original loading of the sound, along with the pointer to the sound in memory, to compute a final address of the sound data (which is beyond the header portion of the sound file itself). That was a mouthful! The function that starts the Sound Blaster and play a digitized sample is shown in Listing 9.5.

496

Listing 9.5. A function to play a sound sample.

```
int Voc_Play_Sound(unsigned char far *addr,
                    unsigned char header_length)
{
// This function plays a preloaded VOC file.

unsigned segm,offm;

segm = _FP_SEG(addr);
offm = _FP_OFF(addr) + header_length;
 // Add in the length of the header.

_asm
   {
   mov bx,6          ; Function 6: play a VOC file
   mov ax, segm      ; We can only move a register into a
                     ; segment, so we need this.
   mov es, ax        ; es gets the segment.
   mov di, offm      ; di gets offset.
   call driver_ptr   ; Call the driver.

   } // end in-line asm

} // end Voc_Play_Sound
```

The `Voc_Play_Sound()` function takes only two parameters:

☐ A pointer to the sound file

☐ The length of the header

Using this information, the function computes the starting address of the actual digitized data and then passes this to the sound driver to be played by the Sound Blaster. The attractive feature of the Sound Blaster in this area (playback) is that, once the sound is initiated, the programmer doesn't have to monitor its progress. The Sound Blaster uses DMA to access the data directly from memory, without the need of programmer or CPU intervention.

We've touched on some of the key functions that are incorporated into our sound library at the end of the day. The rest of the functions are shown in a moment, in a demo program. However, let's list them all out so that we know what each of their functions are. Table 9.6 does that.

Table 9.6. The complete sound library interface for the Sound Blaster's digitized sound driver ct-voice.drv.

Function name and purpose.

`void Voc_Get_Version(void)`

This function prints out the version number of the ct-voice.drv driver.

`int Voc_Init_Driver(void);`

This function initializes the sound driver once the sound driver is loaded.

`int Voc_Terminate_Driver(void);`

This function unloads and terminates the driver.

`void Voc_Set_Port(unsigned int port);`

This function sets the base I/O port the Sound Blaster uses for communications.

`void Voc_Set_Speaker(unsigned int on);`

This function turns the output of the Sound Blaster on and off.

`int Voc_Play_Sound(unsigned char far *addr,unsigned char header_length);`

This function plays a sound.

`int Voc_Stop_Sound(void);`

This function stops a currently playing sound.

`int Voc_Pause_Sound(void);`

This function pauses a sound that's playing.

`int Voc_Continue_Sound(void);`

This function continues a previously paused sound, but not one that has been stopped.

`int Voc_Break_Sound(void);`

This function breaks a sound out of a loop structure, which is used to repeat segments of a digitized sound.

`void Voc_Set_DMA(unsigned int dma);`

This function sets the interrupt used by the Sound Blaster to tell the CPU that a DMA slice is needed.

Function name and purpose.

```
void Voc_Set_Status_Addr(char far *status);
```

This function sets the address of a global variable in C, which is used as the storage area for the driver's internal status.

```
void Voc_Load_Driver(void);
```

This function loads the ct-voice.drv driver into memory.

```
char far *Voc_Load_Sound(char *filename, unsigned char *header_length);
```

This function loads VOC files into memory to be played later.

```
void Voc_Unload_Sound(char far *sound_ptr);
```

This function unloads a previously loaded VOC file and releases the memory back to the operating system.

Also, there are some global variables that track different events and the status of different parts of the system:

```
char far *driver_ptr;        // Pointer to the sound driver
                             // ct-voice.drv
unsigned version;            // Holds the version of the driver
char far *data_ptr;          // Pointer to sound file
unsigned ct_voice_status;    // Global status variable
```

We're now ready to see the functions in action. I've created a demo program for which I recorded household animals to make the sound FX. These sounds are all real, obtained at great personal risk to me. (In fact, my life hung in the balance many times as I recorded these sounds from the wild.) The name of the demo program is snddemo.c; the executable is called snddemo.exe.

The program needs a couple of things to run:

☐ All the VOC files must be in the same working directory as the sound demo program.

☐ The ct-voice.drv driver must be in the same directory.

This has already been taken care of for you; however, you may have a problem. The ct-voice.drv driver I've supplied with all programs and games in this book that create sound use the driver for the Sound Blaster 16. This is the Sound Blaster I own. If you own an older model, the driver may not work. Fortunately, this is not a problem! On the CD there's a directory that has all of the drivers for the different models of the Sound Blaster. You simply copy the correct version of the ct-voice.drv driver into the directory of snddemo.exe, and into the other directories of any other programs that use sound. If

you don't want to hunt on the CD, you can use the ct-voice.drv driver that came on the distribution disks with your particular Sound Blaster or compatible.

The only problem with all this is that all versions of the ct-voice.drv driver have the same name, which makes things confusing. Nevertheless, just make sure you have the proper copy of the driver in the working directory of any of the programs in the book that use sound and you'll at least hear something. (Otherwise, you may be rebooting a lot!)

Now that I've got that out of my system, let's see the demo. The source code is contained in Listing 9.6.

Listing 9.6. A sound library demo program (snddemo.c)

```c
// I N C L U D E S ///////////////////////////////////////////

#include <io.h>
#include <conio.h>
#include <stdio.h>
#include <stdlib.h>
#include <dos.h>
#include <bios.h>
#include <fcntl.h>
#include <memory.h>
#include <malloc.h>
#include <math.h>
#include <string.h>

#include "graph3.h"  // Include our graphics stuff.
#include "graph4.h"

// D E F I N E S ///////////////////////////////////////////

#define NUM_SOUNDS    5  // Number of sounds in this demo

#define DUCK_SOUND    0  // Take a guess, Einstein!
#define BEE_SOUND     1
#define CAT_SOUND     2
#define FROG_SOUND    3
#define EXIT_SOUND    4

// G L O B A L S ///////////////////////////////////////////

char far *driver_ptr;      // Pointer to the sound driver
                           // ct-voice.drv
unsigned version;          // Holds the version of the driver
char far *data_ptr;        // Pointer to sound file
unsigned ct_voice_status;  // Global status variable

char far *sounds[NUM_SOUNDS];      // Array that holds pointers
                                   // to sound files
unsigned char lengths[NUM_SOUNDS]; // The length of each sound
pcx_picture animals_pcx;           // The PCX image loaded
```

```
// F U N C T I O N S /////////////////////////////////////////////

void Voc_Get_Version(void)
{
// This function prints out the version of the driver.

_asm
   {
   mov bx,0         ; Function 0: get the version number
   call driver_ptr  ; Call the driver.
   mov version,ax   ; store in version variable

   } // end in-line asm

printf("\nVersion of Driver = %X.0%X",
      ((version>>8) & 0x00ff), (version&0x00ff));

} // end Voc_Get_Version

//////////////////////////////////////////////////////////////////

int Voc_Init_Driver(void)
{
// This function initializes the driver and returns the status.

int status;

_asm
   {
   mov bx,3         ; Function 3: initialize the driver
   call driver_ptr  ; Call the driver.
   mov status,ax    ; Store in version variable

   } // end in-line asm

// Return the status.

printf("\nDriver Initialized");

return(status);

} // end Voc_Init_Driver

//////////////////////////////////////////////////////////////////

int Voc_Terminate_Driver(void)
{
// This function terminates the driver and deinstalls it
// from memory.

_asm
   {
   mov bx,9         ; Function 9: terminate the driver
   call driver_ptr  ; Call the driver.

   } // end in-line asm
```

continues

Listing 9.6. continued

```c
// Deallocate memory.

_dos_freemem(_FP_SEG(driver_ptr));

printf("\nDriver Terminated");

} // end Voc_Terminate_Driver

/////////////////////////////////////////////////////////////////

void Voc_Set_Port(unsigned int port)
{

// This function sets the I/O port of the Sound Blaster.

_asm
    {
    mov bx,1        ; Function 1: set port address
    mov ax,port     ; Move the port number into ax.
    call driver_ptr ; Call the driver.

    } // end in-line asm

} // Voc_Set_Port

/////////////////////////////////////////////////////////////////

void Voc_Set_Speaker(unsigned int on)
{

// This function turns the speaker on or off.

_asm
    {
    mov bx,4        ; Function 4: turn the speaker on or off
    mov ax,on       ; Move the on/off flag into ax.
    call driver_ptr ; Call the driver.

    } // end in-line asm

} // Voc_Set_Speaker

/////////////////////////////////////////////////////////////////

int Voc_Play_Sound(unsigned char far *addr,
                   unsigned char header_length)
{
// This function plays a preloaded VOC file.

unsigned segm,offm;

segm = _FP_SEG(addr);
offm = _FP_OFF(addr) + header_length;
```

```
_asm
   {
   mov bx,6          ; Function 6: play a VOC file
   mov ax, segm      ; We can only move a register into a
                     ; segment, so we need this.
   mov es, ax        ; es gets the segment.
   mov di, offm      ; di gets offset.
   call driver_ptr   ; Call the driver.

   } // end in-line asm

} // end Voc_Play_Sound

/////////////////////////////////////////////////////////////

int Voc_Stop_Sound(void)
{
// This function stops a currently playing sound.

_asm
   {
   mov bx,8          ; Function 8: stop a sound
   call driver_ptr   ; Call the driver.

   } // end in-line asm

} // end Voc_Stop_Sound

/////////////////////////////////////////////////////////////

int Voc_Pause_Sound(void)
{
// This function pauses a sound that's playing.

_asm
   {
   mov bx,10         ; Function 10: pause a sound
   call driver_ptr   ; Call the driver.

   } // end in-line asm

} // end Voc_Pause_Sound

/////////////////////////////////////////////////////////////

int Voc_Continue_Sound(void)
{
// This function continues a sound that had been paused.

_asm
   {
   mov bx,11         ; Function 11: continue play
   call driver_ptr   ; Call the driver.

   } // end in-line asm
```

continues

Listing 9.6. continued

```
} // end Voc_Continue_Sound

///////////////////////////////////////////////////////////////

int Voc_Break_Sound(void)
{
// This function breaks a sound that's in a loop.

_asm
   {
   mov bx,12       ; Function 12: break a loop
   call driver_ptr ; Call the driver.

   } // end in-line asm

} // end Voc_Break_Sound

///////////////////////////////////////////////////////////////

void Voc_Set_DMA(unsigned int dma)
{
// This function sets the DMA channel for the Sound Blaster.

_asm
   {
   mov bx,2        ; Function 2: set the DMA interupt number
   mov ax,dma      ; Move the DMA number into ax.
   call driver_ptr ; Call the driver.

   } // end in-line asm

} // Voc_Set_DMA

///////////////////////////////////////////////////////////////

void Voc_Set_Status_Addr(char far *status)
{

// This function sets the address of the global status word
// in the driver.

unsigned segm,offm;

// Extract the segment and offset of the status variable.

segm = _FP_SEG(status);
offm = _FP_OFF(status);

_asm
   {
   mov bx,5        ; Function 5: set the status variable
                   ; address
   mov es, segm    ; es gets the segment.
   mov di, offm    ; di gets offset.
```

```
      call driver_ptr    ; Call the driver.

      } // end in-line asm

} // Voc_Set_Status_Addr

///////////////////////////////////////////////////////////////

void Voc_Load_Driver(void)
{
// This functions loads the ct-voice.drv, which allows digitized
// effects to be played.

int driver_handle;

unsigned segment,num_para,bytes_read;

// Open the driver file.

_dos_open("CT-VOICE.DRV", _O_RDONLY, &driver_handle);

// Allocate the memory.

num_para = 1 + (filelength(driver_handle))/16;

_dos_allocmem(num_para,&segment);

// Point the driver pointer to the data area.

_FP_SEG(driver_ptr) = segment;
_FP_OFF(driver_ptr) = 0;

// Load in the driver code.

data_ptr = driver_ptr;

do
 {
 _dos_read(driver_handle,data_ptr, 0x4000, &bytes_read);
 data_ptr += bytes_read;

 } while(bytes_read==0x4000);

// Close the file.

_dos_close(driver_handle);

} // end Voc_Load_Driver

///////////////////////////////////////////////////////////////

char far *Voc_Load_Sound(char *filename,
                         unsigned char *header_length)
{
// This function loads a sound off disk into memory and returns
// a pointer to the data.
```

continues

Listing 9.6. continued

```c
char far *temp_ptr;
char far *data_ptr;

unsigned int sum;

int sound_handle;

unsigned segment,num_para,bytes_read;

// Open the sound file.

_dos_open(filename, _O_RDONLY, &sound_handle);

// Allocate the memory.

num_para = 1 + (filelength(sound_handle))/16;

_dos_allocmem(num_para,&segment);

// Point the data pointer to the allocated data area.

_FP_SEG(data_ptr) = segment;
_FP_OFF(data_ptr) = 0;

// Load in the sound data.

temp_ptr = data_ptr;

do
 {
 _dos_read(sound_handle,temp_ptr, 0x4000, &bytes_read);
 temp_ptr += bytes_read;

 sum+=bytes_read;

 } while(bytes_read==0x4000);

// Make sure it's a VOC file.

    if ((data_ptr[0] != 'C') || (data_ptr[1] != 'r'))
        {
        printf("\n%s is not a voc file!",filename);
        _dos_freemem(_FP_SEG(data_ptr));
        return(0);

        } // end if voc file

    *header_length = (unsigned char)data_ptr[20];

// Close the file.

_dos_close(sound_handle);

return(data_ptr);
```

```
} // end Voc_Load_Sound

/////////////////////////////////////////////////////////////////

void Voc_Unload_Sound(char far *sound_ptr)
{

// This functions deletes the sound from memory.

_dos_freemem(_FP_SEG(sound_ptr));

} // end Voc_Unload_Sound


// M A I N /////////////////////////////////////////////////////

void main(void)
{

int done=0;   // Exit flag
long index;   // Loop counter

// S E C T I O N 1 ////////////////////////////////////////////

// Load the sound driver ct-voice.drv into memory.

Voc_Load_Driver();

// Initialize the driver.

Voc_Init_Driver();

// Set the I/O port of the sound card.

Voc_Set_Port(0x220);

// Set the DMA channel used by the sound card.

Voc_Set_DMA(5);

// Print out the version of the driver.

Voc_Get_Version();

// Set the global status variable in the driver.

Voc_Set_Status_Addr((char far *)&ct_voice_status);

// Load in the sounds.

sounds[DUCK_SOUND ] = Voc_Load_Sound("duck.voc" ,
                                     &lengths[DUCK_SOUND ]);
sounds[BEE_SOUND  ] = Voc_Load_Sound("bee.voc" ,
                                     &lengths[BEE_SOUND  ]);
```

continues

Listing 9.6. continued

```
sounds[CAT_SOUND  ] = Voc_Load_Sound("cat.voc" ,
                                     &lengths[CAT_SOUND  ]);
sounds[FROG_SOUND ] = Voc_Load_Sound("frog.voc",
                                     &lengths[FROG_SOUND ]);
sounds[EXIT_SOUND ] = Voc_Load_Sound("exit.voc",
                                     &lengths[EXIT_SOUND ]);

Voc_Set_Speaker(1);


// S E C T I O N 2 /////////////////////////////////////////////

// Set the video mode to the 320x200, 256-color mode.

Set_Video_Mode(VGA256);

// Load in the background.

PCX_Init((pcx_picture_ptr)&animals_pcx);

PCX_Load("animals.pcx", (pcx_picture_ptr)&animals_pcx,1);

PCX_Show_Buffer((pcx_picture_ptr)&animals_pcx);

PCX_Delete((pcx_picture_ptr)&animals_pcx);

// Main event loop: let the user select a sound to play. Note
// that you can interupt a sound that is currently playing.

// S E C T I O N 3 /////////////////////////////////////////////

while(!done)
    {

    // Has the user pressed a key?

    if (kbhit())
    {
    // Get the key.

    switch (getch())
        {
        case '1':
            {
            Voc_Stop_Sound();
            Voc_Play_Sound(sounds[DUCK_SOUND] ,
                        lengths[DUCK_SOUND]);
            } break;

        case '2':
            {
            Voc_Stop_Sound();
            Voc_Play_Sound(sounds[BEE_SOUND] ,
                        lengths[BEE_SOUND]);
```

```
                        } break;

                case '3':
                        {
                        Voc_Stop_Sound();
                        Voc_Play_Sound(sounds[CAT_SOUND] ,
                                        lengths[CAT_SOUND]);
                        } break;

                case '4':
                        {
                        Voc_Stop_Sound();
                        Voc_Play_Sound(sounds[FROG_SOUND] ,
                                        lengths[FROG_SOUND]);
                        } break;

                case 'q':
                        {
                        done = 1;
                        } break;

                default:break;


                } // end switch

        } // end if keyboard hit

        } // end while

// S E C T I O N 4 /////////////////////////////////////////////

// Say goodbye...

Voc_Play_Sound(sounds[EXIT_SOUND] , lengths[EXIT_SOUND]); ;

// Wait for the end of the sequence to stop. The status variable
// is -1 when a sound is playing, and 0 otherwise.

while(ct_voice_status!=0) {}

// Turn the speaker off.

Voc_Set_Speaker(0);

// S E C T I O N 5 /////////////////////////////////////////////

// Unload sounds.

Voc_Unload_Sound(sounds[DUCK_SOUND ]);
Voc_Unload_Sound(sounds[BEE_SOUND  ]);
Voc_Unload_Sound(sounds[CAT_SOUND  ]);
Voc_Unload_Sound(sounds[FROG_SOUND ]);
Voc_Unload_Sound(sounds[EXIT_SOUND ]);
```

continues

Listing 9.6. continued

```
// Unload the sound driver from memory.

Voc_Terminate_Driver();

// Dissolve the screen...in one line, might I add!

for (index=0; index<=300000; index++,
    Plot_Pixel_Fast(rand()%320, rand()%200, 0));

// Reset the video mode back to text.

Set_Video_Mode(TEXT_MODE);

} // end main
```

Building an Executable: To make an executable of the program in Listing 9.6, you can either type it in or use the source on the companion CD. The name of the source is snddemo.c. The precompiled executable is named snddemo.exe. As before, use the following compile line for Microsoft C:

```
cl -AM -Zi -c -Fc -Gs -G2 snddemo.c
```

After compiling the program in this manner, you can link it to the standard libraries and to our previously generated game library, gamelib.lib, with a link line such as:

```
link /ST:8192 /CO snddemo,,,graphics.lib+gamelib.lib,,
```

This will create a final executable named snddemo.exe.

Let's analyze just the main() section of the program, as all functions in the program are just interfaces to each of the driver functions (which we've already covered).

The general flow of the main() is to:

1. Load in the sound driver.

2. Initialize and set the proper ports on the sound driver.

3. Load in the sound files themselves.

4. Wait in a main loop for the player to press a key that selects a specific sound to be played.

The program also loads a PCX file and displays it; however, we've seen this about a thousand times, so it's nothing new. When the player exits the program, the sound files are unloaded (as is the sound driver), and the program exits gracefully.

The basic idea of the program is to show how to play digitized sounds with the sound library without a lot of extraneous code doing other things. Anyway, let's see what each section of the code does, shall we?

1. In Section 1 the ct-voice.drv driver is loaded, the DMA interrupt is set, the I/O port is set, and the sound files are loaded. We also turn on the output speaker and set the global status variable here. Note that the program always sets the DMA interrupt and I/O port to the same values. In general, in a real game you should load this stuff in using a configuration file. (If you recall, we did something similar in the mechs in Mech War on Day 2. It had a configuration file that was loaded and configured the sound system.)

2. Section 2 is where we put the PC into the 320×200-pixel, 256-color graphics mode (mode 13h) and do all the PCX-file stuff. We load the PCX file that has the animals drawn in it and display it. Then we delete the PCX file from memory and continue.

3. Section 3 is the entrance to the event loop and where the keyboard is tested for a keypress. If any key from 1 through 4 is pressed, the appropriate sound is played by the two function calls Voc_Stop_Sound() and Voc_Play_Sound().

    The first call, to Voc_Stop_Sound(), is to kill any sound currently playing (or, in computer science terminology, Voc_Stop_Sound() *preempts* the current sound). Then a call is made to Voc_Play_Sound(), with the appropriate parameters, to play the actual sound.

4. In Section 4, the player has terminated the program by pressing the Q key. The last sound (a scream saying "Oh no...") plays, and then there's an interesting piece of code we should discuss, which is the famous one-line dissolve!

    When a sound is played, it plays concurrently with the execution stream of the C program that called it. In other words, once the call to Voc_Play_Sound() is made, the program continues to execute instructions after the function call, as the Sound Blaster operates parallel to the system CPU. Figure 9.16 shows the CPU and Sound Blaster working together.

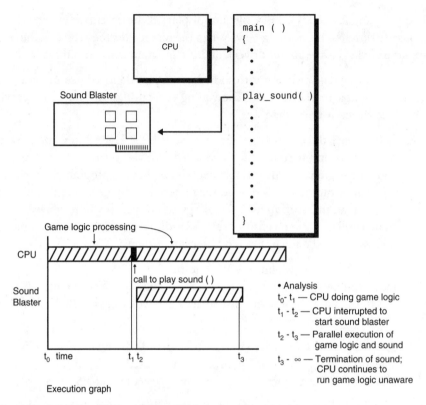

CPU

main ( )
{
 .
 .
 .
 .
play_sound( )
 .
 .
 .
 .
 .
 .
 .
 .
}

Sound Blaster

Game logic processing

CPU

call to play sound ( )

Sound
Blaster

• Analysis
t_0- t_1 — CPU doing game logic
t_1 - t_2 — CPU interrupted to
 start sound blaster
t_2 - t_3 — Parallel execution of
 game logic and sound
t_3 - ∞ — Termination of sound;
 CPU continues to
 run game logic unaware

t_0 time t_1 t_2 t_3

Execution graph

Figure 9.16. *The CPU and Sound Blaster working together.*

This means that, to ensure the sound is done playing, we must poll the status variable until it's zero. When the status variable is zero, there are no sounds being played.

5. Section 5 is the clean-up area of the program. The sound files are unloaded and the driver itself terminated. The program then restores the graphics mode to 80×25 text and returns to the operating system.

That about sums it up for playing digitized sounds using the Sound Blaster, the ct-voice.drv driver, and our own library interface. At the end of the day today we see the final library version, graph9.c (along with graph9.h), which contains the complete sound system we use in our future games.

Now, let's diverge from playing sounds and learn how to manipulate them mathematically in realtime.

Manipulating Sound Files

When a game uses digitized samples for sound FX, there isn't a lot of room for many different versions of the same sample in main memory. This is because the samples themselves take, on average, 8K per second of memory. For example, what if you wanted to have 10 different versions of the same digitized effect, all at different volume levels? Normally, you'd have to create 10 different versions of the sound, each recorded at different levels. On the other hand, you could use the new models of the Sound Blaster to adjust the volume as the sample plays (although the control is not especially fine-grained).

As another example, say you want to play two or more digitized sounds simultaneously. Because the sound channel can only have one data stream at once, you would have to record multiple samples, each with different subsets of the mixed sounds you wanted. Moreover, the software you used to record the sounds would have to support sound mixing.

The solution to all these problems, and more, is to mathematically alter the digitized sounds in memory and use a single sound as the basis for others. Creating effects such as volume changes, mixing, echoing, and so forth can all be done by software quickly, and usually in realtime. Let's take a look at a few examples of this.

Changing the Volume

If we want to change the volume of the sound, or its *intensity*, we must amplify the sound. *Amplification* means to multiply the waveform's amplitude by a constant factor. To accomplish this with a sound file, we must consider a few factors:

☐ First, we must create a secondary buffer in which to do the operation so we don't corrupt the original sound file.

☐ Second, we must make sure to not overflow the data size, which is usually eight bits (-128 to 127) during the amplification operation.

The problem of overflow can be handled a couple of ways:

☐ The first method would be to multiply the sound file by the amplification factor. As amplification is going on, a test is made to see whether the signal has exceeded the range of the digital word. If this is the case, the signal is clipped as shown in Figure 9.17.

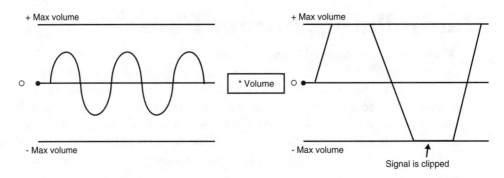

Figure 9.17. *The clipping of a sound signal due to heavy amplification.*

If it looks as though information is lost, it's because it is. Nevertheless, the result sounds reasonable.

☐ The other method of amplifying the sound would be to first find the largest value in the sound file and use it as a basis for the amplification. This way the sound would be amplified, but in a way that it wouldn't be clipped.

We use the first method for our example as it's more to the point. Algorithm 9.1 amplifies a sound.

Given that:

☐ $S_s(i)$ is the source sound file.

☐ $S_d(i)$ is the destination sound file.

☐ V is the amplification factor.

☐ L is the length of the source file.

Then:

Algorithm 9.1. Amplifying a digitized sound with clipping.

```
For (index=0; index<L; index++)
    {

    S_d(index) = S_s(index) * V;
    If (S_d(index) it out of range of word size)
            {
        clip S_d(index) and store the result back in S_d(index);
            } // end if out of range
    } // end for index
```

When Algorithm 9.1 operates on a sound file, the new version of the sound file is generated in the destination buffer and can be played in the normal way. (Of course, the header information would have to be replicated.)

Amplifying sounds is a really basic operation. We need to look at something a little more interesting, such as sound mixing.

Mixing Sounds

Because the Sound Blaster has a single digital channel, only one data stream can be played at once. This means that only one sound can be played at once. What if we want to hear a laser blast along with a gunshot? We can mix the sounds ourselves in a working buffer and then play the result. There are two ways to mix two or more sounds together:

☐ The first method is to take a weighted average that only adds a percentage of each sound to create the resulting sound. This is the *weighted-average technique*.

☐ The second method simply adds the two sounds blindly.

Let's look at each.

The Weighted-Average Technique

The weighted-average technique works in the following way: say we want to mix two sounds. We take the data from each sound and add them together. However, we first multiply each data element from each source by .5. This, in essence, takes only 50 percent of each sound's amplitude. Algorithm 9.2 mixes sounds using a weighted average.

Given that:

☐ $S_{s1}(i)$ is the first source sound file.

☐ $S_{s2}(i)$ is the second source sound file.

☐ $S_d(i)$ is the destination sound file.

☐ L is the length of each source file, which is the same in this case.

Then:

Algorithm 9.2. Mixing sounds using a weighted average.

```
for (index=0; index<L; index++)
    {
    S_d(index) = .5*S_s1(index)+.5*S_s2(index);
```

continues

Algorithm 9.2. continued

```
// Do clipping.

If (S_d(index) it out of range of word size)
            {
        clip S_d(index) and store the result back
        in S_d(index);
        } // end if out of range

} // end for index
```

When Algorithm 9.2 has run on the two sound files, the result in the destination buffer is a mixture of both. If you play the result you hear a laser blast and a scream at the same time.

There's one detail we must take care of in a complete implementation: the length of the sound files. In general, the files won't be the same length. The tactic used in that case is to add the data together until one of the source files ends, and then just copy the remaining portion of the longer file to the destination buffer with its amplitude decreased by 50 percent.

The Simple Mix Technique

As we learned a moment ago, the other method of mixing two sound files together is just to mix them without taking a percentage of each file. This method actually sounds better than the percentage method even though the percentage method seems more mathematically correct. Algorithm 9.3 mixes sound without percentages.

Given that:

☐ $S_{s1}(i)$ is the first source sound file.

☐ $S_{s2}(i)$ is the second source sound file.

☐ $S_d(i)$ is the destination sound file.

☐ L is the length of each source file, which is the same in this case.

Algorithm 9.3. Mixing sound files with simple addition.

```
for (index=0; index<L; index++)
    {
    S_d(index) = S_s1(index)+S_s2(index);
    // Do clipping
    If (S_d(index) it out of range of word size)
```

```
             {
        clip S_d(index) and store the result back
        in S_d(index);
             } // end if out of range
     } // end for index
```

Notice that, in both cases, we clip the resulting sound. If we don't do this, the results are incorrect.

The next spectacular effect we cover is echoes...echoes...echoes...

Echoing Sounds

Echoing means to mix a sound with itself in a recursive manner, so that at some point as the sound plays the same sound is heard again. The calculations for echoing are rather complex and usually cannot be done in realtime. However, you may wish to create an echo for a specific effect, and taking a second or so to do the calculation won't be apparent to the player if that calculation is done during a portion of the game that isn't time-critical. For instance, if the player's character walks into a room with tall walls, any digitized sound should be played with an echo to simulate the acoustic properties of the room the player's character is in.

Let's take a look at how we can create an echo. We want to mix a sound with itself, but with a phase shift or time shift. This means we have a destination buffer into which we first copy the original sound. We then mix in the working buffer sound on top of the original, but with a time lag called the *echo in time*. This is the amount of time before we hear the first echo. During the mixing we can control the amplitude of the mixed echo to make it loud or soft. This process is shown in Figure 9.18.

To continue the echo process, we take the destination file and then mix it again with the original file, using a multiple of the initial time lag. This process is repeated many times to create a final echoed version. Figure 9.19 shows a sound file that has been echoed with a 20-millisecond delay and a 50-percent echo amplitude.

Basically, echoing is analogous to computing compound interest. Algorithm 9.4 echoes a sound.

9

517

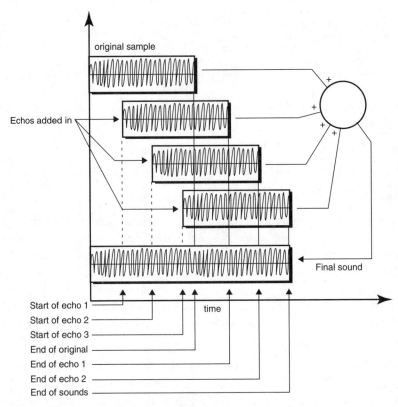

Figure 9.18. *The construction of an echo.*

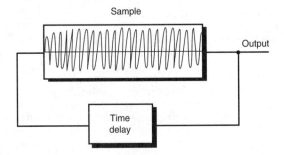

Figure 9.19. *The recursive feedback echo model.*

Given that:

- □ $S_s(i)$ is the source sound file to be echoed.

- □ $S_d(i)$ is the destination sound file or the result of the echo.

- □ L is the length of each source file, which is the same in this case.

- □ Delay is the initial delay, in milliseconds, converted into samples.

- □ Amp is the amplitude of the echo.

Then:

Algorithm 9.4. Echoing a sound file.

```
Copy S_s(i) to S_d(i);

Begin Echo

for (index=0; index<L; index++)
    {
    if (index > Delay)
        {
        S_d(index) = S_s(index-Delay) * Amp + S_d(index);
        }  // end if it's time to echo
    // Clip the signal.
    If (S_d(index) it out of range of word size)
            {
        clip S_d(index) and store the result back in S_d(index);
        } // end if out of range
    } // end for index

// Prepare to echo again.

Delay=Delay+Delay;

Until(Delay>index) Begin Echo

End Echo
```

Algorithm 9.4 echoes the input sound file, but does not take into consideration certain cases, such as expanding the file when you want all echoes to die out. Also, in Algorithm 9.4 the destination file is mixed with the original file; another technique is to mix the destination file with itself for the echo. Each technique gives different results, so experiment.

We've covered all the technical aspects of the Sound Blaster and playing digitized effects. Now we must talk about the proper use of sound in a game.

The Use of Sound in Video Games

I can't remember if I've said this already, somewhere and sometime in the past, but I'll say it again anyway: music and sound are more important that good graphics! There's something magical about music and sound that can go deeper than visual images. Music and sound are probably a part of every human life in way or another. This means that for games to invoke feelings of fear, excitement, and anticipation, we must have music and sound in our games. A game with average graphics and bad game play but good music and sound can really be easy to digest (and will sell more copies!). A good game with good sound can be incredible. There's a synergistic connection between sound and graphics.

I want to give you a few tips on how to make good sound even better. You may write a great game and have awesome graphics, but it could be even better if you take a few advanced concepts into consideration when you write the sound system.

Context-Sensitive Music

Many games play the same music level to level, room to room. Writing a sound system that changes the music depending on the context or environment of the player's character is important. For instance, if a player's character is in a wide-open outside space, we might hear music that's based on wind instruments and is ominous and forbidding. On the other hand, if the character walks into a high-tech room, we might play loud metal or industrial music (heaven forfend a rap video game!). Of course, the transitions from piece to piece should be smooth and unnoticeable: one piece should fade away as the other begins.

Another exciting musical technique is to alter the notes of the music depending on the current situation. For example, if the player's character is weak and dying, we might accentuate the low base tones while de-emphasizing the high happy notes.

Active Tempo Systems

Altering the tempo of music is a relatively new concept that hasn't been implemented much. (Personally, I don't think I've seen it at all.) By an *active tempo system* (ATS, a new acronym I invented), I mean the game software changes the tempo of the music based on the current situation. This tempo change can be a function of a formula that takes into consideration many different factors about the game play.

As a simple example, we could write an ATS system based solely on the distance of the player's character to the exit and the proximity of bad guys. When a character is moving around in the game world and bad guys start getting closer, the beat of the music should increase. In the same way, as the character moves closer to the exit, and to success, the music would pick up.

Digitized Voice

Having digitized voice in a video game is an absolute must. It gives character to the virtual creatures in the computer. For instance, Darth Vader in Star Wars has no face, but his voice defines who he is. Similarly, a video game can use digitized voice to immortalize a creature that doesn't exist and in so doing make it seem real. The problem, of course, is that digitized speech costs a lot memory-wise. This is a setback, but we can work around it by storing all voice on disk, and then loading and fleshing out the samples as necessary. Only frequently used samples need be resident in memory.

Another intriguing possibility is mixing words to create sentences that are generated algorithmically. This is difficult and can sound choppy; however, it can be done. The speaker records his/her voice, saying a few dozen key words and connectives. Then a sentence is generated by mixing these fragments in realtime. The fragments are smoothed by mathematically blending the fragments at their boundaries. Using this technique, you can create complete dissertations and speeches that weren't prerecorded.

These kind of systems are already in use, and have been for years. When you call 411 for directory information (or whatever it is in your area), a computerized voice tells you the number. The number spoken is a concatenation of the single digits that were prerecorded, because the phone company surely hasn't recorded all 350,000,000 phone numbers in digital speech form and placed them on disk!

Adding to the Game Library

As usual, we get a complete library of all the software and functions we've created today. The name of the modules are graph9.c and graph9.h. The modules, along with a precompiled .OBJ version, are on the companion CD. You should add the module to your growing game library gamelib.lib with the library manager.

Summary

Today has been very informative. We've begun to see how complex sound really is. Most of us take it for granted in games; however, we now see that producing and manipulating it is a formidable challenge. We covered the Sound Blaster and talked about all of its important features. We then learned how to record and play digitized samples ourselves using the ct-voice.drv. Furthermore, we learned some hints on how to play music with the SBFMDRV.COM music driver.

Music and sound are interesting topics and I hope you continue educating yourself about them because, as we just learned, they are probably the most important part of a video game.

Q&A

Q How does the FM synthesizer work?

A The FM synthesizer works by creating a pure sine wave—the carrier—and then modulating it by another sine wave called the modulator. By using different amounts of modulation and different attack-sustain-decay-release (ADSR) amplitude envelopes, you can create many complex sounds. In fact, musical instruments and human voices can be realistically synthesized.

Q How much memory do digitized samples consume?

A This depends on the sample rate and the sample size. Here's the formula to compute the amount of memory used by a sample:

```
sample size in bytes = sample time (secs) * sample rate
                    (samples/sec) * sample size (in bytes)
```

Therefore, if we were to sample at 8KHz with single bytes as the sample size, the amount of memory used would be 8,000 bytes per second.

Q Why isn't the ct-voice.drv sound driver accessed using an interrupt?

A This is just a decision Creative Labs made. Maybe they didn't want two different drivers latching onto the system interrupts (that is, both the ct-voice.drv and SBFMDRV.COM drivers).

Q If the sound drivers use the timer interrupt to play music, won't this mess up the system time and the keyboard?

A No. The interrupts are chained so that all the interrupt service routines (ISRs) already being serviced by the interrupt are still serviced at the proper time.

Q How fast do sound waves travel?

A This depends on the medium of transmission. However, in air (on nice day at a temperature of 72 degrees Fahrenheit) at sea level, sound travels at about 650 miles per hour.

Q Can music and digitized sounds be played simultaneously?

A Yes. The DMA takes care of the digital sample, and the interrupt system will play the music.

Q Do I have to digitize samples, or can I create them algorithmically?

A Yes, of course you can create samples with algorithms. This is done all the time. However, you have to create an appropriate header for the sound sample if it is to be loaded into another sound program and interpreted as a VOC file.

Workshop

The Workshop section presents quiz questions to help you cement your new knowledge and exercises to give you experience using what you've learned. Try to understand the questions and exercises before moving on to the next lesson. The answers are in Appendix B.

Quiz

1. What is the Fourier series, and why is it important in sound synthesis?

2. How many digital sound channels does the Sound Blaster have?

3. What is DMA, and how is it used to play sounds?

4. What is the ct-voice.drv driver used for?

5. How is the interrupt vector for the SBFMDRV.COM music driver found?

6. What is the frequency response of normal humans?

7. Can anyone decipher all the words from Prince's song "The Most Beautiful Girl in the World"?

8. What is frequency modulation synthesis?

Exercises

1. Write a function that amplifies a loaded VOC file. The function prototype should look like this:

   ```
   char far *Voc_Amplify(char far *voc_file, int header_length, float
   amplitude);
   ```

   The result of calling the function is that a new buffer is created containing an amplified version of the original VOC file.

2. Digitize your voice with the sample rates of 4KHz to 20KHz. Then listen to the samples and determine where you can start to hear a degradation in the quality of the sample.

3. Write a program that displays a VOC file graphically on the video screen.

4. Create a library of 100 or so digitized samples of all kinds of sounds, such as screams, lasers, explosions (make sure to have supervision!), animals, and so forth.

5. *Extra Credit:* Write a library to play music using the SBFMDRV.COM music driver.

Playing
Dr. Frankenstein

"It's alive, it's alive...!"

—Dr. Frankenstein

Today we explore the world of artificial and synthetic intelligence. In the past week and a half we've been concentrating on graphics, sound, and PC-related topics. Now it's time to talk about creating the brains for our little creations. Learning how to draw graphics, read input devices, play music, and so forth is all important. However, without AI algorithms to control the objects in our games, there isn't going to be much action.

The mathematics behind AI and related subjects is so advanced it takes a Ph.D. to comprehend much of it. Therefore, rather than rattle off Baysian learning algorithms, neural-net models, and a bunch of other abstract rigamarole, we're about to extract the simple from the complex. We learn how to synthesize seemingly complex behaviors with simple rules and simple software.

By the end of today you'll be able to create a "software brain" that actually responds to input, makes decisions, and takes on patterns or *personality*. Here are the topics of today's class on neural-computer synthesis:

- ☐ Introduction to artificial intelligence
- ☐ Tracking and evasion algorithms
- ☐ Fuzzy logic and probability
- ☐ Random movement
- ☐ Taking steps with patterns
- ☐ State machines
- ☐ Implementing personalities
- ☐ Exploration algorithms
- ☐ Building brains from scratch

Introduction to Artificial Intelligence

The term *artificial intelligence* describes techniques used on a computer to emulate logical thinking and decision making. However, the techniques used in classical AI in the past have all been based on deterministic algorithms that use predicate-based rule systems. These systems are based on the "if...then..." structure. A database, or *knowledge base*, is

created in the form of pieces of information that are related to one another by some nature. Then, rules based on logic, semantics, syntax, and so forth are used to solve problems posed to the system, as shown in Figure 10.1.

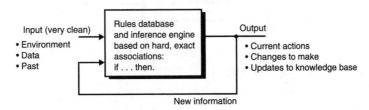

Figure 10.1. *A simple, rule-based AI system.*

The problem with these classical AI systems is that they're almost totally deterministic. Although some systems may use random variables to select between equally likely solutions, in general the AI system is not going to come up with something it hasn't been taught in an indirect way.

The "new" science of artificial intelligence, which I like to call *synthetic intelligence*, is not based on such "crisp" logic. New discoveries in the areas of cellular automata, artificial life, fuzzy logic, neural nets, sparse distributed memory, and more are teaching us that thought is not so deterministic. There's a lot of randomness and personal bias that has no scientific reason. For instance, consider the situation in which you're walking and you take a specific path. You aren't thinking about each and every step as you travel. You simply know that you have a destination and you are trying to get there in the "best" way you can. The "best" is the elusive part. What does your brain do to compute the "best" path? Is it continually computing trajectory vectors and solving for the shortest path? Or is it just pointing you in the general direction and making turns when it "feels" that you're getting too off course?

These kinds of questions and the computational models based on these insights are the basis for the new science of synthetic intelligence. We, as computer scientists and neurologists, are learning that the human mind (and all minds, for that matter) have a "fuzzy" nature to their logic and decision making, and this is one reason we're so complex. Figure 10.2 shows a fuzzy logic system.

Empirical science has been trying for years to measure something that can't be measured, something that can't be counted. The new science is based on "the CE theory," which stands for "close enough."

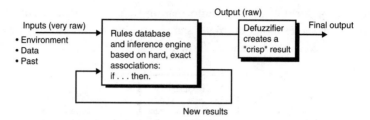

Figure 10.2. *A fuzzy logic system.*

The AI theory we learn today is simple. Nevertheless, it's a starting point from which you can continue to work and make more complex systems. On the other hand, what we learn today is more than enough for the driving AI of video games. By the end of the chapter, you'll understand how to create a model of a brain that's simple to use, programmable, has a personality, and can act and react. This model is something I've been working on for years; it models insects I call *synthesects*. The brains I show you how to make have behavior that's insect-like—which is good enough for a video game, so let's get on with it.

Tracking and Evasion Algorithms

One of the simplest behaviors to model in a video game is the ability of a creature to chase, or track, the player's character. This technique was one of the first AI algorithms used in the early video games and has been a favorite since. Games such as Pac Man use a variation of the tracking algorithm to control the ghosts. Let's see if we can figure out how to accomplish the task of making a creature in a game track or evade the player (or another creature). We begin with the chasing (attacking) algorithm.

Tracking

For our analysis we can use the model of a single player and a single game object or creature. The problem is that we want to make the creature track and chase after the player's character. Both the creature and the character have a pair of coordinates that specifies where each of them are in the game universe, shown in Figure 10.3.

Because we have the position of the character and the position of the creature, we can use this information to calculate a direction for the creature to move that brings it nearer to the player's character. Therefore, the creature looks like it's chasing the player's character. Algorithm 10.1 makes the creature track or attack the player's character no matter where the player moves it.

Video-Game Universe

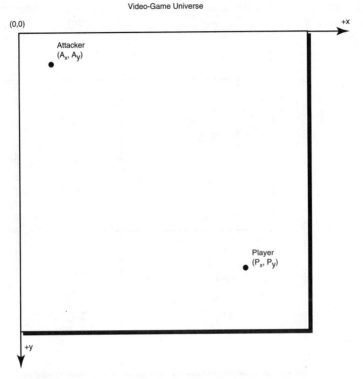

Figure 10.3. *A player's character and opponent in the same world.*

Algorithm 10.1. The tracking algorithm.

```
Given  (Px,Py) - Player's position
       (Cx,Cy) - Creature's position

begin

// Do x tracking.

if (Px>Cx) then Cx++;
else if (Px<Cx) then Cx--;

// Do y tracking.

if (Py>Cy) then Cy++;
else if (Py<Cy) Cy--;

end
```

That's all there is to it: based on each of the coordinates, we move the creature in the direction of the player's character, as shown in Figure 10.4.

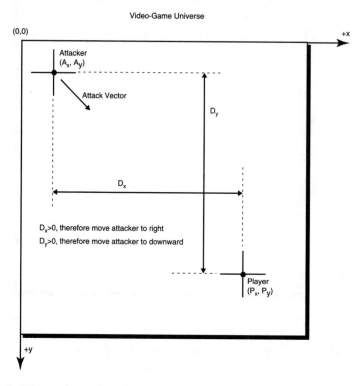

Figure 10.4. *The tracking algorithm in action.*

Algorithm 10.1 is fairly ruthless; it doesn't give up until the creature is right on top of the player's character. This could be just what you have in mind, of course. However, it might be too aggressive. It's like a T1000: it never stops until it gets you. As a further enhancement we might add the following logical premise: when something chases you, it must see you first. In other words, it must be within a certain distance. We could take this into consideration by using a *radius of vision*.

We would test to see whether the creature was within a certain distance of the player's character (its *viewing range* or *sense range*). If this condition were true, we would turn the algorithm on. Otherwise, we would make the creatures do something other than chase the player's character, as it couldn't possibly see the character yet.

Evasion

The inverse of chasing is *evading*. Evasion is done almost exactly the way chasing is done, but everything is reversed. If the creature is on the right side of the player's character, instead of moving to the left (toward the character) the creature moves further to the right, as shown in Figure 10.5.

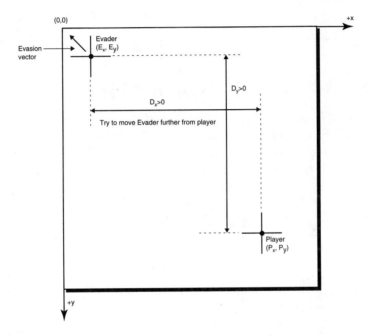

Figure 10.5. *Using the inverse logic of the tracking algorithm to create an evasion algorithm.*

Algorithm 10.2 implements evasion.

Algorithm 10.2. The evasion algorithm.

```
Given  (Px,Py) - Player's position
       (Cx,Cy) - Creature's position

begin

// Do x tracking.
```

continues

Algorithm 10.2. continued

```
if (Px>Cx) then Cx--;
else if (Px<Cx) then Cx++;

// Do y tracking.

if (Py>Cy) then Cy--;
else if (Py<Cy) Cy++;

end
```

A Tracking and Evasion Demo

As an example of implementing these algorithms I've written a demo program, called tracker.exe, which makes a spider chase a poor fly. Then, when you press the T key, the spider evades the fly and the tables are turned. You are the fly—kinda like real life—and you control it using the numeric keypad. (Make sure NumLock is on.) Listing 10.1 contains the source code for tracker.exe.

Listing 10.1. A track and evade demo (tracker.c).

```
// I N C L U D E S /////////////////////////////////////////////

#include <io.h>
#include <conio.h>
#include <stdio.h>
#include <stdlib.h>
#include <dos.h>
#include <bios.h>
#include <fcntl.h>
#include <memory.h>
#include <malloc.h>
#include <math.h>
#include <string.h>

#include "graph3.h"   // Include our graphics stuff.
#include "graph4.h"
#include "graph6.h"

// P R O T O T Y P E S ////////////////////////////////////////

// D E F I N E S //////////////////////////////////////////////

// States the spider (tracker) can be in

#define TRACKER_ATTACK  0    // The spider is attacking the fly.
#define TRACKER_EVADE   1    // The spider is evading the fly.

// S T R U C T U R E S ////////////////////////////////////////
```

```
// G L O B A L S ////////////////////////////////////////////

pcx_picture imagery_pcx,        // The game imagery
            background_pcx;     // The backdrop


// Sprites used in the game

sprite player,                  // The player
       tracker;                 // The spider

// F U N C T I O N S ////////////////////////////////////////

void main(void)
{
// This is the main function.

int done=0;         // Exit flag for whole system

// S E C T I O N 1 //////////////////////////////////////////

// Set the video mode to the 320x200, 256-color mode.

Set_Video_Mode(VGA256);

// Create a double buffer.

if (!Create_Double_Buffer(SCREEN_HEIGHT))
    {
    printf("\nNot enough memory to create double buffer.");

    } // end if

// Clear the double buffer.

Fill_Double_Buffer(0);

// Load the background image into the double buffer.

PCX_Init((pcx_picture_ptr)&background_pcx);

PCX_Load("trackbak.pcx", (pcx_picture_ptr)&background_pcx,1);

// Copy the background into the double buffer.

_fmemcpy((char far *)double_buffer,
         (char far *)(background_pcx.buffer),
         SCREEN_WIDTH*SCREEN_HEIGHT);

PCX_Delete((pcx_picture_ptr)&background_pcx);

Blit_String_DB(0,0,10,"Press Q to exit, T to toggle mode.",1);

// S E C T I O N 2 //////////////////////////////////////////
```

continues

Listing 10.1. continued

```
// Load in imagery for player.

PCX_Init((pcx_picture_ptr)&imagery_pcx);

PCX_Load("trackimg.pcx", (pcx_picture_ptr)&imagery_pcx,1);

// Initialize the player and extract the bit maps.

sprite_width  = 24;
sprite_height = 24;

Sprite_Init((sprite_ptr)&player,0,0,0,0,0,0);

PCX_Grab_Bitmap((pcx_picture_ptr)&imagery_pcx,
                (sprite_ptr)&player,0,0,0);
PCX_Grab_Bitmap((pcx_picture_ptr)&imagery_pcx,
                (sprite_ptr)&player,1,1,0);

player.x          = 160;
player.y          = 180;
player.curr_frame = 0;
player.state      = 1;

// Initialize the tracker and extract the bit maps.

Sprite_Init((sprite_ptr)&tracker,0,0,0,0,0,0);

PCX_Grab_Bitmap((pcx_picture_ptr)&imagery_pcx,
                (sprite_ptr)&tracker,0,0,1);
PCX_Grab_Bitmap((pcx_picture_ptr)&imagery_pcx,
                (sprite_ptr)&tracker,1,1,1);

tracker.x          = 20;
tracker.y          = 20;
tracker.curr_frame = TRACKER_ATTACK;
tracker.state      = TRACKER_ATTACK;

// S E C T I O N 3 /////////////////////////////////////////////

// Scan behind all objects before entering the event loop.

Behind_Sprite_DB((sprite_ptr)&player);
Behind_Sprite_DB((sprite_ptr)&tracker);

// Main event loop

while(!done)
    {

    // Erase all objects.

    Erase_Sprite_DB((sprite_ptr)&player);
    Erase_Sprite_DB((sprite_ptr)&tracker);
```

```
        // Do movement of spider based on mode.

// S E C T I O N 4 ///////////////////////////////////////////

        if (tracker.state==TRACKER_ATTACK)
            {

        // Move the spider toward the player.

        // First, take care of the x components.

        if (player.x > tracker.x)
            tracker.x+=2;
        else
        if (player.x < tracker.x)
            tracker.x-=2;

        // Now take care of the y components.

        if (player.y > tracker.y)
            tracker.y+=2;
        else
        if (player.y < tracker.y)
            tracker.y-=2;

        } // end if spider is attacking

// S E C T I O N 5 ///////////////////////////////////////////

        else
            {

        // Move the spider away from the player.

        // First, take care of the x components.

        if (player.x > tracker.x)
            tracker.x-=2;
        else
        if (player.x < tracker.x)
            tracker.x+=2;

        // Now take care of the y components.

        if (player.y > tracker.y)
            tracker.y-=2;
        else
        if (player.y < tracker.y)
            tracker.y+=2;

        } // end else spider evading

// S E C T I O N 6 ///////////////////////////////////////////

        // Do a boundary collision for the spider.
```

10

continues

535

Listing 10.1. continued

```
        if (tracker.x<0)
            tracker.x = 0;
        else
        if (tracker.x>194)
            tracker.x = 194;

        if (tracker.y<0)
            tracker.y = 0;
        else
        if (tracker.y>174)
            tracker.y = 174;

// S E C T I O N 7 ///////////////////////////////////////////////

        // See whether the player is trying to move.

        if (kbhit())
           {

           // Which key?

           switch(getch())
                {

                // Use the numeric keypad for movement.
                // (Note: NumLock must be activated.)

                case '1':      // Move down and to the left.
                    {
                    player.x-=4;
                    player.y+=4;

                    } break;

                case '2':     // Move down
                    {
                    player.y+=4;

                    } break;

                case '3':      // Move to the right and down.
                    {
                    player.x+=4;
                    player.y+=4;


                    } break;

                case '4':     // Move left
                    {
                    player.x-=4;

                    } break;
```

```
case '6':    // Move right.
   {
   player.x+=4;

   } break;

case '7':     // Move up and to the left.
   {

   player.x-=4;
   player.y-=4;

   } break;

case '8':     // Move up.
   {

   player.y-=4;

   } break;

case '9':    // Move up and to the right.
   {

   player.x+=4;
   player.y-=4;

   } break;

case 't': // Toggle attack mode.
   {

   if (tracker.state==TRACKER_ATTACK)
      tracker.state=tracker.curr_frame =
                        TRACKER_EVADE;
   else
      tracker.state=tracker.curr_frame =
                        TRACKER_ATTACK;
   } break;

case 'q': // Exit the demo
   {
   done = 1;
   } break;


default:break;

} // end switch

// SECTION 8 /////////////////////////////////////////////

   // Do a boundary collision for the player.
```

continues

Listing 10.1. continued

```
        if (player.x<0)
            player.x = 304;
        else
        if (player.x>304)
            player.x = 0;

        if (player.y<0)
            player.y = 184;
        else
        if (player.y>184)
            player.y = 0;

        } // end if kbhit


// S E C T I O N 9 ////////////////////////////////////////////////

    // Do animation.

    if (++player.curr_frame==2)
        player.curr_frame = 0;

    // Scan the background under objects.

    Behind_Sprite_DB((sprite_ptr)&player);
    Behind_Sprite_DB((sprite_ptr)&tracker);


    // Draw all the imagery.

    Draw_Sprite_DB((sprite_ptr)&player);
    Draw_Sprite_DB((sprite_ptr)&tracker);


    // Copy the double buffer to the screen.

    Show_Double_Buffer(double_buffer);

    // Draw the state of spider on top of the video buffer.

    if (tracker.state == TRACKER_ATTACK)
        Blit_String(8,180,12,"Mode=Attack",1);
    else
        Blit_String(8,180,9,"Mode=Evade",1);

    // Wait a sec...

    Delay(1);

    } // end while

// S E C T I O N 10 ////////////////////////////////////////////////

// Reset the video mode to text.
```

```
Set_Video_Mode(TEXT_MODE);

// Free the double buffer.

Delete_Double_Buffer();

} // end main
```

Building an Executable: To make an executable of the program in Listing 10.1, you can either type it in or use the source on the companion CD. The name of the source is tracker.c. The precompiled executable is named tracker.exe. As before, use the following compile line for Microsoft C:

```
cl -AM -Zi -c  -Fc -Gs -G2 tracker.c
```

After compiling the program in this manner you can link it to the standard libraries and to our previously generated game library, gamelib.lib, with a link line such as:

```
link /ST:8192 /CO tracker,,,graphics.lib+gamelib.lib,,
```

This creates a final executable named tracker.exe.

The program is simple: most of it is to load in the PCX files and build the sprites. However, there are a couple of interesting points in it, so let's take a closer look at it.

As usual, the animation is done in a main event loop enclosed by a while(), and the screens are drawn using a double buffer, one frame at a time. We use the standard method of drawing graphics, which is the erase-move-draw sequence discussed on Day 2. These are the most important aspects to get down. If you understand the event loop and the erase-move-draw sequence, the game logic just goes in the middle—and you have a video game!

Anyway, let's see what each section of the main() does.

1. Section 1 is the beginning of the whole program. Here we put the PC into mode 13h, allocate the double buffer, and load in the background image PCX file, which is a spider's web.

2. In Section 2 we load in another PCX file that contains all the imagery for the fly and the spider. We then extract the appropriate bit maps from the PCX files and create the sprite objects used in the game.

3. In Section 3 we're ready to enter into the event loop, but first the background is scanned under all sprites. Then the event loop is entered and the first phase of the animation cycle (erase) is performed.

4. Section 4 implements the chasing algorithm we discussed a moment ago.

5. Section 5 is called in the case where the spider is not chasing the fly—in other words, when it's evading the fly.

6. As the spider is moved to chase or evade the fly, it's possible that it might come in contact with a screen boundary. We must take this into consideration, and that's what Section 6 does. If the spider crosses a screen edge, it's pushed back.

7. Section 7 is where the code for the player's fly begins. In this portion of the code the keyboard is tested to see whether a key has been pressed to move the fly or change the attack mode.

8. Just as the spider was tested against the boundaries of the screen, so is the fly; that's the purpose of Section 8. However, instead of being blocked by the boundaries, the fly can "warp" to the other side.

9. Section 9 is where the fly is animated. There are two frames of animation for the fly. The system toggles between them each frame. Here, also, is where the objects are drawn and the double buffer is copied to the screen buffer. Finally, on top of the video buffer, the state of the spider is displayed using our text blitter.

10. Section 10 ends the program, deallocates everything, and returns the PC to text mode.

As you can see, Algorithms 10.1 and 10.2 are interesting and, surprisingly, between them synthesize a complex behavior.

Next, let's move on to the use of probability and fuzzy logic.

Fuzzy Logic and Probability

As we learned in the introduction today, the behavior of humans and animals is not totally predictable—even for the creatures that are acting out the behaviors themselves. This is where fuzzy logic and probability come into play. Fuzzy logic has been around since the 1960s, but didn't become a mainstream concept until the 1990s. *Fuzzy logic* is based on taking a set of inputs or conditions and then using what's called a *defuzzifier* to come up with a "crisp" solution based on data and probability. For example, if we wrote a program to control street lights using purely deterministic rules, such as "When

there is a car coming the other way, then turn the light red" and so on, the light program would never decide to turn the light on in any other case. This is where fuzzy logic comes into play.

A program that uses fuzzy logic uses a set of rules and then, using statistics and probability, comes up with results that are somewhere between those rules and the solutions it has been programmed with. This may seem like rolling dice to come up with answers, but that's what we do much of the time, so why not make computers do it?

We use a form of fuzzy logic in this chapter to control our creatures. Later, we see a more complex use of fuzzy logic and probability, but for now let's start off simple. We can use a set of rules along with probability to create a simple machine that acts based on a random variable. These actions could determine the movement, direction, and so on of creatures and game objects. As an example, say we want to make a group of alien spaceships attack the player's character. We could use the attack algorithm, Algorithm 10.1. However, this wouldn't give the player much chance. Instead, we could use a random number to select a direction in which to move the alien ship, instead of always making it head toward the player's character like a homing missile.

We could go a step further and use a random number to select one of three rules. The rules could be:

☐ Chase the player's character.

☐ Retreat from the player's character.

☐ Move randomly.

We could use these rules as follows:

1. We would select a random number, from 1–3.

2. Based on the number selected, we would select one of the rules, or *states*. Figure 10.6 shows the use of random numbers to select new states.

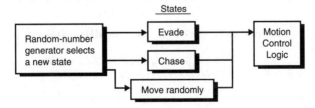

Figure 10.6. *Using random numbers to select new states for the game elements.*

541

In the case of the third rule, we would select a pair of random numbers and then use them for the new trajectory of the creature.

3. We would execute the rule for a period of time (a number of frames).

4. We would then select a new rule and start all over.

This system may seem simple and trivial, but the results are quite impressive. I've made simple, probability driven, rule-based creatures and then have been mesmerized by the complex behaviors they seem to have.

Random Movement

We've seen how to implement the attacking and evading algorithms, but how do we select a random direction? This is as easy as selecting two random variables and assigning them to the velocity components of the creature. Algorithm 10.3 shows this.

Algorithm 10.3. The random-movement algorithm.

```
velocity_x = rand()%MAX_VELOCITY;
velocity_y = rand()%MAX_VELOCITY;
```

The variables `velocity_x` and `velocity_y` then would be used to translate the creature or object in question each frame.

As an example of using random variables to select a direction, I've created a demo that makes a synthetic fly move around the computer screen. (The program was inspired by a fly that was annoying me, and has now gone to that big fly house in the sky.) In any case, a fly brain is pretty easy to simulate, as you'll see. The name of the program is thefly.exe. There are no controls: you just watch a fly buzz around a flower. Press any key to exit the program. Listing 10.2 contains the source code for thefly.exe.

Listing 10.2. A demonstration of probability based behavior (thefly.exe).

```
// I N C L U D E S //////////////////////////////////////////////

#include <io.h>
#include <conio.h>
#include <stdio.h>
#include <stdlib.h>
#include <dos.h>
```

```
#include <bios.h>
#include <fcntl.h>
#include <memory.h>
#include <malloc.h>
#include <math.h>
#include <string.h>

#include "graph3.h"   // Include our graphics stuff.
#include "graph4.h"
#include "graph6.h"

// G L O B A L S ///////////////////////////////////////////

pcx_picture imagery_pcx,      // The game imagery
            background_pcx;    // The backdrop

// Sprites used in the game

sprite thefly;                // The fly

int fly_xv=5,                 // The velocity of the fly
    fly_yv=5,
    fly_clock=10;             // How many cycles of frames the
                              // fly will move in the current
                              // direction

// F U N C T I O N S ///////////////////////////////////////

void main(void)
{
// This is the main function

// S E C T I O N 1 /////////////////////////////////////////

// Set the video mode to the 320x200, 256-color mode.

Set_Video_Mode(VGA256);

// Create a double buffer.

if (!Create_Double_Buffer(SCREEN_HEIGHT))
   {
   printf("\nNot enough memory to create double buffer.");

   } // end if

// Clear the double buffer.

Fill_Double_Buffer(0);

// Load the background image into the double buffer.

PCX_Init((pcx_picture_ptr)&background_pcx);

PCX_Load("flybak.pcx", (pcx_picture_ptr)&background_pcx,1);
```

continues

Listing 10.2. continued

```
    // Copy the background into the double buffer.

    _fmemcpy((char far *)double_buffer,
            (char far *)(background_pcx.buffer),
            SCREEN_WIDTH*SCREEN_HEIGHT);

    PCX_Delete((pcx_picture_ptr)&background_pcx);

    Blit_String_DB(8,8,0,"Press any key to exit.",1);

    // S E C T I O N 2 ///////////////////////////////////////////

    // Load in imagery for the fly.

    PCX_Init((pcx_picture_ptr)&imagery_pcx);

    PCX_Load("flyimg.pcx", (pcx_picture_ptr)&imagery_pcx,1);

    // Initialize the fly and extract bit maps.

    sprite_width  = 36;
    sprite_height = 36;

    Sprite_Init((sprite_ptr)&thefly,0,0,0,0,0,0);

    PCX_Grab_Bitmap((pcx_picture_ptr)&imagery_pcx,
                (sprite_ptr)&thefly,0,0,0);
    PCX_Grab_Bitmap((pcx_picture_ptr)&imagery_pcx,
                (sprite_ptr)&thefly,1,1,0);

    thefly.x          = 160;
    thefly.y          = 100;
    thefly.curr_frame = 0;
    thefly.state      = 1;

    // S E C T I O N 3 ///////////////////////////////////////////

    // Scan behind all objects before entering the event loop.

    Behind_Sprite_DB((sprite_ptr)&thefly);

    // Main event loop

    while(!kbhit())
        {

        // Erase all objects.

        Erase_Sprite_DB((sprite_ptr)&thefly);

        // Move the fly.

        thefly.x+=fly_xv;
        thefly.y+=fly_yv;
```

```
// S E C T I O N 4 //////////////////////////////////////////

    // Check whether it's time to change direction.

    if (--fly_clock==0)
       {

       // Select a new direction.

       fly_xv = -10 + rand()%21;   // -10 to +10
       fly_yv = -10 + rand()%21;   // -10 to +10

       // Select an amount of time to do it.

       fly_clock = 5 + rand()%50;

       } // end if time to change direction

// S E C T I O N 5 //////////////////////////////////////////

    // Do a boundary collision for the fly. If the fly hits an
    // edge, bounce it back.

    if (thefly.x<0 ¦¦ thefly.x>294)
       {
       // Bounce the fly back.

       fly_xv=-fly_xv;
       thefly.x=thefly.x+2*fly_xv;

       } // end if over x boundary

    if (thefly.y<0 ¦¦ thefly.y>164)
       {
       // Bounce the fly back.

       fly_yv=-fly_yv;
       thefly.y=thefly.y+2*fly_yv;

       } // end if over y boundary

    // Do animation of the fly.

    if (++thefly.curr_frame==2)
       thefly.curr_frame = 0;

// S E C T I O N 6 //////////////////////////////////////////

    // Scan the background under objects.

    Behind_Sprite_DB((sprite_ptr)&thefly);

    // Draw all the imagery.

    Draw_Sprite_DB((sprite_ptr)&thefly);
```

continues

Listing 10.2. continued

```
        // Copy the double buffer to the screen.

        Show_Double_Buffer(double_buffer);

        // Wait a sec...

        Delay(1);

        } // end while
// S E C T I O N 7 /////////////////////////////////////////////

// Reset the video mode to text.

Set_Video_Mode(TEXT_MODE);

// Free the double buffer.

Delete_Double_Buffer();

} // end main
```

Building an Executable: To make an executable of the program in Listing 10.2, you can either type it in or use the source on the companion CD. The name of the source is thefly.c. The precompiled executable is named thefly.exe. As before, use the following compile line for Microsoft C:

```
cl -AM -Zi -c -Fc -Gs -G2 thefly.c
```

After compiling the program in this manner you can link it to the standard libraries and to our previously generated game library, gamelib.lib, with a link line such as:

```
link /ST:8192 /CO thefly,,,graphics.lib+gamelib.lib,,
```

This creates a final executable named thefly.exe.

The fly program is much simpler than the previous tracker program. However, we may as well cover the salient points of it. Again, we discuss only the main() module, as that's where all the action takes place and the rest of the graphics library is immaterial, irrelevant, and immoral. (Just kidding. I saw Butthead say that on MTV.)

Game Law: Game programmers must have a twisted sense of humor. Otherwise, they take things seriously and try to teleport entire star systems into black holes, which could be a quick way to trim your waist of those extra pounds.

1. Section 1 places the PC into mode 13h, and loads and displays the initial background image on the screen.

2. Section 2 is responsible for loading the imagery for the fly and creating the sprite object.

3. Section 3 scans the background under the fly and then enters the event loop. Once the event loop is entered, the fly is translated with its current random-direction vector.

4. The fly moves in a random direction for a specific amount of time based on the variable `fly_clock`. When this variable runs out, a new direction is selected in Section 4.

5. The fly tries to fly away if we don't cage it in the virtual world. Section 5 keeps the fly on the screen.

6. Section 6 draws the fly and displays the double buffer. Note how a call to `Delay()` is made. This is to keep the program from running at warp speed.

7. In Section 7, the event loop has been exited. It's time to clean everything up and set the video mode back to the text mode.

The fly program is simple, but I still can't get over how much it looks and acts like a real fly. Of course, it doesn't hunt, eat, mate, or die; however, somehow, we've captured the essence of fly behavior using this extremely simple model. Later today we use probability to drive more complex systems and obtain even more exciting results. For now, on to patterns.

Taking Steps with Patterns

Within our bag of tricks we now have algorithms to:

☐ Track (chase) and evade

☐ Make decisions

☐ Move in random directions

However, many times a behavior displayed by a human or a thinking creature is predetermined and in the form of a *sequence* or *pattern*. For instance, when you start your car in the morning, you follow a predetermined sequence of steps—a pattern—every time to accomplish this task. This pattern was realized either by deduction, logic, or experience, or maybe a mixture of all of them. Nevertheless, the end result is that you follow a pattern.

We're all familiar with patterns for both creatures and players' characters in video games. Many people who play video games figure out patterns that, when used, always beat the computer. The reason for this is that the computer itself is using patterns, and you as a player can figure out the inverse (figuratively speaking) of the computer's pattern and use it to beat the computer.

Using patterns in a game is something we want to do. Personally, I think a game should never be totally pattern-based; that would make it boring. However, we should have the ability to execute patterns as part of our overall brain architecture.

In the example I just mentioned, starting the car is a perfect reason to have patterns. Granted, we could probably figure out how to start a car if we were to use logic and had a knowledge of mechanics and electronics, but using a pattern is much easier. In the case of video games, we can use patterns for anything we wish, such as:

- [ ] Selecting a direction
- [ ] Selecting rules
- [ ] Selecting a behavior

Of course, the list goes on and on and your imagination is the only limiting factor.

Let's talk about how we'd use patterns to move a creature around the screen. We might even select this pattern with a random number from a set of patterns. (Can you see the possibility of nesting these structures?)

Our example scenario is a shoot-'em-up game that places the player's character at the bottom of the screen and the game-controlled creatures at the top in some formation. Now, we might want the creatures to execute certain flight patterns—loops, curls, split S-turns, and so forth—and then find its place back in the formation. The game we played on Day 2 (Mech War) uses such a routine. There's a table of patterns from which the program can select at random, and then the program plays out the table. Here's the actual data structure used in Mech War:

```
// This data structure holds the instructions for the patterns
// the mechs take when in pattern mode.
```

```
int patterns[NUM_PATTERNS][MAX_PATTERN_ELEMENTS]

    = {1,1,1,1,1,1,1,1,1,2,2,2,2,3,3,3,3,3,3,3,4,4,4,4,5,5,5,5,6,
   6,7,7,7,7,8,8,8,8,7,7,7,7,7,7,6,6,7,5,4,4,4,3,3,2,2,1,1,0,0,0,-1,
    1,1,1,1,1,1,1,1,1,1,2,2,3,3,4,4,5,5,5,5,5,5,5,5,5,5,7,7,7,7,7,7,
   7,8,8,8,8,1,1,1,1,1,0,0,0,0,1,1,1,1,1,1,1,1,1,1,0,0,0,-1,
        1,1,8,8,7,7,8,8,7,7,7,7,7,7,7,7,6,6,5,5,4,4,3,3,3,3,3,3,
3,3,4,4,4,4,5,5,6,6,7,7,7,7,7,7,7,6,6,5,5,4,4,3,3,2,2,1,1,0,-1,
1,1,2,2,3,3,3,3,3,3,3,3,4,4,5,5,5,5,5,5,6,6,7,7,7,7,7,7,7,7,8,
8,1,1,1,1,1,1,2,2,3,3,4,4,5,5,6,6,7,7,8,8,1,1,0,0,0,0,-1};
```

As you can see, there are four patterns. Each pattern contains a maximum of 60 instructions. These instructions are translated to directions, and then into actual velocity vectors to control the alien mechs. This kind of pattern use is illustrated in Figure 10.7.

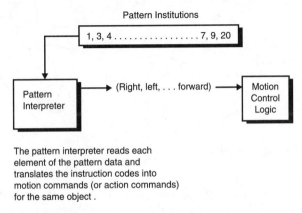

Figure 10.7. *The use of patterns to control game objects.*

In the pattern engine for mechs, I used patterns to move the mechs on the screen. The program reads into the table and then, based on the current element in the table, moves the mech in the proper direction. There are 10 values or instructions the pattern engine understands. The values 1-8 are the directions north (N), south (S), east (E), west (W), northeast (NE), northwest (NW), southeast (SE), and southwest (SW), respectively. The 0 means sit still, and the -1 means the end of pattern. Having a -1 allows me to make patterns smaller than the total size of 60 elements.

The use of patterns isn't connected just to movement. Patterns can be used to select patterns, random numbers, and so on. For instance, you can use a pattern as the seed for a random-number generator, so that as time flows forward the random numbers generated are based on a pattern of different seed values. This could have the effect of changing the probability distributions of the number and, hence, the behaviors of any system that uses random numbers. For the game brains we make, we use patterns only as movement sequences. However, you can use them for anything you wish.

State Machines

The next thing we must add to our brains is a form of memory so the system can move from one behavior to another and know the behavior it's currently performing.

A *state machine* is a device that has a memory and a system of rules that dictate how the state machine changes states as a function of time and input. Figure 10.8 shows a state machine.

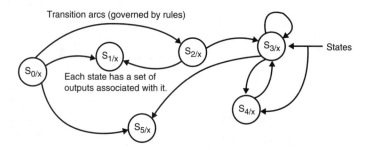

Figure 10.8. *A state machine.*

While state machines are typically used in hardware designs to implement complex logic without the use of a microprocessor, the concept of the state machine is useful in software engineering as well. A video game can have many modes of operation—for example, the initialization mode, the dying-sequence mode, the normal mode, and the termination mode—and state machines can keep track of these in addition to tracking the overall state of the game.

State machines are also useful to control the creatures and game objects in a video game. For example, we might have a state machine that could track the state of the player's character. The character could have the following states:

- State 0: Alive
- State 1: Dying
- State 2: Dead

Based on theses states, the game logic would do different things. If the player's character were in state 0, the logic would allow the character to move, fire, and so forth. However, if the character were in state 1 (dying), the game logic would display the death sequence

and the character wouldn't be able to move or fire anymore. Finally, when the state switches to state 2 (dead), the game logic would go through whatever sequence it had to bring the character back to life.

Of course, there would be logic that would move the player's character from state to state. If the character were in state 0 (alive), the only way to get into state 1 (dying) would be to be shot or hit in some way. Once the character was in state 1 (dying), after a period of time the character would automatically move into state 2 (dead). Therefore, we see that state changes are a result of both the environment of the game—the input—and the state machine itself, meaning the next state is based on the current state in some way. This is illustrated in Figure 10.9.

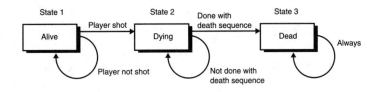

Note: state transition is based on "if/then" events or other rules.

Figure 10.9. *A state machine used to control the different states of a player's character or other object.*

The example we just covered is typical of a video-game state machine used for game objects. In general, a game object may have many states with complex rules governing the state changes, technically called *state transitions*. Moreover, a state can have outputs. For example, in the case of our state model, the dead state might have an output signaling the sound system to play an explosion. This is an example of an output generated by a state machine.

We have an idea of what a state machine is, but how do we make them in the computer? Creating a state machine is easy; although we can't physically create a state machine, we can simulate one in the virtual world of the computer:

1. We create one or more variable(s) to track the state, usually called state (or state_1 if there are more than one state machine in the structure in question).

2. We then give names to the states, such as ATTACKING, EVADING, or whatever, along with values. This is usually done in #define lines.

3. We then make rules based on each of the states and the possible inputs that move the state machine to the desired next state.

Playing Dr. Frankenstein

Using as an example a state machine to track the status of some game object (possibly an alien creature!), here's a pseudocode implementation of the more salient points of state machines:

```
// These are the states

#define ALIVE 0
#define DEAD  1
#define DYING 2

int alien_state = ALIVE; // Start the alien off alive.

// Begin main event loop of game.

while(!done)
    {

    if (alien_state==ALIVE)
       {

       move the alien
       animate the alien

       // Test whether we need to make a state change.

       if (the alien has been shot by player)
           {
           // Change the state of the alien to dying.
           alien_state = DYING;
           } // end if

       } // end if alive

    else
    if (alien_state==DYING)
       {

       show death sequence

      // Test whether the death sequence is done.

       if (death sequence is done)
           {
           // Change state to dead.

               alien_state = DEAD;

           } // end if death is done

       } // end if dying
    else  // Alien must be dead.
       {
       // The alien is dead, so clean up the mess.
```

```
    kill alien data structure and take alien out of game
    } // end else

  } // end main event loop
```

This pseudocode captures the essence of what a state machine does. The basic idea is that there's a variable tracking the current state of the alien. Using this variable, along with input from the game (such as what the player is doing), the state machine can make the proper transitions. Of course, there are a lot of little details that aren't taken into consideration here. For instance, when a state transition is made from "alive" to "dying," we don't take into consideration any housekeeping details, such as setting variables and so on.

Furthermore, state machines may have timers or clocks to help track temporal events or count how many cycles a certain state should execute for. As an example, the "dead" state would really have a clock or timer that timed how long the death sequence would be played and then terminate when this timer expired. The amount of time programmed into this timer would probably have been done when the state machine made a transition from the "alive" state to the "dying" state as part of the housekeeping.

Finally, most actual implementations of state machines have half a dozen or more states. Therefore, a `switch()` statement is a more appropriate logic structure than IF statements.

> **Warning:** When designing a state machine, be sure to think out all states and transition rules carefully and be cautious not to create an "infinite loop" that toggles between one of a pair of states forever.

As far as using state machines in video games, it's unavoidable. Each object in a video game must have a set of states and a set of logical conditions to move that object from state to state. Moreover, many times creatures may be so complex that they have substates, or state machines within state machines, as shown in Figure 10.10.

Nonetheless, a state machine is an abstract virtual implementation of a concept, and there are millions of ways to actually do it. However, the method we've discussed is straightforward and works well, so I suggest using it as a foundation.

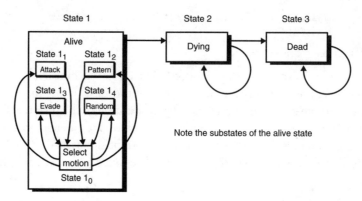

Figure 10.10. *Substates within a state.*

Implementing Personalities

We have almost all the pieces required to create a synthetic computer game brain, so let's talk about the concept of personality and how it ties in with all of our other components.

The word *personality* means the specific traits that one individual has that differ from another individual of the same species. Personalities are what makes everyone different. If we all had the same personality, we'd all be interesting to another race or species, but boring to each other. As game developers, we must try to extrapolate some basics out of this concept of personality and use them to model personality into our synthetic brains.

If we step back and take a look at the actions and reactions of two people (or animals) in the same situation, we see that most of the time the two individuals do roughly the same thing if the situation is primal—hunger, fear, anger, passion—and possibly two completely different things if the situation is intellectual. We aren't going to try to analyze the latter because it's too complex (and, for a video game, most of the game action is of a primal nature anyway).

So in primal or instinctive situations two creatures do roughly the same thing under the same set of conditions. The *roughly* part is what we're interested in. The word "roughly" is a hint to personality. For example, an aggressive creature might stand up to a large predator more often than would a more passive creature. This would manifest itself in what we refer to as personality. If the creatures were human, we might say that one guy is the macho type and the other is more of a wimp. This is the essence of personality.

10

If we were to observe the actions of our two creatures under certain conditions and chart the occurrence of different actions and reactions, we could come up with a statistical model of that individual. This is a valid method of thinking, and is actually used in psychology studies. By observing people, animals, or insects, we can arrive at probability models that infer what the creature will do in a situation as a function of probability.

Using our last example, we might find that 60 percent of the time the tough guy acted tough, while the wimpy guy acted tough only 10 percent of the time. Hence, we can use this probability model in reverse and create a creature in a video game that has a personality that's a composite of the probabilities of performing certain actions. Then, by giving slightly different probabilities to each creature in the game, we can make each creature seem to have a different personality.

The different actions a video-game creature can perform can usually be counted on two hands, and aren't as complex and subtle as those of humans, so it's possible to write them down and assign a probability to them. As an example, we could model the personality of two kinds of alien attackers using a set of five different personality traits. Then, as the game ran, we could select a new state for the alien creature using its probability model. This is illustrated in Figure 10.11.

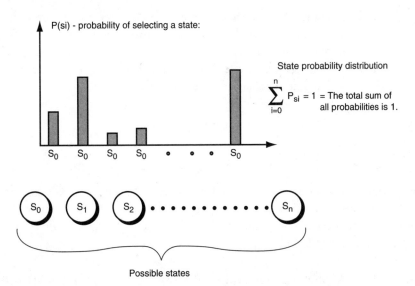

Figure 10.11. *The use of probability distributions to select new states.*

Table 10.1 is a possible list of personality traits that translate to different states.

Table 10.1. A sample personality distribution.

State (trait)	Probability of occurring
Attack mode	50 percent
Random mode	20 percent
Pattern mode	10 percent
Sleep mode	5 percent
Flock mode	15 percent

We see in Table 10.1 that there are five states, or traits, the creature can take on. We would use a random variable along with probability data to select a new state when the time was right.

This is the basis of personality in our final model. We use random variables along with algorithms, state machines, and personality distributions to create realistic models of thought for our game creatures.

As an example of the power of this technique, I've written an ant demo that creates an army of red ants looking for food and marching up and down the screen. When you see the demo, you may be surprised at how much it really looks like an army of ants doing the things that ants do. The model I used consists of a single personality for each ant driving a state machine that can have the following states:

```
// State of ants

#define ANT_MARCH   0
#define ANT_RANDOM  1
#define ANT_PATTERN 2
#define ANT_SITTING 3
```

I elected to have a single personality for each ant because ants don't seem to be terribly different from each other, and having slightly different personalities wouldn't do much for the simulation. Anyway, the name of the demo is antsrus.exe and the source code is antsrus.c. Listing 10.3 contains the listing for you to study.

Listing 10.3. A personality demo (along with the rest of the brain model) to synthesize ants (antsrus.c).

```
// I N C L U D E S /////////////////////////////////////////////

#include <io.h>
#include <conio.h>
```

```
#include <stdio.h>
#include <stdlib.h>
#include <dos.h>
#include <bios.h>
#include <fcntl.h>
#include <memory.h>
#include <malloc.h>
#include <math.h>
#include <string.h>

#include "graph3.h"  // Include our graphics stuff.
#include "graph4.h"
#include "graph6.h"

// D E F I N E S ///////////////////////////////////////////////

#define CELL_WIDTH       20     // Size of bit maps in world
#define CELL_HEIGHT      20

#define NUM_ROWS         10     // Number of rows and columns in
                                // terrain
#define NUM_COLUMNS      16

#define NUM_ANTS         20     // This should be enough. (It has
                                // to be a multiple of 2.)

#define NUM_PATTERNS      3     // There are 3 patterns
#define PATTERN_LENGTH   25     // At most, each pattern has 25
                                // elements.


// Direction of ant

#define ANT_UP       0
#define ANT_DOWN     2
#define ANT_RIGHT    4
#define ANT_LEFT     6

// State of ants

#define ANT_MARCH    0
#define ANT_RANDOM   1
#define ANT_PATTERN  2
#define ANT_SITTING  3

// S T R U C T U R E S ///////////////////////////////////////////

typedef struct ant_typ
        {
        int dir;       // Direction of ant
        int state;     // State of ant
        int count_1;   // Counter one
        int count_2;   // Counter two
        int max_1;     // Maximum count for counter 1
        int max_2;     // Maximum count for counter 2
        int index_1;   // General index
```

continues

Listing 10.3. continued

```
            int index_2;  // General index

        } ant, *ant_ptr;

// G L O B A L S //////////////////////////////////////////////

pcx_picture imagery_pcx,        // The game imagery
            background_pcx;     // The backdrop

// Sprites used in the game

sprite ants[NUM_ANTS],          // The ant sprites
       rock;                    // The rock sprite

ant ant_data[NUM_ANTS];         // Ant data structures


// This array is a probability density of the different states.

int ant_personality[10] = {
                        ANT_MARCH,
                        // 60% of the time, march up and down.
                        ANT_MARCH,
                        ANT_MARCH,
                        ANT_MARCH,
                        ANT_MARCH,
                        ANT_MARCH,
                        ANT_RANDOM,
                        // 10% of the time, randomize.
                        ANT_PATTERN,
                        // 20% of the time, try a pattern.
                        ANT_PATTERN,
                        ANT_SITTING
                        // 10% of the time, sit.
                        };

int terrain[NUM_ROWS][NUM_COLUMNS] =
 {0,0,0,0,0,0,0,0,0,0,0,0,0,0,0,0,0,
0,0,0,0,0,0,0,0,0,0,0,0,0,0,0,0,0,
1,0,0,0,0,0,0,0,0,0,0,0,0,0,0,1,0,
0,0,0,1,0,0,0,0,0,2,0,0,0,0,0,0,0,
0,0,0,0,0,0,0,0,0,0,0,0,0,0,0,0,0,
0,1,0,1,0,0,0,0,0,0,0,0,1,0,0,0,0,
0,0,0,0,0,0,0,0,0,0,0,0,0,0,0,0,0,
0,0,0,0,0,0,1,0,0,0,0,0,0,1,0,0,0,
0,1,0,0,0,0,0,0,0,0,0,0,0,0,0,0,0,
0,0,0,0,0,0,0,0,0,0,0,0,0,0,0,0,1};

int ant_patterns[NUM_PATTERNS][PATTERN_LENGTH]=

{ 0,0,0,4,4,4,2,2,2,6,6,6,2,2,2,0,0,4,2,6,0,-1,0,0,0,
  2,2,2,6,6,0,0,4,4,4,4,4,2,6,0,6,2,2,4,0,6,2,4,-1,0,
  4,4,4,4,4,0,6,6,6,6,6,6,6,2,4,0,6,2,2,2,6,0,2,4,-1};
```

```
// F U N C T I O N S ///////////////////////////////////////////

void Draw_Ants(void)
{
// This function draws all the ants.

int index;

for (index=0; index<NUM_ANTS; index++)
    Draw_Sprite_DB((sprite_ptr)&ants[index]);

} // end Draw_Ants

///////////////////////////////////////////////////////////////////

void Erase_Ants(void)
{
// This function erases all the ants.

int index;

// Loop through and process all ants.

for (index=0; index<NUM_ANTS; index++)
    Erase_Sprite_DB((sprite_ptr)&ants[index]);

} // end Erase_Ants

///////////////////////////////////////////////////////////////////

void Behind_Ants(void)
{
// This function scans behind all the ants.

int index;

// Loop through and process all ants.

for (index=0; index<NUM_ANTS; index++)
    Behind_Sprite_DB((sprite_ptr)&ants[index]);

} // end Behind_Ants

///////////////////////////////////////////////////////////////////

void Init_Ants(void)
{
// This function initializes all the ants, places them in two
// columns on the screen, and sets them all to march.

int index;

// Loop through and process all ants.

// First, the up ants
```

continues

Listing 10.3. continued

```
for (index=0; index<(NUM_ANTS/2); index++)
    {

    // Set up fields in the data structure.

    ant_data[index].dir       = ANT_UP;
    ant_data[index].state     = ANT_MARCH;
    ant_data[index].count_1   = 0;
    ant_data[index].count_2   = 0;
    ant_data[index].max_1     = 100 + rand()%100;
    ant_data[index].max_2     = 0;
    ant_data[index].index_1   = 0;
    ant_data[index].index_2   = 0;

    // Set up fields in the sprite structure.

    ants[index].curr_frame    = ANT_UP;
    ants[index].x             = 165 + rand()%10;
    ants[index].y             = index*CELL_HEIGHT;

    } // end for index

// Now, the down ants

for (index=(NUM_ANTS/2); index<NUM_ANTS; index++)
    {

    // Set up fields in the data structure.

    ant_data[index].dir       = ANT_DOWN;
    ant_data[index].state     = ANT_MARCH;
    ant_data[index].count_1   = 0;
    ant_data[index].count_2   = 0;
    ant_data[index].max_1     = 100 + rand()%100;
    ant_data[index].max_2     = 0;
    ant_data[index].index_1   = 0;
    ant_data[index].index_2   = 0;

    // Set up fields in the sprite structure.

    ants[index].curr_frame    = ANT_DOWN;
    ants[index].x             = 180 + rand()%10;
    ants[index].y             = (index-(NUM_ANTS/2))*CELL_HEIGHT;

    } // end for index

} // end Init_Ants

//////////////////////////////////////////////////////////////

void Draw_Rocks(void)
{
// Based on the terrain array, place a rock on the screen
```

```
// wherever there's a 1.

int x,y;

// Loop through and draw rocks.

for (y=0; y<NUM_ROWS; y++)
    {

    for (x=0; x<NUM_COLUMNS; x++)
        {

        // Is there a rock here?

        if (terrain[y][x]==1)
            {
            // Position the rock sprite.

            rock.x = x*CELL_WIDTH;
            rock.y = y*CELL_HEIGHT;

            Draw_Sprite_DB((sprite_ptr)&rock);

            } // end if

        } // end for x

    } // end for y

} // end Draw_Rocks

// M A I N //////////////////////////////////////////////////////

void main(void)
{
// This is the main function.

int done=0,           // Exit flag for whole system
    index,            // Loop index
    change_state,     // Used to flag when an ant should change
                      // state
    new_dir,          // Local AI variable
    cell_x,cell_y;    // Used to compute what cell the ant is in
                      // for rock collision


// S E C T I O N 1 //////////////////////////////////////////////

// Set the video mode to the 320x200, 256-color mode.

Set_Video_Mode(VGA256);

// Create a double buffer.

if (!Create_Double_Buffer(SCREEN_HEIGHT))
```

continues

Listing 10.3. continued

```
        {
        printf("\nNot enough memory to create double buffer.");

        } // end if

// Clear the double buffer.

Fill_Double_Buffer(0);

// Load the background image into the double buffer.

PCX_Init((pcx_picture_ptr)&background_pcx);

PCX_Load("antbak.pcx", (pcx_picture_ptr)&background_pcx,1);

// Copy the background into the double buffer.

_fmemcpy((char far *)double_buffer,
         (char far *)(background_pcx.buffer),
         SCREEN_WIDTH*SCREEN_HEIGHT);

PCX_Delete((pcx_picture_ptr)&background_pcx);

Blit_String_DB(2,2,10,"Press any key to exit.",1);

// S E C T I O N 2 ///////////////////////////////////////////////

// Load in the imagery for the ants.

PCX_Init((pcx_picture_ptr)&imagery_pcx);

PCX_Load("antimg.pcx", (pcx_picture_ptr)&imagery_pcx,1);

// Initialize the player and extract bit maps.

sprite_width  = 20;
sprite_height = 20;

// Create all the ants...we have a long way to go to create the
// Genesis bomb, but I'm on the job!

for (index=0; index<NUM_ANTS; index++)
    {
    // Initialize the ant sprite.

    Sprite_Init((sprite_ptr)&ants[index],0,0,0,0,0,0);

    // Load the bit maps.

    PCX_Grab_Bitmap((pcx_picture_ptr)&imagery_pcx,
                    (sprite_ptr)&ants[index],0,0,0);

    PCX_Grab_Bitmap((pcx_picture_ptr)&imagery_pcx,
                    (sprite_ptr)&ants[index],1,1,0);
```

```
        PCX_Grab_Bitmap((pcx_picture_ptr)&imagery_pcx,
                    (sprite_ptr)&ants[index],2,2,0);

        PCX_Grab_Bitmap((pcx_picture_ptr)&imagery_pcx,
                    (sprite_ptr)&ants[index],3,3,0);

        PCX_Grab_Bitmap((pcx_picture_ptr)&imagery_pcx,
                    (sprite_ptr)&ants[index],4,4,0);

        PCX_Grab_Bitmap((pcx_picture_ptr)&imagery_pcx,
                    (sprite_ptr)&ants[index],5,5,0);

        PCX_Grab_Bitmap((pcx_picture_ptr)&imagery_pcx,
                    (sprite_ptr)&ants[index],6,6,0);

        PCX_Grab_Bitmap((pcx_picture_ptr)&imagery_pcx,
                    (sprite_ptr)&ants[index],7,7,0);

        // Initialize the ant vars.

        ants[index].curr_frame = 0;
        ants[index].state      = 1;

        } // end for index

// Load up the rock.

Sprite_Init((sprite_ptr)&rock,0,0,0,0,0,0);

PCX_Grab_Bitmap((pcx_picture_ptr)&imagery_pcx,
                (sprite_ptr)&rock,0,0,1);

rock.curr_frame = 0;
rock.state      = 1;  // Alive or dead, it's not doing much!


// S E C T I O N 3 ///////////////////////////////////////////

// Draw all the rocks.

Draw_Rocks();

// Initialize the ants.

Init_Ants();

// Scan the background once before the loop.

Behind_Ants();

// S E C T I O N 4 ///////////////////////////////////////////

// Main event loop

while(!kbhit())
```

continues

563

Listing 10.3. continued

```
    {

    // Erase all objects.

    Erase_Ants();

    // S E C T I O N 5 ///////////////////////////////////////////

    // Begin AI logic

    // At this point we want to move all the ants, change stats,
    // and so on.

    for (index=0; index<NUM_ANTS; index++)
        {

        // Reset the state change flag.

        change_state = 0;

        // What state is the ant in?

        switch(ant_data[index].state)
            {

            case ANT_MARCH:
                {

                // Test whether it's time to change state.

                if (++ant_data[index].count_1 ==
                            ant_data[index].max_1)
                    change_state = 1;

                } break;

            case ANT_RANDOM:
                {
                // Select a new direction for the ant.

                ant_data[index].dir     = 2*(rand()%4);
                ant_data[index].state   = ANT_MARCH;
                ant_data[index].count_1 = 0;
                ant_data[index].max_1   = 50 + rand()%50;

                // Set up fields in the sprite structure.

                ants[index].curr_frame  = ant_data[index].dir;

                } break;

            case ANT_PATTERN:
                {
                // Test whether it's time to use next pattern
```

```
// element.

if (++ant_data[index].count_1 ==
  ant_data[index].max_1)
  {
  // Reset the counter.

  ant_data[index].count_1 = 0;

  // Move to the next element of the pattern.

  ant_data[index].index_2++;

  new_dir =
  ant_patterns[ant_data[index].index_1][ant_data[index].index_2];

  if (new_dir!=-1)
     {

     // Change the direction of the ant.

     ant_data[index].dir =
            ants[index].curr_frame = new_dir;

     } // end if not done with pattern
  else
     {

     change_state = 1;

     } // end else pattern is dead

  } // end if time to change pattern element

} break;

case ANT_SITTING:
  {

  // Test whether it's time to change state.

  if (++ant_data[index].count_1 ==
            ant_data[index].max_1)
     change_state = 1;

  } break;

default:break;

} // end switch

// S E C T I O N 6 /////////////////////////////////////////////

// Check whether there has been a state change.
```

continues

565

Listing 10.3. continued

```
if (change_state)
   {

   // Use the personality table to select a new state.

   ant_data[index].state = ant_personality[rand()%10];

   // Based on the new state, set ant up appropriately
   // (if needed).

   switch(ant_data[index].state)
       {

       case ANT_MARCH:
           {
           // Select up or down.

           ant_data[index].dir     = 2*(rand()%2);
           ant_data[index].state   = ANT_MARCH;
           ant_data[index].count_1  = 0;
           ant_data[index].max_1    = 100 + rand()%75;

           // Set up the current frame.

           ants[index].curr_frame=ant_data[index].dir;

           } break;

       case ANT_PATTERN:
           {

           // Select the pattern and set a pointer to
           // the first element.

          ant_data[index].index_1=rand()%NUM_PATTERNS;
           ant_data[index].index_2 = 0;

           // This time, these two variables are used
           // to count how long to play each pattern
           // instruction.

           ant_data[index].count_1  = 0;
           ant_data[index].max_1    = 2 + rand()%3;

           // Based on the first pattern element, set
           // the initial direction.

           ant_data[index].dir =
             ant_patterns[ant_data[index].index_1][0];

           ants[index].curr_frame=ant_data[index].dir;

           } break;
```

```
            case ANT_RANDOM:
                {

                ant_data[index].state    = ANT_RANDOM;

                // Do nothing; the logic above
                // takes care of it.

                } // Break;

            case ANT_SITTING:
                {

                ant_data[index].state    = ANT_SITTING;
                ant_data[index].count_1   = 0;
                ant_data[index].max_1     = 10 + rand()%10;

                } // Break;

            } // end switch state;

        } // end if we need to move to another state

// S E C T I O N 7 ///////////////////////////////////////////////


        // Check whether the ant has bumped into a rock. If so,
        // set state to random.

        // Obtain the cell location of the ant using the center
        // of the ant as reference.

        cell_x = (ants[index].x+10)/CELL_WIDTH;
        cell_y = (ants[index].y+10)/CELL_HEIGHT;

        // Test whether there's a rock there.

        if (terrain[cell_y][cell_x]==1)
            {
            // Set state of ant to random.

            ant_data[index].dir      = 2*(rand()%4);
            ant_data[index].state    = ANT_MARCH;
            ant_data[index].count_1  = 0;
            ant_data[index].max_1    = 50 + rand()%50;
            ants[index].curr_frame   = ant_data[index].dir;

            change_state = 0;

            } // end if ant hit a rock

// S E C T I O N 8 ///////////////////////////////////////////////


        // No matter what state ant is in, we should move it in
        // the direction it's pointing (unless it is sitting).
```

continues

567

Listing 10.3. continued

```
                    // Don't move the ant if it's sitting.

                    if (ant_data[index].state!=ANT_SITTING)
                    {
                    // Based on direction, move the ant.

                    switch(ant_data[index].dir)
                        {

                        case ANT_RIGHT:
                            {
                            ants[index].x+=4;
                            } break;

                        case ANT_LEFT:
                            {
                            ants[index].x-=4;
                            } break;

                        case ANT_UP:
                            {
                            ants[index].y-=4;
                            } break;

                        case ANT_DOWN:
                            {
                            ants[index].y+=4;
                            } break;

                        default:break;

                        } // end switch direction

// S E C T I O N  9 ////////////////////////////////////////////////

                    // Change the animation frame using a toggle.

                    if ((ants[index].curr_frame % 2)==0)
                        ants[index].curr_frame++;
                    else
                        ants[index].curr_frame--;

                    // Boundary detection

                    if (ants[index].x > 300)
                        ants[index].x = 0;
                    else
                    if (ants[index].x < 0)
                        ants[index].x = 300;

                    if (ants[index].y > 180)
                        ants[index].y = 0;
                    else
```

```
        if (ants[index].y < 0)
            ants[index].y = 180;

    } // end if ant wasn't sitting

    } // end for index

    // End AI logic

// S E C T I O N 10 ///////////////////////////////////////////

    // Scan the background under objects.

    Behind_Ants();

    // Draw all the imagery.

    Draw_Ants();

    // Copy the double buffer to the screen.

    Show_Double_Buffer(double_buffer);

    // Wait a sec...

    Delay(1);

    } // end while

// S E C T I O N 11 ///////////////////////////////////////////

// Reset the video mode to text.

Set_Video_Mode(TEXT_MODE);

// Free the double buffer.

Delete_Double_Buffer();

} // end main
```

10

Building an Executable: To make an executable of the program in Listing 10.3, you can either type it in or use the source on the companion CD. The name of the source is antsrus.c. The precompiled executable is named antsrus.exe. As before, use the following compile line for Microsoft C:

```
cl -AM -Zi -c  -Fc -Gs -G2 antsrus.c
```

After compiling the program in this manner you can link it to the standard libraries and to our previously generated game library, gamelib.lib, with a link line such as:

```
link /ST:8192 /CO antsrus,,,graphics.lib+gamelib.lib,,
```

This creates a final executable named antsrus.exe.

Hopefully, you've run the program in Listing 10.3, and I'll bet you agree that it's pretty neat. It amazes me that such simple rules and models can be used to create such complex systems. Even though each ant alone isn't too exciting, when you place a collection of them into the simulation you've created a system that has orders of magnitude more states than the simple cell on which the system is based. In the case of the ants demo, there are more than 9.536X1013 total system states for the simulation! As you can see, when we start getting into the realm of numbers that are this large and systems that have this kind of complexity, we're definitely on the right track.

The ant simulation is by far the most complex we've seen today, so we definitely want to analyze it.

The main() is where all the logic is performed. However, there are also some functions in this program that you should spend some time reviewing yourself. Nothing complicated, but I throw a couple of tidbits that aren't totally related to the material at hand into all our programs. In this case, the rocks are drawn using a data array containing a matrix of integers that represent where rocks should be placed on the screen. Otherwise, the remaining functions aren't too interesting. Keeping those factors in mind, here is the analysis by section:

1. Section 1 is the startup section of the code, where the PC is put into mode 13h, the double buffer is created, and the PCX file for the background is loaded and copied into the double buffer.

2. Section 2 is where the PCX file that holds the imagery for the ants is loaded. Then the sprite objects are generated from this data, along with a single rock sprite that's used for each rock. Also, each ant had to have a more complex data structure than what the sprite's internal data structure had to offer, so I created an ant data structure that holds more detailed information. Here it is for review; notice the state and counter fields in the structure:

```
typedef struct ant_typ
    {
```

```
    int dir;        // Direction of ant
    int state;      // State of ant
    int count_1;    // Counter one
    int count_2;    // Counter two
    int max_1;      // Maximum count for counter 1
    int max_2;      // Maximum count for counter 2
    int index_1;    // General index
    int index_2;    // General index

    } ant, *ant_ptr;
```

3. Section 3 is responsible for drawing the rocks and initializing the ants' data structures. Also, it scans the background under all the ants before they're rendered so the sprite engine won't replace garbage on the first run through the event loop.

4. Section 4 is the beginning of the main event loop, and the place where the "erase" portion of the erase-move-draw sequence is performed.

5. Section 5 is the beginning of the AI logic. The states of the state machine are tested and, based on the current state of each ant, the proper actions taken. Moreover, this is where the system flags the necessity of making a state change when a state has been completed.

6. If a state change has been requested in the previous section, Section 6 is where it's processed. A new state is selected based on the personality array called ant_personality[]. Housekeeping, such as setting the proper variables, is taken care of for the new state.

7. Section 7 is called the "preemptive" section of the code. If the ant hits a rock, no matter what it's doing it must change directions. (Otherwise, it would kill itself.) This is analogous to when a person is performing some action, such as cooking, and is burned. The person who was cooking instantly stops what he or she is doing and pulls the burned hand away. This is an instinctive, or *reflex*, action, and that's exactly what this "preemption" code models. In any case, the current state is preempted and the ant is given a new random direction by the ANT_RANDOM state.

8. Section 8 uses the ant's current direction variable to determine which way the ant is to move now.

10

9. Section 9 is the final portion of the AI logic. The ant is tested to see whether it has hit a boundary. If it has, it's transported to the other side of the screen. We have seen the technique many times now, and it's standard. Also, a jump is made back to the top of the FOR loop, and the next ant is processed.

10. In Section 10 all the animation and motion of the ants have been completed, so it's time to draw the ants. This section scans the background under the ants, draws them into the double buffer, and then dumps the double buffer to the screen. Finally, there is a call to the Delay() function that locks that maximum frame rate now to no higher than 18.2 frames per second so the demo will run at the same speed on all machines.

11. Section 11 is the end of the simulation, where memory is released and the PC is placed back into text mode.

The model of a brain that we've detailed here is powerful. I can guarantee that it will be more than a formidable opponent for any human player. (Although that's kind of sad when the model can be implemented in a few dozen lines of C code.)

Now let's diverge for a moment and talk about how we would make a creature find its way through a game universe.

Exploration Algorithms

The last class of algorithms that we must discuss are called *exploration algorithms* or *search algorithms*. They're based on a searching algorithm used in data structures such as binary trees, graphs, and other related topologies. We need some kind of algorithm to help our game creatures find their way through game mazes, asteroid fields, or whatever. We can accomplish this by using simple rules that can be referenced by the game brain of a creature to help it traverse the environment at hand.

As an example of exploration and hunting techniques, we can develop an algorithm that allows a game creature to find its way through a 2-D maze while at the same time either looking for its friends or looking for the player's character. We can use a 2-D maze such as the one shown in Figure 10.12 for our discussions.

If you place your finger at the starting location and try to find your way to the exit, it will probably take you about 5-10 seconds to do it. However, if you were actually in the maze yourself and couldn't see the entire thing at once, it might take 5-10 days!

If you were trapped in the maze, you would probably be able to recall places in the maze where you had been already, and at last you would find your way out. However, there's

a better way that uses a simple set of rules to accomplish the same task. For example, if the internal structure of the maze were such that it all looked the same, you might be stuck in there forever. Fortunately, there are algorithms you could use to find your way out of 2-D, 3-D, and even N-dimensional mazes. Some of the algorithms are simple and don't take into consideration all cases, while others are more complex and always work. Our only goal here is to introduce you to the subject, and not to inundate you with it, so we look at only the simplest of algorithms.

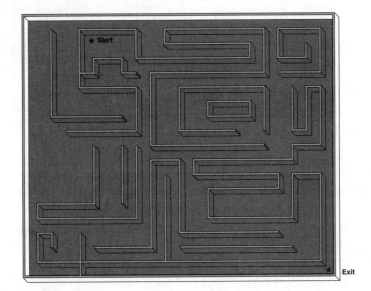

Figure 10.12. *A 2-D maze.*

The algorithm works on the following premise: if you traverse the maze by keeping the wall to your right, and at each intersection always take a right turn, at some point you will find your way out of the maze. Of course, this algorithm has problems in cases of circular submazes, such as the one shown in Figure 10.13.

This problem can be eradicated by using a slightly more complex algorithm that uses memory, or possibly a random variable that randomly selects the direction to go at intersections. A possible random distribution would be, "90 percent of the time turn right, and 10 percent of the time turn left." This slows down the traversal of the maze, but the creature will be able to find its way out.

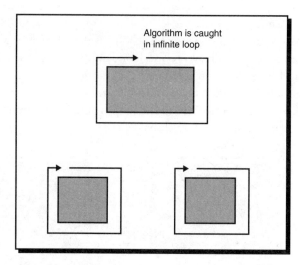

Figure 10.13. *The circular loop problem.*

The next facet of the algorithm we should add is to merge the tracking algorithms we saw earlier today. For example, as the creature was traversing the maze and came to a wide space where it could navigate a little, it would move toward (or away from) the player's character until it hit a wall, and then it would revert back to its exploration mode. Of course, the exploration mode would be worked into the overall model of our brain and would be one of the possible states of the state machine.

Building Brains from Scratch

We've now covered all we need to create complete, autonomous creatures in video games. Moreover, we've learned the basis for assumptions on which the model is based, and they have sound reasoning. As far as the models you use in your video games, I suggest simple random variables for some creatures, state machines for others, and complete personality models for your most complex creatures. Remember, use only what's necessary for any of the creatures in a game. If the creature moves around in an intelligent-looking manner and seems to act and react with the player, it serves its purpose. If the creatures seem too dumb, you'll have to implement a more advanced model.

Finally, the use of separate personalities is an extremely good way to create hundreds of variations of the same brain model. For example, you may create a single brain model and then, by selecting radically different personality distributions, use the results as the brain logic for entirely different creatures in the game.

Summary

Today we've talked about one of the most fascinating parts of a video game: bringing it to life. We learned about random numbers, tracking and evading algorithms, patterns, and the fundamentals of state machines. We also learned how to model the elusive concept of personality into our creatures, and how to make them find their way around the universes we build for them.

I think the reason many game developers create games is that it fascinates them to watch little creatures run around, seemingly alive and aware of their virtual environments. (Who knows? Maybe they really are alive!)

Q&A

Q What is synthetic intelligence?

A Synthetic intelligence is a method of modelling thought instead of trying to enumerate all possible rules of thought (which would be impossible).

Q Why do we need artificial and synthetic intelligence in video games?

A So the games are fun and aren't totally predictable.

Q How smart are the creatures in DOOM?

A They use the tracking algorithm and the exploration algorithm, along with a state machine.

Q How does a chess game work?

A Chess and other strategy-based games are founded on complex, rule-based analytical algorithms that use what are called objective functions, to compute the best possible move. (We don't explore objective functions in this book.) This can be done recursively, so that the computer can try millions of moves, look at all the possible replies, and select the one that has the best overall outcome.

Q Will computers ever really think like we do?

A Yes. Neural nets are being grown on silicon, human memory is being understood better and better, and the physical nature of the electrochemical interactions of the cells in our brain are almost completely mapped. Within the next few years I believe that a learning machine with the ability to be logical and

creative will come to be. It's inevitable based on the geometric growth of our technology. It's really an interesting paradox: our own minds want to understand how they themselves work, and how to replicate themselves. Weird, huh?

Workshop

The Workshop section presents quiz questions to help you cement your new knowledge and exercises to give you experience using what you've learned. Try to understand the questions and exercises before moving on to the next lesson. The answers are in Appendix B.

Quiz

1. What's the difference between classical artificial intelligence and synthetic intelligence?

2. What is fuzzy logic?

3. What is a state variable?

4. How is personality implemented in our brain model?

5. How does the chasing algorithm work?

6. What was the problem with the exploration algorithm we discussed?

Exercises

1. Experiment with the probability distribution array for the ants program. Change the entries in the table and see what the effects are on the ants. Here is the table you should alter:

```
int ant_personality[10] = {
                ANT_MARCH,
                // 60% of the time, march up
                // and down.
                ANT_MARCH,
                ANT_MARCH,
                ANT_MARCH,
                ANT_MARCH,
                ANT_MARCH,
                ANT_RANDOM,
```

```
// 10% of the time, randomize.
ANT_PATTERN,
// 20% of the time try a pattern.
ANT_PATTERN,
ANT_SITTING
// 10% of the time, sit.
};
```

2. Draw a graphical representation of the brain model we've developed.

3. Create a state machine model along with the state transition rules for a creature to fly to one side of the screen, bounce off, turn, and fly in the other direction.

4. Alter the tracker program so it randomly selects between the two states (attack and evade) instead of letting the player control it.

5. *Extra credit:* Go outside and observe some insect or small animal. Then try to model a group of them in the computer.

11

Out of Time

The concept of time in a video game is really important. Unfortunately for us, time is always moving forward. It would be nice if we could stop time, do all our calculations, draw the video image, and *then* start time up again! (I can guarantee that there would be some incredible ray-traced games.) Alas, we can't stop time as of yet. Therefore, we must work with it as we would with any other resource, and use it as efficiently as we can. Today we discuss such time-related topics as interrupts, multitasking, and basic techniques to make the timing of video games easier. Here's what we cover:

- ☐ The flow of time in a video game

- ☐ Introduction to multitasking on the PC

- ☐ Interrupts on the PC

- ☐ Functional programming techniques

- ☐ Self-contained functions

- ☐ Responder functions

- ☐ The game state

- ☐ Using the internal timer

- ☐ Implementing a multitasking kernel

- ☐ Detouring the keyboard

- ☐ Adding to our game library

The Flow of Time in a Video Game

As you've been learning, a video game is responsible for a sequence of tasks that must be completed every cycle at a reasonable rate. In general, this is the sequence:

- ☐ Erase all imagery in the game.

- ☐ Process game logic.

- ☐ Perform transformations of objects.

- ☐ Draw all imagery.

- ☐ Repeat this sequence until the game is over.

Each one of these tasks can further be broken down into many subtasks related by game type, software structure, and so forth. We must come up with methodologies that enable us to build the underlying skeletal structure of a game in such a way that we can facilitate the more important problems in a game, such as the graphics and game logic.

The main idea of what we must learn is how to write programs that are, in a sense, multitasking. Because the PC has only a single processor, we can't really do the graphics of our game on one CPU and the logic on another; we must use a single CPU to do everything. However, we can program it in such a way that it seems to the player as though everything is happening simultaneously. At this point in the game (pun intended), we've seen more than one game loop and a few skeleton games and demos, and we have a grasp of the basic structure of a game. We just need a few special tools and tricks to really take control of the PC in such a way that we can get the real-time performance we need out of it. By the end of today, we'll know everything we need to know about controlling the temporal aspects of the PC and a video game that's running on it.

Introduction to Multitasking on the PC

Any computer can be made to *multitask,* or execute more than one process at a time. However, few computers can multiprocess. A *multiprocessing computer system,* unlike a *multitasking computer,* has multiple processors that can each be performing a different task at the same time. Figure 11.1 shows a multiprocessing computer system.

The PC may not be a multiprocessing computer, but it's so fast that we can accomplish multitasking with it. Multitasking on the PC means that each program or process gets a certain amount of CPU time per second. For example, in Microsoft Windows the user can set how much time is allotted to each process if it's a DOS process. (Windows processes are not preemptive; they get control within the event loop and. When one process is finished, the next Windos process takes its time slice.) Time slices of 50 milliseconds are common. This means that if there are 10 programs, each program executes for 50 milliseconds and then relinquishes control to the operating system, which then selects another process to execute for 50 milliseconds, and so on. When each process has had its own time slice the whole thing repeats, ad infinitum, as shown in Figure 11.2.

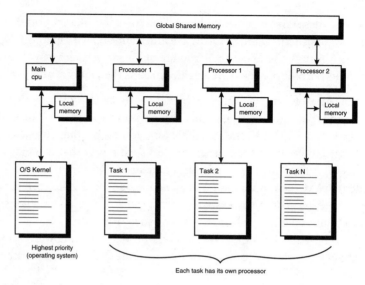

Figure 11.1. *A multiprocessor computer system.*

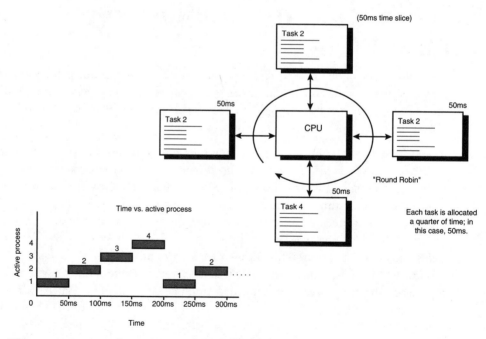

Figure 11.2. *A single processor multitasking.*

The details of implementing multitasking are complex. The state of the system must be retained for each process so the process thinks it's the sole user of the CPU. This "saving of state" is called saving the *context*. When a process has used up its time, the operating system, or *kernel*, saves the state of the CPU registers and locks any other process from accessing the memory area occupied by the terminating process.

This brings up the concepts of memory management and system security, which is the practice of making sure that one process or program does not corrupt another process. For example, if process A has a bug and crashes, process B shouldn't be penalized for this and be halted along with process A. Similarly, process B shouldn't be allowed to write into a memory location occupied by process A's code segment.

Writing a complete multitasking operating system is a little beyond the scope of this chapter, but we can learn the fundamentals of implementing multitasking on the PC based on using interrupts. In reality, we don't need multitasking in a video game. We only need to run each function that composes the game, in a specific order and for a reasonable amount of time, so the player perceives everything as happening simultaneously. The only drawback to this is that the PC has a weak timing structure. That means that it's hard for us, as programmers, to guarantee that something will happen exactly 60 times per second. The only way to accomplish tight timing like this is to create super-tight code and cycle counting—which is impossible on the PC because there are so many variables to take into consideration (such as the CPU, the graphics card, and so on).

A second method is to base timed processes on the internal timer chip, called the 8253. This chip is capable of initiating an interrupt at a given time interval. This is not the only interrupt that we can use; the PC is loaded with interrupts that are generated based on different events. For example, the keyboard generates an interrupt when a key is pressed. However, the timer interrupt is the most commonly used interrupt for game timing, so we focus on it. In essence, we implement multitasking with some kind of interrupt structure based on time or on important events.

Interrupts on the PC

Entire books have been written on dealing with interrupts and writing interrupt-service routines (ISRs) on the PC. However, they make it more complicated then it has to be! We cut straight to the chase here and learn how to implement ISRs on the PC using C and some really simple techniques.

First, we must understand exactly what an interrupt is. An *interrupt* is a request by something to service the requesting party in some way. The PC has two kinds of interrupts:

☐ Hardware interrupts are things such as keyboard requests, "serial port needs data" calls, and so forth.

☐ Software interrupts, on the other hand, are a mechanism to call operating-system resources in such a way that a uniform interface can be created by software engineers and be adaptable to any processor architecture.

Software interrupts are forced by the program. For instance, a popular interrupt is interrupt 10H, which is the video BIOS interrupt. This interrupt is initiated by the assembly language instruction INT XXH, where XXH is in this case 10H. When the processor sees this instruction it stops what it's doing and jumps, or *vectors*, to an interrupt program responsible for processing the interrupt. This process is shown in Figure 11.3.

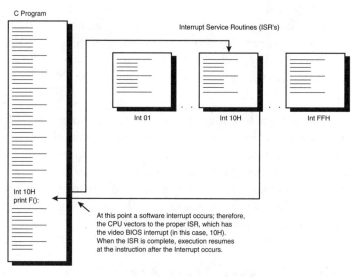

Figure 11.3. *A software interrupt being serviced.*

In the case of video BIOS, there's a collection of routines that can be called through this interrupt. When the interrupt-service routine is complete, control is given to the next instruction after the INT XXH call.

A hardware interrupt works much in the same way. However, no assembly language instruction is needed to initiate the interrupt. The interrupt is initiated by hardware that sends a signal to the *programmable interrupt controller* (PIC) within the PC, which in turn tells the CPU that there's an interrupt (hardware type) that needs processing. At this point the CPU stops what it's doing and, based on the type of interrupt, vectors to the ISR. The interrupt is serviced. When the interrupt-service routine is complete, control is given back to the program that was interrupted and the state of the processor is restored. The program that was interrupted has no idea that an interrupt took place. Again, this process is shown in Figure 11.3.

As video-game programmers, the only thing we need to know how to do is write an ISR to tell the CPU the interrupt at which to install our ISR. We know that when an interrupt is initiated by either hardware or software, the CPU vectors to the ISR. Therefore, there has to be a table containing these *interrupt vectors* so the CPU can jump to the proper ISR. In fact, there is such a table! It lies in the first 1024 bytes of memory on the PC and has 256 entries. Each entry is four bytes long and is a FAR address to the ISR. For example, if interrupt 5H was initiated, the CPU would look in the fifth entry of the table, which would be found at byte offset 20, and then use the four bytes found as the segment and offset of the ISR.

The interrupt has entries for both hardware and software interrupts. Some interrupts are used often, and some shouldn't be touched because they are needed by the operating system or for the PC to function (unless, of course, you *want* to touch them...).

Table 11.1 lists all the interrupts. I've highlighted the interrupts that are the most interesting to us. Although you'll probably only ever use two or three of them, it's good to know just how much havoc we can wreak on the PC with this little table!

Table 11.1. The interrupt table.

Number	Address	Function
0H	**000-003H**	**Divide by zero**
1H	004-007H	Single step
2H	008-00BH	Non-maskable interrupt
3H	00C-00FH	Breakpoint
4H	**010-013H**	**Overflow**
5H	014-017H	Print screen

continues

Table 11.1. continued

Number	Address	Function
6H	018-01BH	Reserved
7H	01C-01FH	Reserved
8H	**020-023H**	**Timer 18.2**
9H	**024-027H**	**Keyboard**
AH	028-02BH	Reserved
BH	02C-02FH	RS-232 port 1
CH	030-033H	RS-232 port 0
DH	034-037H	Hard disk
EH	038-03BH	Diskette
FH	03C-03FH	Reserved
10H	040-043H	Video I/O call
11H	044-047H	Equipment check call
12H	048-04BH	Memory check call
13H	04C-04FH	Diskette I/O call
14H	050-053H	Serial I/O call
15H	054-057H	Cassette I/O call
16H	058-05BH	Keyboard I/O call
17H	05C-05FH	Printer I/O call
18H	060-063H	ROM BIOS entry code
19H	064-067H	Bootstrap loader
1AH	068-06BH	Time of day call
1BH	**06C-06FH**	**Get control on break**
1CH	**070-073H**	**Get control on timer**
1DH	074-077H	Video initialization table
1EH	078-07BH	Diskette parameter table

Number	Address	Function
1FH	07C-07FH	Graphics char table
20H	080-083H	DOS program terminate
21H	084-087H	DOS universal function
22H	088-08BH	DOS terminate address
23H	08C-08FH	DOS Ctrl break
24H	090-093H	DOS fatal error vector
25H	094-097H	DOS absolute disk read
26H	098-09BH	DOS absolute disk write
27H	**09C-09FH**	**DOS terminate and stay resident**
28-3FH	0A0-0FFH	Reserved for DOS
40-7FH	100-1FFH	Not used
80-F0H	200-3C3H	Reserved by Basic
F1-FFH	3C4-3FFH	Not used

In a moment we see how to latch onto the timer interrupt and have an ISR called every 18.2 seconds. First, however, we must take a look at how we can write an ISR with C.

Fortunately, C compilers come with a keyword that allows easy construction of an ISR. The new keyword is _interrupt. You can use this keyword to tell the compiler that a specific function is used as an interrupt-service routine, and that any special prolog or epilog code added to it should be taken care of. With that in mind, all we need to do to create an ISR is write a standard C function that has the keyword _interrupt within the declaration. Listing 11.1 shows a function declaration that has the bare minimum to be an interrupt function.

Listing 11.1. A skeleton ISR routine.

```
void _interrupt far Our_Isr(void)
{

// code

} // end Our_Isr
```

Now, the next thing we want to do is install our ISR into the interrupt table. We do this by figuring out the segment and offset of our ISR function and then changing the appropriate interrupt vector in the interrupt table, as shown in Figure 11.4.

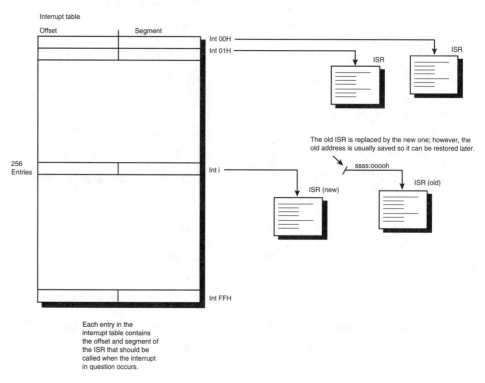

Figure 11.4. *Replacing an interrupt vector.*

This works, but not all the time. What if an interrupt occurred just as we were changing the interrupt vector? The CPU would vector to a nonvalid ISR address and probably hit data or something. Hence, we must do the operation *atomically* (in a single CPU operation) so we're guaranteed an interrupt won't occur when we change the interrupt vector. Moreover, we must store or save the old interrupt vector so we can restore it when our program terminates.

To solve all these problems, we can use a couple of functions that come with the C run-time library. These functions are named _dos_setvect() and _dos_getvect(), and set and retrieve interrupt vectors, respectively.

For example, say we want to change the timer interrupt 1CH. To do this we would first save the old interrupt vector and then set the timer interrupt point to our interrupt vector. The code fragment in Listing 11.2 would do the job.

Listing 11.2. Installing an interrupt vector.

```
void (_interrupt far *old_isr)();

// this will hold the old ISR, take note of the syntax

// this is how you make a function pointer in C

// save old ISR

old_isr = _dos_gegtvect(0x1C);

// now install the new interrupt routine

_dos_setvect(0x1C, Our_Isr);

// .. do game processing

//.. at this point, we just restore the old interrupt

_dos_setvect(0x1C, old_isr);

// That's all there is to it!
```

As an example of installing an ISR that does something reasonably interesting, let's latch onto the timer interrupt, which is entry 1CH in the interrupt table. We can write a simple program that sets the interrupt vector to point to our own ISR instead of to the system ISR. Then, when our ISR is complete, it terminates by calling the old ISR. This technique is called *interrupt chaining*.

To restate this, we can install our own ISRs to perform tasks. However, we may still want the old ISR to do the work it was designed to do *in addition to* what our ISR does. Therefore, we chain the ISRs together. Figure 11.5 shows this graphically.

On the other hand, if we wish, we can elect to not chain interrupt-service routines by not making our function call the old ISR at the end of its operation. This is workable as long as you realize that none of the work done by the old ISR will be done, and the newly installed ISR must take care of any housekeeping chores performed by the old ISR.

The program we see in a moment is the bare minimum needed to install an ISR. The program saves the old timer ISR vector and then installs a new timer ISR that simply updates a global variable. The name of the program is timeint.exe. Listing 11.3 contains the source code.

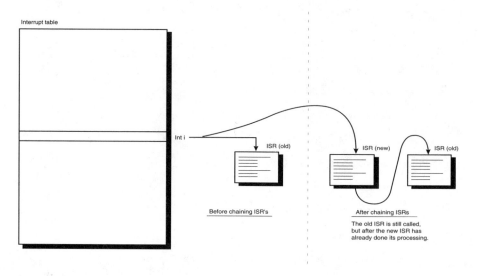

Figure 11.5. *Chaining ISRs together.*

Listing 11.3. A program that takes over the timer ISR (timeint.c).

```
// I N C L U D E S ///////////////////////////////////////////////

#include <dos.h>
#include <bios.h>
#include <stdio.h>
#include <math.h>
#include <conio.h>

#include "graph3.h"  // include graphics our stuff
#include "graph4.h"
#include "graph6.h"

// D E F I N E S ///////////////////////////////////////////////

#define TIME_KEEPER_INT 0x1C // the time keeper interrupt

// G L O B A L S ///////////////////////////////////////////////
//used to hold old interrupt vector

void (_interrupt far *Old_Time_Isr)();


long counter=0;  // global variable to be altered by ISR
```

```
// F U N C T I O N S ///////////////////////////////////////////

void _interrupt far Timer(void)
{

// increment value of counter 18.2 times a second

counter++;

// now call old interrupt handler (if there was one).
// This is only needed
// if you want to chain interrupts handlers.
// In the case that you want
// total control then the next instruction wouldn't be used.

Old_Time_Isr();

} // end Timer

// M A I N ///////////////////////////////////////////////////

void main(void)
{

char string[128]; // working string

// set video mode to 320x200 256 color mode

Set_Video_Mode(VGA256);

// draw instructions

Blit_String(2,2,15,"Press any key to exit.",0);

// install our time keeper ISR while saving old one

Old_Time_Isr = _dos_getvect(TIME_KEEPER_INT);

_dos_setvect(TIME_KEEPER_INT, Timer);

// wait for user to hit a key

while(!kbhit())
    {

    // print out current value of "counter",
    // but note how we don't change it!
    // it is being changed by the ISR

    sprintf(string,"The interrupt has been called %ld times",
            counter);
    Blit_String(2,2+2*8,10,string,0);

    } // end while
```

continues

Listing 11.3. continued

```
// replace old time keeper ISR

_dos_setvect(TIME_KEEPER_INT, Old_Time_Isr);

// reset the video mode back to text

Set_Video_Mode(TEXT_MODE);

} // end main
```

Building an Executable: To make an executable of the program in Listing 11.3, you can either type it in or use the source on the companion CD. The name of the source is timeint.c. The precompiled executable is named timeint.exe. As before, use the following compile line for Microsoft C:

```
cl -AM -Zi -c -Fc -Gs -G2 timeint.c
```

After compiling the program in this manner you can link it to the standard libraries and to our game library, gamelib.lib, with a link line such as:

```
link /ST:8192 /CO timeint,,,graphics.lib+gamelib.lib,,
```

This creates a final executable named timeint.exe.

Here's what happens in Listing 11.3:

1. The program begins in the main() function by placing the PC in mode 13h graphics and then proceeds to save the old time keeper interrupt vector in the variable Old_Time_Isr.

2. At this point, the new interrupt vector is installed. This interrupt vector points to the function Timer(), which has been declared as a C-based interrupt function.

3. The Timer() function does nothing except increment the variable counter, which is printed in the loop body of the main() function. However, there's one small detail of interest: at the end of the Timer() function, a call is made to the old interrupt vector by making a call to Old_Time_Isr(). This chains our ISR to the old ISR and enables us to enhance the functionality of the ISR without

having to rewrite all the housekeeping functions performed by the old ISR. In a case in which we don't want to call the old ISR, the call to `Old_Time_Isr()` would be omitted.

Now, if we focus our attention back on the `main()` function and its loop body, we see that the variable `counter` has not changed; it's only printed. The only place at which it's changed is within the ISR function `Timer()`. Therefore, the `main()` function is multitasking in a crude way with the ISR that we've installed. We could even go so far as to say that the ISR is a message-passing function, "sending messages" to the `main()` function.

 Note: *Message passing* has many meanings. In general, however, it means to change a variable that will cause a "listening" function to take a specific course of action.

A little later today we focus further on the multitasking capabilities of the PC. For now, however, we should take up the topic of functional programming techniques.

Functional Programming Techniques

Functional programming techniques are methods of creating templates or foundations for the functions in a video game. For example, if you analyzed a networking system, you would find that there are some prevalent techniques used in the coding the software, such as certain ways of handling errors, a uniform function prototype, or whatever. These are the kinds of commonalities we want to extract from video-game functions. We want to take a look at about 1,000,000 lines of game code and find the common denominator among different programs. The only problem is that 1,000,000 lines of code would take up a few more pages than we have for today's discussion. Therefore, I'm going to cheat and give you some of the answers.

Ultimately, only you can create the software technology you're most comfortable with. Your games and techniques will undoubtedly be different from mine; nevertheless, there are going to parallels between our techniques that would allow us to look at each other's software and understand it.

Personally, I have many techniques that I use to write the thousands of lines of code needed for a complete game in a reasonable amount of time. I would call all these

techniques "my technology." In this section we look at just a couple of these techniques, which can help immensely in the construction of a real-time video game.

Self-Contained Functions

A *self-contained function* is a function made up of two of more sections. These sections can be broken up into the following groups:

- [ ] Initialization
- [ ] Processing
- [ ] Termination

The interesting thing about these three groups is that the designers of C++ must have been video-game programmers, because this functionality is encapsulated in the language. C++ allows for objects to have *constructors* and *destructors*, which are analogous to the initialization and termination phases of our functions. In any case, we're using C, and we aren't going to switch to C++ for something that can be implemented in C.

As an example, let's say that we have a function that's supposed to rotate a few color registers. We want to call the function from the main game loop and have it perform this task without parameters, and without the main game loop performing any initialization and or termination. We can accomplish this using a self-contained function. A *self-contained function* is just a function with memory that lets it remember its internal state from call to call. This allows it to move from state to state and do the requested processing without the calling function having to worry about housekeeping chores such as variable initialization, memory allocation, and so forth.

We use a simple model (which happens to be my favorite) for a self-contained function. The model has two states:

- [ ] Initialization
- [ ] Normal processing

When the function is entered for the first time, it records the event. Then, when it's entered the second, third, and fourth time, and so on, the function changes to its normal processing state. We accomplish this with the use of local static variables, or *statics*. These statics are local to the function. They can't be accessed by other functions, enabling us to use many of the same naming conventions. Listing 11. 4 contains a basic model of a self-contained function.

Listing 11.4. A self-contained function.

```
int Self(void)
{
static int intialized = 0; // used to track state of function

// test if function has been called before

if (!initialized)
   {
   // allocate variables
   // communicare with hardware
   // etc.
   // set local state flag to reflect that initialization is complete
   initialized = 1;

   } // end if first time
else // function will now do normal processing
   {
   // this code will be executed from now on
   } // end else

} // end Self
```

As you can see, the architecture is simple, yet powerful. The more work each function can do, the less you have to think about in the main control logic. The perfect game would be a collection of "black boxes" controlled by a master control program that didn't need to know how each of the black boxes worked, but knew how to use them. This approach is illustrated in Figure 11.6.

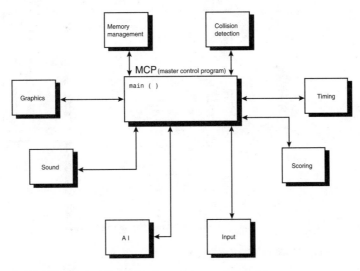

Figure 11.6. *The "black box" approach to video game design.*

Of course, you can further embellish the structure by having more states and parameterize it, but Listing 11.4 is the basic model you can start with.

This leads us back to multitasking. The self-contained function is like a separate task that runs on a single CPU and is permitted its running time when the main game loop makes a call to it. However, the function just needs to be called; it doesn't need its figurative hand held to do its job.

The next kind of functional programming technique I want to discuss is responder functions.

Responder Functions

A responder function is really a function that's listening to some conversation in the system. The conversation could be a timer, a variable, a hardware port, or whatever. The point is that the responder function "watches" the state of the object or event that needs tracking and then, when the appropriate event occurs, performs some action. Figure 11.7 shows a responder function.

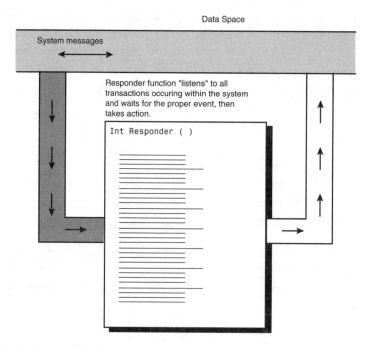

Figure 11.7. *A responder function.*

This action may be causing another event to occur—which yet another responder function is watching. This process could go on forever in one long responder chain, such as the one shown in Figure 11.8.

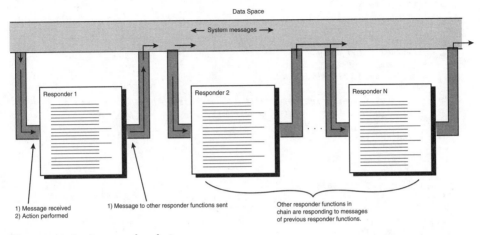

Figure 11.8. *A responder chain.*

The important thing is that the responder function takes a load off the main game loop. The main game loop just makes a call to the responder function and knows that, if the event has happened within the last game cycle, the responder function will do its job.

There's an important point that must be made here. A responder function can also be a self-contained function. The responder function itself may have an initialization phase along with its normal response phase. Keep this in mind.

As an example of a responder function, let's say there's a global variable tracking the amount of fuel a player has. When the fuel level reaches a specific value, we want to hear a digitized message that says "Fuel low." We could accomplish this with the pseudocode responder function in Listing 11.5.

Listing 11.5. A responder function that responds to a low-fuel event.

```
void Low_Fuel(void)
{

static int talked_yet=0;
```

continues

Listing 11.5. continued

```
// first test if the responder function has already provided its response.
// if so then don't respond anymore

if (!talked_yet)
    {

    // test if fuel is low
    if (fuel < low_threshold)
        {
        // play digitized sound

        // set state variable to reflect that message has been played so that
        // "fuel low" is repeated continually

        talked_yet=1;

        } // end if fuel low

    } // end if not talked yet
else
    {
    // do nothing in this case
    } // end else

} // end Low_Fuel
```

Admittedly, this function could be a little cleaner in the logical sense of the term. However, this code successfully merges the essence of a responder function with the power of self-contained functions. This is the basic technique you should use when writing games. Try to encapsulate as much independent functionality in each of the game functions as possible, so the main game loop doesn't have much to do other than call a bunch of functions and act like a multitasking scheduler. This concept is shown in Figure 11.9.

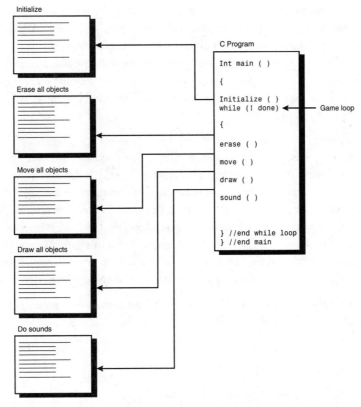

Figure 11.9. *The game loop calling the modules of the game.*

The Game State

The next topic of interest is the game state. By *game state* I mean the overall state of the main event or game loop composing the video game. Here are some of the main states the game can be in:

- [ ] The initialization phase

- [ ] The erase-move-draw cycle

- [ ] The game logic

- [ ] Collisions and special FX

However, we need to step back for a moment and think of the main event loop as a complete system in itself. Metaphorically speaking, just as a human body is composed of cells that make up organs, which in turn make up systems, a video game has much the same architecture. We can think of a video game as being like a collection of cells. Each cell is responsible for a specific set of tasks. The easier we can create these cells and make them do what they're supposed to do, the quicker we'll be able to write our games (and make billions of dollars!).

By designing hierarchical software systems we can encapsulate complexity that, if it were freestanding, would be incomprehensible. For instance, we couldn't build an entire computer with just transistors. (Even if we could, it would take a million years!) However, if we use transistors to make gates that in turn are used for chips that make up functional blocks, we can connect them to create a complete system. Along this line of thought, we must think of the main game loop as the highest level of the systems that make up a video game. There may be many systems in a game, from the graphics system to the AI system, and they may all be fairly autonomous. However, we want the main game loop to basically watch over everything and make global decisions.

To accomplish this functionality, we need a set of game-state variables. These variables are used to track details, including:

☐ The start of a level

☐ The end of a level

☐ The initialization of the entire game

☐ The graceful termination of the game

And more; it's really up to you. However, you'll definitely have a much easier time controlling all the dozens (if not hundreds) of functions if the main game loop itself has a "rough" idea of what's going on, and is the overall master control program. By *master control program* I mean a program that can send a message from the main game loop to all other functions, instructing those functions to stop what they're doing and do something else when the game changes state.

Using the Internal Timer

The main idea of today's lesson is the efficient use of time in a video game. This efficient usage encompasses many areas that may seem unrelated, such as the topic we just discussed. However, a game is a temporal piece of software, and time is its essence. We

must now switch gears and go back to talking about the internal timer and how we can use it to multitask.

The PC is equipped with 8253 chip that contains three counters. These counters can be programmed to count at different rates and can be used to cause interrupts and trigger events.

Interrupt 1CH is directly connected to one of these counters, and the rate at which the interrupt occurs is related to a fixed system value modified by a programmable value. In other words, there are limits to the speed of the counters. By reprogramming the internal timer and latching onto it in the form of an ISR, we can accomplish many things. For example, say we need to update some variable exactly 60 times per second. We could reprogram the internal timer to initiate an interrupt every 1/60th of a second, and then install an ISR into the timer interrupt at location 1CH in the interrupt table. Then, when the ISR was called (60 times per second) it could perform its task, we could rest assured that this was occurring exactly 60 times a second.

Reprogramming the internal timer is easy once you know how (and once you know how not). We aren't going to get into an in-depth discussion about the timer chip because it's rather complex. Instead, in this section we learn how it works in general, see its low-level programming, and then write functions to take care of the details so we never have to think about it again!

We communicate with the internal timer chip using the I/O ports shown in Table 11.2.

Table 11.2. The 8253 timer chips counter allocation.

I/O Port	Counter #	Usage
40h	Counter 0	Timer/disk
41h	Counter 1	Memory refresh
42h	Counter 2	Tape drive/speaker
43h	Control Register	Controlling the timer functions

As you can see, there isn't a terribly large interface to control the chip. However, its programming isn't utterly without problems.

There are three counters, numbers 0–2. We can do anything we wish to them, but I suggest leaving number 1 alone as it's used by the system to control the dynamic RAM refresh rate, and probably will cause a catastrophic crash if altered. We play only with

counter 0, because it's the one already being used as the system timer. The question is, how do we program the timer to count at a certain rate? This is cool, so listen carefully:

1. The PC contains a crystal that oscillates at 1.19318 megahertz. This signal is fed into the counter and used as a time base.

2. The value programmed into the counter's 16-bit count registers is then used to divide this number down to a slower rate.

   For example, if wanted the counter to count at its slowest possible rate, we would divide 1.19318MHz by the largest possible 16-bit number, which is 65,535. The result of the division would be 18.206759. If we chop off a few decimal points, we see that this is the good old 18.2 ticks per second on which the PC runs.

In general, the formula to be used to solve for a desired count rate is the one shown in Formula 11.1.

Formula 11.1. Computing the counter value.

```
                        1.19318mhz
16 bit counter value = -----------------
                        desired frequency
```

Of course, this equation is bounded by two limits:

☐ The upper limit is the fastest the counter can possible count at, which is 1.19318MHz.

☐ The lower limit is the slowest the counter can count at, which (as we've already seen) is 18.2Hz.

Therefore, the range of possible values is [18.2Hz,1.19318MHz]. This is more than enough, and serves our purposes perfectly. In the case in which you want something to occur every second, you can program the timer to run at, say, 20Hz and then have your ISR count up to 20 before it does anything. The result would be an event every second.

Because we're writing PC-based video games, we're mostly interested in a few key event rates. These rates are usually based on the game's *frame rate*, which is the ultimate heartbeat of the game. Table 11.3 shows some common frequencies and the 16-bit values that must be programmed into the counter.

Table 11.3. 16-bit counter values for different clock rates.

Hex Value	Decimal Value	Time Base
4DAE	19886	60Hz
5D37	23863	50Hz
7486	29830	40Hz
965C	39772	30Hz
E90B	59659	20Hz
FFFF	65535	18.2Hz

The next thing we must figure out is how to reprogram the internal timer. We can accomplish this through the control registers we saw in Table 11.2. The 16-bit value is placed into the counter register in a low/high scheme, but the control register must be programmed correctly before this process takes place. Just to be complete, Table 11.4 contains the bit designations for the 8253 control register.

Table 11.4. 8253 Control Register Bit Designations.

Bit 0	
0	Count in binary
1	Count in BCD.

Bits 1-3 select the counter mode.

Bit 3	Bit 2	Bit 1	Mode
0	0	0	0—Interrupt on terminal count
0	0	1	1—Hardware retriggerable one-shot
X	1	0	2—Rate generator
X	1	1	3—Square wave
1	0	0	4—Software retriggerable strobe
1	0	1	5—Hardware retriggerable strobe

continues

Table 11.4. continued

Bits 4 and 5 control the reading and writing.

Bit 5	Bit 4	Function
0	0	Counter latch operation
0	1	Read/write least-significant byte of counter
1	0	Read/write most-significant byte of counter
1	1	Read/write least-, then most-significant byte

Bits 6 and 7 select the counter accessed for the operation.

Bit 7	Bit 6	Counter #
0	0	0
0	1	1
1	0	2
1	1	illegal

Game Law: Don't ask why hardware engineers make everything so complicated. Just accept it as punishment for a previous life.

There are quite a number of nebulous little bits that must be programmed—and, based
on their descriptions, there isn't much that can be determined. Fortunately, I can
magically tell you the proper combination you can use to accomplish counter programming the way we want. We use the binary counting method, square wave waveform, and
load with the least/most significant word as our bit settings. That, along with setting the
bits for the proper counter to be programmed, is all we need do. Therefore, here's the plan
of attack:

1. Create a control word that sets the proper bits to set up the counter in the way
   just described.

2. Write this control word to port 43h, which is the control register.

3. Write the least and most significant bytes of the 16-bit value we previously
   computed in the counter port at 40h.

The counter then is reprogrammed.

Based on the fact that this sequence of steps seems to leave a lot of room for problems,
I've supplied a function in Listing 11.6, along with some #defines that have the most
common rates already computed for you.

Listing 11.6. Software to reprogram the internal timer.

```
#define CONTROL_8253    0x43   // the 8253's control register
#define CONTROL_WORD    0x3C   // the control word to set mode 2,
                               // binary least/most
#define COUNTER_0       0x40   // counter 0
#define COUNTER_1       0x41   // counter 1
#define COUNTER_2       0x42   // counter 2

#define TIMER_60HZ      0x4DAE // 60Hz
#define TIMER_50HZ      0x5D37 // 50Hz
#define TIMER_40HZ      0x7486 // 40Hz
#define TIMER_30HZ      0x965C // 30Hz
#define TIMER_20HZ      0xE90B // 20Hz
#define TIMER_18HZ      0xFFFF // 18.2Hz (the standard count
                               // and the slowest possible)

#define LOW_BYTE(n) (n & 0x00ff)        // extracts the low-byte
#define HI_BYTE(n)  ((n>>8) & 0x00ff)   // extracts the hi-byte


void Change_Timer(unsigned int new_count)
{

// send the control word, mode 2, binary,
// least/most load sequence

_outp(CONTROL_8253, CONTROL_WORD);

// now write the least significant byte to the counter register

_outp(COUNTER_0,LOW_BYTE(new_count));

// and now the the most significant byte

_outp(COUNTER_0,HI_BYTE(new_count));

} // end Change_Timer
```

Analysis

The Change_Timer() function takes as a parameter the 16-bit value to be placed into
counter number zero, which is used as the timing counter and is responsible for
creating the interrupt 1CH. The Change_Timer() function itself is simple and does

exactly what we said it should. It writes the proper control word to the control register, and then writes the low and high byte of the new counter rate into the counter register. Notice, also, that the LOW_BYTE() and HI_BYTE() macros are used to extract the low and high byte of an integer.

As an example of using this function to do something interesting, let's now look at a program that takes the new rate, in hertz, to which you'd like the internal timer reprogrammed. You enter the new rate on the command line. Remember, the value range is [18.2Hz–1.19318MHz], but if you reprogram the timer in a way that causes too many interrupts per second, the system probably will lock. Try numbers from 20–1,000, and then run the timeint.exe program to see that the timer interrupt is actually happening faster or slower than it was with the standard setting of 18.2Hz.

Note that the program does no error checking and only takes integers. If you don't send a parameter, the program resets the internal timer to 18.2Hz. The name of the program, shown in Listing 11.7, is timer.exe.

Listing 11.7. A command-line program to reprogram the internal timer.

```
// I N C L U D E S ///////////////////////////////////////////

#include <dos.h>
#include <bios.h>
#include <stdio.h>
#include <stdlib.h>
#include <math.h>
#include <conio.h>

#include "graph3.h"   // include graphics our stuff
#include "graph4.h"
#include "graph6.h"


// D E F I N E S ///////////////////////////////////////////

#define CONTROL_8253   0x43  // the 8253's control register
#define CONTROL_WORD   0x3C  // the control word to set mode 2,
                             // binary least/most
#define COUNTER_0      0x40  // counter 0
#define COUNTER_1      0x41  // counter 1
#define COUNTER_2      0x42  // counter 2

#define TIMER_60HZ     0x4DAE // 60Hz
#define TIMER_50HZ     0x5D37 // 50Hz
#define TIMER_40HZ     0x7486 // 40Hz
#define TIMER_30HZ     0x965C // 30Hz
#define TIMER_20HZ     0xE90B // 20Hz
#define TIMER_18HZ     0xFFFF // 18.2Hz (the standard count and
                              // the slowest possible)
```

```
// M A C R O S ///////////////////////////////////////////////

#define LOW_BYTE(n) (n & 0x00ff)        // extracts the low-byte
                                        // of a word
#define HI_BYTE(n)  ((n>>8) & 0x00ff)   // extracts the hi-byte
                                        // of a word

// F U N C T I O N S ///////////////////////////////////////////

void Change_Timer(unsigned int new_count)
{

// send the control word, mode 2, binary,
// least/most load sequence

_outp(CONTROL_8253, CONTROL_WORD);

// now write the least significant byte to the counter register

_outp(COUNTER_0,LOW_BYTE(new_count));

// and now the the most significant byte

_outp(COUNTER_0,HI_BYTE(new_count));

} // end Change_Time

// M A I N //////////////////////////////////////////////////////

void main(int argc, char **argv)
{

double rate = 1.1931817E+6;  // system timer clock rate
                             // used as dividend

unsigned int quotient;       // the resulting value to load
                             // into the counter

// test if a parameter was sent;
// if not, flag a error and set timer to 18.2

if (argc==1)
   {
   printf("\nReseting system to 18.2 ticks/second.");

   Change_Timer(TIMER_18HZ);

   return;

   } // end if user didn't send new rate

// compute proper divisor and re-program clock

quotient = (unsigned int)( rate / (double)atoi(argv[1]) );
```

continues

Listing 11.7. continued

```
// re-program timer

Change_Timer(quotient);

printf("\nTimer re-programmed to %d or %s ticks/second",
        quotient,argv[1]);

} // end main
```

Building an Executable: To make an executable of the program in
Listing 11.7, you can either type it in or use the source on the companion
CD. The name of the source is timer.c. The precompiled executable is
named timer.exe. As before, use the following compile line for Microsoft C:

```
cl -AM -Zi -c -Fc -Gs -G2 timer.c
```

After compiling the program in this manner you can link it to the standard
libraries and to our previously generated game library, gamelib.lib, with a
link line such as:

```
link /ST:8192 /CO timer,,,graphics.lib+gamelib.lib,,
```

This creates a final executable named timer.exe.

The program only knows two cases:

☐ A command-line parameter is interpreted as an integer used to compute the
proper counter rate to produce the desired frequency.

☐ If the parameter isn't a command-line parameter, the internal timer is reprogrammed to 18.2Hz by using the value FFFFh or 65535.

Implementing a Multitasking Kernel

All this stuff about timers, interrupts, and special functions has probably seemed a bit
disconnected. Maybe so; however, it's possible to use the timer interrupt to create a

simple, "round-robin" multitasking kernel under DOS that can be used in your video games to automate the calling of a few key time-related functions.

As you know, a video game is a single task that calls many functions, which perform their work and return. This process is repeated forever until the game is terminated in the main game loop. (Refer back to Figure 11.9 for a graphical representation of this.)

In a way, we're using the main() function as a little kernel that calls a bunch of tasks. However, the rate at which these tasks are called is hard to determine: the order in which they're called usually is important, and they usually are tightly coupled to the game at hand.

What if we could pretend that the PC contained 17 processors? In that scenario, the first 16 would be used for simple tasks that don't do much but are important (such as blinking lights, changing variables, acquiring input data, and so on). The 17th task would be the main() function, which has a lot more processing power and could be used for the real meat of the game. This simulation of multiple processors can easily be accomplished on the PC using interrupts and some cool programming. In fact, I supply a complete, round-robin multitasking kernel that you can start from your C program to execute simple tasks for your games. The model I give you is simple, but opens up many possibilities to explore.

The kernel works as follows:

1. An ISR is installed that latches onto the timer interrupt.

2. When the ISR is activated, it makes a call to a function in a table and allows the function to execute one cycle.

3. Then, when the next timer interrupt occurs, the next function in the table gets to execute until each function has had a crack at the CPU. When this occurs then the process starts all over.

This model is shown in Figure 11.10.

The table of functions is simply a table of function pointers, which point to the tasks the user wishes executed. The tasks are installed into the table using a function call, and can consequently be removed if so desired. The multitasking rate is determined my the timer rate (which, as we've learned, can be reprogrammed).

As an example, if we set the timer for 60Hz and then install three tasks, each task gets one-third of the overall rate, or 20Hz. This means each task executes 20 times per second: not bad! The kernel is primitive and doesn't allow preemption or priorities, but it does cycle through the tasks in an orderly manner and never crashes (knock on particle board).

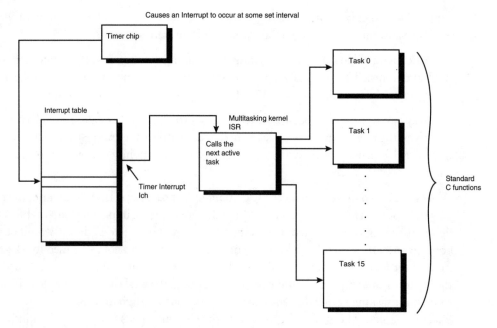

Figure 11.10. *An interrupt-driven multitasking model on the PC.*

Let's take a look at the software modules, and then see a cool demo that runs three tasks plus the main() C function.

The Components of the Multitasking System

We should become familiar with all the components of the multitasking system. First, we have the #define lines:

```
// multitasking kernel defines

#define MAX_TASKS       16  // this should be enough to turn
                            // your brains to mush
#define TASK_INACTIVE   0   // this is an inactive task
#define TASK_ACTIVE     1   // this is an active task
```

These are used to set the maximum number of tasks in the system at one time and to associate reasonable identifiers with active and inactive tasks.

Next is the task structure.

```
// this is a single task structure

typedef struct task_typ
        {

        int id;             // the ID number for this task
        int state;          // the state of this task
        void (far *task)(); // the function pointer to the
                            // task itself

        } task, *task_ptr;
```

The task structure is simple: it contains an ID number, a state, and a function pointer to the task that's called when the scheduler executes the task. (Notice the syntax used to define a function pointer!)

Finally, we have the task array itself, which is just a storage house for all three tasks. (We could have used a linked list, of course—but for 16 elements, I don't think so!)

```
task tasks[MAX_TASKS];  // this is the task list for the system

int num_tasks = 0;  // tracks number of active tasks
```

The array holds 16 task structures and must be initialized before the system is started up.

All we need do to make this whole thing work is initialize the task array, install some tasks, and then (during the timer interrupt) let our ISR execute the next task in the list. Therefore, the first function we should concern ourselves with is the initialization function. Listing 11.8 shows an initialization function for the multitasking kernel.

Listing 11.8. The initialization function for the multitasking kernel.

```
void Initialize_Kernal(void)
{

// this function will set up the task list and prepare for it
// to be populated

int index; // loop variable

for (index=0; index<MAX_TASKS; index++)
    {
    // set ID to current location in list

    tasks[index].id = index;

    // set to inactive

    tasks[index].state = TASK_INACTIVE;
```

continues

Listing 11.8. continued

```
// set function pointer to NULL;

tasks[index].task = NULL;

} // end for index

} // end Initialize_Kernal
```

The function in Listing 11.8 is called with no parameters and returns nothing. The only thing the function does is initialize all the elements in the tasks array.

The next function of interest in the one to add a task to the task list. The code shown in Listing 11.9 does that.

Listing 11.9. Adding a task to the task list.

```
int Add_Task(void (far *function)())
{
// this function will add the task to the task list and
// return its ID number
// which can be used to delete it.
// If the function returns -1 then the
// task list is full and no more tasks can be added

int index;

for (index=0; index<MAX_TASKS; index++)
    {
    // try and find an inactive task

    if (tasks[index].state == TASK_INACTIVE)
        {
        // load new task into this position

        tasks[index].state = TASK_ACTIVE;
        tasks[index].id    = index;
        tasks[index].task  = function; // assign function pointer

        // adjust global task monitor

        num_tasks++;

        // return ID to caller

        return(tasks[index].id);

        } // end if found an inactive task

    } // end for index
```

```
// if we got this far then there are no free spots...bummer

return(-1);

} // end Add_Task
```

The Add_Task() function takes as a parameter the address of the function to be installed in the task list. The function then returns one of the following:

☐ If the task can be installed into the task list, the Add_Task() function returns the task's ID, which can later be used to remove the task.

☐ If the task cannot be installed into the task list, the Add_Task() function returns a -1.

The next important function we need is something to delete a task from the system. Listing 11.10 contains code that does that.

Listing 11.10. Deleting a task from the system.

```
int Delete_Task(int id)
{
// this function will try to delete a task from the task list,
// if the function
// is successful, it will return 1 else it will return 0.

if (tasks[id].state == TASK_ACTIVE)
   {
   // kill task and return success

   tasks[id].task  = NULL;
   tasks[id].state = TASK_INACTIVE;

   // decrement number of active tasks

   num_tasks--;

   return(1);

   } // end if task can be deleted
else
   {
   // couldn't delete task
   return(0);

   } // end task already dead

} // end Delete_Task
```

The `Delete_Task()` function takes as a parameter the ID number of the task to be removed (which was saved from the call to `Add_Task()`). The function then returns one of the following:

☐ If the task can be removed, the `Delete_Task()` function returns a 1.

☐ If the task has already been removed, the `Delete_Task()` function returns a 0.

Warning: The `Delete_Task()` function does no bounds checking on the task ID, so be careful!

Now that we can add and delete tasks, the next thing we would like to do is to start the multitasking kernel and let it do its magic. This is accomplished by the code shown in Listing 11.11.

Listing 11.11. Starting the multitasking kernel.

```
void Start_Kernal(void)
{
// install our time keeper ISR while saving old one

Old_Time_Isr = _dos_getvect(TIME_KEEPER_INT);

_dos_setvect(TIME_KEEPER_INT, Multi_Kernal);

} // end Start_Kernal
```

That's it. All the `Start_Kernal()` function does is point the timer interrupt to our ISR, which is the kernel itself. However, the function makes sure to save the old timer-interrupt vector so it can be replaced when the program is complete and we exit to DOS. Therefore, the next function should be something that stops the multitasking kernel. The code in Listing 11.12 does just that.

Listing 11.12. Stopping the multitasking kernel.

```
void Stop_Kernal(void)
{

// replace old time keeper ISR

_dos_setvect(TIME_KEEPER_INT, Old_Time_Isr);

} // end Stop_Kernal
```

That was a strain on the membrane!

Finally, we're missing one crucial element of this whole discussion: the multitasking kernel itself. Here it is, in Listing 11.13.

Listing 11.13. The multitasking kernel.

```
void _interrupt far Multi_Kernal(void)
{

// this function will call all of the task in a round-robin
// manner such that
// only one task will be called per interrupt.
// note: ther must be at least
// one active task in the task list

static int current_task=0;  // current_task to be executed
                            // by kernel

// test if there are any tasks at all

if (num_tasks>0)
{

// find an active task

while(tasks[current_task].state!=TASK_ACTIVE)
    {
    // move to next task and round robin if at end of task list

    if (++current_task>=MAX_TASKS)
      current_task=0;

    } // end search for active task

// at this point we have an active task so call it

tasks[current_task].task(); // weird looking huh!

// now we need to move to the next possible task

if (++current_task>=MAX_TASKS)
   current_task=0;

} // end if there are any tasks

// chain to old ISR (play nice with the other children)

Old_Time_Isr();

} // end Multi_Kernal
```

11

The `Multi_Kernal()` interrupt function is so simple and does so much that you can't help but be impressed with the capabilities of the PC:

1. The kernel operates by first testing whether there are any active tasks and, if so, executes the next task in the task list for one cycle.

2. The index to the current task then is bumped up by one.

3. During the next interrupt, the next task in the list is executed.

4. The kernel then goes back to the first step.

Let's now reiterate how to use the multitasking system:

1. First, we initialize the system with a call to `Initialize_Kernal()`.

2. Next, we use the `Add_Task()` function to add tasks to the task list.

3. Finally, we make a call the `Start_Kernal()` function. This installs the `Multi_Kernal()` ISR, and multitasking begins.

4. If we wish to kill or remove a task from the task list, we make a call to the function `Delete_Task()` with the ID number of the task we wish removed.

5. Finally, when we're done multitasking, we can stop the system and set everything back to normal with a call to `Stop_Kernal()`.

Realize that this multitasking system is simple: barely able to handle much more than simple tasks. However, it's a good starting point for making a complex system. Furthermore, the simplicity helps you make sure that each task executed isn't too complex and doesn't takes a lot of CPU time.

Warning: Don't make any DOS calls in the tasks. DOS is not reentrant, and this could cause a problem. Try to stick to straight C code and library functions.

There is a final aspect of all this that we should cover: the fact that the rate of multitasking is based on the timer-interrupt rate (which we've already learned how to reprogram). Therefore, if you want your tasks to run faster or slower, you must make a call to `Change_Timer()` to set the proper tasking rate of the PC's internal timer.

The demo of the multitasking system is called mtask.exe, and is very cool. It creates three tasks and shows each of their outputs in a window on the screen. You can then alter the

rate of multitasking with the numeric keys 2 through 6, and kill tasks by pressing the first letter of their names:

☐ Press the S key to kill the star field.

☐ Press the M key to kill the mirror.

☐ Press the B key to kill the balls.

Anyway, play with the program and study the source code until you're comfortable with the whole idea of multitasking using interrupts. Listing 11.14 contains the code.

Listing 11.14. A multitasking demo (mtask.c).

```
// I N C L U D E S //////////////////////////////////////////////

#include <io.h>
#include <conio.h>
#include <stdio.h>
#include <stdlib.h>
#include <dos.h>
#include <bios.h>
#include <fcntl.h>
#include <memory.h>
#include <malloc.h>
#include <math.h>
#include <string.h>

#include "graph3.h"  // include graphics our stuff
#include "graph4.h"
#include "graph5.h"
#include "graph6.h"

// D E F I N E S //////////////////////////////////////////////

// timer defines

#define CONTROL_8253  0x43  // the 8253's control register
#define CONTROL_WORD  0x3C  // the control word to set mode 2,
                            // binary least/most
#define COUNTER_0     0x40  // counter 0
#define COUNTER_1     0x41  // counter 1
#define COUNTER_2     0x42  // counter 2

#define TIMER_60HZ    0x4DAE // 60Hz
#define TIMER_50HZ    0x5D37 // 50Hz
#define TIMER_40HZ    0x7486 // 40Hz
#define TIMER_30HZ    0x965C // 30Hz
#define TIMER_20HZ    0xE90B // 20Hz
#define TIMER_18HZ    0xFFFF // 18.2Hz (the standard count and
                            // the slowest possible)
```

continues

Listing 11.14. continued

```
// interrupt table defines

#define TIME_KEEPER_INT   0x1C  // the time keeper interrupt

// multitasking kernel defines

#define MAX_TASKS      16  // this should be enough to turn your
                           // brains to mush
#define TASK_INACTIVE  0   // this is an inactive task
#define TASK_ACTIVE    1   // this is an active task


// defines for demo tasks

#define NUM_ATOMS 30
#define NUM_STARS 50

// M A C R O S ////////////////////////////////////////////////

#define LOW_BYTE(n) (n & 0x00ff)        // extracts the low-byte
#define HI_BYTE(n)  ((n>>8) & 0x00ff)   // extracts the hi-byte

// S T U C T U R E S ///////////////////////////////////////////

// this is a single task structure

typedef struct task_typ
        {

        int id;            // the ID number for this task
        int state;         // the state of this task
        void (far *task)(); // the function pointer to the
                           // task itself

        } task, *task_ptr;

// structures for demo tasks

typedef struct particle_typ
        {
        int x,y;           // position of particle
        int xv,yv;         // velocity of particle
        unsigned char color; // color of particle
        } particle, *particle_ptr;

// P R O T O T Y P E S /////////////////////////////////////////

void Change_Timer(unsigned int new_count);

// multitasking stuff

void Initialize_Kernal(void);
```

```
void Start_Kernal(void);

void Stop_Kernal(void);

int Add_Task(void (far *function)());

int Delete_Task(int id);

void _interrupt far Multi_Kernal(void);

// G L O B A L S ////////////////////////////////////////////

void (_interrupt far *Old_Time_Isr)();  // used to hold old
                                        // interrupt vector

// multitasking stuff

task tasks[MAX_TASKS];  // this is the task list for the system

int num_tasks = 0;      // tracks number of active tasks

// globals for demo tasks

particle atoms[NUM_ATOMS]; // the balls

particle starfield[NUM_STARS]; // the star field

int star_id, mirror_id, ball_id; // used to hold IDs so
                                 // that tasks can be
                                 // terminated later

// F U N C T I O N S ////////////////////////////////////////

void Initialize_Kernal(void)
{
// this function will set up the task list and
// prepare for it to be populated

int index; // loop variable

for (index=0; index<MAX_TASKS; index++)
    {
    // set ID to current location in list

    tasks[index].id = index;

    // set to inactive

    tasks[index].state = TASK_INACTIVE;

    // set function pointer to NULL;

    tasks[index].task = NULL;
```

continues

Listing 11.14. continued

```c
    } // end for index

} // end Initialize_Kernal

/////////////////////////////////////////////////////////////////

void Start_Kernal(void)
{
// install our time keeper ISR while saving old one

Old_Time_Isr = _dos_getvect(TIME_KEEPER_INT);

_dos_setvect(TIME_KEEPER_INT, Multi_Kernal);

} // end Start_Kernal

/////////////////////////////////////////////////////////////////

void Stop_Kernal(void)
{

// replace old time keeper ISR

_dos_setvect(TIME_KEEPER_INT, Old_Time_Isr);

} // end Stop_Kernal

/////////////////////////////////////////////////////////////////

int Add_Task(void (far *function)())
{
// this function will add the task to the task list
// and return its ID number
// which can be used to delete it.
// If the function returns -1 then the
// task list is full and no more tasks can be added

int index;

for (index=0; index<MAX_TASKS; index++)
    {
    // try and find an inactive task

    if (tasks[index].state == TASK_INACTIVE)
        {
        // load new task into this position

        tasks[index].state = TASK_ACTIVE;
        tasks[index].id    = index;
        tasks[index].task  = function;  // assign function pointer

        // adjust global task monitor

        num_tasks++;
```

```
        // return ID to caller

        return(tasks[index].id);

        } // end if found an inactive task

    } // end for index

// if we got this far then there are no free spots...bummer

return(-1);

} // end Add_Task

////////////////////////////////////////////////////////////

int Delete_Task(int id)
{
// this function will try to delete a task from the task list,
// if the function
// is successful, it will return 1 else it will return 0.

if (tasks[id].state == TASK_ACTIVE)
    {
    // kill task and return success

    tasks[id].task   = NULL;
    tasks[id].state  = TASK_INACTIVE;

    // decrement number of active tasks

    num_tasks--;

    return(1);

    } // end if task can be deleted
else
    {
    // couldn't delete task
    return(0);

    } // end task already dead

} // end Delete_Task

////////////////////////////////////////////////////////////

void _interrupt far Multi_Kernal(void)
{

// this function will call all of the task in a round robin
// manner such that
// only one task will be called per interrupt.
// note: ther must be at least
// one active task in the task list
```

continues

Listing 11.14. continued

```
static int current_task=0;  // current_task to be
                            // executed by kernel

// test if there are any tasks at all

if (num_tasks>0)
{

// find an active task

while(tasks[current_task].state!=TASK_ACTIVE)
    {
    // move to next task and round robin if at end of task list

    if (++current_task>=MAX_TASKS)
      current_task=0;

    } // end search for active task

// at this point we have an active task so call it

tasks[current_task].task(); // weird looking huh!

// now we need to move to the next possible task

if (++current_task>=MAX_TASKS)
   current_task=0;

} // end if there are any tasks

// chain to old ISR (play nice with the other children)

Old_Time_Isr();

} // end Multi_Kernal

////////////////////////////////////////////////////////////////

void Change_Timer(unsigned int new_count)
{

// send the control word, mode 2, binary,
// least/most load sequence

_outp(CONTROL_8253, CONTROL_WORD);

// now write the least significant byte to the counter register

_outp(COUNTER_0,LOW_BYTE(new_count));

// and now the the most significant byte

_outp(COUNTER_0,HI_BYTE(new_count));
```

```
} // end Change_Timer


// D E M O  T A S K S ///////////////////////////////////////

void Rectangle(int xo,int yo,int x1,int y1,unsigned char color)
{

// draw a rectangle using the Bline function

Bline(xo,yo,x1,yo,color);
Bline(x1,yo,x1,y1,color);
Bline(x1,y1,xo,y1,color);
Bline(xo,y1,xo,yo,color);


} // end Rectangle

///////////////////////////////////////////////////////////////

void Stars(void)
{
// this function will animate a star field

int index; // loop variable

static int initialized=0;  // this is the local static
                           // state variable

if (!initialized)
   {

   // initialize all the stars

   for (index=0; index<NUM_STARS; index++)
       {
       // initialize each star to a velocity, position and color

       starfield[index].x     = 226 + rand()%70;
       starfield[index].y     = 26  + rand()%70;

       // decide what star plane the star is in

       switch(rand()%3)
             {
             case 0: // plane 1- the farthest star plane
                 {
                 // set velocity and color

                 starfield[index].xv = 2;
                 starfield[index].color = 8;

                 } break;
```

11

continues

Listing 11.14. continued

```
            case 1: // plane 2-The medium distance star plane
                {

                starfield[index].xv = 4;
                starfield[index].color = 7;

                } break;

            case 2: // plane 3-The nearest star plane
                {

                starfield[index].xv = 6;
                starfield[index].color = 15;

                } break;

            } // end switch

        } // end for index


    // draw working window

    Rectangle(225,25,225+75,25+75,9);

    // set variable to move to next processing state

    initialized=1;

    } // end if being initialized
else
    { // must be nth time in, so do the usual


    // process each star

    for (index=0; index<NUM_STARS; index++)
        {
        // E R A S E ///////////////////////////////////////////

        Plot_Pixel_Fast(starfield[index].x,starfield[index].y,0);

        // M O V E ///////////////////////////////////////////

        if ( (starfield[index].x+=starfield[index].xv)>=225+75 )
            starfield[index].x = 226;

        // D R A W ///////////////////////////////////////////

        Plot_Pixel_Fast(starfield[index].x,starfield[index].y,
                        starfield[index].color);

        } // end for index
```

```
    } // end else

} // end Stars

/////////////////////////////////////////////////////////////

void Mirror(void)
{
// this function will draw a mirrored pixel image

int x,y;

unsigned char color;

static int initialized=0;   // this is the local
                            // static state variable

if (!initialized)
   {

   // draw working window

   Rectangle(125,25,125+75,25+75,9);

   // set variable to move to next processing state

   initialized=1;

   } // end if not intialized
else
   {

   // D R A W /////////////////////////////////////////////////

   // draw a mirrored image

   x       = rand()%38;
   y       = rand()%38;
   color   = (unsigned char)(rand()%256);

   Plot_Pixel_Fast(x+125,y+25,color);
   Plot_Pixel_Fast((75-1)-x+125,y+25,color);
   Plot_Pixel_Fast(x+125,(75-1)-y+25,color);
   Plot_Pixel_Fast((75-1)-x+125,(75-1)-y+25,color);

   } // end else

} // end Mirror

/////////////////////////////////////////////////////////////

void Balls(void)
{
// this function will bounce a collection of balls around
```

continues

Listing 11.14. continued

```
int index; // used for looping

static int initialized=0;   // this is the local
                            // static state variable

if (!initialized)
   {

   // initialize all structures

   for (index=0; index<NUM_ATOMS; index++)
      {
      // select a random position and trajectory for each atom
      // their background

      atoms[index].x      = 26 + rand()%70;
      atoms[index].y      = 26 + rand()%70;

      atoms[index].xv     = -2 + rand()%4;
      atoms[index].yv     = -2 + rand()%4;

      } // end for index

   // draw working window

   Rectangle(25,25,25+75,25+75,9);

   // set initialized flag so process can switch states

   initialized = 1;

   } // end if need to initialize
else
   { // do normal processing

   // E R A S E ////////////////////////////////////////////////

   // loop through the atoms and erase them

   for (index=0; index<NUM_ATOMS; index++)
      {
      Plot_Pixel_Fast(atoms[index].x, atoms[index].y, 0);
      } // end for index

   // M O V E ////////////////////////////////////////////////

   // loop through the atom array and move each atom also
   // check collsions
   // with the walls of the container

   for (index=0; index<NUM_ATOMS; index++)
      {

      // move the atoms
```

```
            atoms[index].x+=atoms[index].xv;
            atoms[index].y+=atoms[index].yv;

            // did the atom hit a wall, if so reflect the
            // velocity vector

            if (atoms[index].x > 98 ¦¦ atoms[index].x < 27)
               {
               atoms[index].xv=-atoms[index].xv;
               atoms[index].x+=atoms[index].xv;
               } // end if hit a vertical wall

            if (atoms[index].y > 98 ¦¦ atoms[index].y < 28)
               {
               atoms[index].yv=-atoms[index].yv;
               atoms[index].y+=atoms[index].yv;
               } // end if hit a horizontal wall

            } // end for index

    // D R A W ///////////////////////////////////////////////////

    // loop through the atoms and draw them

    for (index=0; index<NUM_ATOMS; index++)
        {
        Plot_Pixel_Fast(atoms[index].x, atoms[index].y, 10);
        } // end for index

    } // end else normal processing

} // end Balls

// M A I N ///////////////////////////////////////////////////

void main(void)
{
int trate=20;          // initial timer rate
int done=0;            // exit flag
char string[80];       // used for printing


// SECTION 1 ///////////////////////////////////////////////////

// set video mode to 320x200 256 color mode

Set_Video_Mode(VGA256);

// initialize the multitasking system

Initialize_Kernal();

// load in some processes and save their IDs

star_id   = Add_Task(Stars);
```

continues

Listing 11.14. continued

```
ball_id   = Add_Task(Balls);

mirror_id = Add_Task(Mirror);

// SECTION 2 ///////////////////////////////////////////////////

// set timer rate to 20Hz

Change_Timer(TIMER_20HZ);

// turn on the multitasking kernel, each task will be executed
// every 3
// interrupts since there is a round robin scheduler in place

Start_Kernal();

// SECTION 3 ///////////////////////////////////////////////////

// now do main processing in parallel with other tasks

// draw menu

Blit_String(10,105,10,   "Multi-Tasking Control Menu",1);
Blit_String(10,110+10,2,
            "Press (2-6) to Change interrupt rate.",1);
Blit_String(10,110+20,2,"Press 'B' to kill ball task.",1);
Blit_String(10,110+30,2,"Press 'S' to kill stars task.",1);
Blit_String(10,110+40,2,"Press 'M' to kill mirror task.",1);
Blit_String(10,110+50,2,"Press 'Q' to exit.",1);

Blit_String(25,10,10,"Balls",0);
Blit_String(125,10,10,"Mirror",0);
Blit_String(225,10,10,"Star Field",0);


// SECTION 4 ///////////////////////////////////////////////////

// main event loop

while(!done)
    {

    // test if key was hit

    if (kbhit())
        {

        // get the character and test it

        switch(getch())
            {

                case '2': // set system timer to 20hz
                    {
```

```
                    Change_Timer(TIMER_20HZ);
                    trate = 20;

                    } break;

        case '3': // set system timer to 30Hz
                    {
                    Change_Timer(TIMER_30HZ);
                    trate = 30;

                    } break;

        case '4': // set system timer to 40Hz
                    {
                    Change_Timer(TIMER_40HZ);
                    trate = 40;

                    } break;

        case '5': // set system timer to 50Hz
                    {
                    Change_Timer(TIMER_50HZ);
                    trate = 50;

                    } break;

        case '6': // set system timer to 60Hz
                    {
                    Change_Timer(TIMER_60HZ);
                    trate = 60;

                    } break;

// SECTION 5 //////////////////////////////////////////////////

        case 'b': // kill the ball task
                    {
                    Delete_Task(ball_id);
                    Blit_String(25,10,12,"INACTIVE  ",0);
                    } break;

        case 's': // kill the star field task
                    {
                    Delete_Task(star_id);
                    Blit_String(225,10,12,"INACTIVE  ",0);
                    } break;

        case 'm': // kill the mirror task
                    {
                    Delete_Task(mirror_id);
                    Blit_String(125,10,12,"INACTIVE  ",0);
                    } break;
```

continues

Listing 11.14. continued

```
                    case 'q': done=1; break;

                    default:break;

                    } // end switch

            } // end if kbhit

        // display info

        sprintf(string,"System timer at %dHZ  ",trate);
        Blit_String(10,190,15,string,0);

        } // end while

// SECTION 6 /////////////////////////////////////////////////////

// turn off the multitasking kernel

Stop_Kernal();

// reset system timer to 18.2

Change_Timer(TIMER_18HZ);

// reset the video mode back to text

Set_Video_Mode(TEXT_MODE);

} // end main
```

Building an Executable: To make an executable of the program in Listing 11.14, you can either type it in or use the source on the companion CD. The name of the source is mtask.c. The precompiled executable is named mtask.exe. As before, use the following compile line for Microsoft C:

```
cl -AM -Zi -c  -Fc -Gs -G2 mtask.c
```

After compiling the program in this manner, you can link it to the standard libraries and to our previously generated game library, gamelib.lib, with a link line such as:

```
link /ST:8192 /CO mtask,,,graphics.lib+gamelib.lib,,
```

This creates a final executable named mtask.exe.

Analysis There isn't much to this program; however, we cover its main points as always.

The program's purpose is to create three tasks, add them to the task list, and then start the multitasking kernel. Along the way the timer is reprogrammed and the main() C function is used to control the operation of the multitasking kernel, which is running independently of the main() function itself. In essence, there are four tasks running when the program starts:

☐ The C main() function

☐ Three demo tasks

Let's cover the function of the main() function:

1. In Section 1, as usual, we begin by placing the PC into mode 13h. The kernel is then initialized and the three tasks are added to the task list. The tasks themselves are simple, 20- to 50-line graphic programs that draw stars, bounce pixels, and draw a kaleidoscope on the screen. We aren't interested in them because they could be anything. However, remember: be cautious when selecting the tasks and their complexity. And no calls to DOS functions!

2. In Section 2 the internal timer is reset to 20Hz instead of the absurd rate of 18.2Hz. The multitasking kernel is then started.

3. Section 3 is where some text blitting is done, and the instructions are drawn for the player.

4. In Section 4 the keyboard is queried and, if the player is trying to change the speed of the tasking, a call is made to Change_Timer() with the appropriate parameter.

5. If the player wishes to kill a task, Section 5 is where it's done. This section makes a simple call to the Delete_Task() function and includes the proper task ID number, which was saved during creation of the task list using the calls to Add_Task().

6. Section 6 is the end of the road. The timer is reset to 18.2Hz, the multitasking kernel is stopped, and the PC is reset to text mode.

Detouring the Keyboard

The next topic we discuss is the keyboard. I know we've already covered the keyboard and all the typical game input devices (on Day 7). However, we didn't really learn how the keyboard is used in a professional-quality video game. That's what we do now.

The keyboard is a complex device, and a real pain to understand if you don't have all the pieces to its puzzle. Fortunately, we see exactly how it works in this section, and how we can use it as a set of switches that can all be pressed and released simultaneously.

The problem with reading the keyboard with the functions we've created, or with BIOS, is that only one key can be pressed at a time. There's a stupid buffer that can only hold about 15 characters (don't quote me). We need closer communication with the keyboard; we can't have BIOS or any other interrupt interpreting the keyboard for us and then handing down the information. For example, what if we were to press the up arrow and down arrow at the same time? Using the keyboard-reading methods we learned on Day 7, we would receive one or the other. What if we needed to use the arrows for movement and the Spacebar for firing?

The answer to these problems is that we have to get close to the keyboard hardware itself. We must read the keyboard presses and releases as they occur, and keep track of what keys are down and what keys are up in a table. We can then look into this table and test for simultaneously pressed keys. The question is, how can we read the actual keyboard hardware? The answer is get out the IBM PC/AT Technical Reference book and about bottle of whiskey and prepare for some suffering. I have already done this for both of us (minus the whiskey) and have figured out how to access the keyboard and read the hardware itself.

We can communicate with the keyboard through two I/O ports:

- ☐ The keyboard data registers, which are at I/O location 60h

- ☐ The keyboard control register, which is at I/O location 61h

Using these two ports, we can directly see what the keyboard is doing. We know that the keyboard sends out a scan code when a key is pressed, and that this scan code is converted into ASCII by BIOS and then furnished to us. However, there's more to it. In reality, the scan code is sent when the key is pressed, but another code is sent when the key is released. This other, "phantom" code is called the *break code*, and is equal to the scan code plus 128. In other words, keyboard generates the break scan code by setting the high bit of the original make scan code.

The PC's BIOS takes care of all the details of scan codes, break codes, conversion to ASCII, and so forth. The only problem is that the interface over which we communicate to BIOS is serial. This means we can only track a single keypress at one time. Furthermore, we only get a message when a key is pressed, and not when they key is released. This is not going to suffice for the kind of control we need. Therefore, we must rewrite the keyboard ISR and install a new one specifically designed to use the keyboard as just a big set of switches.

The keyboard interrupt is at location 09h in the interrupt table, so all we need do is write a new keyboard ISR and install it. The only difficulty is that we must know how to control and communicate with the keyboard so we don't lose any information! In a moment we see how to do that, but let's first decide on what the ISR is to do:

☐ The ISR is to be called whenever is key is pressed or released; therefore, we want to record these events in a table. The table is to have an entry for each keyboard key we want to track. If we wanted to track the whole keyboard, the table would have 101 entries.

☐ When an interrupt occurs, we read the code from the keyboard buffer (however that's done) and then test to see whether it's one of the keys we're tracking. At this point, we update the table by either setting the key to "pressed" or "released" in the table. Hence, this keyboard state table is continually updated by the ISR whenever a key is pressed or released.

☐ We make this table global, and thereby can access it in our main game code as if it were a static table. In fact, it's being updated by an ISR.

This is the plan. The only problem we have is: how do we write a keyboard ISR that reads the key scan code when a key is pressed?

When our ISR is activated we know that there must have been a keyboard press or release; therefore, we must read the code from the keyboard buffer and then tell the keyboard that we've read the code so that another interrupt can be issued, and another key pressed. To accomplish this task, we take the following steps:

1. Read the code from the keyboard buffer at I/O port 60h.

2. Read the data from the keyboard I/O port at 61h, do a logical OR operation on it with 82h, and write the result back. This resets the keyboard read flag.

3. Reset the interrupt controller. This step isn't really needed because it's done by the epilog code generated by the C compiler, but "better safe than sorry." Therefore, a 20h is written to I/O port 20h, which is the interrupt controller's control register.

If we follow these three steps and update the key state table properly, everything will work fine. The only detail we must further consider is whether we should chain the interrupts together. In other words, should we call the old keyboard ISR at the conclusion of our ISR? The answer is: NO! We want total control.

As an example of how to implement a new keyboard ISR and how to write a complete set of functions that install and remove it, I've created a simplified version of a keyboard

11

ISR that tracks only a few important keys. The keys tracked are the arrow keys, the Spacebar, the Ctrl keys, the Alt keys, the Enter keys, the Tab key, and the Esc key. The new keyboard ISR is called New_Key_Int(). You can installed it in the usual manner. However, I thought it would be nice to supply functions to install and remove the ISR. Therefore:

☐ To install the new keyboard ISR, you make a call to the function called Install_Keyboard().

☐ To remove the keyboard ISR, you make a call to the function Delete_Keyboard().

Let's take a look at the keyboard ISR and get the main idea behind its operation. To implement our new keyboard ISR and handler software, we need some #defines, a global keyboard state, and some extra functions to make everything work smoothly. Don't worry about the #defines and other details; they're self-explanatory and are taken care of in the library module we create later. Listing 11.15 contains the code.

Listing 11.15. The new keyboard ISR.

```
void _interrupt _far New_Key_Int()
{

// read the key from the hardware and then re-enable
// the keyboard to
// read another key

_asm
   {
   sti                      ; re-enable interrupts
   in al, KEY_BUFFER        ; get the key that was pressed
   xor ah,ah                ; zero out upper 8 bits of AX
   mov raw_key, ax          ; store the key in global variable
   in al, KEY_CONTROL       ; set the control register
   or al, 82h               ; set the proper bits to reset
                            ; the keyboard flip flop
   out KEY_CONTROL,al       ; send the new data back to the
                            ; control register
   and al,7fh
   out KEY_CONTROL,al       ; complete the reset
   mov al,20h
   out INT_CONTROL,al       ; re-enable interrupts
                            ; this is not really needed since
                            ; we are using the
                            ; C _interrupt function type,
                            ; it does this for us,
                            ; however, it's a good habit to get
                            ; into and can't
                            ; hurt
```

```
        } // end in-line assembly

// now for some C to update the arrow state table

// process the key and update the key state table

switch(raw_key)
        {
        case MAKE_UP:    // pressing up
             {
             key_table[INDEX_UP]    = 1;
             } break;

        case MAKE_DOWN:  // pressing down
             {
             key_table[INDEX_DOWN] = 1;
             } break;

        case MAKE_RIGHT: // pressing right
             {
             key_table[INDEX_RIGHT] = 1;
             } break;

        case MAKE_LEFT:  // pressing left
             {
             key_table[INDEX_LEFT] = 1;
             } break;

        case MAKE_ENTER:    // pressing enter
             {
             key_table[INDEX_ENTER]    = 1;
             } break;

        case MAKE_TAB :  // pressing tab
             {
             key_table[INDEX_TAB ] = 1;
             } break;

        case MAKE_SPACE : // pressing space
             {
             key_table[INDEX_SPACE ] = 1;
             } break;

        case MAKE_CTRL : // pressing control
             {
             key_table[INDEX_CTRL ] = 1;
             } break;

        case MAKE_ALT  : // pressing alt
             {
             key_table[INDEX_ALT ] = 1;
             } break;

        case MAKE_ESC  : // pressing escape
             {
```

continues

Listing 11.15. continued

```
                 key_table[INDEX_ESC ]  = 1;
                 } break;

        case BREAK_UP:    // releasing up
                 {
                 key_table[INDEX_UP]    = 0;
                 } break;

        case BREAK_DOWN:  // releasing down
                 {
                 key_table[INDEX_DOWN]  = 0;
                 } break;

        case BREAK_RIGHT: // releasing right
                 {
                 key_table[INDEX_RIGHT] = 0;
                 } break;

        case BREAK_LEFT:  // releasing left
                 {
                 key_table[INDEX_LEFT]  = 0;
                 } break;

        case BREAK_ENTER:    // releasing enter
                 {
                 key_table[INDEX_ENTER]   = 0;
                 } break;

        case BREAK_TAB :  // releasing tab
                 {
                 key_table[INDEX_TAB ]  = 0;
                 } break;

        case BREAK_SPACE : // releasing space
                 {
                 key_table[INDEX_SPACE ] = 0;
                 } break;

        case BREAK_CTRL :  // releasing control
                 {
                 key_table[INDEX_CTRL ]  = 0;
                 } break;

        case BREAK_ALT  : // releasing alt
                 {
                 key_table[INDEX_ALT  ] = 0;
                 } break;

        case BREAK_ESC  :  // releasing escape
                 {
                 key_table[INDEX_ESC ]  = 0;
                 } break;

        default: break;
```

```
    } // end switch

// note how we don't chain interrupts,
// we want total control of the keyboard
// however, if you wanted to chain then you would make
// a call to the old
// keyboard handler right here.


} // end New_Key_Int
```

The `New_Key_Int()` keyboard ISR may seem long, but it's simple. There are two phases to its operation:

☐ During the first phase the key is read from the keyboard I/O ports and the proper manipulations are done to the keyboard control register to allow another interrupt. I used in-line assembly here because it's easier than C (at least for this case).

☐ During the second phase of the function, the key that was just read is tested to see whether it's one of the keys being tracked by the software. If it is, the state of the key (pressed or released) is used to update the keyboard state table `key_table[]`. Also, the key itself is stored in a global variable called `raw_key` just in case you want to do some processing yourself.

As you can see, accessing the keyboard state table can be done through the global array named `key_table[]`. To see whether a key is pressed or released, the table is indexed with a value that represents the location of key in the table. For example, if you wanted to know if the Enter key was down, you would type:

```
if (key_table[INDEX_ENTER]==1)
    {
    // do work
    } // end if
```

Use a similar procedure for ther keys.

As an example of seeing how everything fits together in a complete program, I've written a crude lunar lander game that installs the new keyboard ISR and then queries the `key_state[]` table in the main game loop to figure out what keys are being pressed. The lunar lander ship has four thrusters, which point north, south, east, and west. The thrusters can be activated simultaneously by holding any combination of the keys down. The object of the game is to land the lunar lander on the pad without smashing it.

Out of Time

The lunar lander game doesn't have much in it we haven't seen yet. Study the interface to the keyboard, because it's the main object of these discussions. Listing 11.16 contains the source code.

Listing 11.16. A lunar lander game that uses the new keyboard ISR (lunar.c).

```
// I N C L U D E S ////////////////////////////////////////////

#include <io.h>
#include <conio.h>
#include <stdio.h>
#include <stdlib.h>
#include <dos.h>
#include <bios.h>
#include <fcntl.h>
#include <memory.h>
#include <malloc.h>
#include <math.h>
#include <string.h>

#include "graph3.h"  // include our graphics stuff
#include "graph4.h"
#include "graph5.h"
#include "graph6.h"


// D E F I N E S ////////////////////////////////////////////

#define KEYBOARD_INT    0x09   // the keyboard interrupt number
#define KEY_BUFFER      0x60   // the location of the
                               // keyboard buffer
#define KEY_CONTROL     0x61   // the location of the keyboard
                               // controller
#define INT_CONTROL     0x20   // the location of the interrupt
                               // controller

// make and break codes for the arrow keys
// (note the make codes are the
// same as the scan codes and the break codes are
// just the scan codes plus
// 128.  For example the scan code for the UP key is 72
// which is the make code.
// if we add 128 to this then the result is 128+72 = 200.

// arrow keys

#define MAKE_RIGHT      77
#define MAKE_LEFT       75
#define MAKE_UP         72
#define MAKE_DOWN       80

// some useful control keys

#define MAKE_ENTER      28
```

638

```
#define MAKE_TAB          15
#define MAKE_SPACE        57
#define MAKE_CTRL         29
#define MAKE_ALT          56
#define MAKE_ESC          1

// and now the break codes

#define BREAK_RIGHT       205
#define BREAK_LEFT        203
#define BREAK_UP          200
#define BREAK_DOWN        208

#define BREAK_ENTER       156
#define BREAK_TAB         143
#define BREAK_SPACE       185
#define BREAK_CTRL        157
#define BREAK_ALT         184
#define BREAK_ESC         129

// indices into arrow key state table

#define INDEX_UP          0
#define INDEX_DOWN        1
#define INDEX_RIGHT       2
#define INDEX_LEFT        3

#define INDEX_ENTER       4
#define INDEX_TAB         5
#define INDEX_SPACE       6
#define INDEX_CTRL        7
#define INDEX_ALT         8
#define INDEX_ESC         9

#define NUM_KEYS          10  // number of keys in look up table

// G L O B A L S /////////////////////////////////////////////

void (_interrupt _far *Old_Key_Isr)();   // holds old keyboard
                                          // interrupt handler

int raw_key;  // the global raw keyboard data

// the arrow key state table

int key_table[NUM_KEYS] = {0,0,0,0,0,0,0,0,0,0};


// globals for the demo

int land_sx = 160,    // starting x of the landing pad
    land_ex = 180,    // ending x of the landing pad
    land_y  = 170;    // the y position of the platform

float lander_xv = 0, // the initial velocity of the lunar lander
```

continues

Listing 11.16. continued

```
        lander_yv = 0,
        fuel      = 1000; // initial load of fuel

int right_engine = 0,    // these track which engines
                         // need to be displayed

    left_engine  = 0,
    up_engine    = 0,
    down_engine  = 0;

pcx_picture imagery_pcx,        // the game imagery
            background_pcx;     // the backdrop

// the sprite used in the game

sprite lander;                  // the lunar lander

// F U N C T I O N S ///////////////////////////////////////////

void _interrupt _far New_Key_Int()
{

// read the key from the hardware and then
// re-enable the keyboard to
// read another key

_asm
   {
   sti                     ; re-enable interrupts
   in al, KEY_BUFFER       ; get the key that was pressed
   xor ah,ah               ; zero out upper 8 bits of AX
   mov raw_key, ax         ; store the key in global variable
   in al, KEY_CONTROL      ; set the control register
   or al, 82h              ; set the proper bits to reset the
                           ; keyboard flip flop
   out KEY_CONTROL,al      ; send the new data back to the
                           ; control register
   and al,7fh
   out KEY_CONTROL,al      ; complete the reset
   mov al,20h
   out INT_CONTROL,al      ; re-enable interrupts
                           ; this is not really needed since
                           ; we are using the
                           ; C _interrupt function type,
                           ; it does this for us,
                           ; however, it's a good habit to
                           ; get into and can't hurt

   } // end in-line assembly

// now for some C to update the arrow state table

// process the key and update the key state table

switch(raw_key)
```

```
{
case MAKE_UP:      // pressing up
     {
     key_table[INDEX_UP]    = 1;
     } break;

case MAKE_DOWN:  // pressing down
     {
     key_table[INDEX_DOWN]  = 1;
     } break;

case MAKE_RIGHT: // pressing right
     {
     key_table[INDEX_RIGHT] = 1;
     } break;

case MAKE_LEFT:  // pressing left
     {
     key_table[INDEX_LEFT]  = 1;
     } break;

case MAKE_ENTER:     // pressing enter
     {
     key_table[INDEX_ENTER]    = 1;
     } break;

case MAKE_TAB :  // pressing tab
     {
     key_table[INDEX_TAB ]  = 1;
     } break;

case MAKE_SPACE : // pressing space
     {
     key_table[INDEX_SPACE ] = 1;
     } break;

case MAKE_CTRL :  // pressing control
     {
     key_table[INDEX_CTRL ]  = 1;
     } break;

case MAKE_ALT  : // pressing alt
     {
     key_table[INDEX_ALT  ] = 1;
     } break;

case MAKE_ESC  :  // pressing escape
     {
     key_table[INDEX_ESC ]  = 1;
     } break;

case BREAK_UP:      // releasing up
     {
     key_table[INDEX_UP]    = 0;
     } break;
```

continues

Listing 11.16. continued

```
        case BREAK_DOWN:  // releasing down
                {
                key_table[INDEX_DOWN]  = 0;
                } break;

        case BREAK_RIGHT: // releasing right
                {
                key_table[INDEX_RIGHT] = 0;
                } break;

        case BREAK_LEFT:  // releasing left
                {
                key_table[INDEX_LEFT]  = 0;
                } break;

        case BREAK_ENTER:    // releasing enter
                {
                key_table[INDEX_ENTER]  = 0;
                } break;

        case BREAK_TAB :  // releasing tab
                {
                key_table[INDEX_TAB ]  = 0;
                } break;

        case BREAK_SPACE : // releasing space
                {
                key_table[INDEX_SPACE ] = 0;
                } break;

        case BREAK_CTRL :  // releasing control
                {
                key_table[INDEX_CTRL ]  = 0;
                } break;

        case BREAK_ALT  : // releasing alt
                {
                key_table[INDEX_ALT  ] = 0;
                } break;

        case BREAK_ESC  :  // releasing escape
                {
                key_table[INDEX_ESC ]  = 0;
                } break;

        default: break;

        } // end switch

// note how we don't chain interrupts,
// we want total control of the keyboard
// however, if you wanted to chain then you would make a
// call to the old
// keyboard handler right here.
```

```
} // end New_Key_Int

////////////////////////////////////////////////////////////////

void Install_Keyboard(void)
{

Old_Key_Isr = _dos_getvect(KEYBOARD_INT);

_dos_setvect(KEYBOARD_INT, New_Key_Int);

} // end Install_Keyboard

////////////////////////////////////////////////////////////////

void Delete_Keyboard(void)
{

_dos_setvect(KEYBOARD_INT, Old_Key_Isr);

} // end Delete_Keyboard

// M A I N ///////////////////////////////////////////////////////

void main(void)
{
int done=0,      // system exit flag
    index,       // looping variable
    score;       // used to compute score

char string[80];  // used for printing

// SECTION 1 //////////////////////////////////////////////////////

// install the keyboard driver

Install_Keyboard();

// set video mode to 320x200 256 color mode

Set_Video_Mode(VGA256);

// create a double buffer

if (!Create_Double_Buffer(SCREEN_HEIGHT))
   {
   printf("\nNot enough memory to create double buffer.");

   } // end if

// clear the double buffer

Fill_Double_Buffer(0);
```

continues

643

Listing 11.16. continued

```
// SECTION 2 /////////////////////////////////////////////////

// load in the background image into the double buffer

PCX_Init((pcx_picture_ptr)&background_pcx);

PCX_Load("moon.pcx", (pcx_picture_ptr)&background_pcx,1);

// copy the background into the double buffer

_fmemcpy((char far *)double_buffer,
         (char far *)(background_pcx.buffer),
         SCREEN_WIDTH*SCREEN_HEIGHT);

PCX_Delete((pcx_picture_ptr)&background_pcx);

// load in imagery for lunar lander

PCX_Init((pcx_picture_ptr)&imagery_pcx);

PCX_Load("lander.pcx", (pcx_picture_ptr)&imagery_pcx,1);

// initialize player and extract bit maps

sprite_width  = 16;
sprite_height = 16;

Sprite_Init((sprite_ptr)&lander,0,0,0,0,0,0);

for (index=0; index<5; index++)
    PCX_Grab_Bitmap((pcx_picture_ptr)&imagery_pcx,
                    (sprite_ptr)&lander,index,index,0);

// set position of lander

lander.x          = 100;
lander.y          = 10;
lander.curr_frame = 0;
lander.state      = 1;

PCX_Delete((pcx_picture_ptr)&imagery_pcx);

// scan background under lander

Behind_Sprite_DB((sprite_ptr)&lander);


// SECTION 3 /////////////////////////////////////////////////

// main event loop

while(!done)
     {

     // erase the lander
```

```
      Erase_Sprite_DB((sprite_ptr)&lander);

      // transform the lander,
      // notice how we look at the keyboard state table

      // reset current frame of lander and active engines

      lander.curr_frame = 0;
      right_engine = left_engine = down_engine = up_engine = 0;

      // now we will look into the keyboard table
      // to see what keys are being
      // pressed, note that this table is updated
      // not by the main(), but by
      // the keyboard interrupt, this allows us to
      // track multiple keys simulataneously

// SECTION 4 /////////////////////////////////////////////////

      // test if user is exiting

      if (key_table[INDEX_ESC]) done=1;

      // test the motion keys

      if (key_table[INDEX_RIGHT])
         {

         // increase x velocity

         lander_xv+=.1;

         // limit velocity

         if (lander_xv>3)
             lander_xv=3;

         // set engine flag

         right_engine = 1;

         // expend fuel

         fuel-=.5;

         } // end if

      if (key_table[INDEX_LEFT])
         {
         // decrease x velocity

         lander_xv-=.1;

         // limit velocity
```

continues

Listing 11.16. continued

```
            if (lander_xv<-3)
               lander_xv=-3;

            // set engine flag

            left_engine = 1;

            // expend fuel

            fuel-=.5;

            } // end if

        if (key_table[INDEX_UP])
            {
            // decrease y velocity

            lander_yv-=.1;

            // limit velocity

            if (lander_yv<-3)
               lander_yv=-3;

            // set engine flag

            up_engine = 1;

            // expend fuel

            fuel-=.5;

            } // end if

        if (key_table[INDEX_DOWN])
            {
            // increase y velocity

            lander_yv+=.1;

            // limit velocity

            if (lander_yv>4)
               lander_yv=4;

            // set engine flag

            down_engine = 1;

            // expend fuel

            fuel-=.5;

            } // end if
```

```
// SECTION 5 ///////////////////////////////////////////////////

    // based on current velocity, move lander

    lander.x = lander.x + (int)(lander_xv+.5);
    lander.y = lander.y + (int)(lander_yv+.5);

    // check if lander has moved off screen boundary

    // x tests

    if (lander.x > 320-16)
        lander.x = 0;
    else
    if (lander.x < 0)
        lander.x = 320-16;

    // y tests

    if (lander.y > 190-16)
        lander.y = 190-16;
    else
    if (lander.y < 0)
        lander.y = 0;

// SECTION 6 ///////////////////////////////////////////////////

    // apply gravity

    lander_yv+=.05;

    if (lander_yv>3)
       lander_yv=3;

    // expend fuel

    fuel-=.02;

    // draw the lander

    Behind_Sprite_DB((sprite_ptr)&lander);

// SECTION 7 ///////////////////////////////////////////////////

    // based on the engines that are on, draw the lander

    // always draw the standard lander without engines first

    lander.curr_frame = 0;
    Draw_Sprite_DB((sprite_ptr)&lander);

    // draw any engines that are on

    if (right_engine)
       {
```

continues

Listing 11.16. continued

```
            lander.curr_frame = 2;
            Draw_Sprite_DB((sprite_ptr)&lander);
            } // end if

        if (left_engine)
            {
            lander.curr_frame = 3;
            Draw_Sprite_DB((sprite_ptr)&lander);
            } // end if

        if (up_engine)
            {
            lander.curr_frame = 1;
            Draw_Sprite_DB((sprite_ptr)&lander);
            } // end if

        if (down_engine)
            {
            lander.curr_frame = 4;
            Draw_Sprite_DB((sprite_ptr)&lander);
            } // end if

// SECTION 8 ////////////////////////////////////////////////////

        // draw indicators

        if (fuel<0) fuel=0;

        sprintf(string,"Fuel = %.2f   ",fuel);
        Blit_String_DB(10,2,10,string,0);

        sprintf(string,"XV = %.2f   ",lander_xv);
        Blit_String_DB(10,12,10,string,0);

        sprintf(string,"YV = %.2f   ",lander_yv);
        Blit_String_DB(10,22,10,string,0);

        // show the double buffer

        Show_Double_Buffer(double_buffer);

        // wait a while

        Delay(1);

// SECTION 9 ////////////////////////////////////////////////////

        // test if the lander has landed

        if (lander.x >= 245 &&
            lander.x <= (266-16) && lander.y >= (185-16) &&
            lander_yv < 2.0)
            {
            // print banner
```

```
          Blit_String(2,60,15,
                    "T H E  E A G L E  H A S  L A N D E D!",1);

          // compute score based on fuel and velocity

          score = (int)(fuel*10 - lander_yv * 100);

          if (score < 0) score = 0;

          sprintf(string,"Score was %d",score);
          Blit_String(100,110,15,string,1);

          // wait a second

          Delay(100);

          // fade everything

          Fade_Lights();

          // exit system

          done=1;

          } // end if the lander has landed

      } // end while

// SECTION 10 //////////////////////////////////////////////////

// delete the keyboard driver

Delete_Keyboard();

// reset the video mode back to text

Set_Video_Mode(TEXT_MODE);

// free the double buffer

Delete_Double_Buffer();

} // end main
```

Building an Executable: To make an executable of the program in Listing 11.16, you can either type it in or use the source on the companion CD. The name of the source is lunar.c. The precompiled executable is named lunar.exe. As before, use the following compile line for Microsoft C:

```
cl -AM -Zi -c  -Fc -Gs -G2 lunar.c
```

After compiling the program in this manner, you can link it to the standard libraries and to our previously generated game library, gamelib.lib, with a link line such as:

```
link /ST:8192 /CO lunar,,,graphics.lib+gamelib.lib,,
```

This creates a final executable named lunar.exe.

 Analysis

The main point of this discussion is not to belabor the operation of the lunar lander code, but to understand the use of the keyboard ISR. However, we touch upon the main points of the lunar lander code during the analysis.

1. Section 1 is where the PC is placed into mode 13h, the double buffer is created, and the keyboard ISR is installed.

2. Section 2 is where the background lunar surface and the bit maps for the lunar lander are loaded. Also, the sprite objects are generated, and the background under the initial position of the lander is scanned in preparation for entering the main event loop for the first time.

3. Section 3 is where the lander is erased and its engine state reset to reflect that all engines are off.

4. Section 4 is where we want to focus. The keyboard state table key_table[] is accessed in this section to determine what keys are being pressed. If any of the arrow keys are being pressed, the velocity of the lander is increased appropriately (while expending some fuel in the process). Notice that this is a read-only process. The key_table[] is altered by the keyboard ISR, and we need only look at its contents with the proper indices to determine whether the keys in which we're interested are being pressed.

5. Section 5 is where the lander is translated, and boundary checks are done to see whether it has moved off the visible region of the screen.

6. Section 6 is where gravity is applied, which is just a modification of the vertical component of the velocity. Also, fuel is expended here to reflect internal power usage of the lander. Notice that the gravity is not allowed to translate the lander faster than three pixels per frame.

7. Section 7 may seem a little confusing, but really is simple. Instead of drawing the lander with all possible combinations of thrusters (which would take 16 bit maps) I decided to test which thrusters were on and redraw the bit maps with

the thrusters on one on top of the other. Because this ship always looks the same (save for the thrusters being on), this technique works. Basically, we overlay each version of the ship on top of the same area to make it look as though we have 16 different bit maps, when in fact there are only five!

8. Section 8 is the section that draws all the instrumentation displayed, such as those showing the velocity of the ship and the amount of fuel left.

9. Section 9 is the landing test. The lander's position and velocity are used to determine whether it has landed on the landing pad at a reasonably slow descent rate. If so, this descent rate and the amount of fuel left are used to compute an overall score.

    There's something to be learned here about scoring. I decided that having more fuel when the lander was finished landing would be a good thing, but the faster the lander's decent, the worse. Using these two premises, I created a scoring function that gives reasonable results. In general, you should try to make scoring functions that take a couple of aspects of the environment into consideration. This rewards players who go that extra inch.

    Anyway, if the lander has landed successfully, a score is displayed along with a banner. Then the lights fade and the main event loop is terminated.

10. Section 10 is the end of the game: all resources must be released, deleted, or both. Therefore, the old keyboard driver is reinstalled here. The PC is reset to graphics mode and the double buffer deallocated.

That about sums up the keyboard driver. Remember: it's just a starting point. There are many better ways to track the keys. For instance, you could use a look-up table system to get rid of the switch statement in the keyboard ISR, and so forth.

Adding to Our Library

We haven't really created too many new functions in today's discussions. We have a function to reset the internal timer, some functions to create a multitasking environment, and a way of installing a new keyboard ISR. The source and header files for all these functions are called graph11.c and graph11.h, respectively. As a review, let's see what new functions we now have:

☐ Timer functions

```
void Change_Timer(unsigned int new_count);
```

Use this function to change the rate of the internal timer.

☐ Multitasking Functions

```
void Initialize_Kernal(void);
```

Use this function to initialize the multitasking task list.

```
void Start_Kernal(void);
```

Use this function to start the multitasking kernel.

```
void Stop_Kernal(void);
```

Use this function to stop the multitasking kernel and remove the ISR.

```
int Add_Task(void (far *function)());
```

Use this function to add a task to the task list.

```
int Delete_Task(int id);
```

Use this function to delete a task from the task list.

```
void _interrupt far Multi_Kernal(void);
```

This is the multitasking kernel, which is never directly called by the game code. Instead, it's installed by the Start_Kernal() function.

☐ Keyboard Functions

```
void _interrupt _far New_Key_Int()
```

This is the new keyboard ISR that enables us to record multiple and simultaneous key presses.

```
void Install_Keyboard(void)
```

This function installs the new keyboard interrupt ISR function.

```
void Delete_Keyboard(void)
```

This function removes the new keyboard ISR and reinstalls the old one.

Summary

Today we learned about the timing aspects of a PC-based video game. We covered interrupts, the keyboard, and the internal timer. We learned how to write a multitasking operation system, and we also learned some specific programming techniques that enable use to write game-related functions more easily and make them more autonomous.

Finally, we saw yet another small game (the lunar lander game) that reinforced our knowledge of game loops and graphics.

Q&A

Q Is multitasking necessary for a PC game?

A The answer depends on your definition of multitasking, but in general a game is a form of multitasking or real-time program. Each module in the game must be allowed its runtime during each game loop cycle if the transparency, or illusion of simultaneous execution of all events, is to be achieved.

Q What is the difference between a responder function and a self-contained function?

A A responder function can also be a self-contained function. By *self-contained* I mean the function has some local memory that records its state. This allows the main game logic to do less housekeeping for the functions in the game. A responder function can be self-contained, but is used to react to messages or events occurring in the system.

Q Why does the interrupt controller have to be reset by writing a 20h to location 20h?

A If this isn't done, the peripheral interrupt controller (PIC) continues to ignore all interrupts. The CPU goes on about its business and ignores the keyboard, memory refresh, "divide by zero," and thus your computer goes into a comotose state.

Q Why use the timer to cause an interrupt that occurs at some specific rate?

A A PC has no way of doing tight timing because of its architecture. There are so many PCs with so many different processors, we can't draw any conclusions about how fast our programs will run. Therefore, if we have a time-critical event that must be processed at some specific interval, using interrupts and the timer is the best way to do it.

Workshop

The Workshop section presents quiz questions to help you cement your new knowledge and exercises to give you experience using what you've learned. Try to understand the questions and exercises before moving on to the next lesson. The answers are in Appendix B.

Quiz

1. What is a self-contained function?

2. How many internal timers does the PC have?

3. Why is the timer interrupt so important?

4. What keyboard interrupt is used to take control of the keyboard?

5. What is the difference between a scan code and the break code?

6. What I/O ports are used for the internal timer chip?

7. What is the difference between multitasking and multiprocessing?

Exercises

1. Alter the multitasking kernel code so each task has some form of priority.

2. Add to the lunar lander game an alien that comes out from time to time.

3. Write a more-complex keyboard ISR that saves the state of all the 101 keys on the keyboard.

4. Figure out why the motion of the lander isn't "smooth" and fix it.

5. Try writing an ISR that traps a "divide by zero."

Laying Out the Universe

We've been covering a lot of ground in the past week and a half. Now we slow things down for a few days to talk about some less technical, but more creative, topics. There isn't going to be much material in the next few chapters, but what there is must be thought about carefully. We're nearly to the point where there's nothing more to do but start writing games! As of yet, however, there are still a few more topics and concepts to cover. Today we learn about the following:

- ☐ The game universe
- ☐ Cell-based worlds
- ☐ Vector-based worlds
- ☐ Graphical language-based worlds
- ☐ Representing objects
- ☐ Collision detection

The Game Universe

A video game is basically a color image generated on the video screen. This video image is a representation of a virtual world that is either a subset of reality, an exaggeration of reality, or a synthesis of reality (for example, flight simulators). We're interested in creating games that are 2-D for the most part and are a subset of reality—in other words, surrealistic. The physics in our games don't have to be true, the objects don't have to be real, and the game itself doesn't have to make sense. As long as the game is fun and people like to play it, that's all we're concerned with.

As you've seen in many of the demo programs and examples thus far in the book, the objects in our games can be constructed of lines and polygons or be of the bit-map type. The same goes for the environment. For example, we saw in the demo game Robopunk that the side-scrolling universe was constructed of cells that represented bit maps. This is one way of creating backgrounds. We've also seen that backgrounds can be large bit maps or whole screens. The game Mech War used a PCX file I drew to represent the background of space. Finally, we could generate a universe with a list of polygons that represented the rooms, objects, and other visualizations in the environment.

What we want to do today is take a look at the main methods of representing game universes, and some of the pros and cons of each. Keep in mind that you may do things any way you wish. For example, you may find that mixing methods works best for you. Therefore, keep an open and creative mind. It's time for you to start taking the reins; I'm just going to be your guide from now on.

Cell-Based Worlds

The first kind of world representation to discuss is a classic method of representing 2-D bit-mapped environments. The basic technique is to break the screen area down into a set of rectangles, or *cells*, as shown in Figure 12.1.

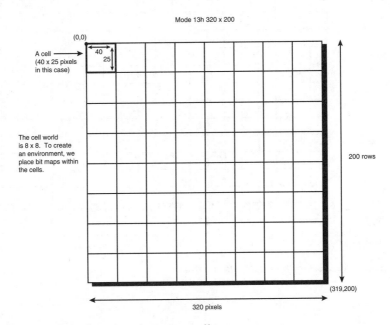

Figure 12.1. *Breaking the screen down into cells.*

The size of each rectangle is up to you; however, the common sizes are 8×8 and 16×16 pixels.

Once you've broken the screen area down into a set of cells, you can paste a collection of bit maps into these cells using some kind of 2-D matrix to represent the bit map that should be placed in each cell. For example, if we use the standard mode 13h resolution of 320×200 pixels and break the screen into 16×16 cells, we'd have a cell-based screen that was 20×12. This would, however, leave eight unused lines of resolution at the bottom of the screen. These lines are shown in Figure 12.2.

These unused lines of resolution could be employed for controls, text, or whatever. Furthermore, there's no reason why the entire screen must be used up by the cell matrix. You may decide to only have 16×10 cells, each being 16×16 pixels. This would take up

256×160 pixels of the entire screen and leave a lot of area for special displays and so forth, as shown in Figure 12.3.

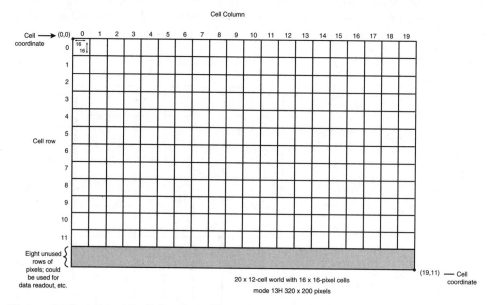

Figure 12.2. *A 20×12 cell-based world.*

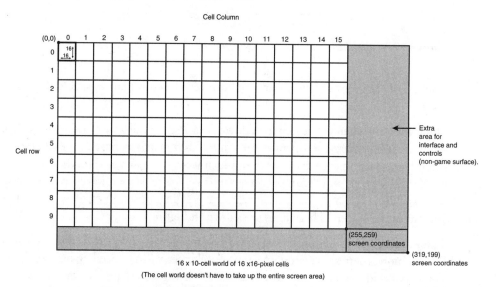

Figure 12.3. *A 16×10 cell-based world.*

As far as the representation of the cells in the cell-based world, a standard 2-D array of integers or an array of strings is usually the best choice. The data structure is referenced not only to draw the actual screen, but also for collision detection. Figure 12.4 shows a cell-based world accessed for collision detection.

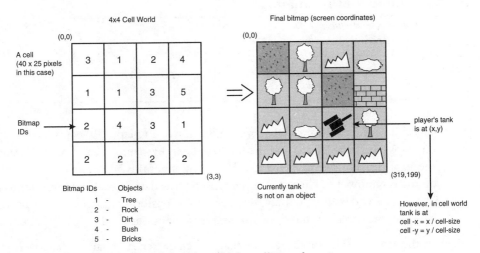

Figure 12.4. *Accessing the cell-based world for collision detection.*

For instance, if you look at the way each screen is represented in Robopunk, you see something like this:

```
char *screen_1[CELL_ROWS] = {"          ",
                             "##*###*####",
                             "##########",
                             "<=========",
                             "######:####",
                             "####<=;=>##"};
```

It probably looks a little messy as printed; however, we can see that screen_1 is a collection of strings, each being 10 characters long. Each character in the string represents a bit map, and there are six rows of these bit maps. The bit maps in this case are all 32×32. Therefore, the entire screen area used up was 320×192 pixels, which is almost the entire screen except for the last eight lines.

Accessing the data structure is easy. You can use the syntax of screen_1[y][x], or you can alias a string pointer to the current row of interest. The important thing is that we now have a compact way of representing a screen in our game.

The next question is: how do we draw the screen using the data structure? Well, we use two for loops that iterate through the data structure, position the proper bit map

12

represented by each of the elements in the matrix (based on the size of each cell), and draw them on the screen. Algorithm 12.1 contains a rough algorithm to do this.

Algorithm 12.1. Drawing a screen represented by a 2-D matrix of bit map IDs.

```
for (y=0; y<NUM_ROWS; y++)
    for (x=0; x<NUM_COLUMNS; x++)
        {
        bitmap_id = world[y][x];
        Draw_Bitmap(bitmap_id,x*CELL_WIDTH,y*CELL_HEIGHT);
        } // end for x
```

Algorithm 12.1 draws a screen out of a collection of bit maps. (Of course, we assume the bit maps have been loaded and the function `Draw_Bitmap()` exists, but the operation of the algorithm is easy enough to see.) Each element of the 2-D matrix is accessed. Based on the ID number or character in the location, the data is used as an index into a table of bit maps with which to draw the screen. (The position of each bit map is computed based on the size of each cell's width and height and the final x,y cell position.)

In the case of Robopunk, you see that the characters *, #, and others were used to represent bit maps. This is totally arbitrary. If you wish, you can use a 2-D array of integers. However, I've found that using ASCII characters is a little easier because there always seems to be a character that looks similar to what the bit map is, or there's some other connection. (For example, if we wrote a game that had ladders in it we might decide to use the letter H for a bit map that was a ladder, and maybe the letter E for the bit map that was a picture of an exit door.) How you decide to do it is up to you; however, I suggest using a character-based world that represents the bit maps that are supposed to be drawn on the screen.

As a simple example to see how this all works, I've provided a program that draws a desert scene on the screen using an array of integers to represent the terrain. In this case the world is 20×12 and each cell is 16×16 pixels. There are four bit maps with the ID numbers shown in Table 12.1.

Table 12.1. Bit map IDs for a cell-based world.

Background Dirt	= 0
Tree	= 1
Rock	= 2
Bush	= 3

There's one detail that we must also take into consideration when using a cell-based world: each cell can have only a single bit map in it. This means if you want to be able to have a rock and tree at the same location, you must do one of the following:

☐ Layer the data structures and draw the screen twice, the first time with the foreground and the second with the background.

☐ Make multiple versions of the bit maps. For example, if you wanted a rock, a tree, and a rock with a tree, you might have a set of bit maps like those shown in Figure 12.5.

Figure 12.5. *Bit maps for a cell-based world.*

Anyway, here is the program. It's called cellw.exe, and the source is shown in Listing 12.1.

Listing 12.1. A demo of drawing a universe with cells (cellw.exe).

```
// I N C L U D E S //////////////////////////////////////////////

#include <io.h>
#include <conio.h>
#include <stdio.h>
#include <stdlib.h>
#include <dos.h>
#include <bios.h>
#include <fcntl.h>
#include <memory.h>
#include <malloc.h>
#include <math.h>
#include <string.h>
```

continues

Listing 12.1. continued

```c
#include "graph3.h"  // include our graphics stuff
#include "graph4.h"
#include "graph6.h"

// D E F I N E S ///////////////////////////////////////////////

#define CELL_WIDTH      16   // size of bit maps in world
#define CELL_HEIGHT     16

#define NUM_ROWS        12   // number of rows and columns
#define NUM_COLUMNS     20   // in terrain

// G L O B A L S ///////////////////////////////////////////////

pcx_picture imagery_pcx;       // the background bit maps

// the sprites used in the demo

sprite objects;

int terrain[NUM_ROWS][NUM_COLUMNS] = {0,0,0,0,0,0,0,0,0,0,0,0,0,1,1,1,3,3,3,3,0,
0,0,0,0,2,0,0,0,0,3,0,0,0,0,0,0,3,0,0,3,0,
0,0,0,0,0,0,0,2,0,0,0,0,0,0,0,3,0,0,3,0,
0,0,0,0,0,0,0,0,0,0,0,0,0,0,0,3,0,0,3,0,
0,0,0,1,0,0,0,0,0,0,0,0,1,0,0,3,3,3,3,0,
0,0,0,0,0,0,0,0,0,0,0,0,0,0,0,0,0,0,0,0,
0,0,0,0,1,0,0,0,1,0,0,0,0,0,0,1,0,0,0,
0,0,0,0,0,0,0,0,0,0,2,0,0,2,0,0,0,0,0,0,
0,0,0,2,2,0,0,0,0,0,0,0,0,2,0,0,0,0,0,0,
0,0,2,2,0,0,0,0,0,0,0,0,0,2,0,0,0,0,0,3,
0,0,2,2,0,0,0,0,0,1,0,0,0,0,0,0,1,0,0,0,
0,0,0,0,0,0,0,0,0,0,0,0,0,0,0,0,0,0,0,0};


// M A I N ///////////////////////////////////////////////////

void main(void)
{
// this is the main function

int x,y;


// SECTION 1 ///////////////////////////////////////////////

// set video mode to 320x200 256 color mode

Set_Video_Mode(VGA256);

// create a double buffer

if (!Create_Double_Buffer(SCREEN_HEIGHT))
   {
   printf("\nNot enough memory to create double buffer.");
```

```
      } // end if

// clear the double buffer

Fill_Double_Buffer(0);

// SECTION 2 //////////////////////////////////////////////////

// load in imagery for the background objects

PCX_Init((pcx_picture_ptr)&imagery_pcx);

PCX_Load("terrain.pcx", (pcx_picture_ptr)&imagery_pcx,1);

// initialize player and extract bit maps

sprite_width  = 16;
sprite_height = 16;

// initialize the object sprite

Sprite_Init((sprite_ptr)&objects,0,0,0,0,0,0);

// load the bit maps

PCX_Grab_Bitmap((pcx_picture_ptr)&imagery_pcx,
                (sprite_ptr)&objects,0,0,0);

PCX_Grab_Bitmap((pcx_picture_ptr)&imagery_pcx,
                (sprite_ptr)&objects,1,1,0);

PCX_Grab_Bitmap((pcx_picture_ptr)&imagery_pcx,
                (sprite_ptr)&objects,2,2,0);

PCX_Grab_Bitmap((pcx_picture_ptr)&imagery_pcx,
                (sprite_ptr)&objects,3,3,0);


objects.curr_frame = 0;
objects.state      = 1;

// SECTION 3 //////////////////////////////////////////////////

// based on terrain array draw world

// loop through data array

for (y=0; y<NUM_ROWS; y++)
    {

    for (x=0; x<NUM_COLUMNS; x++)
        {

        // draw the proper bit map at the proper position
```

12

continues

Listing 12.1. continued

```c
        objects.x = x*CELL_WIDTH;
        objects.y = y*CELL_HEIGHT;

        // extract the cell element

        objects.curr_frame  = terrain[y][x];

        Draw_Sprite_DB((sprite_ptr)&objects);

        } // end for x

   } // end for y


// SECTION 4 //////////////////////////////////////////////////

Blit_String_DB(2,2,10,"Press any key to exit.",1);

// let's see what we drew

Show_Double_Buffer(double_buffer);

// main event loop

while(!kbhit())
    {

    } // end while

// reset the video mode back to text

Set_Video_Mode(TEXT_MODE);

// free the double buffer

Delete_Double_Buffer();

} // end main
```

Building an Executable: To make an executable of the program in Listing 12.1, you can either type it in or use the source on the companion CD. The name of the source is cellw.c. The precompiled executable is named cellw.exe. As before, use the following compile line for Microsoft C:

```
cl -AM -Zi -c  -Fc -Gs -G2 cellw.c
```

After compiling the program in this manner you can link it to the standard libraries and to our previously generated game library, gamelib.lib, with a link line such as:

```
link /ST:8192 /CO cellw,,,graphics.lib+gamelib.lib,,
```

This creates a final executable named cellw.exe.

Analysis The only interesting thing in the whole program is the drawing of the screen, which is done in the `main()` function. The screen drawing is done almost exactly as we saw in Algorithm 12.1: each cell in the 2-D data matrix is accessed, and the data is used as a bit-map ID to index into a sprite structure that had been previously loaded with the bit maps for the screen.

Using a sprite might not be the most efficient way of doing this. However, it's not worth creating an entirely new set of functions and data structures with different names to do what can already be done with the sprite engine. Anyway, let's cover each section of the program:

1. In Section 1, as usual, we set up the graphics mode and allocate the double buffer.

2. Section 2 is where we load in the PCX file containing the images for the four background bit maps that make up the game world. Also, the sprite object is initialized and the bit maps are loaded into the sprite.

3. Section 3 is where the actual terrain is drawn based on the cell definition in the `terrain[][]` array. Each element is accessed and used as an index into the sprite bit map's array to render the screen.

4. In Section 4 we wait for the player to hit a key, and then place the PC back into text mode and exit.

Vector-Based Worlds

The next method of representing worlds is a little older and has its roots in old adventure and action games where there isn't a lot of background imagery. In *vector-based worlds*, the background environment is drawn with polygons or lines. For example, you could have a giant list of polygon vertices and then use these to build polygons to draw to the screen. This kind of representation is shown in Figure 12.6.

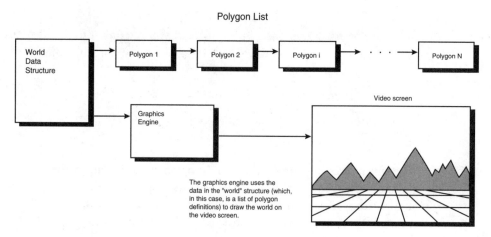

Figure 12.6. *Using a list of polygons to generate a world.*

Later in the book we make an adventure game that has rooms the player's character can walk through. We may decide to draw these rooms with lines instead of bit maps, as doing so might be easier.

The downside to using lines or polygons to draw the universe is that it takes a lot of them to draw anything that looks reasonable. For instance, to fill a 320×200 screen with any background based on bit maps takes, on average, a couple of hundred bytes of storage to hold the 2-D matrix of integers or strings. In the case of using lines or polygons, there could be hundreds of lines or polygons needed to make a scene look realistic.

However, we do gain something by using lines or polygons: the ability to place objects anywhere we wish. In the case of a cell-based, bit-mapped world, we could only place bit maps at cell locations, not at arbitrary locations. When using line- or polygon-based universes, we can place anything anywhere—and that is a real plus.

The other factor we must consider when using line- or polygon-based worlds is that collision detection becomes much more difficult if the objects collide with the background. We must test the game objects to see whether they have any and all of the vectors in the polygon world, which is time-consuming. Although it's possible to forget about the polygons and use the screen bit map, collision detection is still a problem. We talk more about this when we cover collision later today.

As an example of drawing a world with lines, imagine we have a file that contains endpoints. The first element in the file is the number of lines for the screen, and then we have the lines themselves. Each line could have the following format:

```
color,x1,y1,x2,y2
```

The file could be read and the screen rendered by connecting all the lines using the proper color. This is just one way of doing it. Another method could be to load the file into an array first and then process it. The method is up to you as long as it does the job of loading the data. As an example algorithm, imagine that we have a file containing this data format, and we want to process the file for a screen of data. Algorithm 12.2 would do the job.

Algorithm 12.2. Drawing a screen based on lines.

```
// open the file

file = fopen("screen.dat","r");

// read the number of lines in file

fscanf(file,"%d",&number_of_lines);

// read each line from file and draw them

for (lines=0; lines<number_of_lines; lines++)
    {
    // read the strucuture - color,x1,y1,x2,y2
    fscanf(file,"%d %d %d %d %d",color,x1,y1,x2,y2);

    // draw the line
    Bline(x1,y1,x2,y2,color);

    } // end for lines
```

Algorithm 12.2 has a few details missing (but who's counting details?!). The main idea of the algorithm is that a data source (an ASCII file) is read and used to generate the screen. Of course, once the screen is drawn there's no data structure that can be referenced to see the geometry of the screen. To remedy this, we could save each line into a list or an array data structure as the line is drawn. Each element of the data structure would be a line itself. This data structure could then be used for calculations and collision detection.

As an example of this whole process, I've created a program called linew.exe, which uses a file called linew.dat to generate a universe consisting of a set of rooms. This could be used for an adventure game, for example. The program also saves each line as an array element so the lines can be processed later in the program, or the screen could be redrawn, if need be, without reloading the ASCII file. Listing 12.2 contains the source.

12

Laying Out the Universe

Listing 12.2. Drawing a screen with lines (linew.c).

```c
// I N C L U D E S //////////////////////////////////////////////

#include <io.h>
#include <conio.h>
#include <stdio.h>
#include <stdlib.h>
#include <dos.h>
#include <bios.h>
#include <fcntl.h>
#include <memory.h>
#include <malloc.h>
#include <math.h>
#include <string.h>

#include "graph3.h"  // include our graphics stuff
#include "graph4.h"
#include "graph5.h"  // need polygon stuff
#include "graph6.h"

// D E F I N E S //////////////////////////////////////////////

#define MAX_LINES 128

// S T R U C T U R E S //////////////////////////////////////////////

typedef struct line_typ
        {

        int color;      // color of the line
        int x1;         // first endpoint of the line
        int y1;
        int x2;         // second endpoint of the line
        int y2;

        } line, *line_ptr;

// G L O B A L S //////////////////////////////////////////////

// the data structure that holds all the lines

line line_data[MAX_LINES];

// M A I N //////////////////////////////////////////////

void main(void)
{

FILE *fp;

int color,x1,y1,x2,y2,num_lines,lines;  // working variables

// this is the main function
```

668

```
// SECTION 1 ///////////////////////////////////////////////////

// set video mode to 320x200 256 color mode

Set_Video_Mode(VGA256);

// SECTION 2 ///////////////////////////////////////////////////

// open the data file

fp = fopen("linew.dat","r");

// extract number of lines

fscanf(fp,"%d",&num_lines);

// load each line and draw

for (lines=0; lines<num_lines;lines++)
    {
    // load a line structure

    fscanf(fp,"%d %d %d %d %d",&color,&x1,&y1,&x2,&y2);

    // save line in data structure

    line_data[lines].color = color;
    line_data[lines].x1    = x1;
    line_data[lines].y1    = y1;
    line_data[lines].x2    = x2;
    line_data[lines].y2    = y2;

    // render the line

    Bline(x1,y1,x2,y2,color);

    } // end for lines

// SECTION 3 ///////////////////////////////////////////////////

Blit_String(2,2,10,"Press any key to exit.",1);

// main event loop

while(!kbhit())
    {
    // do nothing !
    } // end while

// reset the video mode back to text

Set_Video_Mode(TEXT_MODE);

} // end main
```

 Building an Executable: To make an executable of the program in Listing 12.2, you can either type it in or use the source on the companion CD. The name of the source is linew.c. The precompiled executable is named linew.exe. As before, use the following compile line for Microsoft C:

```
cl -AM -Zi -c -Fc -Gs -G2 linew.c
```

After compiling the program in this manner you can link it to the standard libraries and to our previously generated game library, gamelib.lib, with a link line such as:

```
link /ST:8192 /CO linew,,,graphics.lib+gamelib.lib,,
```

This creates a final executable named linew.exe.

 This program is so simple you're probably getting bored—but better bored than confused. Let's see what each section does, shall we?

1. Section 1 is where the system is put into mode 13h, but notice that a double buffer isn't allocated. This is because the polygon engine doesn't use a double buffer as of yet. It writes directly to screen RAM.

2. Section 2 is the main part of the program. First, the data file linew.dat is opened. Within the file is the line structures that must be processed.

   If you recall, each line consists of a color and the two endpoints, for a total of five elements. The lines are loaded in one by one and saved in a global array called line_data[].

   After each line is loaded and saved, it's drawn.

3. In Section 3 the screen has been rendered and we're waiting for the player to press a key to exit the program. When this occurs the PC is placed back into text mode.

The program in Listing 12.2 doesn't do much other than open the data file, load the lines one by one and draw them. The only improvement we could make on the program or technique is to use higher-level primitives—and that's the next topic of discussion.

Graphical Language-Based Worlds

Each of the techniques already discussed—bit maps, lines, and polygons—has its strengths and weaknesses when it comes to representing worlds:

- ☐ Using bit maps is good for creating a full screen of background with little data storage. Collision detection is easier with cell-based worlds because it's easy to compute the player's cell location and use it to determine, for example, whether there's an obstacle in the cell. The main downfall of using bit-mapped, cell-based worlds is that they have a finite resolution based on the cell size.

- ☐ Polygons and lines are good for creating highly arbitrary worlds, but you need lots of memory to store the database and collision detection becomes quite difficult.

A hybrid of all these techniques is to use a language of primitives, a *graphics language* (GL), that allows a file of commands to be read. This file is a description of the universe and allows for bit maps, polygons, lines, pixels, circles, fills, and so forth. The file is read and the commands are parsed and interpreted.

This file might look something like this:

```
load background stars.pcx
line 12,33,45,34,12
fill 12,67,23,56,123
bitmap imagery.pcx 3,4,120,90
...
```

Using a GL is a high-level way of drawing screens and backgrounds for games. Personally, I admit I've never done it; I like to stick to vector or cell-based worlds. However, it's an intriguing possibility. The only problem with it is that, again, collision detection and access to the data structure would be a nightmare. This isn't a problem on a Silicon Graphics supercomputer, but on the PC we must be a bit more careful.

If you just want a compact way of drawing neat backgrounds quickly, a graphics-language method might be the choice for you. However, if you want to be able to perform a lot of collision detection and your game needs access to the environment, I suggest using cell-based worlds.

Representing Objects

We've been concentrating on the representation of the environment of the game, but what about the objects in the game themselves? Well, the objects (as we've learned) are

going to be sprites most of the time, with the following structure. (This is the same structure you saw in Listing 4.1 on Day 4.)

```
typedef struct sprite_typ
        {
        int x,y;            // Position of sprite
        int x_old,y_old;    // Old position of sprite
        int width,height;   // Dimensions of sprite,
                            //    in pixels
        int anim_clock;     // The animation clock
        int anim_speed;     // The animation speed
        int motion_speed;   // The motion speed
        int motion_clock;   // The motion clock

// An array of pointers to the images
        char far *frames[MAX_SPRITE_FRAMES];
// The current frame being displayed
        int curr_frame;
// The total number of frames
        int num_frames;
// The state of the sprite: alive, dead...
        int state;
// What's under the sprite
        char far *background;
// An auxiliary pointer to more, data if needed
        void far *extra_data;
        } sprite, *sprite_ptr;
```

The sprite structure suffices for most needs; however, you may decide to use something else completely. For example, in the case of using polygons to represent objects in an Asteroids- or Battlezone-type game, you'd have to create a similar structure to hold all the relevant fields to control the game object, which could be a creature, player, or whatever.

The only thing you need worry about when designing a structure is that it contains all the fields you need, such as:

- [ ] Position

- [ ] Color

- [ ] Velocity

- [ ] Auxiliary variables

You don't want any of that information floating around globally (unless you need it to). Each game object should be a self-contained entity that can be completely defined by its own structure. In other words, if you have access to the fields of the structure, you can tell everything about the object and need not reference anything else in the game.

Remember, we must process each game element as quickly as possible so we can get through the game cycle fast. This may mean that we store a few pieces of information to help save time. In general, it's better to eat up more memory than time in real-time applications such as video games.

Collision Detection

The last topic we talk about today is collision detection in cell-based and vector-based worlds. I warn you that collision detection is a kind of voodoo: in many cases game programmers use tricks instead of standard textbook methods. This is because time is of essence—and as long as some way works, who cares if it's the "correct" way?!

Collision Detection in a Cell-Based World

The first kind of collision detection we cover is that done in a cell-based world. Take a look at Figure 12.7; it represents a 16×12 cell-based world where each bit map is 16×16 pixels.

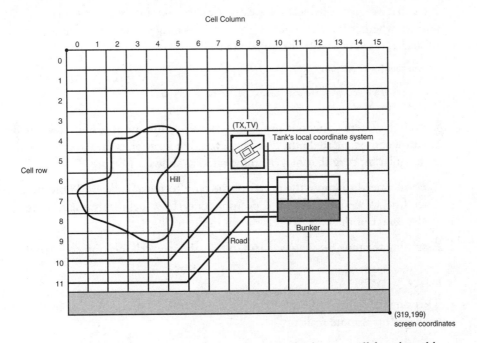

Figure 12.7. *Computing the collision of an object overlaid into a cell-based world.*

We see there's a tank in the world, but the question is: has it hit a wall or other obstacle? This can be resolved easily by using the following technique.

We already know where the tank is in screen coordinates—call it (tx,ty). We know the size of each screen cell, which is 16x16. Finally, we know that some sort of 2-D data matrix represents the screen itself. Assuming that the data matrix is a 2-D array of integers called screen[][], and that it's filled with integers representing the bit maps, we have no problem testing for collision. Here's all we do:

1. Compute what cell the tank is in.

2. Test whether there's an obstacle there by indexing into the screen[][] array.

   We compute a cell location by dividing the tank's screen position by the cell size, as follows:

   ```
   cell_x = tx/16;
   cell_y = ty/16;
   ```

   Note that we divided by 16 in both cases because this is the size, in pixels, of each cell in both the horizontal and vertical axis.

Now that we have a cell location, we can use it to index into the screen[][] data structure and see whether there's something there. Assuming all elements that are non-zero are obstacles, we could write the following code:

```
if (screen[cell_y][cell_x])
   {
   // the tank bumped into something, so back it up
   } // end if
```

Easy, huh? There's only one problem with this technique as it stands. We're using the position of the tank to do the test. However, that position is the upper left corner of the rectangular bit map that makes up the tank, as shown in Figure 12.8.

We really need to know the center of the tank to make collisions a bit more realistic. Therefore, we would bias the tank position (tx,ty) by values that translate the test position to the center of the tank. This is shown in Figure 12.9.

Assuming the tank bit map was 16×16 also, the new cell location code would then be:

```
cell_x = (tx+8)/16;
cell_y = (ty+8)/16;
```

This centers collision detection at the center of the tank instead of in the upper-left corner. This is more realistic.

Tank bit map

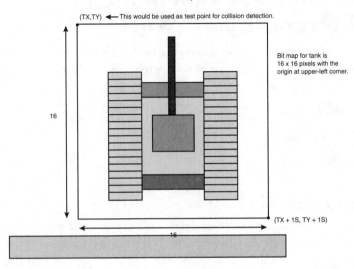

Figure 12.8. *The local coordinate system of a bit map.*

Tank bit map (16 x 16 pixels)

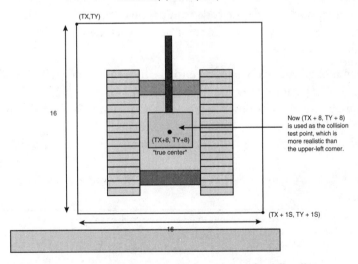

Figure 12.9. *Using the center of a bit map as the test point for cell collision.*

Collision Detection in a Line- or Polygon-Based World

The next kind of collision detection we talk about is used when the environment is based on lines or polygons. There are two ways to test for collision when the universe is based on lines or polygons:

☐ Image space

☐ Object space

Let's talk about each.

Image Space

Image-space algorithms in general deal with the final, bit-mapped image on the screen: the raster image itself. Because the screen is just an array of bytes at some location, we can always look into it for a particular pixel value and use that to determine whether a collision has occurred. For example, the barriers used in Mech War to separate the player's ship from the mechs employed an image-space algorithm for detecting collision with missiles. I drew the barriers using a unique set of color values. Then, when the missile was in motion, I made the code scan the pixel under the missile with the `Get_Pixel()` function and test whether the color of the pixel was that of the barrier. If so, I knew a collision had occurred.

Even though you're not supposed to see the source code for Mech War until the end of the book, I want to show you now the section that does this kind of collision detection. Don't worry if some of the function calls aren't familiar; the only thing that's important here is that you see how the screen pixels themselves are being tested for a certain color, which is the barrier color. Listing 12.3 contains the relevant code.

Listing 12.3. An excerpt from Mech War showing image-space collision.

```
// test for barrier collisions by scanning the pixels
// in the near vicinity
// of the torpedo

        for (pixel_y=miss_y; pixel_y<miss_y+8; pixel_y++)
            {

            pixel=Get_Pixel_DB(miss_x, pixel_y);

            if (pixel>=BARRIER_START_COLOR &&
                pixel<=BARRIER_END_COLOR)
```

```
    {
    // kill missile

    missiles[index].state = MISS_DEAD;

    // start explosion

    Start_Explosion(miss_x, pixel_y,1);

    // smash barrier a bit

    for (index2=0; index2<25; index2++)
        {

        Plot_Pixel_Fast_DB(miss_x-4+rand()%8,
                           pixel_y-4+rand()%8, 0);

        } // end for

    break;

    } // end if barrier hit

} // end for pixel_y
```

I've put the most important lines in the fragment in bold. These lines read the pixel and do the test.

12

Object Space

Image-space collision detection works fine, but has its limitations. For one thing, it severely limits the number of colors that can be used freely, because they may be interpreted as something else (like a mine!). Object-space collision detection is more like the "right" way to detect collisions. Unfortunately, it's also the slower way.

Object-space collision detection uses the actual line segments or polygons that make up the universe as the geometry to be tested for collision with game objects. This means that if there are 1,000 lines on the screen that make up the environment, there are 1,000 tests done. It's true that many of the tests are trivial, because much of the environment can be trivially rejected. However, a test is a test—and if there are 20 game objects running around, there will be 20,000 tests per game cycle...ouch!

The tests done are the typical line-intersection tests we learned to do on Day 5. However, we can do fewer tests if some of the environment is background only. Therefore, we might have two databases:

☐ The first database could hold all the lines that make up the background that is static and doesn't interact with the game in any but a visual way.

☐ The second (smaller) database could hold the lines that must be used for collision detection.

The collision-detection function would therefore have to access only one of the databases, and the number of tests could be greatly reduced.

Summary

Today we learned about some of the more prevalent methods of representing the game universe. We learned about cell-based and vector-based worlds, along with some of the reasoning behind using them. We also took a look at a couple of programs that demonstrated both methods in use. Finally, we learned how to test for collisions in these worlds, because checking whether something has been blown up is one the main ideas in a game!

Q&A

Q Why are world representations important?

A World representations are important because all our game logic and algorithms operate within the virtual environment, whatever it may be. The more efficiently we can access the representation and process it to generate cool screens, the better.

Q What's the difference between using strings or integers to represent cell-based worlds?

A The main difference is that using strings is a little easier for human beings to comprehend, but this only matters if screens are drawn by hand, cell by cell. When screens are generated with some kind of tool, the representation is irrelevant because the human eye never has to see it.

The advantage of using integers is that there's one less translation that must be done, because ASCII characters first must be converted into integers and then into final indices into the array of bit maps.

Q Is there any reason to create cell-based worlds that use 8×8-pixel or 16×16-pixel cells?

A Well, the smaller the cell, the better the resolution of collision and the more detailed a screen can be. However, the larger the cells, the fewer that must be drawn per screen, and therefore the faster the drawing of each screen. For example, if the screen is full of 8×8 cells, there are 40×25 cells—or 1,000 bit maps—that must be blasted to the screen!

Q What if I want to have 20 or so cell-based screens. Should I keep them on disk?

A No, definitely not. You'll need access to all of them during the course of the game in real time for collision detection and so forth. If you're crunched for space, though, at least try to keep as many in memory as possible and then thrash them out to disk when needed.

Workshop

The Workshop section presents quiz questions to help you cement your new knowledge and exercises to give you experience using what you've learned. Try to understand the questions and exercises before moving on to the next lesson. The answers are in Appendix B.

Quiz

1. What's the difference between image space and object space?

2. What is a cell-based world?

3. If a cell-based world is 10×10 and each cell is 16×16, how much memory does it take to represent a screen?

4. Why are vector-based worlds poor for collision detection?

5. Why is the center of a sprite better for collision detection than its upper-left corner?

Exercises

1. Add some more bit maps to the cell-based demo.

2. Add a little man who can walk around in the cell-based demo and bump into rocks.

3. Make little balls bounce around the vector-based demo, bouncing off the blue walls only.

4. On your PC, calculate how much time it takes to draw a cell-based world that is 20×12 using cells that are 16×16 pixels.

5. *Extra Credit:* Try to write a simple graphics language and parser that allows scenes to be drawn based on a description file.

13

The Physics of Games

We're almost to the two-week mark! We've covered a tremendous amount of ground and talked about almost every facet of video-game design that *can* be talked about. For a change of pace, today we talk a little about the physical modeling of different kinds of systems. We've been learning a great deal about I/O, graphics, sounds, AI, and so on, but we need to learn about friction, acceleration, momentum, and other physical quantities and manifestations if we're going to create games that have any kind of realistic action in them. Here's what we see today:

- ☐ Why we need physics in games
- ☐ Velocity, acceleration, and momentum
- ☐ Elastic collisions
- ☐ Modeling gravity
- ☐ Modeling friction
- ☐ Computing trajectories
- ☐ Particle-system explosions

Why Do We Need Physics in Games?

A video game is a simulation, or exaggeration, of reality (in at least some sense of the word). In some cases, a video game makes no sense at all and the laws of physics are meaningless. On the other hand, sometimes the laws of physics are extremely important, such as in a car-racing game where the cars must slide around the track properly. Whatever the situation, we must learn about the basic methods upon which the real universe operates so we can use these methods—or twists on them—to control some of the motion and (virtual) physical traits of the objects in our games.

The universe can be modeled using only a few simple equations, and the rest can be derived from there. For example, one of the most famous physical equations is Newton's force law, shown in Formula 13.1:

Formula 13.1. *Newton's force equation.*

$$F = MA$$

This equation states that the force an object can exert, or the force being exerted on an object, is equal to the mass of the object times the acceleration of the object. Using this equation and a few more simple equations (and a bit of calculus), just about everything in the universe can be explained—as long as the objects aren't too big or too small.

We all know that Newtonian physics is only an approximation of the real universe. The fact is, there are more subtle forces in play: quantum mechanics, space distortion, the strong and weak forces, and so forth. However, Newtonian physics works just fine as long as we can live with errors in the zillionth decimal place, which I think will suffice as most of the math we do is in integers, anyway!

We want to learn how to apply simple physical models to our game objects. These models help us move game objects more realistically, make them collide more reasonably, and in general give us a starting point from which to work so we don't end up re-deriving all the hard work done by physics researchers over the past couple of millennia.

Now, all this doesn't mean that we have to use real physics models to manipulate our game objects. It just means that we should try to find parallels in the real world to help us write the motion-control logic for the objects.

For example, we've all seen an object drop from a given height. If you drop a tank and an apple from the same height, they seem to drop at the same rate. The fact of the matter is, they don't! It's just that the mass of each object relative to the Earth is so small that the force exerted on each object is probably slightly different at only the 20th or 30th decimal place. However, in a video game we may want to exaggerate this and make the tank drop much faster than the apple. We could do this by knowing the basic model of gravity and then making the tank's gravitational constant much higher than that of the apple.

As another example, say you have two objects in a game and you want them to collide and bounce off each other. If you're a physics major, you should know that you set this up as follows:

1. Resolve the momentum of each object into its 2- or 3-D components.

2. Take the direction vectors of each object.

3. Resolve the proper direction and final momentum of each object after the collisions.

However, if you're *not* a physics major you just want to bump each object off the other in a reasonable-looking manner! The key behind making games is to make it look "good." The word "good" doesn't mean correct or proper; if it *looks good*, that's all that matters.

13

What we do in the following pages is look at some physical formulas and see how they relate to making things happen in games. When we get to more complex subjects, such as elastic collisions, we approximate the reality of the situation to a generalization that looks and words reasonably well. All we want to get out of today is a general idea of how to move things around, and to know where to look if we want more details about the laws of motion.

Velocity, Acceleration, and Momentum

Velocity, acceleration, and momentum are common physical quantities with which you should be familiar because you deal with them every day. You may not be able to recite their textbook definitions, but you have an innate understanding of them by virtue of everyday experience.

Velocity

Velocity is probably familiar to everyone. It means *the rate of change of distance per unit time*. For example, when you're driving your car you might drive 85 miles per hour (a common freeway speed for California). This is measure of velocity. It means that in one hour you'll travel 85 miles. We've already seen velocity in the games and demos presented so far in this book. When we use some constant or variable to translate an object, we do it again with every game cycle. In essence, we move an object a certain number of pixels per second, which translates to velocity. The velocity can be measured in pixels per second, if you like.

Take a look at the following code:

```
player_x=player_x + x_velocity;
player_y=player_y + y_velocity;
```

We see that the position of the player (actually, an object representing the player) is at (player_x, player_y), and that the object's velocity is x_velocity in the x-axis and y_velocity in the y-axis. This means that with every game cycle the object representing the player moves x_velocity pixels in the x-axis and y_velocity pixels in the y-axis, as shown in Figure 13.1.

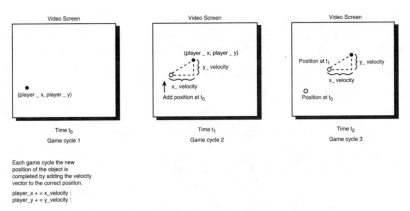

Each game cycle the new
position of the object is
completed by adding the velocity
vector to the correct position.

player_x + = x_velocity :
player_y + = y_velocity :

Figure 13.1. *Moving an object with constant velocity.*

There's an interesting point to make here: we see that velocity can be a 2-D entity, as it is in this case. The player's character has both an x and y velocity. In a 3-D game, objects might have 3-D velocities.

The key to understanding multidimensional quantities that operate in multiple planes at once is to just take one at a time. Don't try to comprehend them all at once. As an example of velocity, I've created a simple program that queries you for the x and y components of the velocity for an object. The program then moves the object at that velocity. The name of the program, shown in Listing 13.1, is velocity.c.

Listing 13.1. Moving an object with constant velocity (velocity.c).

```
// I N C L U D E S ////////////////////////////////////////////

#include <io.h>
#include <conio.h>
#include <stdio.h>
#include <stdlib.h>
#include <dos.h>
#include <bios.h>
#include <fcntl.h>
#include <memory.h>
#include <malloc.h>
#include <math.h>
#include <string.h>

#include "graph3.h"    // include our graphics stuff
#include "graph4.h"
#include "graph6.h"

// P R O T O T Y P E S ////////////////////////////////////////////
```

Listing 13.1. continued

```c
// D E F I N E S ////////////////////////////////////////////////

#define VELOCITY 4    // constant speed of ship

// S T R U C T U R E S ////////////////////////////////////////////

// G L O B A L S ////////////////////////////////////////////////

pcx_picture imagery_pcx,     // the game imagery
            background_pcx;  // the backdrop


// the sprites used in the game

sprite object;                // the object

// F U N C T I O N S ////////////////////////////////////////////

void main(void)
{
// this is the main function

// SECTION 1 ////////////////////////////////////////////////////

// set video mode to 320x200 256 color mode

Set_Video_Mode(VGA256);

// create a double buffer

if (!Create_Double_Buffer(SCREEN_HEIGHT))
    {
    printf("\nNot enough memory to create double buffer.");

    } // end if

// clear the double buffer

Fill_Double_Buffer(0);

// SECTION 2 ////////////////////////////////////////////////////

// load in the background image into the double buffer

PCX_Init((pcx_picture_ptr)&background_pcx);

PCX_Load("velback.pcx", (pcx_picture_ptr)&background_pcx,1);

// copy the background into the double buffer

_fmemcpy((char far *)double_buffer,
        (char far *)(background_pcx.buffer),
        SCREEN_WIDTH*SCREEN_HEIGHT);
```

```
PCX_Delete((pcx_picture_ptr)&background_pcx);

// load in imagery for object

PCX_Init((pcx_picture_ptr)&imagery_pcx);

PCX_Load("viper.pcx", (pcx_picture_ptr)&imagery_pcx,1);

// SECTION 3 //////////////////////////////////////////////////

// initialize player and extract bitmaps

sprite_width  = 50;
sprite_height = 24;

Sprite_Init((sprite_ptr)&object,0,0,0,0,0,0);

PCX_Grab_Bitmap((pcx_picture_ptr)&imagery_pcx,
                (sprite_ptr)&object,0,0,0);

object.x          = 0;
object.y          = 100;
object.curr_frame = 0;
object.state      = 1;

// scan behind all objects before entering event loop

Behind_Sprite_DB((sprite_ptr)&object);

// SECTION 4 //////////////////////////////////////////////////

// main event loop

while(!kbhit())
    {

    // erase all objects

    Erase_Sprite_DB((sprite_ptr)&object);

// SECTION 5 //////////////////////////////////////////////////

    // move object with costant velocity

    object.x+=VELOCITY;

    // test if object is beyond edge of screen, if so send back to
    // other edge

    if (object.x>319-50)
        object.x = 0;

// SECTION 6 //////////////////////////////////////////////////

    // scan background under objects
```

13

continues

Listing 13.1. continued

```
        Behind_Sprite_DB((sprite_ptr)&object);

        // draw all the imagery

        Draw_Sprite_DB((sprite_ptr)&object);

        // copy the double buffer to the screen

        Show_Double_Buffer(double_buffer);

        // wait a sec

        Delay(1);

        } // end while

// SECTION 7 /////////////////////////////////////////////////////

// reset the video mode back to text

Set_Video_Mode(TEXT_MODE);

// free the double buffer

Delete_Double_Buffer();

} // end main
```

Building an Executable: To make an executable of the program in Listing 13.1, you can either type it in or use the source on the companion CD. The name of the source is velocity.c. The precompiled executable is named velocity.exe. As before, use the following compile line for Microsoft C:

```
cl -AM -Zi -c -Fc -Gs -G2 velocity.c
```

After compiling the program in this manner, you can link it to the standard libraries and to our previously generated game library, gamelib.lib, with a link line such as:

```
link /ST:8192 /CO velocity,,,graphics.lib+gamelib.lib,,
```

This creates a final executable named velocity.exe.

 The program in Listing 13.1 demonstrates the simple use of velocity to translate an object, which in this case is a spaceship. The program uses the standard double-buffered scheme along with a nice background image. Here are the main points of the program:

1. Section 1 is where the system is placed into mode 13h and the double buffer created.

2. In Section 2 we load the background and the images for the spaceship. Also, notice how the background image is copied into the double buffer.

3. In Section 3 the spaceship sprite is initialized and its bit map extracted from the PCX file. Also, this is where the background under the sprite is scanned in preparation for entering the game loop.

4. Section 4 is the entrance to the main event loop where the exit variable is tested and all the images erased. In this case, there's only a single object: the spaceship itself.

5. Section 5 is where the object is translated based on the VELOCITY constant. This is done by a simple addition. At the end of the section we do a test to see whether the sprite has flown off the right edge of the screen. If so, it's "warped" back to the left edge.

6. Section 6 is the end of the erase-move-draw cycle; therefore, the data under the object is scanned and the object drawn. Finally, the double buffer is copied to the video buffer and the Delay() function is called to force the demo to run at a maximum of 18 frames per second.

7. In Section 7 the demo is over. This section resets the PC to text mode and relinquishes the double buffer.

Acceleration

Acceleration is velocity's big brother. It's the *rate of change of velocity per unit of time*. For example, when you press the gas pedal down in your car, the velocity of the car continues to change until it stabilizes. You see this by watching your speedometer needle keep moving to your desired speed. If we were to look at a graph of velocity versus time and acceleration versus time of a car accelerating, it would look like Figure 13.2. (Note: this is a fast car—preferably, a Porsche.)

13

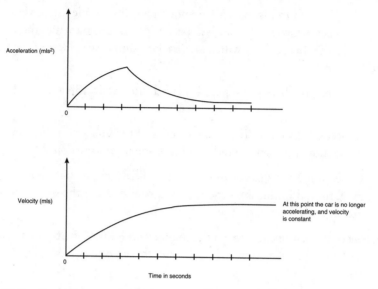

Acceleration (m/s²)

0

Velocity (m/s)

At this point the car is no longer
accelerating, and velocity
is constant

0

Time in seconds

Figure 13.2. *Acceleration and velocity curves for an accelerating car.*

We see that acceleration dies down once it's complete, while velocity stabilizes at a constant value. Modeling this is easy: all we do is add a constant value to the velocity per unit of time. This results in acceleration. Then, when we want to stop the acceleration, we stop adding the constant. The math for acceleration looks like this:

```
velocity = velocity + acceleration;
```

If this operation is done every game cycle, and the velocity is used to translate an object, the object moves faster and faster every cycle because the velocity is building up. Using our previous example of velocity to move the player's character, we can do the same thing with an acceleration:

```
// first add in the acceleration to the velocity
x_velocity = x_velocity + x_acceleration;
y_velocity = y_velocity + y_acceleration;

// now do the translation

player_x=player_x + x_velocity;
player_y=player_y + y_velocity;
```

Again we see that acceleration can have two components; if it's happening in 3-D, it can have three components. In most cases, however, a single value for acceleration is used for the both x- and y-axis instead of a separate value for both. Thus, having two values allows us more freedom.

As an example of acceleration in action, I've created a program that takes as input the acceleration of an object, starts the object off from a dead stop, and accelerates it. The name of the program, shown in Listing 13.2, is accel.exe.

Listing 13.2. Accelerating an object (accel.c).

```
// I N C L U D E S /////////////////////////////////////////////

#include <io.h>
#include <conio.h>
#include <stdio.h>
#include <stdlib.h>
#include <dos.h>
#include <bios.h>
#include <fcntl.h>
#include <memory.h>
#include <malloc.h>
#include <math.h>
#include <string.h>

#include "graph3.h"  // include our graphics stuff
#include "graph4.h"
#include "graph6.h"

// P R O T O T Y P E S /////////////////////////////////////////

// D E F I N E S ///////////////////////////////////////////////

// S T R U C T U R E S /////////////////////////////////////////

// G L O B A L S ///////////////////////////////////////////////

pcx_picture imagery_pcx,     // the game imagery
            background_pcx;   // the backdrop


// the sprites used in the game

sprite object;               // the object

// F U N C T I O N S ///////////////////////////////////////////

void main(void)
{
int accel=0,            // acceleration input by user
    velocity=0,         // current velocity of dragster
    peddle_to_metal=0,  // has the user punched it?
    engine=0,           // state of 500CI engine
    done=0;             // system exit variable

char buffer[80];        // used for printing

// this is the main function
```

continues

691

Listing 13.2. continued

```
// SECTION 1 ////////////////////////////////////////////////////

printf("\nEnter the acceleration of the dragster (1-10) ?");
scanf("%d",&accel);

// set video mode to 320x200 256 color mode

Set_Video_Mode(VGA256);

// create a double buffer

if (!Create_Double_Buffer(SCREEN_HEIGHT))
    {
    printf("\nNot enough memory to create double buffer.");

    } // end if

// clear the double buffer

Fill_Double_Buffer(0);

// SECTION 2 ////////////////////////////////////////////////////

// load in the background image into the double buffer

PCX_Init((pcx_picture_ptr)&background_pcx);

PCX_Load("road.pcx", (pcx_picture_ptr)&background_pcx,1);

// copy the background into the double buffer

_fmemcpy((char far *)double_buffer,
        (char far *)(background_pcx.buffer),
        SCREEN_WIDTH*SCREEN_HEIGHT);

PCX_Delete((pcx_picture_ptr)&background_pcx);

Blit_String_DB(8,8,10,"'Q' to quit, 'G' to start.",1);

// load in imagery for object

PCX_Init((pcx_picture_ptr)&imagery_pcx);

PCX_Load("drag.pcx", (pcx_picture_ptr)&imagery_pcx,1);

// SECTION 3 ////////////////////////////////////////////////////

// initialize player and extract bitmaps

sprite_width  = 36;
sprite_height = 8;

Sprite_Init((sprite_ptr)&object,0,0,0,0,0,0);
```

```
PCX_Grab_Bitmap((pcx_picture_ptr)&imagery_pcx,
                (sprite_ptr)&object,0,0,0);

object.x          = 0;
object.y          = 170;
object.curr_frame = 0;
object.state      = 1;

// scan behind all objects before entering event loop

Behind_Sprite_DB((sprite_ptr)&object);

// SECTION 4 ////////////////////////////////////////////////

// main event loop

while(!done)
    {

    // erase all objects

    Erase_Sprite_DB((sprite_ptr)&object);

    // test if user is tryin to go

    if (kbhit())
       {
       // what key?

       switch(getch())
            {
            case 'g': // g for gas, gone, go!
                 {
                 // we can only start dragster
                 // if it hasn't already started

                 if (!peddle_to_metal)
                    {
                    peddle_to_metal=engine=1;

                    } // end if

                 } break;

            case 'q': // to quit
                 {

                 done=1;

                 } break;

            default:break;

            } // end switch

       } // end if
```

continues

Listing 13.2. continued

```c
// SECTION 5 ////////////////////////////////////////////////////

    // test if it's time to move the dragster

    if (peddle_to_metal && engine)
       {

       // move object with velocity

       object.x+=velocity;

       // apply the horsepower baby (acceleration)

       velocity+=accel;

       // test if dragster has hit end of strip,
       // if so stop it rather abrubtly

       if (object.x > 319-36)
          {
          engine=0; // turn off engine and apply
                    // infinite braking force!

          // push dragster back a bit

          object.x = 319-36;

          } // end if

       } // end if

// SECTION 6 ////////////////////////////////////////////////////

    // scan background under objects

    Behind_Sprite_DB((sprite_ptr)&object);

    // draw all the imagery

    Draw_Sprite_DB((sprite_ptr)&object);

    // show some info

    sprintf(buffer,"Speed = %d   ",velocity);
    Blit_String_DB(110,100,10,buffer,0);

    sprintf(buffer,"Acceration = %d   ",accel);
    Blit_String_DB(110,110,10,buffer,0);

    // copy the double buffer to the screen

    Show_Double_Buffer(double_buffer);

    // wait a sec
```

```
        Delay(1);

    } // end while

// SECTION 7 /////////////////////////////////////////////////

// reset the video mode back to text

Set_Video_Mode(TEXT_MODE);

// free the double buffer

Delete_Double_Buffer();

} // end main
```

Building an Executable: To make an executable of the program in Listing 13.2, you can either type it in or use the source on the companion CD. The name of the source is accel.c. The precompiled executable is named accel.exe. As before, use the following compile line for Microsoft C:

```
cl -AM -Zi -c -Fc -Gs -G2 accel.c
```

After compiling the program in this manner, you can link it to the standard libraries and to our previously generated game library, gamelib.lib, with a link line such as:

```
link /ST:8192 /CO accel,,,graphics.lib+gamelib.lib,,
```

This creates a final executable named accel.exe.

This program is a little more exciting than the velocity.exe one, but not by much. However, it's good that we're really getting a firm grip on the basics, as they really are the most important of all.

Analysis The accel.exe program operates by querying the player for an acceleration factor from 1–10. You can think of this acceleration factor in terms of pixels of acceleration per frame of animation, which is related to time by the factor that relates frames per second. As the player, you're prompted to press the G key to start the dragster. The dragster then pops into gear and runs down the strip until it hits the end and comes to a halt.

13

There are a couple of visual indicators displaying some interesting information on the screen. One indicator shows the selected acceleration. The other shows the velocity as a function of time once the dragster is started. As far as the operation of the program goes, here are the more salient points:

1. In Section 1 you're asked to input an acceleration factor, which is stored in the variable `accel`. The system is then placed in mode 13h, and the double buffer is created.

2. Section 2 is where the background is loaded, along with the bit map for the dragster.

3. In Section 3 the dragster sprite is initialized and the background under it scanned so it can be replaced during the first iteration of the main event loop.

4. Section 4 is where the program enters the event loop and the dragster is erased. Also, the keyboard is tested to see whether you're trying to start the dragster or exit the demo. In either case, appropriate flags are set.

5. In Section 5, if you pressed the G key, the flags named `peddle_to_metal` and `engine` are both set high. When this occurs, Section 5 adds the velocity to the current position of the dragster, and then adds the acceleration to the velocity. This has the effect of causing a linear acceleration curve, as the increase in velocity is constant. Figure 13.3 shows a linear acceleration curve.

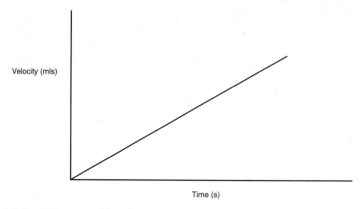

Figure 13.3. *A linear acceleration curve.*

The position of the dragster is tested to see if it's at the end of the strip. If it is, the driver gets the worst case of whiplash ever seen because the dragster is stopped in zero time—in other words, with infinite deceleration. (Bad on the back.)

6. Section 6 is where the background is scanned, the dragster drawn, and the displays rendered. Finally, the double buffer is copied into the video buffer for view and the `Delay()` function is called for synchronization purposes.

7. Section 7 is the end of the program, so all resources (such as the double buffer) are released and the PC is placed back into text mode.

Momentum

In a video game there are objects that are supposed to represent things such as cars, missiles, aliens spaceships, or whatever. Each of these objects is supposed to be made out of virtual matter; therefore, they should have some kind of mass. This mass relates to the amount of matter that makes them up. (Mass is *not* weight. Weight is a force: the result of an acceleration acting upon a mass. People always make the mistake of saying that something weighs "blank" kilograms. Kilograms are mass. Pounds are force. If they wanted to say that they weighed a certain amount in the metric system, they would measure it in newtons! And, by the way, the English measure of mass is called the slug.) Anyway, because the objects in our games should have some kind of mass, that means that they will have momentum when they're in motion.

Trains versus Bullets

Momentum is one of those things that's sort of hard to pin down, but in general it's that property of a moving object that relates to the mass and velocity of the object. If an object is moving at a certain rate, it's going to take a certain amount of force to stop it. For example, a train moving at two miles per hour is going to be a lot harder to stop than a bullet traveling at 1,000 miles per hour. This is because the mass of the train is so much larger than that of the bullet. And, even though you may not think so, if a train hit you at two miles per hour and your mass had nowhere to go (meaning you were fixed in space), you would be instantly compressed. The only reason people survive being hit by cars and trains is that there's a brief contact and then some of the striking object's momentum is transferred to the struck object and sends it sailing through space!

We might want to use momentum in a game to help make an explosion seem realistic. For example, if a ship blows up in any kind of atmosphere, we may want to model the shock wave (which is a collection of air molecules with mass) disturbing the other ships around it. Therefore, we might want to do a *momentum transfer*. This might change the velocity of the other objects relative to their masses. The formula to compute momentum is:

13

Formula 13.2. *Computing momentum.*

```
momentum = mass * velocity;
```

Of course, this doesn't mean anything when comparing the virtual world of the computer to the real world. Objects are relative to the other objects in the game—and we can make their mass anything we like. However, if we want to create a believable game, we should scale all objects in the universe so their virtual-physical properties are relatively correct as far as the simulation goes.

Conservation of Momentum

All this talk about momentum is a lead into computing the results of a collision between two objects in the game world. However, before we do that we must talk about the *law of conservation*. Conservation in the context of physics means that some quantity is conserved after a reaction. The quantity may be transformed but still will exist. This is basically a corollary of the statement that "energy cannot be either created nor destroyed" (although I'm still not sure if I really believe that!).

In the case of momentum when one body collides with another, the momentum is conserved because it can't go anywhere else. (Of course, this statement only makes sense if there's no friction in the system, which would translate to a loss.) Anyway, if there are two bodies and they collide, the equation shown in Formula 13.3 is true:

Formula 13.3. *Conservation of momentum.*

```
M1V1 = M2V2
```

where:

- ☐ $M1$ is the mass of object one.

- ☐ $M2$ is the mass of object two.

- ☐ $V1$ and $V2$ are their respective velocities.

Knowing the actual physical model of momentum conservation can help you model the collisions in your game more realistically, even though you may not follow the model exactly (which is the case in most games).

Elastic Collisions

We're going to see how a straight-line, perfectly elastic collision takes place. First, we must define "elastic." An *elastic collision* is one where there are no energy losses from, or deformation of, the objects. If the objects are deformed, there's an absorption of energy (which causes the deformation), and the collision is not elastic. In this discussion we consider only straight-line collisions, such as the one shown in Figure 13.4.

Figure 13.4. *Two masses about to collide.*

For comparison, Figure 13.5 shows an inelastic collision.

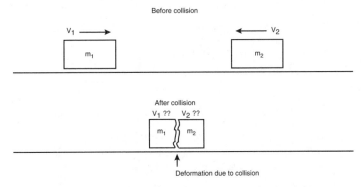

Figure 13.5. *An inelastic collision resulting in energy loss due to deformation.*

Computing the velocities after an arbitrary, angled collision takes too much math and isn't necessary as we're only trying to get a grasp on the subject. Computing the velocities after a straight-line collision is hard enough. The mathematics behind a straight-line elastic collision aren't too terribly complex; just a bit long. However, bear with me.

We know that the momentum of the two colliding objects is conserved after the collision. We also know both of the masses and velocities of the object before the collision. The problem is, we don't know enough to find the velocities after the collision. We must look somewhere else for more information. The answer to our dilemma is to use the kinetic energy of the objects to help solve for their final velocities after collision.

13

Hopefully, you will recall from high school physics that *kinetic energy* is the measure of energy an object possesses because of its motion. The equation for kinetic energy is shown in Formula 13.4:

Formula 13.4. *Kinetic energy of an object in motion.*

```
kinetic energy = (1/2)*M*V²
```

where:

- ☐ M is the mass of the object.

- ☐ V is the velocity of the object.

If we compute the kinetic energy of each object before the collision and use that along with the rule of conservation of momentum, we can write equations that solve for the final velocities of the objects. Doing this takes a bit of algebra—and I don't want to give you anymore headaches than you already have, so I'll do the algebra for you. Take a look at Figure 13.6 first.

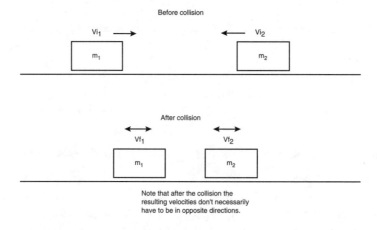

Figure 13.6. *The complete elastic collision.*

Given:

- ☐ Object 1 has initial velocity Vi_1 and mass M_1.

- ☐ Object 2 has initial velocity Vi_2 and mass M_2.

The velocities after the collision are described by Formula 13.5.

Formula 13.5. *The computation of final velocities after a collision.*

```
        2*M₂*Vi₂ + Vi₁*(M₁-M₂)
Vf1 = ----------------------------------
            M₁+M₂

        2*M₁*Vi₁ + Vi₂*(M₁-M₂)
Vf2 = ----------------------------------
            M₁+M₂
```

where Vf1 and Vf2 are the final velocities of the objects.

Now, the values of mass and velocity are only relative to the game universe, and they don't really matter. You can use any values you wish. Just make sure they make sense on a relative basis, and that the results are what you want.

Modeling Gravity

Video games are full of gravity effects that are modeled in some cases, faked in others. For instance, if we wanted to make a little man jump, we might draw a set of frames that made him look as though he was jumping and create a set of positions for him during the jump, such as shown in Figure 13.7.

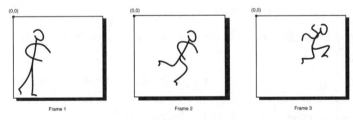

Frame 1   Frame 2   Frame 3

Figure 13.7. *Motion of an object within an animation cell to create motion locally within the bit-map boundaries of the object.*

However, if we want to generate his path using physics, we must learn to model gravity.

Because most video games occur on land, sea, or some sort of massy object (such as a giant starship), the force of gravity should be in play. Gravity is the force that pulls two objects together. The field that does this is called a *gravitron field* (and someday we'll figure out how to create an antigravitron). Anyway, the force of gravity, or the attraction between two objects, is represented in Figure 13.8.

13

We see that there is a force between the two objects, and that this force is in a direct line. Formula 13.6 governs this force.

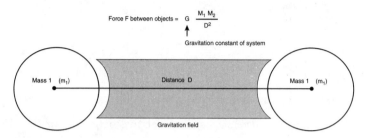

Figure 13.8. *Two masses being attracted to each other.*

Formula 13.6. *The gravitational force between two objects.*

$$\text{Force} = G * \frac{M_1 * M_2}{D_2}$$

where:

☐ D is the distance between the objects.

☐ M_1 and M_2 are the masses of the objects.

☐ G is the gravitational constant of whatever universe in which the whole process is occurring.

Although Formula 13.6 is correct, it's a bit hard to work with. Let's see if we can't extract the basic function of it as it applies to a physical system. As an example, let's drop a ball off a building, as has just happened in Figure 13.9.

We know that the ball will fall faster and faster until it hits the ground. We also know that gravity has an effect only in the vertical direction; that is, the ball doesn't translate horizontally. Therefore, it seems that if we apply an acceleration to the ball's vertical velocity in the downward direction, we will have modeled gravity. This is exactly what we want, and it works perfectly.

Say that an object has an initial velocity, in both the x and y directions; we can call them x_velocity and y_velocity, respectively. To apply a gravity field to the object, we would simply add a constant value to the vertical component each cycle of the game, something like this:

```
x_velocity = x_velocity+ 0; // no gravity on X-axis
y_velocity = y_velocity + gravity;
```

where `gravity` is, in essence, the gravitational strength.

We also can look at gravity another way: we can see the position of an object as a function of time and can compute its velocity and position that way if we wish. Assuming the object started off at (0,0) in the game world, Formula 13.7 and Formula 13.8 describe the velocity and position of the object relative to time.

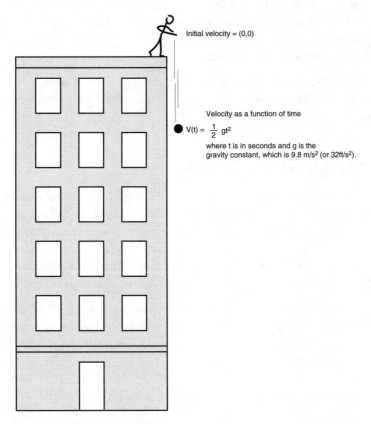

Figure 13.9. *A dropping ball.*

Formula 13.7. *Velocity as a function of time with a given gravitation constant.*

```
x_velocity = x_velocity + 0; // Doesn't change
y_velocity = y_velocity + gravity * time;
```

The Physics of Games

Formula 13.8. *The position of an object with a gravity field.*

```
x_position = x_velocity * time; // Note that the object does
                                // move as there's an x velocity

y_position = y_velocity * time + 1/2 * gravity * time2;
```

Note that `time` is squared in the vertical component of the object's position. However, the `time` variable is not *our* time but game time, which is game cycles. As long as everything we speak of is in the game world, we can think of a single game cycle as a single second for purposes of this discussion.

You can use these two formulas to apply gravity to the objects in your game. The constants you pick are up to you: just make them whatever they need to be for the desired results.

Modeling Friction

We've all seen friction before; it's an unavoidable problem with the universe we live in and makes the cost of living really high! *Friction* can loosely be defined as *the loss of energy due to heat or kinetic energy transfer*. For example, when you're driving your car and lift your foot off the gas pedal, the car slows down. This is because there's friction in both the transmission (the engine, bearings, and so forth) and the environment (wind, the road surface, and so on), all eating up your kinetic or "motional" energy.

Modeling friction mathematically the real way is a bit too complicated; we really don't need to compute energies and forces and then use them to find velocities as a function of time. We just want a simple model that works. To create this model, first take a look at Figure 13.10.

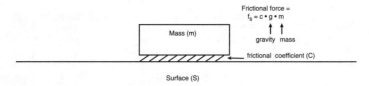

Figure 13.10. *Friction acting on a mass.*

Here we see in a mass, M, resting on a surface, S. A a frictional coefficient, C, relates to the amount of force necessary to move the object initially and at a constant speed. The amount of friction is proportional to the amount of mass of the object, as this mass is causing the acceleration of gravity to push the object down on the surface harder.

704

We can think of friction as the loss of velocity of an object as a function of time. For instance, if we fire a torpedo in water and want the torpedo to come to rest at some point, we might give the torpedo an initial velocity of, say, 1,000 units and then each game cycle subtract a constant value from this velocity. The result of this would be perceived by the player as an apparent frictional force. The code to do something like this would look like this:

```
velocity = velocity - friction;
```

This line of code would be executed every game cycle until the velocity was zero. At that point it would no longer be executed, as the velocity would become negative!

As an example of modeling friction, I've created a demo in which a boat that fires a torpedo and the torpedo comes to a halt before the end of the screen. The name of the demo is friction.exe. Listing 13.3 contains the source. Use the F key to fire the torpedo.

Listing 13.3. A demo of friction (friction.c).

```
// I N C L U D E S ///////////////////////////////////////////

#include <io.h>
#include <conio.h>
#include <stdio.h>
#include <stdlib.h>
#include <dos.h>
#include <bios.h>
#include <fcntl.h>
#include <memory.h>
#include <malloc.h>
#include <math.h>
#include <string.h>

#include "graph3.h"   // include our graphics stuff
#include "graph4.h"
#include "graph6.h"

// D E F I N E S ///////////////////////////////////////////

#define FRICTION 1    // virtual frictional coefficient of water

// G L O B A L S ///////////////////////////////////////////

pcx_picture imagery_pcx,      // the game imagery
            background_pcx;    // the backdrop


// the sprites used in the game

sprite object;                // the object

// F U N C T I O N S ///////////////////////////////////////////
```

continues

Listing 13.3. continued

```c
void main(void)
{

int torpedo_xv=0,   // initial velocities
    torpedo_yv=0,
    fired=0,        // state of torpedo
    done=0;         // exit variable


// SECTION 1 ///////////////////////////////////////////////////////

// set video mode to 320x200 256 color mode

Set_Video_Mode(VGA256);

// create a double buffer

if (!Create_Double_Buffer(SCREEN_HEIGHT))
    {
    printf("\nNot enough memory to create double buffer.");

    } // end if

// clear the double buffer

Fill_Double_Buffer(0);

// SECTION 2 ///////////////////////////////////////////////////////

// load in the background image into the double buffer

PCX_Init((pcx_picture_ptr)&background_pcx);

PCX_Load("ship.pcx", (pcx_picture_ptr)&background_pcx,1);

// copy the background into the double buffer

_fmemcpy((char far *)double_buffer,
        (char far *)(background_pcx.buffer),
        SCREEN_WIDTH*SCREEN_HEIGHT);

PCX_Delete((pcx_picture_ptr)&background_pcx);

// load in imagery for object

PCX_Init((pcx_picture_ptr)&imagery_pcx);

PCX_Load("torpedo.pcx", (pcx_picture_ptr)&imagery_pcx,1);

// SECTION 3 ///////////////////////////////////////////////////////

// initialize player and extract bit maps

sprite_width  = 8;
sprite_height = 8;
```

```
Sprite_Init((sprite_ptr)&object,0,0,0,0,0,0);

PCX_Grab_Bitmap((pcx_picture_ptr)&imagery_pcx,
                (sprite_ptr)&object,0,0,0);

object.x          = 154;
object.y          = 178;
object.curr_frame = 0;
object.state      = 1;

// draw instructions

Blit_String_DB(8,8,15,"Press 'Q' to quit, 'F' to fire.",1);

// scan behind all objects before entering event loop

Behind_Sprite_DB((sprite_ptr)&object);

// SECTION 4 /////////////////////////////////////////////////

// main event loop

while(!done)
     {

     // erase all objects

     Erase_Sprite_DB((sprite_ptr)&object);

// SECTION 5 /////////////////////////////////////////////////

     // test if user is trying to fire torpedo

     if (kbhit())
        {

        switch(getch())
             {

             case 'q': // just exit?
                  {
                  done=1;

                  } break;

             case 'f':
             case 'F': // fire the torpedo
                   {
                   // make sure torpedo hasn't been fired

                   if (!fired)
                   {

                   // set flag that torpedo has been fired
```

continues

Listing 13.3. continued

```
                                    fired=1;

                                    // set initial velocity or torpedo

                                    torpedo_xv = 0;    // no movement X direction

                                    torpedo_yv = -16; // initial velocity,
                                                      // note it is
                                                      // negative since
                                                      // torpedo is moving
                                                      // upward

                            } // end if

                            } break;

                    } // end switch

            } // end if kbhit


// SECTION 6 //////////////////////////////////////////////////////

        // test if torpedo has been fired

        if (fired)
            {

            // do translation

            object.x+=torpedo_xv;
            object.y+=torpedo_yv;

            // apply water friction only to vertical
            // component of velocity

            torpedo_yv+=FRICTION;

            // test if velocity has become postive or zero

            if (torpedo_yv>0)
                torpedo_yv = 0;

            } // end if fired

// SECTION 7 //////////////////////////////////////////////////////

        // scan background under objects

        Behind_Sprite_DB((sprite_ptr)&object);

        // draw all the imagery

        Draw_Sprite_DB((sprite_ptr)&object);
```

```
    // copy the double buffer to the screen

    Show_Double_Buffer(double_buffer);

    // wait a sec

    Delay(1);

    } // end while
// SECTION 8 //////////////////////////////////////////////

// reset the video mode back to text

Set_Video_Mode(TEXT_MODE);

// free the double buffer

Delete_Double_Buffer();

} // end main
```

Building an Executable: To make an executable of the program in Listing 13.3, you can type it in or use the source on the companion CD. The name of the source is "friction.c". The precompiled executable is named "friction.exe". As before use the following compile line for Microsoft C.

```
cl -AM -Zi -c -Fc -Gs -G2 friction.c
```

After compiling the program in this manner you can link it to the standard libraries and to our previously generated game library, gamelib.lib, with a link line such as:

```
link /ST:8192 /CO friction,,,graphics.lib+gamelib.lib,,
```

This creates a final executable named friction.exe.

This program is somewhat similar to the accel.exe program in that there's some force changing the velocity of an object. In the case of accel.exe, the force was a big engine. In the case of this program, the force is that of friction caused by a torpedo moving through water without a propulsion unit.

This program waits for you to press the F key, which is what fires a torpedo. Once the torpedo is fired with its initial velocity, it slowly comes to a halt because of the friction of water. This is modeled by subtracting a frictional value from the initial velocity value each game cycle. (Hopefully, the target was in range!) Here is the analysis:

709

13

1. Section 1 is where—you guessed it—the video mode is set to mode 13h and the double buffer is created.

2. Section 2 loads the PCX files that hold both the watery background and the image of the torpedo.

3. Section 3 is where the sprite for the torpedo is initialized and the directions are blitted on the screen. Also, as usual, the background under the sprite is scanned before entering the event loop.

4. Section 4 is the entrance to the event loop, and where the sprite is erased in preparation for transformation.

5. In Section 5 the keyboard is tested to see whether the player has fired the torpedo. If the torpedo has been fired, the initial velocity of the torpedo is assigned, and a flag that denoting that the torpedo has been fired is set.

6. In Section 6, based on the state of the "fired" flag, the torpedo is moved using the velocity values. When the translation is complete, the velocity is adjusted by the frictional coefficient of water, called FRICTION.

7. In Section 7 the torpedo is drawn, the double buffer is copied to the screen, and a small delay is issued to synchronize the system.

8. Section 8 is the end, and I think by now you know what happens.

Computing Trajectories

Many times when writing a sideview game you may want to fire a projectile and have gravity or some other effect (such as wind) alter the projectile's course after it's been fired. Normally, when a missile, particle beam, laser, or other weapon is fired in a game, an initial velocity is given to the object and the object continues along the same path, translated only by velocity. To model this scenario more realistically, though, we must include the effect of gravity, friction, and any other force that could be acting on the object. For an example, take a look at Figure 13.11 to see a diagram of the different quantities and values involved in a trajectory problem.

As game programmers, we're interested in being able to model this with some simple insights that can be used to make the projectile do what we want it to. For example, say we wanted to fire a projectile in a manner such as shown in Figure 13.12.

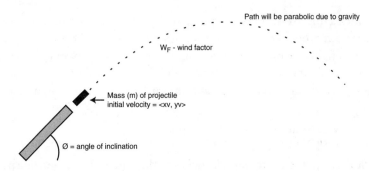

Figure 13.11. *The trajectory of a mass.*

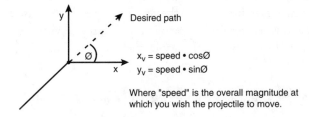

Figure 13.12. *Computing the components of a trajectory problem.*

We would compute the initial velocity by using the cos() and sin() functions as shown in Formula 13.9.

Formula 13.9. *Computing the trajectory of a particle.*

```
xv = cos(θ) * MAGNITUDE;
yv = sin(θ) * MAGNITUDE;
```

where:

- ☐ θ is the angle relative to the horizon.

- ☐ MAGNITUDE is the overall speed of the projectile, in pixels, per game cycle.

The result of applying this trajectory to a particle is that the object follows a straight-line path from its point of origin. This may be the effect we desire, but what if we want the object to feel the effects of gravity, wind, or some other force? The answer to this is that we can use the *theory of superposition*. This theory states that *if there is a collection of electromagnetic or mechanical waves in a system, the result of all the independent waves is the sum of the individual waves.*

We can extend this to our trajectory problem. If we wish to have more than a single force acting upon our projectile's trajectory, we simply add up all the forces. In the case of our motion model, this means we can have more than one component to the velocity values. Normally, we might have just x_velocity and y_velocity, but we can also have x_wind and y_gravity, which could be constants that are added to the translation equation, like this:

```
x_position = x_position + x_velocity + x_wind;
y_position = y_position + y_velocity + y_gravity;
```

To conclude, trajectories are way of modifying the standard, straight-line path an object would take with a constant value for velocity. This modification can be of the form of secondary constants added to the equation, or even functions that take time or screen position as parameters to further alter the velocity values. In any case, trajectories are easy to implement and you can simulate many neat effects—gravity, magnetic fields, winds, water currents, and so forth—with simple math.

Particle System Explosions

The term *particle system* has become a hot one in computer graphics and simulation. In essence, it's a technique of simulating a physical effect by building a simulation out of a collection of small *cells*, each of which are governed by simple rules. These cells individually don't do much, but in unison a more complex system seems to arise. There's an almost synergistic effect going on. For example, it's always been difficult to algorithmically create effects such as rain or fire. With a particle system, however, effects like this become easy to implement.

Here's how it works:

1. A few basic rules are thought up to govern the particles and their motion.

2. Then, using the ability of the computer to replicate the particle hundreds (if not thousands) of times, a complex system can be generated with simpler building blocks.

If we think about this, it makes sense. For example, if we could model atoms in the computer, we could make objects out of virtual atoms and let the objects interact. We could see the results and be oblivious to the actual math or physics taking place. This is the idea of particle system: we don't try to model the outcome of the system, we try to model a system and see its outcome!

As far as games are concerned, there are many interesting ways to use particle systems. One of the most common area is explosions. To make great explosions, we create a collection of particles that have the following rules:

1. Start from a position within a specified radius of the destroyed object.

2. Radiate out at some random velocity.

3. Apply gravity to the particles.

4. Transform the color or intensity of the particles as a function of time.

5. Terminate the particles when they hit the boundary of the screen, or when a timer runs out.

Rules 3, 4, and 5 are somewhat arbitrary and up to you, but the first two rules are the bare minimum needed for the effect.

To implement a particle explosion you'd need some functions to do the work. In general, however, you might use a standard "vanilla" particle structure, such as:

```
typedef struct particle_typ
        {
        int x;                    // x position
        int y;                    // y position
        int xv;                   // x velocity
        int yv;                   // y velocity
        unsigned char color;      // the color of the particle
        unsigned char back;       // the color behind the particle
        int state;                // the state of the particle
        int tag;                  // if the particle is a missile then who
                                  // does it belong to?
        int counter;              // use for counting
        int threshold;            // the counters threshold

        int counter_2;
        int threshold_2;

        } particle, *particle_ptr;
```

This is the actual structure used for the particle explosion in the Mech War game from Day 2. We see that there are fields for velocity, position, color, background pixels, and a couple of counters used to track the lifetime of each particle as it's radiated out from the point of impact.

Implementing a particle explosion in your games takes nothing more than writing a function to erase the particles, move the particles, and draw the particles. The only exciting thing at all about the functions is that each one of them processes tens to hundreds of these little particles instead of the single game object we've seen processed in all of the demos thus far.

13

Summary

Today we've taken a brief course in Newtonian mechanics and seen how the simple models of physical phenomena apply to the objects in our games. We learned about velocity, acceleration, friction, gravity, momentum, and collisions. The most important thing to get out of today's lesson, though, is the realization that as long as something works, who cares whether it's the "correct" or "right" way of doing it? If there's one thing you should remember about writing video games, it's that most of the time nothing is as it seems!

Q&A

Q Why is physical modeling important in video games?

A We need physical models to control the motion of the objects in our games. We don't need to model reality perfectly. However, basing our motion models on the real world helps make things look more realistic.

Q What is the difference between velocity and acceleration?

A Velocity is like speed; it's how fast you're going right now. Acceleration is how fast your speed changes as a function of time.

Q What is inertia?

A Inertia is sort of like momentum, but different. It's the property of an object in motion or at rest that makes it stay at motion or at rest. You could think of it as a force that resists motional changes.

Q How can water be modeled?

A This depends on the context. For example, do you want something to look like water, act like water, or something in between? In any case, water can be modeled using all the techniques we've seen thus far, such as friction and particle-system simulation. (However, you might want to experiment with sinusoidal waveforms in some manner, as water and its motion are a supposition of these types of waveforms.)

Q Is it possible to simulate reality in a computer?

A Yes. However, the computer has to simulate even quantum effects, which would seem to be impossible based on the Pauli Exclusion Principle. Nevertheless, we surely got 99.9 percent of the way today!

Workshop

The Workshop section presents quiz questions to help you cement your new knowledge and exercises to give you experience using what you've learned. Try to understand the questions and exercises before moving on to the next lesson. The answers are in Appendix B.

Quiz

1. What does F=MA mean?

2. What causes friction?

3. Can an object be moving if its acceleration is negative?

4. What is kinetic energy?

5. In what direction does gravity operate?

6. Is the gravitational pull of the Earth the same for all objects, regardless of their mass?

Exercises

1. Write a program that creates a particle explosion.

2. Modify the velocity.c program in Listing 13.1 so you can control the velocity of the object with the keyboard.

3. Write a program that enables you to start two block masses (m1,m2) at some initial velocity toward each other. Have the program compute their collision and recompute the velocity of each mass after the collision.

4. Write a program that makes a single pixel move in a circular path.

Tools of the Trade

At this point we've covered most of the (non-creative) aspects of video-game design. Now let's talk about some of the tools that can be helpful to a video game designer. (Remember, there's more to a video game than the actual program: there's the artwork, the sounds, the "feel" of the game, and more.) Today we talk about some of the tools we need to create a video game, and then polish off the game library we've been constructing for the past two weeks. We also do a final review of all the functions in the library and their usage.

Here are the topics we cover today:

- [ ] Paint programs
- [ ] Animation programs
- [ ] Morphing and transformation programs
- [ ] Video digitizing and models
- [ ] Sound editors
- [ ] Prerecorded sound FX
- [ ] Making music
- [ ] Game tools
- [ ] Map editors
- [ ] World builders
- [ ] The game library
- [ ] A functional description of the library

Paint Programs

Unless you're going to write a text-only game, you need artwork and imagery. One source of this imagery is paint programs. A paint program is a piece of software designed to draw images in a manner similar to how an artist paints on a canvas. Paint programs enable you to draw primitive shapes—such as circles, squares, and curves—and also draw images pixel by pixel with the mouse. Because all the games we plan to write are in mode 13h, it makes sense to use a paint program that can write PCX files for the 320×200-pixel, 256-color mode. Moreover, the paint program you choose should be able to operate in the target mode in which the game will run, which is mode 13h.

The reasoning behind making sure the paint package functions in mode 13h lies in the aspect ratio of the pixels, along with the number of colors. For example, say you used a

mode that had an 800×600-pixel resolution with 24-bit color. When the images were read into your game to be run in mode 13h, they would look distorted and the colors wouldn't be correct. In general, therefore, it's best to select a paint program that allows you to run in many different graphics modes—especially mode 13h.

Of course, if you're using the paint program to do image processing (such as smoothing, filtering, or whatever), the processed image would be good in mode 13h as long as the original image looked fine in mode 13h, with the proper colors and so forth. For example, you may really like Dpaint, but perhaps another program that works only in 640×480 mode has a special effect you like. You could import the Dpaint image into the other program and then, after doing the image processing, export the image back out to Dpaint.

For the most part, all paint programs (and their interfaces) are similar. However, there are some "bare minimums" you should look for:

- [ ] As we've already said, your paint program should support mode 13h.

- [ ] The program should enable you to set any of the 256 color registers.

- [ ] The program should have a lot of image-processing tools, such as blurring, anti-aliasing (removing the "jaggies" from lines), rotation, shearing, and scaling, most of which were discussed on Day 5 (in the chapter called "Polygon Engines").

- [ ] The program should accommodate multiple pages of memory so you can flip back and forth from one page to another.

- [ ] The program should have working areas that can be messy while you're drawing your final images. For example, I always like to have a page on which I draw a collection of texture patches. These textures look like rock, grass, sand, brick, or whatever. Then, when I need a rock texture, I extract it from my working page, switch to my final page, and place the texture where I want it. The main point here is that the video screen is like paper and there is only so much of it, so the more paper you have to work with the better.

As far as suggesting a paint program, I like Dpaint, Deluxe Animation, Fractal Paint, or PC-Paint. All of these programs are good and have more than enough features for you to create some terrific imagery for your games.

Finally, I'm assuming that you're artistic. Many people aren't, and that's fine. However, using the computer as a tool, you would be surprised what can be done once you get the hang of it. These paint programs have so much functionality they can make even the worst artist look good. If you take your time and work with the features of the paint program, you should be able to come up with decent images.

14

Animation Programs

The objects in video games are in constant motion. They're also *animated*, meaning that there's more than one frame of imagery for each game object. As a matter of fact, there could be dozens or hundreds of frames of animation for the objects in games. For example, if you wanted to make an alien in a game, you would draw the frames of animation for it walking to the right, walking to the left, jumping, dying, hissing, and maybe even some frames for when it's stationary. The problem here is twofold:

☐ How do you draw frames of animation?

☐ Once you have the frames of animation, how do you see what they would look like in action?

Drawing Animated Figures

Being able to draw animated figures is rather hard; some people can do it and some can't. The trick to drawing animated figures is imagination. You must be able to see in your mind what something looks like as it turns, jumps, or whatever. If you can't do this, you must rely on logic and physics.

You can use common sense to try to draw something walking. For example, I have always had a problem making my figures look like they were walking, so what I would do is start out with stick figures. Then I would animate their legs, then their arms, and then any other parts of their bodies, like antennas. At that point, I would remake the stick figures into complete drawings by filling in all the parts, as shown in Figure 14.1.

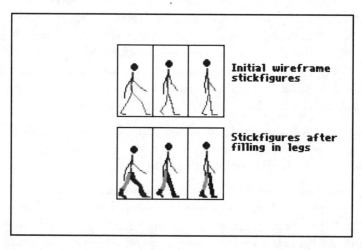

Figure 14.1. *Using simple stick figures to help create complex characters.*

Once you do this a few times it becomes easier to draw the animation without going through the stick-figure phase.

Seeing the Action

We still must find out how we can see the animation before we place it in the game. There are a couple of ways to do this.

The first method is for you to write an animation package that enables you to import PCX files, extract the cells of animation, and then play them out at some specific rate. This solution is reasonable, but you'll have to write a fairly sophisticated package to accomplish it. Many times this is the only solution—and, believe me, all video-game programmers have written their own paint programs and animation packages for an application when they couldn't fit any other commercially available piece of software to the job.

The other way of testing the animation is with an animation package. Now, there aren't a whole lot of animation packages that do what we want them to do. Most animation packages are sophisticated and designed for more complex applications (such as creating short films). Nevertheless, there are some programs that you can use along with the paint program to test the animation cells for your games. A few of the more popular programs are Deluxe Animator (which is also a paint program), Aegis Animator, and Autodesk Animator. All of these programs can do the job.

As you can probably guess, the Autodesk product is top of the line (although you may be willing to pay the price for all its capabilities). My advice is to keep everything simple for your first few games, and maybe you should think about writing your own animation package or using Deluxe Animator.

Morphing and Transformation Software

Computer graphics are a hot topic today and will continue to be for the foreseeable future. There are a ton of commercial products available that can take your PCX files and do all kinds of weird things to them. Manipulations such as morphing, texture mapping, lighting effects, and so on can all be done easily using an *image-processing program*. You can use these image-processing programs to create FX and frames of animation you can use in your games.

14

For example, you may want to morph an alien into a human. (*Morph* means to "blend" images as you change a thing from one form to another.) You could use an image-processing program to do each step of the change, save each frame in a file, and later import them into a game.

A lot of game designers use high-end 3-D packages to create the introductions and in-between scenes in their games. For example, you may have a simple 2-D shoot-'em-up game, but maybe you want a really impressive introduction that's in 3-D. You could use a program such as Autodesk's 3-D Studio to create an introduction sequence in full 3-D, then play it using a special piece of software that comes with 3-D Studio. If you have the budget for high-end graphics software, I suggest purchasing some high-end products to help you generate the imagery for your games. There's nothing better than to have a really cool introduction, but beware: the game had better be good! (We discuss this in more detail in a moment.)

Video Digitizing and Models

The last source of game imagery is real objects. It's possible to use a video camera and a digitizer board (such as the Video Blaster) to digitize video taken of objects for use in a video game. The setup is fairly easy: you purchase a video digitizer and install it into your PC. Then, using some video source (such as a camcorder or VCR), you create and digitize video images. You can use this digitized video in the game directly, or you can grab single frames.

Later, you can even extract objects from these single frames. Many game developers these days are using miniature models of the monsters, ships, and so forth in their games. This is done by creating little video studios and then taking snapshots of the models against a monocolor backdrop (just like the blue screens used in movie production). Such a studio setup is shown in Figure 14.2.

You then import these snapshots of the models into paint programs and touch them up or modify them for your game.

For example, you may want to make a karate game, but aren't a good enough artist to draw the frames of animation for the combat. In this case, you could do the following:

1. Video a martial artist (or even yourself) doing the moves in slow motion.

2. Take the video and extract key frames you wish to use in the game.

3. Finally, you would take the raw imagery and touch it up in a paint program to make the animation cells look as though they're of a game character, and not a human being.

This technique can result in impressive animation that looks real. For example, Disney has been doing this for years. They video real actors dancing, jumping, or whatever, and then use the frames of the live action as a foundation for their animators to work with.

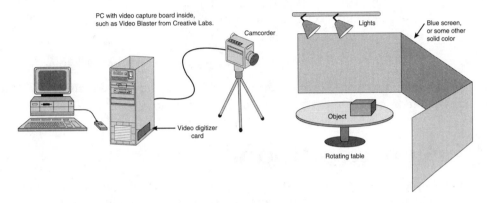

Figure 14.2. *A miniature video studio.*

Sound Editors

We learned on Day 9 how to play digitized sounds in our games, and saw a shareware program called Blaster Master that enables us to record, playback, and manipulate digitized sounds. However, there are many more things that we can do to the sounds we record besides what we've seen. In general, the digitized sounds used in a video game must be quite good: worth their consumption in memory. This means they must sound almost better than real life. Additionally, some sounds are impossible to digitize at a single time; they must be pasted together or edited with software.

Sound-editing software (and associated packages) are a whole other ball game from the graphics software we've been talking about. For our uses we must be able to take some basic sounds and then mix them together and edit them, much as would be done in a recording studio. To accomplish this, you need a piece of software that enables you to record, playback, edit, and perform various effects on the digitized sounds. You'll have to search yourself for the package that meets your needs, but there are a few features to look for as a minimum:

☐ The software must be able to record sounds from multiple sources.

☐ The software must play back sounds.

14

☐ The software must have multiple recording rates.

☐ The software must have sound-processing functions, such as pitch change, echo, volume change, fade, and so on.

☐ The software must accommodate multiple file formats to facilitate easy importing and exporting of sound files.

☐ The software must have the ability the paste sounds together back to back.

If the sound editor you choose has these features as a minimum, you should be able to create sounds that are of the quality needed for video games.

Prerecorded Sound FX

Sometimes the sounds you need in your games just can't be digitized because it's impossible or impractical to do so. Another source of sounds and sound FX are from CDs or tapes. There are many companies that create sound FX CDs offering dozens or hundreds of prerecorded sounds. You can find CDs with explosions, laser blasts, scary sounds, footsteps, and so forth. You can digitize the sounds off the CD and then use them in your games.

In addition to the sound FX CDs, you can also digitize sounds from movies, tapes, and other sources. However, if you use anything in your games that might be registered, trademarked, copyrighted, or protecting in any way, you should find out if there's going to be legal problem with your using that sound. For example, Paramount would probably be a little upset if you digitized Captain Kirk and used him in a game without giving them something. However, if you hear a good explosion or crunch in a movie, chances are you can use that sound effect without any problems.

Making Music

Although we didn't learn exactly how to play music with the Sound Blaster card, we have an idea. I have no doubt that you'll figure it out and then want to add music to your games. However, finding sources of music can be tricky. The music has to be in some format that's convertible into CMF files. This means the music must be in some form of MIDI. In other words, someone has to have converted the music into computer form. Having music on CDs isn't going to help you, because you need the notes and instruments of the music.

There are only two ways we can obtain music for our games:

☐ The first way is to compose and sequence the music ourselves using a synthesizer with a MIDI port, or maybe even the computer itself (if you're a musical genius), and then convert the music into a Sound Blaster-compatible file.

☐ The second method is to look around on BBSs and other sources for songs that have already been converted into PC format. You can take these songs and use them in your games. However, again, you're up against the copyright and protection laws. You must ask the composer or originator of the music if you may use it.

In any case, once you have the music, you might want to change it around a little to make it more appropriate for your particular game. This may mean changing the octaves or tempo, or maybe even changing the instruments used to play the music. These changes and more can be done with different software packages that are designed for sequencing and editing music. There are hundreds of these programs available from the public domain and from commercial manufacturers, but you'll have to search them out for yourself.

Game Tools

We've talked enough about third-party tools to help us write our games. Now we must talk about the tools we write to help us create our games more easily. You see, many times when writing a game there are processes or tasks that must be done with data, sounds, graphics, or something else. Sometimes these operations are so difficult or tedious for humans to do, it makes sense to write a small program, or *tool*, to do it for you.

For example, I'm always using look-up tables in my programs, so one day I wrote a program that could create almost any kind of trigonometric look-up table you could think of and write it out to an ASCII file. As another example, you may have so many graphics images in your game that you may want to make a tool that can store them in some other file format and let you archive them until you need them. These are just a couple of examples of the tools you could create to help write a game.

There are millions of programs already written that could be helpful in the creation of a game, and your own imagination is the only gatekeeper on thinking of clever tools to speed things up. However, a couple of tools are classics, and I want to cover them next.

14

Map Editors

A *map editor* is a piece of software designed to help create the levels for a game you're making. For example, imagine that you decide to create a D&D-type game and you want to have 500 rooms. Each room can contain monsters, treasure, or other objects, and has an entrance and exit. Each of these rooms is represented by some data structure that contains the geometry of the room, along with the objects and their positions within the room. The problem is, how do you generate the data structure? Of course, you could type in thousands of lines of ASCII tokens—but there must be a better way.

The solution is to create a tool that enables you to use some kind of input device, such as a mouse or keyboard, to draw the room and place the objects. The tool then takes the input you give it and generates the proper data file. Once the tool creates the data file, that file can be read in by your game program and used during game play.

The map tool should be able to load rooms and edit them. Then the new room could be rewritten out to a file. This would enable you to quickly create hundreds of rooms once you had the tool written. Granted, it will take some time to write the map editor program, but (believe me!) it will be well worth the savings in frustration caused by doing the job manually. Furthermore, once you've written the tool, someone less technically inclined (such as an artist or designer) can create rooms for your game.

World Builders

World builders are a generalization of map editors. A map editor has a close relationship to the adventure or maze-type games for which it generates the environment. A world builder is something that can be used for anything.

For example, you may want to write a racing game that has a single track per level. In such a case:

☐ You could make a tool that enables you to draw the track in a single screen.

☐ Then you might use the world builder to alter or program in the parameters of the track. (For instance, you may want some areas of the track to have good traction, and others not.)

☐ Finally, you could use the world builder to set switches and flags in the video game. These switches could be logical conditions that, when made true, cause something to happen (such as a sound effect or explosion). For example, in your racing game, you might want to have a digitized sound effect make a

"bump" whenever the car passes over a certain portion of the track. You could point and click at the part of the track on which this effect should take place, and the data would be recorded in the final data structure along with the track itself. Then, when the data structure was loaded in by the game software, it would take into consideration all the extra elements you set up in the world tool.

Again, by having a piece of high-level software with an interface to build up a world, you can have someone other than a programmer make the levels.

A Few Last Additions to the Game Library

We've almost completed our game library. It's time to take a look at all the functions we have at our disposal, along with a description of each. Realize that the game library we've been creating in the past two weeks is quite general, and is only a starting point for you. There are many better ways to do everything, and I'm sure that I left out a lot of things that you might need. However, even using what we have, we should be able to write some good games.

There are a few areas that I'd do over given more time. For instance, the sprite engine's data structure isn't the best for applications that have many creatures with the same animation cells. In the Mech War game, for example, I used the sprite structure we created on Day 6. I soon realized that I was wasting a lot of memory, because all mechs look alike. Nevertheless, we live and learn. In a way it's good that the library isn't perfect, because as you use it to write games you'll realize how it needs to change. This will enable you to make an even more powerful library next time.

Before we start discussing all the functions in the library, I want to make a few final additions to it. On Day 5 we created a polygon engine that drew directly to the video screen and didn't use the double-buffer system. I feel we may use polygons in one or more of the small games we make in the week to come, so I want to add new versions of the polygon functions that have the double-buffer functionality. The final additions to the game library are in the files called graph14.c and graph14.h. The new functions allow lines and polygons to be drawn into the double buffer. As per our agreement on the naming convention for double buffer functions, the new functions have the same names, along with a _db appended to the function name.

Listing 14.1 contains the C module for the last additions to the game library.

Listing 14.1. The last additions to the game library (graph14.c).

```c
// I N C L U D E S ////////////////////////////////////////////

#include <io.h>
#include <conio.h>
#include <stdio.h>
#include <stdlib.h>
#include <dos.h>
#include <bios.h>
#include <fcntl.h>
#include <memory.h>
#include <malloc.h>
#include <math.h>
#include <string.h>

#include "graph3.h"  // include our graphics stuff
#include "graph4.h"
#include "graph5.h"
#include "graph6.h"
#include "graph14.h"

// F U N C T I O N S ////////////////////////////////////////////

void Draw_Polygon_DB(polygon_ptr poly)
{
// this function draws a polygon into
// the double buffer without clipping
// caller should make sure that vertices
// are within bounds of clipping
// rectangle, also the polygon will always
// be unfilled regardless
// of the fill flag

int index,xo,yo;

// extract local origin

xo = poly->lxo;
yo = poly->lyo;

// draw polygon

for (index=0; index<poly->num_vertices-1; index++)
    {

    Bline_DB(xo+(int)poly->vertices[index].x,
            yo+(int)poly->vertices[index].y,
            xo+(int)poly->vertices[index+1].x,
            yo+(int)poly->vertices[index+1].y,
            poly->b_color);

    } // end for index

    // close polygon?

    if (!poly->closed)
```

```
        return;

    Bline_DB(xo+(int)poly->vertices[index].x,
             yo+(int)poly->vertices[index].y,
             xo+(int)poly->vertices[0].x,
             yo+(int)poly->vertices[0].y,
             poly->b_color);


} // end Draw_Polygon_DB

////////////////////////////////////////////////////////////////

void Draw_Polygon_Clip_DB(polygon_ptr poly)
{

// this function draws a polygon into the double
// buffer with clipping
// also the polygon will always be unfilled regardless
// of the fill flag in the polygon structure

int index,  // loop index
    xo,yo,  // local origin
    x1,y1,  // end points of current line being processed
    x2,y2;

// extract local origin

xo = poly->lxo;
yo = poly->lyo;

// draw polygon

for (index=0; index<poly->num_vertices-1; index++)
    {

    // extract the line

    x1 = (int)poly->vertices[index].x+xo;
    y1 = (int)poly->vertices[index].y+yo;

    x2 = (int)poly->vertices[index+1].x+xo;
    y2 = (int)poly->vertices[index+1].y+yo;

    // clip line to viewing screen and
    // draw unless line is totally invisible

    if (Clip_Line(&x1,&y1,&x2,&y2))
        {
        // line was clipped and now can be drawn
        Bline_DB(x1,y1,x2,y2,poly->b_color);

        } // end if draw line

    } // end for index

    // close polygon?          // close polygon
```

14

Listing 14.1. continued

```c
    if (!poly->closed)
      return;

    // extract the line

    x1 = (int)poly->vertices[index].x+xo;
    y1 = (int)poly->vertices[index].y+yo;

    x2 = (int)poly->vertices[0].x+xo;
    y2 = (int)poly->vertices[0].y+yo;

    // clip line to viewing screen and
    // draw unless line is totally invisible

    if (Clip_Line(&x1,&y1,&x2,&y2))
      {

      // line was clipped and now can be drawn

      Bline_DB(x1,y1,x2,y2,poly->b_color);

      } // end if draw line

} // end Draw_Polygon_Clip_DB

///////////////////////////////////////////////////////////////

void Bline_DB(int xo,int yo,int x1,int y1,unsigned char color)
{
// this function uses Bresenham's algorithm IBM (1965)
// to draw a line from
// (xo,yo) - (x1,y1) into the double buffer

int dx,       // difference in x's
    dy,       // difference in y's
    x_inc,    // amount in pixel space to move during drawing
    y_inc,    // amount in pixel space to move during drawing
    error=0,  // the discriminant i.e. error i.e.
              // decision variable
    index;    // used for looping


unsigned char far *vb_start = double_buffer; // directly access
                                             // the double
                                             // buffer for speed


// SECTION 1 //////////////////////////////////////////////////

// pre-compute first pixel address in video buffer
// use shifts for multiplication

vb_start = vb_start + ((unsigned int)yo<<6) +
                        ((unsigned int)yo<<8) +
```

```
                    (unsigned int)xo;

// compute deltas

dx = x1-xo;
dy = y1-yo;

// SECTION 2 ////////////////////////////////////////////////////////

// test which direction the line is going in i.e. slope angle

if (dx>=0)
   {
   x_inc = 1;

   } // end if line is moving right
else
   {
   x_inc = -1;
   dx     = -dx;   // need absolute value

   } // end else moving left

// SECTION 3 ////////////////////////////////////////////////////////

// test y component of slope

if (dy>=0)
   {
   y_inc = 320; // 320 bytes per line

   } // end if line is moving down
else
   {
   y_inc = -320;
   dy    = -dy;   // need absolute value

   } // end else moving up

// SECTION 4 ////////////////////////////////////////////////////////

// now based on which delta is greater we can draw the line

if (dx>dy)
   {

   // draw the line

   for (index=0; index<=dx; index++)
       {
       // set the pixel

       *vb_start = color;

       // adjust the discriminate

       error+=dy;
```

Listing 14.1. continued

```
                    // test if error overflowed

            if (error>dx)
               {

               error-=dx;

               // move to next line

               vb_start+=y_inc;

               } // end if error overflowed

            // move to the next pixel

            vb_start+=x_inc;

            } // end for

      } // end if ¦slope¦ <= 1
else
      {

// SECTION 5 //////////////////////////////////////////////////////////

      // draw the line

      for (index=0; index<=dy; index++)
            {
            // set the pixel

            *vb_start = color;

            // adjust the discriminate

            error+=dx;

            // test if error overflowed

            if (error>0)
               {

               error-=dy;

               // move to next line

               vb_start+=x_inc;

               } // end if error overflowed

            // move to the next pixel

            vb_start+=y_inc;
```

```
        } // end for

    } // end else ¦slope¦ > 1

} // end Bline_DB
```

The new functions in Listing 14.1 are almost identical to the old ones that wrote to the video screen, except that wherever there was a reference to `video_buffer` I changed it to `double_buffer`. This is an inefficient way of doing things, and a more elegant method could have been implemented with pointers. However, the path was already taken, and the easiest (that is, fastest) solution was to just copy the code and make the changes. Furthermore, in this case the replicated functions take only an extra kilobyte or two, so I wouldn't worry about it.

The Game Library: A Functional Description

We now have a complete graphics, sound, multitasking, and input library with which to write games. It seems appropriate that we should have a functional listing, just as you'd see with any run-time library you could purchase commercially. What I do in this section is take the library file and extract all the functions and modules they came from to create a clean, functional listing you can use as a reference when writing your games. This may be boring, but read it at least once. I remember something that a math professor once told me: "There are worse things a man can do than read the *Microsoft C Run-Time Library Reference Book*." (He was correct! You'd really be surprised at all the interesting functions the compiler has.)

Anyway, here is a description of our library.

Day 3—Module Name: graph3.c

Function syntax:

```
void H_Line_Fast(int x1,int x2,int y,unsigned int color);
```

Description:

> This function draws a horizontal line in the video buffer using WORD-sized video writes.

Parameters:

- ☐ *x1*: the starting x position

- ☐ *x2*: the ending x position

- ☐ *y*: the y position on which the line is to be drawn

- ☐ *color*: the color of the line

Return value: None

Function syntax:

```
void V_Line(int y1,int y2,int x,unsigned int color);
```

Description:

This function draws a vertical line directly into the video buffer.

Parameters:

- ☐ *y1*: The starting y position of the line

- ☐ *y2*: The ending y position of the line

- ☐ *x*: The x position of the line

- ☐ *color*: The color of the line

Return value: None

Function syntax:

```
void Set_Palette_Register(int index, RGB_color_ptr color);
```

Description:

This function sets the RED, GREEN, and BLUE components of a palette register in the VGA card.

Parameters:

- ☐ *index*: The color register to set, from 0–255

- ☐ *color*: A pointer to the color structure holding the desired new color

Return value: None

Function syntax:

```
void Get_Palette_Register(int index, RGB_color_ptr color);
```

Description:

This function reads the contents of a color register.

Parameters:

☐ *index*: The color register to be read, from 0–255

☐ *color*: A pointer to the storage structure in which the extracted color is saved

Return value: None

Function syntax:

```
void Blit_Char(int xc,int yc,char c,int color,int trans_flag);
```

Description:

This function draws a character from the 8×8 ROM character set into the video buffer.

Parameters:

☐ *xc*: The x-coordinate of the character in pixels

☐ *yc*: The y-coordinate of the character in pixels

☐ *c*: The ASCII code of the character

☐ *color*: The color of the character, from 0–255

☐ *trans_flag*: Determines whether the background shows through the character: if set to one, the background is visible; if set to zero, the background is obscured

Return value: None

Function syntax:

```
void Blit_String(int x,int y,int color, char *string,int trans_flag);
```

Description:

This function is based on the character function and prints a string to the video buffer.

Parameters:

☐ *x*: The x position of the string

☐ *y*: The y position of the string

☐ *color*: The color of the printed string

☐ *string*: A pointer to a NULL terminated ASCII string

☐ *trans_flag*: Determines whether the background shows through the character: if set to one, the background is visible; if set to zero, the background is obscured

Return value: None

14

Function syntax:

```
void Plot_Pixel(int x,int y,unsigned char color);
```

Description:

This function plots a pixel into the video buffer.

Parameters:

- ☐ *x*: The x-coordinate of the pixel
- ☐ *y*: The y-coordinate of the pixel
- ☐ *color*: The color of the pixel

Return value: None

Function syntax:

```
void Plot_Pixel_Fast(int x,int y,unsigned char color);
```

Description:

This function plots a pixel into the video buffer using a fast shift multiply.

Parameters:

- ☐ *x*: The x-coordinate of the pixel
- ☐ *y*: The y-coordinate of the pixel
- ☐ *color*: The color of the pixel

Return value: None

Function syntax:

```
void Set_Video_Mode(int mode);
```

Description:

This function switches the video mode of the VGA card.

Parameters:

- ☐ *mode*: The new video mode you wish the VGA set to from 0–0x0F.

Return value: None

Function syntax:

```
void Delay(int clicks);
```

Description:

This function makes the system wait for a number of system clock ticks. The internal timer is usually set for 18.2 per second.

Parameters:

☐ *clicks*: The number of clock ticks you wish to wait for

Return value: None

Day 4—Module Name: graph4.c

Function syntax:

```
void PCX_Init(pcx_picture_ptr image);
```

Description:

This function initializes a PCX image structure that is used to load and work with a PCX file.

Parameters:

☐ *image*: A pointer to the PCX image structure you wish initialized

Return value: None

Function syntax:

```
void PCX_Load(char *filename, pcx_picture_ptr image,int enable_palette);
```

Description:

This function loads a PCX file off disk into the local buffer within a PCX structure.

Parameters:

☐ *filename*: The filename of the PCX file you wish loaded off disk

☐ *image*: A pointer to the PCX structure into which you want the image data loaded

☐ enable_palette: If true, indicates to load the color palette information along with the image data; if false, does not load the palette

Return value: None

Function syntax:

```
void PCX_Delete(pcx_picture_ptr image);
```

Description:

>   This function deletes the memory used up by the temporary image buffer that was created during the initialization of a PCX image structure.

Parameters:

☐   *image*: The pointer to the PCX image structure you wish to delete

Return value: None

Function syntax:

```
void PCX_Show_Buffer(pcx_picture_ptr image);
```

Description:

>   This function displays the data loaded into a PCX image structure on the video screen.

Parameters:

☐   *image*: A pointer to a PCX image structure into which a PCX file has been loaded

Return value: None

Function syntax:

```
void Sprite_Init(sprite_ptr sprite,int x,int y,int ac,int as,int mc,int ms);
```

Description:

>   This function initializes a sprite structure.

Parameters:

☐   *sprite*: A pointer to the sprite structure

☐   *x*: The initial x position of the sprite

☐   *y*: The initial y position of the sprite

☐   *ac*: The initial value of the animation counter

☐   *as*: The initial value of the animation speed

☐   *mc*: The initial value of the motion counter

☐   *ms*: The initial value of the motion speed

Return value: None

Function syntax:

```
void Sprite_Delete(sprite_ptr sprite);
```

Description:

This function frees up the memory used by a sprite.

Parameters:

☐ *sprite*: A pointer to the sprite to be deleted

Return value: None

Function syntax:

```
void PCX_Grab_Bitmap(pcx_picture_ptr image,
                     sprite_ptr sprite,
                     int sprite_frame,
                     int grab_x, int grab_y);
```

Description:

This function extracts a rectangular bit map from a PCX file structure and places it into one of the animation cells of a sprite.

Parameters:

☐ *image*: A pointer to the PCX image structure into which an image has been loaded

☐ *sprite*: A pointer to the sprite

☐ *sprite_frame*: The cell number to extract the bit map from

☐ *grab_x*: The x-cell position of the bit map to extract

☐ *grab_y*: The y-cell position of the bit map to extract

Return value: None

Function syntax:

```
void Behind_Sprite(sprite_ptr sprite);
```

Description:

This function scans the background under a sprite and saves it in the sprite structure.

Parameters:

☐ *sprite*: A pointer to the sprite object within which the background is saved

14

Tools of the Trade

Return value: None

Function syntax:

```
void Erase_Sprite(sprite_ptr sprite);
```

Description:

This function erases a sprite that had previously been drawn on the video screen.

Parameters:

□ *sprite*: A pointer to the sprite to be erased

Return value: None

Function syntax:

```
void Draw_Sprite(sprite_ptr sprite);
```

Description:

This function draws a sprite directly into the video buffer.

Parameters:

□ *sprite*: A pointer to the sprite to be drawn on the screen

Return value: None

Function syntax:

```
unsigned char Get_Pixel(int x,int y);
```

Description:

This function extracts a single pixel from the video buffer and returns the color value.

Parameters:

□ *x*: The x-coordinate of the pixel to be extracted

□ *y*: The y-coordinate of the pixel to be extracted

Return value: A byte representing the color of the scanned pixel

Function syntax:

```
int Sprite_Collide(sprite_ptr sprite_1, sprite_ptr sprite_2);
```

Description:

This function tests whether the bounding boxes of two sprites have intersected.

Parameters:

- □ *sprite_1*: A pointer to the first test sprite

- □ *sprite_2*: A pointer to the second test sprite

Return value: If there was an intersection, 1; otherwise, 0

Day 5—Module Name: graph5.c

Function syntax:

```
void Create_Tables(void);
```

Description:

This is an internal function that creates the trigonometric look-up tables for the polygon engine.

Parameters: None

Return value: None

Function syntax:

```
void Rotate_Polygon(polygon_ptr poly, int angle);
```

Description:

This function rotates a polygon a specified number of degrees counter clockwise.

Parameters:

- □ *poly*: A pointer to the polygon structure to be rotated

- □ *angle*: An integer representing the angle to rotate the polygon

Return value: None

Function syntax:

```
void Scale_Polygon(polygon_ptr poly, float scale);
```

Description:

This function scales a polygon by the given scale factor.

Parameters:

- □ *poly*: A pointer to the polygon structure to be scaled

- □ *scale*: The scaling factor by which to scale the polygon

Return value: None

Function syntax:

```
void Translate_Polygon(polygon_ptr poly, int dx,int dy);
```

Description:

This function translates a polygon.

Parameters:

- □ *poly*: A pointer to the polygon structure to translate
- □ *dx*: The amount of translation in the x direction
- □ *dy*: The amount of translation in the y direction

Return value: None

Function syntax:

```
void Draw_Polygon(polygon_ptr poly);
```

Description:

This function draws a polygon to the video buffer.

Parameters:

- □ *poly*: A pointer to the polygon to be drawn

Return value: None

Function syntax:

```
int Clip_Line(int *x1,int *y1,int *x2, int *y2);
```

Description:

This function clips the line segment defined by the endpoints (x1,y1) to (x2,y2) to the view window.

Parameters:

- □ *x1*: A pointer to the first x-coordinate of the line
- □ *y1*: A pointer to the first y-coordinate of the line
- □ *x2*: A pointer to the second x-coordinate of the line
- □ *y2*: A pointer to the second y-coordinate of the line

Return value: If clipping was done on the line, this function alters the sent variables passed as pointers to those of the new clipped line endpoints; otherwise, the line's endpoints are left untouched

Function syntax:

```
void Draw_Polygon_Clip(polygon_ptr poly);
```

Description:

This function draws a clipped polygon directly into the video buffer.

Parameters:

☐ *poly*: A pointer to the polygon to draw

Return value: None

Function syntax:

```
void Bline(int xo, int yo, int x1,int y1, unsigned char color);
```

Description:

This function draws a line directly into the video buffer from (xo,yo) to (x1,y1).

Parameters:

☐ *xo*: The initial x endpoint of the line

☐ *yo*: The initial y endpoint of the line

☐ *x1*: The final x endpoint of the line

☐ *y1*: The final y endpoint of the line

☐ *color*: The color of the line

Return value: None

Function syntax:

```
void Draw_Boundary(int color);
```

Description:

This function draws the clipping rectangle directly into the video buffer.

Parameters:

☐ *color*: The color with which to draw the clipping rectangle

Return value: None

14

Day 6—Module Name: graph6.c

Function syntax:

```
void Show_Double_Buffer(char far *buffer);
```

Description:

This function copies the double buffer to the video buffer so it becomes visible.

Parameters:

☐ *buffer*: A pointer to the double buffer memory

Return value: None

Function syntax:

```
int Create_Double_Buffer(int num_lines);
```

Description:

This function creates a double buffer of a given size.

Parameters:

☐ *num_lines*: The number of scan lines or rows to make the double buffer

Return value: If the double buffer was successfully created, 1; otherwise, 0

Function syntax:

```
void Fill_Double_Buffer(int color);
```

Description:

This function fills the double buffer with a solid color.

Parameters:

☐ *color*: The color with which to fill the double buffer

Return value: None

Function syntax:

```
void Delete_Double_Buffer(void);
```

Description:

This function deletes the double buffer and frees up its memory.

Parameters: None

Return value: None

Function syntax:

```
void Plot_Pixel_Fast_DB(int x,int y,unsigned char color);
```

Description:

This function draws a pixel into the double buffer using a fast multiply technique.

Parameters:

☐ *x*: The x-coordinate of the pixel

☐ *y*: The y-coordinate of the pixel

☐ *color*: The color of the pixel

Return value: None

Function syntax:

```
void Scale_Sprite(sprite_ptr sprite,float scale);
```

Description:

This function scales a sprite and draws it directly to the video buffer.

Parameters:

☐ *sprite*: A pointer to the sprite to be scaled

☐ *scale*: The scaling factor

Return value: None

Function syntax:

```
void Fade_Lights(void);
```

Description:

This function is a self-contained screen transition that has the effect of fading the lights.

Parameters: None

Return value: None

Function syntax:

```
void Disolve(void);
```

14

Description:

> This function is a self-contained screen transition that has the effect of dissolving the screen.

Parameters: None

Return value: None

Function syntax:

```
void Melt(void);
```

Description:

> This function is a self-contained screen transition that has the effect of melting the screen.

Parameters: None

Return value: None

Function syntax:

```
void Sheer(void);
```

Description:

> This function is a self-contained screen transition that has the effect of a "wipe," or shear.

Parameters: None

Return value: None

Function syntax:

```
void Wait_For_Vsync(void);
```

Description:

> This function waits for the next vertical synchronization pulse.

Parameters: None

Return value: None

Function syntax:

```
void Behind_Sprite_DB(sprite_ptr sprite);
```

Description:

> This function scans the background under a sprite in the double buffer.

Parameters:

☐ *sprite*: A pointer to the sprite structure

Return value: None

Function syntax:

```
void Erase_Sprite_DB(sprite_ptr sprite);
```

Description:

This function erases a sprite in the double buffer.

Parameters:

☐ *sprite*: A pointer to the sprite to erase

Return value: None

Function syntax:

```
void Draw_Sprite_DB(sprite_ptr sprite);
```

Description:

This function draws a sprite into the double buffer.

Parameters:

☐ *sprite*: The pointer to the sprite to be drawn into the double buffer

Return value: None

Function syntax:

```
void Blit_Char_DB(int xc,int yc,char c,int color,int trans_flag);
```

Description:

This function draws a single 8×8 character from the ROM character set into the double buffer.

Parameters:

☐ *xc*: The x pixel location at which to draw the character

☐ *yc*: The y pixel location at which to draw the character

☐ *c*: The ASCII code of the character to be drawn

☐ *color*: The color of the character

☐ *trans_flag*: Determines whether the background shows through the character: if set to one, the background is visible; if set to zero, the background is obscured

14

Return value: None

Function syntax:

```
void Blit_String_DB(int x,int y,int color, char *string,int trans_flag);
```

Description:

This function prints an entire screen into the double buffer.

Parameters:

- □ *x*: The x position of the string to be printed

- □ *y*: The y position of the string to be printed

- □ *color*: The color of the string

- □ *string*: A pointer to a NULL terminated ASCII string

- □ *trans_flag*: Determines whether the background shows through the character: if set to one, the background is visible; if set to zero, the background is obscured

Return value: None

Day 7—Module Name(s): graph7j.c, graph7k.c, graph7m.c

Function syntax:

```
unsigned char Buttons(unsigned char button);
```

Description:

This function reads the buttons on the joystick(s).

Parameters:

- □ *button*: A predefined constant that determines which button is being requested

Return value: If the button is down, 1; if the button is up, 0

Function syntax:

```
unsigned int Joystick(unsigned char stick);
```

Description:

This function reads one of the potentiometers of a joystick.

Parameters:

- □ *stick*: A constant that determines which joystick potentiometer to read

Return value: The value of the joystick potentiometer

Function syntax:

```
unsigned int Joystick_Bios(unsigned char stick);
```

Description:

This function uses the system BIOS to read one of the joystick potentiometers.

Parameters:

☐ *stick*: The constant value that determines which joystick potentiometer to read

Return value: The value of the joystick potentiometer

Function syntax:

```
unsigned char Buttons_Bios(unsigned char button);
```

Description:

This function uses BIOS to determine the state of the joystick buttons.

Parameters:

☐ *button*: A constant that determines which button to test

Return value: If the button is down, 1; if the button is up, 0

Function syntax:

```
void Joystick_Calibrate(int stick);
```

Description:

This function calibrates a joystick so the maximum deflection of the yoke can be utilized.

Parameters:

☐ *stick*: The joystick to be calibrated

Return value: None

Function syntax:

```
int Joystick_Available(int stick_num);
```

Description:

This function tests whether a joystick is plugged into the system.

Parameters:

☐ *stick_num*: The joystick to be tested for existence

Return value: A Boolean value determining whether the stick is present.

Function syntax:

```
unsigned char Get_Ascii_Key(void);
```

Description:

This function gets an ASCII key from the keyboard with full translation.

Parameters: None

Return value: The ASCII key in the keyboard buffer

Function syntax:

```
unsigned int Get_Control_Keys(unsigned int mask);
```

Description:

This function gets the control keys of the keyboard such as the shift keys, control keys, alt keys and so on.

Parameters:

☐ *mask*: A binary mask used to select which key is being tested

Return value: If the key is being pressed, a non-zero value; if the key is not being pressed, 0

Function syntax:

```
unsigned char Get_Scan_Code(void);
```

Description:

This function gets the scan code of the key being pressed.

Parameters: None

Return value: The scan code of the last pressed key

Function syntax:

```
int Squeeze_Mouse(int command, int *x, int *y,int *buttons);
```

Description:

This function accesses the mouse position, state, and buttons.

Parameters:

☐ *command*: A constant determining what parameter of the mouse is being set or queried

☐ *x*: A pointer to the x position or x quantity of the mouse

☐ *y*: A pointer to the y position or y quantity of the mouse

☐ *buttons*: The state of the buttons

Return value: The success or failure of function; the meaning depends on the command sent

Day 8—Module Name: graph8.c

Function syntax:

```
fixed Assign_Integer(long integer);
```

Description:

This function assigns an integer to a fixed-point number.

Parameters:

☐ *integer*: The number to be converted into a fixed-point number

Return value: The resulting fixed-point number

Function syntax:

```
fixed Assign_Float(float number);
```

Description:

This function assigns a floating-point number to a fixed-point number.

Parameters:

☐ *number*: The floating-point number to be converted to a fixed-point number

Return value: The resulting fixed-point number

Function syntax:

```
fixed Mul_Fixed(fixed f1,fixed f2);
```

14

Description:

This function multiplies two fixed-point numbers together.

Parameters:

- *f1*: The multiplier
- *f2*: The multiplicand

Return value: The result of the multiplication

Function syntax:

```
fixed Div_Fixed(fixed f1,fixed f2);
```

Description:

This function divides one fixed-point number by another.

Parameters:

- *f1*: The dividend
- *f2*: The divisor

Return value: The result of the division

Function syntax:

```
fixed Add_Fixed(fixed f1,fixed f2);
```

Description:

This function adds two fixed-point numbers together.

Parameters:

- *f1*: The first number to be added
- *f2*: The second number to be added

Return value: The result of the addition

Function syntax:

```
fixed Sub_Fixed(fixed f1,fixed f2);
```

Description:

This function subtracts one fixed-point number from another.

Parameters:

- *f1*: The first number
- *f2*: The number to be subtracted from the first number

Return value: The result of the subtraction

Function syntax:

```
void Print_Fixed(fixed f1);
```

Description:

This function prints out the whole part and decimal part of a fixed-point number.

Parameters:

☐ *f1*: The fixed-point number to be printed out

Return value: None

Day 9—Module Name: graph9.c

Function syntax:

```
void Voc_Get_Version(void);
```

Description:

This function prints out the version number of the VOC driver.

Parameters: None

Return value: None

Function syntax:

```
int Voc_Init_Driver(void);
```

Description:

This function initializes the VOC driver.

Parameters: None

Return value: Success or failure of driver initialization

Function syntax:

```
int Voc_Terminate_Driver(void);
```

Description:

This function terminates the VOC driver and frees its memory.

Parameters: None

Return value: Success or failure of the driver termination

14

Function syntax:

```
void Voc_Set_Port(unsigned int port);
```

Description:

This function sets the I/O port of the Sound Blaster.

Parameters:

☐ *port*: The I/O port for which the Sound Blaster is set

Return value: None

Function syntax:

```
void Voc_Set_Speaker(unsigned int on);
```

Description:

This function enables the Sound Blaster's audio output.

Parameters:

☐ *on*: If 1, the output is turned on; if 0, the output is turned off

Return value: None

Function syntax:

```
int Voc_Play_Sound(unsigned char far *addr,unsigned char header_length);
```

Description:

This function plays a preloaded VOC file.

Parameters:

☐ *addr*: The address of the raw sound data in memory

☐ *header_length*: The length of the header portion of the VOC file

Return value: If successful, 1; otherwise, 0

Function syntax:

```
int Voc_Stop_Sound(void);
```

Description:

This function stops a sound from playing.

Parameters: None

Return value: Success or failure of the termination of sound

Function syntax:

```
int Voc_Pause_Sound(void);
```

Description:

This function pauses a sound that is playing.

Parameters: None

Return value: Success or failure of the pause

Function syntax:

```
int Voc_Continue_Sound(void);
```

Description:

This function continues a sound that had been previously paused.

Parameters: None

Return value: Success or failure of the continuation of a previously paused sound

Function syntax:

```
int Voc_Break_Sound(void);
```

Description:

This function breaks a sound loop.

Parameters: None

Return value: Success or failure of breaking a sound loop

Function syntax:

```
void Voc_Set_IRQ(unsigned int irq);
```

Description:

This function sets the IRQ interrupt request number for the Sound Blaster.

Parameters:

☐ *dma*: The interrupt number

Return value: None

Function syntax:

```
void Voc_Set_Status_Addr(char far *status);
```

14

Description:

> This function sets the status variable in the VOC driver to a globally accessible variable in the C program.

Parameters:

☐ *status*: A pointer to the variable into which the VOC driver should place its status

Return value: None

Function syntax:

```
void Voc_Load_Driver(void);
```

Description:

> This function loads the ct-voice.drv sound driver into system memory.

Parameters: None

Return value: None

Function syntax:

```
char far *Voc_Load_Sound(char *filename, unsigned char *header_length);
```

Description:

> This function loads a VOC file off disk into memory.

Parameters:

☐ *filename*: The name of the VOC file to load

☐ *header_length*: A pointer to a variable in which the header length of the loaded VOC file is stored

Return value: A pointer to the start of the loaded VOC file in memory

Function syntax:

```
void Voc_Unload_Sound(char far *sound_ptr);
```

Description:

> This function frees the memory used up by a loaded VOC file.

Parameters:

☐ *sound_ptr*: A pointer to the beginning of a previously loaded VOC file

Return value: None

Day 11—Module Name: graph11.c

Function syntax:

```
void Change_Timer(unsigned int new_count);
```

Description:

This function reprograms the internal timer.

Parameters:

☐ *new_count*: The new 16-bit counter value that should be programmed into the timer

Return value: None

Function syntax:

```
void Initialize_Kernal(void);
```

Description:

This function initializes the multitasking kernel.

Parameters: None

Return value: None

Function syntax:

```
void Start_Kernal(void);
```

Description:

This function starts the multitasking kernel and loads the ISR that does the multitasking.

Parameters: None

Return value: None

Function syntax:

```
void Stop_Kernal(void);
```

Description:

This function stops the multitasking kernel and unloads the ISR.

Parameters: None

Return value: None

14

Function syntax:

```
int Add_Task(void (far *function)());
```

Description:

This function adds a task into the task list of the multitasking kernel.

Parameters:

☐ *function*: A function pointer to a function that should be multitasked

Return value: The ID number of the task

Function syntax:

```
int Delete_Task(int id);
```

Description:

This function deletes a task from the task list.

Parameters:

☐ *id*: The ID number of the task to remove

Return value: If the task was removed, 1; otherwise, 0

Function syntax:

```
void _interrupt far Multi_Kernal(void);
```

Description:

This is an internal function and is the actual multitasking kernel.

Parameters: None

Return value: None

Function syntax:

```
void Install_Keyboard(void)
```

Description:

This function installs the new low-level keyboard handler that enables you to receive multiple key presses.

Parameters: None

Return value: None

Function syntax:

```
void Delete_Keyboard(void)
```

Description:

This function removes the keyboard handler and restores the previously installed keyboard ISR.

Parameters: None

Return value: None

Day 14—Module Name: graph14.c

Function syntax:

```
void Draw_Polygon_DB(polygon_ptr poly);
```

Description:

This function draws a polygon into the double buffer.

Parameters:

☐ *poly*: A pointer to the poly to draw

Return value: None

Function syntax:

```
void Draw_Polygon_Clip_DB(polygon_ptr poly);
```

Description:

This function draw a clipped polygon into the double buffer.

Parameters:

☐ *poly*: A pointer to the polygon to draw

Return value: None

Function syntax:

```
void Bline_DB(int xo, int yo, int x1,int y1, unsigned char color);
```

Description:

This function draws a line into the double buffer from (xo,yo) to (x1,y1).

14

Parameters:

- ☐ *xo*: The initial x-coordinate of the line
- ☐ *yo*: The initial y-coordinate of the line
- ☐ *x1*: The final x-coordinate of the line
- ☐ *y1*: The final y-coordinate of the line
- ☐ *color*: The color of the line

Return value: None

Summary

Today we covered many topics relating to tools available from commercial vendors, as well as those you may wish to create to help yourself build games more efficiently. We learned about graphics packages and even that there are sources of prerecorded sound FX we can use in our games. We then took a look at some classic tools that often are used when writing games, such as map editors and world builders. Finally, we saw the whole game library listed, function by function—and I'll bet you didn't think we'd written so much code!

Q&A

Q Why are tools necessary?

A Tools are needed to help speed up and automate the creation of a video game. Without them, some tasks would be impossible to do. Imagine drawing bit maps on paper and converting them to pixel values instead of using a paint program!

Q What's the advantage of using a piece of software to draw levels, rather than drawing levels by hand?

A The advantages are that you can use an interface; the levels can be stored in an abstract data form; and a nontechnical person can create levels for the games.

Q Will we add any more functions to the game library?

A We definitely write more functions in the coming week. However, we may not add them to the library, as most of the functions are specific to each game.

Q Can I use the game library to write games and then sell those games commercially?

A Yes. The code is yours to do with as you wish.

Workshop

The Workshop section presents quiz questions to help you cement your new knowledge and exercises to give you experience using what you've learned. Try to understand the questions and exercises before moving on to the next lesson. The answers are in Appendix B.

Quiz

1. What is a map editor?

2. What is a sequencer?

3. Why is it important that the paint program we use be able to run in mode 13h?

4. Is it legal to copy sounds from movies, CDs, or tapes?

Exercises

1. Go to a store and research about a half dozen or so paint programs.

2. See how much it would cost to build a production studio for miniature modeling.

3. Make a library of sound effects.

14

Day 8

Video games are the most performance-intensive applications that exist. On this day, you learned how to avoid writing inefficient code, as well as how to find possible optimizations and then how to make them. Day 8 covered assembly language, loop unrolling, look-up tables, register usage, parameter passing, 32-bit programming, and more.

Day 9

A game is not a game without sound. During this day, you learned about the fundamentals of sound and the architecture of the Sound Blaster. Then you learned how to play digitized sound effects using the CT-VOICE.DRV driver. You were shown the basics of playing MIDI music.

Day 10

You learned how to make the PC think, or seem to think, in order to make the creatures in your games intelligent. You discovered probability techniques, state machines, and personality look-ups, and then used these techniques to create some fairly realistic models.

Day 11

This day was probably one of the most interesting you had. The magic of interrupts and multitasking were covered, as well as how the two most important interrupts of all (keyboard and timer) are controlled. Finally, an entire multitasking kernel was created for you to use in your games.

Day 12

A video game needs to take place in the computer, meaning it needs a simulated environment. On this day, you learned how to efficiently represent this environment with cell-based worlds, vector-based worlds, and a hybrid of both.

Day 13

Whether or not you like physics, you learned that you had better understand physics because it's needed to create video games. On this day, you learned how to model some basic manifestations of the universe, such as velocity, acceleration, momentum, friction, gravity, and collisions.

Day 14

There is more to a video game than the program itself. There are the artwork, the sound, the music, the idea, and many other resources that need to be part of the overall product. Today you learned about all these topics, and then ended the day by looking at the complete game library and creating a functional listing of it.

3

WEEK

AT A GLANCE

15

16

17

18

19

20

21

At this point in the game, you are a master video programmer and are ready to start making games. Hence, you learn some of the details that you need to consider in order to make a complete game. Following those lessons, you see four complete games and analyze their functions. At the end of the week, you learn a little about 3-D games, as well as how to market your creations. (Remember me if you get rich!)

Where You're Going

On Day 15, "Video Game Design Philosophies," you learn the last of the techniques needed to make a complete game. On Day 16, "Blowing Things Up with Sea Shark!," you see the first of the games made using the game library. On Day 17, "Adventuring with Venture," you see how a top-view adventure game is made. On Day 18, "Simulating Cities with Sim-Pizza," you see how a simple autonomous city is created. Day 19, "Adventures in Text," is a treat for everyone and a trip back in history. You learn the much-coveted magic of text-based games and the complex parsing techniques that they employ. During Day 20, "Making the Quantum Leap to 3-D Space," you see what it takes to make a 3-D game. Finally, on Day 21, "Marketing your Creations," you learn how to make it big by selling your games. Who knows, maybe soon you'll be driving around in a Porsche 959. If you do, please give me a ride!

Video-Game Design Philosophies

We're almost ready to start writing games. We've covered all the technical aspects of video game design, and all that's left is the final touches that really are the icing on the cake. Today we talk about a potpourri of topics ranging from game introductions to installation programs. The idea of today's discussion is to introduce you to some of the elements of a video game that are of a more creative nature. Therefore, I want you to relax today and read the following pages like a story instead of a technical manual. Every person reading this material will get something slightly different out of it, because everyone will have their own ideas about how the ideas presented here today will be implemented in their own games. Here's what we cover:

- Introductions and cut scenes
- Setup and installation
- Input devices
- High scores
- Saving the game
- Pausing the action
- User interfaces
- Demo modes
- Setting the difficulty level
- Using memory
- Multiple players
- Add-on modules
- Compatibility
- Copy protection

Introductions

The introduction of a video game is important. Some games have incredible, elaborate introductions that are rendered in 3-D and make the player think that the game that follows is going to be just as good. In other cases, there isn't an introduction scene at all and the game may sit in demo mode or at an introductory scene that's a static image. In this case, the game itself is probably so strong that an introduction with a lot of glitz isn't necessary.

A good rule of thumb to follow when creating introductions to games is to make the introduction tell a story about the game that's about to be played. It's all right to put incredible graphics and animation into the introduction as long as you don't try to suggest to the player that the game will look equally as good. If the player has super-high expectations based on the introduction, he or she may be really let down by the game itself. Therefore, you should endeavor to match the introduction with the game itself, and try to make the introduction tell a little story (even if the story is only made up). By doing this, you place the player into an imaginary land, and their imagination becomes a help instead of a hindrance to the game presentation itself.

Cut Scenes

Any good game should have goals: finding the scroll, solving the puzzle, blowing everything in the level away, and so forth. When the player reaches a point in the game at which something important has been accomplished, or something is about to radically change, there should be some kind of *cut scene*, or extra animation, to tell a little story and reward the player. For example, when the player completes a level, perhaps a creature can appear and talk to the player from the screen. The creature could give the player another hint about the game. Another idea is to have the game go into an autopilot mode, where the character performs a few really cool actions that the player can watch like a movie.

Whatever you decide to do, try to have some extra footage in the game to reward the player and make him or her say, "Wow, that's cool!" Of course, there's a negative side to cut scenes: a player may like the scene the first few times, but at some point the cut scene may get boring. Hence, you should try to keep them short and to the point, and always allow some keyboard stroke to exit the cut scene (and the introduction, for that matter).

Setup and Installation

Every game you play must have some kind of installation procedure to load the game onto the hard drive, or at least create some kind of configuration file. The key to creating a successful installation and setup program is *ease of use*. Don't rely on the user to have all the answers; don't assume that the 5.25-inch drive is drive A; and so forth. You should write software that checks out as much as possible about the system and then asks the user some really simple questions. The user shouldn't have to do more than select the destination drive of the game. The rest should be automated. Moreover, the installation software should take all input from the user only as a suggestion, and make tests to see whether the destination drive has enough memory and so on.

The next important thing is the installation interface. Make it simple, but elegant. Don't create an interface with a million buttons and inputs that are going to confuse the user and prolong the installation. Remember: a player wants to load the game as fast as possible and start playing it. Even if setting up the upper memory blocks a certain way and changing the number of wait states or memory accesses would help the game run faster, these are not the kinds of operations that should be done in an installation program. If your game must take a lot of highly technical aspects of the system into consideration, it might be wise to supply another program specifically for advanced installation. This program would let the more-seasoned users tweak the system to run the game at its fullest capacity.

Once the game is installed it's time to ask the user a few questions about graphics, sound cards, and so forth. As a developer, you should scan the entire *environment string*—a string kept by DOS that describes paths, sets, and related information—and extract as much information as possible from it, asking the user only what you can't get there. The only questions you should ask the user are those to which you can supply a set of possible answers. One thing you don't want to do is stump your users and frustrate them into a frenzy over game options.

Commonly, the most complex part of a setup program is the selection of the sound-system components, and maybe the alteration of the AUTOEXEC.BAT and CONFIG.SYS files. You should endeavor to make any of these selections or modifications reversible.

 Warning: If you modify any system files, always make a backup of them!

Input Devices

We've already covered the control and interface of all the popular input devices that can be used for a video game. However, we must talk about the *art* of interfacing, rather than just the nuts and bolts of it.

As a rule, you should support as many input devices as possible. Even though you may think a joystick is the only appropriate input device for a game, you should nevertheless support the keyboard and even a mouse (as awkward as a mouse may be). Furthermore, you should always allow the user to configure the input device to his or her liking. For example, in the case of a keyboard, you might allow them to select the function of each key.

Finally, the player should be able to change the input device during game play using a keystroke, such as a function key. In general, you should allow the player to access some kind of function menu that allows him or her to change certain aspects of the game as it's being played. These aspects could be the input device, the environment, the volume of the sound, and so forth.

High Scores

Every game should have some method of recording the player's score from previous games. This gives the player a sense of accomplishment while allowing him or her to strive in the next game to beat the highest recorded score.

The interface for entering the player's name is up to you. You can use a simple text-input box or an elaborate matrix of weird characters in a weird font selected by a pointer. In either case, the high-score table should be written to disk in a simple format (ASCII strings) and displayed during the introduction and end of the game.

Another nice touch you might want is to create a system of ranks or names for scores in specific ranges. For example, scores less than 100,000 points you might label as "rookie," and scores over 100,000 points might be called "pro." Remember: a game is an overall presentation from the beginning to end, and the more attention to detail a game has, the more the player will appreciate it.

Saving the Game

One of the biggest drawbacks to playing an arcade game is that you can't save the game! However, this is no problem with computer games. We have the ability to save the game, and we should exploit it. Many players can quickly become frustrated by a game they get half-way through and then have to start all over again. This is one of the fastest ways to lose player interest. (Granted, being able to save a game at any point does take some of the challenge out of it as the player can be more aggressive, knowing that he or she can revert to the saved game of a moment ago.)

Taking everything into consideration, you still should supply a save-game option and let the player make his or her own decision about the morality of continually saving the game. If you don't want to have a save-game option, another solution may be to supply codes to the player every time he or she completes a level. The player can type in these codes and start of at the beginning of that level instead of the beginning of the game. (There was a French game called Astro Marine Corps on the Amiga 500 computer that

I played for days, and every time I completed a level, the game would supply me a code that was a name of a spaceship from various movies.)

As far as the technical implementation of saving a game, it's fairly straightforward: you must create a disk file that contains the state and value of every variable in the game. This may be a tedious function to write, but it's not that hard. You have to make sure that when the game is restored, it's an exact copy of the game that was saved. The format of the data can be in either pure binary or ASCII text. I suggest using pure binary in this case, however, as you can read the data into a giant buffer and then load it into all the structures and variables in the game without translation.

Pausing the Action

There's a point in all games where the action gets to be too much and players need to take a break before their hearts burst! A pause option should be implemented as a keystroke that stops the entire game at the end of the game loop and displays some kind of banner indicating that the game has been paused. Moreover, a new practice I'm seeing more and more is that the lighting is dimmed. In other words, all the color registers' RGB values are decreased by a certain percentage. This makes for a nice effect, and I suggest you use it.

When a game is paused at the end of a game loop, you must make sure the *whole* game is paused. This means that any sounds or music playing on the sound system are terminated and any multitasking events halted until the game is resumed. Therefore, if your game has a complex multitasking system along with interrupt-driven sound, you should send messages to these subsystems and turn them off so the game isn't in a "quasipaused" mode!

Finally, to resume the game, the player should be able to press just about any key other than the pause key itself.

User Interfaces

The issue of user interfaces is definitely a topic on which there are as many opinions as there are interfaces. Nevertheless, the interface you should present to the player should be clean and to the point. The graphics should be nice, with a few extra blinking lights, gauges, or whatever, but the vital information must be easy to access visually. There's nothing worst than a confusing symbolic interface. (I am *so* tired of reading Klingon script in some of these games. For example, there is a D&D-type game that uses a version of the DOOM engine. I'm not going to name the game, but you practically need a linguist to decipher the icons on the screen controls.)

Using icons is fine, but make them look something like what they're supposed to represent. For example, if there's a weapon icon representing the current weapon, it should look like the weapon that's currently active. This means: a gun should look like a gun, not a firestick!

Game Law: Don't use digitized pictures of yourself in the user interface.

Finally, there are the topics of multiple interfaces and pop-up interfaces. *Multiple interfaces* mean that there is a region of the interface that can change with a keystroke. Within this region, the interface information and controls change to allow the player to view and control another aspect of the game. A word of wisdom: keep the number of interfaces down to three to five. If you need more, you should rethink the entire interface scheme because you must encapsulate more information in the displays.

Pop-up interfaces are similar to pop-up windows. They overlay the game surface. For example, you may want to have pop-up interfaces show the player a map of the game area, or a pop-up thermal image of the creature standing in front of you, and so on. You can have as many pop-up interfaces as you wish, as long as they aren't necessary for game play. You don't want the player frantically toggling through dozens of displays looking for the plasma cannon while he or she is being obliterated by a particle beam!

Demo Modes

All games should have a demo mode to give the player a taste of what the game has to offer, and to allow the game to do some advertising of its own.

There are a couple of popular ways to create demo modes:

☐ The first is to digitize yourself playing by recording the input data in a file as you play. Then the game runs, but instead of using a real input device as the input, the game reads a data file that simulates the input device. Figure 15.1 shows how this works.

You do have to take care digitizing this input. I suggest digitizing not the input device itself, but the motions. In other words, wait until the input has filtered all the way down to the control functions. The reason for this is the temporal and interrupt structure of the PC. Sometimes, keystrokes and input data are lost. If you siphon that data off at the point at which you're certain it's going to cause a change (that is, in the actual switch statements and control logic), you're assured that the digitized play will be faithfully reproduced.

☐ The second method of implementing a demo mode is to use a simple AI program to control the input device. The problem with using an AI system in your game's demo mode is that it's an order-of-magnitude more complex than simply digitizing your input and playing it back.

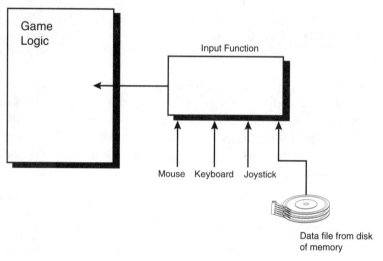

Figure 15.1. *Using a data file as an input device.*

Of course, that last statement depends on the type of game we're talking about. However, in general, writing software that makes the game character fight creatures in the game and successfully traverse a few of the levels is quite a challenge, and I suggest you use the first method of digitizing your own input and during the demo mode the input data is played back.

The format of the digitized records can be anything you like. For example, if you decide to digitize the joystick, you might create a record structure that has both the x and y deflection of the joystick, along with the buttons status. This information could be reconstructed in three bytes, and the digitized file would be a collection of these three-byte records.

Setting the Difficulty Level

Everyone is different, and some players will be able to think faster and move their characters more effectively than others. Therefore, your games should have some kind of difficulty-level setting that takes differences in the range of players into consideration. The difficulty level can be represented as a single variable, and this variable used as the input to many of the functions in the game.

As an example, say we wrote a shoot-'em-up game. We might use the difficulty setting to control the number of alien ships on the screen at a time, the probability of the aliens firing, and maybe even an input in the AI algorithms to control different aspects of the aliens' personalities, such as aggression and so forth. Also, we can use the difficulty setting to control the initial amount of fuel, weapon energy, time to complete each level, and other related factors.

Using Memory

The PC under DOS has 640K of system memory. However, as we all know, most PCs have a minimum of four megabytes of memory. The problem is how to use this extra memory. There are a few choices we can consider to access the full amount of memory of the PC:

- [ ] We can use a DOS extender, which we talked about in Day 8 (in the chapter called "Warp Speed, Anyone?").

- [ ] We can use the extended BIOS functions that support an expanded memory manager.

- [ ] We can use a virtual memory package that comes with some of the C compilers.

- [ ] We can create a RAM drive and use it as memory.

All of these tactics have their strong points and weak points. The most important question to ask is: what is the memory needed for? For example, you'll never be able to execute code of expanded or extended memory without a DOS extender (or manually placing the PC in protected mode yourself). If you need the extra memory for data storage, any of these techniques can be used. However, the data must be paged into the DOS working space by the expanded memory manager for you to have access to it. Figure 15.2 shows extra memory paged into DOS.

This kind of thrashing to memory is fine for loading in new levels and data, but a lot of paging during the game play is going to make the game seem "choppy."

There is no perfect solution to the problem, but there are some guidelines. If the system has more than 640K of memory, you should attempt in some manner to use it to minimize disk access—even if that only means creating a RAM drive and copying the files there. The days of using DOS as an excuse are over, and as game developers, we can no longer say that DOS has only 640K when the PC the game is running on might be equipped with 16 megabytes of memory!

Of course, you should try to minimize the amount of memory needed for a game. You'll get different answers depending on who you ask, but the common denominator is four

megabytes of RAM on a standard PC. As long as you follow this rule, a large majority of PC owners will be able to run your game on their system.

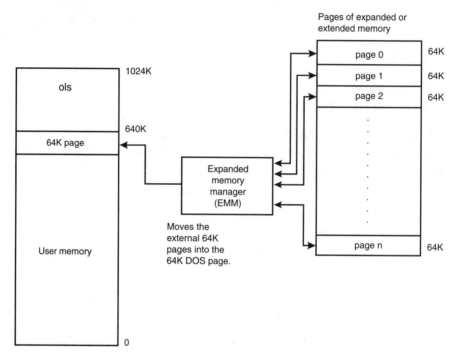

Figure 15.2. *Extra memory paged in to DOS.*

Multiple Players

Video games are great fun, and computer-generated opponents can be quite challenging, but sometimes people just want to destroy their friends or family on the virtual battlegrounds of the computer. Therefore, you should always try to accommodate multiple players in your games. On the PC there are some physical constraints that make more than two players impractical, so we should at least try to figure out ways to implement two players in a game. The players should have the option to play with each other, against each other, or taking turns (depending on game type).

Although we didn't really talk about multiplayer game design, there's nothing too hard about it. You just have two players instead of one, two input sources instead of one, and so on. (Writing networked games is difficult and a whole other ball game, but we aren't going to talk about that this time around.)

Finally, if the game is of the "take a turn" genre, such as a D&D or strategy game, any number of players can play because they can all take the keyboard or input device for their turn, giving it to the next player when their turn is up.

Add-On Modules

One of the greatest marketing ploys of all time is creating a product that can be enhanced by add-on modules or options. For instance, when you purchase an automobile, you are inundated by all the option packages. A video game is much the same. If the game is properly written, you can have add-on packages for extra levels, speech modules, multiplayer support, network support, and more. One of the most impressive uses of this technique has been with Wolfenstein 3-D by ID Software. They get you hooked on Level One of their games and then make you pay through the nose for the rest of the levels or modules.

This technique is now in wide use by most large game developers, such as Origin Systems, Accolade, and Electronic Arts. I suggest you start out simple and make add-on modules for your games only for extra levels. These extra levels should be easy to create if you use the proper tools to write your game, such as the world builders and map editors we discussed yesterday. If you design the game correctly, you can generate new levels and worlds in a matter of days—when the game itself may have taken months!

Compatibility

The sordid topic of compatibility...Taking into consideration that the IBM PC isn't PC compatible, we have to think a little about what this word means. In general, you should write your games using C, with in-line assembler when necessary. Don't use tricks with the VGA card that you're not absolutely sure will work on every PC. Finally, you should try to stay away from playing with the hardware of the PC too much.

Use the following system configuration as a target:

Processor:	386SX-25
Math co-processor:	None
Memory:	4M
Sound System:	Sound Blaster-compatible
Free Hard Drive Space:	20M
Input Devices:	Keyboard, mouse, and joystick

As you'll be using a standard C compiler, I also suggest that you set its option to use at least 286 instructions. Also, if you use any assembly language modules, don't use 486- or 586-specific instructions or registers. Stay compatible with the 386 processor.

Copy Protection

I'm really a good source of information when it comes to copy protection—I was a 15-year-old software pirate—so listen carefully. There's one rule when it comes to copy protection and I will place it in large letters for you:

Everything can be copied.

That sums it up for copy protection. The question is, can we take steps to make it at least a pain or inconvenient to copy a game? The answer is yes. However, there are only two ways to protect games these days and only one of them is worth talking about.

☐ The first method is to use a *dongle*, which is a piece of hardware you must plug into the PC to play the game. This method works, but it can be hacked by finding and hacking the dongle test code or replicating the dongle itself (which I have done many times).

☐ The second method of copy protection is to request the user to type in a word from the manual. This, of course, can be remedied with a copy machine or by hacking the test code, but most average game players may think twice about making a copy of a manual to play a game.

Of course, you can use all the old techniques of bad sectors on the disk, checksums, hidden files, and so on, but they just don't work. Take my word for it. The best thing for you to do is make games that are so good the pirates themselves go out to the store to buy their own copy!

Summary

Today we took a brief look at some of the little details that go into making a complete game (other than the game software itself). The only thing I want you to get out of today's discussion is that there's more to a complete commercial game than the game itself. The entire presentation is important because where video games are concerned, the cover of the book is as important as the contents.

15

Q&A

Q What is a dongle?

A A dongle is a piece of hardware plugged into the PC for copy-protection purposes. Without it, the software in question won't work.

Q What is the difference between expanded and extended memory?

A Expanded memory is from 640K to one megabyte, and extended memory is anything above one megabyte.

Q How many PCs are there that meet our minimum hardware requirements?

A About 50 million as of this morning...

Q How much is a high-end 3-D modeler like 3-D Studio from Autodesk?

A About $2,500 to $5,000, depending on the options you get.

Workshop

The Workshop section presents quiz questions to help you cement your new knowledge and exercises to give you experience using what you've learned. Try to understand the questions and exercises before moving on to the next lesson. The answers are in Appendix B.

Quiz

1. What is the best way to implement a demo mode?

2. What is a pop-up interface?

3. What is an environment string?

4. Can software be executed from extended or expanded memory?

5. Why is it important to make backups of any system files that are changed by your game during installation?

Exercises

1. Take a break. You deserve it!

2. Go back and skim the entire book and refresh your memory on anything you didn't have a good grasp on—because tomorrow we hit warp speed!

Blowing Things Up
with Sea Shark!

WEEK
3

For the next three days you will be looking at some examples of complete games from a high level/designer's point of view. You have already covered the technical details of how to write a complete video game, so now it is time for some real examples. By dissecting a few games, you will see some specific patterns and techniques. These patterns and techniques will be standard no matter what game you make. Today you will begin your exploration of games with a simple "shoot-'em-up" game called Sea Shark (see Figure 16.1). As previously mentioned, we won't discuss issues on a technical level, but rather on a design level where the details of implementation aren't that important. Here are the targets of the day:

- [ ] The initial concept
- [ ] The artwork
- [ ] The sound FX and sound system
- [ ] Playing the game
- [ ] Playing tips
- [ ] The introduction
- [ ] The instructions
- [ ] The player
- [ ] The missiles
- [ ] The "bubble" particle system
- [ ] The enemy boats
- [ ] The explosions
- [ ] The scoring
- [ ] Displaying the end-of-wave information
- [ ] The input system
- [ ] Background animation and FX
- [ ] The end-of-game control
- [ ] What we learned
- [ ] Making the game better
- [ ] BUGS
- [ ] Building the game

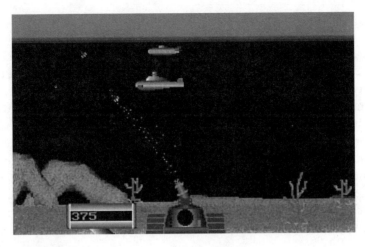

Figure 16.1. *Sea Shark.*

The Initial Concept

On Day 2, we made a combat game, so to avoid presenting you with another space combat game, Sea Shark's environment is set underwater. If you are old enough, you may remember a game called Sea Wolf by Bally Midway. When Sea Wolf was released, it was one of the most popular games of its day. It featured a periscope that the player looked through to target enemy subs and boats that would traverse the screen above and below the water line. The player could fire a torpedo and watch it travel to the target and possibly obliterate it. Sea Shark has much of the same flavor to it, except that Sea Shark is in color and has better graphics and sound.

As soon as I had the initial idea of a type of Sea Wolf game, I started working on the details. Then I weighed what I wanted the game to have against my tight schedule of one week. In the real world you may have six months to two years to complete a game, but you will always have to cut some elements out of the game to meet schedules, costs, and so on. In the end, my game consisted of three different subs, a speedboat that skims above water, a stationary missile cannon controlled by the player, and a few blinking lights. As far as special effects are concerned, the game has a cool "bubble" particle simulator that is used when the underwater missiles are fired by the player. These bubbles are completely passive and have no effect as far as game play is concerned; nevertheless, they add to the overall presentation of the game. Finally, the game is full of interesting digitized sound effects that make the game's personality a little more complex.

The Artwork

The artwork for Sea Shark consists of a set of .PCX files drawn with Deluxe Animation for Electronic Arts (see Figure 16.2). There are two subs that can travel in either a westward or eastward direction and a speedboat that can do the same. There aren't any frames of animation for each of the water boats because there isn't much to animate on a sub or boat. (Maybe a rotating radar could have been put on the boat and some kind of propeller on the subs.) The next major piece of art for the game was the player's cannon. It was difficult to decide what the player's cannon should look like because I hadn't decided on what the player was yet. (The player could have been a sub, an underwater station, or whatever.) I eventually made the player an underwater tank and attached a cannon to the top of the tank (which is a static image). The cannon can be in three positions, thus having three frames of animation.

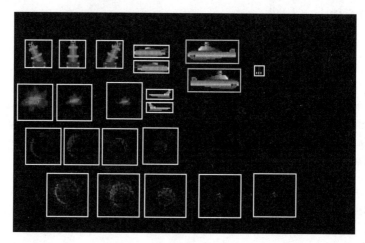

Figure 16.2. *Some of the artwork for Sea Shark.*

Because the player has the ability to fire a missile, I had to create something that looked like a Polaris missile. Then I used Deluxe Animation to rotate the missile bit map and create three different versions of it (one for each direction in which the cannon can point). This is a typical technique used in 2-D games; a paint program is used to prerotate 2-D bit maps, and the bit maps are loaded into the game and displayed consecutively to simulate rotation.

The next imagery that the game needed was some kind of underwater explosion. First I tried to make white explosions, but they didn't look good. I settled on red, spherical

explosions because they looked the best. Finally, all the introduction, instruction, and background screens were drawn as full-screen .PCX files.

The artwork itself is very important; however, the size of the bit maps is also important. The reason for this is twofold. First, the larger the bit maps, the more memory they take up. Secondly, and more important, the larger the bit maps, the slower they will be rendered on-screen and, thus, the slower the overall game will be. These factors must be taken into consideration when creating artwork. The problem is that some objects will be much larger than others. The question then becomes, "Should the size of the largest object in the game be used for all objects, even ones that are smaller?" The answer to this question is *yes* and *no*.

You should try to come up with a few bit-map sizes for the game that allow you to place large sets of bit maps together in the same .PCX file. For example, a good rule of thumb is to have 4–5 different bit-map sizes such as 4×4, 8×8, 16×16, 32×32, 48×48, and if necessary, some sizes that aren't square such as 48×16, 24×8, and so on. These bit-map sizes will be used for objects that don't have square geometry. Take a look at Table 16.1 to see all the different bit-map sizes used in Sea Shark and what they were used for.

Table 16.1. The bit-map sizes used for Sea Shark.

Object	Bit-Map Size in Pixels
Large Subs	48×20
Medium Subs	32×10
Boat	24×8
Missile	8×8
Explosions	32×32
Player's Cannon	24×24

The Sound FX and Sound System

The sound FX for the game were challenging because they had to sound like they were underwater sounds. All the sounds were digitized with the shareware program Blaster Master using my voice or household objects to create the sounds. Table 16.2 lists the sound effects in Sea Shark and how they were made.

Table 16.2. The sound effects for Sea Shark.

Sound Effect	Technique
The missile firing and streaming sound	Human Voice
The explosion sound	Human Voice
The sonar pulse from the large sub	Human Voice
The end-of-wave notice (German accent)	Human Voice
The end-of-game notice	Human Voice

As you can see, all the sound FX were made with vocal cords. It is fairly easy to make sound FX using only a human voice if you have some understanding of the physics of sound and the spectral components and shape of different kinds of sounds. Although the samples from the human-voice actor must be processed by sound software and changed considerably, it is still amazing how many sounds a person can make. Of course, you don't have to make all sound effects with your mouth. Explosions and voice effects are easy, but train sounds, metallic sounds, breaking glass, and so on are sounds for which you will probably need props.

```
int Initialize_Sound_System(void);
```

This function is used to load all the sounds and test if the CT-VOICE.DRV driver is present. It also loads a configuration file that sets the I/O port of the Sound Blaster along with the interrupt.

```
void Close_Sound_System(void);
```

This function unloads all the sound files and removes the sound driver from memory.

```
void Play_Sound(int sound);
```

This function will play the requested sound.

You won't be adding these functions to your library, but you should adopt something similar for your games since it makes the sound interface easier to handle.

Playing the Game

To play Sea Shark, type SEASHARK.EXE, and the game will load in all the sound and graphics files, and then it will begin. Currently, there is a sound driver for Sound Blaster

16 within the working directory of Sea Shark. If you have another model of Sound Blaster, you will have to overwrite this driver with the version of CT-VOICE.DRV for your appropriate Sound Blaster or compatible. Also, the file named SEASHARK.CFG has the Sound Blaster's I/O port and interrupt within it. They are currently set for I/O port 220h and interrupt 5. If you need to change them, you can edit this file. However, the numbers in the file must be in decimal so you will have to convert hexadecimal I/O port addresses into their decimal equivalent. After the introduction and instruction screens, the game will begin and you will be at the bottom of the screen manning your missile cannon. Use the A and S keys to rotate your cannon, and press the spacebar to fire a missile.

You can only have three missiles active at one time, and a small light on your tank will indicate if you have a missile free to be fired. If the light is green, you have a free missile; otherwise, all missiles are in transit, and you will have to wait for one of them to hit a target or detonate at the surface. When you've had enough of the game, you can quit by pressing Q. You will hear a familiar voice (if you've seen the movie *Aliens*); it's actually my voice doing an imitation, but it sounds close enough.

Playing Tips

Sea Shark is basically a point-and-shoot game, but you can increase your performance by leading your targets and continually firing in a sweeping fashion, even if there are no targets you can fire at. By having active missiles moving toward the surface, you will catch enemies many times as soon as they come out of the "chute" if you use this technique.

If you are trying to hit the speedboat, try to make the kill with a vertical shot because the missiles travel the fastest in this direction.

The Introduction

The introduction to Sea Shark consists of a single .PCX file that was originally created by taking a screen shot of the game in progress and placing some text on top of the image. You may elect not to take a screen shot and draw a really cool introduction screen that looks nothing like the game, or you may even render it with 3-D Studio. In any case, the introduction screen is supposed to indicate the type of game to the player and try to create an air of excitement and motivation. After the image is displayed, a screen transition is called and the player is shown the instruction screen.

The Instructions

The instructions for Sea Shark were drawn using a paint program and displayed using mode 13h. But because the resolution of mode 13h is not really for drawing text, a lot of information can't be displayed at once. If need be, you may want to use a pure text mode or a higher resolution graphics mode for the instruction portion of the game; otherwise, you can have multiple instruction screens or scrolling instructions.

The Player

The player in Sea Shark is supposed to be a tank with a missile cannon mounted on top of it. The player has only two controls. He can rotate the cannon into three positions and fire from any position. The imagery for the three positions was prerotated using Deluxe Animation and, therefore, is not done in real time. The software for the player is fairly simple. It checks to see if the player wants to rotate the cannon and tests if a missile has been fired. If the player is rotating the cannon, the new current direction is updated and the appropriate frame of animation is selected for the cannon sprite. If the cannon can no longer rotate in the direction that the player is requesting, nothing happens. Maybe a sound effect of bending or cracking metal could have been played when the player tries to move the cannon too far?

Almost all the logic for the player is in the `main()` function of the game, so you can easily modify and trace the operation of the game. The only two things not done in the `main()` function (as far as the player is concerned) are blinking some indicator lights on the tank and updating the missile state light. The blinking blue lights on the tank are accomplished using color rotation, and the missile indicator light is controlled by changing a single color register based on the number of missiles in the water.

The Missiles

The player has the ability to fire underwater missiles. These missiles are completely autonomous and self-contained. A call is made to a function that starts a missile (if one is free), and from that point on the player's control logic need not concern itself with the missiles' control. The missiles are basically sprites that have a certain x and y velocity. This velocity is looked up in a table that is indexed by the current direction of the player's cannon at the time the missile is fired. This table was created manually by estimating the x and y velocity of a projectile moving at the three different angles that the missiles can travel relative to the horizon.

After the missile is fired, it does its own collision detection and will terminate itself along with any enemy it hits. Furthermore, when a hit is detected, the missile logic will try to start an explosion—that is, if there are any explosions available to start. (The game has only so many explosions that can be active at once to cut down on processing time.) Like the missiles, the explosions are self-contained and self-updating; they need only to be started. From there they will run their course and terminate.

The "Bubble" Particle System

When a missile is fired underwater you will see bubbles that are caused by the rocket engines propelling the missile. You can simulate this effect using a simple particle system, as you read about on Day 13. The bubbles are implemented as single pixels that are randomly placed near the end of the missile as it moves. These bubbles are also given slightly different colors from a set of the grays in the palette. Then the bubbles "age" for a few frames and move upward with a random velocity. After a few more frames the bubbles pop and terminate. You will also notice that the bubbles only occur below a certain depth line. This is a function of the missile code. The missile logic will only start a bubble below a certain vertical position, to simulate the initial "fuel burn." As usual, the bubbles are implemented as a self-contained set of functions and only need to be started; from there they will operate independently.

The Enemy Boats

The enemy boats are all controlled by the same logic. The only difference is that the logic will select a different "water boat" to start up. Once started, however, the same functions control both the subs and the speedboat. The enemies are controlled by the following algorithm.

Algorithm 16.1. The enemy control algorithm.

```
Start the enemy boat from either the right or left side of the screen.
Choose a random vertical position and a random horizontal velocity.
Select an enemy—that is, a medium sub, large sub, or speedboat.
While (enemy is not dead)
    {
    move enemy

    if (enemy has hit edge of screen) then terminate enemy

    if (enemy has been hit by missile) then terminate enemy and start explosion
```
continues

Algorithm 16.1. continued

```
} // end while
```

The Explosions

The explosions are implemented as self-contained functions that can be started anywhere on-screen by making a call to Start Explosion(). After the explosion has started, it will run its course by cycling through all its frames of animation and then terminate. In Sea Shark there are three different sets of explosion frames that can be used for an explosion and they are randomly selected when an explosion is started; moreover, the explosions are further made to look slightly different by controlling their animation speed.

Some explosions will occur more slowly than others. The speed of the explosion is controlled by a parameter that is sent to the function that starts the explosion. The "speed" parameter is used to control the number of game frames that are executed before the next animation frame of the explosion is selected and displayed.

Timing issues are very important because many game animations won't or shouldn't be run at the maximum frame rate. Timing control is accomplished by using counters to count cycles before changing the animation frame. This is the reason why the original sprite structure had the fields `anim_speed` and `anim_clock`. They were included for just such timing considerations.

Listing 16.1. The sprite structure.

```
typedef struct sprite_typ
        {
        int x,y;              // position of sprite
        int x_old,y_old;      // old position of sprite
        int width,height;     // dimensions of sprite in pixels
        int anim_clock;       // the animation clock
        int anim_speed;       // the animation speed
        int motion_speed;     // the motion speed
        int motion_clock;     // the motion clock

        char far *frames[MAX_SPRITE_FRAMES]; // array of pointers to the images
        int curr_frame;                      // current frame being displayed
        int num_frames;                      // total number of frames
        int state;                           // state of sprite, alive, dead...
        char far *background;                // what's under the sprite
        void far *extra_data;                // an auxiliary pointer to more
                                             // data if needed

        } sprite, *sprite_ptr;
```

The Scoring

The scoring for the game is extremely rudimentary. Each enemy has a fixed point value assigned to it, and if the player hits the enemy, his score is appropriately updated. A much better scheme would have taken into consideration the speed of the enemies and the distance between the player's cannon and the enemy. This information could have been used to further scale or add onto the fixed score to reward a player for being a better marksman. For example, a formula such as Formula 16.1 could have been used.

Formula 16.1—A Better Scoring Function

```
points = (fixed point value) + 100*((distance between player and enemy)/200);
```

This formula will reward the player for shooting enemies as a function of distance a maximum of 100 extra points in addition to the fixed point value for the enemy in question. Of course, the speed of the enemy could be worked in as another term in the overall equation.

Displaying the End-of-Wave Information

Because Sea Shark is just a mindless "shoot-'em-up" game without levels or different tasks, a method had to be devised to at least have "waves" of attackers. Therefore, after a specific amount of time, the game will pause and display the process for the current wave. This pause, however, posed a big problem. I wanted the display to be in real time, which meant that the graphics would have to be double buffered. However, if you recall, we didn't write any functions to save an arbitrary region on-screen and restore it. The sprites have this functionality, but they are the only objects that do. Because most of the information displayed at the end of a wave is text, the background under the text had to be saved and restored just like a big sprite.

To accomplish this goal, a simple function was written that could save the background. Although everything worked out fine, this illuminated a problem with the graphics library that we overlooked. We should have written a few functions to get, save, and put rectangular bit maps that are not sprites. After the display problem was solved, the actual information display was the next task. This involved tracking the number of enemies of each type that were hit during the wave, and then displaying that information with the cumulative score. Finally, some visual icons of the enemies, along with a digitized German voice, was added to the end-of-wave sequence to make it more enjoyable.

The Input System

Although we created a complex, interrupt-driven keyboard interface to support multiple key presses and so forth, this kind of functionality wasn't really needed in Sea Shark. There were only three controls (right, left, and fire), and the standard `kbhit()` and `getch()` worked fine for these inputs. So I elected not to make the game more complicated than it needed to be and left out keyboard driver software.

Background Animation and FX

Unfortunately, there isn't much background animation in the game except some blinking lights. The lights on the player's tank cycle is accomplished using color rotation, and there is a missile-ready indicator that is also done using color register animation. In general, if the effect you are trying to achieve is blinking lights, moving lights, or appearing or disappearing objects, then color register animation is your best bet. However, be careful in selecting the color registers with which to accomplish the animation. As a rule, you should use the color registers near the end of the range such as 240–255.

End-of-Game Control

Because the player can't be hit or damaged, he will survive forever. A way had to be devised to end the game under a certain condition. This condition is that 100 enemy ships get away. When this occurs, the screen will be blotted with randomly placed explosions and then the game will end. The end-of-game determination is implemented by tracking the number of enemy ships that make it to the other side of the screen without being terminated. The sum of this calculation is tested every game cycle to the number 100; if it is greater, the main game loop is placed into a "dying" state and random explosions are played and the player is rendered powerless.

What We Learned

You learned how to create a very simple game with all the elements needed to be called complete. Furthermore, you really saw the power of self-contained functions and the use of them. This is probably the most important lesson to be learned; without self-contained functions, video games are too hard to build. The sheer number of running operations and tasks is too complex to be tracked by a single function. Finally, the thought process behind a complete game design was laid out along with the reasoning behind it.

Making the Game Better

First the game needs to have levels with different backgrounds; this would add to the same boring screen being displayed at all times. Then the enemies need to be less passive. A possibility would be to have them drop depth charges toward the player's tank. In addition, the explosions could be more spectacular. The bubble particle system simulator could be used in conjunction with added logic to the enemy software so that when an enemy was hit, explosions would be started and the enemy ship would plummet until it hit the ocean floor in a trail of black particles. Finally, there should be some ranking logic to rank the player at the end and reward him with a medal of some kind for a extraordinary performance.

BUGS

The game only seems to have a problem with the end-of-wave determination. Somehow, it is always off by one or two. The end of wave is determined by counting the number of enemies that are started. How the enemy ends up is irrelevant, but the number of enemies that have entered into the game are counted. Furthermore, for each wave there is a different number of enemies that are to be allowed into the game before ending the wave. This number always seems to be off by two. This bug is unnoticeable to the player, and it is a mystery to me.

Building the Game

Sea Shark consists of the main program (called SEASHARK.C), .VOC sound files, .PCX graphics files, and the SEASHARK.CFG configuration file. These files, along with the game library, are all that is needed to create the final executable and play the game. The following is a complete list and description of the files needed for Sea Shark.

Software

SEASHARK.C—The game software.
SEASHARK.CFG—The sound configuration file.

Graphics

SHARKSB1.PCX—The medium boats.
SHARKSB2.PCX—The large boats.
SHARKEXP.PCX—The explosions.

SHARKGUN.PCX—The player's gun.

SHARKBOT.PCX—The speedboat.

SHARKMIS.PCX—The player's missile.

SHARKBAK.PCX—The background for the game.

SHARKINT.PCX—The introduction screen.

SHARKICN.PCX—The bit-map for the ships icons used for the end-of-wave sequence.

SHARKINS.PCX—The instruction screen.

Sounds

SMISSLIE.VOC—The sound of the missile.

SEXPL.VOC—The explosion.

SWAVE.VOC—The end of wave message.

SSONAR.VOC—A sonar pulse.

SOVER.VOC—The end of game message.

Libraries

GAMELIB.LIB—Our game library.

Building an Executable: To make an executable of the program, you can use the source on the disk. The name of the source is SEASHARK.C. The precompiled executable is named SEASHARK.EXE. As before, use the following compile line for Microsoft C:

```
cl -AM -Zi -c -Fc -Gs -G2 seashark.c
```

After compiling the program in this manner, you can link it to the standard libraries and our game library (gamelib.lib) to create an executable.

Summary

Today was the first day that we took our complete game library and created a complete game. It seems like it actually works! You learned how to take a concept from the drawing board all the way to a complete product. And as a bonus you saw how a particle system can be used to simulate bubbles and help make the underwater fakery more realistic.

Q&A

Q **Why learn how to make shoot-'em-up games when they are so old and primitive?**

A Because the elements of shoot-'em-up games are similar to the elements of any advanced game, and secondly, you must learn to fly before you can teleport.

Q **How were the explosion sounds made?**

A Explosions are mostly "white" noise. I made the explosions by blowing into the microphone and then using Blaster Master to "tweak" the sample.

Workshop

The Workshop section presents quiz questions to help you cement your new knowledge and exercises to give you experience using what you've learned. Try to understand the questions and exercises before moving on to the next lesson. The answers are in Appendix B.

Quiz

1. How are the bubbles in Sea Shark implemented?

2. How many different bit-map sizes are there in Sea Shark?

3. How is the end of game determined?

4. What was the problem with the end-of-wave sequence and how was it solved?

5. Why was the standard C input library used instead of the input library we made?

Exercises

1. Add more enemies to Sea Shark.

2. Fix the end-of-wave bug.

3. Make the enemies drop depth charges.

4. Add some fish swimming around.

5. Make the scoring function more complex to take into consideration distance between the tank and the target.

Adventuring with Venture

Adventuring with Venture

Adventure and Dungeons & Dragons–based games are some of the most popular in the world. These types of games are usually implemented as a collection of rooms or environments that the player can explore. The rooms are usually presented to the player by either "warping" to each room when the player crosses the threshold of a door or by "scrolling" the world. We will use the "warping" technique, which is a very coarse type of scrolling—paged scrolling. You viewed this technique a couple of weeks ago when experimenting with the ROBO PUNK demo. Creating an adventure-type game is an order of magnitude more challenging than a simple shoot-'em-up because of many factors. First, the data structures and graphics are more complex due to the size of the environment. Second, the game actually has to have a goal and plot! Here's what you'll explore today:

- ☐ The initial concept
- ☐ The artwork
- ☐ The sound FX and sound system
- ☐ Playing the game
- ☐ Playing tips
- ☐ The introduction
- ☐ The instructions
- ☐ The representation of the universe
- ☐ The Archer
- ☐ The bow
- ☐ The player's death
- ☐ The Daemons and AI
- ☐ The green fireballs
- ☐ The Daemon death
- ☐ The dreaded bat
- ☐ The objects in the game
- ☐ The dagger of Mosk
- ☐ The Archer's inventory display
- ☐ The exit door

☐ The scoring system

☐ The input system

☐ Background animation and FX

☐ End-of-game control

☐ Closing scene

☐ What we learned

☐ Making the game better

☐ BUGS

☐ Building the game

The Initial Concept

The idea for Venture originally came from an old Atari 2600 game that was a favorite of mine called Adventure. Adventure was an amazing feat for the limited capabilities of the 2600. The game had a set of rooms that used a paged scrolling technique to move throughout the environment. The idea of the game was to find a golden chalice and place it in one of the rooms within the game. Three dragons tried to foil your mission, and a bat would fly around and steal anything you were carrying. Your primary weapon was a sword, but it only worked in one direction! Finally, because the graphics were very limited, the player was represented by a dot instead of an image!

With the elements of Adventure and a few ideas of my own, I finally came up with Venture (see Figure 17.1). Venture is a top-view game, with the objects drawn to make it look 3-D (similar to Gauntlet by Atari). The game consists of 16 rooms that are page scrolled as you reach the edge of the screen. The game has a single monster (called a Daemon) that spits green fireballs and makes very disturbing noises. The hero of the game is called *Archer*; he has a bow and a supply of arrows that he uses to defend himself from the Daemons. His mission is to find the enchanted dagger. This dagger is somewhere within the game domain and glows red. (You can't miss it.) Also within the game is a bat that flies overhead to annoy Archer. Currently, however, the bat does nothing except look scary and make a scary sound.

As with most adventure-type games, the game has many aspects to it other than the main goal of finding the dagger. Archer can find gold and silver and collect it, eat food, and refill his supply of arrows. Archer also can become wounded, and he will die if his health

becomes too low. After Archer finds the dagger, he must proceed to find the exit and leave the game domain. At this point, a message from the King is displayed that describes Archer's next quest.

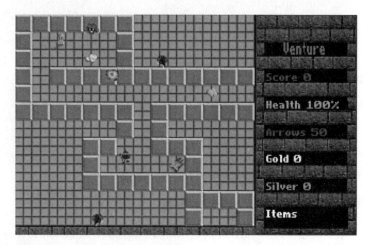

Figure 17.1. *Venture in action.*

Venture is a good example game and will work as an excellent foundation for you to enhance and modify because of its small size (less than 4,000 lines) and because of its modularity.

The Artwork

The artwork for Venture was a nightmare to create. I spent hours trying to draw all the cells for the dungeon. I wanted the game to have a 3-D look; therefore, I had to create bit-maps that had shadows and perspective. This turned out to be a big production because I am not very good at drawing in 3-D; however, I found that looking at other games helped a lot in trying to simulate the 3-D look I was trying to achieve. You should always research other games' artwork and study them before trying to create your own. By doing this you will get a feel for what something should look like at the different angles along with the proper shadow placement. The hardest part of the game was drawing the walls because there are so many different versions of the wall bit-maps that must be drawn. A top wall, bottom wall, left wall, right wall, T-intersection, right angle, left angle, and so on all must be drawn so that the world construction looks consistent. In the end, it was taking too long to draw all the 3-D walls, and I ended up using shaded squares to represent walls. Look at Figure 17.2 to see all the artwork for the game.

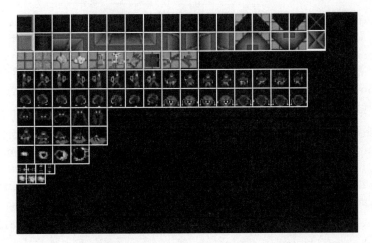

Figure 17.2. *The artwork for Venture.*

As you can see, there are a lot of bit-maps. Of course, I have put them all in a single figure for you to see, but many of them are in separate .PCX files because they have different bit-map sizes. Let's enumerate what the game has as far as artwork. There are the walls that make up the game world, and then there are objects that Archer can pick up such as gold, silver, food, and arrows. Pay close attention to the bit-maps for the objects; you will notice that under them is the bit-map for the floor, which is the standard technique used. Instead of trying to draw the object on top of the game world at runtime, the object is placed on a standard floor tile bit-map and then can be drawn as part of the world (see Figure 17.3).

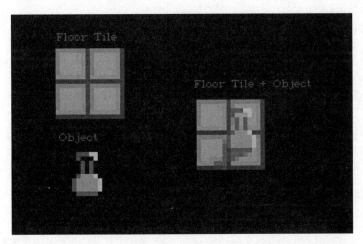

Figure 17.3. *Mixing an object with the floor bit-map.*

Next there are the bit-maps for Archer, which consist of a few frames of animation for the four directions he can move in. Similarly, the Daemons are drawn in the same way, that is a set of cells for motion in each of the four directions. I could have drawn bit-maps for diagonal motion, but that would have been extremely difficult to do, so if the monsters move in a diagonal direction, the frames for vertical or horizontal motion are selected based on how much more the motion is concentrated in one direction.

The next major element of the game is the bat, and it consists of a few frames of animation to make it look like it's flapping its wings. You will notice that the same animation cells are used no matter what direction the bat flies. To make the animation complete, we would supply animations for all of the main directions: north, south, east, and west. But, because the bat is flying in the air, the same animation cells look fine.

Finally, there are the bit-maps for all the special effects such as fireballs, arrows, and explosions. The arrows are the only objects that aren't animated since making an arrow spin in the low resolution of 320×200 would be a waste of time. On the other hand, fireballs and explosions do have a few frames of animation; however, the fireball animation isn't as pronounced as I would like it to be because of its size; oh well. See Table 17.1 for a complete look at all the objects and their respective bit-map sizes.

Table 17.1. The bit-map sizes used for Venture.

Object	Bit-Map Size in Pixels	Animation Frames
Archer	16×16	21
Arrows	8×8	4
Daemons	16×16	16
Fireballs	8×8	3
Explosion	16×16	4
Bat	16×16	5
Basic World Cell	16×16	N/A
Stationary Objects	16×16	N/A

The Sound FX and Sound System

The sound FX for Venture were carefully selected and worked on for quite a while to make them as professional and disturbing as possible. They were all made by my voice and a few household props. The sounds are played using our sound library with the added software interface used in Sea Shark that allows a clean initialization, use of the sound, and termination of the sound system. All the sounds were digitized using no more than 6KHz mono sampling. The samples, after being digitized, were usually echoed to simulate the dungeon's acoustics. After making Venture, I realized that we should have implemented a sound scheduler that would queue sounds and allow them to be played with priorities instead of just preempting the current sound. It can be annoying to hear a digitized sample be interrupted by another one, but you live and learn. Table 17.2 shows all the sounds in the game and how they were made.

Table 17.2. The sound effects for Venture.

Sound Effect	Technique
Archer being hurt	Human Voice
Daemon dying	Human Voice
Daemon spitting a fireball	Human Voice
Bow	A yard stick
Finding gold or silver	Bolts dropped in a can
Finding arrows	Human Voice
Finding potion	Human Voice
Archer eating a meal	Human Voice
Archer dying	Human Voice
Bat	Human Voice
Dagger being picked up	Human Voice
Introduction voice	Human Voice
Low-health warning	Human Voice
End-of-game message	Human Voice

Amazingly enough, almost all the sound effects were made with a human voice!

Playing the Game

To play Venture, type **VENTURE.EXE** in the working directory for today. The game will automatically load all the files and search for the sound configuration file (VENTURE.CFG), load the Sound Blaster I/O port, and interrupt from it. Also, as usual the CT-VOICE.DRV driver will be loaded from the working directory. This is the version of the driver for the Sound Blaster 16, so you will have to overwrite it with your particular Sound Blaster's version of the driver if you don't have a Sound Blaster 16. Change the I/O port or interrupt in the configuration file if you need to, but remember that they must be in decimal format.

When the game begins you see an introduction screen followed by an instruction screen. To exit the instruction screen, press a key and the game begins. You see your character (Archer) standing in the middle of a little green room with some arrows next to him. Pick up the arrows and then proceed to hunt for the dagger. To move Archer, use the arrow keys. To fire an arrow, use the spacebar; however, fire arrows sparingly because you have a limited supply of them, which is indicated along with your score and health on the right side of the screen. As you play the game, try to collect as much gold, potion, and food as possible because Archer will need all the goods he can carry to complete the task of finding the dagger and getting out alive.

When you find the dagger, you are free to exit the game via the exit door (which is located somewhere in the game domain). If you try to exit the game before collecting the dagger, you will be a loohooohooooseehhheeeerr!

Playing Tips

Archer isn't what you would call fast, but he is dangerous with a supply of arrows. So when you enter a room, shoot first and ask questions later. Also, when you enter a room, the monsters will not activate for about 1.5 seconds; this gives you a little time to adjust to the screen warp. You can use this time to see where the monsters are and then back out of the room, come up with an attack plan, and then reenter. Next, if your health is at 100 percent, don't eat any food because it will go to waste; only eat if your health is below 100 percent.

The dagger is located in the bottom left portion of the game grid, and the exit is in the bottom right portion; however, both of them are within a little maze that is full of Daemons, so be careful and make sure you are fully armed with a supply of arrows before trying to find either. Finally, the Daemons for the most part use the simple attack algorithm that you saw on Day 10. So if you sit in one position and shoot, chances are they will run right into the arrows.

The Introduction

The introduction to Venture isn't very spectacular; it simply shows a screen shot with some text on it. I was tempted to digitize 20–30 seconds of live video from a D&D movie and play it on-screen, but I didn't have time. (Maybe you could add this embellishment.) After the introduction screen displays, it dissolves and the instructions are placed on-screen.

The Instructions

The instruction screen is actually pretty good. I'm happy with the way it looks. The paper that the instructions were written on was created using Deluxe Animation with the translucency option. Grays and tans were mixed to make a paper texture. The bit-maps of the creatures and objects of the game were taken from the artwork and placed into the instruction screen so that the player would be able to see the actual objects along with the verbiage that went along with them. This is a good technique to use, and you should use it as much as possible. Always try to add graphics and even animation to the instruction screen because it helps convey information faster and in a more compact form than text does. And most important, it's much cooler to have graphics than text. Finally, you may even want to add digitized speech to add a few key comments to the instructions.

The Representation of the Universe

Here is where Venture takes a hard left turn from Sea Shark. Due to Venture's multiple screens and bit-mapped cell graphics, the game is based on a cell matrix world such as those discussed on Day 12. This allows a small database of cell IDs to be loaded to represent entire screens. In the case of Venture, the universe is a collection of screens where each screen is a 14×12 matrix of bit-map IDs. The data structures that hold the screen data along with other important data items follow in Listing 17.1.

Listing 17.1. The data structures for the screens of Venture.

```
// this is used to track the position of a monster and its state when the
// screen is first paged to, and to recall when the screen is left and
// revisited so that monsters that are killed stay dead and live monsters
// are restarted in their last positions

typedef struct monster_pos_typ
    {
```

continues

Listing 17.1. continued

```
        int state;  // state of monster
        int x,y;    // position of the monster is pixel coordinates

        } monster_pos, *monster_pos_ptr;

// this is the data structure that holds a single screen

typedef struct screen_typ
        {

        int cells[CELL_ROWS][CELL_COLUMNS];    // the data storage for cell IDs

        int num_monsters;                      // number of monsters in the screen

        monster_pos positions[NUM_MONSTERS];   // this holds the state and positions
                                               // of the monsters on entry and exit

        } screen, *screen_ptr;
```

As you can see, each screen consists of an integer matrix of cell IDs along with an array that holds the positions and states of the monsters. This array is needed to record the positions of the monsters when the player leaves the screen so that when the player returns, the monsters can be replaced to their former positions. Of course, the data structure could be eliminated; however, if the player killed all the monsters in a room and then left and came back to the room, they would regenerate. This regeneration is unrealistic and unfair; therefore, using a data structure to recall them is appropriate.

The game universe is based on screens (rooms) that are 2-D arrays of integers; however, there is another level of abstraction. The universe itself is an array of 4–4 screens for a total of 16 rooms. The data structure that holds the entire universe follows:

```
screen world[WORLD_ROWS][WORLD_COLUMNS];   // the game world
```

Amazing that an entire universe can be contained in a single line of C code. Well, that's modern technology for you!

If you remember when we discussed tools on Day 14, you should recall that we talked about map editors and universe builders. Basically, you learned that it is important to create tools so that the game grid can be created and altered easily. Unfortunately, I didn't have time to create a tool to draw the game world and place objects, but I did make the data structure that represents the game world very simple and easy to create and load.

Because the game world for Venture is a 4×4 array of screens, each being 14×12 IDs, it seemed appropriate to make the screen definition file ASCII-based, where different

ASCII characters would stand for different walls and objects in the world. Then a function could be written to load the ASCII file and parse all the data and construct the game world. Also, within the data would be the position of the dagger, the monsters, and all the gold, silver, food, arrows, potions, and so on. A special character would be selected to represent each one of these objects. The function that loads the game world and does this construction is called Load_Screens() and takes the file name as a parameter from which to load the universe. The format of the universe is

Screen 1

Screen 2

.
.
.

Screen 16

where each screen consists of a 14×12 array of characters that represent the bit-maps that should be placed on-screen. Furthermore, the screens are ordered in row major form, meaning that the first four screens make up the first row in the world, and so on. The name of the file that contains this data must always be the same and is called VENTURE.DAT. As an example, take a look at Figure 17.4 to see the entire ASCII game grid with each screen placed properly. You will notice that the plain ASCII characters are used to represent each of the bit-maps in the game. For example, the character *a* is a wall, % is gold, and so forth. Table 17.3 lists the most important bit-maps and the ASCII characters used to represent them.

Table 17.3. The bit maps for Venture and the ASCII characters that represent them.

Object	ASCII Character	Name
Floor tile	.	Period
Quicksand tile	,	Comma
Food tile	+	Plus
Arrows tile	^	Carrot
Potion tile	*	Asterisk
Gold tile	%	Percent
Silver tile	$	Dollar

continues

Table 17.3. continued

Object	ASCII Character	Name
Dagger tile	!	Exclamation Point
Exit tile	?	Question Mark
Monster	~	Tilde

```
aaaaaaa......~   ...............   ...............   ..............
a.*.~.a......    ...............   ...............   ..............
a...%.a.......   ..aaa...aaaaa.   aaaaaaaaaaaaaa   .aaaaaaaaaaaa.
a.aaaaaaaaaaaa   aaa.a..a~..~a.   ...........~...~.  ............a.
a..........$..   ......~.a.+..a.   ....aaaaaaaaa aaa...%%%...a.
aaaaaaa.aaaaa   aa..a..a....a.   ...b.........   ...a.....~~.a.
......a.a.....   .aaaa...a.aaa.   ..b*b...aaaa.   ...aaaaaaaaaa.
....aa..aaa...   ...............   ..b.....a...   ......a,,,,,a.
....a....^a...   .....aaaaa....   ..aaaaaa..a...   ..aaa.a,,,,,a.
....aaaaaa...   ......a...a...   ....aa.~+.a...   ..a..a,.~.,a.
..........aaaa   ....aaa.a.~..   .....a...a...   ..a$.a,.a.,a.
~.........a.a   .........a....   .....a.......   ...aa.a..a..a.

aaaaaaaaaaa..a   ..........a...   ..............   ..a......a..a.
a..........~.a   ..........a...   .......~....aaa aaa......a..a.
a.aaaaaaaaa..a   ..aaaaa..a....   ...a....   ..a.....a+.a.
a.a.......a..a   ......a..aaaaa aaaaaaaa...a.   ..a...aaaaaa.
a.a+.$%$..a..a   ..a..~a.......   .......a...a.   ..aa.aa,,~.$a.
a.a........a.a   ..a.*.a..~....   .....+.a.aaa. aaa,,~,,,,,,a.
a.a.......a..a   ..aaaa.......   ..~.~..a.a...   ..a,,,,,~,,,a.
a.aaaaa...a..a   ...........~..   .......a.a.~.   ..aaaaa,,~,,a.
a.....a...a..a   aaaaaaaaa..aaa aaaaaaaa..a%...   .......a,,,,a.
a~..~+a...a...   ......~.+a..a.   ..........aaaa aaaaa.a$,,$a.
aaaaaaa..aaaa.   aaaaaaaaa..a..   ...~........a.   ....a.*aaaaa..
a...........   ..........a..a.   ..............a..   ...a..a......

A............   ..........A..A..   ..............   ...A..A......
A.A.........   ..........A.~A..   .....+..A..A.   ...A..A.....
A~A.........   ..........A.~A..   .........A..A.   ...A..A.....
A%A.........   ..AAAAAAA..AAA AAAAAAAAA..AAA A..AA...A....
AAAAAAAAAA...   ...$.....%....   ..............   .......AAAAAA
........AA...   ...............   ..............  AAAA...A...%A
..A......AA..   ..AAAAA..AAAAA AAAAAAAAA.~...   ...A.~...AA$A
..A.A.AAAA...   ......A..A....   ......,,A.~..   ...A.~..AA.A
..A.~A..AA...   ......A..AAAAA ......,,A....   ...A+........A
..A..A.~^AA..   ....*..A....~~A ,,,,,.$%A....   ...AAAAAAA~.A
..AAAAAAAAA...   ....AAAAAAAA .....,$%AAAAAA   .........A.~A
...........   ...............   ........,,,,,,,...  ......*....AA.A

...........   ...............   ..............AAAA AAAAAAAAAAAA.A
..........   ...............   ...........A$..   ............A.A
..AAAAAAAAAAA AAAAAAAAAAAA.   .......AAAA AAA..A.....A.A
.............   ...........AA AAAAA.....   ...A..A$%$..A.A
..AAAAAAAAAAA AAA..AAAA.....   .....AAAAAA...   ..A..AAAAAAA~A
..A,,,,,......   ..A..A..AAAAAA AAA.......~AAA AAA.........A.A
..A,$%,..A....   ..A..A.++....A   ...AAAA%.......   .......A...A~A
..A,.%.,..A....   ..A..A....a...   ........AAAAA...   ...AAAAAAA.A
..A,,,,AAAAAAA AAA..AAAAAAAA.   .,,,,,,,,,,..A..   ..A....A~.~.A
..A....A.~..~.   ..~..~.~......A.   .,+..+,....A...   ..A~..A$%$.A
..A....A!.~..   ...~...~+.~.AA   .,~..~,....A...   ..A...A^+.?A
......AAAAAAA AAAAAAAAAAAAAA .,,,,,,,,...AAA AAAAAAAAAAAA
```

Figure 17.4. *The universe data file VENTURE.DAT.*

Although it may not be so, the ASCII characters were chosen to have some kind of relation to what they represent. For example, the $ character represents silver. Alas, there is a point when you will run out of good characters and *F* will have to represent a car!

The only interesting character that we should discuss briefly is the tilde character (~) which is used to place a monster. Whenever the screen-loading software detects one of these characters, the position of the monster is computed and then inserted with a "live" state into the array of monsters within the screen structure. Then, when that particular screen is paged to (by the player hitting a screen edge), the game creates the monster(s) and displays them based on this data. Therefore, if you want to make the game harder, place more ~ characters within the VENTURE.DAT file.

The Archer

Archer (an archer by trade) is the hero of the game. He can move in four directions: east, west, north, and south. He also can fire arrows from his bow. Archer is 16×16 pixels and implemented very simply as a sprite. Whenever Archer walks, he cycles through four frames of animation, which is enough to make the motion look semireal. Along with the sprite structure that is the main data structure for Archer, there are some extra variables that Archer uses to track his inventory and state. These are

```
// players inventory

long players_score  = 0;              // initial score
int players_dir     = PLAYER_SOUTH;   // initial direction of player
int silver_pieces   = 0;              // amount of silver pieces player has
int gold_pieces     = 0;              // amount of gold pieces player has
int number_potions  = 0;              // number of magical potions (smart bombs)
int health          = 100;            // start health off at 100 percent
int num_arrows      = 50;             // player has 50 arrows to start with
int dagger_found    = 0;              // flags if the player has found the dagger
int weak_counter    = 350;            // used to count how many cycles before
                                      // verbal health message is repeated
int start_death     = 0;              // flags if players death sequence has started
```

As Archer moves around the game world, his screen position is converted to cell coordinates on a frame-by-frame basis, and the current cell he is standing on is tested to see if it has an object in it such as gold, food, and so on. If so, the object is taken and the bit-map of the object is replaced with a plain floor tile to indicate that the object has been taken. Archer's collision detection with the walls works in much the same way. If a wall bit-map ID is detected, whichever way Archer was traveling that moved him in the region with a wall is used to back him up; this keeps Archer from walking through walls. In essence, object detection and collision detection for the world geometry are in cell space that is really a 14×12 integer matrix.

17

Finally, Archer's logic is completely controlled in the main() function so that you can track him without function hopping.

The Bow

Archer's only weapon is his bow; however, this is a magical bow and it packs quite a wallop! The bow can fire up to three arrows at a time, which travel in the direction that Archer is pointing when he fires. Therefore, Archer can't run in one direction and fire in another. The arrows are implemented as self-contained autonomous functions which view the arrows as entities that can either hit a wall or a monster. The arrow only needs to be started by Archer, and from there it will travel on its own and do all collision detection itself.

If an arrow detects that it has hit a wall segment, the arrow code terminates the arrow that hits the wall. On the other hand, if an arrow hits a monster, the arrow code sets the monster into its death state and the arrow code terminates the arrow as it is probably stuck in the decaying carcass of the monster. Currently, the arrows travel at 6 pixels per frame, which is 50 percent faster than anything in the game. This guarantees that when Archer takes aim, nothing will escape his fury.

The Player's Death

When Archer's health runs below 20 percent, an intermittent message will be heard notifying the player to find more food and that Archer is about to make his journey to the big game grid in the sky. The intermittent message is accomplished by first testing if Archer's health is below 20 percent and then enabling a counter. When the counter hits a predetermined value, the counter is reset and the message is played. Without the counter, the message would be continually played every cycle since Archer's health could be below 20 percent for a long period of time if food isn't found. The only way to implement this counter is with a global variable or a local static in the function that does the counting. See Listing 17.2 for the code fragment that voices the message.

Listing 17.2. The code fragment that controls the health display and voice.

```
// draw health in red if weak

if (health>=20)
    {
    Blit_String_DB(270+2,78,10,buffer,0);
```

```
    // set counter almost at threshold
    weak_counter=350;
    }
else
    {
    Blit_String_DB(270+2,78,12,buffer,0);

    // test if we have verbally told player he is weak

    if (++weak_counter>400)
        {

        Play_Sound(SOUND_HEALTH);

        // reset counter

        weak_counter=0;

        } // end if speak

    } // end else player weak
```

At some point in the game there is a good possibility that Archer will get killed. When this happens a sequence of "pain" or "death" frames is shown and Archer dies. I always like to make my game characters fall down in a pool of blood (see Figure 17.5), but you may prefer something less graphic. After the death sequence, the game ends and the screen melts and that is it...

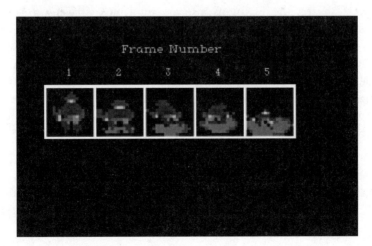

Figure 17.5. *The "death" sequence of Archer.*

The Daemons and AI

Venture has only one enemy in the game; however, it would be very easy to add another enemy with the current software. The Daemons, as I call them (inside joke for UNIX people), are little, round creatures that spit fireballs. The Daemons are implemented using the techniques from Day 10. Each Daemon can be a one of seven states. These states are shown in Table 17.4.

Table 17.4. The states of a Daemon.

State Name	Probability
Sitting Still	10%
Turning	10%
Chasing Archer	40%
Evading Archer	20%
Moving Randomly	20%
Dead	N/A
Dying	N/A

As you can see, the Daemons also are implemented using a skewed probability distribution for selecting their states. This implements a basic "personality" of aggression. The Daemons can move in any direction; however, because there are only animation cells for the four directions (east, west, north, and south), a decision must be made about what cells to use when the Daemon is not moving in a purely horizontal or vertical direction. This is done by looking at the horizontal and vertical translation components. If the diagonal motion has a large horizontal component but a small vertical component, the animation cells for westward or eastward motion are selected. Similar logic is used for inverse code.

The Daemons also have the ability to spit fireballs. The fireballs are spit on an average of once every 60 frames; therefore, the expectation of a fireball being fired based on the number of Daemons on-screen can be computed in the following formula.

Formula 17.1—Computing the Probabilistic Expectation of a Fireball Being Spit

```
P(fireball per frame) = (number of Daemons)/60
```

Therefore, if a screen had four Daemons on it, there would be a fireball spit roughly every second.

The fireballs are implemented with a set of self-contained functions as is most everything in a video game. When a Daemon fires one, the Daemon need not worry about the fireball anymore. The fireball logic tests for collisions and detects collisions with the wall itself.

The Green Fireballs

The green fireballs are magical in nature and are pretty nasty. They travel in whatever direction they are initially given until one of two premises is met. If a wall is hit, the fireball terminates and an explosion is started. The second case occurs when the fireball hits Archer. In this case, the fireball is terminated, an explosion is started at the Archer's current position, and the health of Archer is decreased. The fireballs are animated, although it is hard to see the animation that consists of three frames of animation. The animation cells are supposed to simulate the look of fire, but I think that they could be much better.

The Daemon Death

Archer is equipped with a magical bow and, therefore, the damage done by the arrows shot by this bow should be somewhat magical. I decided to take some of the code from the Mechs game that was used to disintegrate the mechs for the death sequence of the Daemons. The idea behind this was that the magical arrow was sending the Daemon to another dimension. Whatever dimension the Daemon gets sent to when it is hit by an arrow, the Daemon is put into a dying state and, for a few frames, the Daemon bit-map is drawn using a modified bit blitter. This modified bit blitter, instead of taking the actual bit-map and blitting it down unscathed, takes the bit-map and then logically AND the data with random noise. The result is then filtered red and placed into the double buffer. This has the effect of making the bit-map look like it's transporting or disintegrating. We never formally looked at this code, but you can see it now in Listing 17.3.

Listing 17.3. The disintegrating bit blitter.

```
void Draw_Sprite_DBM(sprite_ptr sprite)
{

// this function draws a sprite on the screen row by row very quickly
// note the use of shifting to implement multiplication
// also it is used as a special effect, the sprite drawn is melted by
// using the sprite area as a filter region to place red pixels in

char far *work_sprite;
int work_offset=0,offset,x,y;
unsigned char data;

// alias a pointer to sprite for ease of access

work_sprite = sprite->frames[sprite->curr_frame];

// compute offset of sprite in video buffer

offset = (sprite->y << 8) + (sprite->y << 6) + sprite->x;

for (y=0; y<sprite_height; y++)
    {
    // copy the next row into the double buffer using memcpy for speed

    for (x=0; x<sprite_width; x++)
        {

        // test for transparent pixel i.e. 0, if not transparent then draw

        if ((work_sprite[work_offset+x]))
            double_buffer[offset+x] = RED_BASE+rand()%32;

        } // end for x

    // move to next line in double buffer and in sprite bit-map buffer

    offset      += SCREEN_WIDTH;
    work_offset += sprite_width;

    } // end for y

} // end Draw_Sprite_DBM
```

The Dreaded Bat

After I played Venture for a while, it seemed to be missing something, so I added a bat that would fly over every so often to add to the overall mood of the game. The bat is a sprite that is launched based on a random variable. Its flight pattern and logic are very simple. The bat logic starts the bat from either the left or right edge of the screen. Then the logic selects a starting vertical position and starts the bat on its way. After the bat has started, it can operate in one of two states. The first state is "steady flight." In this state the bat moves in a straight line until it hits the opposite edge of the screen where it self-terminates. The second state of operation is "wave flight." When the bat is in this mode of operation, it follows a SINE wave curve as it flies overhead. This makes it look like it's dipping down and trying to attack poor Archer.

Currently, the bat is passive and has no idea whether it's flying above Venture, Sea Shark, or whatever. It would nice to make it dart down at Archer or to at least make it a target that Archer could shoot. I have to admit that I did have the bat doing something, but I took it out. The screen was getting too cluttered with little black splotches all over the ground!

The Objects in the Game

Within Venture there are many objects that can be collected, such as gold, silver, potion, food, arrows, the dagger, and even an axe. These objects are of the stationary type and they are only images; they have no active role in the game. The only way that the game logic determines whether the Archer has picked one of these up is by converting Archer's coordinates into cell-matrix coordinates and then accessing the screen data structure to see if the cell Archer is on has an object in it, such as a sack of arrows or food. This conversion is done by taking the rough center of Archer and dividing this position by a factor of 16 (as each cell is 16×16). This cell position is then used to access the screen data structure, and the bit-map ID from the data structure is retrieved and compared against the ID for each of the objects in the game. The fragment of code found in Listing 17.4 does just this.

Listing 17.4. The code that determines what Archer is picking up.

```
// obtain cell location of player's feet as this is a pseudo 3-D view
// and his feet are more meaningful than his center

cell_x = (player.x+8)  >> 4;  // divide by 16 as cells are 16x16 pixels
cell_y = (player.y+14) >> 4;
```

continues

Listing 17.4. continued

```
// what is the cell at this location

cell_id = world[screen_y][screen_x].cells[cell_y][cell_x];

// is this cell a wall or obstruction?
```

You will notice that the test point on Archer is skewed toward his feet because they are what would touch an object first. Finally, as objects are collected, variables are updated such as health, arrows, and so on.

The Dagger of Mosk

Venture has one special object that deserves its own explanation. Finding this object is the whole goal of the game and the object is, of course, the enchanted dagger of Mosk. The dagger is implemented the same as all the other objects in the game except that it has a blade that is drawn using a special color register. This color register is manipulated to make the blade (or anything in the color) glow red. This color manipulation is done by a self-contained function that is called every cycle. The function is so simple and compact, I can't resist showing it to you.

Listing 17.5. The dagger glowing function.

```
void Glow_Dagger(void)
{
// this is a self-contained function that makes the dagger glow

static int clock=0,        // used for timing, note: they are static!
           entered_yet=0,
           ci=2;           // used to make color increase or decrease

RGB_color color;           // used to hold color values during processing

// test if function is being called for first time

if (!entered_yet)
   {
   // reset the palette registers to bright blue, dark blue, dark blue
   color.red   = 32;
   color.green = 0;
   color.blue  = 0;
   Set_Palette_Register(254,(RGB_color_ptr)&color);

   // system has initialized, so flag it
   entered_yet=1;
```

```
      } // end if first time into function

// try and glow dagger
   if (++clock==1)  // is it time to rotate
      {
      // get the color
      Get_Palette_Register(254,(RGB_color_ptr)&color);

      // increase or decrease color
      color.red+=ci;

      // test if max or min or range has been hit
      if (color.red>63 ¦¦ color.red<2)
         ci=-ci;

      // set the colors
      Set_Palette_Register(254,(RGB_color_ptr)&color);

      // reset the clock
      clock=0;
      } // end if time to rotate

} // end Glow_Dagger
```

The function is self-contained and self-initializing. During its first call, the function initializes the color register used for the glowing effect (which is 254), and on subsequent calls the register is updated.

The Archer's Inventory Display

No adventure game would be complete without some kind of inventory display to show players what they have (or don't have). Venture's inventory display is positioned on the right side of the screen and takes up the full vertical extent of the screen. The display shows everything that Archer needs to know, including his health, riches, arrows, and magical items on his belt. The display is implemented using simple text blitting and is updated at the end of every game cycle.

Originally, the display was oriented horizontally and positioned at the bottom of the screen, but this just didn't look right. The advantage of this was that the double buffer could be made smaller since the inventory display doesn't have a lot of animation in it and didn't need to be updated flicker free (see Figure 17.6).

However, the game ran fast enough and the added speed wasn't a worthy trade for the way it looked (which was bad).

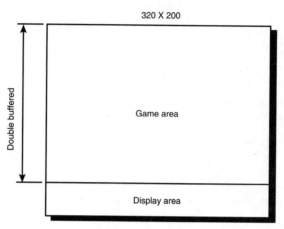

By placing the display area
at the bottom, only the game
area needs to be double
buffered. This can increase
the frame rate from 10 percent
to 30 percent.

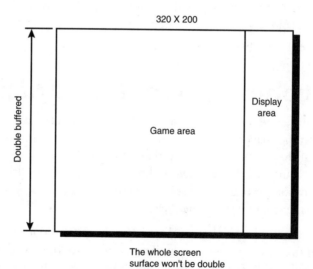

The whole screen
surface won't be double
buffered.

Figure 17.6. *Different screen display setups.*

The Exit Door

Archer needs a way to get out, and the exit door (or tunnel) is his only hope. The exit door is an object just like all the others except that Archer doesn't pick it up. When the software detects that Archer has stepped on the exit object, the game "end sequence" is initiated. If Archer has the dagger, then the game ends in a good way; otherwise, Archer gets a nasty message. The code that tests for the exit door being stepped on is shown in Listing 17.6.

Listing 17.6. A code fragment showing the logic of the exit door.

```
case EXIT_ID: // Archer is trying to exit
              {
              // exit if dagger found

              if (dagger_found)
                  done=1;

              } break;
```

As you can see, the fragment is from a `switch()` statement that actually tests all the possible bit-map IDs that Archer could be standing on. In this case the main loop exit condition is set, and the game moves to the end game sequence, which is either a letter from the King or a hazing by the evil landlord of the dungeon.

The Scoring System

The scoring system for Venture uses a fixed-point value scale as does Sea Shark. The Daemons are worth 250 points, and finding the dagger is worth 1,000 points. The points are recorded in the variable `players_score`. You may want to further embellish this by adding a random factor to the score or taking into consideration distance. For example, to add a random factor when the Archer kills a monster, you might change the current score code

```
players_score+=250;
```

to

```
players_score+=(250+rand()%50);
```

This would add up to an extra 50 points, which you could argue was due because the specific monster the player killed was meaner than the others!

The Input System

The input system for Venture had to have full control of the keyboard. There was no way that Venture would work properly with standard C input. The reason for this was that the player has to be able to press more than one key at a time. For example, the player wants to move forward and fire simultaneously. The second reason for using direct keyboard access is that the BIOS functions supported by the C library buffer keyboard input and have poor real-time response. The keyboard code that we created during Day 11 was used to solve these problems, and after using it, I am very happy with it. We did a good job designing it. Its usage and installation are almost transparent.

The rough version of Venture was made using standard getch(). Then, when the game was near completion, the new keyboard handler was put in. This is a good technique to use because the keyboard handler is kind of greedy and takes the keyboard ISR over completely. This makes it hard for screen-capture software and even debuggers because they are pushed out by the "aggressive" keyboard handler.

To refresh your memory on how the keyboard handler is used, let's go through a quick exercise in it. First, the proper include file (graph11.h) must be included. Then somewhere in the main() function, the keyboard handler should be installed with a call to Install_Keyboard(), and at the end of the game a call should be made to Delete_Keyboard(). As long as these two functions are called, anywhere in between them the keyboard action array can be accessed as a global array (which is declared in graph11.h). For example, to see if the up-arrow key is pressed, you would write the following:

```
if (key_table[INDEX_UP])
    {
    // perform action
    } // end if up
```

That's it.

Please note that when the keyboard handler is installed, the C keyboard functions will most likely malfunction except for the shift-state functions.

Background Animation and FX

Venture has no background animation or effects except for the color register animation that is being done to register 254. I suppose that this could be used to create a few effects in the game grid, but currently there are none.

End-of-Game Control

You have learned that the end of game occurs if Archer dies or if he tries to exit. If he exits with the dagger, the game displays the goal screen; otherwise, the game voices a verbal message. In either case, the main event loop flag (*done*) is set and the main event loop is exited.

Closing Scene

The only closing scene that Venture has is a picture of a page with a message from the King that appears if the game is solved. There is no animation except for the screen transition. It would be nice if the page burned.

What We Learned

We learned how to create a cell-based world that supports paged scrolling. We learned how to detect collisions with moving objects in the world and with stationary objects. Finally, we learned that clean and simple data structures can make everyone's lives easier.

Making the Game Better

First, Venture is just asking to have more levels, which are very easy to implement. All you would have to do is load another .DAT file after the current level was solved. Also, the bat needs to be a more active part of the game. Finally, there should be at least three different monster types in the game. This will be easy to implement since all that is really needed is the artwork.

BUGS

I'm sure I haven't found one tenth of all the bugs in Venture, but here are the ones I have noticed. Archer can get stuck in walls. This occurs sometimes when moving from screen to screen. Next, the monsters oscillate sometimes when chasing Archer. I suspect this is caused by the granularity of their motion.

Building the Game

Venture consists of four main parts: the universe database, the sound configuration file, the sound effects themselves, and all the .PCX files for the artwork. Using these files along with the game library an executable can be created. Here is a complete list of all the files used for Venture.

Software

VENTURE.C	—The source code to Venture.
VENTURE.CFG	—The sound configuration file.
VENTURE.DAT	—The universe database in ASCII format.

Graphics

VENTIMG.PCX	—The main imagery for Venture.
VENTEXPL.PCX	—The animation for the explosion.
VENTBAK.PCX	—The background.
VENTWEAP.PCX	—The arrows and the fireballs.
VENTINT.PCX	—The introduction screen.
VENTINS.PCX	—The instruction screen.
VENTGOAL.PCX	—The goal screen displayed when Archer finds the dagger.

Sounds

VHEALTH.VOC	—The low-health warning.
VHURT.VOC	—The sound that Archer makes when he is hit.
VMONEY.VOC	—The sound of gold and silver being picked up.
VMFIRE.VOC	—The spitting sound of the monsters.
VARROW.VOC	—The sound of an arrow hitting a monster.
VEAT.VOC	—The sound of Archer eating.
VINTRO.VOC	—The introduction message.
VFARROW.VOC	—The message heard when Archer finds arrows.
VPOTION.VOC	—The message heard when Archer finds potion.
VEND.VOC	—The end-of-game message.
VBOW.VOC	—The sound of the bow being pulled.
VBAT.VOC	—The sound of the bat flying.

VMDIE.VOC	—The sound a monster makes when it dies.
VDAGGER.VOC	—The message heard when the dagger is found.
VDEATH.VOC	—The scream of Archer when he dies.
VGOAL.VOC	—The sound heard if Archer does his job.

Libraries

| GAMELIB.LIB | —Our game library. |

Building an Executable: To make an executable of the program, you can use the source on the disk. The name of the source is venture.c. The precompiled executable is named venture.exe. As before, use the following compile line for Microsoft C:

```
cl -AM -Zi -c -Fc -Gs -G2 venture.c
```

After compiling the program in this manner, you can link it to the standard libraries and our game library (gamelib.lib) to create an executable.

17

Summary

Today you saw how a multiscreen adventure-type game can be created and implemented using our library. You learned how to effectively represent the game universe, detect collisions, and have multiple instances of game objects active simultaneously. You also learned the importance of good data structures and the necessity of tools.

Q&A

Q Why is the game universe only 4×4; why not make it bigger?

A There is no reason other than that it would take longer to create the VENTURE.DAT file; however, the game is designed to handle any size universe just by changing a few constants in the code.

Q How long did it take to create Venture?

A It took seven days and seven nights (literally), or about 140 hours.

Q How can I easily change what the monsters look like?

A Simply edit the .PCX files and change what they look like; however, the bit-maps must be the exact same size, 16×16, and the placement of the bit-maps in the .PCX files must be exact.

Q I see that there is artwork for the 3-D walls; why didn't you use it?

A It was too hard to create the world, and it would have taken too long. Feel free, however, to complete the world with the 3-D wall bit-maps yourself.

Workshop

The Workshop section presents quiz questions to help you cement your new knowledge and exercises to give you experience using what you've learned. Try to understand the questions and exercises before moving on to the next lesson. The answers are in Appendix B.

Quiz

1. How many frames of animation does Archer have?

2. Why use Archer's feet to center the object-detection test?

3. What is the effect of having a probability distribution for the selection of the Daemon states?

4. How many arrows can Archer shoot at once?

5. Look at the code for Venture and determine the probability of the bat flying out as a function of time (given that there are 18 frames per second)?

Exercises

1. Fix all the bugs in the game.

2. Make Archer able to shoot down the bat.

3. Add two more monsters to the game.

4. Create an entire new universe for the game to run on—that is, make a new VENTURE.DAT file.

18

Simulating Cities
with Sim-Pizza

In recent years a new breed of video game has become more and more popular: simulation. Granted, simulations have been around for a long time; however, they usually had limited graphics and sounds and were implemented mostly with text. The company Maxis took the concept of simulations one step further and gave the player the ability to act as a minor god who could control and alter factors influencing the simulation. The most popular of the early SIMs was called SIMCITY.

These new simulations are very complex, and an entire book could be written on how to create them. Today you will skim the surface of these capabilities by implementing a game that has a small city with cars, pedestrians, a pizza delivery boy, and customers. Our simulation won't allow us to alter the game universe, change the environment, or build things, but it will allow us to sit back passively and watch it operate. This is one of the facets of simulations: if you choose, you can just sit and watch the simulation rather than take an active role in it.

The challenge of creating even a simple simulation is modeling the objects in the game world. Sim-Pizza is a pizza delivery simulation and is as close to life as you can get. (Yeah, right!) It's a lot of fun and is a welcome change from the standard games we've been writing. Today's agenda contains the following items:

- [ ] The initial concept
- [ ] The artwork
- [ ] The sound FX and sound system
- [ ] Playing the game
- [ ] Playing tips
- [ ] The introduction
- [ ] The instructions
- [ ] The representation of the universe
- [ ] Tony's pizza hut
- [ ] Vinnie the pizza boy
- [ ] The pizzas
- [ ] The order scheduler
- [ ] Vinnie's demise
- [ ] The humans

- [ ] The splats
- [ ] The cars
- [ ] The customers
- [ ] Virtual time in Sim-Pizza
- [ ] The moped's instruments
- [ ] The scoring system
- [ ] The difficulty system
- [ ] The input system
- [ ] The end-of-game control
- [ ] The time card
- [ ] What we learned
- [ ] Making the game better
- [ ] BUGS
- [ ] Building the game

The Initial Concept

The idea for Sim-Pizza was based on the Atari arcade game Paper Boy. I wanted to do something that had an autonomous city running in the background and a main character who had some kind of job to do. My friend Dion and I came up with Vinnie the pizza delivery boy, and the concept for Sim-Pizza emerged (see Figure 18.1). The idea of the game was to have Vinnie deliver pizzas to customers within a small area of the city (Little Italy). The deliveries would be dispatched by a pizza hut owned by Vinnie's uncle Tony. First Vinnie receives an order via the radio-linked communications display mounted on his moped's handlebars. (Yes, Vinnie uses a moped to deliver pizzas.) Then he takes the pizza to the customer's home, which glows or blinks for a couple seconds so that Vinnie can determine its location.

Delivering pizzas is fine, but background animation is needed, so I added an entire city of cars and people to make things more interesting. Therefore, the city block to which Vinnie delivers contains freely moving pedestrians and cars. Moreover, the people can be hit by cars or the moped, and the cars in turn can hit Vinnie. Just as in real life, then,

Vinnie needs to be careful when driving through the city. Finally, to make the game more financially rewarding, Vinnie receives tips from his customers if he makes the delivery promptly, and he is paid a base salary of $4.25 per hour. His daily total is tallied up at the end of the game and displayed on a time card. After you play the simulation for an entire eight-hour day (which is about 10 minutes on the computer), you will have a much greater appreciation for the poor pizza delivery boy who makes stops at your house!

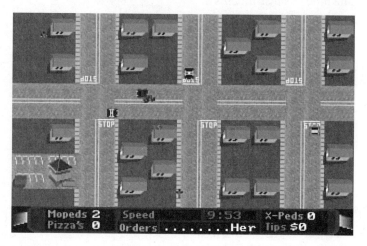

Figure 18.1. *You and your moped in the world of Sim-Pizza.*

The Artwork

The artwork for Sim-Pizza was much easier than that of Venture. Even though Sim-Pizza uses perspective artwork to simulate a 3-D view, the artwork itself was easier to create because there was less of it and there was little animation. The artwork for Sim-Pizza consists of the background bit maps for the city. These include the grass, roads, stop signs, houses, and pizza hut imagery. Then there are the bit maps for the cars that are not animated. Next, the human bit maps—which are animated, but which are so tiny that the minimal animation looks fine. In addition, there are the graphics for Vinnie's moped. The moped is very small but has to look semi-realistic because it can turn in 1 of 16 different directions or at 22.5-degree intervals. Lastly, there are the frames of animation for the pizza that Vinnie can throw and for the pain frames for the humans and Vinnie. See Figure 18.2 for a composite of all the artwork.

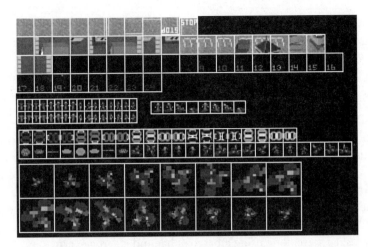

Figure 18.2. *The artwork for Sim-Pizza.*

Vinnie's death sequence is very interesting because it consists of a set of animation frames that were consecutively enlarged to make Vinnie look like he is getting bigger (or is being thrown into the air) as he dies. This enlargement was done prior to the game using Deluxe Animation to scale and rotate the bit maps. We'll cover this feature in greater detail in a few moments. Sim-Pizza probably has more different sized bit maps than any game thus far, which is shown in detail in Table 18.1.

Table 18.1. The bit map sizes used for Sim-Pizza.

Object	Object Size in Pixels	Animation Frames
Vinnie and his moped	12x12	16
Vinnie's death sequence	32x30	16
Humans	6x10	4
Human's death	10x10	4
Cars	12x12	4
Pizza	6x6	8
Basic World Cell	16x16	N/A

As you can see, Sim-Pizza has many different sized bit maps. In general, you should avoid using this many different bit maps; for this game, however, there was no way around it.

The Sound FX and Sound System

Sim-Pizza uses the same enhanced sound interface as Sea Shark and Venture, so I won't belabor the new functionality. The sounds for Sim-Pizza were the most challenging yet because the sounds of cars skidding, pulling away, honking, and so forth had to be digitized using real props. Alas, in the quest for reality my friends and I went into the parking garage, and with a Geo Tracker and a 944 Porsche as props, we made all the sounds that you hear in Sim-Pizza. The Italian accents were done by me (half my family is Sicilian, so I have mastered the accent), and the sound effects of people getting smashed and crushed were done using a baseball bat and a garbage can.

The sound system uses the standard configuration file to set the I/O port and interrupt. Currently, the CT-VOICE.DRV found in today's working directory is for the Sound Blaster 16; hence, if yours is a different model you will have to overwrite this file. Table 18.2 catalogs the different sound effects in Sim-Pizza.

Table 18.2. The sound effects for Sim-Pizza.

Sound Effect	Technique
Car starting	Geo Tracker burning rubber
Car stopping	Geo Tracker skidding
Moped horn	Geo Tracker's horn
Car horn	Porsche's Horn
Human being hit	Baseball bat, garbage can, and human voice
Vinnie being hit	Baseball bat, garbage can, and human voice
Male customer	Male human voice
Female customer	Male human voice
Tony telling Vinnie there's a delivery	Human voice
Tony scolding Vinnie for losing an order	Human voice

Sound Effect	Technique
Tony telling Vinnie the day's over	Human voice
The introduction	Human voice

Playing the Game

To play Sim-Pizza, simply type **SIMPIZZA.EXE** in today's working directory and the game loads an execute. Make sure to have the proper settings in the SIMPIZZA.CFG sound initialization file and the correct CT-VOICE.DRV sound driver for your particular sound driver. When the game launches, you see an introduction screen that dissolves into an instruction screen. To exit the instruction screen, press any key. In a couple seconds the game begins and you find yourself looking at the game area in the upper region of the screen and the handlebars of your moped in the lower region of the screen. Vinnie is sitting on his moped in the parking lot of the pizza hut waiting for you to control him. The moped is controlled by the arrow keys. The up and down arrows are used for throttle and brakes, respectively, and the right and left arrows are used to turn the moped.

The moped has a new gyrosynchronous stabilizer, so you won't fall down no matter how slowly you go. This feature comes in handy when making tight turns. Vinnie's moped has a rack on the back that holds the pizzas; this rack is currently empty. To obtain some pizzas, drive into the pizza hut and make a circle; Tony will be sure to give you some pizzas. At this point you are ready to go. Drive onto the street and wait for an order to be displayed in the "order" window of your control panel. When an order arrives, you see the number of the house, and the house blinks a few times on the game area. At this point, drive to the house and press the space bar to throw a pizza at the customer.

There are a few rules of thumb to follow. First, Vinnie is right handed, so he always throws the pizza from his right side. Next, the pizza will only stay airworthy for about 50 feet, so make sure to be close to the house you are delivering to and try to hit the front door! Also, as you are driving around, you will undoubtedly notice pedestrians and cars. The cars will flatten you if you're not careful, and the moped is hazardous to the lives of the pedestrians. Watch out! If you hit a pedestrian or if you are hit by a car, there will be a mess. Lastly, if you go psycho and decide to go on a Death Race 2000 spree, you have to pay for each injured pedestrian at the end of the day.

Sim-Pizza simulates a working day; therefore, the game lasts from 9:00 a.m. to 5:00 p.m. on the virtual clock on the moped's display. This is about ten minutes of real time. This

18

time will be cut short on two occasions: if you press the Esc key or if you destroy all the mopeds. In either case, the game ends and the time card with a fully annotated listing of the day's work (and carnage) is displayed.

Playing Tips

Sim-Pizza is a very tense game. By the time the afternoon begins, you will be inundated by orders, upset customers. and tons of traffic. Your best strategy is to keep calm and focus on one thing at a time. Don't try to run from one end of the city to another; this will probably result in lost orders. Next, drive in the middle of the roads between lanes; this strategy almost guarantees that you are never hit. Although it is tempting to smash the pedestrians, try to control yourself; they are very costly, and you make only $4.25 per hour! Finally, deliver your orders as quickly as possible, and make sure to approach the homes slowly and take aim; otherwise, you will be throwing pizzas away, which will surely upset Uncle Tony!

The Introduction

The introduction to Sim-Pizza is a standard PCX file that was captured from game play; the file was then drawn on using Deluxe Animation from Electronic Arts. It would have been nice to have Vinnie drive across the bottom of the screen and draw out the title *Sim-Pizza* by throwing pizzas at the screen, and then throw a pizza at the viewer; that final pizza could then drip off the screen. Maybe next time...

The Instructions

The instruction screen was drawn as a PCX file. Because of the complexity of Sim-Pizza, however, I wish that the resolution was higher so that more text could could appear on-screen that describes features of the game—such as how you can press the Alt key to blow the moped's horn.

The Representation of the Universe

Sim-Pizza uses a cell-based universe mixed with a transparent line-based representation that bounds the houses. The main reason I chose a cell-based world was to allow different cities to be easily used for the game and collision detection. Because the cities are constructed from bit-map IDs, just as the screens of Venture were, it is very easy to make

an entire city. If the city was an actual PCX image, then the positions of the houses, the pizza hut, the road, and so on would all have to be recorded somewhere, and the collision detection would become much more complex. Moreover, the current position of the moped couldn't be used to index into a table of bit-map IDs to compute what the moped was bumping into.

One problem occurred when using a purely cell-based world, and it arose when trying to test whether the pizza thrown by Vinnie was hitting the front of a house. The problem is that the front of the houses for both the Eastward and Westward homes takes up different portions of the 16×16 pixel bit map used for the cell; furthermore, the front of the house extends into a portion of another bit map. This is because the homes are created by tiling four bit maps next to each other in a 2×2 grid (see Figure 18.3). Having such an ill-defined front of the house region was going to be a problem for collision detection, so the solution was to create a database of the center of each home as the screen was being drawn. This database, along with the bit-map IDs, could be used to create a bounding box around the front of each home that was more realistic and could be used by the pizza code to determine whether the pizza hit the front of the home. The data structure that holds the positions of the houses along with some other information is shown in Listing 18.1.

18

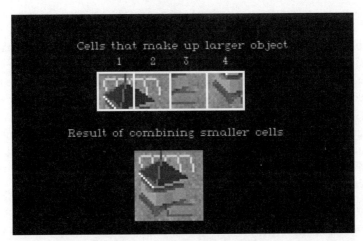

Figure 18.3. *Building a larger object by using bit map cells.*

Listing 18.1. The data structure for a house.

```
// this is the structure used to database all the house
// positions in the city
```

continues

Listing 18.1. continued

```
typedef struct house_typ
        {
        int x;      // position of house
        int y;
        int type; // type of house i.e.east or west front door
        int num;    // house number

        int state;  // is there an order pending

        int timer;  // the current time left to
                    // deliver the pizza

        } house, *house_ptr;
```

The position of the house in screen coordinates is stored in the position fields along with the direction of the house being stored in the type field. The state and timer fields are used by the ordering scheduler to track which homes have pending orders and how long the residents of those houses have been waiting for their pizzas. There is a structure for each house in the game, and an array is used to hold all of them. The array's declaration is as follows:

```
house house_pos[MAX_HOUSES];  // the houses in the city
```

The preceding array is used only to track the positions of the homes—mainly to compute collision detection. However, there is a second reason for creating the array. When the game runs, you will notice that the homes blink with white numbers on their roofs. This is accomplished by drawing number bit maps on top of the homes *after* the screen has been initially drawn using the cell-based bit maps. Because the homes were drawn using the screen-drawing function, the only way that the numbers could be successfully placed on the tops of the homes is by creating the house_pos[] array to track their positions. Then, after the initial bit maps for the house are drawn with the rest of the background, you can draw the numbers.

The house_pos[] array is needed for a couple of important reasons, but the actual drawing of the screen is performed by reading the cell data, and then converting the bit-map IDs into images and blitting them on the screen. The technique used in Sim-Pizza is the same as that used for Venture, except that the data structure holding the screen image in Sim-City isn't loaded from disk; it is part of the program defined globally. The only reason for this difference is that I didn't see us needing different cities at this point. Listing 18.2 includes the name of the data structure and the data within it.

Listing 18.2. The data structure that holds the city.

```
// the city that pizza boy delivers to

char *city_1[CELL_ROWS] = {
                "..45[]0145[]{.45[]01",
                "..76[]3276[]0176[]32",
                "..45[]01.}[]3245[]01",
                "..76s]32.}s]{.76s]32",
                "^^^^##^^^^##^^^^##^^",
                "vvvv##vvvv##vvvv##vv",
                "..45[S{.45[S0145[S{.",
                "..76[]0176[]3276[]01",
                "cd89[]3245[]{..}[]32",
                "feba[]0176[]0145[]01",
                "...}[]32.}[]3276[]32",};
```

The characters selected to define the different bit maps in Sim-Pizza are definitely more cryptic than those of Venture. This was mainly because the characters had to represent different portions of larger objects such as houses, the pizza hut, and different sides of the road. In fact, some of the objects are larger than 16×16 pixels, but they still had to be drawn using 16×16 cells. Of course, the cell size could be increased to 32×32, but this would decrease the overall resolution of the image and the placement of objects. Table 18.3 lists what each of the bit map ID characters represents in the game world.

Table 18.3. The bit maps for Sim-Pizza and the ASCII characters that represent them.

Object	ASCII Character
Grass	'.'
Plain road	'#'
East side of road	']'
West side of road	'['
North side of road	'^'
South side of road	'v'
Northbound stop sign	'S'
Southbound stop sign	's'

continues

Table 18.3. continued

Object	ASCII Character
Cell 1 of westward-pointing home	'0'
Cell 2 of westward-pointing home	'1'
Cell 3 of westward-pointing home	'2'
Cell 4 of westward-pointing home	'3'
Cell 1 of eastward-pointing home	'4'
Cell 2 of eastward-pointing home	'5'
Cell 3 of eastward-pointing home	'6'
Cell 4 of eastward-pointing home	'7'
Cell 1 of pizza hut	'8'
Cell 2 of pizza hut	'9'
Cell 3 of pizza hut	'a'
Cell 4 of pizza hut	'b'
Cell 1 of parking lot	'c'
Cell 2 of parking lot	'd'
Cell 3 of parking lot	'e'
Cell 4 of parking lot	'f'

Note: The larger objects that consist of more than one bit map are constructed by placing the cells in clockwise order in a 2×2 matrix.

Tony's Pizza Hut

The pizza hut is basically a stationary background object and could have just as well been a DMV or a Dairy Queen. The game doesn't know that the hut exists except for a test that is done in the main event loop that checks whether the moped is within a region

located on top of the pizza hut. If the player is in the region, then Vinnie's supply of pizzas is replenished. Therefore, if you move the location of the pizza hut by editing the `city_1[]` data structure, the code will still think that the hut is located in its original spot. The actual C code that does this test is in the `main()` module and is shown in Listing 18.3.

Listing 18.3. The code fragment that computes whether Vinnie has entered the pizza hut to replenish his supply of pizzas.

```
// test if moped has got a new load from the pizza hut

    tx = ((int)(boy.x >> FP_SHIFT))+6;
    ty = ((int)(boy.y >> FP_SHIFT))+8;

    if (tx>=40 && tx<=52 && ty>=136 && ty<=150)
        boy_pizzas = 5;
```

The code works by first converting the moped's position into integers, and then doing a rectangular bounding box test. The conversion to integers is necessary because the moped's position, velocity, and many other variables are in fixed-point representation. Fixed-point math was needed for the complex modeling of the moped such as friction, horse power, braking force, and so on.

Vinnie the Pizza Boy

Vinnie the pizza boy is the main hero in the game and is permanently mounted on a red Riva moped that has had some high-tech modifications made to the instrument panel. Vinnie also has the ability to throw pizzas at his customers. The moped is modeled in a fairly complex way, and most of the math that is done to the moped is done in fixed point with a 24.8 (24 bits whole part, 8 bits decimal part) representation. The fixed-point math was needed to simulate such things as acceleration, braking, and friction. These manifestations couldn't have been modeled properly with standard integral representations. Furthermore, I didn't want to use floating point because I felt it would be too much of a load on the game's performance. In any case, the use of fixed-point math in Sim-Pizza is a good example of the power of the technique, and you should study it very carefully.

The moped is basically a sprite with a large global data structure that contains the state of the moped along with the fields used for timing and event synchronization. The structure used to track all this information is shown in Listing 18.4.

18

Listing 18.4. The data structure for Vinnie the pizza boy.

```
// typedef for the player

typedef struct player_typ
        {
        fixed x;                    // x position
        fixed y;                    // y position

        fixed xv;                   // x velocity
        fixed yv;                   // y velocity

        fixed curr_xv;              // x velocity
        fixed curr_yv;              // y velocity

        fixed max_xv;               // max x velocity
        fixed max_yv;               // max y velocity


        fixed throttle;            // current throttle position
        fixed hp;                   // horse power
        fixed friction;             // the friction of
                                    // the air, bike, ...
        fixed brakes;               // the braking friction

        fixed max_throttle;         // maximum throttle position

        int state;                  // the state of the player
        int direction;
        int counter_1;              // use for counting
        int threshold_1;            // the counters threshold

        int counter_2;

        int threshold_2;

        int counter_3;
        int threshold_3;

        sprite object;              // the sprite

        } player, *player_ptr;
```

I'm sorry for naming the structure *player*, but that's life. The most interesting fields are the ones that deal with the modeling of the moped's motion. The fields related to the moped's motion are the position fields, the velocity fields, and the fields named throttle, hp, friction, max_throttle, and brakes. The position and velocity fields are used to reflect what these variables are doing, so we will focus our discussion on them. The throttle field is used to track the current amount of throttle that is being applied to the moped's velocity. This throttle is basically a multiplier used to control the amount of

horsepower (hp) applied to the final velocity of the moped. The friction variable is used to slow down the moped when there is no throttle being applied. To manually slow down the moped, use the brakes; to engage the brakes, press the down arrow.

The initialization of these variables and their relative magnitudes is rather interesting (see Listing 18.5).

Listing 18.5. The initialization of the moped motion state.

```
// set up state information

boy.state             = BOY_ALIVE;
boy.x                 = Assign_Integer(48);
boy.y                 = Assign_Integer(144);
boy.curr_xv           = 0;
boy.curr_yv           = 0;
boy.max_xv            = 0;
boy.max_yv            = 0;
boy.xv                = 0;
boy.yv                = 0;


boy.throttle          = 0;
boy.hp                = Assign_Float((float).4);
boy.friction          = Assign_Float((float)-.10);
boy.brakes            = Assign_Integer(1);

boy.max_throttle      = Assign_Integer(3);

boy.counter_1         = 0;
boy.threshold_1       = 2;

boy.object.curr_frame = 0;
boy.direction         = 0;
```

Note: The fixed-point fields are initialized using the functions from the fixed-point library that we created on Day 8. Of course, the assignments could have been made inline, but using the functions is cleaner. In addition, speed is not important during initialization, so function calls are fine.

The motion control of the moped is controlled totally in the main() of the program and updates the moped state every frame based on both the inputs and the current state. The last aspect of the moped we will discuss is the rotation of the moped. You accomplish the rotation by having 16 prerotated frames of animation, and then referring to a look-up

table to compute the proper velocity vector for each specific direction. The velocity look-up table was created by writing a small program that computed the SINE and COSINE of an angle as the angle went from 0 to 360 in 22.5-degree increments. This data was then brought into the program and placed into a table. The table is a fixed-point table, and its construction is rather interesting. The floating-point numbers are used with a multiplier and a cast to FIXED right in the definition of the table. This makes things much cleaner than having a floating-point table and then translating it to fixed point. Listing 18.6 shows the fixed-point table that holds the X component of the velocity vector for each of the 16 different angles in which the moped can drive.

Listing 18.6. A fixed-point table made of floating-point numbers.

```
// velocities used to compute trajectory vector of moped

fixed boy_xv[NUM_BOY_FRAMES] =

                    {(fixed)(1.000000*FP_SHIFT_2N),
                     (fixed)(0.923880*FP_SHIFT_2N),
                     (fixed)(0.707107*FP_SHIFT_2N),
                     (fixed)(0.382684*FP_SHIFT_2N),
                     (fixed)(0.000001*FP_SHIFT_2N),
                     (fixed)(-0.382682*FP_SHIFT_2N),
                     (fixed)(-0.707105*FP_SHIFT_2N),
                     (fixed)(-0.923879*FP_SHIFT_2N),
                     (fixed)(-1.000000*FP_SHIFT_2N),
                     (fixed)(-0.923881*FP_SHIFT_2N),
                     (fixed)(-0.707109*FP_SHIFT_2N),
                     (fixed)(-0.382687*FP_SHIFT_2N),
                     (fixed)(-0.000004*FP_SHIFT_2N),
                     (fixed)(0.382679*FP_SHIFT_2N),
                     (fixed)(0.707103*FP_SHIFT_2N),
                     (fixed)(0.923878*FP_SHIFT_2N)};
```

Note: The factor of FP_SHIFT_2N is equal to 256, which is analagous to shifting by eight bits to the left.

The Pizzas

You use the space bar to control the pizzas that Vinnie throws. Vinnie can only hold five pizzas on his moped, and the maximum number of pizzas that can be airborne at once is three. The pizzas were one of the harder animations to create because I haven't

personally seen many pizzas get chucked across a street. The final animation selected for the pizzas was to make them look like a flipping coin with a dark and light side. When in action, the pizzas look very cool and are fun to watch in mid-flight. There are eight frames of animation for the pizza, and the animation is invariant of direction of motion.

The pizzas are implemented as self-contained functions, and once they are started, they operate on their own. The direction of motion of the pizza has an interesting basis. Because Vinnie is right-handed, he must always throw the pizza perpendicular to the direction his moped is pointing. Using this geometric insight, the trajectory of the pizza can be computed by taking the COSINE and SINE of the moped's current direction minus 90 degrees (see Figure 18.4). This is mathematically correct, but a waste of time. Therefore, Sim-Pizza uses a look-up table with these calculations already done in them. The table is indexed by the current direction of the moped, which is one of 16 different positions numbered 0 through 15. Listing 18.7 shows the code that starts the pizza and computes the proper index into the look-up table.

18

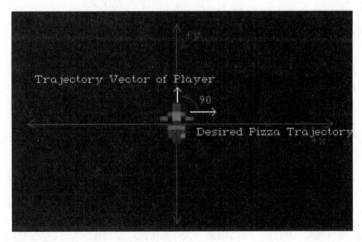

Figure 18.4. *Computing the trajectory of the pizza.*

Listing 18.7. The code that computes the proper direction to start a pizza in.

```
if (key_table[INDEX_SPACE]) // throw pizza
            {
            // throw a pizza

            // are there any pizzas to throw
```

continues

Listing 18.7. continued

```
if (—boy_pizzas<0)
   boy_pizzas = 0;
else
   {
   // send message

 Insert_Message("Here's your pizza mister!",1);

   // rotate pizza direction 90 CC

   direction = boy.direction - 4;

   if (direction<0)
       direction+=16;

   // send a pizza sailing

   Start_Pizza(((int)(boy.x >> FP_SHIFT)+5),
               ((int)(boy.y >> FP_SHIFT)+5),
               pizza_xv[direction],
               pizza_yv[direction],
               0);

   } // end else

} // end if throw a pizza
```

The code operates by first testing whether there are any pizzas to throw. Then it computes the proper index into the velocity look-up table, makes a call to the message display, and starts the pizza on its way.

The Order Scheduler

The order scheduler for Sim-Pizza is probably one of the most complex pieces of software we have seen thus far. The function of the scheduler is simply to send orders to Vinnie. This function might seem simple, but it is fairly complex because not only must the orders be given, but they must be tracked and aged. By *aging*, I mean that once an order has been issued, there must be a finite amount of time at which point the order is lost and is no longer valid. The order scheduler must take care of this aging process, as well as inform Vinnie about lost orders. The order scheduler is also connected to the software that makes the number on a customer's house blink to indicate the location of the house.

Therefore, there are three components to the overall order scheduler. The first component is the scheduler itself that uses a random variable based on the time of day (the later

in the day, the more orders) to send an order. The second component is the data structure and software that tracks and ages orders and terminates the order if too much time passes. Finally, there is a connection between the scheduler and the software that illuminates the numbers on houses. This is needed so that when an order is sent, the player can see the location of the house. The software that illuminates the number on a house can only handle one home at a time, so if another order is sent before the house has completed its cycle, the current house will be pre-empted and the new order will be served. This doesn't mean the order is terminated; it means that the player may not see the house number illuminated for a complete cycle—four blinks.

Vinnie's Demise

If Vinnie drives carelessly, sooner or later he will be hit by a car and thrown a couple hundred feet into the air. This effect was accomplished by taking the bit maps for the moped and enlarging them in steps to make the moped look like it is getting closer—coming toward the screen. These bit maps were then loaded into a sprite structure along with some timing parameters. When the moped is hit by a car, the player or Vinnie (however you want to think of him) is put into a dying state, and the death sequence takes over for a couple seconds.

18

The death sequence works by displaying a total of 16 animation cells. The 16 cells are broken into two blocks of time: the time when the moped is flying upward and the time when the moped is flying downward toward Earth. Also, as the frames are displayed, the moped is translated toward the center of the screen to simulate perspective; when the moped falls back down to where the impact took place, the moped tracks on the point of impact. The sequence thus has a 3-D look to it. After the death sequence is complete, the player is placed back into the normal "alive" mode, and the game continues from the pizza hut. Of course, Vinnie has one fewer moped now, a fact that is recorded and displayed by the moped's instruments.

The Pedestrians

One of the simulation aspects of Sim-Pizza is that pedestrians walk around the city. These pedestrians are implemented much like the monsters in Venture, except that they are more passive. The pedestrians only have two states of operation: alive and dead. The pedestrian software will start a pedestrian on one of the streets and select a direction of motion (East, West, North, or South) for the pedestrian to move in. Some pedestrians are blue and some are red. Once the pedestrian is started, the software continues to

animate the pedestrians' walk, testing for collision with the homes, cars, or a moped. If a collision is detected, a splat is started; this splat is a death sequence, and the pedestrian is removed from the active list.

The Splats

The splats are not part of the pedestrian code and are more like an explosion that looks like a pedestrian getting smashed. The "splats" are self contained and will run for a few frames and then terminate. There can only be four active splats at one time. This should be enough to serve all the pedestrians getting hit, since on average only two are getting converted into pavement simultaneously!

The Cars

The cars in Sim-Pizza weren't as easy to model as I thought they would be. The basic problem was that the cars needed to be able to "see" each other in the virtual world. I soon came to the conclusion that this feature would take too long to implement, so I had to create another strategy. The strategy was to start the cars on the four main roads and place stop signs on the Northward and Southward traveling streets. Then an algorithm was created that would start a car on one of the roads in one of the possible directions. If the car hit a stop sign, it would stop, wait a moment, and accelerate. This method, coupled with a scheduler that minimized the probability of two cars driving down the same road, was the final solution.

In the end, the cars look realistic and their motion is believable. In addition, the sound FX for them stopping, driving, and starting makes them seem alive. Currently, the simulation can have up to eight cars, which is more than enough. If there were any more, then the probability of two cars driving on the same street at the same time would be too high. The cars have no car-car collision detection, and they can't turn. They are basically oblivious to the entire universe around them. A slightly better model of them could be made by testing the space in front of each car as it travels to see if another car is blocking it; if so, the car in the rear would slow down or stop. This added feature would disallow two cars piling on each other, which currently occurs every once in a while. Finally, the cars are full of sound FX. I hope you like these sounds; I almost got carted off to jail making them!

The Customers

The customers in Sim-Pizza only exist as far as the order scheduler is concerned. Each house isn't really able to place an order. The orders are given to a house. This is backward, but for the purposes of a game, it doesn't matter. In any case, once an order is received by a house, a tip is given to Vinnie along with a verbal "thank you" (male or female voice). Subsequently, a text message reiterating the verbal message appears on the order display of the moped. Also, if Vinnie takes too long delivering an order, Tony will haze him verbally; this verbal hazing also appears as a text message in the order display.

Virtual Time in Sim-Pizza

Because I wanted to simulate in Sim-Pizza an entire day within a reasonable amount of real-time, a method had to be devised based on the frame rate to speed up time. The final decision was made that each minute of virtual time be roughly 25 frames, which makes the game last for about 10 minutes. The variable that tracks the current time is in virtual minutes and is called `boy_time`. It is initialized with 540, which is 9:00 a.m. (540/60=9). This variable is incremented every 25 frames and is used to display the time on the moped's digital clock. To display the time, the variable is converted into hours and minutes by division. When 5:00 p.m. arrives, the game ends; this occurs when `boy_time==1020`.

The Moped's Instruments

The instrument panel on the moped is implemented as text except for one item: the digital speedometer. I recently was driving a Corvette and it had a digital speedometer that was very cool, so I decided to place one on the moped. The information shown on the instrument panel is

- ☐ Number of pizzas on moped rack
- ☐ Number of mopeds remaining
- ☐ Time of day
- ☐ Number of injured pedestrians
- ☐ Tips
- ☐ The scrolling order display

18

All of the information displayed by the instruments is tracked in a set of variables that is updated by the game software each frame. Listing 18.8 covers the set of variables that does most of this tracking.

Listing 18.8. The variables that track the player's status.

```
// statistics of boy

int boy_mopeds    = 3,        // number of mopeds
    boy_pizzas    = 0,        // number of pizzas on moped rack
    boy_xpeds     = 0,        // number of peds player has killed
    boy_tips      = 0,        // current tips
    boy_time      = 540,      // the time in minutes
    orders_filled = 0,        // how many orders have been filled
    total_orders  = 0;        // total pizzas ordered
```

The scrolling display and the digital speedometer are handled differently. Let's talk about them.

The digital speedometer is really a set of lights that is implemented with color registers. The moped's current speed is used each frame to compute the number of the lights to illuminate. This is done by setting some of the color registers to bright blue and the others to dark blue. The number of lights to turn on is computed by dividing the maximum speed of the moped into intervals and then comparing the current speed to see what interval it falls within. Of course, this method of display is only approximate, but it didn't bother me in the Corvette, and I bet it won't bother you on the moped. Who cares if it's not practical; it looks good!

The scrolling order display is the most complex information display that we have seen so far. It is actually an entire piece of software that was written separately from the game and then merged. The display had to have the following attributes:

☐ The capability to display large messages

☐ The capability to queue a new message if a message is being displayed and another message is entered into the display

☐ The capability to terminate an existing message and display another message if the second message is important and was entered with a high priority

The solution to all of the these problems was to create a FIFO data structure that serves as a "consumer" of strings. Messages could be inserted into the structure by "producers," and another "consumer" would take the strings from the data structure and send them to a display function that would scroll them.

Note: The words *producer* and *consumer* are from operating system theory and they relate to the words *server* and *client*. However, with the entrance of X-Windows into the computer world, I don't think anyone really knows what a server and client are anymore. And I don't think people sleep as well!

The data structure used to hold the strings is a FIFO queue and is implemented with a stack. The message system is very clean, and a message can be entered into the queue at any time by using the function `Insert_Message(char *string, int preempt)`. If the preempt flag is set then the message will pre-empt anything that is currently being displayed. Take a look at Figure 18.5 to see a graphic representation of the way the pieces of the messaging system are put together and operate.

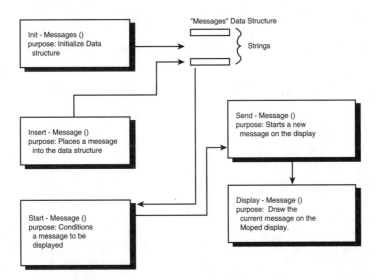

Figure 18.5. *The structure of the order messaging system.*

The Scoring System

Sim-Pizza, because of its simulation nature, doesn't have a system of points, but rather scores the player's overall performance. This performance is based on the number of orders sent out, the number filled, the number of pedestrians hit, the number of mopeds

destroyed, and the average time its takes to fill an order. Also, the player receives a salary of $4.25 per hour. All of these factors are taken into consideration to make up a time card that tallies all the information in a credit/deduction layout.

The Difficulty System

Sim-Pizza is supposed to simulate real life. With this as a motivation, the difficulty system of Sim-Pizza is based on the time of day. As the time of day nears 5:00 p.m., everything gets more hectic. This feature is achieved by updating a variable each hour. This variable is then used in all the probability calculations as a multiplier to compute the range of random variables. Consequently, the game gets harder as time flows forward. As an example, Listing 18.9 is an excerpt of the code that starts some of the objects in the game.

Listing 18.9. The difficulty variable being used to make things harder!

```
// start objects here

    if (rand()%(difficulty)==1)
       Start_Human();

    if (rand()%(difficulty)==1)
       Start_Car();

    if (rand()%(difficulty*5)==1)
       Order_Pizza();
```

Note: The variable `difficulty`, or a multiple of it, is used to control the range of the random variables used to start up different elements of the game.

The Input System

The input system of Sim-Pizza is done through the new keyboard handler. This was absolutely necessary, not because of tracking multiple key presses so much, but because the moped is very hard to steer without having a choppy keyboard interface such as `getch()`. The keys tracked are the arrows, the space bar, Esc, and Alt (the moped horn).

End-of-Game Control

The determination of the end of the game is controlled by two factors. The first is the time of day. At 5:00 p.m., the game ends and the time card is displayed. The other event that can cause an early end-of-game sequence is the destruction of all the mopeds. In this case, Vinnie is promptly taken to the time card screen.

The Time Card

The time card is the icing on the cake and endorses the fact that getting ahead in America for young people is really difficult. The time card displays the events of the day and shows the totals for number of hours worked, tips, injuries, and lost orders, and presents the player with a final pay for the day—usually $0.00. Take a look at Figure 18.6 to see the time card display. The time card function is fairly simple and is based on straightforward calculations (see Listing 18.10).

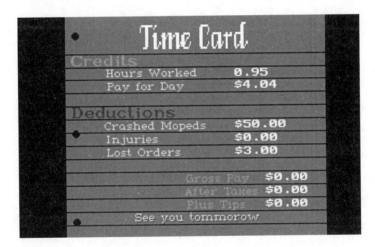

Figure 18.6. *The time card for the day.*

Listing 18.10. The time card function.

```
void Show_Stats(void)
{
// this function displays the stats screen

float hours,          // hours worked
```

continues

Listing 18.10. continued

```
        pay,          // pay due to salary
        cost_mopeds,  // cost of breaking mopeds
        cost_lost,    // cost due to lost orders
        cost_injuries, // cost of hurting peds
        gross,        // gross pay
        net,          // net pay after taxes and deductions
        final;        // total finally pay

char buffer[64];  // used to build up stat strings

// load instruction screen and display it until a key press

PCX_Init((pcx_picture_ptr)&intro_pcx);
PCX_Load("simstats.pcx", (pcx_picture_ptr)&intro_pcx,1);
PCX_Show_Buffer((pcx_picture_ptr)&intro_pcx);

// display stats
// hours worked

hours = (float)(boy_time-540)/(float)60;
sprintf(buffer,"%.2f",hours);
Blit_String(202,48,15,buffer,1);

// total pay

pay = 4.25*hours;
sprintf(buffer,"$%.2f",pay);
Blit_String(202,59,15,buffer,1);

// crashed mopeds

cost_mopeds = 50*(3-boy_mopeds);
sprintf(buffer,"$%.2f",cost_mopeds);
Blit_String(202,95,15,buffer,1);

// injuries

cost_injuries = 100*boy_xpeds;
sprintf(buffer,"$%.2f",cost_injuries);
Blit_String(202,107,15,buffer,1);

// lost orders

cost_lost = 3*(total_orders-orders_filled);
sprintf(buffer,"$%.2f",cost_lost);
Blit_String(202,119,15,buffer,1);

// gross pay

gross = pay - cost_mopeds - cost_injuries - cost_lost;
if (gross<0)
    gross=0;
```

```
sprintf(buffer,"$%.2f",gross);
Blit_String(230,143,15,buffer,1);

// after taxes

net = gross*.7;
sprintf(buffer,"$%.2f",net);
Blit_String(230,155,15,buffer,1);

// plus tips

final = net+boy_tips;
sprintf(buffer,"$%.2f",final);
Blit_String(230,167,15,buffer,1);

// wait for exit

while(kbhit())
     getch();

// let user see it

while(!kbhit()){};
getch();

PCX_Delete((pcx_picture_ptr)&intro_pcx);

} // end Show_Stats
```

The time card function will not display a negative value even if Vinnie's damages cost more than the pay he made for the day. This is because his uncle pays for any damages, although if Vinnie racks up these debts, he's in big trouble when he gets home!

What We Learned

Today we learned that it's possible to build a fairly believable virtual model of a city with some simple programming techniques. The most important thing to be learned today, however, is that complexity can be created out of a collection of simple systems. The cars, humans, and moped of Sim-Pizza are simple when taken separately, but when thrown together, a rich and complex world seems to emerge. Granted, this world is just an illusion, but who cares? Illusion is the business we are in.

Making the Game Better

There are a million things that could be added to Sim-Pizza; I believe if my friends hadn't stopped me I would still be adding to it. First, the game needs to scroll. Scrolling would

allow Vinnie to drive through different parts of the city. Next, the cars should have more intelligent logic and the ability to turn and "see" in front of them. Another neat effect would be to see Vinnie drive into the pizza hut, meaning that when the moped is in the pizza hut reload area, the screen view could change to show a side view of another worker bringing pizzas to Vinnie and putting them on the moped's rack. Finally, the pedestrians need to do more than just walk in a straight line; they should get in fights or chase Vinnie!

BUGS

The word *bug* doesn't do justice to Sim-Pizza because the game needs many more features in order to be complete, but there are some little problems that I have noticed. First, the collision detection for everything just doesn't work right in all cases. This is related to the 3-D view emulation, the selection of test points on objects, and the size of the bounding boxes used in collision tests. The collision detection needs to be tuned up—especially the test for the pizza hitting a house. Next, a complete 8.0 hour day reads as 8.02 hours, which is no big deal, but needs to be fixed to be totally correct.

Building the Game

Sim-Pizza consists of the main program, the graphics, and the sounds. There is no universe database such as in Venture. An executable of the game can be created with these files and the game library GAMELIB.LIB. (Of course, the standard C libraries should be linked in also.) The following sections contain a complete list of software for Sim-Pizza.

Software

SIMPIZZA.C — The main source code for Sim-Pizza.
SIMPIZZA.CFG — The sound configuration file.

Graphics

SIMINT.PCX — The introduction screen.
SIMINS.PCX — The instruction screen.
SIMIMG.PCX — The main imagery for the city.
SIMSTATS.PCX — The time card screen.
SIMBAK.PCX — The moped's instruments.
SIMIMG2.PCX — The cars and the moped.

SIMIMG3.PCX —The imagery for the pedestrians.
SIMIMG4.PCX —The imagery for the pedestrians getting smashed.
SIMIMG5.pcx —The imagery for the flying pizza.
SIMIMG6.pcx —The death animation for the player.

Sounds

SMCSTOP.VOC —The car stopping.
SMCSTART.VOC—The car starting.
SMMHORN.VOC—The moped's horn.
SMCHORN.VOC—The car's horn.
SMMHIT.VOC —The moped being hit.
SMHHIT.VOC —A human being hit.
SMYO.VOC —Tony telling Vinnie there's an order.
SMLOST.VOC —Tony telling Vinnie he lost an order.
SMTHANK1.VOC—Thank you from a customer (male voice).
SMTHANK2.VOC—Thank you from a customer (female voice).
SMTOO.VOC —An upset customer (male).
SMCOME.VOC —Tony telling Vinnie to come home.
SMCAR.VOC —A car driving by in the distance.
SMSTART.VOC —Bada Boom Bada Bing!

Libraries

GAMELIB.LIB —Our game library.

Summary

Today you learned how to make a simulation. The problems of collision detection and world representations were covered. Also, you saw how advanced data structures such as queues sometimes come in handy. Finally, you learned that all video games don't need to be of the standard shoot-'em-up or hunt-'em-down variety. A good game can be created based on some job or process in the real world.

Q&A

Q How long did it take to make Sim-Pizza?

A It took eight days and a lot of Mountain Dew!

Q Will fixed-point math work as fast on a computer without a math coprocessor than one that has a math coprocessor?

A Yes.

Q Can I simply change the `city_1[]` data structure to create a new city?

A Yes and no. As long as you leave the roads and the pizza hut in the same place, there won't be a problem. However, if you want to move the roads and the pizza hut, there are a few hard-coded constants in the game that will have to be changed, such as the code that tests whether the moped is trying to resupply itself at the pizza hut and the code that starts cars and humans.

Q How can I make the moped go faster?

A You hellion! Change the `max_throttle` setting.

Workshop

The Workshop section presents quiz questions to help you cement your new knowledge and exercises to give you experience using what you've learned. Try to understand the questions and exercises before moving on to the next lesson. The answers are in Appendix B.

Quiz

1. Why was the extra data structure needed to track the positions of the houses?

2. How is the speedometer implemented?

3. What are the maximum number of humans that can be alive at once?

4. How many digits of decimal accuracy does the fixed-point representation of Sim-Pizza have?

5. Look through the code. What is the speed of a flying pizza?

Exercises

1. Make the pedestrians able to make 90-degree turns.

2. Fix all the bugs.

3. Add code so that a helicopter flies overhead. (Consider using the bat code from Venture.)

4. Mount a laser cannon on Vinnie's moped for close encounters with cars.

Adventures in Text

Today, you learn about the oldest games around. These are known as *text adventures*, or *text-based games*. A long time ago (the 1970s and early 1980s), computers didn't have the graphics capabilities they have today. Because of this, most games were descriptive in nature rather than graphic. The games used text to convey the state of the game and conversely the player typed in English sentences (actually a subset of it) to command the character in the game. One of the most notable games created in the early '80s was a game called Zork by Infocom. It was incredibly successful because the language interpreter was very advanced and the game environment was very robust. Furthermore, the user could type in almost any sentence and the game could figure out what the player was trying to say.

The material covered today isn't difficult, but it is different from the other material you have learned about. There are quite a few new terms and many of them have meanings that aren't well-defined. By the end of the day, however, you will be able to create your own text adventure! Here are the topics for today:

- [ ] What is a text game?
- [ ] How do text games work?
- [ ] Getting input from the outside world
- [ ] Language analysis and parsing
- [ ] Lexical analysis
- [ ] Syntactical analysis
- [ ] Semantic analysis
- [ ] Putting all the pieces together
- [ ] Representing the universe
- [ ] Placing objects in the world
- [ ] Making things happen
- [ ] Moving around
- [ ] The inventory system
- [ ] Implementing sound, smell, and sight
- [ ] Making it realtime
- [ ] Error handling
- [ ] Creeping around with Shadow Land

What is a Text Game?

A *text game* is a video game without the video— at least without all the cool graphics. Text games are like interactive books that are written as you play. The user gets to use his or her own imagination to make up what he or she thinks the universe being played in looks like. Some of you may never have seen a text game because you are a product of the "GUI Age." The interface to a text game is a simple as the following:

```
What do you want to do? Eat the apple

Yum, that tasted good!

What do you want to do?
.
.
```

What you see here is a short dialogue between the computer and player. In most text games, the computer prompts the player to tell it to do something. Then the computer breaks down the sentence into components and sees if the action is legal, and then proceeds with the action, if possible.

The thing to remember is that there are no images or sounds. The only image is in the player's mind. And the only thing that creates this image is the descriptions given by the game. Therefore, the English language used to describe the game universe should be as "fluffy" and poetic as possible. Suppose that you are designing a text game that contains a bathroom. When the player asks to "see" what the bathroom looks like, one possible description might be

```
...you see a white bathroom with towels hanging on the racks...
```

This is fine, but it's boring. A better response would be

```
...you are stunned by the size of the bathing room that surrounds you. To your West,
you see a large shower enclosed in rose tinted glass. The entrance to which is paved
with small polished stones. To the East, you see a large wash area with marble basins
and silver faucets. From above you are bathed in sunlight from the three overhead
skylights. Finally, at your feet is a pattern of black and white tiles placed with
surgical precision....
```

As you can see, the second version is much better. It creates an image in your mind, and this is the key to text adventures. Although the interface to a text game usually is nothing more than text, the game being played is limited only by the imagination of the designers and that of the player. A text game usually contains hundreds of pages of descriptive text within the universe's database. This text is used as the foundation for the universe when the player asks something about it.

The technology needed for text games is based on compiler techniques coupled with very elegant data structures and algorithms. Remember, computers don't understand English and making them understand what nouns, verbs, adjectives, prepositional phrases, direct objects, and so forth are is a great task to say the least (I wish I would have paid more attention when my teachers were diagramming sentences). Many people may think that creating a text-based adventure is easy, but they are very wrong. Personally, I think that people who write text adventures probably know more about computer science, data structures, and mathematics than the people who write arcade games.

Text game gurus definitely know a lot about compilers and interpreters, which everyone knows is a very difficult subject. Even today, text games are still going strong; however, they have been augmented with incredible graphics. The genre of *RPG* (Role Playing Games) really is the evolved state of text games. Many RPGs have text interfaces so that the player can converse with and ask questions of the characters in the game. Today, you aren't going to take a course in compiler design (which you should do to be a complete person), but you will learn some of the basic concepts and techniques used to create a text-based adventure. You also will see a complete game at the end of the day, called Shadow Land.

How Do Text Games Work?

This is a good question. There are many answers, all of which are correct, but each of these possible answers has some factors in common. First, the interface to the game will be a bi-directional, text-only communications channel. This means that the computer only has the text to say what it wants to say and similarly, the player can only dictate its input, likewise, with text. Also, there are no joysticks, mice, flight sticks, or light pens. Secondly, the game consists of some type of "universe," whether it be the Old West, an apartment building, or a space station. This universe will consist of geometry, descriptions, and rules. The geometry is the actual geometry of the universe, the size and placement of the rooms, hallways, ponds, and so on. The descriptions are the actual text you can call on to describe what a location looks, sounds, or smells like.

The rules of the game are the things that can and cannot be done. For example, you may not be able to eat a rock, but you can eat a sandwich. When the geometry, descriptions and rules of the game are in place, the data structures, algorithms, and software that enables the player to interact with the environment needs to be created. This consists mainly of an *input parser*. The input parser is responsible for translating and making sense of the player's input. The player will communicate with the game using standard English words. You can use these words to create complete sentences, small phrases, or even single commands. The parser and all its components break down the sentence into separate words, analyzes the meaning of the sentence, and then executes the appropriate functions to make happen what the player is asking for.

There is one catch, however. The computer doesn't understand natural language, and giving it a complete understanding of the English language is a Ph.D. thesis, at the very least. As a game programmer, you just want to give the player a subset of the English language and impose a few rules about how sentences are constructed. For example, the game you will see later today, called Shadow Land, has a very limited vocabulary. It can only understand the following words:

Table 19.1. The Shadow Land vocabulary.

Word	Used As
LAMP	Noun
SANDWICH	Noun
KEYS	Noun
EAST	Noun
WEST	Noun
NORTH	Noun/Adjective
SOUTH	Noun/Adjective
FORWARD	Noun/Adjective
BACKWARD	Noun/Adjective
RIGHT	Noun/Adjective
LEFT	Noun/Adjective
MOVE	Verb
TURN	Verb
SMELL	Verb

19

continues

Table 19.1. continued

Word	Used As
LOOK	Verb
LISTEN	Verb
PUT	Verb
GET	Verb
EAT	Verb
INVENTORY	Verb
WHERE	Verb
EXIT	Verb
THE	Article
IN	Preposition
ON	Preposition
TO	Preposition
DOWN	Preposition

The vocabulary of Shadow Land is very small, but you will be surprised at how many legal sentences you can construct. The problem is making sense of these constructions using some general algorithm. This process is called *syntactical analysis* and is very tedious and complex. Entire books, such as the infamous *Dragon Book* by Aho, Sethi, and Ullman, have been written on how to do this in an efficient manner. You don't need (or want) to make things too complex, so we will force rules on our vocabulary that create a little "language." This language will be the one by which the user must abide when constructing sentences.

Once the user has typed something and the game figures out what he or she is trying to say, then the game will proceed to bring the request to fruition and will output the results. For example, if the player asks to "look," then the game will access the universe database along with the current position of the player. Together, this data can be used to print out the general description of the room, which may be static. If there are movable objects within the game, then there is as a second phase of the description. The game logic will test to see of there are any objects within the field of view of the virtual character and then print them out. When the final description prints, however, it must seem fluid and not

choppy. For example, the game software first should test to see if there are any objects in the room and, if so, make note of it and slightly alter the last sentence of the static description to have a conjunction such as "and" so that the objects when listed don't appear from nowhere.

As an example, a room may have this static description.

```
...You are surrounded by tall walls with Roman art hanging upon them.
```

Suppose that a moveable object is in the room, such as a plant. Then the computers response might be

```
...You are surrounded by tall walls with Roman art hanging upon them.

There is a plant in the East corner of the room.
```

A better algorithm for printing out descriptions might take into consideration that there is a moveable object in the room and then print the description out like this.

```
...You are surrounded by tall walls with Roman art hanging upon them and there is a
plant in the East corner of the room.
```

Although, the sentence is slightly artificial, rough, and the computer wouldn't know the difference between a plant and a ogre, at least the sentences somewhat are connected. This is one of the "tricks" in making good text games. You must "work" the output sentences to make them read as if they aren't being printed out from a static database.

There is more than parsing the text and trying to satisfy the request, however. The game must have some type of data structure to represent the universe and the objects within the universe. This representation, whatever it may be, also must have some type of valid geometrical coherence because as the player moves around, he or she will expect to find a key where they dropped it. This means that many times, the universe will have to be modeled as a 2-D vector map or cell map. This allows the player to move around in a data representation that has some geometrical relation to the virtual space the player thinks he or she is in. Next, the game has to have some type of structure that contains the "state" of the player. This could mean his or her health, position, inventory of objects, and position in the game universe.

Finally, other aspects of the game, such as a goal and the enemies (if there are any), must be implemented. The goal might be as simple as finding an enchanted chalice and putting it somewhere; or, the goal may be as complex as solving some a puzzle with a questions and answers dialogue between the player and a creature in the game. The creatures in the game will be implemented as data structures only; however, these data structures can move around the universe data structure, move objects, eat food, and attack the player (possibly). All these aspects of the text game must be implemented in a way so that the

illusion of a real environment is upheld. This means that you should assume that the player can't see the game, but everything better make sense or else!

To reiterate, Figure 19.1 shows all the components of a text game. Referring to the figure, you see that there is an input section that parses the players commands and then tries to execute these commands. The parser only understands a specific vocabulary and, furthermore, the sentences created with this vocabulary are limited by the "language" designed by the game designer. Next, there is a set of data structures holding the representation of the universe, the position of the objects, and the description strings for sights, sounds, and smells. Also, you see the representation of the player and his or her inventory, along with the representation of the enemies in the game. Finally, there is a million or so functions, rules, and little details that make it all work.

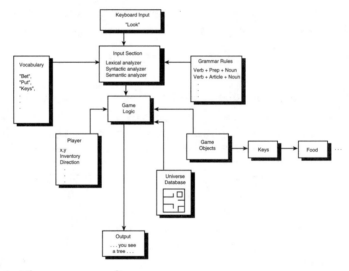

Figure 19.1. *The components of a text game.*

Getting Input from the Outside World

Because a text-based game uses the keyboard as its sole input device, you should take some time to make this as easy as possible. The player will be typing sentences to command the text game to perform an action. This seems simple enough, but the problem is how to read these sentences. The standard scanf() function won't work correctly because of the possibility of whitespace and multiple arguments. You need a function that will get a line of input, regardless of the characters that make up the line. This input will stop if, and only if, the user presses the Enter key. At this point, the sentence is passed to the next piece of software in the parser chain. So, the question is "How do you get a single line of text without DOS, C, or the input line editor making decisions for you?" The answer is to use single-character input and build up a string until the Enter key is pressed. You can do this using the getch() function with a test for backspace and carriage return. Following is a typical line input function:

Listing 19.1. A single line input function with editing capability.

```
char *Get_Line(char *buffer)
{
// this function gets a single line of input and tolerates white space

int c,index=0;

// loop while user hasn't hit return
while((c=getch())!=13)
    {
// implement backspace
    if (c==8 && index>0)
        {

        buffer[-index] = ' ';
        printf("%c %c",8,8);

        } // end if backspace
    else
    if (c>=32 && c<=122)
        {
        buffer[index++] = c;
        printf("%c",c);

        } // end if in printable range

    } // end while

// terminate string
buffer[index] = 0;

// return pointer to buffer or NULL
if (strlen(buffer)==0)
    return(NULL);
else
return(buffer);

} // end Get_Line
```

The function takes as a parameter a pointer to a buffer where the inputted string will be placed after the function executes. During execution, Get_Line() will enable the user to input a line of text and also to edit errors using the Backspace key. As the user inputs the

characters, they are echoed out to the screen so that the user can see what he or she is typing. When the user presses the Enter key, the string is terminated with a NULL and function ends.

After the user inputs the string, the game is ready to parse it. The parsing process has many phases (which is covered shortly). Before you can parse the sentence and see what it means, however, you must know what the language is and how it is constructed.

Language Analysis and Parsing

Before the user can enter anything, you must define a "language" that he or she must stay within. This language consists of vocabulary and a set of rules (grammar). Together, these conventions create the overall language. Now, the whole idea of text game is to use the English language. This means that the vocabulary should be English words and the grammar should be legal English grammar. The first request is easy. The second request is much more difficult. Contrary to the beliefs of many of my English teachers, the English language is a terribly complex language system. It's full of contradictions, points of view, different ways of saying things, and so on. In general, the English language is not robust like computer languages. This means that as a text game programmer, you may have to only allow the user a very small subset of the possible grammatical constructions that could be made with a given vocabulary.

This might seem like a problem, but it's not. A player of a text game becomes comfortable very quickly with a more robust subset of the English language and finds that the sentences are concise and to the point. With all that in mind, the first thing that any game needs is a vocabulary. This is constructed in an ongoing manner as the game is written. The reason for this is that as the game is being written, the designer may feel that another game object, such as a "zot," needs to be added. This means that "zot" would need to be added to the vocabulary if the player was to be able to refer to it. Secondly, the designer might decide that more prepositions are needed to make some sentences more natural. For example, to drop an object the player might type

```
"drop the keys"
```

The meaning of this is very clear. The word "drop" is a verb, "the" is a worthless article, and "keys" is a noun. However, it might be more natural for the player to type

```
"drop down the keys"
or
"drop the keys down"
```

Regardless of whether these two sentences are as "good," the fact of the matter is that this is how people talk, which is what is important. Therefore, the vocabulary will need words

for all the objects (nouns) in the game, along with a few good prepositions. As a rule of thumb, start with everything you can do to a mountain and usually that will suffice. Table 19.2 lists common prepositions used in text games.

Table 19.2. Some good prepositions.

from
on
in
down
up
behind
into
before
at

The next type of words needed in a vocabulary are the action verbs. These are the words that mean "do something." They usually are followed by a word or phrase that describes on what action is taking place. For example, in a text game, the action verb "move" is very useful in navigating the player about the universe. A set of possible sentences using "move" as an action verb might be

```
move north
```

```
move to the north
```

or

```
move northward
```

The first sentence is simply enough. It says to move to the north. The second sentence also says to move to the north, but it has a prepositional phrase "to the north." Finally, the third sentence uses the adjective "northward," to mean the same thing. Technically, it could be argued that each of the sentences could mean different things, but to us as game programmers, all the preceding sentences mean the same thing, which is to take a step in the direction of north. Therefore, we see that the use of articles, such as "the," and prepositions are absolutely needed to give the sentences a little variety, even if the meanings are the same.

Back to the subject of action verbs. The game should have a large list of action verbs (many of which can be used by themselves with implied objects). Suppose that the vocabulary for your game had the action verb "smell." You might say

```
"smell the sandwich"
```

which is clear. The command

```
smell
```

however, isn't so clear. Yes, it is clear what the player wants to do, but to what he or she wants it to be done to is ambiguous. This is where the concept of context comes into play. Because there is no direct or indirect object given to "smell," the game assumes that the player means the exterior environment or the last object acted on, as in the situation in which the player just picked up a rock, and then requested the game to smell, for example. The game then might reply "the rock?" and then the player would say "yes" and the proper description string would be printed. On the other hand, if the player recently has not picked up anything, then the single command "smell" might illicit a general description of the smell within the room in which the player is standing.

After you decide which action verbs, nouns, prepositions, and articles to use, the rules for the language itself must be generated. These rules describe the possible sentence constructions that are legal. This information is used by the syntactical analyzer along with the semantic analyzer to compute the meaning of the sentence as well as its validity. As an example, generate a vocabulary along with the grammatical rules that governs it. Table 19.3 is of a simple language.

Note: If something is referred to as a verb, noun, adjective, preposition, or article, then just accept it because I am going to use the word in that manner, even if it isn't strictly correct to think of it as such. Remember the language we make up for games is *not* English. It is only based on English and a verb in one language may be an adjective in the other!

Table 19.3. A sample vocabulary.

Word	Used As	Type Name
rock	Noun	OBJECT
food	Noun	OBJECT

Word	Used As	Type Name
table	Noun	OBJECT
key	Noun	OBJECT
get	verb	VERB
put	verb	VERB
the	article	ARTICLE
on	preposition	PREP
onto	preposition	PREP

The type name is used to group similar word types, so they can be worked with more efficiently in the program.

Now that you have the vocabulary, you can use it to construct the language. This means creating the rules for legal sentences. Not all of these sentences may make sense, but they all will be legal. These rules usually are referred to as *the syntax of the language* or the *productions*. Table 19.4 is a table for the productions of Glish.

Note: I will refer to the language you will be constructing as *Glish*.

19

Table 19.4. The productions of "Glish."

```
OBJECT->"rock"¦"food"¦"table"¦"key"

VERB->"get"¦"put"

ARTICLE->"the"¦NULL

PREP->"on"¦"onto"¦NULL

SENTENCE->VERB+ARTICLE+OBJECT+PREP+ARTICLE+OBJECT

Where the "¦" means logical OR, "+" means concatenate and NULL means NULL string.
```

Now, if you try to build sentences using the production for SENTENCE, then there are quite a few sentences that can be constructed; however, some of them may not make any semantic sense. For example, the sentence

```
"put the rock onto the table"
```

makes perfect sense, but the sentence

```
"get the rock onto the table"
```

is unclear. It could mean place the rock on the table, but maybe not. This is where you must do one of two things. You must either incorporate more productions into the language to separate specific verbs and their constructions, or the game code must test annually whether sentences make "sense." To make sure you see how the productions are used, let's do a few examples of legal sentences.

Table 19.5. Some sample sentences and their clarity of meaning ranked 1 to 10 (with 10 be very clear).

Sentence	Clarity	Legality
"put rock"	4	Yes
"put the rock"	4	Yes
"get the key"	8	Yes
"put down the food"	10	No (There is no production for placing a preposition after the verb and "down" isn't in the vocabulary.)
"put the food on rock"	7	Yes
"put the rock down onto table"	7	No (There are two prepositions concatenated after each other following the object; there is no production for this form.)

As you can see from Table 19.5, if a production doesn't exist for a particular sentence form, then the sentence is illegal, regardless of whether it makes sense. This is because the computer does not know whether it is a legal sentence unless there is an implementation of the production or syntactic rule that governs the construction of the desired sentence. To put it clearly in English, you must program in every single sentence type as a logical construction of the elements in the vocabulary and you must be able to test each sentence to see if it follows the production rules. Of course, I was joking about the "clearly" part!

Once you break down the sentence and the meaning is starting to become clear, then comes the semantic checking. This phase tests whether a valid sentence makes sense. For example, the sentence

```
"get the key onto the table"
```

is a legal construction, but it is unclear what the user wants. This sentence probably should be flagged as unclear and the user should be requested to say it in another way, such as

```
"put the key on table"
```

The question that should be burning in your mind is "After I figure out what the user wants to say, how do I make the program do what the sentence says to do?". The answer is with *action functions*. Action functions are called based on the action verb of the sentence. These action functions can act as syntax checkers, semantic checkers, or a combination of both or neither (it's a personal preference). One thing the action function will do, however, is make something happen. You accomplish this by having a separate function for each action function. The action functions themselves are responsible for figuring out to which object(s) the action verb is supposed to be applied, and then perform the requested action. For example, the action function for the verb "get" might step through the following set of operations:

1. Extract the *object* (noun) from the sentence.

2. Use *vision* to see if the requested object is to be picked up is within the reach of the player.

3. If the object is within reach, then it is retrieved. At this point, the universe database, along with the player's inventory, are updated to reflect this action.

The first step (extracting the object) is accomplished by "consuming" words that don't change the meaning of the sentence. For example, the prepositions and articles in the Glish language don't change the meaning much of any particular sentence. Look at the following:

```
"put the key"
```

You can take out the article "the" without changing the meaning. This consumption of irrelevant words is transparent to the players, but allows them to write sentences that make more sense from their point of view. Even though the language parser might like

```
"put key on table"
```

a human player may feel more comfortable with

```
"put the key onto the table"
```

In any case, the action function will take care of this logic. Once the action function has figured out what needs to be done, doing it is easy. In the case of the original example of getting something, the object would be taken out of the universe database and inserted into the player's inventory; where the player's inventory might just be an array of characters or structures that list the objects the player is holding. For example, in the game Shadow Land, the player's inventory and everything about him or her is contained within the following single structure:

Listing 19.2. The structure that holds the player in Shadow Land.

```
// this structure holds everything pertaining to the player

typedef struct player_typ
        {
        char name[16];   // name of player
        int x,y;         // postion of player
int direction;   // direction of player, east,west north,south

        char inventory[8]; // objects player is holding (like pockets)
        int num_objects;   // number of objects player is holding

        } player, *player_ptr;
```

The inventory in this case is an array of characters that represent the objects the player is holding. "s," for example, stands for sandwich. This data structure is just an example, you may want to do it differently than this.

Game Law: Text games usually are not played in realtime; hence, they can be slow internally because the game will have years, relatively speaking, to think as the player types in a single sentence!

In essence, all a text game must do is break down a sentence, figure out the action requested, call the appropriate action function(s), and perform the action. Performing the action is done simply by updating data structures, changing coordinates, and printing out text. The major problem in a text game, as you probably have surmised, is the translation of the input command string into something the computer can deal with, such as numbers. This is called *tokenization* or *lexical analysis* and is the next topic of discussion.

Lexical Analysis

When the player types in a sentence using the vocabulary you supply, the sentence must be converted from strings into tokens (integers) so that syntactic and semantic phases of analysis can proceed. The reason lexical analysis is necessary is due to the fact that working with strings is much more difficult, time consuming, and memory intensive than working with tokens (usually which are integers). Hence, one of the functions of the lexical analyzer is to convert the input sentence from string form to token form. There are three parts to this translation. The first part of lexical analysis is simply separating the "words" in a sentence and extracting them. By "words," it is meant strings of characters separated by *whitespace*. Whitespace usually is considered to be the space character (ASCII 32) and the horizontal tab (ASCII 9). For example, the sentence

```
"This      is     a test."
```

contains four words. They are:

1. `This`

2. `is`

3. `a`

4. `test`

You also can see that periods will have to be taken into consideration because they separate sentences. If the user is only going to be inputting a single line at a time, he or she may not put a period at the end of each input sentence. Alas, the period can be thought of as whitespace. On the other hand, if it is legal for the player to type multiple commands separated by a period or other phrase separator, such the colon (:) or semicolon (;), then extra logic may be needed because the sentences should be parsed separately. For example, if the period is assumed to be whitespace in a single sentence construction as in

```
"This is a test."
```

then the meaning to the parser is the same as

```
"This is a test"
```

However, when two sentences are placed next to each other with the period being interpreted as whitespace, then the following problem can occur. The following sentence

```
"This is a test. Get the book."
```

will be interpreted as

19

```
"This is a test get the book"
```

which has no meaning.

The moral of the story is be careful what you elect to call whitespace.

Now you need to figure out a way to extract from a sentence the "words" separated by whitespace. The C library actually has a string function to do this called `strtok()`, but it doesn't work properly on some compilers. Because we like to reinvent the wheel, we will summarily dismiss it.

Game Law: Game programmers like to rewrite everything—even the operating system!

What you need is a function that will separate the words out for you. This actually is a fairly easy function to write as long as you take your time and take into account all the cases that can occur, such as NULL terminators, whitespace, and the return character. Following is one such implementation of a token extraction function:

Listing 19.3. A function to extract tokens from an input sentence (excerpted from Shadow Land).

```c
int Get_Token(char *input,char *output,int *current_pos)
{

int index,    // loop index and working index
    start,    // points to start of token
    end;      // points to end of token

// set current positions
index=start=end=*current_pos;

// eat white space
while(isspace(input[index]) ¦¦ ispunct(input[index]))
    {
    index++;
    } // end while

// test if end of string found
if (input[index]==NULL)
    {
    // emit nothing

    strcpy(output,"");
    return(0);

    } // end if no more tokens
```

```
// at this point, we must have a token of some kind, so find the end of it
start = index; // mark front of it
end   = index;

// find end of Token
while(!isspace(input[end]) && !ispunct(input[end]) && input[end]!=NULL)
    {
    end++;
    } // end while

// build up output string
for (index=start; index<end; index++)
    {

    output[index-start] = toupper(input[index]);

    } // end copy string

// place terminator
output[index-start] = 0;

// update current string position
*current_pos  = end;

return(end);
} // end Get_Token
```

The function takes three inputs. An input string to be parsed, an output string that holds the extracted token, and the current position in the string that is being processed. For example, let's see how a string can be parsed using the function. First you need to declare a couple of variables.

```
int position=0;  // used as index from call to call to keep track of current string
                 // position

char output[16];  // output string

// begin program

Get_Token("This is a test",output,&position);
```

After this call the variable output would have a "This" in it and position would be equal to 4. Let's do one more call...

```
Get_Token("This is a test",output,&position);
```

Now, the variable output would have is in it, and position would be updated to 7. If Get_Token() is repeatedly called in this fashion, then each "word" in the sentence will be extracted and placed in the buffer output (and each previous string in output will be overwritten by the next token word). Consequently, you now have a method of obtaining the "words" that make up a sentence.

19

The next task is to convert these strings into integer tokens so that you can work with them more easily. This is done with a function that has a table of strings along with the token for each of the vocabulary words. A search through the table is done for each word and when, and if, the string is found in the table, it then is converted to an integer token (see Figure 19.2).

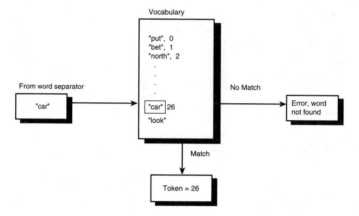

Figure 19.2. *A word being tested to see if it's in the vocabulary of the game.*

During this phase of lexical analysis is where the vocabulary checking is done. If a word is not in the vocabulary then, it is not in the language, and hence, is illegal. As an example, the game Shadow Land has the following data structure to hold each word in the vocabulary:

Listing 19.4. The data structure for a token in Shadow Land.

```
// this is the structure for a single token

typedef struct token_typ
        {
        char symbol[16];   // the string that represents the token
        int value;         // the integer value of the token
        } token, *token_ptr;
```

This structure has a place for both the string and a value to be associated with it. The string is the actual vocabulary word while the value is arbitrary. However, the values for tokens must be mutually exclusive unless you want to make words synonymous. Using the preceding structure and some defines, you can create a vocabulary table in very compact

form that can be used as a reference in the lexical analysis to convert words to tokens and to check their validity. Following is the vocabulary table used in Shadow Land.

Listing 19.5. The static initialization of the vocabulary table for Shadow Land.

```
// this is the entire "language" of the language in Shadow Land.

token language[MAX_TOKENS] = {

    {"LAMP",      OBJECT_LAMP      },
    {"SANDWICH",  OBJECT_SANDWICH },
    {"KEYS",      OBJECT_KEYS      },
    {"EAST",      DIR_1_EAST       },
    {"WEST",      DIR_1_WEST       },
    {"NORTH",     DIR_1_NORTH      },
    {"SOUTH",     DIR_1_SOUTH      },
    {"FORWARD",   DIR_2_FORWARD    },
    {"BACKWARD",  DIR_2_BACKWARD   },
    {"RIGHT",     DIR_2_RIGHT      },
    {"LEFT",      DIR_2_LEFT       },
    {"MOVE",      ACTION_MOVE      },
    {"TURN",      ACTION_TURN      },
    {"SMELL",     ACTION_SMELL     },
    {"LOOK",      ACTION_LOOK      },
    {"LISTEN",    ACTION_LISTEN    },
    {"PUT",       ACTION_PUT       },
    {"GET",       ACTION_GET       },
    {"EAT",       ACTION_EAT       },
    {"INVENTORY", ACTION_INVENTORY},
    {"WHERE",     ACTION_WHERE     },
    {"EXIT",      ACTION_EXIT      },
    {"THE",       ART_THE          },
    {"IN",        PREP_IN          },
    {"ON",        PREP_ON          },
    {"TO",        PREP_TO          },
    {"DOWN",      PREP_DOWN        },
};
```

As you can see, there are character strings followed by defined symbols (the value of which are irrelevant as long as they are different). Notice that the defined symbols have familiar prefixes, such as PREP (preposition), ART (article), and ACTION (verb).

Note: I have been using example code excerpts from Shadow Land. If you haven't seen the game or the code for it, don't worry. You are only trying to grasp concepts at this point and using specific implementation examples will not degrade the lesson because the techniques are so standard.

Once a table like this exists in some such form, the token strings can be compared to the elements in the table, the character strings representing the tokens can be converted to integers, and finally, the input sentence will be a string of numbers which can be processed in a more convenient fashion. Following is a sample "tokenizer." It also is from the game Shadow Land, but if you have seen one, you have seen them all. Don't worry about the defined constants, just concentrate on the overall operation of the function.

Listing 19.6. A function that converts token strings of an input sentence into integer tokens.

```
int Extract_Tokens(char *string)
{
// this function breaks the input string down into tokens and fills up
// the global sentence array with the tokens so that it can be processed

int curr_pos=0,       // current position in string
    curr_token=0,     // current token number
    found,            // used to flag if the token is valid in language
    index;            // loop index

char output[16];
// reset number of tokens and clear the sentence out
num_tokens=0;

for (index=0; index<8; index++)
    sentence[index]=0;

// extract all the words in the sentence (tokens)
while(Get_Token(string,output,&curr_pos))
    {
    // test to see if this is a valid token
    for (index=0,found=0; index<NUM_TOKENS; index++)
        {
        // do we have a match?
        if (strcmp(output,language[index].symbol)==0)
            {
            // set found flag
            found=1;

            // enter token into sentence
            sentence[curr_token++] = language[index].value;
            break;
            } // end if

        } // end for index

    // test if token was part of language (grammar)
    if (!found)
        {
        printf("\n%s, I don't know what \"%s\" means.",you.name
                                                ,output);

        // failure
```

```
            return(0);

        } // end if not found

    // else
    num_tokens++;
    } // end while
} // end Extract_Tokens
```

The function operates with an input string passed to it containing the users commands. The function then proceeds to break down the sentence into separate "words" using the Get_Token() function. Each word then is scanned for in the vocabulary table and when a match is made, the word is converted into a token and inserted into a token sentence which basically is a version of the input sentence in token form (integers rather than strings). If the "word" is not found in the vocabulary table, then there is a problem and the code will emit an error. I have highlighted this section in the preceding function, so that you can see how easy it is.

Let's take a brief detour for a moment to cover two topics. The first is *error handling*. This always is an important part of any program, and I cannot emphasis how important it is, especially in a text-based game in which a bad input can "trickle" down into the bowels of the game engine and logic, and really mess things up. Therefore, it can't hurt to have too much error checking in a text game. Even if you are 99-percent sure an input to a function should be of the correct form, always test it that one last time.

Secondly, notice that I use very primitive data structures. I don't do this because I don't know how to implement multi-level balanced AVL trees with interconnecting adjacency lists. It's because I do (I'm being facetious). Sure, a linked list or binary tree might be a more elegant solution, but is it really worth it for a dozen or so vocabulary words? The answer is "No." My rule of thumb is the data structure should fit the problem and arrays fit a lot of small problems. When the problems get large, then it's time to bring in the big guns, such as linked lists, B-trees, graphs, and so on. For small problems, however, get the code working with simple data structures or you will be forever trying to figure out why you keep getting NULL pointer errors, GP-faults, and other bothersome features!

All right, now that you finally know how to convert the sentence into tokens, it's time for the syntactic and semantic analysis phases.

Syntactical Analysis

Hold on tight, because this is where things start getting a bit cloudy. Strictly speaking, *syntactic analysis* as defined in compiler texts is the phase in which the input token stream is converted into grammatical phrases so that these phrases can be processed. Because the

19

languages you have been considering for implementation are fairly simple and have simple vocabularies, this highly general and elusive definition needs to be pruned to mean something in your context. As far as you are concerned, syntactic analysis will mean "making sense out of the sentence." This means applying the verbs, determining the objects, extracting the prepositions and articles, and so on.

The syntactic analysis phase of your games will occur in parallel with the action(s) meant by the sentence. This is totally fine and many compilers are interpreters are designed this way. The code is generated or interpreted on-the-fly. You already have seen what the syntactic phase of analysis looks like. It is accomplished by calling functions responsible for all the action verbs in the language. Then these action functions further process the remainder of the input sentence, which already is in token form, and then attempts to do whatever is supposed to be done. For example, a syntactic parser for a text game might begin by determining which action verb began the sentence and then calling an appropriate action function to deal with the rest of the sentence. Of course, the rest of the sentence could be processed and tested for validity before the call to the action function, but this isn't necessary. I prefer to place the burden of further processing on the action functions. My philosophy is this: each action function is like an object that operates on a single type of sentence. This single sentence is one that begins with a specific word. You should not hold a single function responsible for checking the syntax of all the possible sentences before making the call to the appropriate action function.

As an example, the following function is used in Shadow Land to dispatch each sentence to the proper action function. The single mission of this function is to look at the first word in the sentence (which is a token), and then vector to the correct action function. At that point, it is the job of the action function to check the remainder of the syntax of the sentence. Following is the action dispatcher:

Listing 19.7. The function used in Shadow Land to call the action functions based on the action verb used in the input sentence.

```
void Verb_Parser(void)
{
// this function breaks down the sentence and based on the verb calls the
// appropriate "method" or function to apply that verb
// note: syntactic analysis could be done here, but I decided to place it
// in the action verb functions, so that you can see the way the errors are
// detected for each verb (even though there is a a lot of redundancy)

// what is the verb?

switch(sentence[FIRST_WORD])
    {
    case ACTION_MOVE:
        {
```

```
      // call the appropriate function
      Verb_MOVE();
      } break;

case ACTION_TURN:
      {
      // call the appropriate function
      Verb_TURN();
      } break;

case ACTION_SMELL:
      {
      // call the appropriate function

      Verb_SMELL();
      } break;

case ACTION_LOOK:
      {
      // call the appropriate function
      Verb_LOOK();
      } break;

case ACTION_LISTEN:
      {
      // call the appropriate function
      Verb_LISTEN();
      } break;

case ACTION_PUT:
      {
      // call the appropriate function
      Verb_PUT();
      } break;

case ACTION_GET:
      {
      // call the appropriate function
      Verb_GET();
      } break;

case ACTION_EAT:
      {
      // call the appropriate function
      Verb_EAT();

      } break;

case ACTION_WHERE:
      {
      // call the appropriate function
      Verb_WHERE();
      } break;

case ACTION_INVENTORY:
      {
```

Listing 19.7. continued

```
                          // call the appropriate function
                          Verb_INVENTORY();
                          } break;

                  case ACTION_EXIT:
                          {
                          // call the appropriate function
                          Verb_EXIT();
                          } break;

                  default:
                          {
                          printf("\n%s, you must start a sentence with an action verb!",
                                  you.name);
                          return;
                          } break;

                  } // end switch

} // end Verb_Parser
```

The function is simply beautiful. It looks at the first word in the sentence (which by definition of the language better be a verb) and then calls the corresponding action function. For a graphical representation of this, look at Figure 19.3.

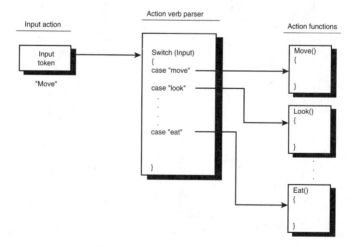

Figure 19.3. *An action verb being dispatched to the proper action function.*

The next part of parsing analysis is the semantic analysis phase.

Semantic Analysis

Semantic analysis is where most of the error checking takes place. Because you are doing the syntactic analysis "on-the-fly" along with making things happen in the game, however, this responsibility is merged into the action function during syntactic analysis. Syntactic analysis is supposed to break down the sentence into its meaning and then semantic analysis is used to determine if this meaning makes sense (getting confused yet?). As you can see, this business of syntactic and semantic analysis seems to be almost circular and, therefore, again I will cut to the quick and make a hard fast rule. In a text-based game, the syntactic and semantic analysis are done simultaneously. As the sentences meaning is being computed, the sentence is tested for sense.

I hope you understand this very subtle concept. If it helps, it's kind of similar to turning on snow skis. Once you can do it, it's easy, but until then, you have no idea how to do it.

Putting All the Pieces Together

You have all the components of the complete parser and text interpreter engine. Now you get to see how all the pieces go together to form the backbone of a text game (see Figure 19.4).

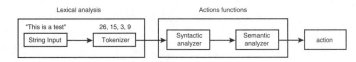

Figure 19.4. *The sections of the input parser.*

Referring to the figure, you see that the input stream is broken into words by the front end of the lexical analyzer, then the word strings are converted into integer tokens. The token stream then is fed into the front end of the syntactic parser which "sends" the sentence of tokens to the proper action function. The action function then tries to apply the action requested by the player to the object(s) in the sentence. As the action is being applied, syntax checking and semantic integrity also are being tested simultaneously by the action function.

The important concept to grasp is that all the input parsing, syntax checking, and so forth, are for the single reason of trying to figure out what the player wants to do. Once you determine this, the coding is straightforward and similar to what you have done in

arcade games. The only caveat is that the actions performed are acted on internal data structures, and the only output is text. Remember, the player only "views" the game universe by way of strings of static or synthesized text that the game outputs as each "move" is made. Hopefully, you have a grasp of how the text input phase of a text game works. If I were to leave the subject now, you should be able to create a text game. Rather than concluding, however, let's cover some techniques to control and manipulate other aspects of a text game. (Be warned, these techniques are illustrative only and I'm sure there are better, different, and more clever ways of doing them.)

Representing the Universe

The universe in a text game can be represented in many ways. Whatever representation is used should have some type of geometrical relationship to the virtual environment the player is running around in. For example, if you create a full 3-D space text adventure, then you might have a 3-D world modeled in a database. Even though the player would never see the world visually, all collision detection and motion would be done within the 3-D model. Since this book is about 2-D games, however, the representations are flatter. For a moment, think of a one-story house. Imagine that the roof is removed and you are looking down at the house from above (you're in a hovercraft) (see Figure 19.5). You can see the rooms of the house, the objects, and the people moving around. This is the type of representation you want to use for your text games.

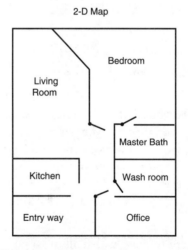

Figure 19.5. *A top down "blue print" view of an environment.*

How do you implement a data structure of such a model? You can do it in two ways. You could use a vector-based model based on lines and polygons. There would be a database of this geometry and the game code would use it to move the game objects around. This technique is fine, but a bit difficult to visualize since you would be working in pure "vector space." A better approach would be to have a 2-D matrix of cells that represented the game universe. This is the same technique used to create cell-based worlds in many of the games you have seen (Venture, Sim-Pizza, and Robo Punk, for example). Admittedly, we will never "see" the world, but having an actual 2-D floor map that can be accessed very simply will make the game code very simple to write. The game Shadow Land, for example, uses a 2-D matrix of characters to represent the game universe (which is my apartment). Take a look at the following to see the actual data structure used in the game.

Listing 19.8. The data structure used to represent the game universe of Shadow Land.

```
// this array holds the geometry of the universe

// l - living room
// b - bedroom
// k - kitchen
// w - washroom
// h - hall way
// r - restroom
// e - entry way
// o - office

//                      ^
//                     NORTH
// < WEST          EAST >
//                     SOUTH
//                      v

char *universe_geometry[NUM_ROWS]={"********************************",
                    "*lllllllll*bbbbbbbbbbbbbbbbbbb*",
                    "*lllllllll*bbbbbbbbbbbbbbbbbbb*",
                    "*lllllllllll*bbbbbbbbbbbbbbbbb*",
                    "*lllllllllll*bbbbbbbbbbbbbbbbb*",
                    "*lllllllllll*bbbbbbbbbbbbbbbbb*",
                    "*lllllllllll*bbbbbbbbbbbbbbbbb*",
                    "*lllllllllll*bbbbbbbbbbbbbbbbb*",
                    "*lllllllllll*bbbbbbbbbbbbbbbbb*",
                    "*lllllllllll*bbbbbbbbbbbbbbbbb*",
                    "*lllllllllll*bbbbbbbbbbbbbbbbb*",
                    "*lllllllllll*bbbb*rrr*********",
                    "*lllllllllllhhhhhh*rrrrrrrrrrr*",
                    "*lllllllllllhhhhhh*rrrrrrrrrrr*",
                    "*lllllllllhhh******rrrrrrrrrrr*",
                    "*********hhhh*rrrrrrrrrrrrrrrr*",
                    "*kkkkkkk*hhhh*rrrrrrrrrrrrrrrr*",
```

continues

Listing 19.8. continued

```
                               "*kkkkkkk*hhhh*rrrrrrrrrrrrrrrrrr*",
                               "*kkkkkkk*hhhh*rrrrrrrrrrrrrrrrrr*",
                               "*kkkkkkkhhhhh******************",
                               "*kkkkkkkhhhhhhhhhhhhwwwwwwwwwwww*",
                               "*kkkkkkkhhhhhhhhhhhhwwwwwwwwwwww*",
                               "*kkkkkkk*hhhhhhhhhhwwwwwwwwwwww*",
                               "*kkkkkkk*hhhh*ooooo************",
                               "*kkkkkkk*hhhh*ooooooooooooooooo*",
                               "*kkkkkkk*hhhh*ooooooooooooooooo*",
                               "*kkkkkk*hhhhh*ooooooooooooooooo*",
                               "*******hhhhhh*ooooooooooooooooo*",
                               "*eeeeeeeeeeee*ooooooooooooooooo*",
                               "*eeeeeeeeeeee*ooooooooooooooooo*",
                     "*eeeeeeeeeeee*ooooooooooooooooo*",
                               "******************************",};
```

It might be a bit difficult to see the rooms due to the printer font, but if you sqint your eyes a bit, you can see all the rooms. Notice that walls are built with the * character and different rooms are defined by placing a single character within the confines of the room, such as o for *office*. Placing in the each room characters that describe the room type is helpful in determining where at any time the player is. If the player is placed at any (x,y) position in the map, then the code that prints out "where" the player is only has to index into the array and look at the character on which the player is standing. Using this information, the appropriate text strings then can be displayed.

Placing Objects in the World

Objects in the game world can be created using two main techniques. The first technique is to use an array or linked list of objects, in which each element defines the object, its position, and any other relevant properties. The only problem with this technique is that when a player is in a room and asks to "look," then the object list must be accessed and visibility of each object must be determined. Also, collision detection, "putting" and "getting," are more complex when the objects are stored in this way. An easier method that is related to the way the universe is defined is to have another 2-D matrix of characters with the same geometry as the universe map. Rather than walls and floor tiles within it, however, the objects are placed in it. Then you can imagine that both data structures are synthetically overlaid by the game code. The following, for example, is the object placement map for Shadow Land.

Listing 19.9. The object placement database for Shadow Land.

```
// this array holds the objects within the universe

// l - lamp
// s - sandwich
// k - keys
//                      ^
//                      NORTH
// < WEST               EAST >
///                     SOUTH
//                      v

char *universe_objects[NUM_ROWS]={"                                  ",
                                  "  l                            k  ",
                                  "                                  ",
                                  "                                  ",
                                  "                                  ",
                                  "                                  ",
                                  "                                  ",
                                  "                                  ",
                                  "                                  ",
                                  "  l                               ",
                                  "                                  ",
                                  "                                  ",
                                  "                                  ",
                                  "                                  ",
                                  "                                  ",
                                  "                                  ",
                                  "                                  ",
                                  "                                  ",
                                  "                                  ",
                                  "                                  ",
                                  "                                  ",
                                  "                                  ",
                                  "     s                            ",
                                  "                                  ",
                                  "                                  ",
                                  "                                  ",
                                  "                                  ",
                                  "              s               l  ",
                                  "                                  ",
                                  "                                  ",};
```

As you can see, the object map is very sparse, and it should be because it contains only the objects in the universe. Determining if the player is near an object or even on top of one, however, is very simple because there is a one-to-one relationship between the geometry of the universe, the universe of objects, and the position of the player. The only drawback to using the "cell" technique to represent a game universe for a text game is that the cell world has only a finite number of cells and thus positions within the universe, but this is really a small inconvenience and the player will never know!

Making Things Happen

You learned previously that making things happen merely means to print out some text or change some values in data structures, such as the position of the player. A text game really is just a "live" database that is accessed and modified as the game is played. Frankly, an arcade game is also, but there is a more complex output device being used (the screen) and arcade games must be in realtime. Text games wait for the user to input a text string before doing anything. When this "waiting" is taking place, the code is stuck in the line input function and the game universe is "motionless" during this period.

Moving Around

Motion in a text game is accomplished by changing the position of the player's character in the game. This usually is as simple as modifying a couple variables. For example, if the player typed

```
"move north"
```

the computer's output would be

```
"You take a few steps..."
```

The game code might decrement the y- position of the player's character (North is in the negative y-direction), and then that would be it. The players position would be tested to see if the player stepped on something, hit a wall, or fell of a cliff, but the actual motion is done with only a couple variable changes. This simplicity stems from the fact that the player is plopped down in the 2-D map and is just a square that can move east, west, north, or south.

The Inventory System

The *inventory system* is a text game list that contains a description and tally of all the objects the player is holdin. This list can be an array or a linked list. If the objects are complex, then the list might be a list of structures. In Shadow Land, the inventory is so simple that nothing more than an array of characters was used to hold the inventory. The player can have a sandwich (s), a set of keys (k) and a lamp (l). If the player is holding one or more of these objects, then in a character array called inventory[], the characters representing these objects are stored. Then when the player asks to see what he or she is holding, a simple traversal of this list and a few output strings is all that is needed.

But how does the player get the objects? Well, he or she picks them up from the game universe. If a player was in a room and "saw" the keys, for example, then he or she might request the game to "get" the keys. The game then would "pick up" the keys by removing the k from the object universe, replacing the spot the keys were in with a blank and then inserting a k into the inventory list of the player. Of course, making the computer "see" what's in a room and ascertain if the player is within reach is a bit complex, but you get the idea.

Implementing Sound, Smell, and Sight

The implementation of the human senses in a text game is the most challenging of all because the player can't really see, hear, or smell items within the text game. This means that apart from the algorithmic considerations, the output descriptions must be full of adjectives, descriptives, qualifiers, and so on to create mental images. Implementing sounds and smells are the easiest because they are not focused senses. By focused, I mean that if a specific room has a general smell, then the player should smell it at any location of the room. Similarly, the same goes for sounds. If the room has music playing, then the music will be heard in any part of the room. Vision is the most complex because it is more focused than sound and smell, and is much harder to implement. The following sections take a look at all three senses and show you how to implement them.

Sound

There are two types of sounds in a text game; static and dynamic. *Static* sounds are the sounds that are always in a room. *Dynamic* sounds are sounds that can enter and leave a room. First, let's discuss static sounds. To implement static sounds, there should be a data structure that contains a set of descriptive strings for each room. When the player asks to "listen," these strings are printed out by testing the room the player is in and using this information to select the correct set of strings. For example, if the player types listen while in a machine shop, then the following monologue might be presented:

```
What do you want to do? Listen

...You hear the sounds of large machines all around you. The sounds are so strong and
piercing you feel them in your teeth. However, beyond all the sounds of the large
machines, somewhere in the background you hear a peculiar hum and you're not sure what
it is?
```

The data structure containing these static strings is up to you, but I suggest an array of strings with a field that describes which room the string is for, or an array of structures with a structure for each room. For example, following is the static string structure data structure used for Shadow Land, along with the sounds for the game.

Listing 19.10. The static data structure used to contain the informational strings in Shadow Land along with the static sounds in the game.

```
// this is the structure used to hold a single string that is used to
// describe something in the game like a smell, sight, sound...

typedef struct info_string_typ
        {
        char type;        // the type of info string i.e. what does it describe
        char string[100]; // the actual description string
        } info_string, *info_string_ptr;

// these info strings hold the smells in each room
info_string smells[]={

{'l',"You smell the sweet odor of jasmine with an undertone of potpourri. "},
{'b',"The sweet smell of perfume dances within your nostrils...Realities possibly. "},
{'k',"You take a deep breath and your senses are tantalized with the smell of"},
{'k',"tender breasts of chicken marinating in a garlic sauce. Also, there is "},
{'k',"a sweet berry smell emanating from the oven.                          "},
{'w',"You are almost overwhelmed by the smell of bathing fragrance as you"},
{'w',"inhale.                                                             "},
{'h',"You smell nothing to make note of. "},
{'r',"Your nose is filled with steam and the smell of baby oil... "},
{'e',"You smell pine possible from the air coming thru a small orifice near"},
{'e',"the front door.                                                     "},
{'o',"You are greeted with the familiar odor of burning electronics. As you inhale"},
{'o',"a second time, you can almost taste the rustic smell of aging books.       "},
{'X',""}, // terminate
};
```

As you can see, there are strings for each room in the game and the end of each string is delineated with a X character. This is just one way to do things, but it works for me!

Dynamic sounds are more complex to implement than static sounds because they can move around the environment. Shadow Land has no dynamic objects, but I will explain how to implement dynamic sound.

Each object that can move around the universe has a sound attached to it which is just a string that describes the sound the object makes. Hence, when a player asks to listen to the sounds in a room, first the static sound is printed out, it then is determined what objects are in the room and then their sounds also are printed out after the static portion of the text. Of course, you should try and make the sentences "connect" together with some type of conjunction so that the sounds don't look like a bulleted list!

Smell

The sense of smell is done in the exact same way sounds are except that the text strings should describe the smells in the room rather than the sounds. Moreover, dynamic smells are implemented in the same way as described previously, as an "attachment" to the dynamic objects. An ogre, for example, might have a bad smell attached to it that is described with the static smell of the room. This would be done by testing if the ogre is in the same room as the player. This is easy because you can look at the position of the ogre and of the player, index into the universe map, and see if they are on the same cell type.

Tip: There is one artistic aspect of describing smells you should know about. If something smells bad, then try to make it sound as if it smells bad in a good way, get my drift?

Sight

Implementing vision in a text game is an interesting problem. You want to make a virtual character "see" in a virtual world that isn't even visible to the player! Well, being the software sorcerer that you are, this is no problem at all if you use the correct data structures and approach.

First, the easiest data structure with which to implement sight is the map world because it is a 2-D version of the world the player hypothetically is walking around in. The algorithm also is easy—all you have to do is understand how you (yourself) see, and then implement a version of your sight within the text game that is based on the data structures in the game.

To begin with, there is static vision and dynamic object base vision. The *static vision* is taken care of (as you have seen) and is very general. If a player asks to "look" at a room, then the first part of the description would be a static one that is always the same. The second part of the description then might focus on what's within the player's *virtual field of view* or *VFOV* (I like acronyms). This is the hard part. You somehow must scan in front of the player and detect whether objects are within the scan space. Unlike the smell and sound test, you can't just check whether the dynamic object is within the room because it might be behind the player. You instead must see if it is within the room in conjunction with being within the VFOV.

19

To test if an object is within the VFOV of the player, you need to know five things:

1. The position of the player.

2. The direction of the player.

3. The positions of all the dynamic objects.

4. The depth of the scan (distance).

5. The view angle of the scan.

Steps 1, 2, and 3 are easy. You can find that information by looking at the data structures for the player and all the dynamic objects. Questions arise when you consider steps 4 and 5. First, the *depth* means how far should the player be able to see. This is relative, but as a rule of thumb, the player should be able to see at least the length of the largest room. The second factor, *view angle*, really is the field of view and simply means the angle at which the scan will take place (see Figure 19.6).

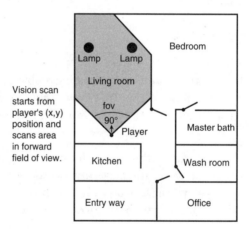

Figure 19.6. *The virtual vision system in action.*

Now, because the player can only be facing four directions (north, south, east or west), the scan become very simple. All that is needed are two `for` loops to accomplish the scan.

The scan will have a shape of an upside down pyramid and the view and or field of view will be 90 degrees. This is close enough to a normal human's field of vision and is realistic for a game. Hence, the scan will emanate from the players position and test each cell in the scan (see Figure 19.7).

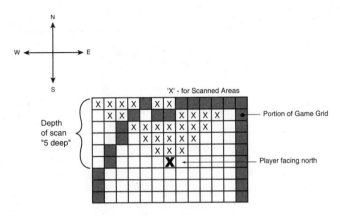

Figure 19.7. *A close up of the player's vision scan.*

In general, one `for` loop will control the x-axis deflection of the scan and one `for` loop will control the y-axis deflection. The scan will continue until a specified depth is reached (which is the distance) and then the vision scan will be complete.

As the vision scan is running, tests are made to see if any of the blocks within vision contain a dynamic object. If this is true, then each object is "tagged" and placed in a list. Then when the vision strings print out, the list is referred to and the specific visual strings for each dynamic object is printed out, along with the general static view.

Shadow Land uses this technique to "see" in a room. As an example, following is the vision code that takes care of vision in the northern direction. Pay close attention to the structure of the `for` loops and the tests. Don't worry if some of the variables or defines are not visible; just try to understand the overall operation of the code fragment.

Listing 19.11. A code fragment from Shadow Lands that produces a vision scan in the Northern direction.

```
case NORTH:
        {
        // scan like this
        //    .....
        //     ...
        //      P
        for (y=you.y,scan_level=0; y>=(you.y-depth); y—,scan_level++)
            {
            for (x=you.x-scan_level; x<=you.x+scan_level; x++)
                {
                // x,y is test point, make sure it is within the universe
                // boundaries and within the same room
                if (x>=1 && x<NUM_COLUMNS-1 &&
                    y>=1 && x<NUM_ROWS-1 &&
                    universe_geometry[y][x]==universe_geometry[you.y][you.x])
```

continues   891

Listing 19.11. continued

```
                              {
                              // test to see if square has an object in it
                              if (universe_objects[y][x]!=' ')
                                  {
                                  // insert the object into object list
                                  stuff[*num_objects].thing = universe_objects[y][x];
                                  stuff[*num_objects].x    = x;
                                  stuff[*num_objects].y    = y;

                                  // increment the number of objects
                                  (*num_objects)++;

                                  } // end if an object was found
                              } // end if in boundaries
                          } // end for x
                    } // end for y

            // return number of objects found
            return(*num_objects);

            } break;
```

The function operates by scanning the area in front of the player and testing each block in the scan to see if it is within the universe. If the block is within the universe, then the object's data structure is referred to to see if an object is sitting on the block. If so, then the object is inserted into a list and the code proceeds until the scan is done. Pay close attention to the bounding code that determines whether the scanned block is within the universe. This is absolutely needed, because as the scan takes places in a given distance, the code has no way of determining whether it has gone out of bounds of the array or in the negative direction. This is why a *filter* is needed to condition and test each test block position generated by the double for loops. Finally, when you print out the dynamic objects after the static visual, make sure they read in a fluid manner!

Making It Realtime

The text game technology you have been considering thus far is not realtime. This is because the game logic waits for the user to input the text string, the string is processed, the game logic is executed, and the cycle starts over. The problem is that during the text input phase, the game logic is in a wait state. This has two effects on the game. First, time stops until the player inputs a string and presses Enter. Secondly, dynamic objects in the game can't move around; in essence, the game universe cannot evolve while the player is "thinking." This may or may not be desired. There are some text games that stop and wait and others run while waiting for text input.

In a realtime text game, for example, players might sit at the command prompt for ten minutes, but as they do this, they might become surrounded by orcs! To make a game realtime is very easy; all you need to do is slightly change the input function so that it resembles a keyboard handler that only sends the string to the input parser when users press the Enter key. So, the game event loop might look like the following.

```
while(!done)
    {
    Get_Next_Input_Character();
    if (user has typed in a whole string)
        {
        Parser_Logic();
        } // end if an input was entered
    // whatever happened above, let's move all the objects in the game universe
    Move_Objects();
    } // end main loop
```

The realtime aspect of this structure is that players don't have to wait for the input character. If there is one, fine; otherwise, game logic continues in realtime.

Note: The game Shadow Land doesn't have any "living" objects in the universe, so a realtime implementation is not needed.

Error Handling

A text game must have *error handling*, just as arcades do. Most of the error handling, however, is done in the text parsing. There are lexical tests, syntax tests, and semantic tests that must be performed. Lexical tests are easy because they have to do with string comparisons and vocabulary checks. The syntax and semantic tests are more complex because the game logic must start using language productions and rules to check whether the sentence is valid. This is complex and usually there are many special cases you must consider. Similarly, when writing a compiler or interpreter, the code starts off clean, but contains many kludges at the completion. Text games are very similar; you may find yourself doing some lexical testing in the string input function and some syntax checking in the lexical analyzer. Better to be safe than sorry, however! Consequently, the more filters, traps, and tests the input parser has, the better!

Creeping Around with Shadow Land

Well, at this point, I know you are an expert text game writer, but I wanted to show you an example of such a game. As you probably have deduced, the name of the game is *Shadow Land*, which is a fully operational text game that enables full interaction with the environment. The idea behind the game is simple: you must find your keys and drop them in the office. The environment in which you will be playing is my apartment, here in Silicon Valley. I have completely modeled my apartment for you, including the sights, sounds, and smells that usually are within it.

The idea behind the game is that you are an invisible shadow that can move around freely without being detected by me or anyone else in the house. The vocabulary and grammar of the game is very simple, as are the actions you can perform. If you understand Shadow Land, then, with the proper planning, data structures, and algorithms, you shouldn't have a problem creating a game like Zork.

The Language of Shadow Land

Table 19.1 listed the vocabulary of Shadow Land. Now take a look at the productions or syntax rules. Rather than stating them in a rigorous manner, they are listed in a more relaxed way. The following lists again all the words in the vocabulary.

Objects in the game
LAMP, SANDWICH, KEYS

Nautical directions
EAST, WEST, NORTH, SOUTH

Relative directions
FORWARD, BACKWARD, RIGHT, LEFT

Actions or verbs of the language
MOVE, SMELL, LOOK, LISTEN, PUT, GET, EAT, INVENTORY, WHERE, EXIT

Articles or connectives of the language
THE

Prepositions of the language
IN, ON, TO, DOWN

Begin with the legal form of the action verbs. Some of the verbs need no object to mean something. These are `smell`, `listen`, `inventory`, `where`, and `exit`. If you type any of these action verbs singularly, they will work. Furthermore, if you place prepositional phrases, articles, and objects after the verbs, they will have the effect of causing warnings. Following is the outcome of entering any of these verbs:

```
"smell" - This will describe the smell of the room you are in.
"listen" - This will describe the sounds of the room you are in.
"inventory" - This will tell you what you are carrying.
"where" - This will describe your location in the house along with the direction you
are facing.
"exit" - This will end the game.
```

The next set of action verbs can be further qualified by either objects, adjectives, or complete prepositional phrases. These verbs are `move`, `put`, `get`, `look`, and `eat`. Following are the legal forms using some of the earlier production rule syntax in which the parentheses ( ) mean that the word(s) are optional and ¦ means logical OR.

```
"move" + (relative direction) ¦ "move" + "to" + relative direction ¦
"move" + "to the" + relative direction
```

Using the preceding production, the following sentence would be legal:

```
"move to the right"
```

This would have the effect of having the player parry right (sidestep). Another possibility would be

```
"move"
```

This would have the effect making the player walk in the direction he or she currently was facing. An illegal sentence would be

```
"move to the east"
```

This is illegal because *east* is a nautical direction rather than a relative direction. The next interesting action verb is `look`.

```
"look" +(nautical direction) ¦ "look"+"to"+nautical direction ¦
"look"+"to the"+nautical direction
```

Using this verb, the player can "see" objects in the room. For example, if the player just typed `look` and did not include a direction, then the game would only print out the static visual. To see objects in a room you *must* use `look` combined with a nautical direction. For example, to see the northern part of the room, you would type

```
"look to the north"
```

or

19

```
"look north"
```

or

```
"look to north"
```

All the preceding forms all equivalent and the results will be the objects within the players view being described.

Players begin the game facing north, so you need to find way for them to turn. This is done with the `turn` action, which is similar to the `look` verb (as far as the productions rules go).

```
"turn" +(nautical direction) ¦ "turn"+"to"+nautical direction ¦
"turn"+"to the"+nautical direction
```

Hence, to turn east you can type

```
"turn to east"
```

The next two action verbs relating to object manipulation are `put` and `get`. These verbs are used to put down and pick up objects. The only valid objects in the game are the `keys`, `lamp`, and `sandwich`. Following are the production rules for each action verb.

```
"put"+object ¦ "put" + "down" +"object" ¦ "put"+"down the"+object
"get"+object ¦ "get" + "the" +"object"
```

You use the `put` and `get` to move objects around the environment. If you saw a set of keys in front of you, for example, then you might say

```
"get the keys"
```

Warning: When getting objects, you must be near them, so even though you can see an object, you may not be able to grasp it until you move close enough.

Later, you may want to drop the keys. This could be accomplished with the following:

```
"put down the keys"
```

The final most important action verb is `eat` and I'm sure you know what it does. It makes you eat whatever you tell it to, as long as you have the object in your possession. The rule for `eat` is

```
"eat"+object ¦"eat"+"the"+"object"
```

If you wanted to eat the lamp, for example, you would type

```
"eat the lamp"
```

after which you will have satisfied your iron requirements for the day!

At first, you will find the grammar and limited vocabulary tedious, but after a few moments of playing the game, it will become very natural to you. Feel free to add to the vocabulary and grammar rules. One final detail: the input parser is case insensitive, so you can use upper- and lowercase characters at will.

Building and Playing Shadow Land

Shadow Land is the only game so far that is almost totally portable. This is due to the fact that the game is text only. The only two things that might change this statement is that Shadow Land uses `kbhit()` and the ANSI color text driver. Other than that, the code is straight C without any graphics or machine-dependent calls. To build the program, use the source module within today's directory, called `SHADOW.C`. Compile it and link it the standard C library and that's all you need to do! If you don't want to compile and link the program, you can use SHADOW.EXE, which I have created for you.

You already know just about everything you need to play; however, here are a few tips.

The game will begin by asking you your name. It then will ask you what you want to do. At this point in the game, you are standing in the entry way to my apartment. To your left is a kitchen and to the north is a hallway. Use the `move` command to move around in the environment and be sure to `listen` and `smell` everything. Remember that `move`, by itself, always moves you in the direction you are currently facing and `look` needs to be qualified by a nautical direction if you want to see the objects in the room.

Shadow's Game Loop

Following is the game loop for Shadow Land, which is extremely simple because it's not in realtime.

Listing 19.12. The game loop of Shadow Land.

```
void main(void)
{

// call up intro
Introduction();
```

continues

Listing 19.12. continued

```
printf("\n\nWelcome to the world of  S H A D O W  L A N D...\n\n\n");

// obtain users name to make game more personal
printf("\nWhat is your first name?");
scanf("%s",you.name);

// main event loop,note: it is NOT real-time
while(!global_exit)
    {
    // put up an input notice to user

    printf("\n\nWhat do you want to do?");

    // get the line of text
    Get_Line(global_input);

    printf("\n");
    // break the text down into tokens and build up a sentence
    Extract_Tokens(global_input);

    // parse the verb and execute the command
    Verb_Parser();

    } // end main event loop

printf("\n\nExiting the universe of S H A D O W  L A N D...see you later
%s.\n",you.name);

// restore screen color
printf("%c%c37;40m",27,91);

} // end main
```

Note: Be sure to look at the use of the ANSI screen driver, which is activated by sending out ESC followed by [and the appropriate commands.

Analysis

The main() begins by printing an introduction screen and then asking you for your name. At this point the game falls into the main event loop which is static. The loop will wait for you to enter a string, which is returned from Get_Line(). Then the string is tokenized by Extract_Tokens() and finally is parsed and acted upon by the verb parser named Verb_Parser(). That's all there is to it. Until you type exit, this cycle will occur every time you enter a line of text.

Winning the Game

I think that I have already told you how to do this but, if I didn't, then good luck figuring it out!

Summary

Today has definitely been a burn for both of us. You have taken a crash course in compiler design, along with learning the details of implementing a text game. You learned about universe representations, how to implement the senses, and how to make the descriptions in a text game "fluffy" and fun. Finally, you got to see where I live!

Q&A

Q Are text games still popular?

A The answer is yes. Text games augmented with graphics are extremely popular, and pure text games are the only games on text output terminals, so they definitely are popular.

Q Is it possible to make the computer understand the entire English language and all its nuances?

A Yes, but it would be very difficult to implement and would have to be done using an expert system of a neural net since many rules of grammar are still argued over.

Q Is it possible to make the computer generate different description strings for each game?

A Yes—this is a common technique. A pool of strings are used to build up a view, smell, and so on, and the rules governing this construction ensure that the description makes sense.

Q Where are the keys in Shadow Land?

A They are in the bedroom!

19

Workshop

The Workshop section presents quiz questions to help you cement your new knowledge and exercises to give you experience using what you've learned. Try to understand the questions and exercises before moving on to the next lesson. The answers are in Appendix B.

Quiz

1. What is a token?

2. What is a lexical analyzer?

3. What is a production?

4. What are some of the most common whitespace characters?

Exercises

1. Add more vocabulary to the game.

2. Create a cat that runs around the apartment.

3. Make the game realtime.

4. Add sound effects to the game.

20

Making the Quantum Leap to 3-D Space

Today we are going to slow things down and discuss the "state of the art" in video games. This, of course, is *3-D* video games. The basic algorithms and techniques used to write 2-D games are applicable to 3-D, but the graphics techniques are not! Successfully pulling off a 3-D video game on a PC takes a lot of skill, math, and patience. You won't be learning how to create the incredible 3-D graphics for these games today; however, you will take a look at the technologies you can use to create a 3-D game. Following are your target vectors:

☐ What is a 3-D game?

☐ Sprite scaling and parallax scrolling

☐ Polygon technology

☐ Ray casting techniques

☐ Voxel graphics

☐ The new "ellipsoidal" technology

What is a 3-D Game?

A *3-D game* is still a video game except that the graphic view is rendered to simulate a 3-D perspective, as you would see in real life or on a movie screen. Games such as Pac-Man, Asteroids, and Street Fighter, for example, are all 2-D games. They exist in a flat 2-D plane; moreover, the player can only move in two directions, horizontally or vertically. A full 3-D game on the other hand enables the player to "see" objects as they would look in real life, that is, in full 3-D perspective. Furthermore, most 3-D games enable the player to move in all three dimensions. You might be asking, How can a 2-D computer monitor display a 3-D view?" The answer is this is accomplished by using a "projection."

A 3-D image can be projected mathematically onto a 2-D plane, such as the computer screen. Of course, the objects don't truly induce a 3-D effect and your brain knows something is wrong, but at least the images look like their 3-D as seen on TV or in the movies. In essence, 3-D games are more realistic that 2-D games. Good examples of 3-D games are Wing Commander, DOOM, Tie Fighter, Dark Forces, System Shock, Armored Fist, Alone in the Dark I, and Alone in the Dark II. All these games are 3-D; however, they all use different 3-D technologies to accomplish the 3-D illusion.

Sprite Scaling and Parallax Scrolling

Some of the first 3-D games weren't in full 3-D; they were only in partial 3-D. This means that some aspects of the game were 3-D while others were 2-D. A good example of this is the classic Atari racing game, Pole Position. Pole Position was a pseudo-3D racing game released in the 1980s. It wasn't truly 3-D, however. The illusion of 3-D was synthesized using a couple of "tricks." The first trick was called *parallax scrolling*. This was a method of having multiple backgrounds in the distance scroll horizontally at different rates. This would simulate perspective. For example, when you are driving a car and look out the window, you see the mountains in the distance moving slowly while the objects closer to you are moving quickly.

This technique was used to draw the mountains and terrain far in the distance and make them move as if they were 3-D. The next trick was to use a technique called *sprite scaling* to make the race cars become larger as they approached the player and smaller as they moved farther away. Sprite scaling is a technique of scaling the pixels in a 2-D bitmap to synthesize a 3-D effect. Together, these techniques made Pole Position a mega hit and Atari very popular (at the time).

As time moved on 3-D, technology started becoming popular on PCs because the processing power was starting to grow to the point that 3-D graphics on the PC was a possibility. The first and one of the most incredible 3-D games was called Wing Commander by Chris Roberts and was a shock to everyone's system. The technology the game used was known (sprite scaling), but no one had pulled it off as successfully as Chris did. Wing Commander was a full 3-D space combat game that really made the player feel like he or she was in a 3-D universe.

Sprite scaling is a technique to simulate 3-D games. True 3-D graphics meant that the models of the objects in the game and the representation of the universe actually was in 3-D space, mathematically. This is the true form of 3-D graphics.

20

Polygon Technology

It was learned that the public didn't really care if a game was truly 3-D or not, as long as it looked good. After a while, the public wanted more realistic-looking games and the

only answer was to go to the flight simulator and high-end 3-D technology of polygon rendering. Polygon rendering is a technique of creating a full 3-D universe that is both mathematically 3-D and visually 3-D. There are two problems with this technique, however. First, all objects must be approximated with a finite number of polygons, and second, the mathematics used to accomplish the 3-D transformations and rendering is complex and time consuming. These two factors make polygon-based graphics slow to make their way into the arena of video games.

The only successful polygon games still are, for the most part, flight and driving simulators. The problem is that polygon graphics still are computationally expensive and always will be until PCs have built-in hardware graphic engines that can render 3-D graphics without intervention of the system CPU. There are many boards that can do this, of course, but it will be a while before there is a VGX3D card in every PC! Alas, the game companies and other young bright programmers set out to try and find other ways of obtaining polygon quality (or better) using other techniques that aren't so computationally expensive.

Ray Casting Techniques

One day not so long ago, a small company released a game called Wolfenstein 3-D and the world changed forever. Wolfenstein 3-D was mind blowing at the time. The way in which it worked was almost magical. Analysts tried to figure it out, but it seemed that a fully-textured 3-D video game at the time was impossible on the PC. This probably was true; however, the technique used to render the 3-D universe in the game was not standard 3-D polygon graphics but a form of *ray tracing*. Ray tracing is something that creates totally photo-realistic images at the expense of hours, days, or weeks. Ray casting was only the first phase of ray tracing and only computed two things about a 3-D universe: the size of an object and the visibility of an object. This, however, was all that was needed to create a fully textured mapped game in a room-based world.

Ray casting works by casting out rays of light from the user's viewpoint and testing where they intersect with the game universe. From this intersection, the distance between the user and each element of the environment can be computed. At the same time, the hidden surface removal problem is taken care of automatically because walls that are farther from the player are occluded by the nearer walls that the rays first intersect. Basically, ray casting creates a 3-D view in the reverse of how the real world works. In the real world, light reflects off objects from a light source and finally into your eyes. In a ray-casted world, "light feelers" are projected to see what you could possibly see if there is a light

source. Whether it works in reverse or not, it works, and it works wonders because it has opened up a completely new rendering technology to create 3-D games on the PC.

Voxel Graphics

Another 3-D technology that has its roots in medical imaging is called *voxel* graphics, or *volume rendering*. Voxel graphics is a technique used to render a 3-D image that is composed of atoms or voxels. These voxels can be used to create a full volume space image. The technology of voxel graphics is still in its infancy and is computationally expensive. One of the leaders in this technology is Nova Logic, the makers of Commanche and Armored Fist. They have found that using assembly language with this technology is still the only way to get the needed of performance out of the PC.

The main drawback of voxel graphics is that it's well-suited for volume rendering or rendering objects and environments that are volumetric. This is unlike a normal environment that we are used to, such as walls, ceilings, and floors, which are planar. However, voxel graphics is great for making killer terrain and outside landscapes, which is what it is mostly used for.

The New "Ellipsoidal" Technology

It seems that when you think you've heard it all, you hear about something else. Well, there is a new technology called *ellipsoidal* rendering that is in the experimental phase. This technology is a method of creating 3-D imagery and environments using ellipsoids (stretched spheres) as the basic image elements. There are many reasons why this technology is hopeful. First, the ellipsoid is well-defined mathematically and transformations consequently are very simple. Next, objects drawn with ellipsoids have a very "round" and natural look to them. Finally, hidden surface removal, lighting, and rendering of ellipsoids is much like that of spheres, which is much like that of points, which is very simple! Hence, you'll be seeing some games that have a very different look to them in the near future (or if it is the future, then you'll see them now...).

Summary

Today, you covered the technologies and techniques behind 3-D games. You learned about ray casting, polygon graphics, and voxel graphics, and you went a few "rounds" with the new ellipsoidal technology, soon to hit the streets.

20

Q&A

Q Is DOOM done with ray casting?

A I don't think so. I think it uses a scan line Z-Buffer algorithm, coupled with a polygon based world and pre-computed polygon visibility via a binary space partition.

Q How many frames per second do most 3-D games run at?

A They should run at 30 frames a second, but in reality, an average frame rate is 12 frames per second with 15 fps being "high quality."

Q I've heard the term *Gouraud shading* before. What does it mean?

A It is a method of shading polygon faces by using an averaging technique to make the flat surface look more curved.

Q Are there any games that use all the 3-D technologies together?

A Not that I know of.

Workshop

The Workshop section presents quiz questions to help you cement your new knowledge and exercises to give you experience using what you've learned. Try to understand the questions and exercises before moving on to the next lesson. The answers are in Appendix B.

Quiz

1. What is a polygon?

2. What is a voxel?

3. How does sprite scaling work?

4. Look up the equation for an ellipsoid.

Exercises

1. Implement a parallax scrolling game.

2. Use color rotation to simulate the trench from Star Wars.

3. Try to figure out a new 3-D technology yourself!

Marketing Your Creations

You have traveled a long way and periled many obstacles to get this far. You must really want to write video games! Today you will learn how to sell the games you make and maybe become rich, famous, popular, and get a lot of free magazine subscriptions! Your first games probably will not be competitive with professional-quality games created by Lucas Arts, id, or Electronic Arts, but they will be good enough to sell in one shape or another. Today you look at some of the aspects of selling your games and the pros and cons of each method. Here's the price list:

- The final presentation of your game
- Protecting your work
- The marketing channels open to you
- Selling the game to a publishing company
- Distributing the game yourself
- Shareware

The Final Presentation of Your Game

Before you can sell your game, you must compile it into a professional form that is easy to install and play. Just as the software you purchase has an installation program, setup system, READ.ME file, and so on, so must your game. You must make installing and configuring your game very easy for the user. Moreover, you shouldn't assume anything. The user may or may not be a computer expert, so create the installation and setup software for the complete beginner.

Next, you should allow for options as far as sound cards and input devices are concerned. This may not be appropriate in all cases, but you should endeavor to make your game work on as many platforms as possible. This can only help your target market size.

Another factor often overlooked when games are released is the "play testing" phase. This means putting your game through the trials and tribulations of every possible situation to flush out all the bugs. You definitely don't want to release a product that is full of bugs. Doing this will have a long-lasting effect. If you don't, not only will the game you release be received poorly, but any of your future games will be looked at with jaded eyes! Now, to get on the right foot, following is a list of some of the things you should include with your game:

- [ ] The game itself and all the graphics and sound files that go along with it.

- [ ] Any drivers that are needed for the game that the user might not have.

- [ ] An instruction manual in ASCII form along with the instructions that are in the game itself.

- [ ] An installation program that will decompress any files, create directories, and so on, for your game.

- [ ] A setup program so the user can adjust the game to his/her own tastes and hardware configuration.

- [ ] A READ.ME file with the latest bug fixes and/or general comments about the game.

After you have all the preceding information, you may want to compress it into a single file using a compression program such as PKZIP (which is shareware). This is a good idea because it keeps all the files together in a single place and makes distribution much easier.

Protecting Your Work

After you create a game and release it in one way or another, there undoubtedly will be software pirates copying and distributing your game. You can, of course, use copy-protection schemes, but they usually fail. The only thing you really can do is make it as illegal as possible for the pirates to copy your game, so that if you catch them, they won't have a foot to stand on. You can do this by copyrighting your game. Technically, any work you create is automatically copyrighted if you place the word *Copyright* in a conspicuous position along with your name or company. The following examples would be valid copyright notices:

```
Copyright 1995 Andromeda Industries
Copyright (c) Andre' LaMothe 2001
©1999 Megasoft Corporation
```

Although simply displaying the copyright notice on the game itself and relevant files makes it illegal to copy, it's also a good idea to "register" your copyright with the government. This can be done by writing to the copyright office at:

Publications Section
Copyright Office
Library of Congress
Washington, DC 20559
Phone: (202) 707-9100

Request the copyright forms for copyrighting computer programs. The entire process costs $20 to $30.

The Marketing Channels Open to You

Now that you have a complete game disk in your hand and it's protected, you are ready to sell it. The question is: how? Well, there are three approaches to this. Each approach has its pros and cons, but in the end it seems that shareware is the quickest solution for most authors. You be the judge.

Selling the Game to a Publishing Company

You can attempt to sell your game to a large game company such as Electronics Arts, Origin Systems, BrØderbund, Interplay, and so on. This is accomplished in a very strict manner. First, you must call the company(s) that you are interested in and ask for a product submission packet. Within the packet, you will find their terms as far as submissions are concerned and a nondisclosure agreement. The nondisclosure agreement is to indemnify the company from liability in the case that you claim they have stolen your game. So, it is to protect you and them, but in reality it's for them!

After you get the submission packet and fill out the documents and send everything in along with your game, a few weeks will pass and the publisher will notify you as to whether they like the game and think it's a good idea (or a bad one). If they don't like the game, then they will send everything back and that's it! (You may, however, see your idea stolen in the near future; this has happened to me many times.) On the other hand, the publisher might like your game and want to begin negotiations with you. This is when you need a lawyer or legal advisor to ensure that you are not negotiated right out of your game. They may give you $50,000 for it and you may think this is all the money in the world—wrong! The publisher will make 100 times that if it's a good game. The rule of thumb these days is $150,000 up front plus royalties. These types of numbers are for high-quality games; rest assured, if they are bothering with you, then you should feel confident that they like your game and think that it could make a lot of money for them.

Distributing the Game Yourself

If you really feel entrepreneurial, then you might want to package, market, and distribute the game yourself. This is possible, but you had better have a ton of money to capitalize your little endeavor. Advertising costs alone will make your hair white. Self distribution is just too costly to do for a first game.

Shareware

The word *shareware* almost has a magical sound to it. It opens up infinite possibilities. So what exactly is shareware? you ask. Well, it's an honor system—an honor system of software. You give away your game for free and if people like it, then they pay you for it. That probably seems about as possible as monkeys growing wings, but it works! And by the way, monkeys *will* have wings someday. It works because, believe it or not, there are a lot of honest people left in the world. I know that you can't believe that after someone obtains your game, that person would pay for it, but let me tell you a little story. When I wrote my previous book, *Tricks of the Game Programming Gurus*, I had a few conversations with John Carmack of id software. I asked John the very same question about shareware and John replied to me "Well Andre, I'm driving around in a turbo red Ferrari; does that answer your question?" It answered mine and it should answer yours!

To become a shareware author, you can take two routes: the real one and the unreal one. Let's talk about the unreal method first, because it's the easiest. To become an unreal shareware author, all you need to do is upload your game to a few BBSs (Bulletin Board Systems) and place it up on CompuServe. Before you do this, however, you will have to set up your operation and alter your game a bit. To set up shop, you should do the following:

- ☐ Go down to your local County Clerk's office and file a fictitious business name for your new company. You can start a small company as a sole proprietorship for about $50.

- ☐ Open a bank account at a nearby bank under your new business name. This is to hold all the funds that will be rolling in. You probably will have to open the account with $50.

- ☐ Lease a P.O. Box at your local post office to receive mail (you don't want the whole world knowing your address). This will cost about $25 every six months.

- ☐ Install another phone line at your house dedicated to your new business. This will cost about $35 for the installation and $10 a month for local service only. This will suffice since most of the calls will be incoming.

21

☐ Purchase some letter head, envelopes, and business cards. This will cost $80 to $100 for a couple hundred of each.

If you follow the preceding suggestions, then you will have yourself a small company!

Now, you need to make a few adjustments to your software before letting it loose on the networks, so it can migrate, multiply, and spread like a virus. Make a shareware version of your game that is slightly crippled, missing some levels or not fully functional in some way. This is to help motivate your potential customers to pay you (register) for the complete version.

Next, you need to put a screen in the game that indicates that the game is shareware. The screen should look something like the following:

```
Cyber Warrior
(c) 1994 EnCom

This game is Shareware
To register and obtain a fully operational copy,
please send $25.00 to:

EnCom
8086 Silicon Way, #486
Santa Clara, CA 95123

Please indicate if you want 3.5 or 5.25 inch disks
```

You also might want to supply the customer with source code as an added incentive to purchase the game.

Lastly, in addition to the initial registration screen, the game should end with a similar nag screen, and within the files you should supply an ASCII registration form that the customer can print out, fill in, and send to you.

After the registrations start rolling in, send the customer the complete version of the game (maybe with a personalized header), put the check in the bank, and go on your merry way. You probably should supply customers with technical support (that's what the phone is for) for a period of three to six months. This can be yet another selling point of your game.

The "real" way of becoming a shareware author works in much the same way, but you join a group called *ASP* (Association of Shareware Professionals). Members of this group can help you more widely distribute your game, and they publish booklets that list all shareware authors and their titles. This can help you, but there are a few strings attached. You must be a good guy. No cheating, no forgetting to send registrants their complete software, and so forth. Also, you must guarantee to give technical support for a specific period. To find out more, you can contact them at:

Association of Shareware Professionals

545 Grover Road

Muskegon, MI 49442-9427

CompuServe 72050,1433

Phone(616) 788-5131

FAX (616) 788-2765

Give them a call or send them a letter to obtain more information and details about becoming a real shareware author.

Summary

Today you learned that it not only is possible, but it is very easy to sell a game. You learned some of the routes you can take and some of the pitfalls with each of these routes. Remember, you have to start somewhere, so don't worry if your first games are simple in nature. There always is someone who will like them, in spite of their simplicity. Just make sure to continue to improve your games, and in no time you will be creating the most incredible games.

Well, this is it for our journey. I truly hope that you have learned something from reading this book because I have learned a lot from writing it. If you want to get in touch with me, you can reach me at

Andromeda Industries

P.O. Box 641744

San Jose, CA 95164-1744

Time stands still for no one, so make each moment an infinity...

Q&A

Q How many registrations can I expect with the Shareware technique?

A Anywhere from one or two a week to hundreds a week—it depends on the game, but I'm sure your games will do well!

Q Can I be sued by registrants?

A Possibly. If your game damages their computer in some way, but if you place a disclaimer regarding this possibility, then you somewhat protect yourself.

21

Q What is the most successful shareware game in history?

A DOOM—at least at this point in time.

Workshop

The Workshop section presents quiz questions to help you cement your new knowledge and exercises to give you experience using what you've learned. Try to understand the questions and exercises before moving on to the next lesson. The answers are in Appendix B.

Quiz

1. What is so good about distributing your game using the shareware technique?

2. I'm out of questions!

3. I'm still out of questions!

Exercises

1. Write an awesome video game.

2. Sell it.

3. Move to Hawaii.

4. Live happily ever after.

Day 15

On this day, you took a look at the details of making a complete game. Aspects such as demo modes, high score tables, and multiple players were some of the highlights. You learned that a complete video game is more than the graphics and sounds; it must be a polished product. The day ended with a discussion about copy protection.

Day 16

On this day, you finally got to take a break and play some games. The game was Sea Shark, and you walked through its operation, creation, and architecture—millimeter by millimeter.

Day 17

Sea Shark was good, but it was fairly simple. Today you saw a relatively advanced game called Venture. Venture is full of useful lessons such as scrolling, database management, and AI algorithms.

Day 18

On this day, you took a slight detour from the standard shoot-'em-up games and uncovered some of the mysteries behind simulations. The name of the game was Sim-Pizza. You learned about the real power of autonomous functions and that hitting pedestrians is both immoral and costly. (But in cyberspace, it's kinda fun.)

Day 19

This day really came from left field but was a refreshing change. You learned about the oldest games around—text adventures—and how to create them. The topics covered were parsing, universe representations, and to use words to emote mental images. The day was capped off with a complete text game, Shadow Land, that is a model of my apartment. (Did you ever find the keys?)

Day 20

Throughout this book you learned about 2-D graphics and games, but in the depths of your mind, I'm sure you wanted to learn something about 3-D games. On this day, that's what you did. Day 20 covered the technologies used to create games such as Doom and Tie Fighter, and discussed the fundamental concepts behind those games.

Day 21

You learned how to become rich and famous on this day by selling your games. The details of marketing, shareware, and doing deals was touched upon. Also, you learned about all the components that go into a final, marketable game.

The Mech War Challenge

If you've gotten this far in the book, you are definitely a video-game guru! As I said on Day 2, there is a contest to see who is the best of the best, the top gun, the king of the hill, the master of his or her castle. The object of the contest is to take the game Mech War and make it better, bigger, and more fun. To accomplish this, you can do anything you want; however, you must use Mech War as a foundation for the game that you make. (You can't start from scratch.) The contest will be judged twice a year, and the deadlines are June 14 and January 1. To enter the contest, send your submission along with full source code, graphics, sounds, and so forth to me. I will then judge the entries and select the best submission. The entries will be judged mainly on game play and creativity, so awesome artwork isn't a must (since most people aren't artists).

The winner of the contest will be selected within a month after each deadline and will receive a check for $100. Here are the rules of the contest:

1. There are two deadlines each year. They are June 14 and January 1.

2. All submissions prior to the nearest deadline will be entered into the contest for the upcoming deadline.

3. All submissions must have the words "Public Domain" on the introductory screen of the game.

4. All contestants must be humans (no aliens please).

5. All submissions must contain complete source code, graphics, sounds, and any other necessary files to recompile and run the game.

6. All submissions must be accompanied with a self-addressed envelope including postage if you want to be notified that your submission was received.

7. The winner will receive a check within 30 days of the entry deadline.

8. Losers will not be notified.

9. The contest will run through the year 2001.

10. Each contestant can enter only one game per deadline.

11. Send your submission to

    Andromeda Industries
    P.O. Box 641744
    San Jose, CA 95164-1744

    Attn: Mech Challenge

Now let's talk about the software you will need to create Mech War.

The graphics and sound files needed to run the game are within the directory for this appendix and Day 2. The source code for Mech War is within the directory for this appendix. Finally, Mech War uses the standard game library functions you have been writing. Specifically, it uses these modules:

GRAPH3.C/H
GRAPH4.C/H
GRAPH6.C/H
GRAPH9.C/H

You will see these included in the `includes` section of the actual source.

That is all you need to know to enter the contest. Good luck, and may the force be with you!

B

Answers

 **Answers**

This appendix contains answers to selected quiz questions from each day. Because there is more than one correct solution to the exercises in each chapter, "answers" to the exercises are not included in this appendix.

Answers for Day 1, "Lights, Camera, Action!"

Quiz

1. The Atari 800, Apple II, Commodore 64, and TRS-80 Color Computer were the most popular game platforms in the 80's. (But the Atari was the best...)

2. First-person 3-D walkthroughs, simulators, sports games, side scrollers, combat games, and role-playing games.

3. A 2-D game is flat and allows the player to move within—at most—two dimensions. A 3-D game is more realistic and allows the player to move within three dimensions.

4. No. The Sound Blaster will play the sound sample using DMA (Direct Memory Access).

5. About 15, but 12 will usually do.

6. The 386 is a full 32-bit processor with the exception of its data bus being 16 bits wide in the SX model.

7. Speed, Speed, Speed!

8. If I told you, it would ruin it!

Answers for Day 2, "The Components of a Complete Game: Mech War"

Quiz

1. The resolution is 320×200, which is mode 13h.

2. The PCX files contain the imagery for the game and the VOC files contain the digitized samples.

3. Yes, if you think of each of the game elements to be a separate task or process.

5. Mech War runs a maximum of 18 FPS.

Answers for Day 3, "Painting the Screen with the VGA Card"

Quiz

1. VGA stands for Video Graphics Array.

2. The resolution is 320x200 with 256 colors.

4. The pixel address of 100,100 would be 100*256+100 + A000:0000h, which is A000:6464h.

6. Video memory is slow because the CPU must "wait" to access it if the video hardware is accessing the video buffer to draw the screen.

8. Bit blitting means "block image transfer" and is a standard technique used to map a rectangular bitmap onto the video screen.

9. Mode X has a resolution of 320×240.

Answers for Day 4, "Getting Sprite to the Point"

Quiz

1. Because there is an IF statement in the inner loop, there would be a total of 64*64 or 4,096!

2. A bounding box is the smallest rectangle that contains a bitmapped or polygon image; it is generally used for collision-detection algorithms.

3. Delay() is called to synchronize the game to some time base so that it will run at the same speed on all PCs.

4. Using mathematics to rotate each point or by sampling methods based on line algorithms.

5. Flickering means the video image is not stable.

7. It is important to compress graphical images because they are so large, and if uncompressed, they would take up too much memory.

Answers for Day 5, "Polygon Engines"

Quiz

1. A polygon is an N-sided object constructed of line segments.

2. It was invented formally in 1965 and used to quickly draw lines on a raster-based device.

3. `(y-y1) = M(x-x1)...M = (y-y1)/(x-x1). Q.E.D.`

4. The endpoints being totally within the clipping region, totally out of the clipping region, and, in the last case, one endpoint in and one out of the clipping region.

5. Image-space clipping deals with the final pixel image and works at the raster level; object-space clipping tries to use the geometrical properties of the object to clip it.

6. The unit circle is a circle with radius one, and the cosine and sine of an angle as the angle increments from 0 to 360 will trace out a unit circle.

Answers for Day 6, "Real-Time Animation and Effects"

Quiz

1. A double buffer is used to draw the screen image in an off-screen area and then, in one memory-move operation, copy the double buffer into the video buffer. This procedure eliminates flicker.

2. The change is making the array `video_buffer[]` into `double_buffer[]`.

3. The input status word that is at 0×3DAh and the bit to test is the fourth bit from the right, or d3.

4. *Animotion* is the synchronization of animation and motion to make objects move smoothly instead of skipping or sliding.

5. It's used as the additive operand to access the next row or column of the bit map.

6. No. They are copied into the starting color of the color-rotation color set. For example, if we were going to do this: Color 5 <— Color 6 <— Color 7, then we would move Color 5 into Color 7 to make the rotation complete.

7. Because with it we can detect when the video hardware is not accessing the video RAM and do faster updates; furthermore, it is a good time base to lock on to.

8. 70 times per second or at 70Hz.

9. Smooth scrolling and paged scrolling.

10. Page scrolling is moving the entire screen at once.

Answers for Day 7, "Reading the Minds of Devices"

Quiz

1. The joystick port is at 0×201h.

2. They make up the 32-bit value of the current time.

3. It is called with a set of parameters placed in registers describing the function to execute, and then vectored to with an interrupt call.

5. They operate by a charge/discharge circuit that is timed. The amount of time it takes for the charge is proportional to the current position of the joystick, which is really the number of turns of a small variable resistor (potentiometer).

6. Serial.

7. Because each joystick will have slightly different maximum and minimum deflection values due to the construction and the types of potentiometers used.

8. The BIOS can be used, or else a "timeout" program can be written that counts how long it takes for the joystick-charging circuit to charge; if it takes too long, then no joystick is present.

9. The code sent by the keyboard for a key. There is only one scan code for every key on the keyboard, even if there are two characters on the key.

10. $V(t) = V_0 e^{-t/RC}$ is the equation for a discharge, and RC is the time constant, so the capacitor will reach almost 99 percent charge in about 5*RC seconds.

Answers for Day 8, "Warp Speed, Anyone?"

Quiz

1. The MEDIUM memory model has a single 64K NEAR data segment and multiple 64K FAR code segments. The LARGE memory model has multiple 64K FAR data segments and multiple 64K FAR code segments. In most cases, the MEDIUM model is your best bet.

2. Local variables are created in the stack.

3. Because the format of a floating-point number is in an encoded form that must be decoded in order to do any mathematical operations.

4. The 80286 has a maximum memory addressing range of one megabyte.

5. SI and DI are used on Microsoft C compilers.

7. Loops should be unrolled from 8 to 16 times.

Answers for Day 9, "Making the PC Rock!"

Quiz

1. The Fourier Series is a series of sinusoidal terms that, when summed up, can represent any waveform. By taking the inverse of the concept, any waveform can be synthesized by a number of sine waves.

2. It depends on the model, but usually 1.

3. DMA is Direct Memory Access and is used by the Sound Blaster to access digital sound samples. It also uses the data so that the system CPU does not have to retrieve and send data to the Sound Blaster.

4. It is a software driver used to record and play back digitized samples.

5. By scanning all the interrupt vectors and searching for the characters FMDRV at offset $0\times103h$ from where the interrupt vector points to.

6. About 20Hz to 20,000Hz.

7. Using one sine wave to modulate the frequency of another and create harmonics.

Answers for Day 10, "Playing Dr. Frankenstein"

Quiz

1. Artificial intelligence is making the computers seem as though they are thinking; synthetic intelligence is trying to model simple thought processes to synthesize thought.

2. I'm a bit fuzzy on this.

3. A state variable simply holds the state of some object or process; it's like memory.

4. Personality is implemented by selecting new states based on probability distributions.

Answers for Day 11, "Out of Time"

Quiz

1. A function that has local static variables to track its state.

2. The standard PC-AT has three internal timers.

3. Because it is used for the keyboard interrupt and it is a good time base to latch onto for multitasking.

4. The keyboard handler is at INT 0×09h.

5. There is a single scan code for every key on the 101 keyboard; the break code is generated by adding 128 to this value.

6. The timer's control register is at 0×43h and the three counters are at 0×40h, 0×41h, and 0×42h.

Answers for Day 12, "Laying Out the Universe"

Quiz

1. Image space is at the pixel or raster level, while object space deals more with the geometrical construction of the objects.

2. A cell-based world is constructed of tiles that each represent a bitmap.

3. There would be 100 tiles regardless of the pixel size, so the memory required would still be 100 words.

4. Vector-based worlds are poor for collision detection because they are so hard to work. These worlds are difficult to work with because a lot of math must be used to compute the intersections between the world geometry and the game objects.

5. The center of an object is always the best place to center the bounding box because it is the natural center of mass.

Answers for Day 13, "The Physics of Games"

Quiz

1. F=MA is Newton's famous force equation, and it means that the force exerted upon an object is equal to the mass of the object multiplied by the acceleration of the object.

2. Friction is caused by molecules rubbing against each other, which translates into energy losses and heat transfer.

3. Yes. For example, when you hit the brakes your car has a negative acceleration.

Answers for Day 14, "Tools of the Trade"

Quiz

1. A map editor is a program that allows you or your game designer to quickly generate game levels.

2. A sequencer is a musical device or piece of software that allows you to generate a sequence of musical notes.

3. Because when we draw the objects we would like them to look the same as they would in the final game.

4. Technically, no. However, no one is going to notice the use of an explosion, wind, or car sound. But you can't digitize and use sounds such as the famous "I'll be back" without licensing.

Answers for Day 15, "Video-Game Design Philosophies"

Quiz

1. The best way to implement a demo mode is by digitizing yourself playing and then feeding the data into the input function.

2. A pop-up interface is a menu or control that can pop up based on a user selection. In general, it is not always visible.

3. The environment string is a string of data maintained by the operating system that describes various system settings such as paths, set variables, and so forth.

4. Only if the CPU is in protected mode.

Answers for Day 16, "Blowing Things Up with Sea Shark"

Quiz

1. The bubbles are single particles that have an upward velocity and a "lifetime" that are both selected randomly to make the particles move as if they were bubbles.

2. There are six different bit-map sizes.

3. When 100 ships have passed by without being obliterated.

4. The standard C input library was used because the input control was very limited and didn't need to take into consideration multiple key presses.

Answers for Day 17, "Adventuring with Venture"

Quiz

1. Archer has 21 frames of animation!

2. Archer's feet are used for collision detection instead of the center of his body because Venture is supposed to be a 2.5-D game and the view is slanted.

3. Using probability to select the states of the Daemons synthesizes personality.

4. Archer can shoot three arrows simultaneously.

5. The random variable in the bat control logic ranges from 0 to 249; hence, there are 250 discrete values for a probability of success of 1/250. The bat control function is called 18 times per second, so the overall probability of a bat coming out per second is 18/250 = 7.2 percent. Therefore, on average, every 13.8 seconds a bat will come out.

Answers for Day 18, "Simulating Cities with Sim-Pizza"

Quiz

1. So that the numbers can be drawn on them later and to increase the accuracy of the pizza-to-house collision detection.

2. It is implemented using color register effects. There are six color registers that are turned on/off in sequence depending on the speed of the moped.

3. There can be eight humans alive at once.

4. There are eight binary digits used for the decimal portion of the fixed-point numbers, which is about three decimal digits of accuracy.

Answers for Day 19, "Adventures in Text"

Quiz

1. A token is a single "chunk" of a sentence separated by white space. Tokens can be numbers, words, or symbols.

2. The lexical analyzer is responsible for tokenizing the input sentence.

3. A production is a rule that describes how some aspect of the syntax of a given language or grammar works.

4. The space character, the horizontal tab, the line feed, the vertical tab, and the carriage return.

 **Answers**

Answers for Day 20, "Making the Quantum Leap to 3-D Space"

Quiz

1. A polygon is an N-sided object composed of line segments.

2. Technically, a voxel is a 3-D pixel that has volume; in our case, however, a voxel is a single point in 3-D space that represents a finite volume, but really has none.

3. $F(x,y,z) = x^2/a^2 + y^2/b^2 + z^2/c^2 = 1$, where a, b, and c are the lengths of each of the major axes.

Answers for Day 21, "Marketing Your Creations"

Quiz

1. Because it's practically free, very easy, and a quick way to make money!

2. About $500 to start things up and $50 a month for phones and other miscellaneous expenses.

Index

16-bit code

listings

Add to Your Sams Library Today with the Best Books for Programming, Operating Systems, and New Technologies

The easiest way to order is to pick up the phone and call

1-800-428-5331

between 9:00 a.m. and 5:00 p.m. EST.
For faster service please have your credit card available.

ISBN	Quantity	Description of Item	Unit Cost	Total Cost
0-672-30507-0		Tricks of the Game-Progamming Gurus (book/CD-ROM)	$45.00	
0-672-30448-1		Teach Yourself C in 21 Days	$24.95	
0-672-30471-6		Teach Yourself Advanced C in 21 Days (book/disk)	$34.95	
0-672-30309-4		Programming Sound for DOS and and Windows (book/disk)	$39.95	
0-672-30468-6		C Programmer's Guide to Serial Communications, 2nd Edition	$39.95	
0-672-48470-6		Assembly Language: For Real Programmers ONLY!	$44.95	
0-672-30361-2		Virtual Reality and the Exploration of Cyberspace (book/disk)	$26.95	
0-672-30365-5		C for Fun and Profit (book/disk)	$29.95	
0-672-27395-0		Microsoft C/C++ 7 Developer's Guide (book/disk)	$49.95	
0-672-30308-6		Tricks of the Graphics Gurus (book/disk)	$49.95	
0-672-30319-1		The Waite Group's New C Primer Plus, 2nd Edition	$29.95	
0-672-30292-6		Programming Windows Games with Borland C++ (book/disk)	$34.95	
0-672-30313-2		Programming Games for Beginners for Windows (book/disk)	$26.95	
0-672-30311-6		Borland C++ 4 Object-Oriented Programming	$39.95	
		Shipping and Handling: See information below.		
		TOTAL		

❏ 3 ½" Disk

❏ 5 ¼" Disk

Shipping and Handling: $4.00 for the first book, and $1.75 for each additional book. Floppy disk: add $1.75 for shipping and handling. If you need to have it NOW, we can ship product to you in 24 hours for an additional charge of approximately $18.00, and you will receive your item overnight or in two days. Overseas shipping and handling adds $2.00 per book and $8.00 for up to three disks. Prices subject to change. Call for availability and pricing information on latest editions.

201 W. 103rd Street, Indianapolis, Indiana 46290

1-800-428-5331 — Orders   1-800-835-3202 — FAX   1-800-858-7674 — Customer Service

Book ISBN 0-672-30562-3

CD-ROM Install

What's on the CD-ROM

The *Teach Yourself Game Programming in 21 Days* CD-ROM contains

- [ ] A 2-D game library that you can use to develop your own games.

- [ ] All the source code, libraries, utilities, and support files discussed and developed in the book. Using these tools, you can develop powerful and professional games.

- [ ] Hot games that showcase the techniques taught in this book. The games include DOOM 1.666, Wolfenstein 3-D, Blake Stone, Pinball Super Android, and many more.

Installing the CD-ROM

To install the files to your hard drive, complete the following steps:

1. At the DOS prompt, change to the CD-ROM drive containing the installation disc. For example, if the disc is in drive E:, type **E:** and press Enter.

2. Type **INSTALL** and press Enter.

 Note: To install the files on the disc, you'll need at least 40M of free space on your hard drive.

You will then see a menu from which you can choose to install all the programs on the disc, or any one of the programs individually. The installation program will copy the selected files to a directory named \TYGAME, which will be created automatically. The files are arranged in two main subdirectories: /SOURCE, which contains the source files and utilities, and /GAMES, which contains the sample games.